W9-CLM-321

The Linux® Networking Architecture

Design and Implementation of Network Protocols in the Linux Kernel

Klaus Wehrle • Frank Pählke • Hartmut Ritter
Daniel Müller • Marc Bechler

An Alan R. Apt Book

PEARSON

Prentice
Hall

Upper Saddle River, New Jersey 07458

Library of Congress Cataloging-in-Publication Data
CIP DATA AVAILABLE.

Vice President and Editorial Director, ECS: *Marcia J. Horton*
Publisher: *Alan Apt*
Associate Editor: *Toni Dianne Holm*
Editorial Assistant*: Patrick Lindner*
Vice President and Director of Production and Manufacturing, ESM: *David W. Riccardi*
Executive Managing Editor: *Vince O'Brien*
Managing Editor: *Camille Trentacoste*
Production Editor: *Irwin Zucker*
Director of Creative Services: *Paul Belfanti*
Creative Director: *Carole Anson*
Art Director and Cover Manager: *Jayne Conte*
Managing Editor, AV Management and Production: *Patricia Burns*
Art Editor: *Gregory Dulles*
Manufacturing Manager: *Trudy Pisciotti*
Manufacturing Buyer: *Lisa McDowell*
Marketing Manager: *Pamela Hersperger*
Translator: *Angelika Shafir*

© 2005 Pearson Education, Inc.
Pearson Prentice Hall
Pearson Education, Inc.
Upper Saddle River, NJ 07458

Authorized translation from the German language edition entitled *Linux Netzwerkarchitektur: Design und Implementierung von Netzwerkprotokollen im Linux-Kern* published by Addison-Wesley, an imprint of Pearson Education Deutschland GmbH, München, ©2002.

Printed in the United States of America

10 9 8 7 6 5 4 3 2 1

ISBN 0-13-177720-3

Pearson Education Ltd., *London*
Pearson Education Australia Pty. Ltd., *Sydney*
Pearson Education Singapore, Pte. Ltd.
Pearson Education North Asia Ltd., *Hong Kong*
Pearson Education Canada, Inc., *Toronto*
Pearson Educación de Mexico, S.A. de C.V.
Pearson Education—Japan, *Tokyo*
Pearson Education Malaysia, Pte. Ltd.
Pearson Education, Inc., *Upper Saddle River, New Jersey*

Contents

Preface

This book deals with the architecture of the network subsystem in the Linux kernel. The idea for this book was born at the Institute of Telematics at the University of Karlsruhe, Germany, where the Linux kernel has been used in many research projects and its network functionality is modified or enhanced, respectively, in a targeted way. For instance, new services and protocols were developed for the next-generation Internet, and their behavior was studied. In addition, existing protocols, such as the TCP transport protocol, were modified to improve their behavior and adapt them to the new situation in the Internet.

In the course of these research projects, it has been found that the Linux kernel is very suitable for studying new network functionalities, because it features a stable and extensive implementation of the TCP/IP protocol family. The freely available source code allows us to modify and enhance the functionality of protocol instances easily. In addition, the enhancement of the kernel functionality is very elegantly supported by the principle of the kernel modules. However, many studies and theses in this field showed that familiarization with the Linux network architecture, which is required before you can modify the behavior of a protocol instance, demands considerable work and time. Unfortunately, this is mainly due to the facts that the network subsystem of the Linux kernel is poorly documented and that there is no material that would explain and summarize the basic concepts.

Although there are a few books that deal with the Linux kernel architecture and introduce its basic concepts, none of these books includes a full discussion of the network implementation. This situation may be due to the following two reasons:

- The network subsystem in the Linux kernel is very complex. As mentioned above, it implements a large number of protocols, which is probably one good reason for the enormous success of Linux. Both [BoCe00] and [BBDK+01] mention that the description of all these protocols and their concepts would actually fill an entire book. Well, you are reading such a book now, and, as you can see, it has eventually turned out to be quite a large volume, although it describes only part of the network functionality, in addition to the basic concepts of the Linux network architecture.

- Operating-system developers normally deal with the classical topics of system architecture—for example, the management of memories, processes, and devices, or the synchronization of parallel activities in a system—rather than with the handling of network packets. As you go along in this book, you will surely notice that it has been written not by system developers, but by computer-science specialists and communication engineers.

While considering the facts that there was little documentation covering the Linux network architecture and that students had to familiarize themselves with it over and over again, we had the idea of creating a simple documentation of the Linux network architecture ourselves. Another wish that eventually led to the more extensive concept of this book was a stronger discussion of important communication issues: *design and implementation of network protocols in real-world systems*. Networking courses teach students the most important concepts and standards in the field of telecommunication, but the design and implementation of network functionality (mainly of network protocols) by use of computer-science concepts has enjoyed little attention in teaching efforts, despite the fact that this knowledge could have been used often within the scope of studies and theses. The authors consider the description of the implementation of the Linux network architecture and its structure, interfaces, and applied concepts a step towards strengthening the informatics component in networking classes.

The authors hope that this book will help to make the processes and structures of the Linux network architecture easier to understand, and, above all, that our readers will have fun dealing with it and perhaps learn a few things about the networking concept and its practical implementation.

The content of this book corresponds to our knowledge of the Linux network architecture. This knowledge is neither comprehensive nor exhaustive. Nevertheless, we have tried to represent the processes and structures of the Linux network architecture in a fashion as easily understandable and detailed as possible. We are thankful for all hints, suggestions for improvement, ideas, and comments, and we will try to consider them in later editions. Updated information about the Linux network architecture and this book is available online at `http://www.Linux-netzwerkarchitektur.de`.

ORGANIZATION OF THIS BOOK

Chapter 1 will deal intensively with the motivation behind Linux in general and the Linux network architecture in particular; Chapter 2 is an introduction into the basic mechanisms and components of the Linux kernel. To keep the volume of this book manageable, we will discuss only those components that are important for understanding the Linux network architecture. With regard to the other components of the Linux kernel, we refer our readers to other books (e.g., [BBDK+01]).

Chapter 3 is an introduction to the general architecture of communication systems and the functionality of protocols and protocol instances. It includes an introduction to the popular TCP/IP and ISO/OSI layering models.

Chapters 4 and 5 discuss fundamental concepts of the Linux network architecture, including the representation and management of network packets in the Linux kernel (see *Socket Buffers*—Chapter 4) and the concept of *network devices* (Chapter 5). Network devices form the links between the protocol instances on the higher layers and hide the particularities of the respective network adapters behind a uniform interface.

Chapter 6 gives an overview of the activity forms in the Linux network architecture and the flow of transmit and receive processes. In addition, this chapter introduces the interface to the higher-layer protocol instances.

Chapters 7 through 12 discuss protocols and mechanisms of the *data link layer*. More specifically, it describes the *SLIP*, *PPP*, and *PPP-over-Ethernet* protocols and how the *ATM* and *Bluetooth* network technologies are supported in Linux. Finally, we will describe how a Linux computer can be used as a *transparent bridge*.

Our discussion of the TCP/IP protocols starts with an overview of the *TCP/IP protocol family* in Chapter 13. We will begin with a brief history of the Internet, then give an overview of the different protocols within the TCP/IP protocol family. Chapter 14 will deal with the *Internet Protocol* and its mechanisms in detail. In addition, it introduces the *IP options* and the *ICMP protocol*. Chapters 15 through 23 discuss the following protocols and mechanisms on the network layer: *ARP*, *routing*, *multicasting*, *traffic control*, *firewalls*, *connection tracking*, *NAT*, *KIDS*, and *IPv6*.

Chapters 24 and 25 describe the *TCP* and *UDP* transport protocols, respectively. We will close our discussion of the kernel with an explanation of the *socket interface*, in Chapter 26, then end with a short overview of the *programming of network functionality* on the application level.

The appendix includes additional information and introduces tools facilitating your work with the Linux network architecture. The issues dealt with include the *LXR source code browser*, *debugging work in the Linux kernel*, and *tools* you can use to manage and monitor the Linux network architecture.

ADDITIONAL SOURCES OF INFORMATION

This section lists a few useful sources of information where you can find additional information about the Linux network architecture.

Magazines

- The *Linux Magazine* (`http://www.Linux-mag.com`) is probably the best-known Linux magazine. It features articles about all issues that are of interest when you deal with Linux. Of special interest is the *Kernel Corner* column, which regularly publishes articles about the architecture and implementation of components of the Linux kernel—most of them by developers themselves.

- *Linux Focus* (`http://www.linuxfocus.org`) is an online magazine publishing articles in many different languages. It also includes a *Kernel Corner*.

- The *Linux Gazette* (`http://www.linuxgazette.com`) is another online magazine dedicated to Linux.

Useful Links in the World Wide Web

▓ Linux Headquarters: `http://www.linuxhq.com`

▓ Linux Documentation Project: `http://www.linuxdoc.org`

▓ Linux Weekly News: `http://www.lwn.net`

Other Information

▓ *Howtos* include a lot of information about different Linux issues. Most deal with the configuration and installation of various Linux functionalities. Especially for the Linux kernel, there are also a few howto documents—for example, how to use locks in the kernel [Russ00b], and general information on *hacking* in the Linux kernel [Russ00c]. Of course, we should not forget to mention the networking howto, which includes a wealth of tips and information about configuring the network functionality in Linux [Drak00].

▓ The source code of the current kernels is found at `ftp.kernel.org`. There are also mirrors of this FTP server, a list of which can be found at `http://www.kernel.org/mirrors/`.

▓ Information about components and drivers of the Linux kernel are also included directly in the source code of a kernel version, in the Documentation subdirectory. In addition, the file Documentation/kernel-docs.txt includes a list of current information about the Linux kernel—for example, documentation, links, and books. (It's worth taking a look at this file!)

CONVENTIONS USED IN THIS BOOK

This book uses the following typographical conventions to emphasize various elements of the Linux kernel, source texts, and other things.

Functions

A gray bar denotes important functions. A bar describes the function name on the left and the file name (within the kernel's source-code tree) on the right.

When giving a function name in such a place and throughout the body of this book, we normally leave out the parameters, because they would take up much space and impair the readability and text flow.

In general, when introducing a function, we describe the entire parameter set and give a brief description. The variable type is normally left out. For example, the description of the function `int ip_rcv(struct sk_buff *skb, struct net_device *dev, struct packet_type *pt)` from the file `net/ipv4/ip_input.c` is denoted as follows:

`ip_rcv()`	**net/ipv4/ip_input.c**

Throughout the body of this book, we would then refer to this function as `ip_rcv()` or `ip_rcv(skb, dev, pt)`.

Variables, Function Names, Source Text Excerpts, and so on

A sans-serif font is used for excerpts from the source code, variable and function names, and other keywords referred to in the text.

Commands, Program Names, and so on

A sans-serif font is used for the names of programs and command-line tools. Parameters that should be passed unchanged are also printed in sans-serif; those parameters that have to be replaced by values are printed in *sans-serif italic*.

Direct input in the command line is often denoted by a leading shell prompt—for example,

Files, Directories, Web Links, and so on

A sans-serif font is used for files and directories. We generally give the relative path in the kernel source code for files of the Linux kernel (e.g., net/ivp4/ip_input.c). Web links are also printed in sans-serif font (e.g., http://www.Linux-netzwerkarchitektur.de).

Other Conventions

Italic text denotes emphasis, or an introduction to a key term or concept.

ACKNOWLEDGMENTS

Many people's contributions were indispensable in the creation and production of this book. First and foremost, we would like to thank all students who studied the structure of the Linux network architecture in their papers and theses. They contributed enormously to collecting knowledge about the Linux network architecture at the Institute of Telematics:

Nasieh Abdel-Haq, Paul Burczek, Michael Conrad, Frank Dinies, Paul Hankes Drielsma, Jérôme Freilinger, Carolin Gärtner, Stefan Götz, Karsten Hahn, Artur Hecker, Tobias Hinkel, Michael Hofele, Verena Kahmann, Vera Kießling, Stefan Klett, Andreas Kramm, Jan Kratt, Eckehardt Luhm, David Metzler, Ulrich Mohr, Rainer Müller, Sven Oberländer, Vincent Oberle, Jan Oetting, Torsten Pastoors, Christian Pick, Christian Schneider, Steffen Schober, Marcus Schöller, Achim Settelmeier, Uwe Walter, and Jürgen Walzenbach.

The authors wrote this book mainly for their students.

Much appreciation is due to Professor Gerhard Krüger, who has always supported our activities, given us the freedom necessary to write this book, and assisted us with valuable advice. His support also allowed us to procure a Linux test network, which served as the basis for our research activities at the Institute of Telematics in the field of services for the next-generation Internet.

Our special thanks go to all the folks at the publishing houses who published the original German version of this book and the English translation that you are currently reading. Particularly, we would like to thank our editors, Sylvia Hasselbach and Toni

Holm. Their admirable patience helped shepherd us through this book-writing process. The English translation was done by Angelika Shafir, whom we would also like to thank in this place. We also thank all the people who read the manuscript, especially Mark Doll, Sebastian Döweling, Thomas Geulig, Thorsten Sandfuchs, Marcus Schöller, Bernhard Thurm, Uwe Walter, Anja Wehrle, Kilian Weniger, and Friederike Daenecke.

Last but not least, we gratefully acknowledge the support, encouragement, and patience of our families and friends.

KARLSRUHE • BERKELEY • BERLIN • BRAUNSCHWEIG

KLAUS WEHRLE • FRANK PÄHLKE • HARTMUT RITTER • DANIEL MÜLLER • MARC BECHLER

The Linux® Networking Architecture

## PART I

The Linux Kernel

CHAPTER 1

Motivation

Digital data transmission and processing form the basis of our today's information society. Within a short time, the Internet has penetrated all areas of our daily lives, and most of us can surely not imagine everyday life without it. With its new services, it offers us ways to communicate, fascinating all social strata, but corporations and organizations also use the possibilities of the Internet as a basis for internal exchange of information and for communication and handling business with customers and partners.

The technique of the Internet has been developed during the past twenty years; the actual boom began with the introduction of the World Wide Web at the beginning of the nineties. Development has progressed since then; new protocols and standards have been integrated, improving now both the functionality and the security in the "global net."

As developments in the Internet progressed, so did the technologies of the underlying network: The first e-mails were sent over telephone lines at 1200 bits/s in the eighties, but we can now communicate over gigabit or terabit lines. In addition, new technologies for mobile communication are emerging, such as UMTS and Bluetooth.

All these technologies have one thing in common: They are integral parts of digital communication systems, allowing spatial communication and interaction of distributed applications and their users. Modern communication systems decompose these extremely complex tasks into several layers, and the instances of these layers interact via predefined protocols to supply the desired service.

Telematics[1] is a field that handles both the development and research of telecommunication systems (and their basic mechanisms) and the implementation and realization of these systems by using means of computer science. This means that, in addition to the design of communication systems and protocols, the implementation of these mechanisms is an important task within the telematics discipline. Unfortunately, many universities and academic institutions neglect this point. For example, during coverage

---

[1] *Telematics* is the subdiscipline of informatics that deals with the design and implementation of telecommunication systems by use of information technologies.

of the basics and the current standards with regard to communication protocols in detail, only very little knowledge is conveyed as to how these principles can be used (e.g., which basic principles of computer science can be used when implementing communication protocols).

With this book, the authors—who themselves teach computer-science students—attempt to contribute to promoting the computer-science component in telematics. Using the Linux operating system as an example, which the authors employ mainly for research purposes, in addition to the usual office applications (e-mail, World Wide Web, word processing, etc.), we will introduce the practical realization of communication systems and communication protocols. Essentially, the structuring of the network subsystem in the Linux kernel, the structuring of interfaces between network components, and the applied software methods will be used to show the reader various ways to implement protocols and network functionality.

In addition to its teaching use, of course, this book is also intended to address all those interested in the architecture of the network subsystem in the Linux kernel, taking a look behind the scenes at this poorly documented part of the Linux kernel. The following section discusses the Linux operating system and the reasons for its use in offices, companies, networks, and research.

1.1   THE LINUX OPERATING SYSTEM

Linux is a freely available multiuser, multitasking, multiprocessor, and multiplatform UNIX operating system. Its popularity and the number of users increase continually, making Linux an increasingly serious factor in the operating-systems market. Thanks to the freely available source code that everybody can obtain over the Internet and to the fact that everybody can participate in and contribute to the further development of the Linux system, many developers, all over the world, are constantly busy further developing this system, removing existing errors, and optimizing the system's performance.

The fact that most developers do this very time-consuming work for free in their spare time is a sign of the great fun working with Linux and mainly with the Linux kernel can be. As we progress in this book, we will try to pass some of this enthusiasm on to our readers. The large number of research projects at the University of Karlsruhe that have used, enhanced, or modified the Linux network architecture experienced a high motivation of all participating students. The reason was mainly that this offered them a way to participate in the "Linux movement."

The development of Linux was initiated by a student by the name of Linus B. Torvalds, in 1991. At that time, he worked five months on his idea of a new PC-based UNIX-like operating system, which he eventually made available for free on the Internet. It was intended to offer more functions than the Minix system designed by Andrew S. Tanenbaum, which was developed for teaching purposes only [Tane95]. With his message in the Minix newsgroup (see page 1), he set a movement in motion, the current result of which is one of the most stable and widely developed UNIX operating systems. Back then, Linus Torvalds planned only the development of a purely experimental system, but his idea further developed during the following years, so that Linux is now used successfully by many private people, corporations, and scientists alike.

Mainly, the interoperability with other systems (Apple, MS-Windows) and the ability to run on many different platforms (Intel x86, MIPS, PA-RISC, IA64, Alpha, ARM, Sparc, PowerPC, M68, S390) make Linux one of the most popular operating systems.

Not only the extensive functionality of Linux, but also the freely accessible source code of this operating system, have convinced many private people and companies to use Linux. In addition, the German government, with its program for the support of open-source software, promotes the use of freely available programs with freely available source code. The main reason for this is seen not in the low procurement cost, but in the transparency of the software used. In fact, anyone can view the source code and investigate its functionality. Above all, anyone can check what—perhaps security-relevant—functionalities or errors are contained in an application or operating system. Especially with commercial systems and applications, there are often speculations that they could convey information about the user or the installed applications to the manufacturer.

You do not have such fears with freely developed software, where such a behavior would be noticed and published quickly. Normally, several developers work concurrently on an open-source project in a distributed way over the Internet, monitoring themselves implicitly. After all, free software is not aimed at maximizing the profit of a company or its shareholders. Its goal is to develop high-quality software for everybody. Linux is a very good example showing that freely developed software is not just the hobby of a handful of freaks, but leads to serious and extremely stable applications.

The authors of this book use Linux mainly for research work in the network area. The freely available source texts allow us to implement and evaluate new theories and protocols in real-world networks. For example, Linux was used to study various modifications of the TCP transport protocol [WeRW01, Ritt01], to develop a framework for the KIDS QoS support [Wehr01b], and to develop the high-resolution UKA-APIC timer [WeRi00].

1.2 WHAT IS LINUX?

Originally, the term *Linux* described only the operating-system kernel that abstracts from the hardware of a system, offering applications a uniform interface. Over time, the term *Linux* has often come to mean the kernel (the *actual* Linux) together with the entire system environment, including the following components:

- the operating-system kernel (currently version 2.0, 2.2, or 2.4);
- the system programs (compiler, libraries, tools, etc.);
- the graphical user interface (e.g., XFree) and a window manager or an application environment (KDE, Gnome, FVWM, etc.);
- a large number of applications from all areas (editors, browsers, office applications, games, etc.).

Different components not forming part of the kernel originate largely from the GNU project of Free Software Foundation, which explains why the complete system environment is often called "GNU/Linux system." A characteristic common to the

Linux kernel and GNU programs is that they may all be freely distributed under the GNU Public License (GPL), provided that the source text is made publicly available. To the extent that enhancements or modifications have been effected to the programs, then these are automatically governed by the GNU license (i.e., their source text must also be made freely available). Since the advent of Linux, this has had the effect that the system has been further developed free from corporate policy interests and that it has been more strongly oriented to word its users' needs than are other, commercial operating systems. Anyone can participate in the development and implement new capabilities, ones based on the freely available source texts. This means that Linux is always involved in the support of international standards, and no attempt is made to enforce corporate or proprietary standards to secure a market position.

Errors made during the development of a piece of software are normally removed quickly. In addition, there is a continual effort to keep the system performing as well as possible. This has become very clear in the example of the network implementation in the last kernel version: After it had become known that the performance of Linux in the area of protocol handling on multiprocessor systems suffers from a few flaws, the network part was extensively rewritten to remove these faults. This means that Linux is an example that clearly shows the benefits of open-source projects:

- stability,
- performance, and
- security.

1.3 REASONS FOR USING LINUX

The previous section introduced the important properties and objectives of Linux as a free software project. This section will discuss a number of general properties of the Linux kernel, offering more reasons for its use:

- Linux supports *preemptive multitasking*: All processes run independently in different protected memory spaces, so that the failure of one process does not in any way impair the other processes. When a process claims too much computing time, its processor can be taken and allocated to another waiting application. Preemptive multitasking is a fundamental requirement for stable systems.
- *Multiprocessor*: Linux is one of the few operating systems supporting several processors in SMP (*Symmetric MultiProcessing*) operation. This means that several processes can be handled concurrently by different CPUs. Since kernel version 2.0, multiprocessor systems with Intel and Sparc processors are supported. Version 2.2 and the current Version 2.4 additionally improved the performance and parallelism in the Linux kernel.
- *Multiuser*: Several users can work concurrently in one system, when they are logged in over different consoles. In addition, users can work easily on several graphical user interfaces.

- *Multiplatform*: Linux was originally developed only for the personal computer (Intel 80386), but it runs on more than ten processor architectures today. The bandwidth of supported platforms extends from small digital personal assistants over the standard personal computer to mainframe architectures: Intel x86, MIPS, PA-RISC, IA64, Alpha, ARM, Sparc, PowerPC, M68, and so on.

- *Linux is a UNIX system*: It is compatible with the POSIX-1300.1 standard[2] and includes large parts of the functionality of UNIX System V and BSD. This means that you can use UNIX standard software under Linux.

- *Rich network functionality*: The Linux network architecture makes available an extensive choice of network protocols and functionalities in the networking area. The development of the Internet and its services is inseparably linked to UNIX systems. This is why the properties of the TCP/IP protocol family and its behavior can best be studied and controlled in a UNIX system. Other PC operating systems would be unsuitable for this, especially those with source code not publicly available.

- *Open source*: The source code of the entire Linux kernel is freely available and can be used according to the GNU Public License. A large number of programmers work on the further development of the Linux kernel all over the world, continually enhancing and improving it. Linux is distributed over the Internet so that each user can test the kernel and make improvements or enhancements. The development of Linux in this dimension would not have been possible without the Internet.

Formerly, users had to put up with defects in software they purchased; Linux now allows everyone to remove such defects. And it really works. An often heard criticism has been that the driver support for Linux is one of its major problems. This situation has changed dramatically during the past years. For instance, all actually available network cards are supported by Linux. In fact, we can rely to the Linux community to such an extent that there will soon be a matching driver for each new device.

- *Efficient network implementation*: Meanwhile, the Linux kernel makes available a well-structured implementation of the network functionality, which will be our main focus of discussion in the next 27 chapters of this book. The functions can be adapted to the special requirements of the desired system and meet the specifications of the Internet Engineering Task Force (IETF), IEE, and ISO better than many other systems.

In the creation of a new kernel, its desired functionality can be individually configured. For instance, you can enable a large number of optimization options or add specific functionalities (e.g., multicast support and various protocols). While the system is running, you can also use the Proc file system (see Section 2.8) to

---

[2]*Portable Operating System Interface based on UniX—POSIX 1300.1* defines a minimum interface that each UNIX-like operating system must offer.

change parameters—For example, various timeout values for the TCP transport protocol or configuration parameters of other protocol instances. There is even a way to use the Proc file system to enable and disable certain functions at runtime, such as packet forwarding.

- *IP Next Generation*: Since Version 2.1.38, the Linux kernel provides a stable and relatively complete implementation of the new Internet Protocol IPv6. (See Chapter 23.)

- And, finally, the best argument: *Linux is free of charge*. Everyone can download it from the Internet or buy it on CD for a few dollars, usually with a few gigabyte applications (some of them being more useful, some less) and with extensive installation instructions and free support. This means that, for very little money, you can get a high-performing, extremely stable, and easily adaptable operating system that turns a Pentium PC into a high-performing workstation, a highly reliable server, or an individually configurable Internet router.

This chapter has been a brief introduction to Linux; the next chapter will introduce the internal structure of the Linux kernel. We will then discuss the basic structure of communication systems in general and the structure of the Linux network architecture in particular.

# CHAPTER 2

The Kernel Structure

This chapter deals with the basic architecture of the Linux kernel and its components. It provides an overview of the most important areas of the kernel, such as the different forms of activity in the kernel, memory management, device drivers, timers, and modules. Each of these issues will be discussed briefly in this book, to give you an insight into the tasks and processes of each component. Detailed information about each of these issues is found in other books and references. A choice of corresponding sources is given in the bibliography, where we particularly recommend [RuCo01], [BBDK+01], and [BoCe00].

The goal of this chapter is to describe the framework in which the Linux network architecture operates. All areas described below offer basic functions required to offer network services in the first place. This is the reason why knowing them is an essential prerequisite for an understanding of the implementation of the Linux networking architecture.

Figure 2–1 shows the structure of the Linux kernel. The kernel can be divided into six different sections, each possessing a clearly defined functionality and offering this functionality to the other kernel components. This organization is reflected also in the kernel's source code, where each of these sections is structured in its own subtree.

Here we briefly describe these components.

- *Process management*: This area is responsible for creating and terminating processes and other activities of the kernel (software interrupts, tasklets, etc.). In addition, this is the area where interprocess communication (signals, pipes, etc.) takes place. The scheduler is the main component of process management. It handles all active, waiting, and blocked processes and takes care that all application processes obtain their fair share of the processor's computing time.
- *Memory management*: The memory of a computer is one of the most important resources. A computer's performance strongly depends on the main memory it is equipped with. In addition, memory management is responsible for allowing each process its own memory section, which has to be protected against access by other processes.

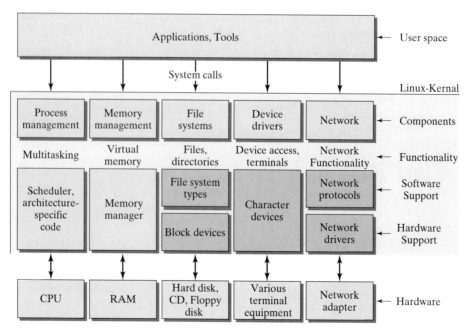

FIGURE 2–1
Structure of the Linux kernel according to [RuCo01].

- *File systems*: In UNIX, the file system assumes a central role. In contrast to other operating systems (e.g., Windows NT), almost everything is handled over the file-system interface. For example, device drivers can be addressed as files, and the Proc file system (see Section 2.8) allows you to access data and parameters within the kernel. These two functionalities can be used very effectively and elegantly, so that they are often used for debugging purposes. (See Appendix B.)

- *Device drivers*: Device drivers abstract from the underlying hardware in every operating system, and they allow you to access this hardware. The modular concept of Linux we will introduce in Section 2.4 offers a way to add or remove device drivers during a running operation, despite its monolithic kernel.

- *Network*: All network operations have to be managed by the operating system, because certain network operations cannot be allocated to a specific process, such as handling an incoming packet. Incoming packets are asynchronous events. They have to be collected, identified, and forwarded before a process can handle them. This is the reason why the kernel is responsible for the handling of packets across program and network interfaces.

Within the kernel, defined interfaces are used to facilitate the design of new functionalities. For instance, there is an interface to the virtual file system, which can be used to add new file systems. The availability of more than a dozen supported file systems shows clearly that this interface was a good design decision by the Linux developers, because no other operating system provides such a large supply of supported file systems. The Linux network architecture also includes many interfaces supporting the dynamic enhancement of the wealth of protocols and network drivers.

The components shown on dark background in Figure 2–1 provide interfaces for the dynamic registration of new functionalities, so that such functionalities can be easily implemented in modules.

2.1   MONOLITHIC ARCHITECTURES AND MICROKERNELS

In contrast to current operating-system developments tending toward a microkernel architecture, the Linux operating system is based on a monolithic kernel. In microkernel architectures, such as the Mach kernel [Tane95] or the Windows NT kernel, the operating system kernel represents merely the absolute necessary minimum of functionality. Good examples are interprocess communication (IPC) and memory management (MM). Building on the microkernel, the remaining functionality of the operating system is moved to independent processes or threads, running outside the operating system kernel. They use a defined interface to communicate with the microkernel, generally via system calls.

In monolithic kernels, to which the Linux kernel belongs, the entire functionality is concentrated in one (large) kernel. In addition to the basic mechanisms known from microkernels, the Linux operating system kernel also includes device drivers, file system drivers, most instances of the network protocols, and much more. (See Figure 2–1.) Compared to microkernel architectures, the use of a monolithic kernel has both benefits and drawbacks, as we will see below.

The benefits include the fact that the entire functionality of the operating system is concentrated in the kernel, allowing the system to work more efficiently. You can access resources directly from within the kernel, so costly system calls and context changes are needed less frequently. One major drawback is that the source code for the operating system kernel can quickly become rather complex, even messy, because no defined interfaces are required within the kernel. In addition, the development of new drivers can be made more difficult by the lack of an interface definition. For example, if you install a new device, you have to retranslate the entire kernel to ensure that this device driver can be compiled with the kernel, a need avoided by microkernel architectures.

That Linux is based on a monolithic operating-system kernel is due to historical reasons. A system that had not been planned to become such a big project, at the beginning, has continually been developed further, so that it became impossible, at some point in time, to migrate to a microkernel architecture. However, since Version 2.0, Linux has made a step towards microkernel architectures. More specifically, the possibility was created of moving certain functionalities into modules, which are loaded into the kernel at runtime, from which they can be removed again.

This removed an important drawback of monolithic kernels and opened the way to loading drivers or other functionalities at runtime. In addition, modularization offers another benefit: Uniform interfaces are defined. This feature had previously been characteristic only of microkernel architectures. Linux has a number of such interfaces, allowing the kernel to be dynamically enhanced by a number of functionalities. This very flexibility and openness of its interfaces is one of the most important benefits of Linux.

TABLE 2–1 Interfaces in the Linux kernel to embed new functionalities.

Functionality	Functions for Dynamic Registration
Character devices	`(un)register_chrdev( )`
Block devices	`(un)register_blkdev( )`
Binary formats	`(un)register_binfmt( )`
File systems	`(un)register_filesystem( )`
Serial interfaces	`(un)register_serial( )`
Network adapters	`(un)register_netdev( )`
Layer-3 protocols	`dev_add_pack( )`, `dev_remove_pack( )`
Layer-4 protocols (TCP/IP)	`inet_add_protocol( )`, `inet_del_protocol( )`
Console drivers	`tty_(un)register_driver( )`
Symbol tables	`(un)register_symtab( )`
Modules	`init_module( )`, `cleanup_module( )`

Table 2–1 shows a selection of the most important interfaces, including the pertinent methods used to register and unregister functionalities.

Despite its modularization, Linux has preserved a major benefit of monolithic kernels: All functions implemented in modules run in protected kernel mode, which means that they do not require any context change when called from within the kernel. This can be seen as a clever combination of the benefits from both main operating-system architectures.

The following sections briefly introduce the kernel components, to better explain the Linux network architecture. You should know the structure and properties of these components to understand how the Linux network architecture works. We refer again to [RuCo01, BBDK+01, BoCe00] for an in-depth study of the Linux kernel components described below.

2.2 ACTIVITIES IN THE LINUX KERNEL

Linux is a multitasking system. This means that several application processes can be active, and several applications can be used, simultaneously. In multiprocessor systems, which have been supported since kernel Version 2.0, even several applications or their processes can be processed in parallel. However, a process is not the only form of activity you can execute in the Linux kernel.

2.2.1 Processes and System Calls

Processes are normally activities that are started to run a specific application, and they are terminated once the application is through. Creating, controlling, and destroying of processes are tasks handled by the kernel of an operating system. Processes operate exclusively in the user address space (i.e., in unprotected mode) of a processor, where they can access only the memory section allocated to them. An attempt to access memory sections of other processes or the kernel address space leads to an *exception*, which has to be dealt with by the kernel.

However, when a process wants to access devices or use a functionality of the operating-system kernel, it has to use a system call to do this. A system call causes the processor to change to the protected mode, and access to the kernel address space is a function of the system call. All devices and memory sections can be accessed in protected mode, but only with methods of the kernel.

The work of processes and system calls can be interrupted by other activities. In such a case, their current state (contents of CPU registers, MMU registers, etc.) is saved; then it is restored when the interrupted process or system call resumes its work. Processes and system calls can be stopped voluntarily or involuntarily. In the first case, they cede processing voluntarily—for example, when they wait for a system resource (external device, semaphore, etc.) and go to sleep until that resource becomes available. Involuntary cession of processing is caused by interrupts, which tell the kernel that an important action has taken place, one that the kernel should be dealing with. This could be a notification about availability of a previously busy resource.

In addition to normal processes and to processes within a system call, we distinguish between further forms of activity in the Linux kernel. These forms of activity are of decisive importance for the Linux network architecture, because the network functionality is handled in the kernel. We will explain the following forms of activity in more detail in the next sections, when we will be discussing mainly their tasks within the Linux network architecture:

- Kernel threads;
- interrupts (hardware IRQs);
- software interrupts (soft IRQs);
- tasklets; and
- bottom halves.

When thinking of the different forms of activity in the kernel (except processes in the system call and kernel threads), an important point will be the parallel execution of the respective form of activity. On the one hand, this concerns the question of whether the instance of a form of activity can be executed concurrently on several processors; on the other hand, of whether two different instances of one form of activity can be executed concurrently on several processors. Table 2–2 shows an overview of these possibilities.

Another interesting thing about the individual forms of activity is to know by what other forms of activity they can be interrupted; Table 2–3 gives an overview. This information is important mainly for protection from undesired side effects caused by concurrent or overlapping operations of two activities on a jointly used data structure. This problem and possible solutions are discussed in detail in Section 2.3. That section will introduce locking mechanisms that, though offering protection against undesired side effects, can reduce a system's performance when used too cautiously. For this reason, it is important to know when which locking mechanisms are required. Note that the possible parallelism and interruptability of different forms of activity play an important role.

TABLE 2–2   Concurrent execution of same activities on several processors.

	Same Activity	Different Activities
HW IRQ	—	•
Soft IRQ	•	•
Tasklet	—	•
Bottom half	—	—

TABLE 2–3   Interruption of activities by other forms of kernel activities.

	HW-IRQ	Soft-IRQ	Tasklet	Bottom Half
HW IRQ	$+/-^1$	–	–	–
Soft IRQ	+	–	–	–
Tasklet	+	–	–	–
Bottom half	+	–	–	–
System call	+	+	+	+
Process	+	+	+	+

[1]Only slow interrupts can be interrupted by other interrupts, as we will see in Section 2.2.2.

2.2.2   Hardware Interrupts

Peripherals use hardware interrupts (often abbreviated as HW IRQs) to inform an operating system about important events (e.g., that the mouse has been moved, a key has been pressed, or a packet has arrived in the network adapter). Hardware interrupts interrupt the current activity in one of the processors and execute the pertinent interrupt-handling routine.

The handling routine for a specific interrupt can be registered at runtime by using the function request_irq(). Details about the registration and management of interrupts are described in [RuCo01]. free_irq() is used to release the handling routine of an interrupt, so that it is no longer executed.

We distinguish between two types of interrupts in the Linux kernel:

- *Fast interrupts* are characterized by the fact that they have a very short interrupt-handling routine and so interrupt the current activity only very briefly. One characteristic of fast interrupts is that all other interrupts in the local CPU are locked while it is executed, so that the interrupt-handling routine cannot be interrupted. Fast interrupts are designated by the flag SA_INTERRUPT when they are registered with request_irq().

- *Slow interrupts* can be interrupted by other interrupts during their execution. They normally have a much longer-interrupt handling routing than fast interrupts and so would claim the processor for too long. This is the reason why only the repeated execution of that interrupt is stopped when a slow interrupt is executed.

Interrupts can generally stop all other activities when they are executed. (See Table 2–3.) At the same time, various interrupts in several CPUs can be handled concurrently, but the interrupt-handling routine of a specific interrupt can be executed only in one CPU at a time.

You can call the function `in_irq()` (`include/asm/hardirq.h`) to check whether the current activity is an interrupt-handling routine (see details in [Russ00b]).

Top Halfs and Bottom Halfs   Interrupt-handling routines should be executed as soon as possible after the interrupt was triggered and interrupt the current activity only briefly. But not every task can be executed by few instructions. For example, handling of a packet arrived in a network adapter requires several thousand ticks, until the packet can be passed on to the relevant process in the user address space. Though it is triggered by an interrupt, this task cannot be done in an interrupt-handling routine.

To keep interrupt handling as short as possible, such time-consuming tasks are divided into two parts:

- The so-called *top half* runs only the most important tasks after a triggered interrupt. The top half corresponds to the interrupt-handling routine. As we will see in Chapter 6, for example, the interrupt-handling routine of a network adapter might just copy the arrived packet to the kernel, where it will be buffered in a queue pending detailed handling by the corresponding protocol instances.
- The *bottom half* runs all operations that are not time-critical and which could not be executed within the interrupt-handling routine for time reasons. The bottom half is scheduled for execution while the top half is running, and, as soon as the scheduler is called again upon completion of the interrupt, it will most likely run the bottom half (depending on the bottom half's type).

For example, if a packet arrives, then the tasks of the bottom half are run by the software interrupt `NET_RX_SOFTIRQ`. (See Chapter 6.)

The following sections introduce three possible activities that can be used as the bottom half in the interrupt-handling process.

2.2.3 Software Interrupts

Software interrupts (or soft IRQs for short) are actually a form of activity that can be scheduled for later execution rather than real interrupts. Software and hardware interrupts differ mainly in that a hardware interrupt actively interrupts another form of activity: Triggering the interrupt causes the (immediate) interruption of the running activity (but, of course, only if the triggering of interrupts is currently allowed).

In contrast, a software interrupt is scheduled for execution by an activity of the kernel and has to wait until it is called by the scheduler. Software interrupts scheduled for execution are started by the function `do_softirq()` (`kernel/softirq.c`). This means that the running activity is not interrupted when a soft IRQ is activated by `__cpu_raise_softirq()`. The corresponding handling routine is triggered when `do_softirq()` is called. This occurs currently only when a system call (in `schedule()`) or a hardware interrupt (in `do_IRQ()`) terminates.

A maximum of 32 software interrupts can be defined in the Linux kernel. Note that only four were defined in the Versions 2.4.x. This includes the soft IRQs NET_RX_SOFTIRQ and NET_TX_SOFTIRQ, which have ensured efficient protocol handling since kernel Version 2.4, and the soft IRQ TASKLET_SOFTIRQ, which is used to implement the concept of tasklets, further described later in this chapter.

Software interrupts differ clearly from the *tasklet* and *bottom half* forms of activity, as we have seen in Tables 2–2 and 2–3. The most important properties of software interrupts are the following:

- A software interrupt can run concurrently in several processors. This means that the handling routine has to be implemented reentrantly (e.g., with net_rx_action). If critical sections exist in a software interrupt (e.g., any global variable it accesses), then these have to be protected by locks.
- A software interrupt cannot interrupt itself while running on a processor.
- A software interrupt can be interrupted during its handling on a processor only by a hardware interrupt.

Calling in_softirq() (include/asm/softirq.h) causes a function to check immediately on whether it is currently in a software interrupt; see details in [Russ00b].

2.2.4   Tasklets

Tasklets are a combination of parallel executable (but lock-intensive) software interrupts and the old bottom halfs,[1] where we can talk neither of parallelism nor of performance. Tasklets were introduced to replace the old bottom halfs.

Tasklets have the following properties:

- The function tasklet_schedule(&tasklet_struct) can be used to schedule a tasklet for execution. A tasklet is run only once, even if it was scheduled for execution several times.
- A tasklet can run on one processor only at any given time.
- Different tasklets can run on several processors concurrently.

The macro DECLARE_TASKLET(name, func, data) can be used to define a new tasklet, where name denotes a name for the tasklet_struct data structure and func denotes the tasklet's handling routine. When the tasklet is to run, then the pointer data, pointing to private data, if applicable, are passed to the function func().

Tasklet_schedule() is used to schedule a tasklet for execution; tasklet_disable() can be used to stop a tasklet from running, even when it is scheduled for execution. It remains scheduled for execution or can be rescheduled. Tasklet_enable() is used to reactivate a deactivated tasklet. However, if that tasklet was not scheduled for execution, it will not run when you activate it.

---

[1] In this connection, we have to differentiate between the general concept of a bottom half that can be implemented by a tasklet (a soft IRQ) and a bottom half in the Linux kernel. In contrast, the form of activity of a bottom half is Linux-specific and denoted by sans-serif font in this text.

The following example shows how easy it is to define and activate a new tasklet:

```
#include <linux/interrupt.h>
/* Handling routine of new tasklet */
void test_func(unsigned long);
/* Data of new tasklet */
char test_data[] = "Hello, I am a test tasklet";
/* Definition of tasklet_struct structure of tasklet */
DECLARE_TASKLET (test_tasklet, test_func, (unsigned long) &test_data);
void test_func(unsigned long data)
{
        /*Do here what you think you have to do, e.g.:*/
        printk(KERN_DEBUG "%s\n", (char *) data);
}
...
/* Use an activity to activate the tasklet */
tasklet_schedule(&test_tasklet);
```

2.2.5   Bottom Halfs

Bottom halfs (BHs) had been the main form of activity in the kernel in early kernels. For example, NET_BH was responsible for handling of network protocols and sending of packets. There can be a maximum of 32 BHs, which are scheduled for execution by the mark_bh() function.

BHs are the form of activity with the smallest parallelism in the kernel, as mentioned in previous sections. The following property shows the major drawback of BHs:

◾ Only one bottom half can run concurrently on all processors of a system at one time.

Because BHs are inflexible and because they are to be replaced by tasklets or software interrupts in future Linux kernel versions, we will not discuss them further here. Information on BHs is found in the literature (e.g., [RuCo01], [BBDK+01] or [BoCe00]).

2.3   LOCKING—ATOMIC OPERATIONS

Several different forms of activity can operate and interrupt each other in the Linux kernel. (See Section 2.2.) In multiprocessor systems, different activities even operate in parallel. This is the reason why it is very important for the stability of the system that these operations run in parallel without undesired side effects.

As long as the activities in the Linux kernel operate independently, there will not be any problem. But as soon as several activities access the same data structures, there can be undesired effects, even in single-processor systems.

Figure 2–2 shows an example with two activities, A and B, trying to add the structures skb_a and skb_b to the list queue. At some point, activity A is interrupted by activity B. After some processing of B, A continues with its operations. Figure 2–3 shows the result of this procedure of the two activities. Structure skb_b was added to the list correctly.

A
B
skb_a->next = queue->next;
skb_b->next = queue->next;
queue->next = skb_b;
queue->next = skb_a;

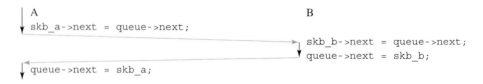

FIGURE 2–2
Activity *B* interrupts activity *A* in the critical section.

queue
next
...
skb_c
next
...
queue
next
...
skb_a
next
...
skb_c
next
...
skb_b
next
...

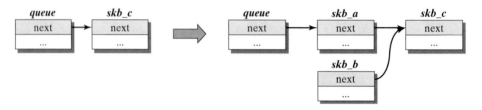

FIGURE 2–3
(Undesired) result of the unprotected operations of activities *A* and *B*.

A
skb_a->next = queue->next;
queue->next = skb_a;
B
skb_b->next = queue->next;
queue->next = skb_b;

FIGURE 2–4
Parallel operations of the activities *A* and *B* in the critical section.

Undesired results can also occur in multiprocessor systems when the two activities *A* and *B* run quasi-in-parallel on different processors, as in the example shown in Figure 2–4.

To avoid these problems when several activities operate on a common data structure (the so-called *critical section*), then these operations have to be *atomic*. Atomic means that an operation composed of several steps is executed as an undividable operation. No other instance can operate on the data structure concurrently with the atomic operation (i.e., no other activity can access a critical section that's already busy [Tan95]).

The next four sections introduce mechanisms for atomic execution of operations. These mechanisms differ mainly in the way they wait for entry into a potentially occupied critical section, which implicitly depends on the size of the critical section and the expected waiting time.

2.3.1 Bit Operations

Atomic bit operations form the basis for the locking concepts *spinlocks* and *semaphores*, described in the following subsections. Locks are used to protect critical sections, and they are normally implemented by variables, which manage the status of locks (i.e., they remember how many activities there currently are in a critical section.

This means that, first of all, the status of locking variables has to be checked and then set, before entry into a critical section. In a processor, this generally adds up to two machine commands to be executed, one after the other. However, it can now happen that a situation like the one described above can occur exactly between these two machine commands (i.e., the activity is interrupted and another activity of the kernel changes the state of variables). For this reason, atomic test and set machine commands are required to support critical sections. Modern processors support these commands and many more. (It would go beyond the scope of this book to describe each one in detail.)

Some of these atomic machine operations, as well as useful operations to manipulate single bits or integer variables, which are often useful to handle protocol headers, are listed in the following examples. Another benefit of these atomic operations is that no additional locks are required for their operations. They run in one single (very fast) machine command.

- `test_and_set_bit(nr, void *addr)` sets the bit with number `nr` in the unsigned long variables of the pointer `addr`. The previous value of the bit is returned as return value.
- `test_and_clear_bit(nr, void *addr)` deletes the specified bit and also returns that bit's previous value.
- `test_and_change_bit(nr, void *addr)` inverts bit `nr` and resets it to its original value.
- `set_bit(nr, void *addr)` sets the bit with number `nr` at address `addr`.
- `clear_bit(nr, void *addr)` deletes the specified bit.
- `change_bit(nr, void *addr)` inverts bit number `nr`.
- `test_bit(nr, void *addr)` returns the current values of the bits.

Integer Operations   Operations can also be run atomically on integers. To do this, however, you have to use the `atomic_t` data type, which corresponds to the `int` data type in all supported architectures.

- `atomic_set(atomic_t *var, int i)` sets the variables to value `i`.
- `atomic_read(atomic_t *var)` reads the variables.
- `atomic_add/atomic_sub(int i, atomic_t *var)` adds or subtracts.
- `atomic_inc/atomic_dec(atomic_t *var)` adds or subtracts in increments of 1.
- `atomic_...._and_test(...)`: see *Bit Operations*.

All of these atomic operations are implemented by one single machine command. However, critical sections often cannot be reduced to one single command, but consist of several operations. Using the atomic bit or integer operations introduced in this section, you can implement locks to protect larger ranges for exclusive access. These *spinlocks* and *semaphores* are introduced in the following subsections.

2.3.2   Spinlocks

Spinlocks are also called *busy wait locks* because of the way they work. When a critical section begins and the lock—in this case the spinlock—has already been set, then the processor waits actively until the lock is removed. This means that the processor continues testing the locking variable in a continuous loop until that locking variable is released by the locking activity.

Though this wastes computing time because the processor seems to continually test the locking variable "meaninglessly," it can prove more effective to continually test the lock for a brief moment and then be able to enter the critical section upon its release rather than call the scheduler and grant the computing time to another activity. A lot of time can elapse until the waiting activity will get its turn after the lock's release. In addition, a change of activity caused by calling the scheduler could eventually take more computing time than a brief wait in the *busy wait loop*. For this reason, we observe the principle that spinlocks represent the best locking method for small critical program points (i.e., points with short locking times).

In the Linux kernel, spinlocks are implemented by the variable `spinlock_t`, which consists of one single integer locking variable. To use a spinlock, you have to create and initialize a `spinlock_t` structure, as in the following example:

```
#include <linux/spinlock.h>
spinlock_t my_spinlock = SPIN_LOCK_UNLOCKED;
/* You can also use spin_lock_init(&my_spinlock) instead of
   an assignment in the definition. */
```

You can now use a set of different functions to request, set, or release spinlocks. Each of these functions is especially suited for certain application cases. First, let's look at how we can set a spinlock:

- `spin_lock(spinlock_t *my_spinlock)` tries to set the spinlock `my_spinlock`. If it is not free, then we have to wait or test until it is released. The free spinlock is then set immediately.
- `spin_lock_irqsave(spinlock_t *my_spinlock, unsigned long flags)` works similarly to `spin_lock()`, but it additionally prevents interrupts and stores the current value of the CPU status register in the variable flags.
- `spin_lock_irq(spinlock_t *my_spinlock)` works similarly to `spin_lock_irqsave()`, but does not store the value of the CPU status register. It assumes that interrupts are already being prevented.
- Similar to `spin_lock()`, `spin_lock_bh(spinlock_t *my_spinlock)` tries to set the lock, but it prevents bottom halfs (see Section 2.2.5) from running at the same time.

The following functions can be used to mark the end of the critical section, depending on the application. Each of them releases an occupied spinlock.

- `spin_unlock(spinlock_t *my_spinlock)` releases an occupied spinlock.
- `spin_unlock_irqrestore(spinlock_t *my_spinlock, unsigned long flags)` releases the specified spinlock and allows interrupts, if there were any activated interrupts when the CPU status register was saved to the variable flags; otherwise it doesn't allow interrupts.
- `spin_unlock_irq(spinlock_t *my_spinlock)` releases the specified spinlock and allows interrupts.
- `spin_unlock_bh(spinlock_t *my_spinlock)` also releases the lock and allows immediate processing of bottom halfs.

The functions introduced above can be used to protect critical sections to avoid undesired side effects from parallel operations on the critical sections from occurring. The example shown in Figures 2–2 and 2–4 can be used as follows, where the use of a spinlock prevents undesired side effects:

```
#include <linux/spinlock.h>
spinlock_t my_spinlock = SPIN_LOCK_UNLOCKED;
// Activity A
spin_lock(&my_spinlock);
skb_a->next = queue->next;
queue->next = skb_a;
spin_unlock(&my_spinlock);

...
// Activity B
spin_lock(&my_spinlock);
skb_b->next = queue->next;
queue->next = skb_b;
spin_unlock(&my_spinlock);
```

The following useful functions are available to handle spinlocks, in addition to the methods used to set and release spinlocks:

- `spin_is_locked(spinlock_t *my_lock)` polls the current status of the lock, without changing it. For a set lock, a value unequal to zero is return; for a free lock, zero is returned.
- `spin_trylock(spinlock_t *my_lock)` sets the spinlock, if it is currently unoccupied; otherwise, the functions immediately returns a value unequal to zero.
- `spin_unlock_wait(spinlock_t *my_lock)` waits for the lock to be released, if the lock is occupied, but the lock is not set.

2.3.3 Read–Write Spinlocks

Spinlocks represent a simple and useful element to protect parallel operations on common data structures from undesired side effects. However, they slow down the progress of activities, because these activities have to wait *actively* for locks to be released. Active waiting is not always necessary in certain situations. For example, there are data structures with frequent read, but few write accesses. A well-known example from the Linux network architecture for this situation would be the list of registered network devices, dev_base. It is rarely changed during a system's runtime (in fact, only by registering a network device), but it is subject to many read accesses.

During accessing of such a jointly used data structure, it is absolutely necessary to use a spinlock, but reading activities do not have to be stopped when no write activity currently operates on that data structure. This is the reason why so-called *read–write spinlocks* are used. They allow several read activities to enter a critical section while there is no write activity operating on it. As soon as an activity with write intention occupies the lock, then no read activities must be in or enter the critical section until the write lock is released.

When we are adding a new net_device structure in our above example of the dev_base list, the undesired effect demonstrated in Figures 2–2 and 2–4 could occur. For this reason, we use the read–write spinlock dev_base_lock to protect our dev_base list. The data structure rwlock_t is used to implement read–write spinlocks.

The following functions are available to set and release read–write spinlocks. Note that we distinguish them according to whether the lock should be entered for read or for write purposes. Again, RW spinlock functions come in different variants with regard to how they handle interrupts and bottom halfs (..._irq(), ..._bh() etc.). We will not repeat a description of their differences here, because their behavior corresponds to the spin_lock() functions.

- read_lock...() tries to access a critical section for reading purposes. If it contains no activities or only reading activities, then the section is accessed immediately. If there is a write activity in the critical section, then we have to wait until that activity releases the lock.
- read_unlock...() leaves the critical section, which it entered for reading purposes only. If a write activity is waiting and there is no other read activity in that section, then it can access the section.
- write_lock...() tries to occupy the critical section for writing purposes. If there is already a (write or read) activity in the critical section, then the activity waits for all activities to leave that section. Subsequently, it puts an exclusive lock on the critical section.
- write_unlock...() releases the (write) lock and thus the critical section.

2.3.4   Semaphores

In addition to active locks, there is a way to avoid waiting until a critical section can be accessed when a lock is set. Instead of waiting, the activity releases the CPU by calling the scheduler. This means that the computing time can be used by other activities. This concept is known by the term *semaphore* or *mutex* in computer science.

The Linux kernel offers semaphores. However, they are not frequently used in the Linux network architecture. Therefore, instead of describing here in detail, we refer our readers to [BBDK+01].

2.4   KERNEL MODULES

We explained in Section 2.1 that monolithic operating-system kernels, including the Linux kernel, have the drawback that all functionality of the operating system is accommodated in a large kernel, making this kernel big and inflexible. To add a new functionality to the operating-system kernel, you first have to create and install a new kernel. This is a rather cumbersome task and can also be expensive, because running applications have to be interrupted and the system has to be restarted. Moreover, using an operating-system kernel that includes all possible kinds of functions, drivers, and protocols is not recommended either, because the kernel would then become huge and consume an unnecessary amount of memory. In addition, there are always new functionalities we would like to integrate into the kernel, or newer versions of existing functionalities, where errors have been removed. In fact, we can assume that the set of functions of an operating-system kernel will change over time. For this reason, monolithic kernels have to be continually updated—with the problems described above.

Linux is based on the monolithic approach, but it has used a different method to solve the problems noted, since kernel Version 2.0. Note that it does not opt for the microkernel-based approach, which also has drawbacks. The solution are *kernel modules*. These modules can be easily added to the kernel at runtime and they behave as if they had belonged to the monolithic kernel since the system started. When the functionality of a module is no longer needed, then it can simply be removed and the memory space it used is freed.

We saw in Figure 2–1 in which components of the kernel we can use modules: *device drivers, file systems, network protocols*, and *network drivers*. The use of modules is actually not limited to these components. Modules can normally be used on an individual basis. However, adding some functionality means that you need a corresponding kernel interface to inform the rest of the kernel about the new components. The interfaces of the Linux network architecture and the possibilities to expand it by new functionalities are one of the central issues of this book.

When compiled as kernel modules, new functionalities can be added as needed and removed once you don't need them anymore. (See Section 2.4.1.) This means that the principle of modularization is very similar to the flexibility of microkernels, the only difference being that Linux modules run in the kernel address space, components of microkernel systems in the user address space. More specifically, the Linux module concept combines the benefits of both operating-system variants. On the one hand, it avoids the expensive change of address spaces known from the microkernel-based approach; on the other, it lets you expand the kernel functionality individually at runtime at the same time.

The following sections take a closer look at the structure and management of kernel modules, because modules are the best and most flexible option to enhance the Linux network architecture. Unfortunately, a detailed description of kernel modules would go beyond the scope of this book; we refer mainly to [RuCo01] and [BBDK+01] instead.

2.4.1 Managing Kernel Modules

A kernel module consists of object code, which is loaded into the kernel address space at runtime, where it can be executed. When the system starts, it is not known which modules with what functionalities should be loaded, so the module has to make itself known to the respective components of the kernel. A module should also remove all references to itself when it is removed from the kernel address space. There are two methods available for these tasks, which each kernel module should implement—namely, init_module() and cleanup_module(). We will have a closer look at these methods in Section 2.4.2; first, however we need some general information about the management of kernel modules outside the kernel.

The following tools are used to manually load a module into the kernel, or remove it from the system:

- insmod Modulename.o [arguments]—This command tries to load a kernel module into the kernel address apace. In a successful case, the object code of the module is linked to the kernel; the module can now access the symbols (functions and data structures) of the kernel. Calling insmod causes the following system calls to run implicitly:

    - sys_create_module() allocates memory space to accommodate the module in the kernel address space.
    - sys_get_kernel_syms() returns the kernel's symbol table to resolve the missing references within the module to kernel symbols. (See Section 2.4.4.)
    - sys_init_module() copies the module's object code into the kernel address space and calls the module's initialization function (init_module()).

When loading a module, we can also pass parameters (e.g., values for device names, name, interrupt lines, irq, and I/O ports, io_addr). In the module itself, these parameters should be designated by the macro MODULE_PARM(arg, type). When the module is loaded, then these parameters are simply passed by module name—for example:

```
root@tux # insmod wvlan_cs eth=1 network_name="myWavelan"
```

- rmmod Modulename removes the specified module from the kernel address space. For this purpose, we use the system call sys_delete_module(), which, in turn, calls the module's method cleanup_module().

    The module can now be removed, if the module's reference counter is zero, which means that the module is currently not used in any point within the kernel. (See details in [RuCo01].)

- lsmod lists all currently loaded modules and their dependencies and reference counters.
- modinfo shows information about a module (e.g., its functionality, parameters, and author). This information cannot be generated automatically; it has to be set by the macros MODULE_DESCRIPTION, MODULE_AUTHOR, and so on in the module's source text.

```
# Aliases - specify your hardware
alias eth0  wvlan_cs
options wvlan_cs eth=1 network_name="MyNet" station_name="neo"

alias char-major-4          serial
alias char-major-5          serial
alias char-major-6          lp
alias char-major-9          st

alias tty-ldisc-1           slip
alias tty-ldisc-3           ppp
```

FIGURE 2–5
Configuration file of the module loader: /etc/modules.conf.

Loading Modules Automatically   In addition to via the command-line tools described above, kernel modules can also be loaded into the kernel automatically when needed. To enable the automatic loading of modules, the corresponding support has to be activated when creating the kernel (CONFIG_KMOD).

Using the tools described in the previous section to add and remove modules always requires a user's intervention—more specifically, the intervention of root. For security reasons, only the system administrator is authorized to load and remove kernel modules. Though this approach is secure, it is somewhat inflexible—for example, when a user requires the functionality of a module that is currently not loaded in the kernel. For this reason, a means was created for reloading modules automatically into the kernel upon demand.

Normally, the kernel generates an error message when a resource or a specific driver is not registered. You can ask for this component in advance by use of the kernel function request_module(). To use this function, you have to first activate the option Kernel Module Loader when configuring the kernel. Request_module() will then try to use the modprobe command to automatically reload the desired module (and any additionally required modules). You can select such options in the file /etc/modules.conf.

Figure 2–5 shows an example of the configuration file /etc/modules.conf. This file specifies that the network device eth0 is currently represented by the module wvlan_cs and that, for loading of this module, the specified parameters should be passed to this module. If modprobe cannot find the module, then printk() generates an error message. (See Appendix B.1.1.)

Though this mechanism runs automatically, it can load only those modules the administrator has specified in the configuration files, to ensure that no user can load system-critical modules. Modules loaded automatically can also be removed automatically after some time. More configuration options of the Kernel Module Loader and the modprobe tool are described on the man pages and in [RuCo01].

2.4.2 Registering and Unregistering Module Functionality

In contrast to an application that runs its tasks after its start, a module normally provides functions used by other parts of the kernel in the course of the system operation. The kernel is enhanced by a new functionality, which may be removed after its use. It is not known upon system start which functionalities will be added to the kernel by modules, so we need interfaces for a module to register its functionality. The different set, of kernel components (see Figure 2–1) have such interfaces (e.g., to register and unregister network drivers, file systems, protocols, etc.). (See Table 2–1.)

These interfaces can most easily be identified by function names. They generally begin with `register_...` and `unregister_...`, respectively. Table 2–1 showed a few examples.

The functionality of a module is registered and initialized in the module's own method `init_module()`. As described earlier, it is called directly after successful integration of the module in the kernel. `Init_module()` should run all initialization tasks, such as reserving memory, creating entries in the /proc directory, initializing data structures, registering and unregistering the functionality, and so on.

Upon successful execution of `init_module()`, the functionality of the module should be known in the kernel, and all initialization steps required for it should have run. However, if something goes wrong during the initialization, all actions done up to this point should be undone in any event. The reason is that, when `init_module()` returns with an error code, the object code of the module is removed from the kernel address space, and all attempts to access methods of the module lead to a memory access error. [RuCo01] includes several tips to solve this problem.

Appendix D shows a kernel module that adds a fictitious functionality to the kernel. In the further course of this book, we will introduce many elements of the Linux network architecture that can be implemented in the form of kernel modules (e.g., network drivers and protocols). You can use the module from Appendix D as a framework for modules you design yourself to enhance the Linux network architecture.

One of the module's own methods, `cleanup_module()`, is used to remove that module from the kernel address space. It should be used to clean up the work environment of the module (i.e., to unregister the module's functionality, free the memory it used, and remove dependencies between the module and other parts of the kernel).

Once you have called and run `cleanup_module()`, there should be no more references by the kernel or other modules to the module concerned. Otherwise, this would lead to a memory access error, causing the computer to crash.

The method `cleanup_module()` is called only if the reference counter (*use counter*) of the module is equal to zero. Otherwise, it is assumed that the module's functionality is currently needed, so that it cannot be removed. The macro `MOD_IN_USE` can be used to check the *use counters*.

A good example for the use of the reference counter is a module-based network driver. As soon as the relevant network device is opened, it is possible to access the driver's methods (and thus the module's methods) asynchronously. For this reason, the reference counter (for module-based drivers) is always incremented by the macro `MOD_INC_USE_COUNT` in the method dev->open(). When the network device is closed, so that driver methods can no longer be accessed, then `MOD_DEC_USE_COUNT` decrements the reference counter by one.

2.4.3   Passing Parameters When Loading a Module

We mentioned in Section 2.4.1 that parameters can be passed during loading of a kernel module. These parameters are specified either directly by `insmod` when loading or by `modprobe` in the configuration file. To be able to pass parameters to a module, you have to have previously declared these parameters in the module's source text. The following macros are available for this purpose:

- `MODULE_PARM(var, type)` designates the variable *var* as a parameter of the module, and a value can be assigned to this parameter during loading. It needs to be previously declared, of course. The second parameter of the macro (*type*) specifies the data type of the module parameter. The following types can be specified:

  - `b:` `byte`
  - `h:` `short` (two bytes)
  - `i:` `integer`
  - `l:` `long`
  - `s:` `string` (or a pointer to a string)

  If the parameter is an array, then this can be specified as such by stating the array size before the type. For example, 1–3i means that the parameter is an array with integer values, and between one and three values can be assigned to this array. More information about this topic are included in the header file `<linux/module.h>`.

- `MODULE_PARM_DESC(var, desc)` allows you to add a description (*desc*) for the parameter *var*. For example, this description is displayed when the tool `modinfo` is called. The description of a parameter should be short, but descriptive enough to make clear the task of that parameter.

In addition, the following macros can be used to output additional information, which can be called by use of the command-line tool `modinfo`. It is recommended that one use this informative option, because there could often be situations where the user of a module does not provide the source text:

- `MODULE_AUTHOR(name)` can be used to specify the author of a module. It is recommended to also state an e-mail address, in addition to names, for easy contact in the event that the module contains errors (and, of course, to be able to accept the large number of thank-you messages for your generous contribution to the open-source movement :-)).
- `MODULE_DESCRIPTION(desc)` should contain a description of the module's functionality. Ideally, you describe the basic functionality and include reference to further information (e.g., a URL).
- `MODULE_SUPPORTED_DEVICE(dev)` is currently not used. However, it might be used in future kernel versions to load the module automatically when the device *dev* is required.

The sample module in Appendix D shows how to use the macros described above.

2.4.4   Symbol Tables of the Kernel and Modules

Kernel modules are object code, which is added to the kernel at runtime. Once it has been embedded, the module is in the kernel address space. Before the embedding of a

```
c01e2640    register_netdevice
c01e2888    unregister_netdevice
c01e0ef8    netdev_state_change
c01ddf94    skb_clone
c01de20c    skb_copy
c01e147c    netif_rx
c01e0b40    dev_add_pack
c01e0b8c    dev_remove_pack
c01e0d78    dev_get
c01e0e94    dev_alloc
d0a03ec4    ppp_register_channel        [ppp_generic]
d0a03f98    ppp_unregister_channel      [ppp_generic]
d0a08660    ppp_crc16_table             [ppp_async]
```

FIGURE 2–6
Symbol table of the Linux kernel (excerpt).

module, however, several aspects have to be observed. As the module will probably have to call functions of the actual kernel and want to use its data structures, we first have to resolve the addresses of these functions and data structures. The Linux kernel includes a table, the ksym symbol table,[2] for this purpose. This table includes all required information. Each row of the table contains the name and memory address of a function or variable. Information about the data type or parameters is not saved to the table. Note that the programmer has to ensure correct mapping.

You can see in Figure 2–6 that a module can access only functions and data structures saved in the kernel's symbol table. Other parts of the kernel are not accessible to a module. This has the benefit that modules cooperate with the kernel exclusively over defined interfaces, as is true for the microkernel architectures described in Section 2.1.

The instruction EXPORT_SYMBOL(xxx) from the file kernel/ksyms.c adds a function or variable of the kernel to the symbol table. From then on, each module can access these variables or call functions. In addition, modules can export references to functions and variables from the module into the symbol table. The macro EXPORT_SYMBOL can be used to allow modules to export selected function and data pointers into the symbol table of the kernel. A module that does not want to export methods or variables can simply use the macro EXPORT_NO_SYMBOLS to express its wish.

A module can normally access only those symbols that are listed in the symbol table when the module loads. For this reason, a situation where two modules loaded consecutively into the kernel want to access each other's symbols may cause problems. The module loaded first cannot access the symbols of the second module, because they are not yet known. Since Linux kernel Version 2.4, however, there is a solution to this problem. This solution is called *intermodule communication* and is introduced in [RuCo01] and [BBDK+01].

---

[2]You can use the command-line call ksyms –a to view the contents of the current symbol table.

2.5   DEVICE DRIVERS

UNIX has its own way of handling physical devices. They are hidden from the user and accessible only over the file system, without limiting their functionality. For example, an application programmer can use the simple file operations `read()` and `write()` to access the driver's hardware, while the `ioctl()` command can be used to configure properties of a device.

Device drivers in the form of modules can be added or removed in Linux at any time. This offers you a comfortable tool to develop and test new functionalities. Figure 2–7 shows an excerpt from the /dev directory, where all devices are listed. In Linux, network adapters are not treated as normal devices and so they are not listed in the /dev directory. Linux has a separate interface for them. The reasons are described in [RuCo01]. Chapter 5 will discuss network devices in detail.

We can see in Figure 2–7 that the entries for device drivers differ from regular directory entries. Each entry includes two numbers used to identify the device and its driver.

■ The *major number* identifies the driver of a device. For example, Figure 2–7 shows that the PS/2 driver has major number 10 and the hard disk driver (hdxx) has major number 3.

The major number can be specified when you register a device driver, but it has to be unique. For drivers you think you will use less often, it is recommended that you let the kernel assign a major number. This ensures that the numbers are all unique. See details in [RuCo01].

■ The *minor number* is used to distinguish different devices used by the same driver. In Linux, a device driver can control more than one device, if the driver is designed as a reentrant driver. The minor number is then used as an additional number to distinguish the devices that driver controls. For example, the hard disk driver with major number 3 in Figure 2–7 controls three hard disks, distinguished by the minor numbers 1, 2, and 65.

Figure 2–7 also shows that the type of each driver is specified at the beginning of each row. Linux differs between two types of physical devices:

■ *Block-oriented* devices allow you optional access (i.e., an arbitrary set of blocks can be read or written consecutively without paying attention to the order in

```
brw-rw----    1 root    disk    3,     0 May 12 19:23 hda
brw-rw----    1 root    disk    3,     1 May 12 19:23 hda1
brw-rw----    1 root    disk    3,     2 May 12 19:23 hda2
brw-rw----    1 root    disk    3,    64 May 12 19:23 hdb
brw-rw----    1 root    disk    3,    65 May 12 19:23 hdb1
crw-rw----    1 root    uucp    4,    64 May 12 19:23 ttyS0
crw-rw----    1 root    uucp    4,    65 May 12 19:23 ttyS1
crw-rw-r--    1 root    root   10,     1 Sep 13 08:45 psaux
```

FIGURE 2–7
Excerpt from the /dev directory.

which you access them). To increase performance, Linux uses a cache memory to access block devices. File system can be accommodated only in block devices (hard disks, CD-ROMs, etc.), because they are required for optional or random access. Block devices are marked with a b in the /dev directory.

A block-oriented driver can be registered with the kernel function register_blkdev(). If the function was completed successfully, then the driver can be addressed by the returned major number. Release_blkdev() is used to release the device.

■ Character-oriented devices are normally accessed in sequential order. They can be accessed only outside of a cache. Most devices in a computer are character-oriented (e.g., printer and sound card). Character-oriented devices are marked with a c in the /dev directory. You can use register_chrdev() to register and release_chrdev() to release character-oriented devices.

The virtual file /proc/devices lists all devices currently known to the kernel. This file is used to find the major number of a driver in the user address space, in case none has been specified during the registration.

To be able to use a device that has not been registered yet, you need to first select a driver and generate an entry in the /dev directory. To create this entry, you use the command mknod /dev/*name typ major minor*, which is passed the name, the type (b or c), the major number of the driver, and the selected minor number for that device. If the command is successful, then you can now use the usual file operations (read(), write(), ioctl(), ...) to access that device.

Figure 2–8 shows how the data structure is passed when you register a character-oriented driver. A driver is addressed over a virtual file in UNIX, so these are all regular file operations. We will briefly describe here only the most important functions, to give you an overview:

■ owner refers to the module implemented by the driver (for a module-based driver);
■ lseek() sets the position pointer in a file. This function can be used for other purposes for non-file-oriented devices;

```
struct file_operations
{
        struct module      *owner;
        int                (*lssek) (file, offset, origin);
        int                (*read) (file, buffer, count, pos);
        int                (*write) (file, buffer, count, pos);
        int                (*readdir) (file, dir);
        int                (*poll) (file, poll_table);
        int                (*ioctl) (inode, file, cmd, unsigned arg);

        ...

        int                (*open) (inode, file);
        int                (*release) (inode, file);

        ...
}
```

FIGURE 2–8
File operations on a device driver.

- ▨ read() transfers data from the driver to the user address space. The driver has to have previously confirmed that the desired buffer is available in the user address space and whether this memory page is currently outsourced. Subsequently, the function copy_to_user() can be used to copy data to the user address space.

- ▨ As with to read(), write() is used to transfer data, but, in this case, from the user address space to the kernel address space (with copy_from_user()). Here again, before you can copy, you have to check the validity of the data range in the user address space. The memory range in the kernel does not have to be verified, because the kernel segment is never outsourced.

- ▨ ioctl() offers the most extensive functionality. It is used to set certain parameters of a driver or device. A constant that represents the desired command[3] and a pointer to the data to be passed with this command are passed to the ioctl() command. This can be arbitrary data. The power of this function is such that the ioctl() command could actually replace all other file operations of a driver.

- ▨ open() and close() are used to prepare (or postedit) a driver for subsequent (or completed) commands. This function must not be confused with similar functions used to configure a driver. Such tasks are normally executed by the ioctl() command. open() is called by a process to inform the driver that it wants to use the device. If a process can be made available only exclusively, then this is policed by the open() function. For this purpose, open() checks on whether another process has already *opened* that device and, if so, denies access to it.

  close() releases the device. Whether exclusive use is desired depends on the type of device.

When a device driver is accessed, certain things can happen at the interface of the device driver. For example, if you use the C library function fopen() to open a device file from the /dev directory, then the open() function of the driver is called in the kernel. If you use fprintf() to write data to the device file, then the write() function of the driver will run in the kernel. Not all operations of a driver have to be supported; only those that the driver really needs.

2.6   MEMORY MANAGEMENT IN THE KERNEL

Memory management is one of the main components in the kernel of any operating system. It supplies a virtual memory space to processes, often one much larger than the physical memory. This can be achieved by partitioning memory pages and outsourcing memory pages that are temporarily not needed to the swap memory on the hard disk. Access to an outsourced page by an application is intercepted and handled by the kernel. The page is reloaded into the physical memory and the application can access the memory without even noticing anything about insourcing and outsourcing of things.

The memory residing in the kernel cannot be outsourced because, if the memory management were to move the code to the swap memory, it would not be available later

---

[3]The commands and their constants are specified arbitrarily by the programmer, but they should be unique within the kernel. For this reason, it is recommended to use a hierarchical coding. (See [RuCo01].)

2.7.1 Standard Timers

In addition to measuring intervals in the microsecond range, we also need a way to run a function at a specific point in time to implement a traffic shaper [WeRi00], which sends packets at specific points in time. The resolution of such a *timer* should be at least in the 100-μs range. However, due to the fact that a PC has only *one* timer component, you can use only this one. As described above, the interrupt is triggered HZ times per second. In addition to updating jiffies, Linux uses the timer interrupt to run functions at specific points in time (i.e., the *timer handler*).

A *timer queue* can be used when a function of the kernel should run at a specific point in time (e.g., switching off the floppy motor). At each occurrence of a timer interrupt, the timer interrupt routine updates the jiffies variable and also checks the timer queue for timer handling routines, as may be present. Each timer_list structure within the timer queue stands for one function (timer handling routine), which is to run at a specific point in time (expires). The exact process of the timer resolution and of subsequent checking of the timer queue is described in [RuCo01].

The following functions are available to manage the timer queue:

- add_timer() adds a timer_list structure to the timer queue according to the time specified by expires. A timer_list structure represents a timer handling routine (i.e., a function to be executed). The kernel runs this function at the specified time.

  Note, however, that the timer interrupt is triggered only HZ times per second. This means that the method can run only when *expires* reaches the value of jiffies. Therefore, there is a small difference between time *t* when the function should theoretically run and the next possible value of jiffies. This difference can take up to $\frac{1}{HZ}s = \frac{1}{100}s$. But 10 ms is too long to allow reasonable traffic shaping.[5]

- del_timer() deletes a timer_list structure from the timer queue. The corresponding function will then no longer run.

- init_timer() initializes a timer_list structure. This function should always be called when a timer_list structure was created.

2.7.2 Using the APIC for High-resolution Timers

The current Linux kernel does not support any freely programmable timers with an accuracy in the microsecond range. As explained above, such high-resolution timers are required to support various functionalities (e.g., for traffic shaping in high-speed networks and to synchronize multimedia contents playback), but additional usages are conceivable. On the other hand, there is the problem that modern processors become increasingly faster, while the accuracy of timers remains at the state of the eighties for downward compatibility with vintage PCs.

---

[5]10 ms corresponds to the transmission time for approximately eighty packets of maximum length over a 100Mbps network.

There are two basic usages for high-resolution timers:

- *Periodic shot*: A timer with a specific interval is initialized and then periodically triggers an interrupt when this interval expires. This corresponds to the behavior of the timer interrupt in the Linux kernel, which always triggers an interrupt after 10 ms.

  This type of timer is suitable for all scenarios where actions have to run frequently and normally after fixed intervals. If the accuracy of these intervals is within the range of milliseconds, then the standard timers described in the previous sections can be used.

- *One shot*: Exactly one action needs to run at a specific time, regardless of other events. Such an action is, for example, when you send a packet at a pre-calculated time or represent an image from a video.

Until recently, one-shot and periodic-shot timers had been available only on the basis of timer interrupts, offering an accuracy of not more than $\frac{1}{HZ}$ seconds. The timer functionality introduced next is based on the APIC component (in short *APIC timer*) to avoid the problems outlined above. The UKA-APIC timer was developed at the Institute for Telematics at the University of Karlsruhe, Germany, and can be downloaded from [ObWe01].

Technical Basis of the APIC Timer   Intel's x86 processor family originally used the *PIC 8259A Programmable Interrupt Controller* to manage triggered interrupts. It was used since the first personal computer at the beginning of the eighties and met its tasks without problem. However, multiprocessor capability needs to distribute triggered interrupts among several processors of an SMP computer. For this reason, Intel introduced the so-called *APIC* (*Advanced Programmable Interrupt Controller*). More specifically, there are the following two different chips, as shown in Figure 2–9:

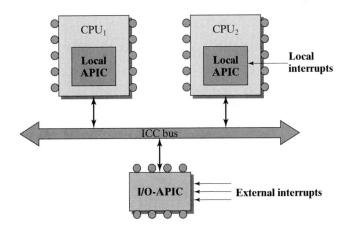

FIGURE 2–9

Use of an Advanced Programmable Interrupt Controller (APIC) in multiprocessor systems.

- The *local APIC* has been integrated in all Pentium processors (since Pentium P54C), and cooperates with the I/O APIC described below in multiprocessor systems. In addition to communicating with the I/O APIC and handling of incoming interrupts, a local APIC offers interesting possibilities, so it will be described here in more detail. Each local APIC has several 32-bit registers, an internal clock, an internal timer, 240 interrupt vectors, and two additional interrupt lines that can be used for interrupts generated locally.

- The *I/O APIC* is a separate component, collecting external interrupts and distributing them to the set of processors of a system. An I/O APIC is generally present only in multiprocessor systems, where such systems may indeed use more than one I/O APIC, which is supported in Linux since Version 2.4 [BoCe00]. The I/O APIC connects to the local APIC components of each installed processor over an interrupt Controller Communication Bus (ICC).

The internal timer of a local APIC is the most interesting part for the tasks discussed in this section. The internal timer works in bus-clock accuracy and can be initialized to a specific value. Subsequently, the value of the timer is decremented at each bus clock, and an interrupt is triggered when zero is reached. This means that the internal timer of the APIC component can be used to implement a high-resolution timer with almost bus-clock accuracy.

In contrast, single-processor systems do not integrate I/O components, and their local APICs are not activated when the system starts in most operating systems. In older P5 processors, you could activate the local APIC component only when the system started, and hardware manipulation was the only way to initialize it again. Since the P6 processor generation (Pentium Pro and successors), you can activate the integrated local APIC also during operation by use of software commands. This means that it can be used to implement a high-resolution timer.

Functionality of the UKA-APIC Timer   We emphasize here once more that the local APIC can be used for a freely programmable timer only in single-processor computers, because the timer of the local APIC in multiprocessor systems is used for interprocessor synchronization.

Some versions of the Linux kernel 2.3 allowed you to reactivate the local APIC component over a module. Unfortunately, this module is no longer present in the 2.4 versions. However, there is a patch [Pett01] you can use to activate the local APIC in single-processor systems at runtime. Based on an activated local APIC and its integrated timer, a high-resolution timer support was developed, featuring a programming interface similar to that of the standard timer of the Linux kernel [ObWe01, WeRi00].

The APIC timer also consists of a patch, integrating the interfaces required in the kernel and from a kernel module that manages the timers. One of the goals set when developing the APIC timer was to pack as much functionality and tasks as possible into one module to keep the understanding and maintenance simple. Unfortunately, there is no way around changes to the kernel for two reasons: First, you first have to activate the APIC component; second, there is no interface to register an interrupt handling routing for the APIC timer interrupt; `request_irq()` does not help either. For this reason, the

APIC timer handling routing, `smp_apic_timer_interrupt()`, normally used in an SMP configuration, is overwritten by another one, which allows entry into the use as a freely programmable timer (`set_apic_timer_up_handler()`). This method can be used only to set a new handling routine for the APIC timer interrupt.

The UKA APIC Timer Module   The UKA APIC Timer module offers the interface required to register individual handling routines. The module consists mainly of management functions for the timer and methods to achieve as high a timer accuracy as possible.

Registered handling routines are managed in a linked list, similar to the management of the standard timer of the Linux kernel. The individual elements are structured as follows:

```
struct apic_timer_list
{
        struct apic_timer_list *next, *prev;
        unsigned long long expires;
        unsigned long data;
        void (*function)(unsigned long long, unsigned long)
};
```

- next and prev are used to link the `apic_timer_list` entries.
- The variable `expires` contains a value for the timestamp counter register, which specifies the time when the handling routine should run. Note that the TSC register operates with the processor clock and not with the bus clock (like the local APIC). The linked list is ordered by trigger points (`expires`) for performance reasons.
- data is a pointer that can be used to point to private data contained in the handling routine. This can be useful for reentrant functions to point to a specific instance.
- function is the function pointer pointing to the handling routine to be executed. Function() is called as soon as the time specified by expires is reached. The parameter data is also passed at this point in time.

The UKA-APIC timer module offers the following interface to the outside. The header file `uka_apic_timer.h` should be embedded to use this interface. To make things simpler for the programmer, the structure of the UKA-APIC timer interface is almost identical to the interface of the standard kernel timer:

- init_apic_timer(struct apic_timer_list *timer) initializes the passed structure of type `apic_timer_list`. Currently, only pointers for the linking are set to NULL.
- add_apic_timer(struct apic_timer_list *timer) registers a structure of type `apic_timer_list` and adds it to the linked list of the registered timers. The handling method `timer->function()` runs when the timer reaches `timer->expires`.
- del_apic_timer(struct   apic_timer_list   *timer) removes an `apic_timer_list` structure from the list of registered timers. This means that the handling routine will no longer run when the timer reaches `expires`.

▓ mod_apic_timer(struct apic_timer_list *timer, unsigned long long expires) modifies the time when a registered timer should run. This change can mean that the apic_timer_list structure may have to be put in another place within the list.

The following code fragment is a simple example to show how you can use the UKA-APIC timer. The following steps are required to register the handling routine test_timer_handler() so that it will run within two microseconds:

```
#include <asm/timex.h>
#include "uka_apic_timer.h"
#define SYS_CLOCK 500000000 //(500 MHz)
static struct apic_timer_list test_timer;
unsigned long long timestamp;
static struct egal_daten data1;
void test_timer_handler(unsigned long long exp, unsigned long data)
{
        /* Do here what you think you have to do :-) */
        * e.g., use hard_start_xmit to send a packet */
}
/* ... This is a routine, in which the timer is activated ... */
/* Initialize the apic_timer_list structure */
init_apic_timer(&test_timer);
/* Read the current time (status of the TSC register) */
timestamp = get_cycles();
/* Set the values... */
timer.function = (void*) &test_timer_handler;
timer.expires = timestamp + (SYS_CLOCK * (2 / 1000000));
timer.data = (unsigned long) &data1;
/* Register the timer */
add_apic_timer(&timer);
```

2.8   THE PROC FILE SYSTEM

All files in the /proc directory are virtual files. They do not exist on any memory medium, but are generated directly by the kernel upon each read access. A proc file is normally a text file showing information about specific parts of the kernel. For example, the commands lspci or apm show you information from the proc files /proc/pci und /proc/apm, respectively, and information about the current devices on the PCI bus or the state of the notebook battery.

The possibilities of the proc file system to display information on the kernel easily in the user mode are used by many system developers. Files and directories in the /proc directory can be easily implemented. In addition, you can register and unregister dynamically, so that the proc directory is often used by modules.

The files and directories in the /proc directory are essentially based on the proc_dir_entry structure, shown in Figure 2–10. Such a structure represents either a directory or a file. The directory *proc* is represented by the variable proc_root. The attributes and methods of the proc_dir_entry structure have the following meaning:

```
struct proc_dir_entry
{
        unsigned short                  low_ino;
        unsigned short                  namelen;
        const char                      *name;
        mode_t                          mode;
        nlink_t                         nlink;
        uid_t                           uid;
        gid_t                           gid;
        unsigned long                   size;

        ...
        struct proc_dir_entry           *next, *parent, *subdir;
        void                            *data;
        int                             (*get_info)(buffer, start, off, count);
        int                             (*read_proc) (buffer, start, off, count, eof, data);
        int                             (*write_proc)(file, buffer, count, data);
        int                             (*readlink_proc)(proc_dir_entry, page);
        unsigned int                    count;   /* use count */
        int                             deleted; /* delete flag */
};
```

FIGURE 2–10
Structure of `proc_dir_entry`.

- `low_ino` is the file's Inode number. This value is filled automatically by `proc_register` when the file is initialized.
- `namelen` specifies the length of the file or directory name, `name`.
- `name` is a pointer to the name of the file (or directory).
- `mode` specifies the file's mode; this value is set to S_DIR for directories.
- `nlink` specifies the number of links to this file (default = 1).
- `uid` or `gid` specifies the user or group ID of the file.
- `size` specifies the length of the file as shown when the directory is displayed.
- `data` is a pointer that can point to private data.
- `next`, `parent`, and `subdir` are pointers to link the proc directory structure.
- `read_proc()` runs when you read-access a proc file. The only task of this function is to fill the `buffer` with the file's output and return the number of written characters as result.
- `write_proc()` is called when you write-access the proc file.

In earlier kernel versions, a `proc_dir_entry` structure had to be created and initialized for each entry to be added to the proc directory. As we have seen above, many of the variables in the structure are needed only after registration.

The following functions were defined to simplify handling of proc entries.

create_proc_entry( )	fs/prof/generic.c

`create_proc_entry(name, mode, parent)` creates a file with name in the proc directory. The relative path to /proc/ can be specified in a name, or a pointer to the `proc_dir_entry` structure of the directory, in which the file should appear, can be set in the parameter parent. References to the /proc and /proc/net directories can be obtained from the pointers `proc_root` and `proc_net`. The parameter mode lets you pass flags for file properties of the proc file you want to create. Normally, this is filled with value 0.

As a result of this function, you obtain a pointer to the `proc_dir_entry` structure created. Now you can enter handling routines for read and write operations on the proc file. You can also set the pointer `data` to private data of a proc entry. This is necessary especially when a read or write function is used for several proc files.

The following source text is a good example to show you how a proc file, /proc/net/test, is created and initialized:

```
test_entry = create_proc_entry("test", 0600, proc_net);

test_entry->nlink = 1;
test_entry->data = (void *) &test_data;
test_entry->read_proc = test_read_proc;
test_entry->write_proc = test_write_proc;
```

`remove_proc_entry( )`	**fs/proc/generic.c**

`remove_proc_entry(name, parent)` removes the proc file specified in name. As with `create_proc_entry()`, you can either state the relative path to /proc or the `proc_dir_entry` structure of the directory where the file name is located.

`proc_mkdir( )`	**fs/proc/generic.c**

Though `create_proc_entry()` can be used to create directories in the proc directory, the kernel offers a simpler way with `proc_mkdir(name, parent)`. The parameters name and parent can be used as in the functions described above. The result of this function is a pointer to the `proc_dir_entry` structure of the directory you created. The example in Appendix D shows how you can create the directory /proc/test by using this function.

`create_proc_read_entry( )`	**include/Linux/proc_fs.h**

We often want to create files in the proc directory merely to display certain information. This means that it is sufficient to register a function to handle a read access to the proc file. Though you can use `create_proc_entry()` and then register the read function, as in our example above, the kernel offers another function to achieve this in one step.

The function `create_proc_read_entry(name, mode, base, get_info)` creates the proc file name and uses the function `get_info()` to initialize read accesses. The parameters name, mode, and base are used as in `create_proc_entry()`.

When there is no write access to the proc file proc/net/test and no private data has to be passed in the above example, then this function can be simplified as follows, where `get_info()` is the method used to handle read access to the proc file:

```
test_entry = create_proc_read_entry("test", 0600, proc_net, test_get_info);
```

`create_proc_info_entry( )`	**include/linux/proc_fs.h**

`create_proc_info_entry(name, mode, base, read_proc, data)` creates a file in the proc directory, just as `create_proc_read_entry()`$$$, but it additionally sets the parameter `data` in the `proc_dir_entry` structure. This variant is used when the read function `read_proc()` is needed more than once. Note that it has to be reentrant, and the pointer data to the private data passed corresponds to the proc file called.

This means that the above example can be replaced by the following function call:

```
test_entry = create_proc_read_entry("test", 0600, proc_net, test_read_proc,
&test_data);
```

2.9   VERSIONING

The Linux kernel is subject to constant improvement and development, and new versions (releases) are published regularly. To prevent users from getting confused and to identify stable versions, we distinguish between so-called *hacker* and *user* kernels. The version of a Linux kernel is denoted by a tuple composed of three letters, x,y,z:

* A *hacker kernel* is not a kernel version used by malicious people to break into highly classified computers. The very opposite is the case; in fact, a hacker kernel is the prototype of a Linux kernel under further development. Normally, new concepts and functions have been added to such a prototype and some errors of the previous version have been (hopefully) removed. Hacker kernels are in the testing phase, and faulty behavior or system failure has to be expected at any time. They mainly serve to integrate and test new drivers and functionalities.

  Once a sufficient number of new drivers and technologies have been added to a hacker kernel, Linus Torvalds will proclaim a so-called *feature freeze*. This means that no new functionality can be integrated, and the only change allowed to that prototype is to remove errors. The objective is a stable user kernel. You can identify a hacker kernel by its odd y version number (e.g., 2.3.z, where z denotes the consecutive number of the kernel version). The next version (e.g., 2.3.51), will then have removed some errors of 2.3.50.

* *User kernels* are stable kernel versions, where you can assume that they are normally free from errors. A user kernel is denoted by an even version number, e.g., 2.2.z. Such versions are recommended to normal users, because you don't have to fear that the system might crash. For example, when version 2.3.51 is very stable and the feature freeze has already been proclaimed, then the kernel will be declared user kernel 2.4.1. New drivers and properties will then be added to hacker kernel 2.5.1.

## PART II

Architecture of Network Implementation

# CHAPTER 3

The Architecture
of Communication Systems

This chapter discusses basic models used to structure communication systems and architectures. The ISO/OSI reference model introduced in Section 3.1.1 failed in practice because of its complexity, especially that of its application-oriented layers. Nevertheless, it still has some fundamental significance for the logical classification of the functionality of telecommunication systems. Though it was less successful in proliferating than expected, this model offers the proposed structure of telecommunication systems in similar form in the field of telematics.

Currently, the technologies and protocols of the Internet (TCP/IP reference model; see Chapter 13) have made inroads and are considered the de facto standards. The architecture of the Internet can easily be paralleled to the ISO/OSI reference model, as far as the four lower layers are concerned. The other layers are application-specific and cannot be compared to the ISO/OSI model.

However, the architecture and protocols of the Internet also represent a platform for open systems (i.e., no proprietary solutions supported by specific manufacturers are used in the network). In addition, the development process for new protocols in the Internet by the Internet Engineering Task Force (IETF) is open for everyone and is designed so that the best and most appropriate technical proposals are accepted.

3.1 LAYER-BASED COMMUNICATION MODELS

Telecommunication systems bridge the spatial distance between distributed computers. The implementation of this task is extremely complex for a number of reasons, so it is not recommended to use a monolithic architecture, which could prove very inflexible and difficult to maintain. This is the reason why communication systems are normally developed as *layered architectures*, where each layer assumes a specific task, offering it in the form of services. The ISO/OSI reference model is probably the best known example of such a layered architecture.

To solve its task, a layer, N, must use only the services provided by the next lower layer $(N - 1)$. More specifically, layer N expands the properties of layer $N - 1$ and abstracts from its weaknesses. For this purpose, the instance of layer N communicates with the instances of the same layer on other computers. This means that the entire functionality of the communication system is available in the top layer. In contrast to a monolithic structure, layering a communication system means a more expensive implementation, but it offers invaluable benefits, such as the independent development of single partial components, easy exchange of single instances, better maintainability, and higher flexibility. Figure 3–1 shows the principles of communication in a layered system.

We can deduce two central terms for layer-oriented communication models from the current section, which will be discussed in more detail in Section 3.2:

- Communication between two instances of the same layer on different computers is governed by predefined rules. These rules are called *protocols*.
- The set of functions offered by a layer, N, to its higher-order layer $(N + 1)$, is called *its service*. The interface through which this service is offered is called *service interface*.

This means that an instance is the implementation of a communication protocol and the service provided within one layer on a computer. The theoretical basis of services and protocols are discussed in Section 3.2.

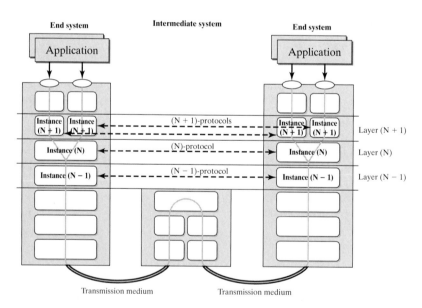

FIGURE 3–1
Communication in layered systems.

3.1.1   The ISO/OSI Reference Model

At the end of the seventies, experts observed increasingly that the interconnection of several computer networks was difficult (because of vendor-specific properties of these networks), if not impossible, so it was found hard to ensure interoperability between the large number of networks in place. This situation led to the proposal to create a uniform and standardized platform for computer-based communication networks.

Open vendor-independent communication required the definition and observance of general standards. The *ISO/OSI reference model* (in short, ISO/OSI model) proposed by the International Organization for Standardization (ISO) for *open systems communication* (OSI) [ITU-94] describes a general abstract model for communication between computer-assisted systems based on digital data. It serves as a framework for the development of communication standards to achieve open communication systems. This reference model has the character of a functional standard for other standards, i.e., it does not represent a specification for implementation, but refers merely to the mutual use of standardized methods for the exchange of data.

The ISO/OSI model consists of seven layers (see Figure 3–2), where one layer offers specific services to its higher-order layer. The ISO/OSI model does not describe a real implementation of a specific system, but merely defines the tasks of each layer. For this reason, it has become the basic model for telecommunication systems during the past decade. That's why the ISO/OSI model is often referred to as the *basic* reference model. In fact, knowledge of the ISO/OSI is normally the basis for the design and structuring of modern computer networks, although it is not a perfect model. It has certain strengths and weaknesses, as we will see later when comparing it to the more *streamlined* TCP/IP model.

The seven layers of the ISO/OSI reference model and their purposes are as follows:

- *Physical layer*: The physical layer handles the transmission of single bits over a physical medium. More specifically, (unstructured) bit sequences are converted to physical signals and transmitted over a physical medium (copper cables, fiber glass, wireless, etc.). The physical layer defines special coding methods, hardware connections, and media types.

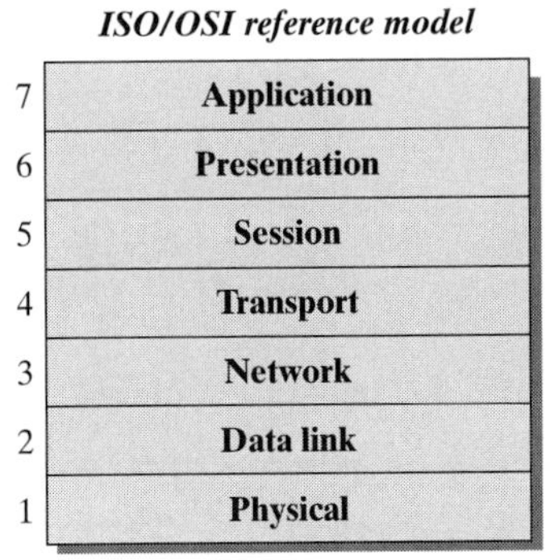

ISO/OSI reference model

7	**Application**
6	**Presentation**
5	**Session**
4	**Transport**
3	**Network**
2	**Data link**
1	**Physical**

FIGURE 3–2
The ISO/OSI basic reference model.

▓ *Data link layer*: This layer specifies how data should be transmitted between two stations directly connected over a medium. The sending system organizes the data in frames and transmits them back to back. If errors occur, then the data link layer is responsible for detecting such errors and retransmitting the data frames. Moreover, the data flow between the two systems should be regulated so that the receiver does not get overloaded (flow control). Examples of data-link-layer protocols are HDLC (High-level Data Link Control), SLIP (Serial Line IP), and PPP (Point-to-Point Protocol); the latter two offer the described functions to only a limited extent.

In local networks, the data link layer often assumes the task to regulate access to a shared medium. In such cases, the data link layer is divided into the *Medium Access Control (MAC)* layer and the *Logical Link Control (LLC)* layer.

▓ *Network layer*: The network layer is responsible for establishing connectivity between all systems of a telecommunication network. For this reason, the network layer deals mainly with switching and forwarding of data (e.g., routing, adapting data units to the admissible size of the respective data link layer (fragmenting), or ensuring various service qualities). Within the scope of this book, we will mainly discuss the Internet protocols Versions 4 and 6.

▓ *Transport layer*: The transport layer regulates the transport of data between applications (i.e., between the sender and the receiver application). Among other things, it is responsible for addressing applications, for controlling the data flow between the end systems, and for securing both the correctness and the order of data.

▓ *Session layer*: The session layer handles the structured exchange of messages over transport links. For example, it can control within a session whether the transfer of data should be concurrently in both directions or only one of the communicating partners should have the right to transmit. In the latter case, the session layer manages the right to transmit.

▓ *Presentation layer*: The presentation layer regulates the presentation of transmitted data in a form independent of the communicating computer systems. Many operating systems use different forms of representation for characters (e.g., ASCII, Unicode), numbers (big-endian, little-endian), and so on. To ensure that this data can be exchanged between the systems involved, the representation layer transmits it in a standardized form (e.g., by using Abstract Syntax Notation (ASN.1) or Basic Encoding Rules (BER)).

▓ *Application layer*: This layer uses specific protocols for different applications, using the lower-level layers to fulfill their tasks—for example, the application layer includes protocols for electronic mail, file transferred, and remote procedure call.

3.1.2   The TCP/IP Reference Model

The naming convention for the Internet reference model is based on the two most important Internet protocols—the Transmission Control Protocol (TCP) and the Internet Protocol (IP). The 7-layer ISO/OSI reference model described earlier was devised before internetworking was invented. Furthermore, the 7-layer reference model devotes an entire layer to session protocols, which have become much less important as

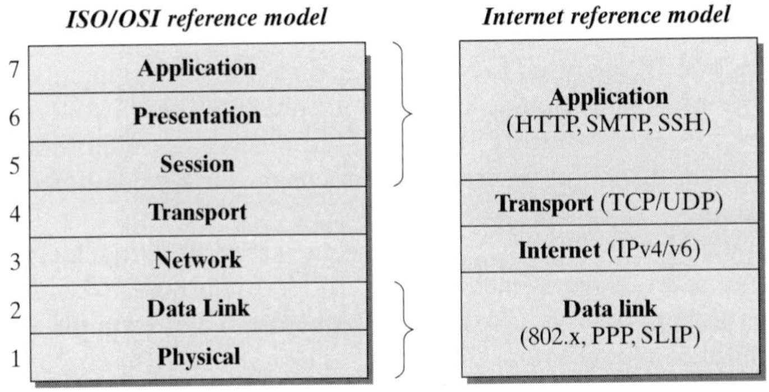

ISO/OSI reference model   *Internet reference model*

7	Application	
6	Presentation	Application (HTTP, SMTP, SSH)
5	Session	
4	Transport	Transport (TCP/UDP)
3	Network	Internet (IPv4/v6)
2	Data Link	Data link (802.x, PPP, SLIP)
1	Physical	

FIGURE 3–3

Comparing the ISO/OSI reference model and the TCP/IP reference model.

computer systems have changed from large mainframe systems to private workstations. As a result, researchers who developed TCP/IP invented a new layering model. This section describes the new layering model briefly.

The TCP/IP layering model, which is also called Internet Reference Model, contains the following layers (shown in Figure 3–3):

- *Application layer*: The application layer combines all application-specific tasks (i.e., the properties of layers 5 to 7 of the ISO/OSI model). The protocols of the application layer include Telnet (for virtual terminals), FTP (file transfer), and SMTP (to transmit e-mail). More recent protocols include DNS (Domain Name System) and HTTP (Hypertext Transfer Protocol).

- *Transport layer*: As in the ISO/OSI model, the transport layer of the TCP/IP reference model allows end-system applications to communicate. The TCP/IP reference model defines two basic protocols for this purpose: the Transmission Control Protocol (TCP) and the User Datagram Protocol (UDP). TCP is a reliable connection-oriented protocol and can transmit a byte stream without errors over the Internet to another computer. UDP is unreliable and connectionless, but is preferred over the more complex TCP in many situations (e.g., to transmit multimedia data).

- *Internet layer*: The Internet layer of the TCP/IP reference model defines the Internet Protocol (IP), including two auxiliary protocols, the Internet Control Message Protocol (ICMP) and the Internet Group Management Protocol (IGMP). The main purpose of the Internet layer is to forward IP packets from the sender to the receiver over the network, where routing of the packets plays an important role. The Internet Control Message Protocol (ICMP) is an integral part of each IP implementation; it serves to transmit diagnostics and error information for the Internet Protocol. The Internet Group Management Protocol (IGMP) is used to manage communication groups.

- *Interface layer*: This layer combines the two lower layers of the ISO/OSI reference model. It handles network adapters and their drivers, which are used to exchange data packets in a specific maximum length over a local area network (Ethernet, Token Ring, etc.) or over a wide area network (ISDN, ATM).

3.2   SERVICES AND PROTOCOLS

Services and *protocols* were briefly discussed in Section 3.1; they are basic elements of layered communication systems. This section describes the meaning of these two terms and the functionality of services and protocols. These two terms serve as a theoretical basis for further explanations in this book, where we will focus on services and protocols used in real-world systems.

We know from the models described in the previous sections that modern telecommunication systems consist of several layers. Each layer has different purposes (depending on the reference model) and offers services to the next higher layer. For example, the IP layer in the TCP/IP reference model offers the following services: *forwarding data units (without guarantees) from a local computer to another computer, specified by its IP address*. This service is used by the transport layer (e.g., by TCP) and expanded so that a byte stream can be transmitted free from errors and in the correct order.

We can say that a service describes the set of functions offered to the next higher layer. In addition, a service defines single service elements, used to access the entire range of services. In other words, the service definition defines the extent and type of service and the interface used to call that service. The definition of a service refers only to the interaction between two neighboring layers and the interfaces concerned. The literature describes this often as *vertical communication*. Exactly how a layer provides its service is not part of the service definition; it only deals with what an implementation has to offer the service user at the interface.

To be able to use the services of a layer, the participating systems have to overcome the spatial separation and coordinate their communication. This is achieved by use of *communication protocols*, which run by *instances* of a layer in the communicating systems. A protocol regulates the behavior of the distributed instances and defines rules for their coordination. For example, it defines messages to be exchanged between the instances to regulate distributed handling between these instances. More specifically, a layer, N, provides its service by distributed algorithms in the respective instances of layer N and by exchanging protocol messages about their coordination. (See Figure 3–1.) Coordination between the instances by protocol messages is also called *horizontal communication*. The service of the lower layer ($N - 1$) is used to exchange protocol messages.

The specification of a service describes the behavior of a layer versus the next higher layer (*vertical communication*), but says nothing about how a service is implemented. It merely defines the format and dynamics at the interfaces to the layer that uses the service. A service is rendered by instances of a layer, which use protocols to coordinate themselves (*horizontal communication*). The protocol specification describes the syntactic and dynamic aspects of a protocol. The protocol syntax describes the format of the *protocol data units* (*PDUs*) to be exchanged and the protocol dynamics describe the behavior of the protocol. The goal of this book is to explain how all of these elements can be designed and implemented in a communication system. Using Linux as our example operating system, we will see what the interfaces between the different layers can look like and what design decisions play a role, mainly from the perspective of efficiency and correctness of the protocols. In addition, we will see how different protocols use their instances, to show the technologies used to implement network protocols.

3.2.1 Interplay of Layers, Instances, and Protocols

After our brief introduction to services and protocols in the previous sections, this section describes the horizontal and vertical processes involved when protocol instances provide a service. The description of these processes forms the basis for understanding how network protocols work, mainly the principles of horizontal and vertical communication. The terms introduced earlier will help us better classify and distinguish structures and parameters involved in the interaction of different layers at the interfaces.

Instances are the components offering services within a layer. To offer a service, the instances of a layer communicate (horizontally). This communication is realized by exchanging protocol data units (PDUs) of layer N. However, data is not exchanged directly between the two instances, but indirectly, over the next lower layer. This means that the instance of layer N uses the service of layer $(N - 1)$ to exchange a PDU with its partner instance. Figure 3–4 shows the interplay of layers and the elements involved.

- *Protocol Data Unit (PDU)*: A PDU is a message exchanged between two instances of a layer to coordinate their behavior. It represents the basic element of horizontal communication. A PDU consists of the following two elements:

  - ▶ The *Protocol Control Information (PCI)* contains control information used to coordinate the two protocol instances and is also called the *packet header*. A PCI carries protocol-specific data and is created by the sending instance, depending on its state. The information is then evaluated and removed from the PDU in the receiver instance.
  - ▶ The *Service Data Unit (SDU)* contains the payload to be transmitted at the order of the higher-level layer. The SDU of layer N normally consists of the PCI of layer $(N + 1)$ and an SDU of layer $(N + 1)$ (i.e., of the $(N + 1)$ PDU).

In certain states of a protocol, it can happen that the PDU does not contain any SDU at all (e.g., to establish a connection or in pure acknowledgment packets). In such cases, merely information needed to coordinate the protocols, but no payload, is exchanged.

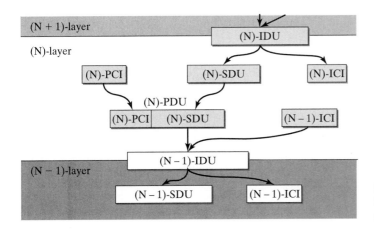

FIGURE 3–4
Data units for vertical and horizontal communication.

▓ Interface Control Information (*ICI*) is created by an instance and forwarded to the next lower layer together with a PDU (vertical communication). This information is needed by the service-rendering layer $(N - 1)$ to offer that service. For example, an ICI can contain the address of the partner instance that should receive the (N) PDU. The (N) PDU are pure payload data for layer $(N - 1)$, so that it cannot evaluate the elements of the (N) PCI included in the (N) PDU, but has to rely on the ICI contents.

▓ The *Interface Data Unit* (*IDU*) of layer $(N - 1)$ is composed of the PDU and the ICI of layer N. The IDU is delivered to layer $(N - 1)$ at the service access point and forms the basis for horizontal communication.

Note that, in the case of a vertical communication between two layers, this communication can take place only in defined *service access points* (*SAPs*), serving to distinguish different service users. SAPs are identified by service-access-point addresses, based on the rule that a service access point addresses exactly one service user. The principle of a service access point will come up often in the following chapters in connection with different environments (e.g., IP address for IP, ports for TCP, etc.).

The further course of this book will show how the dynamic aspects of a network protocol can be implemented (i.e., which programming elements there are and how they can be used in Linux. In addition, we will introduce interfaces and data structures of different instances and explain which parameters play a role as interface control information for different protocols. In this connection, we will explain that the theoretical model of a communication instance described above and the strict separation of the individual layers have to be given up if we want to achieve better performance of the entire protocol stack. When compared with a standard telecommunication work (e.g., [Tane97]), this book deals not only with the specification of protocols and their horizontal communication, but also with vertical communication and implementation aspects of different network protocols.

CHAPTER 4

Managing Network Packets in the Kernel

One of the most important tasks of the network subsystem of an operating system is to process data packets according to the protocols used. In the designing of such a system, the multitude and flexibility of available methods play an important role, in addition to the performance and correctness of these protocols. Many network protocols differ a lot externally, but, when you implement them within an operating system, you can see quickly that the algorithms and operations on data packets are similar, and most of them can be reused. This chapter uses a Linux system as an example to show how data packets can be realized and what general methods are available to manipulate them.

One main reason for the flexibility and efficiency of the Linux network implementation is the architecture of the buffers that manage network packets—the so-called *socket buffers*, or *skb* for short. This central structure of the network implementation represents a packet during its entire processing lifetime in the kernel, representing one of the two basic elements of this network implementation, in addition to network devices. This means that a socket buffer corresponds to a sending or received packet.

This chapter introduces buffer management (i.e., the structure of *socket buffers*) and the operations used to manage or manipulate them. Beginning with an introduction to the sk_buff structure, we will use an example to show how an IP packet is represented in this structure and how it changes along its way across different protocols and layers. In addition, this chapter introduces functions used to manage and change the structure.

4.1 SOCKET BUFFERS

The network implementation of Linux is designed to be independent of a specific protocol. This applies both to the network and transport layer protocols (TCIP/IP, IPX/SPX, etc.) and to network adapter protocols (Ethernet, token ring, etc.). Other protocols can be added to any network layer without a need for major changes. As

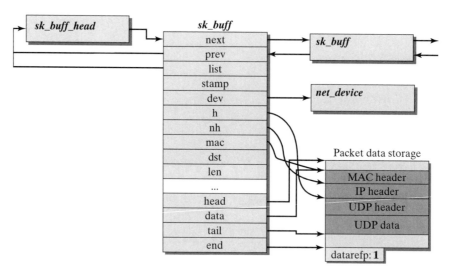

FIGURE 4–1
Structure of socket buffers (`struct sk_buff`) with packet storage locations.

mentioned before, socket buffers are data structures used to represent and manage packets in the Linux kernel.

A socket buffer consists of two parts (shown in Figure 4–1):

- *Packet data*: This storage location stores data actually transmitted over a network. In the terminology introduced in Section 3.2.1, this storage location corresponds to the protocol data unit.

- *Management data* (`struct sk_buff`): While a packet is being processed in the Linux kernel, the kernel requires additional data that are not necessarily stored in the actual packet. These mainly implementation-specific data (pointers, timers, etc.). They form part of the interface control information (ICI) exchanged between protocol instances, in addition to the parameters passed in function calls.

The socket buffer is the structure used to address and manage a packet over the entire time this packet is being processed in the kernel. When an application passes data to a socket, then the socket creates an appropriate socket buffer structure and stores the payload data address in the variables of this structure. During its travel across the layers (see Figure 4–2), packet headers of each layer are inserted in front of the payload. Sufficient space is reserved for packet headers that multiple copying of the payload behind the packet headers is avoided (in contrast to other operating systems). The payload is copied only twice: once when it transits from the user address space to the kernel address space, and a second time when the packet data is passed to the network adapter. The free storage space in front of the currently valid packet data is called *headroom*, and the storage space behind the current packet data is called *tailroom* in Linux.

When a packet is received over a network adapter, the method dev_alloc_skb() is used to request an sk_buff structure during the interrupt handling. This structure is

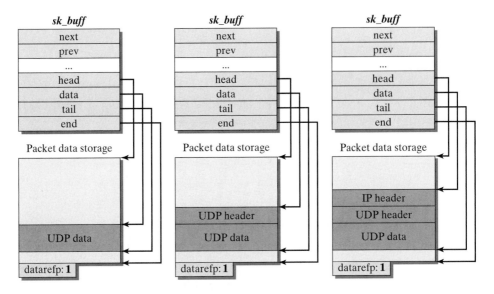

FIGURE 4–2

Changes to the packet buffers across the protocol hierarchy.

then used to store the data from the received packet. Until it is sent, the packet is always addressed over the socket buffer created.

We now explain briefly the parameters of the sk_buff structure (Figure 4–3):

- next, prev are used to concatenate socket buffers in queues (struct skb_queue_head). They should always be provided by special functions available to process socket buffers (skb_queue_head(), skb_dequeue_tail(), etc.) and should not be changed directly by programmers. These operations will be introduced in Section 4.1.1.

- list points to the queue where the socket buffer is currently located. For this reason, queues should always be of the type struct sk_buff_head, so that they can be managed by socket buffer operations. This pointer should point to null for a packet not assigned to any queue.

- sk points to the socket that created the packet. For a software router, the driver of the network adapters creates the socket buffer structure. This means that the packet is not assigned to a valid socket, and so the pointer points to null.

- stamp specifies the time when the packet arrived in the Linux system (in jiffies).

- dev and rx_dev are references to network devices, where dev states the current network device on which the socket buffer currently operates. Once the routing decision has been taken, dev points to the network adapter over which the packet should leave the computer. Until the output adapter for the packet is known, dev points to the input adapter. rx_dev always points to the network device that received the packet.

```
struct sk_buff
{
    struct sk_buff          *next,*prev;
    struct sk_buff_head     *list;
    struct sock             *sk;
    struct timeval          stamp;
    struct net_device       *dev, *rx_dev;

    union /* Transport layer header */
    {
        struct tcphdr       *th;
        struct udphdr       *uh;
        struct icmphdr      *icmph;
        struct igmphdr      *igmph;
        struct iphdr        *ipiph;
        struct spxhdr       *spxh;
        unsigned char       *raw;
    } h;

    union /* Network layer header */
    {
        struct iphdr        *iph;
        struct ipv6hdr      *ipv6h;
        struct arphdr       *arph;
        struct ipxhdr       *ipxh;
        unsigned char       *raw;
    } nh;

    union /* Link layer header */
    {
        struct ethhdr       *ethernet;
        unsigned char       *raw;
    } mac;

    struct dst_entry        *dst;
    char                    cb[48];
    unsigned int            len, csum;
    volatile char           used;
    unsigned char           is_clone, cloned, pkt_type, ip_summed;
    __u32                   priority;
    atomic_t                users;
    unsigned short          protocol, security;
    unsigned int            truesize;
    unsigned char           *head, *data, *tail, *end;
    void                    (*destructor)(struct sk_buff *);

    ...
};
```

FIGURE 4–3

The sk_buff structure, including management data for a packet.

- h, nh, and mac are pointers to packet headers of the transport layer (h), the network layer (nh), and the MAC layer (mac). These pointers are set for a packet as it travels across the kernel. (See Figure 4–2.) For example, the h pointer of an IP packet is set in the function ip_rcv() to the IP protocol header (type iphdr).

- dst refers to an entry in the routing cache, which means that it contains either information about the packet's further trip (e.g., the adapter over which the packet is to leave the computer) or a reference to a MAC header stored in the hard header cache. (See Chapters 15 and 16a.)

▩ cloned indicates that a packet was cloned. Clones will be explained in detail later in this chapter. For now, it is sufficient to understand that clones are several copies of a packet and that, though several sk_buff structures exist for a packet, they all use one single packet data location jointly.

▩ pkt_type specifies the type of a packet, which can be one of the following:

▶ PACKET_HOST specifies packet a sent to the local host.

▶ PACKET_BROADCAST specifies a broadcast packet.

▶ PACKET_MULTICAST specifies a multicast packet.

▶ PACKET_OTHERHOST specifies packets not destined for the local host, but received by special modes (e.g., the promiscuous mode).

▶ PACKET_OUTGOING specifies packets leaving the computer.

▶ PACKET_LOOPBACK specifies packets sent from the local computer to itself.

▶ PACKET_FASTROUTE specifies packets fast-forwarded between special network cards (fastroute is not covered in this book).

▩ len designates the length of a packet represented by the socket buffer. This considers only data accessible to the kernel. This means that only the two MAC addresses and the type/length field are considered in an Ethernet packet. The other fields (preamble, padding, and checksum) are added later in the network adapter, which is the reason why they are not handled by the kernel.

▩ data, head, tail, end: The data and tail pointers point to currently valid packet data. Depending on the layer that currently handles the packet, these parameters specify the currently valid protocol data unit.

head and end point to the total location that can be used for packet data. The latter storage location is slightly bigger to allow a protocol to add protocol data before or after the packet, without the need to copy the packet data. This avoids expensive copying of the packet data location. If it has to be copied in rare cases, then appropriate methods can be used to create more space for packet data.

The space between head and data is called *headroom*; the space between tail and end is called *tailroom*.

▩ The other parameters are not discussed here, because they are of minor importance. Some of them are discussed in other chapters (e.g., netfilter in Section 19.3).

The pointer datarefp is actually not part of the sk_buff structure, because it is located at the end of the packet data space and not defined as a variable of a structure. (See Figure 4–1.) datarefp is a reference counter; it can be easily addressed and manipulated by use of the macro skb_datarefp(skb).

The reference counter was arranged in this way because, during cloning of socket buffers, several sk_buff structures will still point to the same packet data space. If a socket buffer is released, then no other references to the packet data space should also release the packet data space. Otherwise, this would quickly lead to a huge storage hole. The only location where the number of references to packet data can be managed is the packet data space itself, because there is no list managing all clones of a packet. For this reason, and to avoid having to create another data type, we simply reserve a few more bytes than specified by the user when allocating the packet data space. Using the macro skb_datarefp, it is easy to access and test the reference counter to see whether there are other references to the packet data space, in addition to the own reference.

4.1.1 Operations on Socket Buffers

The Linux kernel offers you a number of functions to manipulate socket buffers. In general, these functions can be grouped into three categories:

- *Create, release, and duplicate socket buffers*: These functions assume the entire storage management for socket buffers and their optimization by use of socket-buffer caches.
- *Manipulate parameters and pointers* within the sk_buff structure: These mainly are operations to change the packet data space.
- *Manage socket buffer queues.*

Creating and Releasing Socket Buffers

`alloc_skb()`	**net/core/skbuff.c**

alloc_skb(size, gpf_mask) allocates memory for a socket buffer structure and the corresponding packet memory. In this case, size specifies the size of the packet data space, where this space will be increased (*aligned*) to the next 16-bit address.

In the creation of a new socket buffer, no immediate attempt is made to allocate the memory with kmalloc() for the sk_buff structure; rather, an attempt is made to reuse previously consumed sk_buff structures. Note that requesting memory in the kernel's storage management is very expensive and that, because structures of the same type always require the same size, an attempt is first made to reuse an sk_buff structure no longer required. (This approach can be thought of as simple recycling; see Section 2.6.2.)

There are two different structures that manage consumed socket buffer structures:

- First, each CPU manages a so-called skb_head_cache that stores packets no longer needed. This is a simple socket buffer queue, from which alloc_skb() takes socket buffers.
- Second, there is a central stack for consumed sk_buff structures (skbuff_head_cache).

If there are no more sk_buff structures available for the current CPU, then kmem_cache_alloc() is used to try obtaining a packet from the central socket-buffer cache (skbuff_head_cache). If this attempt fails, then kmalloc() is eventually used. gfp_mask contains flags required to reserve memory.

Using these two caches can be justified by the fact that many packets are created and released in a system (i.e., the memory of sk_buff structures is frequently released), only to be required again shortly afterwards. The two socket buffer caches were introduced to avoid this expensive releasing and reallocating of memory space by the storage management (similarly to first-level and second-level caches for CPU memory access). This means that the time required to release and reserve sk_buff structures can be shortened. When kmem_cache_alloc() is used to reserve an sk_buff structure, the function skb_header_init() is called to initialize the structure. It will be described further below.

Naturally, for the sk_buff structure, a socket buffer requires memory for the packet data. Because the size of a packet is usually different from and clearly bigger than that of an sk_buff structure, a method like the socket-buffer cache does not provide any benefit. The packet data space is reserved in the usual way (i.e., by use of kmalloc()).

The pointers head, data, tail, and end are set once memory has been reserved for the packet data. The counters user and datarefp (number of references to these socket buffer structure) are set to one. The data space for packets begins to grow from the top (data) (i.e., at that point, the socket buffer has no headroom and has tailroom of size bytes).

dev_alloc_skb()	include/linux/skbuff.h

dev_alloc_skb(length) uses the function alloc_skb() to create a socket buffer. The length of this socket buffer's packet data space is length + 16 bytes. Subsequently, skb_reserve(skb, 16) is used to move the currently valid packet data space 16 bytes backwards. This means that the packet has now a headroom of 16 bytes and a tailroom of length bytes.

skb_copy()	net/core/skbuff.c

skb_copy(skb, gfp_mask) creates a copy of the socket buffer skb, copying both the sk_buff structure and the packet data. (See Figure 4–4.) First the function uses alloc_skb() to obtain a new sk_buff structure; then it sets the attributes. Note that only protocol-specific parameters (priority, protocol, ...), the relevant network device (device), and an entry in the route cache are accepted. All pointers dealing with the concatenation of socket buffers (next, prev, sk, list) are set to null.

Memory needed for the payload of the new socket buffers is allocated by kmalloc() and copied by memcopy(). Subsequently, pointers to the new data space are set in the new sk_buff structure. The result of skb_copy() is a new socket buffer (with its own packet data space), which exists independently of the original and can be processed independently. This means that the reference counter of the created copy also shows a value of one, in contrast to a using skb_clone() to replicate a packet.

skb_copy_expand()	net/core/skbuff.c

skb_copy_expand(skb, newheadroom, newtailroom, gfp_mask) also creates a new and independent copy of the socket buffer and packet data; however, a larger

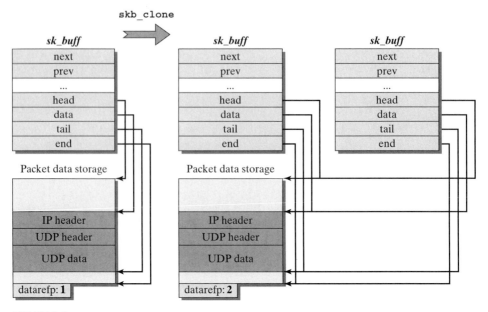

FIGURE 4–4
Copying socket buffers.

space before and after the packet data can be reserved. `newheadroom` and `newtailroom` specify the size of this space before and behind the packet data space, respectively.

`skb_clone()`	**net/core/skbuff.c**

`skb_clone()` also creates a new socket buffer; however, it allocates only one new `sk_buff` structure, and no second memory space for packet data. The pointers of the original `sk_buff` structure and of the new structure point to the same packet data space. There is no backward reference from the packet memory to the references `sk_buff` structures, so the packet memory should be read-only. Figure 4–5 shows the situation before and after `skb_clone()` is called. Among other things, this function is required in multicast implementation. (See Chapter 17.) This allows us to prevent the time-intensive copying of a complete packet data space when a packet is to be sent to several network devices. The memory containing packet data is not released before the variable `datarefp` contains a value of one (i.e., when there is only one reference to the packet data space left).

`kfree_skb()`	**include/linux/skbuff.h**

`kfree_skb()` does the same thing as `kfree_skbmem()` and is called by `kfree_skb()`, but it additionally tests whether the socket buffer is still in a queue (if so, an error message is output). In addition, it removes the reference from the route cache and, if present, calls a `destructor()` for the socket buffer. `kfree_skb()` should be preferred over other options because of these additional security checks.

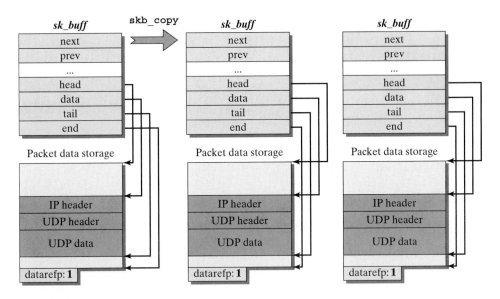

FIGURE 4–5
Cloning socket buffers.

dev_kfree_skb()	include/linux/skbuff.h

dev_kfree-skb(skb) is identical to the method kfree_skb() and is mapped to kfree_skb() by a preprocessor macro.

kfree_skbmem()	include/linux/skbuff.h

kfree_skbmem() frees a socket buffer, provided that it was not cloned and that no instance in the kernel refers to it (datrefp - 1). The variable skb_cloned is tested for null, and datarefp is tested for one. If everything is okay, kfree() first releases the packet memory. Then skb_head_to_pool() is used to insert the sk_buff structure into the socket-buffer cache of the current processor for further use. This means that the memory of the socket-buffer structure is not released for general use (kfree()), but instead is buffered for recycling.

skb_header_init()	include/linux/skbuff.h

skb_header_init() initializes some fields of the sk_buff structure with standard values. Most fields are set to null or NULL, and PACKET_HOST is registered as the packet type.

Manipulating the Packet Data Space   The following functions are declared in the include file <Linux/skbuff.h>. Most of them are defined as inline and have only little functionality; nevertheless, they are important and are used often.

| `skb_get()` | include/linux/skbuff.h |

This increments the number of `user` references to the `sk_buff` structure by one.

| `skb_unshare()` | include/linux/skbuff.h |

`skb_unshared(skb)` uses `skb_cloned` to check for whether the socket buffer is available for exclusive use. If it isn't, then a copy of `skb` is created and returned, so that an exclusive socket buffer is available. In the original packet, the reference counter is decremented by a value of one.

| `skb_put()` | include/linux/skbuff.h |

`skb_put(skb, len)` is an `inline` function that appends data to the end of the current data range of a packet. Though this occurs seldom, because most protocols write their PCI (Protocol Control Information) before the current protocol data unit, there are a few protocol, that require this. More specifically, `skb_put()` increments the pointer `tail` and the parameter `skb->` by `len`. Note that `skb_put()` merely sets the pointers again; the caller is responsible for copying the correct data to the packet data space. The return value is the old value of `skb->tail`, so as to be able to add new packet data to the correct place. Before calling `skb_put()`, we should confirm that the *tailroom* is sufficient; otherwise, the kernel will output an error message and call `skb_over_panic()`.

| `skb_push()` | include/linux/skbuff.h |

`skb_push(skb, len)` works like `skb_put()`, but increases the current packet data space at the beginning of the packet by `len` bytes. This means that the `data` pointer is decremented by `len`, and `skb->len` is incremented by this amount. The return value of `skb_push()` points to the new data space (`skb->data`, in this case). Again, we should first check the *headroom* size.

| `skb_pull()` | include/linux/skbuff.h |

`skb_pull(skb, len)` serves to truncate `len` bytes at the beginning of a packet. The pointer `skb->data` is adjusted, and the length of the packet (`skb->len`) is reduced accordingly—but, first, we check on whether there are still `len` bytes in the free part of the packet data space.

| `skb_tailroom()` | include/linux/skbuff.h |

`skb_tailroom(skb)` returns the bytes still free at the end of the data space. If `skb_put()` requests more data in this space than `skb_tailroom` states, then this will lead to a *kernel panic*.

skb_headroom()   **include/linux/skbuff.h**

skb_headroom(skb) returns (data – head). This corresponds to the amount of free bytes in the front space of the packet data memory. Exactly skb_headroom bytes can still be inserted into the packet by skb_push().

skb_realloc_headroom()   **include/linux/skbuff.h**

skb_realloc_headroom(skb, newheadroom) is required when the memory space between skb->data and skb->head is getting too small. This function can be used to create a new socket buffer with a *headroom* corresponding to the size newheadroom (and not one single byte more). The data part of the old socket buffer is copied into the new one, and most parameters of the sk_buff structure are taken from the old one. Only sk and list are set to NULL. skb_realloc_headroom() is implemented by calling the function skb_copy_expand().

skb_reserve()   **include/linux/skbuff.h**

skb_reserve(skb, len) shifts the entire current data space backwards by len bytes. This means that the total length of this space remains the same. Of course, this function is meaningful only when there are no data in the current space yet, and only if the initial occupancy of this space has to be corrected.

skb_trim()   **include/linux/skbuff.h**

skb_trim(skb, len) sets the current packet data space to len bytes, which means that this space now extends from the initial occupancy of data to tail - data + len. This function is normally used to truncate data at the end (i.e., we call skb_trim() with a length value smaller than the current packet size).

skb_cow()   **include/linux/skbuff.h**

skb_cow(skb, headroom) checks on whether the passed socket buffer has still at least headroom bytes free in the front packet data space and whether the packet is a clone. If either of the two situations is true, then skb_alloc_headroom(skb, headroom) creates and returns a new independent packet. If none of the two tests is true, then the socket buffer skb is returned. skb_cow() is used when a protocol requires an independent socket buffer with sufficient *headroom*.

4.1.2 Other Functions

skb_cloned()   **include/linux/skbuff.h**

skb_cloned(skb) specifies whether this socket buffer was cloned and whether the corresponding packet data space is exclusive. The reference counter datarefp is used to check this.

skb_shared()	include/linux/skbuff.h

skb_shared(skb) checks whether skb->users specifies one single user or several users for the socket buffer.

skb_over_panic(), skb_under_panic()	include/linux/skbuff.h

These functions are used as error-handling routines during an attempt to increase too small a headroom or tailroom of a socket buffer. A debug message is output after each function, and the function BUG() is called.

skb_head_to_pool()	net/core/skbuff.c

skb_head_to_pool(skb) is used to register a socket buffer structure with the socket-buffer pool of the local processor. It is organized as a simple socket-buffer queue, so this product is simply added to the front of the queue by skb_queue_head(). This means that the memory of the socket buffer is not released, but buffered for use by other network packets. This method is much more efficient than to repeatedly allocate and release the memory of a socket buffer by the more complex memory management of the kernel.

The queue skb_head_pool[smp_processor_id()].list cannot grow to an arbitrary length; it can contain a maximum of sysctl_hot_list_len. As soon as this size is reached, additional socket buffers are added to the central pool for reusable socket buffers (skbuff_head_cache).

skb_head_from_pool()	net/core/skbuff.c

This function is used to remove and return a socket buffer from the pool of used socket buffers of the current processor.

4.2 SOCKET-BUFFER QUEUES

When a packet is currently not handled by a protocol instance, it is normally managed in queues. Linux supports the management of packets in a queue structure (struct sk_buff_head) and in a number of operations on this structure. The programmer can use these functions to abstract from the actual implementation of a socket buffer and queues to easily change the underlying implementation of the queue management.

Figure 4–6 shows that the socket buffers stored in a queue are dual-concatenated in a ring structure. This dual concatenation allows quick navigation in either of the two directions. The ring structure facilitates concatenation and prevents the occurrence of NULL pointers.

A queue header consists of the following skb_queue_head structure:

```
struct sk_buff_head
{
        struct sk_buff *next;
        struct sk_buff *prev;
```

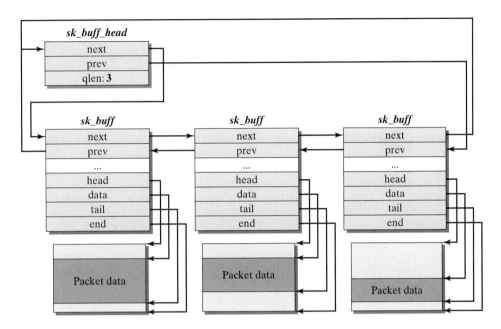

FIGURE 4–6
Packet queues in the Linux kernel.

```
    __u32 qlen;
    spinlock_t lock;
};
```

- **next** and prev are used to concatenate socket buffers; **next** points to the first and prev to the last packet in the queue.
- qlen specifies the current length of the queue in packets.
- lock is a spinlock (see Section 2.3.2) and can be used for atomic execution of operations on the queue. When a critical access occurs, if the spinlock is not free, the access will have to wait until it is released.

4.2.1   Operations on Socket-Buffer Queues

Socket-buffer queues are a powerful tool to arrange packets in Linux. The power of this functionality is complemented by a large number of methods to manage socket buffers in queues.

Most operations on socket buffers are executed during critical phases, or they can be interrupted by higher-priority operations (interrupt handling, soft-IRQ, tasklet, etc.). For this reason, packet data and pointer structures should be processed in an atomic way. Though this introduces some additional cost, because certain mechanisms (e.g., spinlocks and semaphores) have to be used to achieve save states, it is the only way to prevent inconsistent states, which could endanger the stability of the network subsystem and thus of the entire operating system. Security and stability are always more important than performance or benchmarks in Linux.

For example, a fault concatenation could be produced by consecutive nested operations on a queue. The consequence would be a memory access error and eventually a system crash (kernel panic). For this reason, (mainly) the multiprocessor capability of Linux requires atomic handling of such critical processes.

Most queue operations are defined as *inline* procedures in the *include* file <linux/skbuff.h>. This *inline* definition means that there are no real procedures; instead, procedures are built into the body of the calling function, similarly to macros. This reduces overhead of a function call and tolerates a slightly larger kernel. During each function call, we would otherwise have to pack the registers onto the stack and initialize the variable environment of the new function. For the smaller socket-buffer functions, this is far too costly; that's why they are declared inline. The role of each function is still maintained to keep the source code easy to understand and maintain.

Managing Queue Structures

skb_queue_head_init()	include/linux/skbuff.h

skb_queue_head-init(list) initializes an skb_queue_head structure so that it can be used as a queue. Essentially, pointers are set to the structure, and the length is set to null (i.e., next and prev in an empty queue point to the queue list and not to NULL).

skb_queue_empty()	include/linux/skbuff.h

skb_queue_empty(list) checks on whether the queue (list) is empty or still contains buffers. The queue length list->qlen is returned for the sake of simplicity. If it is null, then it is considered to be false; otherwise, it is true.

skb_queue_len()	include/linux/skbuff.h

skb_queue_len(list) returns the actual length of the specified queue, in packets.

Managing Socket Buffers in Queues   The following functions are available to manage packets in queues. These are mainly different strategies for arranging or removing socket buffers in a socket-buffer queue. When a packet is inserted into a queue, then the parameter skb->list of the socket-buffer structure points to this queue. Of course, a packet can always be in one queue only.

Each of the following functions exists in two different versions one with and a second without locked interrupts. This means that, when a function already disabled interrupts, we don't have to do this in queue functions. Functions without locked interrupts are marked by two leading underlines, e.g., __skb_dequeue().

skb_queue_head()	include/linux/skbuff.h

skb_queue_head(list, skb) orders a packet at the header of the specified queue and increments the length of the queue, (list->qlen), by one.

`skb_queue_tail()`	**include/linux/skbuff.h**

`skb_queue_tail(list, skb)` appends the socket buffer `skb` to the end of the queue and increments its length, (`list->qlen`), by one.

`skb_dequeue()`	**include/linux/skbuff.h**

`skb_dequeue(list)` removes the top packet from the queue and returns a pointer to it. The length of the queue is decremented by one. If there is no packet in the queue, then the `NULL` pointer is returned.

`skb_dequeue_tail()`	**include/linux/skbuff.h**

`skb_dequeue_tail(list)` removes the last packet from a queue and returns a pointer to it. If there is no packet in the list, then `NULL` is returned.

`skb_queue_purge()`	**include/linux/skbuff.h**

`skb_queue_purge` empties the queue list: All packets are removed from the list and released by `kfree_skb()`.

`skb_insert()`	**include/linux/skbuff.h**

`skb_insert(oldskb, newskb)` orders the socket buffer `newskb` *in front* of the buffer `oldskb` in the queue. In addition, it sets the `list` pointer of the new socket buffer to the list of the next buffer and increments the queue length.

`skb_append()`	**include/linux/skbuff.h**

`skb_append(oldskb, newskb)` places the socket buffer `newskb` *behind* `oldskb` in the queue of `oldskb`. Additionally, the `list` pointer is set to the queue of the previous buffer and the queue length is incremented by one.

`skb_unlink()`	**include/linux/skbuff.h**

`skb_unlink(skb)` removes the specified socket buffer from its queue (it is not explicitly passed as parameter) and decrements the queue length. `skb_unlink()` checks explicitly for whether the list exists; the function `__skb_unlink(skb, list)` does not run this test, which means that we have to ensure that the buffer is actually in a list.

`skb_peek()`	**include/linux/skbuff.h**

`skb_peek(list)` returns a pointer to the first element of a list, if this list is not empty; otherwise, it returns `NULL`. If a socket buffer is in the queue, then only a pointer to this socket buffer is returned; the socket buffer is not removed from the queue. This is to ensure that no other activities in the kernel can remove that buffer from the queue while operations run on the socket buffer, which can lead to inconsistencies. There is no interrupt-save version of skb_peek().

skb_peek_tail()	include/linux/skbuff.h

skb_peek_tail(list) returns a pointer to the last element of a queue. If this queue is empty, then NULL is returned. Again, the buffer remains in the queue and should be protected. (See skb_peek().)

C H A P T E R   5

Network Devices

Each (tele)communication over a network normally requires a physical medium, which is accessed over a network adapter (network interface). Together, the network adapter and the medium eventually allow bridging of the spatial distance, so that data can be exchanged between two or more communication systems. If we use the ISO/OSI reference model introduced in Section 3.1.1, then the tasks of a network adapter extend over layers 1 and 2a: They include all tasks dealing with data–signal–data conversion (and media access in the case of shared media). All higher-order protocol functions are handled by the protocol instances of the respective operating system.[1] This interface is characterized by the following properties:

- interfacing between specialized hardware in the network adapters and software-based protocols;
- asynchronous input and output point of the protocol stack in the operating system kernel.

In the network architecture of the Linux operating systems, this interface between software-based protocols and network adapters is implemented by the concept of *network devices*. A network-device interface primarily should meet the following requirements:

- *Abstract from the technical properties of a network adapter*: Network adapters might implement different layer-1 and layer-2 protocols and are manufactured by different vendors. This means that their configurations are individual and specific to each network adapter. For this reason, we need a piece of software for each adapter to communicate with the hardware: the *driver* of a network adapter (which is, by the way, also a protocol).

---

[1]This view is limited to software-based communication systems on PC basis. More instances are normally implemented in hardware for dedicated systems.

◼ *Provide a uniform interface for access by protocol instances*: In a system like Linux, there are several protocol instances using the services of network adapters. To be consistent with the principle of layered communication systems (see Section 3.1), these instances should be implemented independently of a specific type of adapter. This means that network adapters should have a uniform interface to the higher layers.

In the Linux kernel, these two tasks are handled by the concept of network devices and are often seen as one single unit. However, it makes sense to distinguish between the two views of network devices and discuss them separately. For this reason, the following section introduces the network-device interface visible from the "top," which offers a uniform interface to the higher protocol instances for physical transmission of data. Later on, Section 5.3 will discuss the "lower" half: the adapter-specific functions that are the actual network driver. Subsequently, Chapter 6 will introduce an example describing how a packet is sent and received on the level of network devices interfacing to the higher protocols.

Not every network device in the Linux kernel represents a physical network adapter. There are network devices, such as the loopback network device, that offer a logical network functionality. The interface of network devices is also often used to bind protocols, such as the point-to-point protocol (PPP).

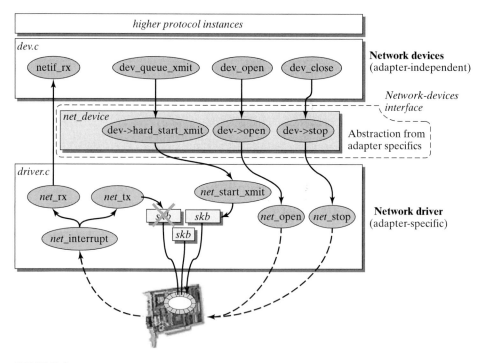

FIGURE 5–1
The structure of a network device interface.

5.1   THE net_device INTERFACE

In addition to character and block devices, network devices represent the third category of adapters in the Linux kernel [RuCo01]. This section describes the concept of network devices from the perspective of higher-layer protocols and their data structures and management.

Network adapters differ significantly from the character and block devices introduced in Section 2.5. One of their main characteristics is that they have no representation in the device file system /dev/, which means that they cannot be addressed by simple read-write operations. In addition, this is not possible because network devices work on a packet basis; a behavior comparable to character-oriented devices can be achieved only by use of complex protocols (e.g., TCP). For example, there are no such network devices as /dev/eth0 or /dev/atm1. Network devices are configured separately by the ifconfig tool on the application level. More recently, another tool available is ip, which can be used for extensive configuration of most network functions.

One of the reasons why network devices are so special is that the actions of a network adapter cannot be bound to a unique process; instead, they run in the kernel and independently of user processes [RuCo01]. For example, a hard disk is requested to pass a block to the kernel: The action is triggered by the adapter (in the case of network adapters), and the adapter has to explicitly request the kernel to pass the packet.

5.1.1   The net_device Structure

struct net_device	include/linux/netdevice.h

```
struct net_device
{
    char                    name[IFNAMSIZ];
    unsigned long           rmem_end, rmem_start, mem_end, mem_start, base_addr;
    unsigned int            irq;
    unsigned char           if_port, dma;
    unsigned long           state;
    struct net_device       *next, *next_sched;
    int                     ifindex, iflink;

    unsigned long           trans_start, last_rx;
    unsigned short          flags, gflags, mtu, type, hard_header_len;
    void                    *priv;
    struct net_device       *master;
    unsigned char           broadcast[MAX_ADDR_LEN], pad;
    unsigned char           dev_addr[MAX_ADDR_LEN], addr_len;
```

```
    struct dev_mc_list    *mc_list;
    int                   mc_count, promiscuity, allmulti;

    int                   watchdog_timeo;
    struct timer_list     watchdog_timer;

    void                  *atalk_ptr, *ip_ptr, *dn_ptr, *ip6_ptr, *ec_ptr;
    struct Qdisc          *qdisc, *qdisc_sleeping, *qdisc_list, *qdisc_ingress;
    unsigned long         tx_queue_len;

    spinlock_t            xmit_lock;
    int                   xmit_lock_owner;
    spinlock_t            queue_lock;
    atomic_t              refcnt;

    int                   features;
    int                   (*init)(struct net_device *dev);
    void                  (*uninit)(struct net_device *dev);
    void                  (*destructor)(struct net_device *dev);
    int                   (*open)(struct net_device *dev);
    int                   (*stop)(struct net_device *dev);
    int                   (*hard_start_xmit) (struct sk_buff *skb,         \
                            struct net_device *dev);
    int                   (*hard_header) (struct sk_buff *skb,struct net_device \
                            *dev,unsigned short type,void *daddr,void *saddr,  \
                            unsigned len);
    int                   (*rebuild_header)(struct sk_buff *skb);
    void                  (*set_multicast_list) (struct net_device *dev);
    int                   (*set_mac_address) (struct net_device *dev, void *addr);
    int                   (*do_ioctl)(struct net_device *dev, struct ifreq *ifr,\
                            int cmd);
    int                   (*set_config)(struct net_device *dev, struct ifmap \
                            *map);
    int                   (*hard_header_cache) (struct neighbour *neigh, struct \
                            hh_cache *hh);
    void                  (*header_cache_update) (struct hh_cache *hh, struct  \
                            net_device *dev, unsigned char *haddr);
    int                   (*change_mtu)(struct net_device *dev, int new_mtu);
    void                  (*tx_timeout) (struct net_device *dev);
    int                   (*hard_header_parse) (struct sk_buff *skb, unsigned  \
                            char *haddr);
    int                   (*neigh_setup) (struct net_device *dev, struct      \
                            neigh_parms *);
    struct net_device_stats* (*get_stats) (struct net_device *dev);
    struct iw_statistics* (*get_wireless_stats) (struct net_device *dev);

    struct module         *owner;
    struct net_bridge_port *br_port;
};
```

The `net_device` structure forms the basis of each network device in the Linux kernel. It contains not only information about the network adapter hardware (interrupt, ports, driver functions, etc.), but also the configuration data of the network device with regard to the higher network protocols (IP address, subnet mask, etc.).

As was mentioned at the beginning of this chapter, the `net_device` structure represents a general interface between higher protocol instances and the hardware used. It allows you to abstract from the network components used. For an efficient implementation of this abstraction, we once again use the concept of function pointers. For this reason, the `net_device` structure contains a number of function pointers, which are called by higher protocols by using their global names, and then the hardware-specific methods of the driver are called from each network device.

For example, `el3_start_xmit()` is used to actually call the function `hard_start_xmit()` for a network adapter of type 3Com/3c509.

In general, the parameters of the `net_device` structure can be divided into different areas, as described below.

General Fields of a Network Device The following parameters of the `net_device` structure (see previous subsection) are used to manage network devices. They have no significance with regard to special layers or protocol instances.

- `name` is the name of the network device. In general, device types are numbered from 0 to *n* (e.g., `eth0`–`eth4`). Some network devices, such as the loopback device (`lo`), occur only once, which means that they have fixed names.

  When registering a network device, you can suggest a name, which should be unique. However, you can also let the system assign the `ethn` name automatically. (See `init_etherdev`.) The naming convention for network devices will be described in detail in Section 5.2.3.

- `next` is used to concatenate several `net_device` structures. We will see in Section 5.2 that all network devices are managed in a singly linked linear list that starts with the pointer `dev_base`.

- `owner` is a pointer to the module structure of the module created by the `net_device` structure of this network device.

- `ifindex` is a second identifier for a network device, in addition to the name. When a new network device is created, `dev_get_index()` assigns a new unused index to this device. This index allows you to quickly find a network device from the list of all devices, which is much faster, compared to search by name.

- `iflink` specifies the index of the network device used to send a packet. This is normally the index `ifindex`, but, for tunneling network devices, such as `ipip`, `iflink` includes the index of the network device that is eventually used to send the enveloped packet.

- `state`: The field `dev->state` contains status information about the network device and the network adapter. It was added to the kernel for the first time in version 2.3.43 and replaces the previous fields `start` (network adapter is open), `interrupt` (driver handles an adapter interrupt), and `tbusy` (all packet buffers are busy). These functions are now replaced by the following flags in the field `state`:

▶ `LINK_STATE_START` shows whether the network adapter was opened with `dev->open()` (i.e., whether it was activated and can be used). However, a `LINK_STATE_START` state set does not automatically mean that packets can be sent. In fact, all buffers on the adapter could be busy. (See next flag.) The flag `LINK_STATE_START` should have read access only, because it should be modified only by the methods used to manage network devices. The method `netif_running(dev)` is available to test this flag.

▶ `LINK_STATE_XOFF` shows whether the network adapter can accept socket buffers for transmission or its transmit buffers (which are normally organized as ring buffers) are already busy. The method `netif_queue_stopped(dev)` can be used to test for this state. Again, only read access to this flag should be allowed.

`LINK_STATE_XOFF` replaces the previous field `dev->tbusy`. Older drivers could take either of three different situations, which accessed the `tbusy` flag. The latter was replaced by the following functions, which make the programming style much easier to read:

▶ *Stopping a transmission*: When the packet buffers of a network adapter are busy, `dev->tbusy = 1` was previously used to stop sending packets to the adapter. Now, there is the (inline) function `netif_stop_queue(dev)`, which sets the `LINK_STATE_XOFF` flag in `dev->state`. This means that no packets are removed from the queue and passed to this adapter. Normally, `netif_stop_queue()` is called by the driver of an adapter, and then the driver is responsible for restarting the transmission. (See Section 5.3.)

▶ *Resuming a transmission*: Once a network adapter has sent a packet from the (ring) packet buffer, it can resume accepting packets from the kernel. The method `netif_start_queue(dev)`, which deletes the `LINK_STATE_XOFF` flag, is used for this purpose. In general, `netif_start_queue(dev)` is used by the driver methods. (See Section 5.3.) This corresponds to `dev->tbusy = 0` in older kernel versions.

▶ *Starting a transmission*: The method `netif_start_queue(dev)` is used to resume passing socket buffers to the network adapter.

▶ In addition, the method `netif_wake_queue(dev)` is used to resume passing packets and, at the same time, to trigger the NET_TX software interrupt, which handles the passing of packets to the network adapter.

▶ The field `interrupt` has no counterpart in the new kernel versions. It was previously used to prevent concurrent handling of interrupt methods. The new and SMP-improved kernels have special methods to control parallel processes. (See Section 2.3.) A driver should use these methods and manage their lock variables in its private data structures as needed.

■ `trans_start` stores the time (in jiffies) when the transmission of a packet started. If, after some time, the driver still hasn't received an acknowledgment to send the packet (ack interrupt), then it can introduce appropriate actions. For these purposes, kernel versions 2.4 and higher use a timer called `watchdog_timer`.

- `last_rx` should include the time (in jiffies) when the last packet arrived.
- `priv` is a pointer to the private data of a network device or to the private data of its driver. Private data contains those variables and structures that are required to manage a network adapter. They are not stored in the `net_device` structure, but they are normally specific to an adapter.
- `qdisc` refers to a structure of the type `Qdisc`, which mirrors the serving strategy of the current network device. Chapter 18 will discuss this issue in detail.
- `refcnt` stores the number of references to this network device.
- `xmit_lock`, `xmit_lock_owner`, and `queue_lock` are used to protect against parallel handling of a transmit process or parallel access to the transmit queue. For example, `xmit_lock_owner` includes the number of the processor, which is currently in the transmit function `hard_start_xmit()`. When no processor is currently transmitting, then `xmit_lock_owner` takes the value −1.

Hardware-Specific Fields

- `rmem_end`, `rmem_start`, `mem_end`, `mem_start`: These fields specify the beginning and end of the common memory space that the network adapter and the kernel share. The location (`mem_start` − `mem_end`) designates the buffers for packets to be sent, and (`rmem_start` − `rmem_end`) designates the location for received packets. The size of the buffers indicates the amount of storage available on the card. When using `ifconfig` to initialize a network adapter, you can specify the addresses of memory locations.
- `base_addr`: The I/O basic address is also set in the driver's *probing* routine during a search for a device. `ifconfig` can be used to display and set the value. In addition, the I/O basic address can be specified when loading most of the modules and as a kernel boot parameter.
- `irq`: The number of the interrupt of a network adapter is also set during the so-called *probing phase* of the driver or by explicitly specifying it when loading the module or starting the kernel. In addition, `ifconfig` can be used to modify the interrupt number during operation.
- `dma` contains the number of the DMA (Direct Memory Access) channel, if the device supports the DMA transfer mode.
- `if_port` stores the media type of the network adapter currently used. For Ethernet, we distinguish between BNC, Twisted Pair (TP), and AUI. There are no unique constants; instead, each driver can use its own values.

Data on the Physical Layer   The values of the following fields are set by the `ethersetup()` function for Ethernet cards. They are generally identical for all Ethernet-based cards, except for the `flag` field, which has to be set to match the card's capability.

There are similar functions to set standard values for token-ring and FDDI adapters (fddi_setup(), tr_setup()). These fields have to be set manually for other network types.

- hard_header_length specifies the length of the layer-2 packet header. This value is 14 for Ethernet adapters. This does not correspond to the length of the actual packet header on the physical medium, but only to the part passed to the network adapter. In general, the network adapter adds additional fields (e.g., the preamble and checksum for Ethernet).

- mtu is the *maximum transfer unit*, which specifies the maximum length of the payload of a layer-2 frame. Layer-3 protocols have to consider this value; they must not pass more octets to the network device. Ethernet has an MTU of 1500 bytes.

- tx_queue_len specifies the maximum length of the output queue of the network device. ether_setup() sets this value to 100. tx_queue_len should not be confused with the buffers of the network adapter. A network adapter normally has an additional ring buffer for 16 or 32 packets.

- type specifies the hardware type of the network adapter. The values are specified in RFC 1700 for the ARP protocol, which has to state the hardware type for address-resolution purposes. Linux defines additional constants not defined in FRC 1700. (See Figure 5–2.)

- addr_len, dev_addr[MAX_ADDR_LEN], broadcast[MAX_ADDR_LEN]: These fields contain the data of the layer-2 address. addr_len specifies the length of the layer-2 address, which is stored in the dev_addr field. The third field contains the broadcast address, which can be used to reach all computers in the local network.

- dev_mc_list points to a linear list with multicast layer-2 addresses. When the network adapter receives a packet with a destination address included in dev_mc_list,

```
ARPHRD_NETROM       0    /* NET/ROM pseudo              */
ARPHRD_ETHER        1    /* Ethernet 10Mbps             */
ARPHRD_EETHER       2    /* Experimental Ethernet       */
ARPHRD_AX25         3    /* AX.25 Level 2               */
ARPHRD_PRONET       4    /* PROnet token ring           */
ARPHRD_CHAOS        5    /* Chaosnet                    */
ARPHRD_IEEE802      6    /* IEEE 802.2 Ethernet/TR/TB   */
ARPHRD_ARCNET       7    /* ARCnet                      */
ARPHRD_APPLETLK     8    /* APPLEtalk                   */
ARPHRD_DLCI        15    /* Frame Relay DLCI            */
ARPHRD_ATM         19    /* ATM                         */

    /* Dummy types for non-ARP hardware */
ARPHRD_SLIP       256
ARPHRD_CSLIP6     259
ARPHRD_PPP        512
ARPHRD_LOOPBACK   772    /* Loopback device             */
ARPHRD_IRDA       783    /* Linux-IrDA                  */
```

FIGURE 5–2
Hardware types defined in RFC 1700 and Linux-specific constants.

then the network adapter has to pass this packet to the upper layers. The driver method set_multicast_list is used to pass the addresses of this list to the network adapter. The hardware filter of this network adapter (if present) is responsible for passing to the kernel only those packets of interest to this computer.

- mc_count contains the number of addresses in dev_mc_list.

- watchdog_timeo and watchdog_timer are used to detect problems an adapter may incur when sending packets. For this reason, the watchdog_timer is initialized when a network device starts and always called after watchdog_timeo time units (jiffies). The handling routine dev_watchdog() checks whether or not watchdog_timeo time units have passed since the last transmission of a packet (stored in trans_start). If this is the case, then there were problems in the transmission of the last packet, and the network adapter has to be checked. To check the network adapter, the driver function tx_timeout() is called. If not much time has passed since the last start of a transmission, then nothing is done, except the watchdog timer is started.

Data on the Network Layer

- ip_ptr, ip6_ptr, atalk_ptr, dn_ptr, and ec_ptr point to information of layer-3 protocols that use this network device. If the network device was configured for the Internet protocol, among others, then ip_ptr points to a structure of the type in_device, which manages information and configuration parameters of the relevant IP instance. For example, the in_device structure manages a list with IP addresses of the network device, a list with active IP multicast groups, and the parameters for the ARP protocol.

- family designates the address family of the network device. In the case of the Internet protocol (IP), this field takes the constant AF_INET.

- pa_alen specifies the length of the addresses of the protocol used. IP addresses of the class AF_INET have the length four bytes.

- pa_addr, pa_braddr, and pa_mask describe the addressing of a network device on the network layer. pa_addr contains the address of the computer or network device. pa_baddr specifies the broadcast address, and pa_mask includes the network mask. All three values are set by ifconfig when a network device is activated.

- pa_dstaddr specifies the address of the other partner in a point-to-point connection (e.g., PPP or SLIP).

- flags includes different switches. Some of them describe properties of the network device (IFF_ARP, IFF_MULTICAST, ...); others output the current state (IFF_UP). Table 5–1 lists the meaning of these switches, which can be set by use of the ifconfig command.

Device-Driver Methods   As mentioned earlier, one of the tasks of the network device interface is to abstract a network device from the underlying hardware. The set of methods available for network driver functions have to be mapped to a uniform interface so

TABLE 5–1   IFF flags of a network device.

Flag	Meaning
IFF_UP	The network device is activated and can send and receive packets.
IFF_BROADCAST	The device is broadcast-enabled, and the broadcast address pa_braddr is valid.
IFF_DEBUG	This flag switches the debug mode on (currently not used by any driver).
IFF_LOOPBACK	This flag shows that this is a loopback network device.
IFF_POINTOPOINT	This is a point-to-point connection. If this switch is set, then pa_dstaddr should contain the partner's address.
IFF_NOARP	This device does not support the Address Resolution Protocol (ARP) (e.g., in point-to-point connections).
IFF_PROMISC	This flag switches the *promiscuous* mode on. This means that all packets currently received in the network adapter are forwarded to the upper layers, including those not intended for this computer. This mode is of interest for tcpdump only.
IFF_MULTICAST	This flag activates the receipt of multicast packets. ether_setup() activates this switch. A card that does not support multicast should delete this flag.
IFF_ALLMULTI	All multicast packets should be received. This is required when the computer is to work as multicast router. IFF_MULTICAST has to be set in addition.
IFF_PORTSEL	Setting of the output port is supported by the hardware.
IFF_AUTOMEDIA	Automatic selection of the output medium (*autosensing*) is enabled.
IFF_DYNAMIC	Dynamic change of the network device's address is enabled (e.g., for dialup connections).

that higher protocols can be accessed. This functionality is implemented exactly by the function pointers of the net_device structure (see above) described in this section. These pointers let you use individual functions for different instances of the net_device structure, which are eventually addressed over a common name.

Some of these functions depend on the hardware of the network adapter and have to be set in the initialization function of the network driver. The other functions are specific to the MAC protocol used by the network adapter and can be initialized by special methods (e.g., eth_setup()). A function pointer not required can be initialized to NULL.

We will next discuss the tasks of the methods of a network device. More specifically, we will describe their basic tasks from the view of the higher protocols. These methods are implemented by the network driver used. The exact implementation in general will be discussed in Section 5.3, using the skeleton network driver as an example.

- init() is used to search and initialize network devices. This method is responsible for finding and initializing a network adapter of the present type. Primarily, a net_device structure has to be created and filled with the driver-specific data of the network device or network driver. Subsequently, the network device is registered by register_netdevice(). (See Section 5.3.1.)

- uninit() is called when a network device is unregistered (unregister_netdevice()). This method can be used to execute driver-specific functions, which may be necessary when a network device is removed. The uninit() has been introduced to the net_device structure since version 2.4 and is currently not used by any driver.

- destructor() is also new in the net_device structure. This function is called when the last reference to a network device was removed (dev->refcnt) (i.e., when no protocol instances or other components in the Linux kernel point to the net_device structure). This means that you can use the destructor() function to do cleanup work (e.g., free memory or similar things). The destructor() function is currently not used by any driver.

- open() opens (activates) a named network device. During the activation, the required system resources are requested and assigned. Note that this method can open only network devices that were previously registered. Normally, dev->open() is used in the dev_open() method which, in turn, is called by the ifconfig command. Upon successful execution of open(), the network device can be used.

- stop() terminates the activity of a network adapter and frees the system resources it has used. The network device is then no longer active, but it remains in the list of registered network devices (net_devs).

- hard_start_xmit() uses a packet (in the form of a socket buffer) over the network device. If successful (i.e., the packet was delivered to the adapter), then hard_start_xmit() returns with the return value 0; otherwise, 1.

- get_stats() gets statistics and information about the network device and its activities. This information is returned in the form of a net_device_stats structure. The elements of this structure will be introduced in the course of this chapter.

- get_wireless_stats() returns additional information for wireless network adapters. This information is forwarded in a structure of the type iw_statistics. The tool iwconfig can be used to display this specific information.

- set_multicast_list() passed the list with multicast MAC addresses to the network adapter, so that the adapter can receive packets with these addresses. This list is called either when the multicast receipt for the network device is activated (IFF_MULTICAST flag) or when the list of group MAC addresses to be received has changed. (See also Section 17.4.1.)

- watchdog_timeo() deals with problems during the transmission of a packet across the network adapter (not when the socket buffer is passed to the network adapter). If no acknowledgment for the packet is received after dev->tx_timeout, then the kernel calls the method watchdog_timeo() to solve the problem.

- do_ioctl(): This method is generally not used by higher protocols, because they have no generic functions. It is normally used to pass adapter-specific ioctl() commands to the network driver.
- set_config() is used to change the configuration of a network adapter at run-time. The method lets you change system parameters, such as the interrupt or the memory location of the network adapter.

The methods for a network device described above depend on the network adapter used, which means that they have to be provided by the driver, if their functionality is required. The methods described below depend less on the hardware of a network adapter, but rather on the layer-2 protocol used. For this reason, they don't necessarily have to be implemented by driver-specific methods, but can run on top of existing methods (e.g., those for Ethernet and FDDI).

- hard_header() creates a layer-2 packet header from layer-2 addresses for source and destination.
- rebuild_header() is responsible for rebuilding the layer-2 packet header before a packet is transmitted. This function was the entry point to the ARP protocol in earlier versions of the Linux kernel. The conversion to the neighbour cache (see Section 15.3.1) should create a stored layer-2 packet header, so that rebuild_header() is called only when the hard header cache contains wrong information.
- hard_header_cache() fills a layer-2 packet header in the hard header cache with passed data. This means that subsequent transmission processes can access a prepared layer-2 packet header.
- header_cache_update() changes the layer-2 destination address in a stored layer-2 packet header in the hard header cache.
- hard_header_parse() reads the layer-2 sender address from the layer-2 packet header in the packet data space of a socket buffer and copies it to the passed address, haddr.
- set_mac_address() can be used to change the layer-2 address of a network adapter, if it supports alternative MAC addresses.
- change_mtu() changes the MTU (Maximum Transfer Unit) of a network device and implements all necessary changes.

5.2   MANAGING NETWORK DEVICES

Now that we know how a network device can be represented by the net_device structure in the Linux kernel, this section discusses the management of network devices. First, we will describe how network devices can be linked, then we will introduce methods that can be used to manage and manipulate network devices. As was mentioned earlier, this section will look at network devices only from the "top"—their uniform interface for protocol instances of the higher-order layers.

All network devices in the Linux kernel are connected in a linear list (Figure 5–3). The kernel variable dev_base represents the entry point to the list of registered network

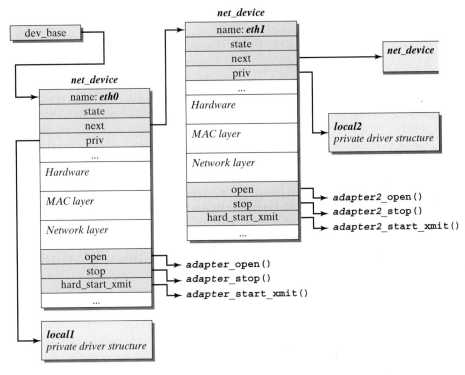

FIGURE 5–3
Linking net_device structures.

devices, pointing to the first element in the list, which, in turn, uses **next** to point to the next element. Each `net_device` structure represents one network device.

The proc directory (`/proc/net/dev`) or the (easier to read) command `ifconfig -a` can be used to call the list of currently registered devices. (See Appendix C.1.)

5.2.1   Registering and Unregistering Network Devices

We know from the previous section that network devices are managed in the list dev_base. This list stores all registered network devices, regardless of whether they are activated. When `register_netdevice()` is used to add a new device to this list, then we first have to create and initialize a `net_device` structure for it. This process can be done in two different ways:

- If we specified in the kernel configuration that the driver of a network device should be integrated permanently into the kernel, then there is already a `net_device` structure. A clever mechanism with preprocessor definitions creates different instances of the `net_device` structure during the translation, depending on the kernel configuration, and these instances are used for the existing network adapters when booting.

  For example, to integrate the driver of an Ethernet card into the kernel, eight `net_device` structures are created for Ethernet network devices, and these structures are initially not allocated to any card.

If the driver was translated as a kernel module, then the driver itself has to create a net_device structure for each existing network adapter. This can be done by the module itself or, for Ethernet drivers, by use of the function init_etherdev().

The list of network devices is used to store entries for those network adapters actually existing. For this reason, before an entry is added to this list, we check for whether a network adapter can be found for a driver. To check this, each of these drivers has an init() or probe() function. It is very specific to each adapter and will be described in more detail in Section 5.3. Among the exception, are logical network devices, such as loopback (lo) and PPP (ppp0), which don't have to rely on underlying hardware.

The following discussion assumes that we want to register a network device based on an Ethernet adapter. During booting of the system or loading of the driver module, the appropriate adapter was found. However, before the network device can be added to the list of known network devices (dev_base), the net_device structure should have been initialized so that the network device can actually be activated and used. The kernel has certain functions (mainly for Ethernet adapters) that facilitate the driver programmer's work.

init_netdev()	**drivers/net/net_init.c**

init_netdev(dev, sizeof_priv, mask, setup) initializes the most important elements from the general range of the net_device structure. (See Section 5.1.1.) First, however, we have to check on whether there is a net_device structure at all. If the value null was entered for dev in the call, then init_alloc_dev() is used to create a new net_device structure, which is also added to the list of network devices by register_netdevice() at the end of the initializing process. If the net_device structure existed already before the call, then the caller has to register it.

Subsequently, the name of the network device is verified. If the array dev->name consists of an empty string or begins with a blank, then the kernel uses the method dev_alloc_name() to allocate a name. In this case, there is an option to use the mask parameter to specify a prefix, which is extended to a valid name for a network device by the known scheme. For example, the prefix test%d produces the name test0, test1, and so on, depending on the network devices already existing with this prefix. If the prefix does not contain a formatting character (%d), then the name should be unique; otherwise, consecutive numbering is not possible, and the function will return an error. Consequently, the network device cannot be initialized.

Once a network device has a unique name, we verify that parameters for its hardware configuration have been stated when the system boots. For this purpose, the list dev_boot_setup in the method netdev_boot_setup_check() is searched for an entry with the name of the new network device. If there is such an entry, then the parameters irq, mem_start, mem_end, and base_addr are taken and added to the net_device structure of the network device.

Now the general part of the initialization of the net_device structure is completed. In the calling of init_netdev, a pointer in the setup parameter has to be passed to a function, which can be used for individual configuration. In general, the setup function handles layer-2 initialization tasks. When one is using `init_etherdev()`, reference is made to the `ether_setup()` method, which initializes the Ethernet-specific function pointers in the `net_device` structure. Finally, `init_netdev()` returns with a pointer to the network device.

`init_etherdev()`	**drivers/net/net_init.c**

`init_etherdev(dev, priv_size)` can be used by Ethernet-based network devices. The function does nothing but call `init_netdev()` with the correct parameters. Similar functions are also available for other MAC protocols (FDDI, HIPPI, etc.).

```
struct net_device *init_etherdev(struct net_device *dev, int sizeof_priv)
{
    return init_netdev(dev, sizeof_priv, "eth%d", ether_setup);
}
```

`ether_setup()`	**drivers/net/net_init.c**

`ether_setup(dev)` is called in `init_netdev()` to initialize the Ethernet-specific parameters and methods of a network device. It adds the pointers of the MAC protocol-specific functions for Ethernet adapters to the `net_device` structure (hard_header, mtu, ...). In addition, it sets the flags (dev->flags) of the network device to `IFF_BROADCAST|IFF|MULTICAST`.

```
dev->change_mtu          = eth_change_mtu;
dev->hard_header         = eth_header;
dev->rebuild_header      = eth_rebuild_header;
dev->set_mac_address     = eth_mac_addr;
dev->hard_header_cache   = eth_header_cache;
dev->header_cache_update = eth_header_cache_update;
dev->hard_header_parse   = eth_header_parse;
dev->type                = ARPHRD_ETHER;
dev->hard_header_len     = ETH_HLEN;
dev->mtu                 = 1500;       /* eth_mtu */
dev->addr_len            = ETH_ALEN;
dev->tx_queue_len        = 100;        /* Ethernet wants good queues */
memset(dev->broadcast,0xFF, ETH_ALEN);
dev->flags               = IFF_BROADCAST|IFF_MULTICAST;
```

`register_netdevice()`	**net/core/dev.c**

`register_netdevice(dev)` is responsible for registering the network device represented by the passed `net_device` structure with the kernel. If the function `dev->init()` exists, then the network adapter is first searched and initialized by the driver function `init()`. Subsequently, there is a check on whether a network device with the requested name is already available. If so, then `register_netdevice()`

returns an error message; otherwise, the network device is simply appended to the end of the linked list dev_base, so that it is available for general use.

In addition, the state dev->state is set to LINK_STATE_PRESENT in register_netdevice(), and dev_init_scheduler() sets the scheduling process for the new network device to the standard FIFO mechanism. This method is also used to cause the function dev_watchdog_init() to initialize the timer to detect transmission problems (dev->watchdog_timer; see Section 5.3.4). However, this timer is not started before the network adapter is activated (dev_open(); see Section 5.2.2).

Finally, the network device obtains a new number (dev->ifindex), and notifier_call_chain(&netdev_chain, NETDEV_REGISTER, dev) calls all registered methods in the notification chain netdev_chain.

`unregister_netdevice()`	**net/core/dev.c**

unregister_netdevice(dev) removes the net_device structure passed as parameter from the list of registered network devices (dev_base). If the network device is still in active state (IFF_UP), it is now closed by the driver function dev->close(). Subsequently, it is searched in the list dev_base and removed. If it is not found, then the function returns an error message.

Once the structure has been removed, unregister_netdevice() synchronizes itself to the NET-RX software interrupt by the big reader lock BR_NETPROTO_LOCK. Subsequently, the queuing discipline is released by dev_shutdown(), and all registered functions in the notification chain netdev_chain are informed about the NETDEV_UNREGISTER event. Subsequently, the destructor of the network driver is called, if it exists. Only the more recent network drivers have destructors, so we have to check periodically on whether existing references to the network device (dev->refcnt) disappeared for older drivers to be able to actually remove the network device.

5.2.2   Opening and Closing Network Devices

The previous section described how a network device is registered; the current section explains how one can be activated and deactivated. As with other device types in the Linux system, activating and deactivating is also referred to as *opening* and *closing*. To open and close a network device, the administrator can use the command ifconfig. It is used not only to activate and deactivate network devices, but also to configure them. More specifically, this command is used to set protocol-specific parameters, such as addresses and subnet masks, and to modify interface parameters for the network adapter (hardware parameters).

In addition, ifconfig can be used to change the flags of a network device. The syntax of ifconfig and its options are listed in Appendix C.1. Naturally, before a network device can be activated, it has to be registered.

Activating a Network Device   When we use ifconfig *name address* up to activate a network device, ifconfig uses the ioctl() command SIOCSIFADDR *(Socket I/O Control Set InterFace ADDRess)* to allocate the specified address to the network device *name*. The handling routine for the INET address family is devinet_ioctl.

Subsequently, the ioctl() command SIOCSIFFLAGS (*Socket I/O Control Set InterFace FLAGS*) is used to set the IFF_UP flag for the network device in the handling method dev_ifsioc(). To manipulate the flag, we use the method dev_change_flags(dev, flags), which also causes the method dev_open(dev) to be called when the IFF_UP flag is set.

dev_open()	net/core/dev.c

The function dev_open(dev) opens a network device (i.e., the network device is activated and can be used). If the network device is already active (IFF_UP), or if it has not been registered ((!netif_device_present(dev)), then the function returns an error message.

The actual initialization (i.e., the device-specific functions) is executed by the open() function of the network driver, if it exists. If this initialization is successful (i.e., no error occurred), then the net_device specific states are set as follows:

- dev->flags assumes the state IFF_UP.
- dev->state is set to LINK_START_START.
- The multicast state is activated by dev_mc_upload().
- The queue and the scheduler of the network device are activated (dev_activate(dev)). At the same time, the method dev_watchdog_up(dev) starts the timer to detect transmission problems. (See Section 5.3.4.) The timer calls the method dev_watchdog() every dev->watchdog_timeo ticks to check that the network adapter works properly.
- The notification chain netdev_chain is informed about the event NETDEV_UP.

Deactivating a Network Device   When we use the command ifconfig *name down* in dev_ifsioc to deactivate a network device, the method dev_change_flags(dev, flags) in the variable dev->flags deletes the IFF_UP flag. The general part of transferring the network device into the inactive state is done by dev_close(). The adapter-specific actions are executed in the driver method dev->stop().

dev_close()	net/core/dev.c

If the network device dev is in the IFF_UP state, then it is deactivated by dev_close(dev) in the following steps:

- All methods in the notification chain netdev_chain are informed about the up-coming deactivation of the network device (NETDEV_GOING_DOWN) and can act accordingly.
- Next, dev_deactivate(dev) removes the packet scheduler dev->qdisc, and the LINK_STATE_START bit in dev->state is deleted. In addition, dev_watchdog_down() stops the timer used to detect transmission problems.
- The driver function dev->stop() deactivates the network adapter.

- Next, all protocols concerned are notified that the network device was stopped (`notifier_call_chain(.., NETDEV_DOWN, ..)`).
- Finally, the reference counter that points to the `net_device` structure is decremented by one.

5.2.3   Creating and Finding Network Devices

`dev_alloc_name()`	**net/core/dev.c**

Each network device in Linux has a unique name. As mentioned earlier, network devices are not represented in the file system, in contrast to character and block devices, which means that they are not addressed by `major` and `minor` numbers. In general, network devices are named by the network type. Table 5–2 shows a few of the names currently used. In addition, devices of the same type are shown and numbered in ascending order, starting from zero (e.g., `isdn0, isdn1`, etc.).

Notice, however, that there are exceptions in allocating network adapters to a category. Linux is strongly oriented to Ethernet, and some functions in the kernel facilitate handling of Ethernet-like adapters, so some (non-Ethernet) adapters also use the category `ethn`, including some ISDN cards.

The convention used in Linux to name network devices has several benefits:

- When one is designing applications and creating configuration scripts, it is simpler to address network devices without knowing their manufacturers and their hardware parameters (interrupt number, port number).
- When replacing equal-type hardware, for example to upgrade an Ethernet adapter from 10 Mbit/s to 100 Mbit/s, we don't have to change the network setting; simply accessing `ethn` is sufficient.

TABLE 5–2   Naming convention for Linux network devices.

Name	Network Device Type
eth	Ethernet (802.3, Ethernet V2), 10 Mbit/s or 100 Mbit/s
tr	Token Ring (802.5)
atm	Asynchronous Transfer Mode
sl	SLIP (Serial Line Interface Protocol)
ppp	PPP (Point-to-Point Protocol)
plip	PLIP (Parallel Line Interface Protocol)
tunl	IPIP Tunnel
isdn	ISDN (Integrated Services Digital Network)
dummy	Dummy-Device
lo	Loopback-Device

dev_alloc()   **net/core/dev.c**

dev_alloc(name, err) reserves memory for a net_device structure. Subsequently, a name is assigned to the network device. As described in connection with init_netdev(), we can use name to specify a prefix. In both cases, the method dev_alloc_name() is used to construct the name.

The parameter err is a pointer to an integer variable, which is contained in the return value of dev_alloc_name() wherever an error occurs. If an error occurs, then dev_alloc() always returns a NULL pointer. Naturally, if the if is successful, it returns a pointer to the new net_device structure.

dev_get...()   **net/core/dev.c**

Various kernel components need to access a specific network device from time to time. We can search for the right net_device structure in different ways. net/core/dev.c has several functions that facilitate this search. These functions step through the linear list of network devices, starting with dev_base, and, when they find it, they return a pointer to the net_device structure we looked for:

- dev_get_by_name(name) searches for the network device specified by name.
- dev_get(name) also searches for the device specified by name.
- dev_get_by_index(ifindex) uses the index of the network device as search criterion.
- dev_getbyhwaddr(type, ha) searches for the network device by the MAC address ha and the type.

dev_load()   **net/core/dev.c**

When a network device is unavailable (i.e., not present in the list of registered devices), then we can use dev_load(name) to request the corresponding driver module. To request a driver module, the kernel has to support the automatic loading of modules. Also, the process in which the request for the network device originates has to have privileges to load the module (CAP_SYS_MODULE):

```
if (!dev_get(name) && capable(CAP_SYS_MODULE))
            request_module(name);
```

5.2.4 Notification Chains for State Changes

As mentioned above, network devices can be registered and removed dynamically. Also, their state can change in the course of time. For example, a network device can change its hardware address or name.

On the network-device level, a state change did not cause problems, but protocol instances in the higher layers use the services of network devices. For efficiency and simplicity reasons, these protocol instances often store references to the network devices

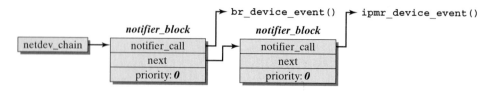

FIGURE 5–4
Notification chain for network devices.

they use. When the state of a network device changes, then these stored states become invalid. The protocol instances concerned should be notified about this fact. Unfortunately, a network device does not normally know the protocols that use its services, or what references they store.

For this reason, protocols can register themselves to be notified of state changes in network devices. This concept is called *notifier chains*; it consists of a list (netdev_chain) of notifier_block structures. Figure 5–4 shows an example of how they are structured. Each of these notifier_block elements includes a request for notification when the state of a network device changes:

- notifier_call() is a pointer to a handling routine, which handles the notification about a network device's state change. Each protocol instance that stores states of network devices should have such a function. For example, the method bridge_device_event() is used for the instance of a transparent bridge described in Chapter 12.

  If a state change occurs in a network device, then all handling routines stored in the list netdev_chain are called, where the following arguments are passed:

  - a pointer to the notifier_block structure, the handling routine of which is actually called;
  - a pointer to the network device (net_device) that changed its state;
  - the state representing the cause for this notification.

- priority specifies a priority for processing of notifications.
- next points to the next notifier_block element in the list and is used for concatenation.

The concept of notifier chains is used not only for network devices, but also for other states that can change. For this reason, the implementation of these notifier chains is generic and can easily be used for other purposes. For example, there is a reboot_notifier_list chain informing that the system is about to reboot.

In the networking area, the concept of notifier chains is used for state changes in network devices. The following list shows possible causes for notifications. Subsequently, we introduce three important functions of this concept.

- NETDEV_UP activates a network device (by dev_open).
- NETDEV_DOWN deactivates a network device. As a consequence of this message, all references to this network device should be removed.
- NETDEV_CHANGE informs that a network device changed its state.

- NETDEV_REGISTER means that a network device was registered but no instance of it has yet been opened.
- NETDEV_UNREGISTER informs that a network driver was removed.
- NETDEV_CHANGEMTU means that the MTU (Maximum Transfer Unit) changed.
- NETDEV_CHANGEADDR means that the hardware address of a network device changed.
- NETDEV_CHANGENAME means that the name of a network device changed.

When a registered handling routine is called, it can use the appropriate functions based on the type passed. For example, when a network device is deactivated (NETDEV_DOWN) in KIDS (see Chapter 22), the corresponding hook is deleted. The method notifier_call_chain(&netdev_chain, *EVENT*, dev), which will be described below, is used to call the notifier chain.

`notifier_call_chain()`	**net/core/dev.c**

notifier_call_chain(&netdev_chain, *EVENT*, dev) informs all handling methods registered in the list netdev_chain about the *EVENT*, where the events described above can occur. notifier_call_chain() is very simple. The linking in the list is used to call all registered functions, one after the other. If one of the functions called returns the constant NOTIFY_STOP_MASK, then the notification is stopped. This is useful to prevent there being several reactions to one event. Otherwise, all registered handling routines are always informed about the event each time this function is called. The registered handling method alone decides whether the message is meaningful for it.

`register_netdevice_notifier()`	**net/core/dev.c**

register_netdevice_notifier(nb) is merely another representation of the method notifier_chain_register(&netdev_chain, nb), which inserts the notifier_block structure passed to the list netdev_chain. The position within the list is determined by the priority.

`unregister_netdevice_notifier()`	**net/core/dev.c**

unregister_netdevice_notifier(nb) removes the specified notifier_block structure from the list netdev_chain. The function notifier_chain_unregister() is used for this purpose.

5.2.5 Transmitting Over Network Devices

`dev_queue_xmit()`	**net/core/dev.c**

dev_queue_xmit(skb) is used by protocol instances of the higher protocols to send a packet in the form of the socket buffer skb over a network device, which is specified by the parameter skb->dev in the socket buffer structure. Section 6.2.2 explains how a packet is transmitted in detail.

5.3   NETWORK DRIVERS

The large number of different protocols in the Linux network architecture leads to considerable differences in the implementations of drivers for different physical network adapters. As was mentioned in the section that described the `net_device` structure, the properties of different network adapters are hidden at the interface of network devices, which means that they offer a uniform view upwards.

Hiding specific functions (i.e., abstracting from the driver used) is achieved by using function pointers in the `net_device` structure. For example, a higher-layer protocol instance uses the method `hard_start_xmit()` to send an IP packet over a network device. Notice, however, that this is merely a function pointer, hiding the method `el3_start_xmit()` in the case of a 3c509 network adapter. This method takes the steps required to pass a socket buffer to the 3c509 adapter. The upper layers of the Linux network architecture don't know which driver or network adapter is actually used. The function pointer can be used to abstract from the hardware actually used and its particularities.

The following sections provide an overview of the typical structuring and implementation characteristics of the functions of a network driver, without discussing adapter-specific properties, such as manipulating the hardware registers or describing the transmit buffers. In general, these tasks depend on the hardware, so we will skip them here. Readers interested in these details can use the large number of network drivers included in the `drivers/net` directory as examples. We use the `skeleton` driver to explain how driver methods work. This is a sample driver used to show usual processes in driver methods rather than a real driver for a network adapter. For this reason, it is particularly useful for explaining the implementation characteristics of network drivers.[2]

Some of the methods listed below are not implemented by some drivers (e.g., `example_set_config()` to change system resources at runtime); others are essential, such as `example_hard_start_xmit()` to start a transmission process.

5.3.1   Initializing Network Adapters

Before a network device can be activated, we first have to find the appropriate network adapter; otherwise, it won't be added to the list of registered network devices. The `init()` function of the network driver is responsible for searching for an adapter and initializing its `net_device` structure with patching driver information. Because we search for a network adapter, this function is often called *search function*.

The argument of the `init()` method is a pointer to the initializing device `dev`. The return value of `init()` is usually 0, but a negative error code (e.g., `-ENODEV`) when no adapter was found.

`net_init()`/`net_probe()`	**net/core/dev.c**

The tasks of the method `dev->init(dev)` are explained in the source text of our example driver, `isa_skeleton`. There is an example driver in `drivers/net/pci_skeleton.c` for PCI network adapters, but we will not describe it here.

---

[2]At this point, we would like to thank Donald Becker, who implemented most of the network drivers for Linux, greatly contributing to the success of Linux. Donald Becker is also the author of the `skeleton` driver used here.

As was mentioned earlier, the main task of the `init()` method is to search for a matching network adapter (i.e., it has to discover the I/O port, especially of the basic address stored in `dev->base_addr`).

We distinguish between two different cases of searching for a network adapter:

■ *Specifying the basic address*: In this case, the previously created `net_device` structure of the network device is passed as parameter to the `init()` method. The caller can use this structure to specify a basic address for I/O ports in advance. When no matching adapter is found in this address, then the `init()` method returns the error message `-ENODEV`. The basic address can be specified in either of the two following ways:

▶ For modularized drivers, parameters can be passed when loading the module, including the I/O basic address (e.g., `io=0×280`). In this case, it should be transferred to the `net_device` structure of the network device in the `init_module()` method of the driver module, so that it will be considered during the search for the network adapter.

▶ For drivers permanently integrated in the kernel, we can also pass parameters when the system boots; these parameters are maintained in the list `dev_boot_setup`. They are transferred to the `net_device` structure of a network device in the method `init_netdev()` (see Section 5.2) and can be used when the network adapter is initialized.

■ *Searching in known basic addresses*: A network adapter generally supports a set of defined port addresses. If no basic address is specified when calling the `init()` method, then the addresses in this list can be probed one after the other. If no adapter can be found in any of these basic addresses in the list, then `-ENODEV` is returned.

The following source code of the `init()` method for the skeleton driver handles only the selection of basic addresses where we want to search (by the methods described above). The actual verification of a specific basic address and the initialization of the `net_device` structure takes place in the method `netcard_probe1(dev, ioaddr)`, which is actually part of the `init()` method and was implemented separately to keep the code simple and easy to understand.

```
/* The name of the card. Is used for messages and in the requests for
 * io regions, irqs and dma channels */
static const char* cardname = "netcard"

/* A zero-terminated list of I/O addresses to be probed. */
static unsigned int netcard_portlist[] __initdata =
        { 0x200, 0x240, 0x280, 0x2C0, 0x300, 0x320, 0x340, 0};

/* The number of low I/O ports used by the ethercard. */
#define IO_NUM 32
```

```
/* Information that needs to be kept for each board. */
struct net_local {
    struct net_device_stats stats;
    long open_time;          /* Useless example local info. */

        /* Tx control lock. This protects the transmit buffer ring
         * state along with the "tx full" state of the driver. This
         * means all netif_queue flow control actions are protected
         * by this lock as well. */
    spinlock_t lock;
};


/* The station (ethernet) address prefix, used for IDing the board. */
#define SA_ADDR0 0x00
#define SA_ADDR1 0x42
#define SA_ADDR2 0x65


int __init netcard_probe(struct net_device *dev) {
    int i;
    int base_addr = dev->base_addr;

    SET_MODULE_OWNER(dev);

    if (base_addr > 0x1ff)    /* Check a single specified location. */
        return netcard_probe1(dev, base_addr);
    else if (base_addr != 0) /* Don't probe at all. */
        return -ENXIO;

    for (i = 0; netcard_portlist[i]; i++) {
        int ioaddr = netcard_portlist[i];
        if (check_region(ioaddr, IO_NUM))
            continue;

        if (netcard_probe1(dev, ioaddr) == 0)
            return 0;
    }
    return -ENODEV;
}
```

Once we have selected a basic address for the network adapter in the above method, the method netcard_probe1(dev, ioaddr) tests whether the adapter we searched for is really at this basic address. For this purpose, the method has to check specific properties of the card, where access should be limited to read access on the I/O ports to ensure that no other adapters will be involved. At this point, it is still unknown whether the adapter we're searching for is really present in the basic address ioaddr.

A very simple method to identify the adapter compares the manufacturer identification with the MAC address. Each network adapter has a unique MAC address, where the first three bytes identify the manufacturer. This identification must correspond with the manufacturer code of the searched card. In any event, additional checks should be done, but they are adapter-specific and are not described in detail here.

Once we are sure that the network adapter we searched for is present in the basic address ioaddr, this address is stored in the net_device structure (dev->base_addr), and the network device is initialized. The I/O ports, starting from the basic address, are reserved by request_region(ioaddr, IO_NUM, cardname) at the end of the initialization function to ensure that no other initialization method can get write access to it.

The initialization process can be divided into the following three phases:

- If the network adapter does not support dynamic interrupt allocation, then the interrupt set by jumpers on the network adapter should be determined and reserved at this point. The kernel supports the search for the interrupt number. Calling the method autoirq_setup() makes the kernel remember interrupt lines not currently registered in a variable. Subsequently, the network adapter should be caused to trigger an interrupt. We can then use the method autoirq_report() to discover, from the previously stored and the actual interrupt vectors, which interrupt was actually active. Next, the interrupt found is reserved for the network adapter by the method request_irq(). In addition, the DMA channel is determined and reserved by request_dma().

  For modern adapters that do not necessarily require specific interrupt or DMA lines, the two system resources are allocated not at this point, but rather when the device is opened. This is necessary to avoid conflicts with other devices.

- Once system resources have been allocated (for older adapters only), memory is reserved for the private data structure of the network device dev->priv and is initialized. This data structure stores the private data of the network driver and statistic information collected during the operation of the network device (net_device_stats structure).

- Finally, the references to driver-specific methods are set in the net_device structure, so that they can be used by the higher layers and protocols. The adapter-specific methods (see also Section 5.1.1) have to be set explicitly. Methods specific to the MAC protocol used (e.g., Ethernet) can be set by special methods (e.g., ether_setup()).

If the network adapter was found and all data structures were initialized correctly, then dev->init() returns 0.

```
/* This is the real probe routine. Linux has a history of friendly device
 * probes on the ISA bus. A good device probe avoids doing writes, and
 * verifies that the correct device exists and functions.*/
static int __init netcard_probe1(struct net_device *dev,int ioaddr) {
    struct net_local *np;
    static unsigned version_printed = 0;
    int i;
```

```
    /*
     * For Ethernet adaptors the first three octets of the station address
     * contains the manufacturer's unique code. That might be a good probe
     * method. Ideally you would add additional checks.
     */
    if (inb(ioaddr + 0) != SA_ADDR0
        ||   inb(ioaddr + 1) != SA_ADDR1
        ||   inb(ioaddr + 2) != SA_ADDR2) {
        return -ENODEV;
    }


    if (net_debug && version_printed++ == 0)
        printk(KERN_DEBUG "%s", version);

    printk(KERN_INFO "%s: %s found at %#3x, ", dev->name, cardname, ioaddr);

    /* Fill in the 'dev' fields. */
    dev->base_addr = ioaddr;

    /* Retrieve and print the Ethernet address. */
    for (i = 0; i < 6; i++)
        printk(" %2.2x", dev->dev_addr[i] = inb(ioaddr + i));

#ifdef jumpered_interrupts
    /* If this board has jumpered interrupts, allocate the interrupt
     * vector now. There is no point in waiting since no other device
     * can use the interrupt, and this marks the irq as busy. Jumpered
     * interrupts are typically not reported by the boards, and we must
     * used autoIRQ to find them. */

    /* ... REMOVED for this book, details see in drivers/net/isa-skeleton.c */
#endif /* jumpered interrupt */
#ifdef jumpered_dma
    /* If we use a jumpered DMA channel, that should be probed for and
     * allocated here as well. See lance.c for an example.*/

    /* ... REMOVED for this book, details see in drivers/net/isa-skeleton.c */
#endif /* jumpered DMA */

    /* Initialize the device structure. */
    if (dev->priv == NULL) {
        dev->priv = kmalloc(sizeof(struct net_local), GFP_KERNEL);
        if (dev->priv == NULL)
            return -ENOMEM;
    }
```

```
memset(dev->priv, 0, sizeof(struct net_local));

np = (struct net_local *)dev->priv;
spin_lock_init(&np->lock);

/* Grab the region so that no one else tries to probe our ioports. */
request_region(ioaddr, IO_NUM, cardname);

dev->open = net_open;
dev->stop = net_close;
dev->hard_start_xmit = net_send_packet;
dev->get_stats = net_get_stats;
dev->set_multicast_list = &set_multicast_list;

dev->tx_timeout = &net_tx_timeout;
dev->watchdog_timeo = MY_TX_TIMEOUT;

/* Fill in the fields of the device structure with Ethernet values. */
ether_setup(dev);

return 0;
}
```

Helper Functions to Allocate System Resources

`request_region()`, `release_region()`, `check_region()`	**kernel/resource.c**

`request_region(port, range, name)` reserves a region of I/O ports, starting with the address port, and marks them as allocated. The kernel manages these reserved port ranges in a linear list. This list can be output from the proc file /proc/ioports, where name is the output name of the reserved instance.

We reserve ports to prevent a driver that searches for an adapter from accessing the ports of another device, causing that device to take an undefined or unintended state. For this reason, before port ranges are assigned, we should always use check_region() to check on whether that range is already taken. The address of the first I/O port of an adapter is stored in the variable dev->base_addr.

release_region(start, n) can be used to release allocated port ranges.

`request_irq()`, `free_irq()`	**kernel/irq.c**

request_irq(irq, handler, flags, device, dev_id) reserves and initializes the interrupt line with number irq. At the same time, the handling routine handler() is registered for this interrupt.

Similarly to what it does with I/O ports, the kernel manages a list of reserved interrupts and can output this list in the proc directory (/proc/interrupts). Again, the string device tells you who reserved this interrupt. The parameter flags can be used to output options when reserving an interrupt. For more information, see [RuCo01].

A reserved interrupt can be released by free_irq(irq, dev_id).

request_dma(), free_dma()	kernel/dma.c

request_dma(dmarr, device_id) tries to reserve the DMA channel dmarr. free_dma(dmarr) can be used to release a reserved DMA channel.

5.3.2   Opening and Closing a Network Adapter

We know from Section 5.2 that network devices are activated and deactivated by the command ifconfig. More specifically, ioctl() calls invoke the methods dev_open() or dev_close(), where the general steps to activate and deactivate a network device are executed. The adapter-specific actions are handled in the driver methods dev->open() and dev->stop(), respectively, of the present network adapter. We use the skeleton sample driver to explain these steps.

net_open()	drivers/net/isa_skeleton.c

The open() method is responsible for initializing and activating the network adapter. At the beginning, the system resources required (interrupt, DMA channel, etc.) are requested. To make available these system resources, the kernel offers various methods you can use as helpers. These methods were introduced briefly in the previous section. System resources are reserved in the open() method for modern adapters, which do not have fixed values for IRQ and DMA lines. For older cards, the resources are searched for and reserved in the init() method. (See init().)

Once a network adapter has been initialized successfully, the use counter of the module should be incremented for modularized drivers, to prevent inadvertent loading of the driver module from the kernel. We can use the macro MOD_INC_USE_COUNT for this purpose.

The network adapter is initialized when all system resources have been allocated successfully. Each adapter is initialized in an individual manner. Normally, a specific value is written to a hardware register (I/O port) of the adapter, which causes the adapter to initialize itself.

The transmission of packets over the network device is started by netif_start_queue(dev). Finally, the value 0 is returned if the transmission was successful; otherwise, a negative error code is returned.

```
/*
 * Open/initialize the board. This is called (in the current kernel)
 * sometime after booting when the 'ifconfig' program is run.
 *
 * This routine should set everything up anew at each open, even
 * registers that "should" only need to be set once at boot, so that
```

```
 * there is non-reboot way to recover if something goes wrong.
 */
static int net_open(struct net_device *dev) {
    struct net_local *np = (struct net_local *)dev->priv;
    int ioaddr = dev->base_addr;
    /*
     * This is used if the interrupt line can turned off (shared).
     * See 3c503.c for an example of selecting the IRQ at config-time.
     */
    if (request_irq(dev->irq, &net_interrupt, 0, cardname, dev))
        return -EAGAIN;
    }
    /*
     * Always allocate the DMA channel after the IRQ, and clean up on failure.
     */
    if (request_dma(dev->dma, cardname)) {
        free_irq(dev->irq, dev);
        return -EAGAIN;
    }

    MOD_INC_USE_COUNT;

    /* Reset the hardware here. Don't forget to set the station address. */
    chipset_init(dev, 1);
    outb(0x00, ioaddr);
    np->open_time = jiffies;

    /* We are now ready to accept transmit requests from
     * the queuing layer of the networking.
     */
    netif_start_queue(dev);
    return 0;
}
```

Deactivating a Network Adapter

example_stop()	drivers/net/isa_skeleton.c

During deactivation of a network adapter, all operations done when the adapter was opened should be undone. This concerns mainly allocated system resources (interrupts, DMA channels, etc.), which should now be freed.

For modularized drivers, the use counter has to be decremented with MOD_DEC_USE_COUNT, and the network device must not accept any more packets from higher layers (netif_stop_queue). Again, the return value is either 0, if successful, or a negative error code.

```
/* The inverse routine to net_open(). */

static int net_close(struct net_device *dev) {
```

```
struct net_local *lp = (struct net_local *)dev->priv;
int ioaddr = dev->base_addr;

lp->open_time = 0;

netif_stop_queue(dev);

/* Flush the Tx and disable Rx here. */

disable_dma(dev->dma);

/* If not IRQ or DMA jumpered, free up the line. */
outw(0x00, ioaddr+0); /* Release the physical interrupt line. */

free_irq(dev->irq, dev);
free_dma(dev->dma);

/* Update the statistics here. */
MOD_DEC_USE_COUNT;

return 0;
}
```

5.3.3   Transmitting Data

Each data transmission in the Linux network architecture occurs over a network device, more specifically by use of the method hard_start_xmit() (start hardware transmission). Of course, this is a function pointer, pointing to a driver-specific transmission function, ..._start_xmit(). This method is responsible for forwarding the packet in the form of a socket buffer and starting the transmission. Before we discuss the usual steps involved in the driver method dev->hard_start_xmit() in this section, we will briefly describe the common architecture of network adapters.

A network adapter is an interface adapter that automatically transmits and receives network packets according to a defined MAC protocol (Ethernet, token ring, etc.). This means that a network adapter has an independent logic that works in parallel to the regular central processor(s). The network adapter and a system processor interact over I/O ports (hardware registers) and interrupts. When a processor wants to pass data to the network adapter, then the processor writes its data to the appropriate I/O ports and starts the desired action. When the adapter wants to pass data to the processor (e.g., a packet it received), then the adapter triggers an interrupt, and the processor uses the interrupt-handling routine of the network adapter to serve the network adapter. This shows clearly that system processors have a leading role versus interface adapters (master–slave relationship).

Transmitting Data Packets

net_start_xmit()	**drivers/net/isa_skeleton.c**

dev->hard_start_xmit(skb, dev) is responsible for forwarding a data packet to the network adapter so that the latter can transmit it. The packet data of the socket buffer is copied to an internal buffer location in the network adapter, and the time stamp `dev->trans_start = jiffies` is attached, marking the beginning of that transmission. If this copying action was successful, it is also assumed that the transmission will be successful. In this case, `hard_start_xmit()` has to return a value of 0. Otherwise, it should return 1, so that the kernel knows that the packet could not be sent.

When forwarding network packets between the operating system and the network adapter, we can distinguish between two different techniques:

- Older network adapters (e.g., 3Com 3c509) have an internal buffer memory on the adapter for packets to be sent. This means that the kernel can always forward only one single packet to the adapter at a time. If a buffer is free, a packet is copied to the adapter right away and the kernel can delete the corresponding socket buffer.

- More recent network adapters work differently. The driver manages a ring buffer consisting of 16 to 64 pointers to socket buffers. When a packet is ready to be sent, then the corresponding socket buffer is arranged within this ring, and a pointer to the packet data is passed to the network adapter. Subsequently, the socket buffer remains in the ring buffer until the network adapter, using an interrupt, has notified that the packet was transmitted. Finally, the socket buffer is removed from the ring buffer and freed.

If the transmission was successful, then the socket buffer is no longer required, and it can be freed by `dev_kfree_skb()`. (See Section 4.1.1.) If an error occurred during the transmission, then the socket buffer should not be touched, because the kernel will most likely try to retransmit the packet.

When the method `hard_start_xmit()` is called, we can assume that there is currently at least one free place in the ring buffer. Whether this is true is checked by `netif_queue_stopped(dev)` before the call. Once the socket buffers have been arranged within the ring buffer, which `add_to_tx_ring` indicates as an example, we should check for whether there are more free buffer places. If this is not the case, i.e., if the ring buffer is fully occupied, then we have to use `netif_stop_queue()` to prevent more packets from being forwarded to the network adapter. The network device is stopped until there will be free places in the ring buffer. The kernel is notified about this situation by an interrupt, as explained in the following section.

```
/* This will only be invoked if your driver is _not_ in XOFF state.
 * What this means is that you need not check it, and that this
 * invariant will hold if you make sure that the netif_*_queue()
 * calls are done at the proper times.
 */
static int net_send_packet(struct sk_buff *skb, struct net_device *dev) {
    struct net_local *np = (struct net_local *)dev->priv;
    int ioaddr = dev->base_addr;
    short length = ETH_ZLEN < skb->len ? skb->len : ETH_ZLEN;
    unsigned char *buf = skb->data;
```

```
/* If some error occurs while trying to transmit this
 * packet, you should return '1' from this function.
 * In such a case you _may not_ do anything to the
 * SKB, it is still owned by the network queuing
 * layer when an error is returned. This means you
 * may not modify any SKB fields, you may not free
 * the SKB, etc.
 */

#if TX_RING
/* This is the most common case for modern hardware.
 * The spinlock protects this code from the TX complete
 * hardware interrupt handler. Queue flow control is
 * thus managed under this lock as well.
 */
spin_lock_irq(&np->lock);

add_to_tx_ring(np, skb, length);
dev->trans_start = jiffies;

/* If we just used up the very last entry in the
 * TX ring on this device, tell the queuing
 * layer to send no more.
 */
if (tx_full(dev))
    netif_stop_queue(dev);

/* When the TX completion hw interrupt arrives, this
 * is when the transmit statistics are updated.
 */

spin_unlock_irq(&np->lock);
#else
/* This is the case for older hardware which takes
 * a single transmit buffer at a time, and it is
 * just written to the device via PIO.
 *
 * No spin locking is needed since there is no TX complete
 * event. If by chance your card does have a TX complete
 * hardware IRQ then you may need to utilize np->lock here.
 */
hardware_send_packet(ioaddr, buf, length);
np->stats.tx_bytes += skb->len;

dev->trans_start = jiffies;

/* You might need to clean up and record Tx statistics here. */
if (inw(ioaddr) == /*RU*/81)
    np->stats.tx_aborted_errors++;
```

```
    dev_kfree_skb (skb);
#endif

    return 0;
}
```

Receiving Packets and Messages from a Network Adapter

`net_interrupt()`   **drivers/net/isa_skeleton.c**

A network adapter uses interrupts and its driver-specific interrupt-handling routine to communicate with the operating system. More specifically, the network adapter triggers an interrupt to stop the current processor operation and notify it about an event. When a network adapter uses an interrupt, we generally distinguish between three different events:

- *Receive a data packet*: The network adapter has accepted and buffered a data packet and now wants to forward this packet to the operating system.
- *Acknowledge a packet transmission*: The network adapter uses this interrupt to acknowledge that a packet previously forwarded by the operating system was sent and that there is now space available in the ring buffer. However, this acknowledgment does not mean that the receiver received the packet successfully; it merely means that the network adapter has put the packet successfully to the medium.
- *Notify an error situation*: Depending on the network adapter used, an interrupt can be used to notify the driver of error situations.

Figure 5–5 shows how the interrupt handling routine of a network driver works. First, we should set an IRQ lock to prevent the function from being executed more than once at the same time. In older versions of the Linux kernel, the flag

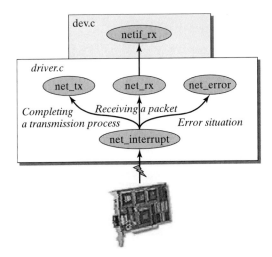

FIGURE 5–5
A network adapter uses an interrupt to send messages.

dev->interrupt was used to this end. From version 2.4 and higher, the driver should have its own lock variable.

Next, we want to know the cause of the interrupt. For this purpose, we normally read a state value from a state register, which shows whether a new packet has been received, whether a transmission was completed, and whether an error situation occurred. If a packet was received, then the driver-specific receive function net_rx() is called. If a packet transmission was fully completed, then the statistics are updated first; then netif_wake_queue(dev) (or dev->busy = 0; mark_bh(NET_BH) in earlier versions) announces the end of transmission and marks the NET_RX software interrupt for execution.

The NET_RX soft IRQ handles all incoming packets. Because it interrupts the normal work of a processor, an interrupt should complete its job quickly. Unfortunately, handling an incoming packet can be very complex, mainly because many protocols (e.g., PPP, IP, TCP, and FTP) normally participate in the process. To ensure that a processor's work is not interrupted for an excessive duration, the interrupt-handling routine carries out only those steps absolutely required to receive a packet. The more intensive part of protocol handling is done in the NET_RX software interrupt, which has a lower priority than interrupt handling.

```
static void net_interrupt(int irq, void *dev_id, struct pt_regs * regs) {
    struct net_device *dev = dev_id;
    struct net_local *np;
    int ioaddr, status;

    ioaddr = dev->base_addr;

    np = (struct net_local *)dev->priv;
    status = inw(ioaddr + 0);

    if (status & RX_INTR) {
        /* Got a packet(s). */
        net_rx(dev);
    }
#if TX_RING
    if (status & TX_INTR) {
        /* Transmit complete. */
        net_tx(dev);
        np->stats.tx_packets++;
        netif_wake_queue(dev);
    }
#endif
    if (status & COUNTERS_INTR) {
        /* Increment the appropriate 'localstats' field. */
        np->stats.tx_window_errors++;
    }
}
```

Acknowledging a Transmission Process

`net_tx()`	**drivers/net/isa_skeleton.c**

With more recent network adapters, the network driver manages a ring buffer of socket buffers, which should be used to transmit over the network adapter. These socket buffers remain in the ring buffer until the network adapter uses an interrupt to acknowledge their transmission. The method `net_tx()` shows the tasks to be executed when a network adapter acknowledges a transmission. The method `net_tx()` is actually part of the interrupt-handling routine and normally is implemented as a separate function only for clarity.

First, we should set a lock (normally a spinlock) to ensure that parallel access attempts cannot cause inconsistent states in data structures. Subsequently, the adapter is repeatedly asked which packets have been sent, until all sent packets have been recorded. Next, the packets are removed from the ring buffer and freed by `dev_kfree_skb_irq(skb)`.

Finally, we should check on whether the network device has been briefly halted by a full ring buffer. At least one buffer place has now been released, so the network can be freed by `netif_wake_queue(dev)`. To free the network device, the flag `LINK_STATE_XOFF` is deleted, as described in Section 5.1.1.

```
void net_tx(struct net_device *dev) {
    struct net_local *np = (struct net_local *)dev->priv;
    int entry;

    /* This protects us from concurrent execution of
     * our dev->hard_start_xmit function above.
     */
    spin_lock(&np->lock);

    entry = np->tx_old;
    while (tx_entry_is_sent(np, entry)) {
        struct sk_buff *skb = np->skbs[entry];

        np->stats.tx_bytes += skb->len;
        dev_kfree_skb_irq (skb);

        entry = next_tx_entry(np, entry);
    }
    np->tx_old = entry;

    /* If we had stopped the queue due to a "tx full"
     * condition, and space has now been made available,
     * wake up the queue.
     */
    if (netif_queue_stopped(dev) && ! tx_full(dev))
        netif_wake_queue(dev);

        spin_unlock(&np->lock);
}
```

Receiving a Data Packet   In contrast to sending a data packet, receiving a data packet from the network is an unforeseeable event for the operating system. The network adapter receives a packet in parallel to processor operations and wants to forward this packet to the kernel. In general, there are two methods to inform the kernel that a packet has arrived.

First, the system could periodically ask the network adapter whether data has been received; this is the so-called *polling principle*. One major problem of this method is the size of the time interval in which the network adapter should be asked. It this interval is too short, then unnecessary computing time is wasted, but, if it is too long, then the data exchange is unnecessarily delayed and the network adapter might be unable to buffer all incoming packets.

The second and better method uses an interrupt and an appropriate interrupt-handling routine to inform the operation system about an incoming packet. A processor of the system is briefly interrupted in its current work, accepts the packet received, and stores it in a queue. Next, the packet is further handled as soon as the processor has time. This *interrupt principle* clearly performs better than the polling principle, and it adapts itself better to the current system load. For this reason, each modern network adapter works by this principle (i.e., the receive function of the network driver is called by its interrupt-handling routine).

net_rx()	drivers/net/isa_skeleton.c

The driver method used to handle incoming packets is responsible for requesting a socket buffer and for filling the packet data space with the packet received. The method dev_alloc_skb() can be used to request a new socket buffer. This method attempts to get a used socket buffer from the socket-buffer cache to avoid slow memory management. Section 4.1.1 introduced the way how dev_alloc_skb() works.

Occasionally, more than one packet arrives. In the example discussed in this section, we use up to ten packets that are accepted by the network adapter and introduced as socket buffers to the Linux network architecture. The status of a received packet can generally be verified from specific hardware registers (i.e., whether the packet was received correctly and, if not, which error occurred). If errors occur, then these are generally collected in a net_device_stats structure, which is not part of the net_device structure; it has to be managed in the private data space (dev->priv) of the network device.

Once a packet has been received correctly and the packet data has been transferred to the packet data range of the socket buffer, the receiving network device **dev** is registered in the sk_buff structure, and the protocol type present in the packet is learned. Notice that this information cannot be carried out from the payload of the MAC packet, so it has to be learned here, before the packet is forwarded to the higher layers. For Ethernet packets, the method eth_type_trans() handles this task and extracts this information from the protocol field of the Ethernet frame. (See Section 6.3.1.)

Subsequently, netif_rx(skb) can place the socket buffers in the input queue. Finally, the statistics for the network device are updated, and the interrupt-handling routine either continues handling the next packet received or terminates the interrupt handling.

```
/* We have a good packet(s), get it/them out of the buffers. */
 static void net_rx(struct net_device *dev) {
    struct net_local *lp = (struct net_local *)dev->priv;
```

```
int ioaddr = dev->base_addr;
int boguscount = 10;

do {
    int status = inw(ioaddr);
    int pkt_len = inw(ioaddr);

    if (pkt_len == 0)        /* Read all the frames? */
        break;               /* Done for now */

    if (status & 0x40) {     /* There was an error. */
        lp->stats.rx_errors++;
        if (status & 0x20) lp->stats.rx_frame_errors++;
        if (status & 0x10) lp->stats.rx_over_errors++;
        if (status & 0x08) lp->stats.rx_crc_errors++;
        if (status & 0x04) lp->stats.rx_fifo_errors++;
    } else {
        /* Malloc up new buffer. */
        struct sk_buff *skb;

        lp->stats.rx_bytes+=pkt_len;

        skb = dev_alloc_skb(pkt_len);
        if (skb == NULL) {
            printk(KERN_NOTICE "%s: Memory squeeze, dropping packet.\n",
                    dev->name);
            lp->stats.rx_dropped++;
            break;
        }

        /* 'skb->data' points to the start of sk_buff data area. */
        memcpy(skb_put(skb,pkt_len), (void*)dev->rmem_start,
                pkt_len);
        /* or */
        insw(ioaddr, skb->data, (pkt_len + 1) >> 1);

        skb->dev = dev;
        skb->protocol = eth_type_trans(skb, dev);

        netif_rx(skb);
        dev->last_rx = jiffies;
        lp->stats.rx_packets++;
        lp->stats.rx_bytes += pkt_len;
    }
} while (-boguscount);
return;
}
```

5.3.4   Problems In Transmitting Packets

Even when a packet was passed to the network adapter, it is not yet certain whether the packet can be transmitted. The network adapter could be faulty, or the interrupt with the acknowledgment of the transmission process could have been lost. For this reason, a *watchdog timer* is used to detect errors.

During the registration of a network device (`register_netdevice()` — see Section 5.2.1), the watchdog timer `dev->watchdog_timer` is initialized in the function `dev_watchdog_init()`. The handling routine of the timer is set not to the function `dev->tx_timeout()`, but to `dev_watchdog()`. Also, the `net_device` structure of the network device is entered as the timer's private data.

When the network device is activated (`dev_open()`) at a later point in time (see Section 5.2.2), then the watchdog timer is started by the method `dev_activate()` or `dev_watchdog_up()`. The time when the timer should be triggered is set to `jiffies + dev->watchdog_timeo`. If no valid value was stated for the interval when the network device was registered, then `dev_watchdog_up()` takes 5 · HZ.

This means that the handling routine of the watchdog timer has completed all `dev->watchdog_timeo` ticks. At the same time, `dev_watchdog()` is tested to check on whether the network device is active and usable at all. And, if the transmit buffers of the network adapter are still full (`netif_queue_stopped(dev)`) and the condition (`jiffies − dev->trans_start > dev->watchdog_timeo`) is met, then there is a problem. The driver method `dev->tx_timeout()` is called to solve this problem, as is described later in this chapter.

If no problem occurred, or if the network device is not active, then the timer is registered again to be executed in `dev->watchdog_timeo` ticks.

In earlier kernel versions, the drivers of network devices were responsible themselves for implementing and managing a watchdog timer. This mechanism assumes that task now in the newer versions. This means that only the adapter-specific reset method `dev->tx_timeout()` has to be implemented.

`net_timeout()`	**drivers/net/isa_skeleton.c**

When a problem situation occurs during the transmission of data packets, then the above described watchdog timer of the network device (`dev->watchdog_timer`) detects the problem. As soon as more than `dev->watchdog_timeo` ticks have passed since the last packet start (`trans_start`), then the handling routine `dev->tx_timeout()` should take care of this problem.

This handling routine is responsible for analyzing the problem and for handling it. Often, the only way to solve the problem is to reset and reinitialize the complete hardware of the network adapter. In any event, an attempt should be made to send the packets waiting in the queue.

```
static void net_tx_timeout(struct net_device *dev) {
    struct net_local *np = (struct net_local *)dev->priv;

    printk(KERN_WARNING "%s: transmit timed out, %s?\n", dev->name,
           tx_done(dev) ? "IRQ conflict" : "network cable problem");

    /* Try to restart the adaptor. */
    chipset_init(dev, 1);

    np->stats.tx_errors++;

    /* If we have space available to accept new transmit
     * requests, wake up the queuing layer. This would
```

```
 * be the case if the chipset_init() call above just
 * flushes out the tx queue and empties it.
 *
 * If instead, the tx queue is retained then the
 * netif_wake_queue() call should be placed in the
 * TX completion interrupt handler of the driver instead
 * of here.
 */
if (!tx_full(dev))
    netif_wake_queue(dev);
}
```

5.3.5 Runtime Configuration

`example_set_config()`   **drivers/net/isa_skeleton.c**

In certain situations, it can be necessary to change the configuration of the system resources used by a network adapter at runtime—for example, when the interrupt cannot be identified automatically, or when there are conflicts with other devices. The driver method `set_config()` can be used to manipulate the configuration of system resources (i.e., interrupt, DMA, etc.) at runtime.

When the current configuration is polled on the application level, then the `irq`, `dma`, `base_addr`, `mem_start`, and `mem_end` parameters can be read directly from the `net_device` structure. However, when one of these parameters has to be changed, then we need a driver-specific method to effect the changes in the adapter. We will use the method `net_set_config()`, which allows us to change only the interrupt line, as an example to show how system resources can be changed in general.

The driver method `set_config()` is called when an application process invokes the `ioctl()` command SIOCSIFMAP (*Socket I/O Control Set InterFace MAP*). Beforehand, however, the process should have read the current configuration by use of the `ioctl()` command SIOCGIFMAP (*Socket I/O Control Get InterFace MAP*). The reason is that, when it wants to change a value, the other parameters should have the current values.

For both `ioctl()` commands, the system parameters are passed in a structure of the type `ifmap`. The `ifmap` structure has the following fields, corresponding to the fields with the same names in the `net_device` structure.

```
struct ifmap
{
    unsigned long mem_start;
    unsigned long mem_end;
    unsigned short base_addr;
    unsigned char irq;
    unsigned char dma;
    unsigned char port;
};
```

The method's return value is also used as return value for the `ioctl()` call. Drivers that don't implement `set_config()` return -EOPNOTSUPP.

```
static int net_set_config(struct net_device *dev, struct ifmap *map){

    if (dev->flags & IFF_UP)        /* no changes on running devices */
        return -EBUSY

    /* we don't allow to change the port address */
    if (map->base_addr != dev->base_addr) {
        return -EOPNOTSUPP;
    }

    /* changing the irq is o.k. */
    if (map->irq != dev->irq) {
        dev->irq = map->irq;
    }

    /* ... */
    return 0;
}
```

5.3.6   Adapter-Specific ioctl() Commands

ioctl() commands are extremely useful tools to start certain actions from within the user address space. Normally, executing the system call ioctl() in a socket causes an ioctl() command of a network protocol to be invoked. The corresponding symbols are defined in the file include/linux/sockios.h and normally relate to a specific protocol instance. However, when an ioctl() command of higher protocol instances cannot be processed, then the kernel forwards it to the network devices, which can then define their own commands in the driver method do_ioctl().

net_do_ioctl()	drivers/net/isa_skeleton.c

The ioctl() implementation for sockets knows 16 additional ioctl() commands, which can be used by drivers. More specifically, these are the commands SIOCDEVPRIVATE to SIOCDEVPRIVATE + 15. When one of these commands is used, then the method dev->do_ioctl() of the relevant network device is invoked.

When called, do_ioctl(dev, ifr, cmd) gets a pointer to a structure of the type ifreq. This pointer (ifr) points to an address in the kernel address space, which contains a copy of the ifreq structure passed by the user. After the loopback from the do_iotcl() method, this structure is copied back to the user address space. This means that a network driver can then use its own ioctl() commands both to receive and to output data. Examples for driver-specific ioctl() commands include reading or writing special registers, such as the *MII* register of some modern network adapters (eepro100, epic100, etc.).

We use the following basic example to demonstrate a driver-specific ioctl() implementation:

```
static int net_ioctl(struct net_device *dev, struct ifreq *ifr, int cmd)
{
    struct net_local *lp = (struct net_local *)dev->priv;
    long ioaddr = dev->base->addr;
```

```
    u16 *data = (u16 *)&ifr->ifr_data;
    int phy = lp->phy[0] & 0x1f;

    switch(cmd) {
        case SIOCDEVPRIVATE:    /* Get the address of the PHY in use */
            data[0] = phy;
        case SIOCDECPRIVATE+1: /* Special ioctl command 1 */
            special_ioctl_1();
        case SIOCDEVPRIVATE+2: /* Special ioctl command 2 */
            special_ioctl_2();

        /* ... */
        default:
            return -EOPNOTSUPP;
    }
}
```

5.3.7 Statistical Information About a Network Device

In most cases, we could want to obtain statistical information about the operation of a network device or its network adapters. Detailed logging of the events can help us find and troubleshoot errors and faulty configurations easily. For this purpose, we always use the data structure `net_device_stats` in the Linux kernel.

`struct net_device_stats`	include/linux/netdevice.h

- `rx_packets` and `tx_packets` contain the total number of packets successfully received and transmitted, respectively, over this network device.
- `rx_errors` and `tx_errors` store the number of faulty packets received and unsuccessful transmissions, respectively. Typical receive errors are wrong checksums or wrong packet sizes. Transmit errors are mainly due to physical problems or faulty configurations.
- `rx_dropped` and `tx_dropped` give the number of incoming and outgoing packets that were dropped for various reasons (e.g., memory unavailable for packet data).
- `multicasts` shows the number of multicast packets received.

The `net_device_stats` structure has a number of additional fields you can use to specify occurring errors in more detail, such as the number of ring buffer overflows, CRC errors, and synchronization errors. The exact structure and content of the `net_device_stats` structure can be found in `<linux/netdevice.h>`. In addition, there is a separate structure (`iw_statistics`) for wireless network adapters, containing radio connection data. (See the file `include/linux/wireless.h`.)

`net_get_stats()`	drivers/net/isa_skeleton.c

Interestingly, there is no pointer to the `net_device_stats` structure for statistical data in the `net_device` structure. The structure for statistical data has to be accommodated in the private data space of a network driver and is invoked by the driver method `get_stats()`.

get_stats(dev)() returns a pointer to the statistical data of a network device (dev). A sample implementation might look like this:

```
/*
 * Get the current statistics.
 * This may be called with the card open or closed.
 */
static struct net_device_stats *net_get_stats(struct net_device *dev) {
    struct net_local *lp = (struct net_local *)dev->priv;
    short ioaddr = dev->base_addr;

    /* Update the statistics from the device registers. */
    lp->stats.rx_missed_errors = inw(ioaddr+1);
    return &lp->stats;
}
```

5.3.8   Multicast Support on Adapter Level

net_set_multicast_list()	drivers/net/isa_skeleton.c

A network adapter uses the MAC destination address of a data packet to decide whether it will accept or ignore it. This process runs on the network adapter, so it doesn't interfere with the central processor's work. The central processor will be interrupted in its work only if the network adapter triggers an interrupt because it wants to forward the packet to higher protocol instances. In general, a network adapter accepts only packets intended for it, to ensure that the processor is not unnecessarily interrupted. Of course, an exception to this rule is the *promiscuous* mode, where all packets are accepted for analytical purposes.

For unicast packets, it is relatively easy to see whether the computer is interested in a packet. The network adapter merely has to detect its own MAC address as the destination address contained in the layer-2 packet header. Broadcast packets are also accepted without exception. However, the situation is different when detecting the correct multicast packets. How can the card know whether the computer is interested in the data of that group? In case of doubt, the card accepts the packet and passes it on to higher protocols, which should be able to know the groups subscribed. Though this method is very expensive, because the central processor has to check each multicast packet, it is the only way for some (older) network adapters to receive the *correct* multicast packets.

A better support for multicast on the MAC level is offered by modern network adapters. Such adapters manage a list of MAC addresses from which they want to receive packets. If only the packets of a specific multicast group should be received, then the corresponding MAC group address is passed to the network adapter, which will then receive the multicast packets. Section 17.4.1 describes the connection between groups and group addresses on the MAC and IP levels.

A network device stores the list of active MAC group addresses in a list (dev->mc_list). Whenever a new address is added or the state of the network device changes, then the driver method dev->set_multicast_list transfers this list to the adapter. The accompanying example illustrates how this method works.

When the network device is in promiscuous mode, then this mode is activated on the card. If all multicast packets should be received or if the list of MAC multicast addresses is bigger than the filter memory on the adapter, then all multicast packets are received; otherwise, the desired MAC addresses are transferred to the adapter—for example, as expressed by `hardware_set_filter`.

```
/*
 * Set or clear the multicast filter for this adaptor.
 * num_addrs == -1 Promiscuous mode, receive all packets
 * num_addrs == 0 Normal mode, clear multicast list
 * num_addrs > 0 Multicast mode, receive normal and MC packets,
 * and do best-effort filtering.
 */
static void set_multicast_list(struct net_device *dev) {
    short ioaddr = dev->base_addr;
    if (dev->flags&IFF_PROMISC)
    {
        /* Enable promiscuous mode */
        outw(MULTICAST|PROMISC, ioaddr);
    }
    else if((dev->flags&IFF_ALLMULTI) || dev->mc_count > HW_MAX_ADDRS)
    {
        /* Disable promiscuous mode, use normal mode. */
        hardware_set_filter(NULL);

        outw(MULTICAST, ioaddr);
    }
    else if(dev->mc_count)
    {
        /* Walk the address list, and load the filter */
        hardware_set_filter(dev->mc_list);

        outw(MULTICAST, ioaddr);
    }
    else
        outw(0, ioaddr);
}
```

## PART III

Layer I + II—Medium Access and Logical Link Layer

CHAPTER 6

Introduction to the Data-Link Layer

In the following chapters, we will leave the hardware area and move on to the world of network protocols. Chapters 7 through 24 discuss the structure and implementation of network protocols in the Linux kernel.

The previous chapters introduced the most important basics of the Linux network architecture, including the general structure of communication systems and protocol instances (Chapter 3), representation of network packets in the Linux kernel (socket buffers, Chapter 4), and the abstraction of physical and logical network adapters (network devices, Chapter 5). Before we continue discussing the structure and implementation of network protocols in detail, this chapter gives a brief introduction to the structuring of the data-link layer, which represents the connecting layer between network devices and higher network protocols. Of primary interest is the background where network protocols run. Another important topic of this chapter is the interplay of different activities (hardware and software interrupts, tasklets) of the Linux network architecture.

The transition between the different activities in the data-link layer (layers 1 and 2 of the OSI model) occurs when packets are sent and received; these processes are described in detail in Sections 6.2.1 and 6.2.2. First, we will describe the path a packet takes from its arrival in a network adapter until it is handled by a protocol instance in the network layer; then we will describe how a packet is sent from the network layer until it is forwarded to the network adapter.

6.1   STRUCTURE OF THE DATA-LINK LAYER

Chapter 3 introduced two reference models where the lower layers up to the network layer were structured in a different way. In the Internet reference model (TCP/IP model) there is only the data-link layer with the network adapter, and no other instance underneath the Internet protocol (network layer). In the ISO/OSI basic reference model, there are two different layers (*physical layer* and *data-link layer*), where the data-link layer is expanded by the media-access layer (Layer 2a) when using local area networks.

This book deals mainly with the protocols of the Internet world, and one assumes that the Internet reference model would best describe the structure of the Linux network architecture. Interestingly, the classification of the ISO/OSI reference model matches the structure of communication systems in local area networks much better. When taking a closer look at the IEEE 802 standards for local area networks, which are actually always used in the Internet, and their implementation in the Linux kernel, we can clearly recognize the structuring of the ISO/OSI model.

For this reason, the following discussion assumes a structuring as shown in Figure 6–1:

▨ The *OSI layers 1* (physical layer) and *2a* (media-access control layer — MAC) are implemented in network adapters.

▨ The *logical-link control* (LLC) layer is implemented in the operating system kernel; network adapters are connected to the operating system kernel by the network devices described in Chapter 5.

6.1.1   IEEE Standard for Local Area Networks (LANs)

With its IEEE 802.x standards, the IEEE (Institute of Electrical and Electronics Engineers) found a very extensive proliferation for local area networks (LANs). The best known LAN technologies are 802.3 (CSMA/CD), 802.5 (Token Ring), and 802.11 (wireless LANs). Figure 6–1 gives a rough overview of the 802.x standards and classifies them within the ISO/OSI layer model. As mentioned above, the data-link layer is divided into a logical-link control (LLC) and a media-access control (MAC) layer for networks with jointly used media. The LLC layer hides all media-specific differences and should provide a uniform interface for protocols to the higher layers; the MAC layer reflects the differences between different transmission technologies.

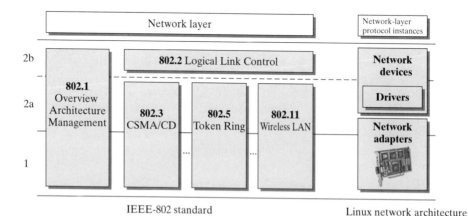

FIGURE 6–1
Standardization of layers 1 and 2 in IEEE 802 and their implementation in the Linux network architecture.

To hide the characteristics of the underlying transmission technology, the LLC layer should offer three services, regardless of this technology:

- *Unreliable datagram service* (LLC type 1): This very simple service offers no flow control or error control, so it doesn't even guarantee that data is transmitted. The removal of errors is left to the protocols of the higher layers.
- *Connection-oriented service* (LLC type 2): This service establishes a logical connection between the sender and the receiver, and it supports flow control and error control.
- *Reliable datagram service* (LLC type 3): This service combines LLC types 1 and 2—it is connectionless, but it supports both flow control and error control.

The very simple service (LLC type 1) is used mainly in local area networks, probably for its simplicity. No connection has to be established, and the higher-layer protocols offer an integrated error-handling feature (e.g., TCP in the transport layer). The protocol header of the LLC type-1 protocol consists of three fields:

- *DSAP* and *SSAP* specify the service access points in the sender and receiver. It is unclear why a protocol identification is stated for both the sender and the receiver, especially because no example is known where the two values would be different. Both fields have a width of only eight bits, so very few protocols can be defined. For this reason, the SNAP extension described below was defined.
- The *Control* field always takes the value 0x03 for LLC type 1. This corresponds to an *Unnumbered Information Frame* in the HDLC protocol, on which the LLC protocols are based.

For these reasons, the LLC layer and the relevant protocol-control information (LLC packet header) can no longer be recognized in some variants of local network protocols, because they were integrated into the packet headers of MAC PDUs. The best-known example is probably 802.3, which has the protocol control information (PCI) of the LLC layer in its protocol field.

One major drawback of this integrated solution is that many organizations and companies try to integrate their proprietary standards into a MAC PDU. To ensure that duplicate assignments of some identifications by different organizations are prevented, the IEEE invented a packet format for the LLC PDU, which allows each organization to define its own packet types. This packet format is called the SNAP extension of the LLC protocol.

In the SNAP extension, the *SSAP* and *DSAP* fields take the constant 0xAA, indicating that they expand the LLC packet header by five bytes (SNAP extension). These five bytes can be used to identify a large number of new protocols. In addition, the extension field is divided into a part for the assigning organization and another part for the actual protocol identification, to prevent conflicts in the assigning of protocol identifiers.

6.2   PROCESSES ON THE DATA-LINK LAYER

As was mentioned in the beginning of this chapter, the data-link layer forms the connecting layer between drivers or network devices and the higher world of protocol removed and processed from the queue. This prevents the protocol-handling routine from blocking the remaining activities of the computer and thereby inhibits denial-of-service attacks.

The first action in the continuous loop is to request a packet from the input queue of the CPU by the method __skb_dequeue(). If a socket buffer is found, then the reference counter of the socket buffer is first incremented in skb_bond(). Subsequently, the socket buffer is transferred to instances of the handling protocols.

First, the socket buffer is passed to all protocols registered in the list ptype_all. (See Section 6.3.) In general, no protocols are registered in this list. However, this interface is excellently suitable for inserting analytical tools.

If the computer was configured as a bridge (CONFIG_BRIDGE) and the pointer br_handle_frame_hook() was set, then the packet is passed to the method handle_bridge(). It will then be processed in the bridge instance. (See Chapter 12.)

The last action (which is generally the most common case) passed the socket buffer to all protocols registered with the protocol identifier (dev->protocol). They are managed in the hash table (ptype_base). Section 6.3 will explain the details of how layer-3 protocols are managed.

For example, the method eth_type_trans() recognizes the protocol identifier 0x0800 and stores it in dev->protocol for an IP packet. In net_rx_action(), this identifier is now mapped by the hash function to the entry of the Internet Protocol (IP) instance. Handling of the protocol is started by a call of the corresponding protocol handling routine (func()). In the case of the Internet Protocol, this is the known method ip_rcv(). If other protocol instances are registered with the identifier 0x0800, then a pointer to the socket buffer is passed to all of these protocols one after the other.

This means that the actual work with protocol instances of the Linux kernel begins at this point. In general, the protocols that start at this point are layer-3 protocols. However, this interface is also used by several other protocols that instead fit in the first two layers of the ISO/OSI basic reference model. The following section describes the inverse process (i.e., how a data packet is sent).

6.2.2   Transmitting a Packet

As is shown in Figure 6–3, the process of transmitting a packet can be handled in several activity forms of the kernel. We distinguish two main transmission processes:

- *Normal* transmission process, where an activity tries to send off ready packets and send them over the network device immediately after the placing of a packet in the output queue of that network adapter. This means that the transmission process is executed either by NET_RX soft-IRQ or as a consequence of a system call. This form of transmitting packets is discussed in the following section.

- The second type of transmission is handled by NET_TX soft-IRQ. It is marked for execution by some activity of the kernel and invoked by the scheduler at the next possible time. The NET_TX soft-IRQ is normally used when packets are to be sent outside the regular transmission process or at a specific time for certain reasons. This transmission process is introduced after the section describing the normal transmission process.

The Normal Transmission Process

dev_queue_xmit()	net/core/dev.c

dev_queue_xmit(skb) is used by the protocol instances of higher protocols to send a packet in the form of a socket buffer, skb, over a network device. The network device is specified by the parameter skb->dev of the socket buffer structure. (See Figure 6–4.)

First, the socket buffer is placed in the output queue of the network device. This is done by use of the method dev->qdisc->enqueue(). In general, packets are handled by the FIFO (First In — First Out) principle. However, it is also possible to define several queues and introduce various mechanisms for differentiated handling of packets. (See Chapters 18 and 22.)

Once the packet has been placed in the queue by the desired method (qdisc), further handling of packets ready to be sent is triggered. This task is handled by qdisc_run().

There is one special case: that a network device has not defined methods for queue management (dev->enqueue == NULL). In this case, a packet is simply sent by dev->hard_start_xmit() right away. In general, this case concerns logical network devices, such as loopback, or tunnel network devices.

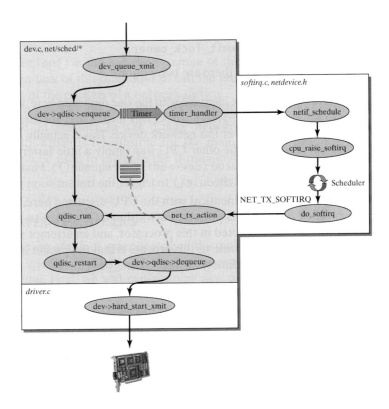

FIGURE 6–4
The process involved when sending a packet by dev_queue_xmit().

6.3.1 Logical Link Control—Determining the Layer-3 Protocol Identifier

`eth_type_trans()`	**net/ethernet/eth.c**

`eth_type_trans(skb, dev)` is the second important part of the Logical Link Control (LLC) implementation in the Linux kernel, in addition to managing the network-layer protocols described in Section 6.3. Two important tasks are executed for this purpose:

◾ Recognize the LLC protocol type used and the protocol identifier of the layer-3 protocol from the protocol control information contained in the layer-2 data frame.

◾ Identify the packet type (unicast, multicast, broadcast) and check on whether the packet is addressed to the local computer.

The method `eth_type_trans()`, which can be used for all Ethernet-compatible network adapters, is called by the network driver in the packet-receive method. (See Section 5.3.) It is responsible for extracting protocol-control information of the LLC layer and handling it appropriately. For this reason, all network devices of a MAC protocol type use the same `type_trans()` method. There are similar methods for token ring and FDDI devices (`tr_type_trans()`, `fddi_type_trans()`).

In general, Ethernet networks do not use any of the LLC standards, but transmit the layer-3 protocol identifier directly in the MAC frame. The only protocol mechanism is thus demultiplexing of different layer-3 protocols. This is the reason why `eth_type_trans()` is relatively simple and easy to understand. However, you can use an LLC protocol based on IEEE 802.2.

First, `skb_pull(skb, dev->hard_header_length)` takes the layer-2 packet header from `eth_type_trans()`. Next, the type of the packet is identified and registered in `skb->pkt_type`. The following mutually exclusive types are possible:

◾ `PACKET_BROADCAST`: The packet was sent to the broadcast address of the local network and is intended for all connected computers.

◾ `PACKET_MULTICAST`: The packet was sent to a layer-2 group address, which means that it is intended for a group of computers.

◾ `PACKET_HOST`: The packet is intended for the local computer (i.e., it was sent to the layer-2 address of the receiving network adapter).

◾ `PACKET_OTHERHOST`: The packet is not intended for the local computer and was received only because the computer is in promiscuous mode.

Subsequently, the protocol identifier of the incoming packet is recognized. In local networks based on the IEEE 802 standard, there are several options, but this book considers only Ethernet-compatible networks:

◾ If a value in the length or protocol field of the Ethernet packet header is bigger than the maximum frame length (1536 bytes), then it is assumed that it is an 802.3-compatible Ethernet adapter. As mentioned earlier, the 802.3 protocol

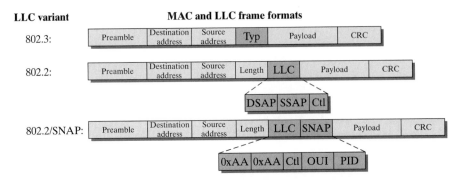

FIGURE 6–7
Variants for LLC protocol control information in Ethernet networks.

integrates the protocol-control information of the LLC layer in the protocol field of the 802.3 frame, thus sparing any need for a separate LLC packet header. This means that the field value contains the protocol identifier of the layer-3 protocol and is registered in skb->type.

■ Older Ethernet adapters store the length of the frame rather than the protocol identifier of the layer-3 protocol in the length or protocol field. For this reason, the protocol-control information of the LLC layer has to be contained in the payload of the Ethernet frame (i.e., an explicit LLC packet header based on the 802.2 standard, SSAP and DSAP—see Figure 6–7).

eth_type_trans() does not verify the LLC-PDU any further, but returns ETH_P_802_2 as the layer-3 protocol identifier. The 802.2 LLC protocol instance is treated as a layer-3 protocol instance. (See Section 6.3.) It is also registered as a layer-3 protocol instance in the hash table ptype_base. Though this conflicts with the layer model, it allows a simpler implementation in this case, because most Ethernet adapters use the integrated LLC variant mentioned previously, and 802.2 is rather an exceptional case. Finally, the demultiplexing process to the layer-3 protocol takes place in the handling routine of the 802.2 protocol (p8022_rcv(), net/802/p8022.c).

Layer-3 protocols can register themselves with the 802.2 protocol instance by use of the method register_8022_client(). For example, the SNAP protocol extension (net/802/psnap.c) can register itself with register_8022_client(0xAA, snap_rcv). From then on, the method snap_rcv(), which links to the corresponding layer-3 protocol, is invoked for all SNAP frames.

Figure 6–7 shows a summary of the frame formats used for different LLC variants in Ethernet:

■ 802.3: LLC-PCI, integrated in the MAC-PCI.
■ 802.2: LLC-PDU in the MAC payload.
■ 802.2/SNAP: SNAP extension in the LLC-PDU.

C H A P T E R   7

The Serial-Line Internet Protocol (SLIP)

7.1   INTRODUCTION

The packet-oriented IP protocol is used to communicate over the Internet. However, a modem can transmit only a continuous byte stream. For this reason, to establish a connection from your local PC over an analog telephone line to the worldwide Internet, we need a protocol that encapsulates network packets so that they can be transmitted over a modem connection between a local computer and a point of presence (PoP). The two endpoints of the modem connection can then communicate over IP. The point of presence itself is directly connected to the Internet and routs IP packets between the local PC and the Internet. (See Figure 7–1.)

Another possible use of such a protocol is for the IP communication of two computers over the serial V.24 interface, which is available in most PCs. This use lets you build an IP network at little cost (and very low speed) without the need to install additional interfaces, such as Ethernet cards.

RFC 1055 [Romk88] specifies the SLIP (Serial Line IP) for the V.24 task. SLIP represents an intermediate layer within the network architecture: At its upward face, packets are taken from or forwarded to the IP layer; at its downward face, data are sent to or received from a serial interface driver.

As compared with the more recent PPP protocol (see Chapter 8), SLIP is very simple, but offers a rather limited functionality:

■ SLIP includes no mechanisms for establishment of a controlled connection: As soon as SLIP has been started on both ends, the connection is implicitly established. For this reason, no parameters, such as IP address, DNS information, or the SLIP operating mode used, can be negotiated. These parameters have to be set manually or by use of a script before SLIP is started.

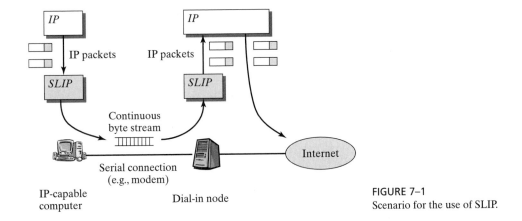

FIGURE 7–1
Scenario for the use of SLIP.

- SLIP serves exclusively for the transmission of Version-4 IP packets. Other network protocols (e.g., IP version 6 or X.25) are not supported.
- SLIP has no mechanisms to detect or correct errors; these functions have to be handled by higher network layers.
- In contrast to PPP, the payload in transmitted IP packets cannot be compressed. The CSLIP operating mode (described in the next bullet) allows you to compress the IP packet headers only.

In addition to the standard operating mode, SLIP supports the following modes:

- In *CSLIP* (Compressed SLIP), the packet headers in transmitted IP packets are compressed by the Van–Jacobson algorithm to utilize slow modem connections better.
- *SLIP6* uses only printable ASCII characters for data transmission. This is necessary when the underlying modem connection cannot transmit all control characters of the ASCII alphabet—for example, because the XON and XOFF control characters are used for flow control. However, a maximum payload of 6 bits per character can be transmitted in this way, and so the transmission rate drops by one-quarter.

7.1.1 Packet Detection and Character Stuffing

A serial interface or a modem connection is designed for the transmission of continuous byte sequences. To be able to send data packets of the IP protocol over such a connection, the sender has to insert special markings, which are then used by the receiver to detect the end of each packet. In SLIP, this is implemented so that the END control character (byte code 192) is inserted before and after each packet.

- To ensure unique detection of packet boundaries, the END character must never occur inside a packet. Of course, this constraint is undesirable, because we want to be able to transmit arbitrary data packets transparently. To maintain this *code*

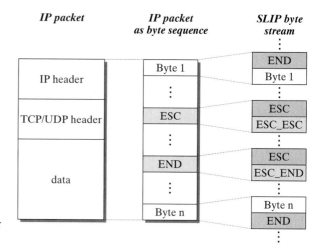

FIGURE 7–2
SLIP marks packet boundaries and uses character stuffing at the sender side.

TABLE 7–1   SLIP control characters.

Character	Byte Code
END	192
ESC	219
ESC_END	220
ESC_ESC	221

transparency, three additional control characters (ESC, ESC_END, and ESC_ESC) are used to implement a so-called *character stuffing* (shown in Figure 7–2):

- Each occurrence of END in packet data is replaced by the ESC ESC_END string.
- Each occurrence of ESC in packet data is replaced by the ESC ESC_ESC string.

The receiver can reverse character stuffing as follows to reconstruct the original IP packet:

- If the ESC character occurs, then the next character is ESC_ESC or ESC_END. In this case, the first ESC is deleted, and the second character is replaced by ESC or END.
- If the END character occurs, then this is the end of that packet, and so the packet can be forwarded to the IP layer.

Table 7–1 lists the four control characters used by SLIP and their byte codes.

7.2   SLIP IMPLEMENTATION IN THE LINUX KERNEL

Before we describe the SLIP implementation in the Linux kernel, we will first discuss the concept of TTY devices and TTY line disciplines, the better to illustrate how SLIP is implemented in Linux. Subsequently, this section will give an overview of the most

TABLE 7–2   Examples of TTY devices.

/dev Entry	Meaning
tty0–tty7	virtual consoles
pty#	pseudo-terminals—e.g., xterm window
ttyS#	serial interfaces

important functions of the SLIP implementation before we describe the steps involved in implementing SLIP in detail.

7.2.1   TTY Devices and Line Disciplines

In Linux, all devices that can act as terminals are grouped under the collective term TTY (Teletype or Terminal Type). Table 7–2 shows several examples. A TTY device is a *character device* offering special functions to control a terminal. This includes, for example, the flag for whether the terminal should produce an echo and commands to position the cursor and change color.

A TTY device can generally switch between different *TTY line disciplines*. This means that, in the Linux kernel, each system call to read (read()), write (write()), or control (ioctl()) invokes a routine specific to this line discipline. More specifically, the implementation of a TTY line discipline is inserted between the TTY device driver (*low-level driver*), which is in charge for the actual input and output, and the user process that wants to access the TTY device. (See Figure 7–3.)

One possible use for a TTY line discipline is the automatic conversion of all line ends between UNIX and Windows computers (LF versus CR/LF). In addition, TTY line disciplines offer an elegant means whereas serial interfaces can intercept and change all data transmitted over a serial interface without the need for the TTY line discipline driver to open and close the serial interface or to establish a modem dialup connection.

To register a new TTY line discipline with the Linux kernel, the driver has to first create a tty_ldisc structure (declared in <include/linux/tty_ldisc.h>) and set the

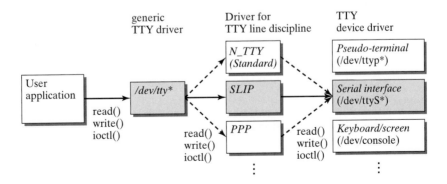

FIGURE 7–3
Interplay between TTY line disciplines and TTY device drivers.

function pointers contained in it. Subsequently, this data structure is registered by `tty_register_ldisc()` with the kernel to make the new TTY line discipline available for user programs.

struct tty_ldisc	include/linux/tty_ldisc.h

The `tty_ldisc` structure includes a number of function pointers, which have to be set by the driver of the TTY line discipline. The following code briefly explains the most important function pointers.

```
struct tty_ldisc {
        int     magic;
        char    *name;
        int     num;
        int     flags;
        /*
         * The following routines are called from above.
         */
        int     (*open)(struct tty_struct *);
        void    (*close)(struct tty_struct *);
        void    (*flush_buffer)(struct tty_struct *tty);
        ssize_t (*chars_in_buffer)(struct tty_struct *tty);
        ssize_t (*read)(struct tty_struct * tty, struct file * file,
                        unsigned char * buf, size_t nr);
        ssize_t (*write)(struct tty_struct * tty, struct file * file,
                        const unsigned char * buf, size_t nr);
        int     (*ioctl)(struct tty_struct * tty, struct file * file,
                        unsigned int cmd, unsigned long arg);
        void    (*set_termios)(struct tty_struct *tty, struct termios * old);
        unsigned int (*poll)(struct tty_struct *, struct file *,
                        struct poll_table_struct *);

        /*
         * The following routines are called from below.
         */
        void    (*receive_buf)(struct tty_struct *, const unsigned char *cp,
                        char *fp, int count);
        int     (*receive_room)(struct tty_struct *);
        void    (*write_wakeup)(struct tty_struct *);
};
```

The following functions are called from "above" (i.e., by the program or module accessing the TTY device):

- The function `open()` is called as soon as the TTY device switches to this line discipline.
- The function `close()` is called when the current TTY line discipline is deactivated. This happens when a TTY device switches from this line discipline into another

one (where the device is first reset to the standard line discipline N_TTX by the Linux kernel) and when the TTY device itself is closed.

- The function `read()` is called when a program wants to read data from the TTY device.
- The function `write()` is called when a program wants to send data to the TTY device.
- The function `ioctl()` is called when a program uses the system call `ioctl()` to change the configuration of the TTY line discipline or of the actual TTY device, but only provided that the higher-layer generic driver for TTY devices was unable to process the `ioctl()` call (as is the case, for example, when the device switches to another TTY line discipline).

The following functions are called from "below" (i.e., from the actual device driver of the TTY device):

- The function `receive_buf()` is called when the device driver has received data and wants to forward this data to the higher-layer program (i.e., to the driver of the TTY line discipline in this case). The parameters passed include the address and length of data.
- The function `receive_room()` is called by the device driver to request the maximum number of bytes that the TTY line discipline can accept with `receive_buf()`.
- The function `write_wakeup()` optionally can be called by the device driver as soon as it has finished sending a data block and is ready to accept more data. However, this happens only provided that it has been explicitly requested by the flag TTY_DO_WRITE_WAKEUP `<linux/tty.h>`.

7.2.2   General Procedure

The lifetime of a SLIP connection under Linux consists of the following phases; the sections below will explain how they are implemented in the Linux kernel:

1. *Initialize the SLIP driver*: the driver is initialized either when the system boots or when the driver module `slip.o` is loaded. At the same time, it registers the new TTY line discipline SLIP.
2. *Establish the connection*: A user program (e.g., `dip` or `slattach`) uses a modem connected to a serial interface (e.g., `/dev/ttyS0`) to dial to an Internet provider, and then switches the TTY line discipline of this serial interface to SLIP. At the same time, the SLIP operating mode (e.g., `CSLIP` or `SLIP6`) has to be set correctly.
3. *Activate and configure the network device*: Once the TTY line discipline has been switched to SLIP, a new network device is available, and the name of this device begins with "sl" (e.g., `sl0`). `ifconfig` can then be used to activate and configure this network device (e.g., by assigning valid IP addresses to both ends of the SLIP connection).
4. *Exchange data*: As soon as the network device has been configured correctly, the SLIP connection is available for sending IP packets.
5. *Deactivate the network device*: Before the SLIP connection is torn down, the network device has to be deactivated by `ifconfig`.

6. *Tear down the connection*: The user program (`dip` or `slattach`) separates the underlying modem connection, which causes the network device to be deregistered.

7. *Deinitialize the SLIP driver*: As soon as the driver module `slip.o` has been removed from the Linux kernel, it frees its memory and undoes the registration of the SLIP TTY line discipline.

7.2.3   Functions and Data Structures

The files `drivers/net/slip.c` and `drivers/net/slip.h` contain the source code for the SLIP implementation in the Linux kernel. Compression of the IP packet headers by the Van–Jacobson method (CSLIP) is implemented in `drivers/net/slhc.c`. However, this implementation will not be discussed in detail in what follows.

`struct slip`	`drivers/net/slip.h`

▨ The SLIP driver represents each SLIP connection by a `slip` structure. This structure includes pointers to the `net_device` structure of the relevant SLIP network device and to the `tty_struct` structure of the underlying TTY device. (See Figure 7–4.) The `slip` structure includes buffer pointers and counters to send and receive data. In addition, it stores the SLIP mode (e.g., CSLIP or SLIP6). In total, the `slip` structure consists of the following fields:

▨ `tty` points to a structure of the type `tty_struct`, which represents the TTY device allocated to this SLIP channel. This structure also includes a `tty_ldisc` structure with the TTY line discipline currently active (in this case, naturally, SLIP).

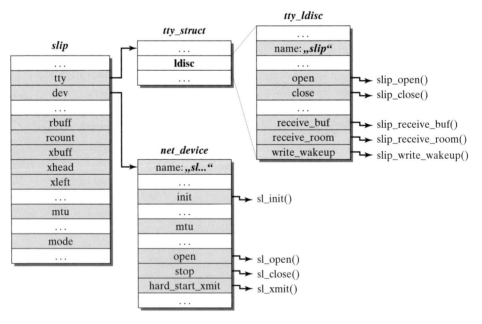

FIGURE 7–4
Important data structures of the SLIP implementation.

- dev points to the net_device structure with the data of the network device allocated to the SLIP connection.
- mtu is the MTU (*Maximum Transmission Unit*) of the SLIP connection, which is additionally stored in the net_device structure.
- mode specifies the active SLIP operating mode (e.g., SL_MODE_SLIP, SL_MODE_CSLIP, or SL_MODE_SLIP6).
- rbuff points to the receive buffer, which is used to buffer data incoming over the TTY device.
- rcount is the number of data bytes currently present in the receive buffer.
- xbuff points to the transmit buffer, which buffers data ready to be output over the TTY device.
- xhead points to the first character in the transmit buffer that has yet to be sent.
- xleft specifies the number of bytes still waiting in the transmit buffer (from xhead).

The SLIP functions can be divided into three categories: general management functions, functions to implement the SLIP TTY line discipline, and functions to implement SLIP network devices. The functions used to implement network devices can be recognized by the prefix "sl_"; the other functions have the prefix "slip_". Figure 7–5

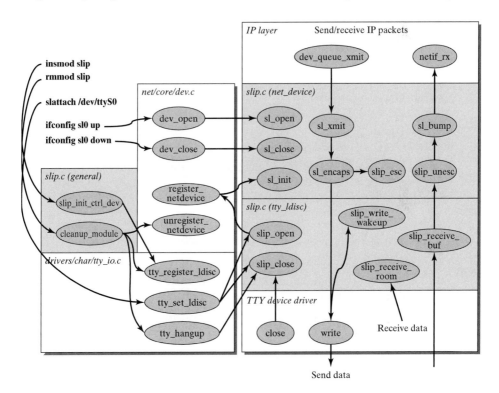

FIGURE 7–5
Functions of the SLIP implementation and their integration in the Linux kernel.

gives an overview of the functions discussed below. The following section also explains their interplay with other parts of the Linux kernel.

`slip_init_ctrl_dev( )`	**drivers/net/slip.c**

This function is called by `init_module()` when the SLIP module is loaded, and it uses the function `tty_register_ldisc()` to register the SLIP TTY line discipline with the Linux kernel.

`slip_open( )`	**drivers/net/slip.c**

This function is invoked by the function pointer `open()` in the `tty_ldisc` structure as soon as a user program wants to switch a TTY device to the SLIP line discipline. It reserves memory for the transmit and receive buffers and registers the new network device for the SLIP connection with the Linux kernel.

`sl_init( )`	**drivers/net/slip.c**

This function is invoked by the Linux kernel whenever a new network device is registered, and it does a complete initialization of the network device and the appropriate `net_device` structure.

`sl_open( )`	**drivers/net/slip.c**

This function is invoked by the function pointer `open()` of the `net_device` structure as soon as the SLIP network device is activated (e.g., by the command `ifconfig up`).

`sl_close( )`	**drivers/net/slip.c**

This function is invoked by the function pointer `stop()` of the `net_device` structure as soon as the SLIP network device is deactivated (e.g., by the command `ifconfig down`).

`slip_close( )`	**drivers/net/slip.c**

This function is invoked by the function pointer `close()` of the `tty_ldisc` structure whenever the underlying TTY device is switched from the SLIP line discipline to another line discipline.

`cleanup_module( )`	**drivers/net/slip.c**

This function is invoked whenever the SLIP module is removed. Among other things, it ensures that all buffers are freed and all SLIP network devices are deregistered. Finally, the registration of the SLIP TTY line discipline with the Linux kernel is removed by calling `tty_register_ldisc(N_SLIP, NULL)`.

`sl_xmit( )`	**drivers/net/slip.c**

This function is invoked by the IP layer, which uses the function pointer `hard_start_xmit()` of the `net_device` structure to output an IP packet over the SLIP network device. The actual work is delegated to the function `sl_encaps()`.

`sl_encaps( )`	**drivers/net/slip.c**

This function is invoked by `sl_xmit()`. As explained in section 7.1.1, it converts the IP packet into a byte sequence. Depending on the SLIP operating mode (CSLIP, etc.), other functions may be called in addition (e.g., the function `slip_esc()`). Subsequently, `sl_encaps()` invokes the function `write()` of the underlying TTY device driver, which eventually sends the byte sequence previously created over the TTY device.

`slip_esc( )`	**drivers/net/slip.c**

This function is invoked by `sl_encaps()` and does the character stuffing described in Section 7.1.1. A similar function called `slip_esc6()` exists for the SLIP operating mode SLIP6, which additionally divides the data into 6-bit blocks and converts it into printable characters.

`slip_write_wakeup( )`	**drivers/net/slip.c**

This function is invoked by the underlying TTY device driver over the function pointer `write_wakeup()` of the `tty_ldisc` structure (see Section 7.2.1) as soon as the TTY device is ready to accept more data. (See also Section 7.2.7.)

`slip_receive_room()`	**drivers/net/slip.c**

This function is invoked by the underlying TTY device driver over the function pointer `receive_room()` of the `tty_ldisc` structure and simply returns the value 65536, because the SLIP implementation can process a maximum of 65536 bytes per call of `slip_receive_buf()`.

`slip_receive_buf()`	**drivers/net/slip.c**

This function is invoked by the underlying TTY device driver over the function pointer `receive_buf()` of the `tty_ldisc` structure to transfer data from the TTY device to the SLIP driver. The function `slip_unesc()` (`slip_unesc6()`, for the SLIP6 operating mode) is invoked to convert the incoming byte stream back into IP packets.

`slip_unesc()`	**drivers/net/slip.c**

This function is invoked by `slip_receive_buf()`; it converts the incoming byte stream into IP packets, using the method described in Section 7.1.1. The function sl_bump() is invoked as soon as the END control character specifies that a complete IP packet was received. There is a corresponding function (slip_unesc6()) for the SLIP6 operating mode.

sl_bump()	drivers/net/slip.c

This function is invoked by slip_unesc() (or slip_unesc6()) as soon as a complete IP packet was reconstructed from the byte stream received. It generates a corresponding sk_buff structure and invokes the function netif_rx() to forward the packet to the IP layer.

7.2.4 Initializing the Driver and Establishing a Connection

The initialization function of the SLIP driver (slip_init_ctrl_dev()) is invoked when the SLIP driver is loaded into the Linux kernel (by the command insmod slip, by the kernel daemon, or, if the SLIP driver is permanently integrated into the Linux kernel, during booting). This initialization function registers the SLIP TTY line discipline with the Linux kernel. For this purpose, a tty_ldisc structure, sl_ldisc, is created, which contains pointers to the functions of the SLIP driver, and tty_register_ldisc (N_SLIP, &sl_ldisc) registers the new line discipline.

A modem connection is established by a user program (e.g., dip) regardless of the SLIP driver. To establish a modem connection, the dip program can call a script, which registers with the system at the other end of the line (i.e., with the PoP of the Internet provider) and also starts a SLIP implementation at that end. Subsequently, it uses the system call ioctl (tty, TCIOCSETD, N_SLIP) to switch the corresponding TTY device (e.g., /dev/ttyS0) to SLIP. Alternatively, the user program slattach can be used to switch an existing modem connection to SLIP line discipline.

The above ioctl() call causes the function tty_set_ldisc() to be invoked in the generic TTY driver; that function, in turn, invokes the routine slip_open of the SLIP driver. The latter reserves memory for a slip structure and for the transmit and receive buffers and uses the system call register_netdevice() to register a new network device, by the name of sl#, with the system kernel. A net_device structure is passed to this system call (see Section 5.1.1), and the function pointer init() in this structure points to the function sl_init().

To initialize the new network device, the Linux kernel invokes the function sl_init() immediately after the above actions. The function sl_init() initializes the net_device structure—for example, by setting the function pointers remaining in the net_device structure (including pointers to the functions sl_open(), sl_close(), and sl_xmit()).

7.2.5 Activating and Deactivating a Network Device

A user can now use the command ifconfig up to activate the new network device. This activation invokes the function sl_open() in the Linux kernel. The user program passes parameters (e.g., the IP address or the MTU) during that action. Subsequently, packets can be sent over the SLIP network device or received from that device. However, to be able to actually transmit packets, we have to set an appropriate route (either automatically, by ifconfig, or by another user program).

The above steps are done in reverse order to tear down a SLIP connection. More specifically, ifconfig is used to deactivate the network device. Any route registered for this device is now deleted automatically by the Linux kernel, so that no more data can be sent over this network device. The user can then use the command ifconfig down to cause the routine sl_close() to be invoked in the Linux kernel. This routine informs the driver that the network device was deactivated, but it doesn't free the relevant data structures just yet. Subsequently, no more data can be sent or received over this SLIP device.

7.2.6   Tearing Down a Connection and Deinitializing the Driver

The SLIP TTY line discipline might need to be terminated for several reasons: First, it is possible that a user program calls the system call close() or the Linux kernel calls the function tty_hangup() to close a serial connection. In the latter case, the Linux kernel resets the line discipline of the relevant TTY device automatically to the standard value N_TTY. Second, it can happen that the TTY device is switched to another line discipline by the function tty_set_ldisc(). Each of these cases invokes the routine slip_close() in the SLIP driver. This routine does some cleanup work (e.g., it decrements the usage counter of the SLIP module).

When the SLIP module is removed (by the command rmmod slip, or automatically), then the function cleanup_module() is invoked. First of all, this function ensures that all open SLIP connections are closed by the function tty_hangup() and that all SLIP network devices are removed. Subsequently, it deregisters the SLIP TTY line discipline by calling tty_register_ldisc (N_SLIP, NULL). After that, the SLIP TTY line discipline is no longer known in the system, and user programs can no longer use it.

7.2.7   Transmitting IP Packets

To transmit an IP packet, the IP layer invokes the function sl_xmit() and passes an sk_buff structure to this function. This causes sl_encaps() to be invoked, which uses the function slip_esc() to do character stuffing and marks packet boundaries. (See Section 7.1.1.) Subsequently, the converted packet is in the transmit buffer, and the pointer xbuff in the slip structure points to this buffer.

To output data to the TTY device, sl_encaps() invokes the write() routine of the relevant device driver. This routine returns the number of bytes that can actually be transmitted in one shot. Subsequently, the xleft variable is set to the number of bytes still missing, and the xhead pointer is set to the first of these bytes.

Because the function sl_encaps() has set the flag TTY_DO_WRITE_WAKEUP, the TTY device driver invokes the function slip_write_wakeup() as soon as it has transmitted the announced number of bytes. Next, the function slip_write_wakeup() tries to transmit the remaining xleft bytes, starting from the position xhead. The write() routine of the device driver, once more, returns the number of bytes to be actually transmitted, which causes xhead and xleft to be adapted accordingly. This process is repeated until the complete IP packet has been transmitted successfully, so that xleft equals null.

7.2.8   Receiving IP Packets

As soon as data have arrived over the TTY device, the device driver invokes the function slip_receive_buf() of the SLIP driver. The maximum number of bytes passed to slip_receive_buf were previously polled (65536 for the SLIP driver) by the function slip_receive_room().

The function slip_receive_buf() invokes the function slip_unesc() for each single buffer character, to undo the character stuffing described in Section 7.1.1 and detect the boundaries of IP packets. More specifically, for a normal character, slip_unesc() writes the character passed to the receive buffer, rbuff, and increments the counter rcount. If the special character ESC is detected, then it is understood that the next character (ESC_ESC or ESC_END) has to be treated appropriately.

If the END character is found, then slip_unesc() forwards the ready packet to sl_bump() and deletes the rbuff receive buffer by resetting rcount to null. The function sl_bump() reserves memory for an sk_buff structure, copies the readily reconstructed IP packet into this structure, and calls the function netif_rx() to pass the sk_buff structure to the IP layer for further processing.

CHAPTER 8

The Point-to-Point
Protocol (PPP)

8.1 INTRODUCTION

The Point-to-Point protocol (PPP) can be used by two computers connected directly (i.e., not over a local area network) to communicate. PPP is defined in RFC 1661 [Simp94a]. A typical application for PPP is dialing into the Internet over a modem; see Figure 8–1. In this case, it increasingly replaces the older SLIP protocol (see Chapter 7), which has proven to be not as flexible as modern applications demand.

In contrast to SLIP, PPP is *multiprotocol enabled*. In addition to IPv4, IPv6, and a large number of other network protocols, PPP also supports several subprotocols, which handle authentication and configuration tasks (e.g., negotiating important connection parameters and allocating dynamic IP addresses).

The architecture of PPP is basically designed for peer-to-peer communication. Nevertheless, in the case of a dialup connection to the Internet, the point of presence is

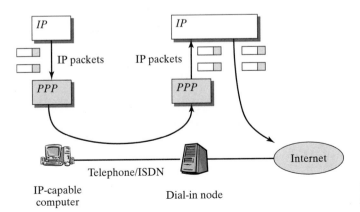

FIGURE 8–1
Scenario for the use of PPP.

often called server and the dialing computer is called client. Though the protocol allows both ends of a connection to expect that the peer authenticate itself and allocates it a dynamic IP address, this would naturally not make much sense when dialing into the Internet.

Linux distinguishes between synchronous and asynchronous PPP, depending on whether the underlying TTY device supports packet-oriented data transmission (synchronous—for example, in ISDN with HDLC as the layer-2 protocol) or it works with a continuous byte stream (asynchronous—e.g., in a modem connection).

We will discuss the asynchronous transmission over a serial interface in more detail later, because it requires more protocol functionality than synchronous PPP. The ISDN subsystem of Linux has its own, independent PPP implementation, which is not discussed here.

8.1.1 Subprotocols

Figure 8–2 shows the structure of a (synchronous) PPP packet. Synchronous PPP always processes entire frames of the lower-layer protocol, which is the reason why it is not necessary to specify the length. Asynchronous PPP additionally requires a frame detection, similar to SLIP. (See Section 7.1.1.) Section 8.3.5 describes how this frame detection is implemented in PPP.

The first 16 bits of a PPP packet specify the content encapsulated in the payload field. Table 8–1 gives an overview of the protocol numbers used. These numbers are built by the address-extension scheme of the HDLC protocol [ISO93], so that the protocols most frequently used can be encoded in one single byte. This means that all protocols have numbers where the first bit of the higher-order byte is deleted and the first bit of the lower-order byte is set (i.e., all have odd numbers). However, truncating the protocol field to 8 bits means that both communicating peers have to support this mode. Linux doesn't know this short version, and such configuration attempts of the peer are blocked off.

FIGURE 8–2
Structure of a PPP packet.

| Protocol 8/16 Bit | Payload | Padding |

TABLE 8–1 Protocol numbers for PPP packets.

Number	Protocol
0x0001-0x3FFF	network-layer protocols (e.g., IPv4, IPv6, IPX)
0x4001-0x7FFF	transmission of small payload amounts without network-layer protocol (low-volume traffic)
0x8001-0xBFFF	subprotocols to configure the network layer (network-control protocols—e.g., IPCP)
0xC001-0xFFFF	subprotocols to establish a PPP connection (link-layer control protocols—e.g., LCP, PAP, CHAP)

The current PPP implementation in Linux can transport four layer-3 protocols: IP, IPv6, IPX, and AppleTalk—which are exactly the protocols that the network layer can handle. The higher-layer network protocol of PPP is handled transparently, so it is easy to add new protocols.

In addition, PPP has so-called subprotocols, which are handled directly by the PPP instance, rather than by forwarding them to the network layer. The most important subprotocols are the following:

- *LCP (Link Control Protocol)*: Subprotocol to configure PPP instances.
- *PAP (Password Authentication Protocol)*: Authenticates the user by clear-text password (often used by Internet service providers).
- *CHAP (Challenge Handshake Authentication Protocol)*: Secure user authentication over a challenge-response mechanism, where the user's password is not transmitted in clear text.
- *IPCP (IP Configuration Protocol)*: Subprotocol to configure the IP layer (e.g., to allocate IP addresses once a PPP connection has been established).

8.1.2 Components of the Linux Implementation

The Linux PPP implementation is composed of four parts: a generic PPP driver, one TTY line discipline (see Section 7.2.1) each for asynchronous and synchronous TTY devices, and a user-space daemon, pppd.

Figure 8–3 gives a rough overview of how these components interact. Some of the communication channels represented in this figure are used, if at all, only during the establishment and teardown of connections; they are shown by dashed lines in the figure.

While the generic PPP driver is communicating with the network layer and one of the drivers (for asynchronous or synchronous PPP) is serving the underlying TTY device, pppd is responsible for the correct interaction of all components. It is also responsible for establishing and tearing down connections and handling the subprotocols described in Section 8.1.1.

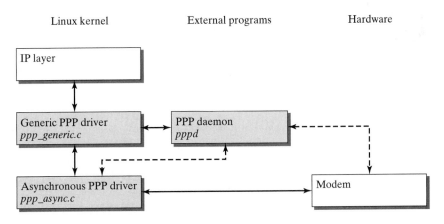

FIGURE 8–3
Interaction of the PPP components.

Each instance of pppd corresponds to exactly one PPP network device (ppp0, ppp1, etc.). This allows several independent PPP interfaces, each having its own settings. To let the PPP daemon communicate with the generic PPP driver, a special character-oriented device with *major number* PPP_MAJOR (108) is set up; normally, it is embedded under /dev/ppp in the file system.

The close interaction of all of these components makes it absolutely necessary to always use the pppd matching the Linux kernel. Otherwise, pppd will report a version conflict when the system starts.

8.2   PPP CONFIGURATION IN LINUX

PPP drivers in the Linux kernel have comparatively few configuration options. The reason is that most settings were moved to pppd, which means that they can be changed at runtime or even set separately for different devices.

It is important to note that PPP over ISDN requires different settings, which have nothing to do with the settings discussed in this section, because the ISDN subsystem includes its full PPP implementation. This applies particularly to the kernel options, but also to the pppd configuration. To be able to use PPP over ISDN, for example, it is not necessary to activate the "normal" PPP in the configuration of the Linux kernel.

8.2.1   Kernel Options

The Linux kernel version 2.2 included only one option that could be used to enable or disable the full PPP support. Version 2.3 introduced three additional setting options (shown in Table 8–2).

The payload compression by the deflate option is preferred over the BSD compression algorithm, because it is free from patents and more effective. By the way, the deflate algorithm is also used in gzip.

8.2.2   pppd—the PPP Daemon

As was mentioned before, most settings are effected by pppd. The configuration files required for these settings are normally stored in the directory /etc/ppp/. See also the manpage of pppd, *Files* section, for details.

Upon startup, pppd reads first the general configuration file options and then a device-specific configuration file (e.g., options.ppp0). In addition, there is a possibility

TABLE 8–2   PPP driver options in the Linux kernel.

Option	Meaning
CONFIG_PPP	Activates the generic PPP.
CONFIG_PPP_ASYNC	Activates the asynchronous PPP.
CONFIG_PPP_DEFLATE	Supports payload compression.
CONFIG_PPP_BSDCOMP	Supports alternative payload compression.

of adding user-specific settings in $HOME/.ppprc. These files include information about the serial interface to be used, about whether configuration requests of the peer should be accepted, and about which user name will be used to log into the peer. The following represent some important entries in the configuration file; however, they do not represent a full configuration:

```
# Options for pppd over a serial line
# /etc/ppp/options
modem                       # use the modem control lines
crtscts                     # use hardware flow control
lock                        # create lockfile to ensure exclusive access
defaultroute                # set default route to this interface
debug                       # enable connection debugging facilities
user egon
```

The user name in the last line serves as key for the entry in the pap-secrets and chap-secrets files, which include the passport of each user in a PAP or CHAP authentication. Both files have the same structure and include clear-text passwords, so the user root should have exclusive read access to these files:

```
# Secrets for authentication using PAP
# /etc/ppp/pap-secrets
# client          server    secret         IP addresses
"egon"            *         "mypassword"
"hugo"            *         "myotherpassword"
```

The structure of the underlying physical connection is left to an external program. For modem connections, this program has to deal particularly with the modem initialization, dialing of the correct phone number (perhaps from a choice of several numbers), and appropriate handling of error messages output by the modem. chat is a program especially suitable for this task; it processes a special script (the so-called *chatscript*) and is included in the pppd package. Of course, you don't need a chatscript to connect two neighboring computers over a null-modem cable.

pppd offers a way to run shell scripts after successful establishment of a connection or before a connection is torn down. The most popular scripts are ip-up and ip-down. The ip-up script is invoked as soon as an IP address was allocated to the end system. It can be used, for example, to send all waiting mails automatically. It is less well known that a number of different scripts can be invoked, in addition to ip-up and ip-down. For example, auth-up is invoked as soon as the user authentication over PPP or CHAP was successful, but before the network protocol used (e.g., IP) is initialized, and ipv6-up and ipx-up are the counterparts to ip-up for IP Version 6 and IPX, respectively. Of course, there is a corresponding "down" script to each of these "up" scripts.

8.2.3   Dial on Demand

Since Version 2.3, pppd supports the dial-on-demand mode directly (i.e., no additional program, such as diald, is required).

The dial-on-demand mode means that a PPP connection is established automatically when needed (i.e., when IP packets are ready to be output from the corresponding network device). If the connection remains idle for a specific (configurable) period, then pppd tears it down automatically. This means that the expensive telephone line is used only upon demand, and the user does not have to dial. The only drawback of this mode is that it introduces a certain delay until the connection is up.

This functionality is implemented by the state PHASE_DORMANT. (See Section 8.4.2.) pppd assumes this state before a peer dialed, if the option demand is stated in its configuration file. In this case, the generic PPP driver in the Linux kernel sends outgoing IP packets for the respective PPP device directly to pppd, which dials into the provider, rather than to the asynchronous driver.

To better control the cost, the option active-filter can be used to specify a filter to decide which network traffic is important enough to establish a connection. Detailed information about this functionality is found in the manpage of pppd in the *Options* section.

8.2.4   Automatic Callback

The automatic callback function means that the client first dials normally to a remote server. During the configuration phase, however, the client uses the PPP subprotocol *CBCP (Call Back Configuration Protocol)* to request a callback. Subsequently, the connection is torn down, and pppd terminates with return value 14. If the server is configured appropriately, then it calls back the client, so that the client and the server, in effect, switch their roles. This functionality is suitable, for example, when a company wants to assume the cost for its teleworkers dialing into company computers.

8.3   PPP IMPLEMENTATION IN THE LINUX KERNEL

As mentioned before, the PPP implementation in Linux is divided into four different tasks: three kernel modules and the pppd user space daemon. During design of this division, care was taken to move as little functionality as possible into the Linux kernel. For this reason, the kernel modules are rather simple. pppd includes 13,000 lines of code (2,100 lines alone in main.c), which means that it is four times the size of the three kernel modules (ppp_generic.c, ppp_synctty.c, and ppp_async.c) together. In the following sections, we will first discuss the generic PPP driver and then the driver for the asynchronous PPP TTY line discipline. The driver for the synchronous PPP line discipline is relatively simple, so we will not discuss it here.

8.3.1   Functions and Data Structures of the Generic PPP Driver

Figure 8–4 shows the most important data structures of the generic PPP driver. There is a separate ppp structure with general management information for each PPP device. Some important entries, particularly the transmit and receive queues, xq and rq, are in a substructure of the type ppp_file. This substructure is also found in the channel structure, which is used to manage single channels in *multilink PPP*, which will not be discussed here, for the sake of simplicity.

There is a PPP device for each network device, the net_device structure of which refers to the related ppp structure in the field priv. In addition, the PPP daemon can send

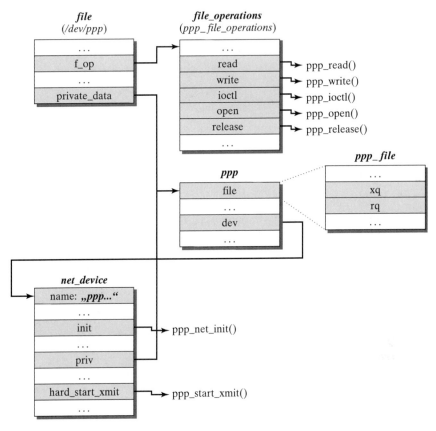

FIGURE 8–4
Important data structures of the generic PPP driver.

and receive control packets of subprotocols (see Section 8.1.1) over the device /dev/ppp. For this purpose, it must first bind the device /dev/ppp to a specific PPP device by use of an ioctl() call. This binding means that a pointer to the ppp structure is entered into the field private_data of the relevant file structure.

ppp_init()	drivers/net/ppp_generic.c

This function is invoked by init_module() whenever the PPP module is loaded: It uses the function devs_register_chrdev() to register the character-oriented device /dev/ppp (see Section 8.1.2) with the Linux kernel.

ppp_cleanup()	drivers/net/ppp_generic.c

This function is invoked whenever the PPP module is removed. It frees all data structures used and deregisters the device /dev/ppp.

`ppp_open()`	**drivers/net/ppp_generic.c**

This function is invoked by the function pointer `open()` in the `file_operations` structure as soon as the PPP daemon opens the device /dev/ppp.

`ppp_release()`	**drivers/net/ppp_generic.c**

This function is invoked by the function pointer `release()` in the `file_operations` structure as soon as the device /dev/ppp is closed again.

`ppp_write()`	**drivers/net/ppp_generic.c**

This function is invoked by the function pointer `write()` in the `file_operations` structure when the PPP daemon sends a PPP control packet over the device /dev/ppp. For this, a matching `ppp_file` structure is determined and passed to the function `ppp_file_write()` as the pf parameter. First, an `sk_buff` structure with the data to be sent is created in this function and appended to the transmit queue pf->xq by `skb_queue_tail()`; then it is output to the underlying network device by `ppp_xmit_process()`.

`ppp_read()`	**drivers/net/ppp_generic.c**

This function is invoked by the function pointer `read()` in the `file_operations` structure when the PPP daemon wants to receive PPP control packets over the device /dev/ppp. As with `ppp_write()`, a matching `ppp_file` structure first is located and passed to the function `ppp_file_read()` as the pf parameter. In this function, `add_wait_queue()` first waits for packets to arrive in the receive queue pf->rq; then the incoming packets are read by `skb_dequeue()`.

`ppp_ioctl()`	**drivers/net/ppp_generic.c**

This function is invoked by the function pointer `ioctl()` in the `file_operations` structure when the PPP daemon uses an `ioctl()` call for the device /dev/ppp to change various parameters of the PPP drivers in the Linux kernel.

`ppp_unattached_ioctl()`	**drivers/net/ppp_generic.c**

This function is invoked by `ppp_ioctl()` when the device /dev/ppp has not yet been bound to a PPP device and so (the `private_data` field of the related file structure has the value 0). Its tasks include the `ioctl()` call PPPIOCNEWUNIT, which creates a new PPP device and writes a pointer to the relevant ppp structure in the field file->private_data.

`ppp_net_init()`	**drivers/net/ppp_generic.c**

This function is invoked by the Linux kernel whenever a new PPP network device is registered. It initializes the `net_device` structure; in particular, the function pointers described below are set.

`ppp_start_xmit()`	**drivers/net/ppp_generic.c**

This function is invoked by the function pointer `hard_start_xmit()` in the `net_device` structure of the IP layer to output an IP packet over the PPP network device. First, the required PPP header is added, then `skb_queue_tail()` adds the complete packet to the transmit queue (similarly to the function `ppp_write()`), and finally `ppp_xmit_process()` outputs the packet to the underlying network device.

`ppp_xmit_process()`	**drivers/net/ppp_generic.c**

This function is responsible for outputting all packets waiting in the transmit queue `ppp->file.xq` to the underlying device. The auxiliary function `ppp_send_frame()`, which can optionally compress the PPP packets, is used for the actual output.

`ppp_input()`	**drivers/net/ppp_generic.c**

This function is invoked by the driver of the underlying TTY line discipline (asynchronous or synchronous) as soon as a PPP packet has been received. After a defragmenting of the packets, if necessary, the function `ppp_do_recv()` is invoked for further processing; then this function forwards the packet to `ppp_receive_frame()`.

`ppp_receive_frame()`	**drivers/net/ppp_generic.c**

This function checks for whether multilink PPP is activated and forwards an incoming PPP packet to either the function `ppp_receive_mp_frame()` (with multilink PPP) or `ppp_receive_nonmp_frame()` (without multilink PPP).

`ppp_receive_nonmp_frame()`	**drivers/net/ppp_generic.c**

When a PPP packet arrives, this function first undoes the compression, if applicable, and then checks for whether it is a data packet or a control packet of a subprotocol. (See Section 8.1.1.) If it is a control packet, then `skb_queue_tail()` adds the packet to the receive queue, where it can be read by the PPP daemon over the device /dev/ppp. If it is a data packet, then the payload is packed in an `sk_buff` structure with the correct protocol identifier and passed to the network layer by calling `netif_rx()`.

8.3.2   Functions and Data Structures of the Asynchronous PPP Driver

The asynchronous PPP module essentially supplies a new TTY line discipline (see Section 7.2.1), by the name of N_PPP, and representing an intermediate layer between the generic PPP driver and the driver of the underlying TTY device.

Figure 8–5 gives an overview of the most important data structures. The driver's state information is maintained in an `asynctty` structure. As in the SLIP implementation (see Section 7.2.3), there is a reference to the `tty_struct` structure of the underlying TTY device, which contains a `tty_ldisc` structure for the PPP TTY line discipline.

A `ppp_channel` structure (which will not be discussed in detail here) is used to reach both the ppp structure of the relevant generic PPP driver and a structure of the type `ppp_channel_ops`, which includes function pointers to, among others, the function

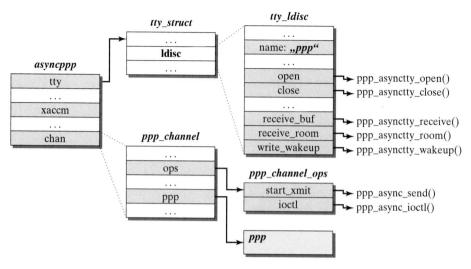

FIGURE 8–5
Important data structures of the asynchronous PPP driver.

ppp_async_send() described further below. Inversely, the ppp structure of the generic PPP driver can be used to reach the relevant ppp_channel structure (and thus the function pointers in ppp_channel_ops) over several detours (which will not be described here, to keep things simple). This is important for being able to pass outgoing packets to the function ppp_async_send() in case of asynchronous PPP.

ppp_async_init()	drivers/net/ppp_async.c

This function is invoked whenever the ppp_async.o module loads. It uses tty_register_ldisc() to register the PPP TTY line discipline with the Linux kernel.

ppp_async_cleanup()	drivers/net/ppp_async.c

This function is invoked whenever the ppp_async.o module is removed. It calls tty_register_ldisc(N_PPP, NULL) to deregister the PPP TTY line discipline.

ppp_async_send()	drivers/net/ppp_async.c

This function is invoked by the function ppp_push() of the generic PPP driver over the function pointer start_xmit() in the ppp_channel_ops structure (see Figure 8–5) as soon as a PPP packet is ready to be sent. It forwards the packet to the function ppp_async_push().

ppp_async_push()	drivers/net/ppp_async.c

This function is invoked by the function ppp_async_send() to transmit a PPP packet. The function uses the auxiliary function ppp_async_encode() to prepare the packet for asynchronous transmission and then sends it to the driver of the underlying TTY device by repeatedly calling `tty->driver.write()`.

`ppp_async_encode()`	**drivers/net/ppp_async.c**

This function uses the character stuffing described in Section 7.1.1 to transmit a PPP packet over an asynchronous device.

`ppp_async_input()`	**drivers/net/ppp_async.c**

This function is invoked by `ppp_asynctty_receive()` as soon as new data was supplied by the underlying TTY device. As with the SLIP functionality (see Section 7.1.1), it undoes character stuffing and detects the beginning and end of PPP packets. As soon as a packet has been read completely, it is forwarded to the function `process_input_packet()`.

`process_input_packet()`	**drivers/net/ppp_async.c**

This function is invoked by `ppp_async_input()` as soon as a PPP packet has been read completely. First, the packet checksum (*Frame Check Sequence—FCS*) is checked. After a number of additional checks, `ppp_input()` is called eventually, to forward the packet to the generic PPP driver.

`ppp_asynctty_open()`, `ppp_asynctty_close()`	**drivers/net/ppp_async.c**

These functions are invoked by the function pointers `open()` and `close()` of the `tty_ldisc` structure as soon as a user program switches a TTY device to the PPP line discipline or resets it to another line discipline. Essentially, an `asynctty` structure is created in `tty_asynctty_open()` for the state data of the TTY line discipline, then initialized, and finally released in `tty_asynctty_close()`.

`ppp_asynctty_read()`, `ppp_asynctty_write()`	**drivers/net/ppp_async.c**

These functions are invoked by the function pointers `read()` and `write()` of the `tty_ldisc` structure whenever a program attempts to send data to a TTY device in PPP line discipline or read from it. Its only functionality is that it returns an error message, because all inputs and outputs of the asynchronous PPP driver run over the device /dev/ppp.

`ppp_asynctty_room()`, `ppp_asynctty_receive()`, `ppp_asynctty_wakeup()`	**drivers/net/ppp_async.c**

These functions correspond largely to the functions `slip_receive_room()`, `slip_receive_buf()`, and `slip_write_wakeup()` of the SLIP implementation. (See Section 7.2.3). When data arrives, then `ppp_asynctty_receive()` invokes the function `ppp_async_input()` (as described earlier).

8.3.3   Initialization

When the PPP module `ppp_generic.o` is loaded, then `ppp_init()` first registers a character-oriented device with the major number 108, which is normally embedded under /dev/ppp into the system. In the next step, the module uses `ppp_async_init()` to register a new TTY line discipline (see Section 7.2.1) by the name "ppp" for the asynchronous PPP driver (`ppp_async.o`). This TTY line discipline is an intermediate layer between the device driver of the underlying device and the `ppp_async.o` module, which facilitates access to all incoming data packets. Once the /dev/tty device and the PPP TTY line discipline have been registered, the first initialization phase is completed.

The second phase is initiated by the calling of pppd. After a brief test of whether its version number matches the kernel driver version, it opens the device /dev/ppp. It then obtains a file descriptor, which is required later to communicate with the generic PPP driver; at first, however, only the reference pointer USAGE_COUNT of the PPP device is incremented.

Next, a user process has to establish a physical connection (e.g., the chat program could dial the number of a dialup server). If this action was successful, then pppd uses the system call `ioctl(tty_fd, TIOCSETD, N_PPP)` to change the TTY line discipline to N_PPP. It then uses `ioctl(ppp_dev_fd, PPPIOCNEWUNIT)` to request the generic PPP driver to create a new network device and then uses `ioctl(fd, _PPPIOCATTACH)` to bind the new network device to the underlying TTY device.

These steps complete the establishment of the actual PPP connection; now the PPP subprotocols, such as LCP, can start authenticating the user and configure higher layers. (See Section 8.4.)

8.3.4   Transmitting IP Packets

The generic PPP driver accepts packets ready for transmission over two different routes: The network layer sends payload packets over the matching network device (pppX), and the PPP daemon sends control packets over the character-oriented device /dev/ppp.

Each data packet to be sent is passed to the function `ppp_start_xmit()` by the network layer in an `sk_buff` structure. (See Section 4.1.) This function appends a 2-byte PPP header (see Figure 8–2) to the beginning of the packet and stores the packet in the transmit queue ppp->xq. Virtually the same thing happens in `ppp_write()`, the function that accepts packets from pppd.

Finally, the function `ppp_xmit_process()` is invoked in each case. It takes packets from the transmit queue and forwards them to the function `ppp_send_frame()` for further processing. Depending on the setting, the packet headers might be compressed by the Van–Jacobson method and the deflate or BSD-Compress method might be used for payload compression. After a forwarding to the function `ppp_async_send()_` of the asynchronous PPP driver (or to the corresponding function of the synchronous PPP driver), the generic PPP driver has completed its processing.

8.3.5   Detecting Frame Boundaries

Frame synchronization (*framing*) is implemented as a TTY line discipline in the asynchronous PPP driver (`drivers/net/ppp_async.c`) and follows the standard specified in [Simp94b]. Basically, this is an easily modified and streamlined *HDLC* (*High Level Data Link Control*; see [ISO93]).

Section 7.1.1 briefly explained why framing is necessary: An asynchronous TTY device (e.g., a modem connection) can process only unstructured byte streams and not full packets, so it is necessary to mark the beginning and end of a packet specially. In PPP, this is done by use of the special control character PPP_FLAG with the binary representation 01111110.

Of course, the remaining data stream should not inadvertently contain such special characters. To prevent special characters from occurring, we use *character stuffing*. This means that all payload bytes corresponding to a control character, such as PPP_FLAG, are prefixed by the character PPP_ESCAPE (binary 01111101). There are more control characters; see include/linux/ppp.defs.h for a complete list.

Framing and character stuffing are largely implemented in the function ppp_async_encode(). A bit vector in the field xaccm in the struct asyncppp structure is used to detect the characters that should have a PPP_ESCAPE prefix. Each of the 32×8 bits in this vector corresponds to one of the 256 available 8-bit characters.

The following program dump from drivers/net/ppp async.c shows how you can convert payload into a data stream:

```
#define PUT_BYTE(ap, buf, c, islcp)            do {           \
        if ((islcp && c < 0x20) || (ap->xaccm[c >> 5] & (1 << (c & 0x1f)))) {\
                *buf++ = PPP_ESCAPE;                           \
                *buf++ = c ^ 0x20;                             \
        } else                                                 \
                *buf++ = c;                                    \
} while (0)
```

In this code, islcp is a flag set only for special LCP commands, which have to work even when the bit vector ap->xaccm has not yet been initialized or has been wrongly initialized.

To protect against transmission errors, a 2-byte CRC checksum (*Frame Check Sequence—FCS*) is appended to the PPP packet before the closing end character (PPP_FLAG). If the packet was fully converted into a data stream, then the driver of the underlying TTY device, which is called by tty->driver.write(), assumes the remaining work.

8.3.6   Receiving IP Packets

Receiving PPP packets over the asynchronous PPP driver works much as does sending packets, just in opposite direction: Incoming data is first sent to the function ppp_asynctty_receive() of the asynchronous PPP driver by the driver of the underlying TTY device. Then the function ppp_async_input()_searches for frame boundaries and undoes character stuffing. The function process_input_packet() tests for whether the checksum (FCS; see Section 8.3.5) is correct. Finally, the fully restored packet is passed to the function ppp_input() of the generic PPP driver.

is closed again, all subprotocols are notified accordingly by the function pointer `close()`. For the authentication protocols PAP and CHAP, the value NULL each is entered for `open()` and `close()` as callback function.

8.4.2   States

The protocol logic of most subprotocols can be represented elegantly in the form of a *finite state machine* (*FSM*). To save cost and avoid errors, the PPP daemon implements a generic FSM, which handles things like state transitions and timers. It is implemented in `pppd/fsm.c` and primarily takes care that the correct callback functions are invoked at the right time. Examples for subprotocols with an implementation that accesses this generic finite state machine include LCP and IPCP.

PPP itself, and thus the PPP daemon, also know different states; however, these states have little to do with the states of subprotocols. These so-called phases are listed in Table 8–3. The PPP daemon behaves differently, depending on the state. For example, it would be fatal to admit configuration protocols for the network layer, such as IPCP, before a successful authentication.

A callback function can be invoked upon request in each of these state transitions. To this end, the callback function need only be added to the otherwise unused global variable `new_phase_hook`.

TABLE 8–3   States (phases) of the PPP daemon.

State	Meaning
PHASE_INITIALIZE	Initial state: pppd initialization.
PHASE_DORMANT	Waiting for activity (for dial-on-demand).
PHASE_SERIALCONN	Establish physical connection.
PHASE_ESTABLISH	Physical connection is up and running.
PHASE_AUTHENTICATE	Authentication in progress.
PHASE_CALLBACK	CBCP (see Section 8.2.4) is running.
PHASE_NETWORK	Network protocols are being configured.
PHASE_RUNNING	Higher layers can start working.
PHASE_TERMINATE	LCP requested connection to be torn down.
PHASE_DISCONNECT	Program to tear down connection has started.
PHASE_HOLDOFF	Wait a little before the next connection is established.
PHASE_DEAD	Connection was interrupted.

CHAPTER 9

PPP over Ethernet

9.1 INTRODUCTION

Chapter 8 introduced the Point-to-Point protocol (PPP). Today, it is most frequently used in access networks that use ADSL as the access technology.

The ADSL (Asymmetric Digital Subscriber Line) access technology offers high-speed Internet access for private or commercial customers. From the technical viewpoint, this is a dedicated line (i.e., a permanent connection). Dedicated lines are normally billed on the basis of transmission volumes. In contrast, private Internet links are billed on a time basis. To enable ADSL to support time-specific billing as well, a new protocol, PPPoE, was developed. PPPoE is based on two accepted standards—PPP and Ethernet.

More specifically, an ADSL modem (NTBBA—Network Termination Point Broad-Band Access), installed behind a so-called splitter, is connected to the computer over Ethernet. This means that the computer has to be equipped with an Ethernet network card. This dedicated Ethernet line between the PC of the home user and the dialup computer of the access network operator is used to establish a PPP connection, which allows the access network operator to identify the user and bill for the usage time between the PPP dialup and the termination of that PPP session. This PPP connection can be used to exchange IP packets.

Figure 9–1 shows the resulting protocol stack. This chapter first introduces the PPPoE (PPP over Ethernet) protocol described in [MLEC+99]. Then, it introduces the implementation in the user space, which is used in kernel Versions 2.2 and 2.3. Finally, this chapter discusses the implementation in the kernel from kernel version 2.4 and up.

9.2 PPPOE SPECIFICATION IN RFC 2516

To be able to transport PPP protocol units over Ethernet, they are inserted as payload in Ethernet frames. For this purpose, two new ethertype values were defined, which show the receiver that the Ethernet frame contains PPP payload.

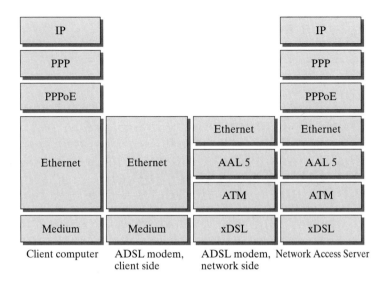

FIGURE 9–1
Protocol stack for the use of PPP over Ethernet.

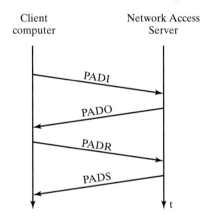

FIGURE 9–2
Typical sequence for PPPoE Active
Discovery.

The two different types serve to distinguish between two phases within PPoE: the discovery stage, and the session stage. A typical discovery stage consists of four steps, which appear as follows (in Figure 9–2): The host sends a PADI (PPPoE Active Discovery Initiation) packet to the Ethernet broadcast address to find out which access concentrators are available in the Ethernet. One (or several) of these access concentrators replies by sending a PADO (PPPoE Active Discovery Offer) packet, informing the host about the Ethernet address where an access concentrator is available, which may specify additional services. The host selects one from the available access concentrators and requests that this concentrator establish a connection by sending a PADR

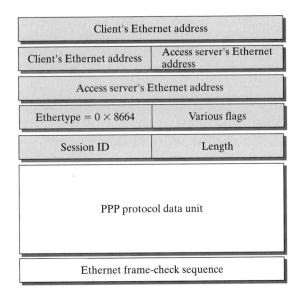

FIGURE 9–3
Protocol data unit of the PPPoE session stage.

(PPPoE Active Discovery Request) packet. The access concentrator replies by sending a PADS (PPPoE Active Discovery Session Confirmation) packet.

Subsequently, the discovery stage is left behind and the session stage begins, where PPP payload is packed transparently in Ethernet frames having ethertype value 0x8864 (in contrast to packets in the discovery stage, which have ethertype value 0x8863). Figure 9–3 shows what a PPPoE packet looks like in the session stage. The underlying Ethernet already forms frames, so PPPoE does not require character stuffing, in contrast to the asynchronous case described in Chapter 8.

The PPP protocol should generally initiate a PPPoE connection to be torn down, but there is also a PADT (PPPoE Active Discovery Terminate) packet, which can be used to terminate a PPPoE connection. Once a PADT packet has been sent or received, not even a normal PPP connection termination packet may be sent.

9.3 IMPLEMENTATION IN THE USER SPACE

The kernels of Versions 2.2 and 2.3 do not support PPPoE. Instead, another daemon is started in the user space, in addition to pppd. This daemon is called pppoed; it processes PPP packets of the Ethernet card and forwards them to pppd. pppd, and pppoed communicate over a pseudo-terminal, as shown in Figure 9–4.

FIGURE 9–4
pppd and pppoed communicate in the user space.

There are various implementations in the user space, including the Roaring Penguin implementation [Roar01], which appears to be the most elaborate. The major drawback of this approach and similar approaches is that the intermediate pseudo-terminal requires an additional transition between the kernel and the user space, which reduces the performance considerably. For this reason, we will consider only the kernel implementation available from kernel Version 2.4 in the following discussion.

9.4 IMPLEMENTATION IN THE LINUX KERNEL

Together with kernel Version 2.4, PPPoE support was integrated in the pppd daemon, and the kernel was expanded by a connection between the generic PPP driver and the Ethernet network card.

Figure 9–5 shows the interaction between these components. The PPPoE driver assumes several functions within the kernel. To the lower layer (i.e., the Ethernet card and the driver software), the PPPoE driver plays the role of a layer-3 protocol. As we will see later in more detail, incoming Ethernet packets are allocated to a protocol matching the type identifier in the Ethernet frame (e.g., the IP protocol or the PPPoE protocol for the ethertype values 0x8863 and 0x8864 mentioned earlier). Towards the higher-layer generic PPP driver, which was described in the previous chapter, the PPPoE driver behaves much as does the asynchronous PPP driver. In contrast to that driver, however, the PPPoE driver does not implement a tty operating mode.

To initiate the PPPoE discovery stage of pppd in the user space, it is additionally necessary to have the PPPoE driver and pppd communicate directly. Section 9.4.2 discusses this communication in detail.

9.4.1 Changes to the Kernel

The PPPoE driver, which is included in kernel Version 2.4 and higher in experimental form, consists of the file drivers/net/pppoe.c. In addition, there is a file called drivers/net/pppox.c, which is intended to harmonize present and future PPP implementations in the kernel. General functions that previously were used only by the

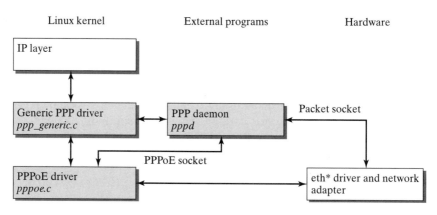

FIGURE 9–5
Communication between pppd and the PPP and PPPoE drivers.

PPPoE implementation were moved to the file pppox.c, and other PPP implementations over other networks should be available in the future.

Functions and Data Structures of the PPPoE Driver   In the first step, the PPPoE driver registers the PPPoE protocol with the kernel. This can be seen in the following piece of source text:

`pppoe_init()`	**drivers/net/pppoe.c**

```
{
Use a function from drivers/net/pppox.c to register the PPPoE protocol:
int err = register_pppox_proto(PX_PROTO_OE, &pppoe_proto);
if (err==0) {
        dev_add_pack(&pppoes_ptype);
        /*Add a packet handler
        for incoming packets of type ETH_P_PPP_SES
        (PPPoE session packets), which points to pppoe_rcv */
        dev_add_pack(&pppoed_ptype);
        /*Add a packet handler for incoming packets of type
        ETH_P_PPP_DISC (PPPoE connection setup packets), which
        points to pppoe_disc_rcv */
        register_netdevice_notifier(&pppoe_notifier);
        /*Add to netdevice notification chain */
        proc_net_create("pppoe", 0, pppoe_proc_info);
        /*Generate an entry in the proc directory */
}
return (err);
}
```

Subsequently, the PPoE driver provides functions that can be used by pppd to access the PPPoE protocol functionality over a PPPoE socket. The structure struct proto_ops pppoe_ops in driver/net/pppoe.c is used to bind the functionality of the PPPoE socket to general socket functions (e.g., connect(), sendmsg(), rcvmsg(), and bind()). Chapter 26 includes a more detailed description of how sockets are implemented in the Linux kernel.

`pppoe_create()`	**drivers/net/pppoe.c**

This function is invoked whenever a new PPPoE socket is opened. The function is exported and announced over the structure pppoe_proto and the function register_pppox_proto().

`pppoe_connect()`	**drivers/net/pppoe.c**

This function calls connect() at the PPPoE socket interface. If the call is successful, then PPPoE packets that have previously been sent or received over the specified Ethernet card can be accessed over the PPPoE socket in the application layer.

`pppoe_sendmsg()`	**drivers/net/pppoe.c**

The function `pppoe_sendmsg()` is used to pack data sent by `pppd` to the PPPoE socket into PPPoE packets and send them over the Ethernet.

`pppoe_rcvmsg()`	**drivers/net/pppoe.c**

This function serves to receive PPPoE packets over the PPPoE socket. However, only packets belonging to the discovery stage of the PPPoE protocol are processed; all other packets are instead forwarded to the generic PPP driver. Information about whether the PPPoE protocol is in the discovery stage or in the session stage is saved in `sk->state`.

Finally, once the PPPoE discovery stage is completed, incoming packets are forwarded to the generic PPP driver. (The case of PPPoE relay is not discussed here.) Various functions can be used to receive packets:

`pppoe_rcv()`	**drivers/net/pppoe.c**

This function is executed within the NET_RX tasklet. It handles error cases and passes packets to the function `pppoe_rcv_core()` for further processing.

`pppoe_rcv_core()`	**drivers/net/pppoe.c**

This function determines the dependency on the phase of the PPPoE protocol stored in `sk->state`, which means that an incoming packet is either forwarded to the generic PPP driver (by the function `ppp_input()`) or appended to the queue of the PPPoE socket by the function `sock_queue_rcv_skb()`, where it will be further processed by the above mentioned function `pppoe_rcvmsg()`.

`pppoe_disc_rcv()`	**drivers/net/pppoe.c**

This function is invoked whenever a packet of the PPPoE discovery stage was received (ethertype 0x8863 or ETH_P_PPP_DISC, as defined in `linux/if_ether.h`). However, the function `pppoe_disc_rcv()` serves only to receive PADT packets; all other packets are rejected. If an incoming packet is a PADT packet, then the PPPoE connection is disconnected and the socket is released.

`pppoe_xmit()`	**driver/net/pppoe.c**

This function is invoked by the generic PPP driver. It serves as wrapper for the function `__pppoe_xmit()`.

`_pppoe_xmit()`	**driver/net/pppoe.c**

This function is used to pack transmit data of the generic PPP driver into a PPPoE frame and send it over the specified Ethernet network card.

9.4.2   Tasks of the ppp Daemon

A data connection is established in several phases. The phase of the PPPoE discovery stage is fully handled by the ppp daemon, avoiding the pppoe driver. Special `packet sockets` are included in kernel Version 2.4 (see Chapter 26) and can be used to send or receive packets specified in RFC 2516 directly to or from the network card. If the discovery stage is successful, then the ppp daemon sets up a ppp interface in the kernel. The ppp daemon achieves this by opening a PPPoE socket and binding this socket to the PPPoE driver. Finally, the ppp daemon uses an `ioctl()` call with the parameter PPPIOCGCHAN (implemented in `driver/net/pppox.c`) to set the field `sk->state` to PPPOX_BOUND.

As was described in the previous section, this causes the PPPoE driver to forward all incoming packets to the generic PPP driver, except for the PPPOE relay case, which is not considered here, and for PADT packets, which are handled by the function `pppoe_disc_rcv()` (as already described). The ppp daemon can use different `ioctl()` calls over the PPPoE socket to change other parameters. However, the data path always leads over the generic PPP driver, from which the PPPoE driver now accepts PPP packets (data and control packets); it packs them and, eventually, passes them to the network card.

9.4.3   Configuration

To be able to use PPPoE in Linux from kernel Version 2.4 and higher, the option `PPPoverEthernet` and the option `Packet Socket` have to be activated in the kernel configuration upon compilation (via activation of the support for experimental drivers). If the PPPoE support is compiled as a module, then we additionally have to add the line "`alias net-pf-24 pppoe`" to the file `/etc/modules.conf`. This line is used to allocate the protocol with identifier 24 to the pppoe module. A package that integrates PPPoE extensions is available for pppd. All we have to do is to complete the file `/etc/ppp/options` by adding the line `plugin pppoe`; pppd can then be started with `pppd eth0`. [Ostr01] includes more installation instructions.

# CHAPTER 10

Asynchronous Transfer Mode—ATM

10.1   INTRODUCTION

Initially, the Asynchronous Transfer Mode (ATM) was introduced to provide a uniform protocol for the transmission of voice and data, offering guarantees for the required QoS (Quality of Service) parameters (such as data rate and delay) [McSp95]).

In contrast to initial expectations and forecasts, the ATM network technology has not established itself in end systems, but it is widely used in core networks. First of all, ATM offers a uniform concept to support QoS (Quality of Service) in networks; QoS was attempted much later in IP-based networks.

The ATM network technology is connection-oriented, which means that a connection has to be established before data can be transmitted. There are two types of connections: In a Permanent Virtual Connection (PVC), the connection throughout the network is established by the network management; a network management station extends the forwarding tables within the forwarding nodes between two endpoints of an ATM connection so that the ATM cells created by the endpoints are forwarded to the other endpoint. The second type of ATM connection is a Signaled Virtual Connection (SVC); in this connection type, the connection is established by the communicating end systems, which send connection requests and respond to such requests.

In ATM jargon, packets are called *cells*. In contrast to IP protocol data units, an ATM cell has a fixed size, 53 bytes: 5 bytes for the packet header, 48 bytes for the payload. The 5-byte packet header includes forwarding information, as for IP frames, which allocates a cell to a connection. The ATM network technology uses a hierarchical connection concept, which distinguishes between paths and channels. Each cell is allocated to exactly one virtual path, and to exactly one virtual channel within that path, as shown in Figure 10–1. This allocation to a path and a channel is specified in two bit fields in the cell header: an 8-bit field for the Virtual Path Identifier (VPI), and a 16-bit field for the Virtual Channel Identifier (VCI).

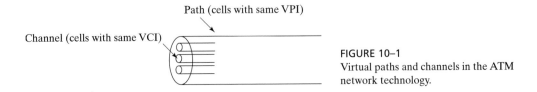

FIGURE 10–1
Virtual paths and channels in the ATM
network technology.

10.2   IMPLEMENTING ATM IN LINUX

Figure 10–2 shows how the ATM support is structured in the Linux kernel. This implementation comprises two major parts:

- Extension of the socket interface to support the ATM protocol. We will not further discuss this part in this chapter, because the socket interface will be described in detail in Chapters 26 and 27.

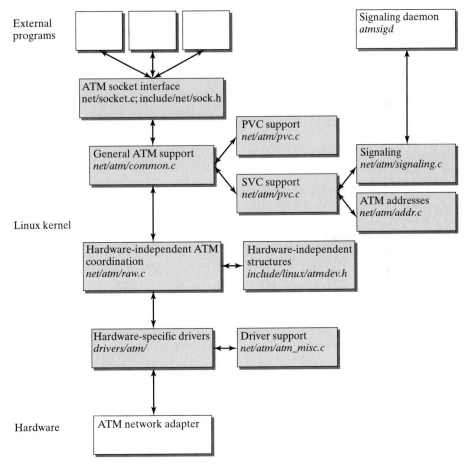

FIGURE 10–2
Structure of the ATM support in the Linux kernel.

- General ATM support within the operating system kernel. Various additional functions are available, depending on whether a connection is a permanent or a signaled virtual connection. This part will be described in detail below.
- Support of various ATM network cards. Again, this is divided into a general part, which is independent of the type of hardware used, and a part that includes the driver for the respective network card and some support functions.

The following sections begin with a description of the data transmission over a permanent virtual channel (PVC). Subsequently, we describe how the signaled virtual channel (SVC) is supported in the Linux kernel.

10.2.1 Permanent Virtual Channels

An application accesses a permanent virtual channel (PVC) over a socket. A PVC socket can take any of four states; closed, created, connected, and connecting (as shown in Figure 10–3).

First, an application creates a socket. When an application creates a socket, the following functions in the kernel are addressed:

pvc_create()	net/atm/pvc.c

In this function, the operations that belong to the protocol family PF_ATMPVC and should be available over the socket are announced. This is done by the allocation

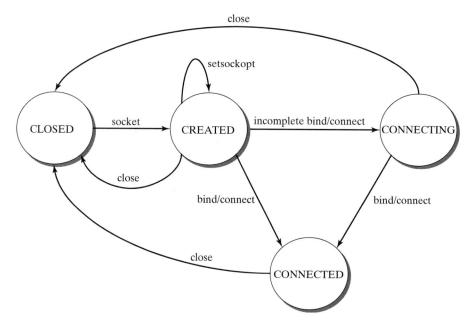

FIGURE 10–3
State transition diagram when opening a socket for a permanent virtual channel.

`sock->ops   =   &pvc_proto_ops;`. Subsequently, `atm_create(sock,protocol,` `PF_ATMPVC)` is used to create a new socket.

`atm_create()`	net/atm/common.c

This function handles a number of memory reservations and initializations required for an ATM socket. In particular, it initializes the structure `atm_vcc` specified in `include/linux/atmdev.h`. The following code fragment was taken from this structure:

```
struct atm_vcc {
      atm_vcc_flags_t flags;              /* VCC flags (ATM_VF_*) */
      unsigned char   family;            /* address family; 0 if unused */
      short           vpi;               /* VPI and VCI (types must be */
      int             vci;               /* equal with sockaddr) */

      unsigned long   aal_options;       /* AAL layer options */
      unsigned long   atm_options;       /* ATM layer options */
      struct atm_dev  *dev;              /* device back pointer */
      struct atm_qos  qos;               /* QOS */
      atomic_t        tx_inuse,rx_inuse; /* buffer space in use */
      void (*push)(struct atm_vcc *vcc,struct sk_buff *skb);
      void (*pop)(struct atm_vcc *vcc, struct sk_buff *skb);  /* optional */
      struct sk_buff *(*alloc_tx)(struct atm_vcc *vcc,unsigned int size);
                                         /* TX allocation routine can be */
                                         /* modified by protocol or by */
                                         /* driver. NOTE: */
                                         /* this interface will change */
      int (*send)(struct atm_vcc *vcc,struct sk_buff *skb);
      void            *dev_data;         /* per-device data */
      void            *proto_data;       /* per-protocol data */
      struct timeval  timestamp;         /* AAL timestamps */
      struct sk_buff_head recvq;         /* receive queue */
      struct k_atm_aal_stats *stats;     /* pointer to AAL stats group */
      wait_queue_head_t sleep;           /* if socket is busy */
      struct sock     *sk;               /* socket backpointer */
      struct atm_vcc  *prev,*next;
};
```

Most entries in this structure are set to null when they are created (e.g., the values for VPI and VCI, the `atm_options`, and the `aal_options`).

In the next step, the application can specify QoS parameters for the socket previously created. To this end, an application calls `setsockopt()` and uses the options SOL_ATM and SO_ATMQOS.

`atm_do_setsockopt()`	net/atm/common.c

In the function `atm_do_setsockopt()`, the values specified by the application are entered in the structure struct `atm_qos` (from `include/linux/atm.h`) contained in the structure `atm_vcc`. The structure `atm_qos` includes two additional structures and one value:

```
struct atm_qos {
        struct atm_trafprm txtp;    /* parameters in TX direction */
        struct atm_trafprm rxtp;    /* parameters in RX direction */
        unsigned char aal;
};
```

The structure `atm_trafprm` (also from `include/linux/atm.h`) is used to specify traffic parameters for the ATM connection. This structure includes the following entries:

```
struct atm_trafprm {
        unsigned char   traffic_class;  /* traffic class (ATM_UBR, ...) */
        int             max_pcr;        /* maximum PCR in cells per second */
        int             pcr;            /* desired PCR in cells per second */
        int             min_pcr;        /* minimum PCR in cells per second */
        int             max_cdv;        /* maximum CDV in microseconds */
        int             max_sdu;        /* maximum SDU in bytes */

        ...
        /* A number of parameters for the ABR service class follows here. */
};
```

The parameter `traffic_class` can take the following values, which are defined in `include/linux/atm.h`: ATM_NONE (no traffic class specified), ATM_UBR (UBR—Unspecified Bit Rate), ATM_CBR (CBR—Constant Bit Rate), ATM_VBR (VBR—Variable Bit Rate), ATM_ABR (ABR—Available Bit Rate), and ATM_ANYCLASS (any traffic class).

The function `atm_do_setsockopt()` is used to run a few checks on the socket status. Subsequently, the function `check_qos()` is invoked.

`check_qos()`	**net/atm/common.c**

This function merely checks on whether the parameters of the transmit and receive directions are identical or are specified for one direction only (different parameters are currently not supported); subsequently, the function `check_tp()` is invoked.

`check_tp()`	**net/atm/common.c**

This function is used to check a few combinations of QoS parameters with regard to their admissibility. If these checks run successfully, then the function `atm_do_setsockopt()` invokes the function `atm_change_qos()`, which uses the function `adjust_tp()` to run further checks. For a PVC, `vcc->dev->ops->change_qos()` is used to invoke the function supplied by the driver to change QoS parameters. For an SVC, the function `svc_change_qos()` defined in `net/atm/svc.c` is called to change QoS parameters.

`pvc_bind()`	**net/atm/pvc.c**

Next, the function `pvc_bind()` is invoked when the application wants to open the socket to send or receive data. The implementation does not distinguish between the socket calls `bind()` and `connect()`. The function `pvc_bind()` is used to initialize the address structure `struct sockaddr_atmpvc`, which is used for PVC only. The other functions are located in the file `net/atm/common.c`, because they are used both for PVC and for SVC.

`atm_connect()`, `atm_connect_vcc()`, `atm_do_connect()`, `atm_do_connect_dev()`	**net/atm/common.c**

These functions are used in the order shown here. First, `atm_connect()` checks the socket status. Next, the function `atm_do_connect()` or the function `atm_do_connect_dev()` is invoked, depending on whether a network interface was specified. If no network interface was specified, then `atm_do_connect()` is invoked, and the function `atm_find_dev()` available in `net/atm/resources.h` is used to search the list of ATM network cards for an interface with the matching identifier. If this search is successful, then the `open()` function supplied by the driver (over `dev->ops->open()`) is invoked, much as for the function `atm_do_connect_dev()`.

`atm_sendmsg()`	**net/atm/common.c**

The transmission of data is identical over PVC and SVC, so this functionality is maintained in the file `net/atm/common.c`. First, the function `atm_sendmsg()` waits for a transmission possibility; next, the transmit data are sent by the driver-specific transmit routine, which is addressed over `vcc->dev->ops->send()`.

`atm_recvmsg()`	**net/atm/common.c**

Like the function `atm_sendmsg()`, the function `atm_recvmsg()` is used for both PVC and SVC connections. The function waits in a loop for incoming data, which is then copied from the socket buffer into the user space by the function `copy_to_user()`.

`atm_release()`, `atm_release_vcc_sk()`	**net/atm/common.c**

We mention the function for orderly release of an ATM socket for the sake of completeness. This is done by the two functions, `atm_release()` and `atm_release_vcc_sk()`, which eventually use the `close()` function supplied by the driver to release all pertinent resources in the driver.

10.2.2 Signaled Virtual Channels

As with PPPoE, a large part of the connection management for the support of signaled virtual channels was moved into a daemon in the user space, as shown in Figure 10–4.

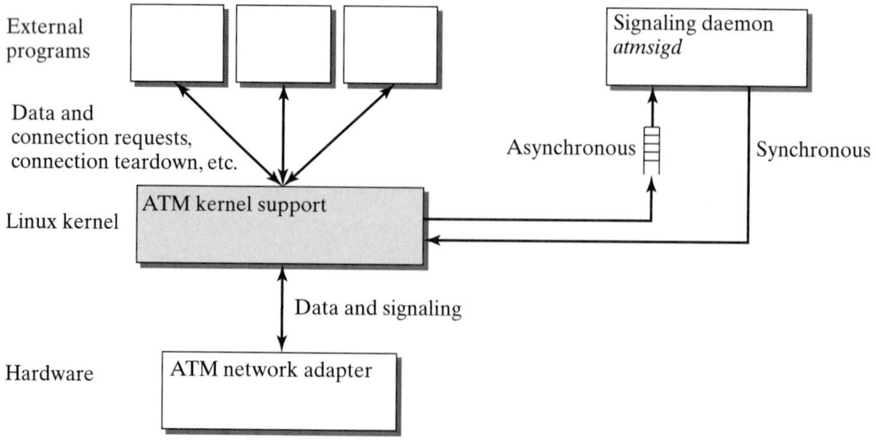

FIGURE 10–4
SVC support in Linux.

Requests to establish or tear down connections and other tasks pertaining to connection management are handled by the signaling daemon, atmsigd. More specifically, all corresponding requests, which can originate both from applications and from the network, are forwarded to the signaling daemon. Requests are put asynchronously into a message queue, from which the signaling daemon fetches messages. In most cases, the kernel performs a synchronous (i.e., blocking) wait for the daemon's response.

Many of the functions available in the file net/atm/svc.c correspond to the previously introduced functions in net/atm/pvc.c, so we will not describe them here in detail. For example, as with the function pvc_create(), the function svc_create() is initially used to announce operations that belong to the protocol family PF_ATMSVC and should be made available over the socket. Subsequently, atm_create(sock, protocol, PF_ATMSVC) creates a new socket.

| svc_bind()   net/atm/svc.c |

The function svc_bind(), which is normally invoked at this point of the procedure, serves as an example for the communication between the kernel and the signaling daemon. The following code fragment was taken from the source code:

```
...
sigd_enq(vcc,as_bind,NULL,NULL,&vcc->local);
add_wait_queue(&vcc->sleep,&wait);
while (vcc->reply == WAITING && sigd) {
       set_current_state(TASK_UNINTERRUPTIBLE);
       schedule();
}
remove_wait_queue(&vcc->sleep,&wait);
...
return vcc->reply;
```

First, the function `sigd_enq()` for the input queue of the signaling daemon, defined in `net/atm/signaling.c`, is passed the message type `as_bind`, together with a pointer to the structure `atm_vcc`, which belongs to the connection. Subsequently, the relevant process remains in the `TASK_UNINTERRUPTIBLE` state until the signaling daemon has fetched the message from the input queue and changed the field `vcc->reply` from WAITING to another value (say, 0 when the action was successful). This value is returned to the function `svc_bind()`.

The full set of messages that can be exchanged between the kernel and the signaling daemon is specified in the `atmsvc_msg_type` structure, stored in the file `include/linux/atmsvc.h`:

```
enum atmsvc_msg_type {
        as_catch_null,as_bind,as_connect,as_accept,as_reject,
        as_listen,as_okay,as_error,as_indicate,as_close,as_itf_notify,
        as_modify,as_identify,as_terminate };
```

The following message types are used for connection control:

- `as_okay`

  The signaling daemon acknowledges a previous message.

- `as_error`

  The signaling daemon reports an error.

- `as_close`

  The kernel informs the daemon that a connection is to be closed.

- `as_bind`

  The kernel sends this message to obtain a local address.

- `as_connect`

  The kernel sends a request to establish a connection to the signaling daemon.

- `as_listen`

  The kernel uses this message to notify that an endpoint was opened, where it will wait for a connection-establishment request.

- `as_indicate`

  The kernel informs the signaling daemon that a connection-establishment request has arrived.

- `as_accept`

  The kernel notifies the signaling daemon that it wants to accept a connection.

- `as_reject`

  The kernel informs the signaling daemon that an incoming connection-establishment request was rejected.

The parameters for these message types are specified in the structure atmsvc_msg in the file include/linux/atmsvc.h. They include addresses and QoS parameters for SVC connections.

10.2.3 ATM Device Drivers

In contrast to Ethernet network cards, ATM network cards handle a large part of the protocol-processing work themselves. Normally, an ATM network card is responsible not only for forming ATM cells, but also for composing these cells into protocol data units for the higher ATM adaptation layer (AAL). This means that the operating system is relieved from these tasks. On the other hand, it means that ATM network cards are more expensive, because the hardware is more costly.

For ATM device drivers, we distinguish between one part that manages the physical layer (PHY driver) and another part that reserves resources and coordinates the protocol and hardware.

The structure atm_dev (in include/linux/atmdev.h) groups device-independent parameters:

```
struct atm_dev {
        const struct atmdev_ops *ops;   /* device operations; NULL if unused */
        const struct atmphy_ops *phy;   /* PHY operations, may be undefined */
                                        /* (NULL) */
        const char      *type;          /* device type name */
        int             number;         /* device index */
        struct atm_vcc  *vccs;          /* VCC table (or NULL) */
        struct atm_vcc  *last;          /* last VCC (or undefined) */
        void            *dev_data;      /* per-device data */
        void            *phy_data;      /* private PHY date */
        atm_dev_flags_t flags;          /* device flags (ATM_DF_*) */
        struct atm_dev_addr *local;     /* local ATM addresses */
        unsigned char   esi[ESI_LEN];   /* ESI ("MAC" addr) */
        struct atm_cirange ci_range;    /* VPI/VCI range */
        struct k_atm_dev_stats stats;   /* statistics */
        char            signal;         /* signal status (ATM_PHY_SIG_*) */
        int             link_rate;      /* link rate (default: OC3) */
#ifdef CONFIG_PROC_FS
        struct proc_dir_entry *proc_entry; /* proc entry */
        char *proc_name;                /* proc entry name */
#endif
        struct atm_dev  *prev,*next;    /* linkage */
};
```

These structures are linked in a list by the pointers prev and next. The structure serves as an interface between the kernel and the driver; this is where all parameters required by the driver for further protocol handling are made available, plus those that the driver must make available to the kernel (e.g., the MAC address of the ATM card). The entries vccs and last are used to manage a list of descriptors for virtual connections, which are known to the ATM network card. The first two elements of the structure atm_dev point to the driver operations supplied by the driver over the structure atmdev_ops and to the PHY driver operations, which are available from the structure atmphy_ops. (Both structures are also defined in include/linux/atmdev.h.)

The most important operations available from the structure atmdev_ops are the following:

- open() reserves resources on the hardware for a new virtual connection; the VPI and the VCI for the connection are passed to the driver.
- The function ioctl() is used to pass ioctl() commands to the driver. If the driver does not know these commands, then it forwards them to the PHY driver.
- The function send() passes data units for transmission.
- The function phy_put() and phy_get() are used by the PHY driver to write a byte to or read one from a hardware register of the network card.

10.2.4 Further ATM Support

The support of "pure" ATM described above (i.e., the support of applications that access ATM sockets directly) was extended by the support of protocols, which convert IP packets to ATM, in a very early stage.

This support includes the following protocols:

- *Classical IP*: Classical IP [Laub94] is the simplest form for transporting IP data traffic over ATM networks. The functions included in net/atm/clip.c are used to support Classical IP.
- *LAN Emulation*: The LAN Emulation [Foru95] represents a second approach to IP over ATM, which, in contrast to Classical IP, uses signaled virtual connections rather than permanent virtual connections. The Linux kernel includes functions for this emulation in the file net/atm/lec.c.
- *MPOA*: The abbreviation "MPOA" [Hein93] stands for "Multiple Protocols over ATM" and represents a more recent approach for the support of IP over ATM. The Linux kernel includes functions for MPOA in the files net/atm/mpc.c, mpoa_caches.c, and net/atm/mpoa_proc.c for corresponding entries in the proc directory.

The functions used by all of these approaches are grouped in net/atm/ipcommon.c.

10.3 CONFIGURATION

ATM support has been part of the Linux kernel since kernel Version 2.4 and requires no additional patches; however, configuring of the kernel requires the entry "Prompt for development and/or incomplete driver" to be activated to provide selection of the desired ATM support.

The signaling daemon described above is not part of the Linux kernel; it has to be installed additionally in the user space. It can be downloaded from [BlAl01], where you will also find other utilities that complete the ATM support in Linux. The current development of the ATM support for Linux can be followed up from the mailing list available at [BlAl01].

CHAPTER 11

Bluetooth in Linux

In connection with the enormous proliferation of portable devices such as laptops, PDAs (Personal Digital Assistants), and mobile phones, it becomes increasingly important to find ways to network these devices. Wireless technologies appear to be an ideal solution to this problem, because they don't need a permanently installed infra-structure and facilitate fast establishment and tear-down of networks (so-called ad-hoc networks). In 1998, a number of manufacturers, including Ericsson, Nokia, IBM, Toshi-ba, and Intel, cooperated in the development of a standard for wireless communication over short distances for consumer electronics. The result of this joint effort is the Blue-tooth technology, which operates in the 2.4 GHz frequency range. The Bluetooth con-sortium specified the radio interface and the higher protocol layers (Bluetooth *core*), plus so-called profiles (Bluetooth *profiles*), each of which defines procedures and parameters of the protocol stack for a specific application field (e.g., telephones, headsets, and file transfer). This standardization effort was intended to ensure interoperability of all Bluetooth devices. The Bluetooth specifications are available at [Group01].

The core specifications include the elements shown in Figure 11–1. The three bot-tom layers are implemented in the Bluetooth hardware (*firmware*). The radio interface deals with frequency bands, signal outputs, transmission channel parameters, and other mobile properties. The baseband processing includes both additional transmission-specific aspects and media-access aspects (e.g., detection of devices in the neighborhood and initialization of synchronous or asynchronous communication channels).

The higher-layer *Link Management Protocol* (LMP), which is implemented by the Link Manager, serves to exchange control data between the higher layers and the baseband processing. The Bluetooth technology is primarily designed for cellular de-vices, so the standard defines an audio interface on a very low layer. However, this audio interface does not play an important role for networked computers. In addition, the standard defines a protocol stack above the three layers mentioned above, which are implemented in hardware. This protocol stack normally runs in software on a client (e.g., a PDA or a laptop).

The bottom layer of this protocol stack—the optional *Host Controller Interface* (HCI)—lets you access device parameters directly, regardless of the interface to the

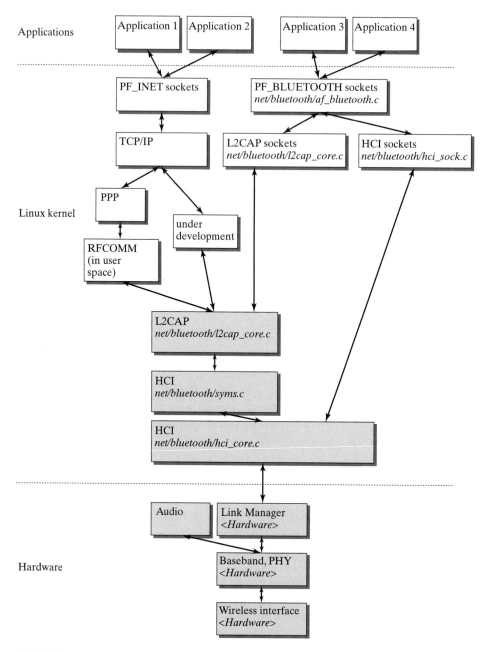

FIGURE 11–1
The Bluetooth protocol stack in the Linux kernel.

device (USB, serial interface), to change or view device parameters. However, it does not serve for data transmission over a Bluetooth device.

The *Logical Link Control and Adaptation Protocol* (L2CAP) is used for each data transmission. It represents the data-link layer of the Bluetooth protocol stack. More specifically, L2CAP is used to send higher-layer packets to the other end of the layer-2 link in another device within the Bluetooth network and to receive from this device. Notice that this is a connection-oriented layer, except for group communication. This means that, if a Bluetooth device moves into the receiving range of another Bluetooth device, then L2CAP has to establish a connection before higher layers can transmit data. This requirement makes the implementation of IP directly over L2CAP more difficult; no such implementation has yet been specified and implemented in the Linux kernel. To find an intermediate solution, the RFCOMM was specified for a virtual RS232 link over the L2CAP protocol of Bluetooth. This means that a virtual COM port is available; it can be used, for example, by PPP (see Chapter 8) to transmit data. The PPP protocol can then also support the use of the TCP/IP protocol suite.

Linux kernel Version 2.4 introduced *Bluez*, a Bluetooth implementation developed by Qualcomm. You can follow up on how Bluez is further developed at `http://sourceforge.net/projects/bluez`. In addition, there are other implementations, among them the Axis stack (`http://sourceforge.net/projects/openbt/`).

11.1   HOST CONTROLLER INTERFACE (HCI)

The Host Controller Interface (HCI) forms the interface between the software protocol stack and the Link Manager underneath it, which is implemented in the firmware of a Bluetooth device. Notice that this is a packet-oriented communication between HCI and the Link Manager rather than a device driver. The difference is that HCI does not access the register and the memory locations of a Bluetooth device directly. Instead, it sends command and data packets to the device and receives data packets and event-message packets from this device. This means that the Host Controller Interface offers a uniform interface for accessing the hardware.

11.1.1   Command Packets

There is a uniform packet format for command packets sent by HCI to the Link Manager. All packets are ordered in groups. In the command group (opcode group), we distinguish between individual commands (opcode commands). Each command packet consists of a 10-bit OCF (Opcode Command Field) and a 6-bit OGF (Opcode Group Field). There are the following command groups:

- *Link control commands* serve to establish a connection to other Bluetooth devices and to control the connection.
- *Link policy commands* serve to change parameters, which are used by the Link Manager to manage connections. For example, such commands can cause connections to switch into the hold mode.

▪ *Host controller and baseband commands* allow you to specify additional parameters for the behavior of the Link Manager (e.g., to filter event messages or to activate the flow control discussed further below).

▪ *Information parameters* offer a pure read access to values of a Bluetooth device, such as the size of the transmit buffer, the version number, and the 48-bit Bluetooth device address.

In addition to these groups, there are the following groups: *status parameters, testing commands, Bluetooth logo testing*, and *vendor-specific debug commands*.

The following sections describe how command packets can be sent within the Bluetooth implementation in the Linux kernel.

`hci_send_cnd()`	net/bluetooth/hci_core.c

This function is used to compose a command packet in the form of an `sk_buff` out of the passed data, the OCF and OGF values, the length, and a pointer to parameters. The function `skb_queue_tail` then appends this packet to the end of the command queue of the `struct hci_dev` of the Bluetooth device.

The structure `hci_dev` is defined in `include/net/bluetooth/hci_core.h`. In addition to the command queue, it contains queues for transmit data. In addition to a number of other parameters, it includes four function pointers, to the functions `open()`, `close()`, `flush()`, and `send()` made available by the Bluetooth device.

Finally, the function `hci_send_cmd()` invokes the function `hci_sched_cmd()`, which marks the `hdev->cmd_task` as ready to be executed. This tasklet was assigned to the device by the function `tasklet_init()` within the function call `hci_register_init()` (net/bluetooth/hci_core.c) when the HCI support was initialized. In addition, there is a `hdev->rx_task` to receive data and another `hdev->tx_task` to send data. When the tasklet `hdev->cmd_task` runs, then the function `hci_cmd_task()` is invoked. This function invokes `hci_send_frame()`.

`hci_send_frame()`	net/bluetooth/hci_core.c

This function serves as a central transmit function for the HCI. This function serves not only to send command packets, but also to send data packets. It uses the entry `int (*send)` from the structure `hci_dev` to invoke the transmit function of the Bluetooth device, to which it passes the `skb`.

11.1.2 Event Packets

The time it takes to process different HCI commands can be different, Bluetooth implements asynchronous communication. The results of a command are announced to HCI in the form of an event packet. In most cases, this is merely an event of the type *Command Complete*, which means that the command was successfully completed. A Bluetooth device can receive arbitrary packets by activating the tasklet `hci_rx_task` when the interrupt triggered by the incoming packet is handled. This tasklet invokes the function `hci_rx_task()`.

`hci_rx_task()`	**net/bluetooth/hci_core.c**

This function is used to distinguish an incoming packet further by type. Incoming event packets are further processed by the function `hci_event_packet()`; accordingly, the functions `hci_acldata_packet()` and `hci_scodata_packet()` are invoked for the ACL and SCO data described further below.

Event packets are further distinguished by type of event in the function `hci_event_packet()`. For example, the type *Number of Completed Packets* invokes the function `hci_num_comp_pkts_evt()`. This function evaluates the content of the event packet, which includes the number of packets actually sent per connection by the Bluetooth device. A handle negotiated between the Link Manager and HCI can be used to map the reported number of sent packets to a specific connection (an `hci_conn` structure). This is done via a hash table in the HCI layer. The counter `acl_cnt` of `struct hci_dev` is incremented by one for each acknowledged packet. Feedback on the number of packets sent serves the flow control described in the following section.

11.1.3   Data Packets

We distinguish between asynchronous connectionless (ACL) and synchronous connection-oriented (SCO) data packets. Both data types are sent when the tasklet `hdev->tx_task` becomes active, and then the function `hci_sched_acl()` (`net/bluetooth/hci_core.c`) is executed. If flow control for ACL data runs between HCI and the Link Manager, then we first have to check on whether ACL data may be sent.

Flow control is used to prevent the transmit buffer of the Bluetooth device from overflowing. This can happen, for example, when an application sends data faster than the Bluetooth device can transport it further—for instance, because the communication partner is temporarily not reachable. The initial size of the output buffer can be polled from HCI. The current size of the output buffer can be derived from event packets of the type *Number of Completed Packets*, described above. HCI assumes that the free output buffer becomes smaller with each packet it passes to the Link Manager. The actual current size can be learned only upon receipt of a new event packet.

Flow control in the Bluetooth protocol stack of the Linux kernel is handled by the function `hci_sched_acl()`. In turn, this function invokes the function `hci_low_acl_sent()`:

`hci_low_acl_sent()`	**net/bluetooth/hci_core.c**

First, this function finds out the total number, num, of all connections known to the specified network device. For each connection (represented by the structure `hci_conn`), the field `acl_sent` includes the number of ACL data packets sent over this connection. This field is incremented during a transmission, but decremented by the number of acknowledged packets over this connection when the described event packet *Number of Completed Packets* is received. In addition, the function `hci_low_acl_sent()` identifies the connection with the smallest number of ACL packets sent, which has to be smaller than 0xffff. If none of the existing connections meets these conditions, then the function's return value is set to null. If there is such a connection, then the total number of acknowledged packets (`acl_cnt` entry in `struct hci_dev`) is divided by the number (`num`) of connections. The result is returned by the parameter `quote`, and the identified connection is the return value of the function. The number of acknowledged packets forms the transmit credit, which is distributed over all ready-to-send connections.

`hci_sched_acl()`	**net/bluetooth/hci_core.c**

Using the `quote` calculated by the function `hci_low_acl_sent()`, this function tries to send ACL data packets over the specified connection (by using the function `hci_send_frame()`). ACL data packets may be sent as long as the queue is not empty, as long as the number of ACL packets to be formed from one `skb` does not exceed the transmit credit of the Bluetooth device, and as long as `quote` is not yet null. Both `quote` and the transmit credit stored in the `hci_dev` structure are decremented by one for each packet sent. At the same time, the number of packets sent over this connection is incremented.

`hci_sched_sco()`	**net/bluetooth/hci_core.c**

Only the transmit credit for SCO packets, included in the field `sco_cnt` of `struct hci_dev`, is considered in the case of SCO data packets. There is no distribution over several connections for SCO connections. SCO data packets are simply sent until the transmit credit is used up.

11.1.4 Accessing the Host Controller Interface

The functionality of the Host Controller Interface (HCI) in Linux is available in different ways. Figure 11–1 shows that HCI can be accessed directly from the user space over a socket. This is normally a socket of the `PF_BLUETOOTH` socket family with protocol identifier `BTPROTO_HCI` und type `SOCK_RAW`. These sockets are created in the file `net/bluetooth/hci_sock.c`. The socket interface is used to supply the usual BSD socket functions. An application can use these functions to send and receive data directly over HCI from and to the network.

Alternatively, an application can use `ioctl()` calls to access the Bluetooth device (e.g., to open, close, or reset the device).

For higher protocol layers to be implemented in the Linux kernel, HCI functions are available over the macro `EXPORT_SYMBOL`. For example, the L2CAP protocol described in the next section accesses these functions, including functions to register and deregister the HCI device (`hci_register_dev()` and `hci_unregister_dev()`) and interfaces to higher protocols. For example, the functions `hci_register_proto()` and `hci_unregister_proto()` serve to register the higher-layer protocol (e.g., L2CAP) that supplies a receive function or other functions to the HCI. The function `hci_register_notifier()` is used by the higher-layer protocol to register itself with the notifier chain of the device. (See Chapter 5.) The function `hci_connect()`, which sends a command packet from HCI to the Link Manager (`net/bluetooth/hci_core.c`), is used to establish a connection. The counterpart of this function is the function `hci_disconnect()`. The functions `hci_send_acl()`, `hci_send_sco()`, and `hci_send_raw()` are used to transmit, and the function `hci_recv_frame()` is used to receive.

11.2 L2CAP

The Logical Link Control and Adaptation Protocol (L2CAP) handles tasks on the data-link layer in the Bluetooth protocol stack. It establishes ACL connections for the next lower layer, but does not transport pure audio data, which primarily is transported over SCO connections. In particular, the L2CAP protocol is responsible for multiplexing data streams from higher layers to an ACL connection, because there must always be at most one ACL connection at a time between two Bluetooth devices. Other important tasks include the segmenting and reassembling of data packets to be able to send and receive the much larger packets of the higher-layer protocols despite the small packet sizes of the baseband layer. L2CAP supports packet sizes of up to 64 Kbytes.

To multiplex several data streams, L2CAP uses the abstraction of the channel. Each channel is allocated to one specific protocol. There are connection-oriented channels for point-to-point communication and connectionless channels used for group communication. A simple signaling method is used to establish an L2CAP connection. The L2CAP protocol can also be accessed directly from the user space over a socket. This is normally a socket from the `PF_BLUETOOTH` socket family with protocol identifier `BTPROTO_L2CAP`.

Now, when HCI receives an ACL packet, then it is passed to the receive function `l2cap_recv_frame()`. If the channel identifier in the packet header is 0x0001, then it is a signaling packet. Subsequently, the function `l2cap_sig_channel()` is invoked; otherwise, the function `l2cap_data_channel()` is invoked.

`l2cap_sig_channel()`	**net/bluetooth/l2cap_core.c**

The type of signaling packet is recognized within this function and, depending on the type, an appropriate handling function is invoked:

```
switch (cmd.code) {
    case L2CAP_CONN_REQ:
        err = l2cap_connect_req(conn, &cmd, data);
        break;
    case L2CAP_CONN_RSP:
        err = l2cap_connect_rsp(conn, &cmd, data);
        break;
    case L2CAP_CONF_REQ:
        err = l2cap_config_req(conn, &cmd, data);
        break;
    case L2CAP_CONF_RSP:
        err = l2cap_config_rsp(conn, &cmd, data);
        break;
```

```
case L2CAP_DISCONN_REQ:
        err = l2cap_disconnect_req(conn, &cmd, data);
        break;
case L2CAP_DISCONN_RSP:
        err = l2cap_disconnect_rsp(conn, &cmd, data);
        break;
```

The following section uses the example of an incoming connection request from a remote communication partner in the Bluetooth network to describe how the L2CAP protocol implementation works.

11.2.1 Connection Establishment Phase

When a request to establish a connection arrives from a remote communication partner, then the signaling code L2CAP_CONN_REQ is detected, and the function l2cap_connect_req() is invoked.

l2cap_connect_req()	net/bluetooth/l2cap_core.c

This function first checks on whether there is a waiting socket for this connection request that matches exactly the source address of the Bluetooth device from which the connection request originates and which concurrently matches the PSM field. The PSM (Protocol/Service Multiplexer) field specifies the desired higher protocol (e.g., RFCOMM).

Such a socket has to have been previously created by an application with the command listen and the function l2cap_sock_listen(), and it has to be in blocking wait state after the function accept() was invoked. This wait state is implemented in the function l2cap_sock_accept(), which uses the function l2cap_accept_dequeue() to wait until the state sk->state switches from BT_LISTEN to BT_CONNECTED.

The function l2cap_get_sock_listen(), which searches all sockets listening to the L2CAP protocol, checks for a socket waiting for an incoming connection request. Subsequently, it ensures that there is not already a connection with the source address of the requesting Bluetooth device. Next, the pertinent sock structure is initialized. The state sk->state in BT_CONFIG and the new channel with the function l2cap_chan_add() are added to the list of channels, conn->chan_list. Subsequently, the function l2cap_send_rsp(), which, in turn, accesses the function hci_send_acl() supplied by HCI, returns a L2CAP_CONN_RSP message to acknowledge the connection request.

11.2.2 Configuration Phase

If there are no errors, then the next step walks through the configuration phase, before the connection can be used for data transmission. First, both ends send a configuration request (signaling code L2CAP_CONF_REQ). The configuration phase can be completed successfully only if the configuration request of the other end has been acknowledged and a positive acknowledgement of its own configuration request was made.

The end that received the connection request waits for a configuration request after successful completion of the connection establishment phase. When the connection request arrives, the function l2cap_sig_channel() invokes the function l2cap_config_req().

l2cap_config_req()	net/bluetooth/l2cap.core.c

This function first uses l2cap_parse_conf_req() to evaluate the configuration options of the peer and store them in the protinfo structure of the sock structure. However, the QoS option is currently not evaluated. Next, the function l2cap_build_conf_rsp() is invoked. This function uses l2cap_conf_output() to discover whether the peer's configuration options (currently only the MTU) can be accepted. The function l2cap_send_rsp() is used to return a response. Subsequently, the function l2cap_send_req() uses the function l2cap_build_conf_req() to create and send a configuration request to the other end. Currently, only the MTU is considered.

l2cap_config_rsq()	net\bluetooth\l2cap.core.c

This function handles the peer's response to the configuration request. If the peer sends a nonempty response, then the current implementation disconnects immediately. Otherwise, the configuration phase can be abandoned. The field sk->state is set to BT_CONNECTED and, starting with the function call l2cap_chan_ready() (net/bluetooth/l2cap_core.c), the function pointer sk->state_change() is used to invoke the function sock_def_wakeup() (both in net/core/sock.c), which eventually marks the process waiting at the socket as an executable process.

11.2.3 Data Transmission Phase

This section describes the data transmission.

l2cap_data_channel()	net/bluetooth/l2cap.core.c

The function l2cap_data_channel() is invoked when data packets are received. The first step is to check for whether a connection is present in the list of channels, conn->chan_list, for the SCID (Source Connection IDentification). This check is done by the function l2cap_get_chan_by_scid(). After further checks, the data packet is put into the receive queue, and the function data_ready() of the sock structure is invoked, which then informs the application that new data is ready.

Looking at things from the BSD socket interface, data is received at the socket interface over the socket call recvmsg, which is mapped to the function l2cap_sock_recvmsg(). In this respect, there are no major differences from the implementations of other protocols that also use the function skb_recv_datagram() (net/core/datagram.c). This function causes a blocking or nonblocking wait for data in the input queue sk->receive_queue.

When sending, the socket call sendmsg() invokes the function `l2cap_sock_sendmsg()`, which uses the function `l2cap_chan_send()` to prepare a packet and then uses `hci_send_acl()` to send it.

11.3   OTHER PROTOCOLS

The L2CAP functionality is currently available for `BTPROTO_L2CAP` sockets only. An interface to higher protocol layers, such as RFCOMM, or for future developments that will allow you to run TCP/IP directly over L2CAP, was not available in the Linux kernel implementation at the time of writing. However, the L2CAP sockets allow you to install these protocols in the user space. The SDP (Service Discovery Protocol) protocol is not integrated in the Linux kernel either. RFCOMM might be implemented in the kernel in the future, but this is currently not intended for SDP.

# CHAPTER 12

Transparent Bridges

12.1   INTRODUCTION

Local area networks (LANs) are limited both in their reach and in the number of stations that can be connected. For example, only a maximum of 30 stations per segment can be connected to Ethernet based on the *10Base2* standard; and even if you connect fewer than the maximum number of stations, but use an extremely traffic-intensive application, it can happen that the traffic in a LAN is so high that the throughput of the entire network drops rapidly.

This degradation is due mainly to the fact that local area networks are broadcast networks—when station A sends a data frame to station B, then the data packet is concurrently transported to all other stations. The bandwidth in a local area network is used only by the sending station at that time (asynchronous time division multiplexing—TDM). The more stations there are in a local area network, the smaller is the share of each single station. Depending on the network technology, a lot of additional time might be used to decide which station may send next (Medium Access Control).

For the above reasons, it is meaningful to divide a heavily loaded or very large local area network into several subnetworks. Similarly, several local area networks can be linked by single coupling elements to form one large internetwork. In this regard, the parts of the original local area network should not be split into different subnetworks (as is possible in IP), but should always represent themselves as one single (sub)network to the network layer. The two networks are connected transparently, for the network layer.

One coupling element that can link different local area networks to form one single logical LAN is called a *bridge*. A bridge connects several local area networks on the data-link layer (layer 2 in the OSI reference model) and distributes the traffic over the subnetworks. Stations that communicate often are generally grouped into one subnetwork. Grouping frequently communicating stations within the same subnetwork means that the entire network has less load to carry, because these stations can exchange traffic within their subnetwork regardless of the traffic in other subnetworks.

12.2   BASICS

As was mentioned above, a bridge is a coupling element that links several local area networks on the data link layer [BaHK94]. For this purpose, a bridge has two or more network adapters (*ports*), which are used to connect to a local area network. In contrast to a repeater, which can merely extend the distance of a LAN, and which simply forwards packets as it received them, a bridge can evaluate certain information in a packet and decide whether that packet should be forwarded.

Bridges come in different variants and with various properties, which will be briefly introduced below:

■ *Local or remote bridges*: Local bridges connect two or more neighboring local area networks—see Figure 12–1. These local area networks are normally linked on the MAC layer.

Remote bridges connect two local area networks physically separated by another network, normally a Wide Area Network (WAN). This bridge type interconnects local area networks on the LLC layer. [BaHK94] includes a detailed description of local and remote bridges. This chapter considers only local bridges.

■ *Translation or nontranslation bridges*: A translation bridge is capable of connecting several local area networks over different media-access protocols (e.g., Ethernet and token ring). Linux is limited in supporting this property, because there could be problems during the transition from one standard to another one. For example, 802.3 supports a limited maximum frame size of 1,500 bytes, but 802.5 supports a much bigger size. For this reason, we cannot feed large 802.5 packets into an 802.3 network.

■ *Source-routing or transparent bridges*: Source-routing bridges represent an extension of the token-ring standard and must be used in token-ring networks only. We will not consider them any further.

In contrast, transparent bridges can be used in all 802.x networks. They mainly handle the transparent interconnection of different 802.x LANs, where the participating stations do not know that there is a bridge in the LAN. In other words, the bridge is not visible to the stations in the interconnected LANs—it is transparent. The bridge functionality under Linux corresponds exactly to the type of a transparent bridge.

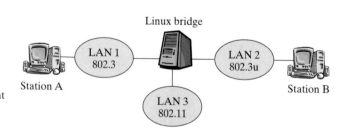

FIGURE 12–1
A Linux computer acts as a transparent bridge, connecting several local area networks.

12.2.1 Properties of Transparent Bridges

In accord with the definition in Section 12.2, a Linux system can be used to implement a *local transparent translation*[1] bridge, which can interconnect different 802.x LANs. Figure 12–1 shows an example in which the Linux computer acts as a bridge, connecting three LANs of different types: one Ethernet (IEEE 802.3), one Fast Ethernet (IEEE 802.3u), and one wireless LAN (IEEE 802.11).

When we use a translation bridge to link different 802.x LANs, then the properties of the different sets of protocols have to be adapted. For example, the bridge should consider the different access methods of the interconnected LANs; it should also consider and convert different packet formats. In addition, we have to consider that properties could be lost during the transition from one LAN type to another type. Examples include priorities or acknowledgments in 802.5 networks, which are lost in 802.3 networks, because the latter don't have anything comparable. Linux currently supports only the interconnection of local area networks that use an Ethernet-compatible frame format on MAC level.

The transparent bridge in Figure 12–1 is responsible for switching data packets between the three networks used in this example to allow the stations in these three networks to communicate. Data packets (which are also called frames on layer 2) with their destination within one local area network are not transported to the other two LANs—internetwork and intranetwork traffic is separate.

The bridge need forward only those data packets intended for another LAN. This translates into a considerable reduction of the network load, because internal traffic loads remain within the LANs and parallel communication is possible internally in each of these LANs. If a computer in one LAN wants to send data to another LAN, then only those LANs required for the transport are used. In addition, the bridge ensures that faulty data packets are filtered and prevented from being transported to the other networks. The *filtering* concept supported by bridges will be described in Section 12.2.2.

Transparent bridges are characterized mainly by the fact that they are hidden from the stations in the network. In addition, they forward frames from one LAN into another LAN independently. To both the inside and the outside, it seems like there is one large local IEEE-802-compatible network. The bridge does not consider protocols used on the network layer; you can select arbitrary protocols.

To achieve transparency, each bridge maintains a table (*forwarding database*) that stores the output line used to reach a station for each layer-2 address. We will see in Section 12.4.2 how this forwarding table is implemented in Linux.

The properties of a Linux bridge introduced above will be discussed in more detail in the next sections.

---

[1] ... however, with the limitation that the 802.x networks be compatible, mainly with regard to their maximum frame lengths. For example, 802.3 and 802.11 can easily be combined, but problems could arise when you use 802.5 LANs.

12.2.2 Forwarding Function

The main task of a bridge is its filter function to separate the traffic between local area networks from the traffic within one local area network. For this function, the bridge is not addressed explicitly; it is transparent for the communication partners. None of the computers in the local area networks knows that the bridge is present. For this reason, the bridge receives each data packet as it passes each network adapter, interprets its destination address, and uses the filter criterion to decide whether the packet should be forwarded to another LAN or not be handled. In the latter case, the addressed station is in the LAN that received the data packet. The bridge can assume that the destination station has already received the packet, so that it does not have to forward it.

As mentioned earlier, a transparent bridge uses a *forwarding table* which stores forwarding information. It also uses positive filters, which are entered as a result of the learning function. (See Section 12.2.3.) The forwarding table provides general information how each computer can be reached over the outputs. If only one LAN is connected to each bridge adapter, then the decision about the LAN on which a computer resides is obvious. If this is not the case, then the LAN and an output adapter are specified to reach the LAN of a computer (the so-called *next hop*).

The example in Figure 12–2 shows how the forwarding function of a bridge works. Station A sends a data packet to station B. Though the bridge was not addressed directly, it receives the packet and searches the forwarding table for destination address B. It finds an entry that refers to LAN2, and eventually sends the packet to this LAN. Packets addressed to computers within the same LAN are not forwarded by the bridge. (See Figure 12–3.)

If the bridge cannot find a destination address in the forwarding table (i.e., if the bridge does not know to which LAN the destination station is connected), then it sends the packet over all of its outputs, except the input port (*flooding*). Figure 12–4 shows this process. Flooding means that the bridge can reach all stations, including those with yet unknown location.

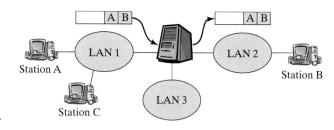

FIGURE 12–2
A transparent bridge forwards a packet.

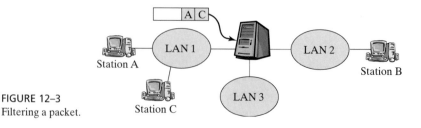

FIGURE 12–3
Filtering a packet.

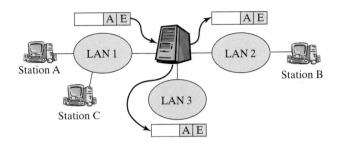

FIGURE 12–4
Forwarding a packet to all outputs.

MAC addresses are not structured hierarchically and hence cannot provide information about the LAN of a destination station, so packets would have to be sent to all outputs of a bridge in a group of interconnected LANs. Unfortunately, flooding packets when the destination network is not known shouldn't be done often. For this reason, transparent bridges have a way to learn the location or direction of an unknown station.

12.2.3   Learning Function

One major problem of transparent bridges relates to how the bridge is structured and how it maintains its forwarding table. Though the system administrator could simply use a static data configuration, this is not desirable for the following reason: A static configuration of the forwarding table cannot respond to changes in the network topology—all tables in all bridges would have to be changed manually as soon as a new station is added to one of the LANs. In addition, there would be consistency problems if one station moves from one LAN to another LAN. For this reason, transparent bridges use a learning algorithm, allowing a bridge to learn the location of an unknown station and to be able to respond to a change in location (i.e., forget the old location and learn the new one).

For this purpose, a bridge follows the entire traffic in all LANs connected to it. For each data packet sent to one LAN, the bridge stores its sender MAC address and the LAN that transported the packet in its forwarding table. The bridge assumes that the LAN that received the packet is the home network of the sending station or at least the best path to reach its home network. The method used to learn routing information by looking at the sender address and the input network is also called *backward learning* in the literature [Tane97].

Backward learning allows a bridge to learn the location of each station that sent a packet. If the bridge receives a packet for a currently unknown station, then it has to use flooding; but it is assumed that a response or acknowledgment will follow from this packet, so the destination address can be found from this reply packet. This means that flooding is normally done only once for each destination address.

To keep the entries in the forwarding table of a bridge up to date, they are extended by a time stamp (activity time). This time value states how long this entry will be valid. This activity time is updated each time that the bridge receives a packet with a sender MAC address it had previously learned. When the activity time of an entry expires, then this entry is deleted (aging mechanism). It is also assumed that the station was either disconnected from the network or no longer exists. On the other hand, if a packet with a previously unknown source address arrives, then the bridge assumes that this station is new to the network. The address of this system and the network adapter that received the packet are added to the forwarding table, and the activity time is initialized.

12.2.4 Spanning-Tree Protocol

There are often redundant connections in a large local internetwork. For example, there could be several bridges running in parallel to connect two LANs, for load-distribution and failure-safety reasons. Figure 12–5 shows an example with redundant connected networks. In this example, if station A in LAN 2 sends a packet to computer B in LAN 5, then bridge 1 floods this packet to LAN 1, and bridge 3 floods it to LANs 3 and 5. Bridge 3 learns that it can reach station A in LAN 2. In the meantime, bridge 2 receives the packet in LAN 1 and floods it to LANs 3 and 4. This means that bridge 3 receives the same packet again, only this time over a different network adapter. Using its learning function, this bridge changes that entry in the forwarding table and floods the packet to the other networks. We could continue this example endlessly to see that, with this network topology, the forwarding tables of all stations would change continuously, and packets would be duplicated and travel around in the network. The bridges have no way to recognize and destroy duplicate packets.

Transparent bridges uses the so-called spanning-tree protocol to solve this problem. This protocol should detect redundant connections in a cyclic topology and build a tree structure that does not include any more cycles. Redundant connections are made inactive and can be reactivated when needed. This means that the LAN internetwork maintains its redundancy. Special messages are used by the bridges in the internetwork to work out the tree structure and to build this structure in a decentralized way.

The spanning-tree method is known from graph theory [OTWi96]. Normally, a spanning tree with minimum total cost can be constructed with an undirected connected graph, where the edges are used as weights to allocate costs. Several algorithms have been introduced as minimum spanning tree (MST) methods to handle this task. The spanning-tree method described here and the MST method have in common that a connected graph is used to form a tree structure. However, the spanning tree in a LAN internetwork is not always the minimum spanning tree from the MST method. This is shown by the example in Figure 12–6.

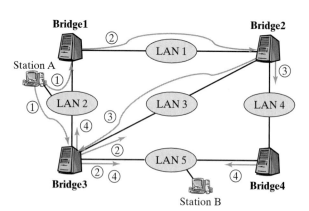

FIGURE 12–5
The effect of cycles.

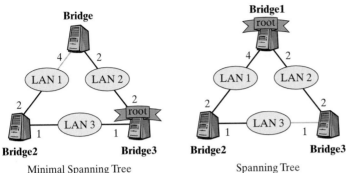

FIGURE 12–6
Spanning-tree protocol versus the MST method.

Minimal Spanning Tree   Spanning Tree

Under the spanning-tree protocol, the root of the tree topology is not determined by the least total cost; instead, the bridge with the smallest bridge identifier is selected. The reason is that the spanning-tree algorithm operates in a decentralized way—it is not calculated centrally in one station. This means that, first of all, all bridges have to agree on the bridge to be selected as the root of the tree. Subsequently, working from the root, the branches of the tree with "minimum" path cost are calculated. These minimum-cost paths do not necessarily have to correspond to the tree structure with the least total cost.

Prerequisites and Terminology   Bridges need certain parameters and values to be able to run the spanning-tree algorithm. These values are then used to manipulate the resulting spanning tree. The following parameters are required by the spanning-tree algorithm:

- Each bridge requires a unique 6-byte identifier, the *bridge ID*.
- Each network adapter (*port*) of a bridge obtains a unique identifier, the *port ID*.
- *Port cost* is assigned to each network adapter. This cost influences the structure of the tree topology, because the total cost should be minimized by the spanning-tree algorithm. For example, the port cost can reflect the load on or speed of a local area network.
- When two LANs can be reached over several paths, then a priority for each network adapter (*port priority*) can be considered when selecting a path. The spanning-tree algorithm will then select the adapter with higher priority and equal path cost.

The following are other important terms:

- *Root bridge*: This is the bridge representing the root of the tree topology.
- *Root port*: This is the port of a bridge with the least transmission cost to the root bridge.
- *Root-path cost*: This is the sum of the cost of all root ports on the path from a LAN within the internetwork to the root bridge. The objective is to find the path with the least root-path cost.

Figure 12–7 shows these terms in an example of the topology described above, where Bridge1 is the root of the tree structure shown in Figure 12–8.

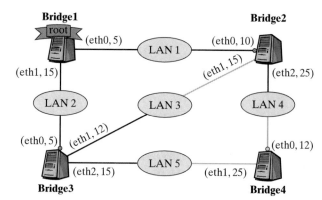

FIGURE 12–7
Topology after running the spanning-tree
protocol.

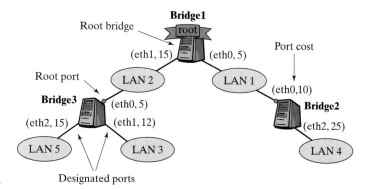

FIGURE 12–8
Tree topology of the LAN internetwork.

Special packets in the form of so-called *Bridge Protocol Data Units* (BPDUs) are exchanged to determine the root bridge and distribute path or port cost. There are two types of BPDUs:

- *Configuration BPDUs* are also called hello packets or configuration messages. They are used to announce the root-bridge identifier, the cost currently accumulated, and certain timer values. Section 12.4.5 will describe the format of this configuration BPDU.

- *Topology change notification BPDUs* (TCN BPDUs): These packets are exchanged when changes occur in the topology. This can happen when a component has failed and when the execution of the spanning-tree method causes certain network adapters of bridges to move into the blocking state.

Bridge PDUs are sent with a special group MAC address. This means that each bridge that receives such a packet can identify a bridge PDU.

Running the Spanning-Tree Algorithm The spanning-tree algorithm is defined in IEEE standard 802.1d. It specifies the principle used to build a noncyclic topology from a partly meshed or cyclic LAN internetwork. This method operates in an absolutely decentralized way.

The spanning-tree algorithm runs in three steps:

1. *Select the root bridge*: The root bridge is the root of the tree topology we want to build. The problem is now to select one of the bridges as the root bridge. To this end, we use a principle similar to the one used in token-ring networks: The bridge with the smallest identifier (bridge ID) is selected as the root bridge.

   At the beginning, the bridges in the LAN internetwork send configuration BPDUs periodically with their own identifiers as root ID to all other bridges. When a bridge receives a BPDU, it is immediately compared with its own bridge ID. If the received root ID is smaller, then the BPDU is forwarded. In contrast, if the own bridge ID is smaller, then it is registered as the root ID and distributed to the other bridges. Eventually, the bridge with the smallest identifier becomes the root bridge.
       One major benefit of this principle is its decentralized property. This means that no central management unit is required. However, the path cost in a LAN internetwork does not play any role in determining the root bridge. This means that you won't necessarily select the best topology, such as in the Minimal Spanning Tree method.

2. *Determine the root port of each bridge*: Each bridge selects the network adapter with the smallest path cost on the path to the root bridge as its root port (root-path cost, RPC). If several paths have the same cost, then the port with the highest priority or (if no priorities are set) the port with the smallest port ID is selected as the root port.

3. *Select the designated bridge for a LAN*: When one subnetwork within the LAN internetwork is connected to several bridges, so that at least one route over each of these bridges leads to the root bridge, then one of these bridges has to be selected for traffic forwarding to the root bridge. This is the only way to create a tree topology. In a local area network, the bridge with the smallest path cost to the root bridge (the so-called *root-path cost*) is normally selected. The network adapter used to connect this designated bridge to the local area network is called the *designated port*. Consequently, there is only one single designated port for each LAN. All adapters of the root bridge are designated ports.

   All output adapters that were not selected as root ports or designated ports are locked (i.e., they take the blocking state). Though no payload packets will be transported over these ports, they can continue receiving BPDUs. This means that a deactivated adapter can detect a component failure and reactivate itself when needed.

Behavior When a Component Fails   When an active bridge (i.e., a root bridge or a designated bridge or an active port) fails, then this can be discovered by a message-age mechanism. To this end, each bridge manages a *max age* value. If the message age value of a BPDU (see Section 12.4.5) exceeds this value, then the spanning-tree algorithm is reactivated to check for which bridges should be active in the new topology. More specifically, bridges where network adapters change states send the topology-change notification BPDUs described above over the path to the root bridge. This means that all other bridges are informed about a change in topology, so that they can respond accordingly.

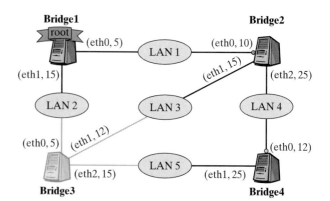

FIGURE 12–9
Topology of Figure 12–7 after bridge 3 has failed.

The message-age value of a bridge PDU is incremented after each forwarding action. If a failure or the adding of a new bridge causes a cycle, then the message-age value increases continually as the packet cycles, eventually reaching the threshold that triggers the spanning-tree algorithm (to reconfigure the LAN internetwork).

Figure 12–9 shows the topology from Figure 12–7, but with a change: Bridge 3 has failed. This means that the connection from LAN 3 to the root bridge over bridge 2 has to be restored, and LAN 5 is reached over bridge 4. The blocked ports of bridge 4, eth0 and eth1, are activated in this situation, allowing proper communication, even though bridge 3 failed.

Avoiding Temporary Loops   The decentralized operation of the spanning tree algorithm makes it possible that some bridges have not stored the globally correct information (i.e., they have only local knowledge). For this reason, the interfaces could be in a "wrong" state, causing loops that can be removed during the further procedure.

For example, if one interface is the designated port, and if no configuration message from a higher-order bridge has arrived in this bridge yet, then data packets would be forwarded on the basis of their local information. Globally, this would cause a loop and the wrong behavior described earlier.

To solve this problem, the standard includes two intermediate states between the blocking and the forwarding states. The transition from one state to another occurs when the so-called *forward delay timer* expires. In the listening state, a bridge must neither learn addresses nor forward packets. It receives configuration messages only if

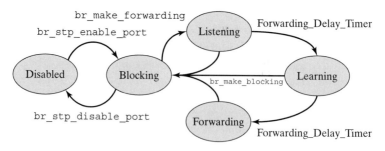

FIGURE 12–10
State automaton of a bridge port.

these messages reset the interface into the blocking state. The next state allows the bridge to enter addresses in the forwarding table (learning function); this state is called the `learning` state. In the `forwarding` state, which is reached after another expiry of the forward delay timer, data packets can be forwarded. Figure 12–10 shows the state transitions of a network adapter.

12.3 CONFIGURING A BRIDGE IN LINUX

A bridge interconnects several local area networks on the data-link layer, simulating the behavior of one large single network to the outside. To connect several local area networks in a Linux system, we need only install several network adapters in the computer. Linux also allows you to manage several bridges within one system, which can operate independently of one another. Each bridge instance has a logical name. One network adapter can always belong to exactly one bridge instance. This allows the system administrator to build virtual local networks (VLANs), which previously required expensive VLAN switches.

The following sections introduce options to configure and control Linux bridges.

12.3.1 Configuring the Kernel and the Network Adapter

To be able to use a Linux system as a bridge, the Linux kernel has to contain the bridge functionality. This is normally not the case, so we have to create a new kernel. When configuring the kernel, you should select the BRIDGING option from the Networking Options. You can integrate it into the kernel either as a module or permanently.

Once you have booted your new kernel (and loaded the module, if applicable), you can use the bridge functionality. Sometimes, you might incur problems when trying to activate several network adapters. If this happens, you can specify the boot parameters `linux ether=0,0,ethx` for each card when you start the system. If you use the LILO boot loader, you can also have the boot parameter passed automatically.

If the bridge functionality resides in the loaded kernel and all network adapters are activated, you can use the `brctl` tool to create and configure the desired bridge instances. `brctl` will be introduced in the next section.

12.3.2 Using the `brctl` Tool to Configure Linux Bridges

You can use the `brctl` (Bridge Control) tool to configure a bridge in Linux. This tool is part of the `bridge-utils` package and can be obtained from [Buyt01].

This tool can be used by the administrator to pass control commands to the bridge implementation in the kernel by using `ioctl()` commands. This section gives an overview of how you can use this program. [BoBu01] includes a detailed description of these commands and several examples.

The `brctl` tool lets you use the following commands to activate and deactivate a bridge. The commands are passed as parameters when `brctl` is called:

- `addbr bridge`: This command creates a new instance of a bridge with the identifier *bridge*.
- `addif bridge device`: This command adds the network adapter *device* to *bridge*. A network adapter can always belong to one bridge only.

- `delbr bridge`: This command deletes the instance of the specified bridge.
- `delif bridge device`: This command deletes the adapter *device* from *bridge*.

The following commands are available in the `brctl` tool to change the default parameters of a bridge:

- `setaging bridge time`: This command sets the *max age* parameter to the specified value. The topology of the LAN internetwork is recalculated when a BPDU with a larger aging time arrives.
- `setbridgeprio bridge prio`: This command sets the bridge priority, not to be confused with the port priority.
- `setfd bridge time`: This command sets the *bridge forward delay* parameter. This value is added to the *aging timer* parameter of a BPDU in each bridge.
- `setgcint bridge time`: This command sets the duration of the *garbage collection* (GC) *interval* for a bridge. Once a GC interval expires, there is a check for whether the forwarding table includes old entries. If it does, then these entries are deleted.
- `sethello bridge time`: This command is used to change the time interval in which hello packets are sent.
- `setmaxage bridge time`: This command sets the *max age* parameter. (See Section 12.2.4.)
- `setpathcost bridge port cost`: This command can be used to change the path cost for a network adapter of the specified bridge.
- `setportprio bridge port prio`: This command changes the priority of a network adapter in a bridge.
- `stp bridge [en|dis]`: This switch can be used to enable (`en`) or disable (`dis`) the spanning-tree protocol in a bridge.

12.3.3 Checking the Bridge Functionality

The following commands are included in the `brctl` tool to check the operation of a bridge and control its functionality:

- `show`: This command shows a list of all bridge instances currently existing in the computer.
- `showbr bridge`: This command outputs the current configuration of the specified bridge. The output for bridge 3 from the example in Figure 12–11 will be shown later.
- `showmacs bridge`: This command outputs the current filter or forwarding table, including the MAC addresses of all known stations (as shown below).

In addition, you can use the `tcpdump` tool to monitor the traffic in each of the interconnected LANs. To monitor LANs, you start `tcpdump -i ethn` and `tcpdump -i ethm` each in a separate window. You should see packets being forwarded in both adapters. In contrast, packets for computers in the same LAN should appear in one adapter only.

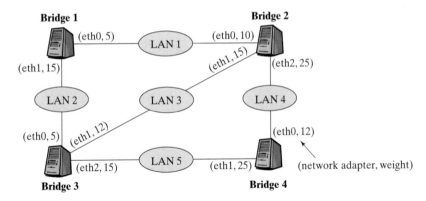

FIGURE 12–11
Redundant LAN internetwork.

12.3.4 Sample Configuration

The following example shows how you can add a bridge based on the configuration of bridge 1 from the LAN internetwork shown in Figure 12–11:

```
root@tux:   #   brctl addbr bridge1
root@tux:   #   brctl addif bridge1 eth0
root@tux:   #   brctl addif bridge1 eth1
root@tux    #   brctl setpathcost bridge1 eth0 5
root@tux    #   brctl setpathcost bridge1 eth1 15
root@tux:   #   ifconfig eth0 0.0.0.0
root@tux:   #   ifconfig eth1 0.0.0.0
root@tux:   #   ifconfig bridge1 129.13.42.100 netmask 255.255.255.0 up
```

In this example, we first create a bridge, bridge1. Subsequently, we add network adapters. The IP addresses are deleted, because the network adapters are allocated to the bridge and should actually forward or filter packets in the LAN internetwork independently of a protocol.

Nevertheless, it is possible to address the bridge (regardless of a network adapter) by using an IP address. This address is allocated to the virtual adapter, bridge1, as shown in the last command. Each bridge instance has such a virtual network device, which has the same name as its bridge instance.

The outputs of brctl showstp bridge3 and brctl showmacs bridge3 are as follows:

```
root@tux # brctl showmstp bridge 3
bridge3
      bridge id          0003.00902744822b
      designated root    0002.00902744da29
      root port          1                     path cost            10
      max age            20.00                 bridge max age       20.00
      hello time         2.00                  bridge hello time    2.00
      forward delay      15.00                 bridge forward delay 15.00
```

```
aging time            300.00              gc interval         4.00
hello timer           0.00                tcn timer           0.00
topology change timer                     0.00 gc timer       0.99
flags                 TOPOLOGY_CHANGE

eth0 (1)
    port id           8001                state               forwarding
    designated root   0002.00902744da29   path cost           5
    designated bridge 0006.009027d1362b   message age timer   1.98
    designated port   8002                forward delay timer 0.00
    designated cost   5                   hold timer          0.00
    flags

eth1 (2)
    port id           8002                state               blocking
    designated root   0002.00902744da29   path cost           12
    designated bridge 0002.00902744da29   message age timer   1.98
    designated port   8002                forward delay timer 0.00
    designated cost   0                   hold timer          0.00
    flags

eth2 (3)
    port id           8003                state               forwarding
    designated root   0002.00902744da29   path cost           15
    designated bridge 0003.00902744822b   message age timer   0.00
    designated port   8003                forward delay timer 0.00
    designated cost   10                  hold timer          0.00
    flags

root@tux # brctl showmacs bridge3
    port no mac addr     is local?        aging timer
    2                    00:90:27:44:82:2b  yes               0.00
    1                    00:90:27:72:0c:31  yes               0.00
    3                    00:90:27:cb:a3:cd  yes               0.00
```

12.4   IMPLEMENTATION

The implementation of the bridge functionality discussed here is relatively new. It has been integrated into the Linux kernel since Version 2.2.14 and 2.3.x and replaces the former and in many ways less flexible implementation. This version includes several new functions (e.g., the capability of managing several bridges in one system, and better options to configure the bridge functionality).

In addition, several details of the implementation have changed to provide more efficient handling. Among other things, the forwarding table is no longer stored in the form of an AVL tree, but in a hash table. Though AVL trees are data structures with a relatively low search cost, $O(\log n)$, hash tables are generally faster when the collision domain remains as low as possible. This means that a well-distributed hash table has the cost $O(1)$. We can assume that a Linux bridge has to store several hundred reachable systems at most, so a hash table is probably the better choice, especially considering that it is much easier to configure.

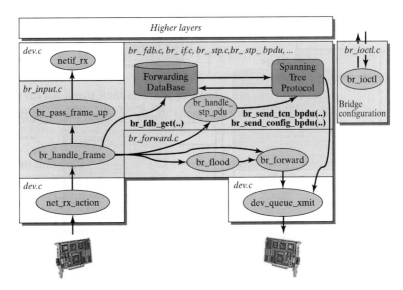

FIGURE 12-12
Integrating the bridge implementation into the Linux network architecture.

The following sections describe in more detail how you can implement the bridge functionality in Linux. We will first introduce the most important data structures and how they are linked, then discuss the algorithms and functions.

12.4.1 Architecture of the Bridge Implementation

Figure 12-12 shows the architecture of the bridge implementation in the Linux kernel. The individual components are divided, by their tasks and over several files. This makes the program text easier to understand and forces the programmer to define the interfaces between the individual components well.

12.4.2 Building and Linking Important Data Structures

The most important data structures of a Linux bridge include information about the bridges themselves and information about the network adapters (ports) allocated to them. We want to repeat here that you can use the new bridge implementation to construct several logically separated bridges in a Linux system. For example, this allows you to easily configure virtual local area networks (VLANs) that are not mutually accessible. In addition to information about the bridge and its ports, you need to store the forwarding table (filter table) for each bridge.

The forwarding table stores the IDs of each reachable station and the port used to reach that station. In addition, a transparent bridge also manages information for the spanning-tree protocol.

The file net/bridge/br private.h defines the structures used to manage the information about bridges and their ports. Figure 12-13 shows how they are built and generally interlinked.

The packet type is set to PACKET_HOST (arrived in the destination system), and the Ethernet header is removed. Subsequently, the packet is passed to the function netif_rx(), which invokes the protocol-handling routine of the appropriate layer-3 protocol.

br_fdb_get()	net/bridge/br_fdb.c

br_fdb_get() searches the forwarding table in the hash table of the specified bridge instance for a MAC destination address passed as a parameter. It first calculates the hash value and searches the hash row to see whether there is an entry with the desired MAC address. If there is an entry, then the desired information for the MAC address is found, and a pointer to the output port used to reach that station is returned. If no entry is found, then the route to the destination station is unknown and the value **null** is returned.

12.4.4 Learning New MAC Addresses

The learning of new MAC addresses is a characteristic of a transparent bridge. It can be achieved only provided that the port is in learning or forwarding state. (See Section 12.2.4.) As was described earlier, the learning function is invoked for each data packet. The source address is added to the forwarding table. If an address already exists in the table, then the information of the net_bridge_fdb_entry structure is updated and the pointer to the entry is returned.

Functions

br_fdb_insert()	net/bridge/br_fdb.c

br_fdb_insert() includes the entire learning function of a transparent bridge. The MAC sender address is entered in the forwarding table for each incoming packet in the BR_STATE_LEARNING and BR_STATE_FORWARDING states. To this end, the hash value of the MAC address is calculated (br_mac_hash()), and the hash row is searched for the appropriate entry. If this entry is found, then both the entry for the input adapter and the aging_timer are updated. This means that the bridge will also learn when a station has moved.

If no entry can be found in the hash row, then br_fdb_insert() creates a new net_bridge_fdb_entry structure and uses hash_link() to add it to the hash row.

br_fdb_cleanup()	net/bridge/br_fdb.c

The forwarding table should be updated whenever a station is no longer active or the network has changed. Unfortunately, a bridge cannot see such an action, because it responds actively to a station's packets only by remembering the origin of a packet in the forwarding table. This means that, when a station has not sent anything for a certain period of time, then the bridge assumes that the station was deactivated or moved. For this purpose, the `gc_timer` is set in a bridge instance. This timer starts the function `br_fdb_cleanup()` periodically in a specific interval, `gc_interval`. It checks all entries in the hash table of a bridge instance and removes all entries with an aging value exceeding timeout.

12.4.5 Implementing the Spanning-Tree Protocol

This section describes how the spanning-tree protocol according to IEEE 802.1d and the relevant functions are implemented. The spanning-tree protocol is used to prevent cycles in a redundant LAN internetwork. The algorithm operates in a decentralized way: Each station has to work out the current state in the LAN internetwork from the information contained in control packets (BPDUs). For example, each bridge assumes initially that it is the root bridge, and it probably has to learn that this is not so from incoming BPDUs.

For this reason, the implementation of the spanning tree protocol is based on the fact that the currently "best" configuration is stored in each port. This means that each new incoming message is verified to see whether the information it contains is better than the information currently stored, so that the currently best configuration is accepted. By comparing the configuration message most recently received with the information available on the bridge itself, it is easy to figure out the root bridge, the root port, and the designated ports.

This also means that all steps are executed consecutively for each configuration message with better information. This means that the root bridge is not defined in all bridges to then compute the least cost for all bridges, and so on; instead, the bridges decide first on the basis of their own knowledge, and subsequently the knowledge of the immediate neighbors is added, and so on, until the configuration messages have eventually visited the entire LAN internetwork, so that the bridges can make their optimal choice for the LAN internetwork. This shows clearly that a real-world implementation does not necessarily have to correspond to the theoretical model to be efficient.

One major benefit of this implementation is that relatively few configuration messages have to be exchanged. How fast a tree structure can be built also depends on the bridges that send their configuration messages first. It is normally more beneficial when bridges with smaller identifiers or higher priorities send configuration messages earlier. However, bridges do not immediately change from the blocking into the forwarding state; they take various intermediate states where no data packets may be forwarded, so that the probability of temporary cycles is low.

The following subsections describe the important aspects of how the spanning-tree protocol is implemented.

Initialization   A bridge in the kernel is initialized by the functions `br_add_bridge()` and `new_nb()` when a bridge instance is created by the `brctl addbr ...` command. As the instructions in this command are processed, the bridge is set as the designated root bridge. When `brctl addif ...` adds ports to the bridge, then these ports are initially put into the `BR_STATE_BLOCKING` state. All timers are initially set to inactive (`br_stp_enable_port()`). Subsequently, the information currently available is verified to see the state the new port can now take.

When a bridge instance is initialized, the bridge timer is also initialized. This timer is a `timer_list` type (see Section 2.7.1); it invokes the `br_tick()` function each second. This function is used to control all timer functions of the bridge instance and the spanning-tree protocol. This means that each bridge instance uses only one single system timer. All internal time-controlled processes run over this timer. (See more information in the later subsection *Timer Handling*.)

Processing BPDUs   The function `br_handle_stp_pdu()` of `br_handle_frame()` is invoked as soon as a BPDU is received. When topology-change packets (TCN) arrive, then `br_received_tcn_bpdu()` assumes all further handling. When configuration packets (Config BPDU) arrive, then the packet content is copied into a `br_config_bpdu` structure, and some of the fields are converted into the internal representation format. For example, time values are stored in jiffies rather than in ticks. Subsequently, the BPDU is further handled by the function `br_received_config_bpdu()`.

Steps of the Spanning-Tree Algorithm   The individual steps of the spanning-tree algorithm were described in Section 12.2.4. As mentioned in that section, the spanning-tree mechanism runs for each configuration message received that changes something in the current configuration.

Whether a new configuration message has information that is better than that currently stored is a decision implemented by logic functions, as are the selection of a root port and the naming of a designated port. Notice that these actions normally use few comparisons.

`br_received_config_bpdu()`	**net/bridge/br_stp.c**

This function initially invokes `br_is_root_bridge()` to check on whether it has been the root bridge itself. Notice that the bridge does not have a global view of the LAN internetwork, as mentioned earlier. There could indeed be other bridges that classify themselves as the root bridge. This situation will change gradually as the spanning-tree algorithm runs its steps, and one bridge will eventually become the only root bridge.

When a new configuration message is better than the current information (a result of calling `br_supersedes_port_info()`), then the following things happen:

- First, the invocation of `br_record_config_information()` causes the data of the configuration BPDU to be written to the `net_bridge_port` structure.
- Next, the `br_configuration_update()` function is invoked. It selects the root ports and designated ports. This action could cause the information structures of the bridge and its ports to change.
- Subsequently, `br_port_state_selection()` recognizes the state of a port. The hello timer is stopped, if the bridge was the root bridge before the new information was stored, but now if it is no longer the root bridge. If a change to the topology is discovered in additional, then the `topology_change_timer` is stopped, the `tcn_timer` is started, and a topology-change message is sent (`br_transmit_tcn()`).

■ If the input port was marked as the root port, then the timeout values of the configuration BPDU are added to the `net_bridge` structure and a configuration BPDU is generated (by `br_config_bpdu_generation()`). In addition, the function `br_topology_change_acknowledged()` is invoked, if the `topoplogy_change_ack` flag was set in the configuration BPDU.

In contrast, if nothing changes in response to the configuration BPDU, then `br_reply()` is invoked, provided that the input port is the designated port. This means that a configuration message with locally stored values is sent.

`br_supersedes_port_info()`	**net/bridge/br_stp.c**

This function checks for whether the stored `net_bridge_port` structure changes in response to a configuration BPDU received (i.e., if the new configuration BPDU includes "better" information). This is the case in either of the following situations:

■ The root bridge in the BPDU has a smaller ID than the root bridge currently stored in the structure.
■ The two IDs are equal, but the path cost in the BPDU is less.
■ The path cost is equal, but the ID of the sending bridge is smaller than the ID of the bridge itself.
■ The IDs of the bridges match, but the port ID of the sending bridge is smaller than the ID of the input port.

The first two points in the above list are normally decisive, but if two local area networks are connected by parallel bridges, then the port ID could also play a role.

`br_record_config_information()`	**net/bridge/br_stp.c**

This function is invoked if the configuration message is better than the information currently stored. The root bridge ID and the cost over the path to the root bridge (RPC) are stored in the `net_bridge_port` structure as designated root and cost, respectively. The bridge sending the configuration message and its output port serve as the designated bridge and port.

The message-age timer is started with the value from the configuration message, to be able to detect potential failures of a component.

`br_record_config_timeout_values()`	**net/bridge/br_stp.c**

An invocation of this function causes the values for expiry of the timers to be copied from the configuration message to the information memory of the bridge. This ensures that critical timers in all bridges of the LAN internetwork have the same time-out values, which are determined by the root bridge.

br_root_selection()   **net/bridge/br_stp.c**

    This function selects the root port of a bridge. The function iterates over all ports, starting with the smallest port number, and it checks for whether the conditions for the root port are met (br_should_become_root_port()). The port must not be a designated port, it must not have the BR_STATE_DISABLED state, and the bridge must not be the root bridge. Subsequently, the path cost to the root bridge is compared. If the costs are equal, then the information from the net_bridge_port structure is considered. Figure 12–14 shows the algorithm used for this procedure.

    If the loop was fully walked through, but no root port was assigned, then the bridge itself becomes the root bridge. Finally, the selected root bridge and the root path cost (RPC) are entered in the net_bridge structure.

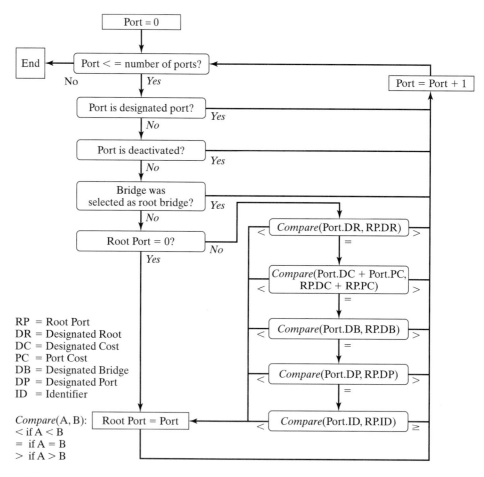

FIGURE 12–14
Selecting a root port.

`br_designated_port_selection()`	**net/bridge/br_stp.c**

This function also checks the ports one after the other. A port becomes the designated port if the configuration message that arrived on this port is better than the configuration message received (and stored in the `net_bridge_port` structure). The configuration message consists mainly of the root bridge ID, the path cost to the root bridge, and the bridge and port IDs, so the corresponding fields in the `net_bridge` structure and in the `net_bridge_port` structure have to be compared. Figure 12–15 shows the algorithm used to implement this condition.

`br_become_designated_port()`	**net/bridge/br_stp.c**

This function is invoked in `br_designated_port_selection()` for each designated port. The port in the bridge whose number is called in this function becomes the designated port. This means that the corresponding information is stored in the `net_bridge_port` structure.

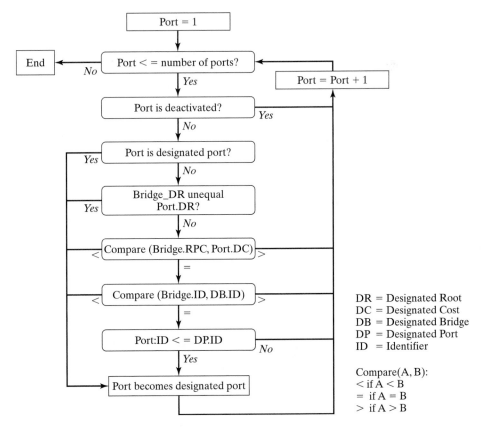

FIGURE 12–15
Selecting a designated port.

`br_port_state_selection()`   **net/bridge/br_stp.c**

The future state is determined for each port, and appropriate functions are invoked. If the port is in the BR_STATE_DISABLED state, then nothing is done. If a port is the root port or a designated port, then `br_make_forwarding()` is invoked to put that port in the forwarding state.

Remember that the intermediate states, BR_STATE_LISTENING und BR_STATE_LEARNING, are used first, as described in Section 12.2.4. The forward delay timer controls this procedure.

In all other cases, `br_make_blocking()` is invoked to put the port in the blocking state. In addition, a topology-change request is caused by `br_topology_change_detection()`, if the port has been in the forwarding or learning state.

`br_transmit_config()`   **net/bridge/br_stp.c**

This function initially checks whether for the hold timer is active. If so, then `config_pending` is set to 1, and the function returns immediately.

If the hold timer has not always been active, then a configuration BPDU with the corresponding values is filled in from the `net_bridge` structure; then the function `br_send_config_bpdu()` is invoked, and the hold timer is started. Figure 12–16 shows how a configuration message is built from the `net_bridge` structure.

Example—Running the Spanning-Tree Protocol   The initialization of the bridges results in the configuration shown in Figure 12–17. However, this figure shows only the most important fields in the structures. Each bridge is initialized as a root bridge. Though the interfaces are in blocking state, configuration messages are sent, because the ports are defined as designated ports.

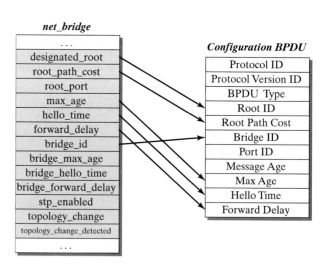

FIGURE 12–16
Example of a configuration message.

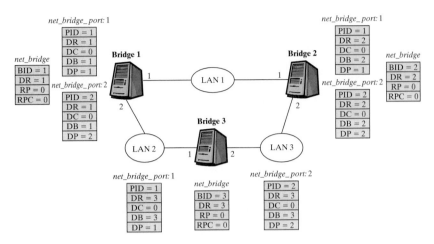

FIGURE 12–17
Initializing bridges for the spanning-tree protocol.

After the bridge initialization, configuration messages are sent over all network adapters. In this example, bridge 1 sends the first configuration message. This information is better than the information stored in the input ports of bridges 2 and 3 (in this case), so the new information is stored in the `net_bridge_port` structures of these ports. Figure 12–18 shows this procedure.

From this information, the root port is selected in bridges 2 and 3. In the example shown in Figure 12–18, port 1 is selected in both bridges, because it is the only port that stored the root bridge with the smallest ID. This selection causes the `net_bridge` structure to change, as shown in Figure 12–19.

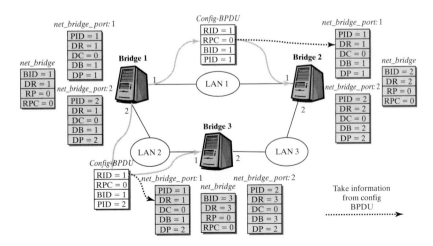

FIGURE 12–18
Storing information from a configuration message.

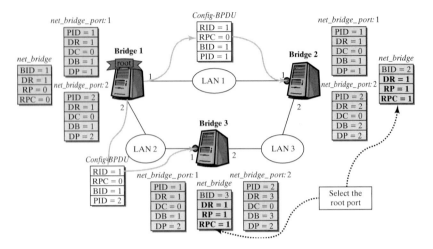

FIGURE 12–19
Selecting a root port.

The next step selects designated ports in the bridges. Port 2 is defined as the designated port in each of the two bridges, because the information about the root bridge in the `net_bridge_port` structure of this port differs from the information in the `net_bridge` structure. The selecting of designated ports changes the `net_bridge_port` structure of these ports, so the new root bridge and its path cost are entered. Figure 12–20 shows this procedure.

Two paths to the root bridge exist for LAN 3 in this example, and so there is a cycle; hence, we have to select a bridge as designated bridge for this LAN. We opt for bridge 2 as the designated bridge, because it has the smaller ID. Notice that this selection, too, depends on the order of the exchanging of configuration messages. For example, if bridge 3

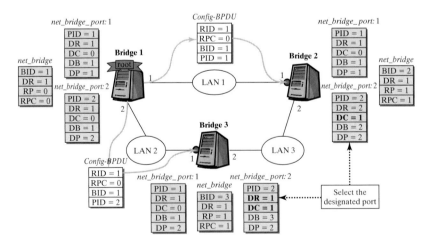

FIGURE 12–20
Selecting designated ports.

sends the first configuration message over its designated port, then bridge 2 will check for whether it is better than the stored configuration. Such would not be the case in this example, so bridge 2 would return a configuration message with its own values. The information in this message would be better than the configuration stored on port 2 in bridge 3. Consequently, this bridge would run the spanning-tree algorithm. Port 1 would remains the root port, but port 2 would no longer be a designated port and would be put into the blocking state. (See Figure 12–21.)

Timer Handling   Each bridge has a function, `br_tick()`, to handle timers. This section describes the seven defined timers. To implement these timers, only one system timer of the type `timer_list` is used. This is the variable tick in each `net_bridge` structure.

The timer `tick` is invoked once every second (`expires = jiffies + HZ`) This causes the function `br_tick()` to be invoked each time. This function defines the behavior of the timers in the following list. Whether a timer has expired is checked for each timer (`br_check_timers()`). In addition, the timers are incremented. The appropriate behavior function is invoked as soon as a timer expires.

- *Hold timer*: The hold timer starts after the configuration BPDU has been sent. When it is active, no configuration BPDU can be sent over the same port. The hold timer expires when its value reaches or exceeds the stored `hold_time`. Then the function `br_transmit_config()` is invoked, if no BPDU has been sent yet. Once it has expired, the hold timer is not restarted. It is stopped explicitly when a port is disabled.
- *GC timer*: The garbage collection timer does cleanup work in the forwarding table. It checks periodically (`gc_interval`) on whether there are old entries in the forwarding table. If there are, then these entries are deleted, to respond to moving stations. In addition, this cleanup work prevents the forwarding table

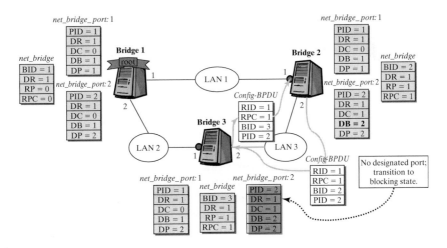

FIGURE 12–21
Configuration for LAN 3.

from filling up with entries for inactive stations. The function `br_fdb_cleanup()` is responsible for this check.

- *Hello timer*: The hello timer is used to send hello packets (configuration BPDUs) at regular intervals. This timer is started after the call of `br_config_bpdu_generation()`, while the spanning-tree protocol is running. It is incremented until its value has reached the stored hello time. Subsequently, `br_config_bpdu_generation()` is invoked again, and the hello timer is restarted.

- *TCN timer*: The TCN timer is used once a TCN BPDU has been sent. This timer causes TCN BPDUs to be sent at regular intervals until the topology change has been acknowledged. The intervals are identical to those for configuration BPDUs.

- *Topology-change timer*: This timer is used exclusively by the root bridge. It specifies the period for which the flags for a topology change request are set (i.e., the period during which configuration messages may be passed). The fields `topology_change_detected` and `topology_change` in the `net_bridge` structure are set to null as soon as this timer expires. This timer is not restarted.

- *Message-age timer*: There is one message-age timer for each network interface in each bridge. This timer is started when the values of a configuration BPDU are written to the `net_bridge_port` structure. The expiry of the message-age timer means that a component has failed. For this reason, the spanning-tree protocol is restarted, where the port with the expired timer is set to be the designated port. Subsequently, the spanning-tree algorithm runs its normal procedure.

- *Forward-delay timer*: The forward-delay timer is used to move the ports of a bridge from the blocking to the forwarding state. This is the reason why there is one such timer for each port. This timer specifies the time interval between two states. It is started by the function `br_make_forwarding()`, and the state of a port is set to BR_STATE_LISTENING in this function.

When in the BR_STATE_LISTENING, the port is switched to the BR_STATE_LEARNING state, and the forward-delay timer is restarted. When the timer expires again, then the state changes from BR_STATE_LEARNING to BR_STATE_FORWARDING. This requires the `br_topology_change_detection()` function to be invoked, if any of the ports stored this bridge is the designated bridge. Figure 12–11 shows these transitions.

Topology Changes   When a new bridge is added to the LAN internetwork, then the spanning-tree protocol (STP) runs as described above: The bridge is initialized as root bridge. If it is actually the (new) root bridge, then its configuration messages will win across all bridges in the internetwork. Otherwise, it receives configuration messages from neighboring bridges, which it will then use to configure its interfaces.

As was mentioned previously, if a bridge or an active port fails, then the message-age timer in the neighboring bridge expires. Figure 12–22 shows this procedure in an example. The port owning the expired timer is set to be the designated port. This means that the current configuration of this port is overwritten. Subsequently, the spanning-tree mechanism runs once more in this bridge.

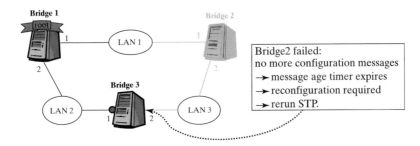

FIGURE 12–22
Example for a topology change: The message-age timer expires.

Functions Used to Display a Topology Change As previously described, the execution of the spanning-tree protocol in a LAN internetwork could cause changes to the topology. TCN BPDUs are sent over the path to the root bridge to ensure that all bridges are informed about such a topology change. In turn, the root bridge sends then configuration BPDUs with the `topology_change` field set, and these BPDUs are transported across all paths within the tree topology.

It is interesting to note that MAC addresses are not added to the forwarding table when the topology is reconfigured. Instead, this is done exclusively by the learning function. However, the entries in the forwarding table can become invalid after a relatively short time, so packets are sent to the relevant stations over all ports so that they will eventually reach their destination.

`br_received_tcn_bpdu()`	**net/bridge/br_stp.c**

If the port that received a BPDU is a designated port, then the function `br_topology_change_detection()` is invoked. `br_topology_change_acknowledge()` is used to send a configuration message with the `topology_change_ack` field set over the input port.

`br_topology_change_detection()`	**net/bridge/br_stp.c**

If the bridge is the root of the tree topology, then the `topology_change` field in the `net_bridge` structure is set to one, and the topology-change timer is started. Unless the topology change has been detected, all other bridges use the `br_transmit_tcn()` function to send a TCN BPDU over their root ports and start their TCN timers. Finally, it is marked that the topology change was detected, to limit the number of TCN BPDUs announcing the same topology change.

`br_topology_change_acknowledged()`	**net/bridge/br_stp.c**

The marking for a topology change is reset, and the TCN timer is stopped. This function is invoked by `br_received_config_bpdu()`, if the flag `topology_change_ack` is set in the incoming configuration message.

## PART IV

Network Layer

CHAPTER 13

The TCP/IP Protocols

This chapter introduces the TCP/IP protocol suite, which represents the basis of the popular Internet. Chapter 3 introduced the TCP/IP reference model. The sections in this chapter and the following chapters begin with an introduction of the tasks of each of these protocols and then describe how they operate and how they are implemented in Linux.

The history of the Internet and its protocols began in 1961, when Leonard Kleinrock developed packet-switching theory at MIT. His work was based on the idea of splitting data into many small packets and sending them to the destination separately, without specifying the exact path. After initial skepticism, the principle was eventually used in a research project of ARPA (Advanced Research Projects Agency), a division of the United States Department of Defense. In 1968, ARPA granted a budget of more than half a million dollars for a heterogeneous network, which was called *ARPANET*.

In 1969, this experimental network connected the four universities of Los Angeles (UCLA), Santa Barbara (UCSB), Utah, and the Stanford Research Institute (SRI) and expanded very quickly. Later, satellite and cellular links were successfully connected to the ARPANET. In one impressive demonstration, a truck in California was connected with the next university over a radio link and used the satellite network to access a computer based in London, UK.

This system was used intensively in the years following. On the basis of the knowledge gained from this system, a second generation of protocols was developed. By 1982, a protocol suite with the two important protocols, TCP and IP, had been specified. Today, the name TCP/IP is used for the entire protocol suite. In 1983, TCP/IP became the standard protocol for the ARPANET. The TCP/IP protocols proved particularly suitable for providing a reliable connection of networks within the continually growing ARPANET. ARPA was very interested in establishing the new protocols and convinced the University of California at Berkeley to integrate the TCP/IP protocols into its widely used Berkeley UNIX operating system. They used the principle of sockets to design applications with network functionality. This helped the TCP/IP protocols to soon become very popular for the exchange of data between applications.

In the following years, the ARPANET had grown to a size that made the management of all computers IP addresses in one single file too expensive. As a consequence, the

Domain Name Service (DNS) was developed and is used to hide IP addresses behind easy-to-remember computer and domain names. Today, the Internet protocol Version 4 is the most frequently used network-layer protocol. However, it was not designed for such an enormous proliferation and has already hit its capacity limits, so a new version had to be developed. The new Internet Protocol Version 6 is also called IPv6 or IPng.

13.1   THE INTERNET PROTOCOL SUITE

Each protocol of the TCP/IP protocol suite handles certain tasks within the TCP/IP protocol stack. Figure 13–1 gives an overview of the TCP/IP protocol stack and its protocols.

- On the data-link *layer* in the Internet model, you find network adapters and their drivers. They allow you to exchange data packets having a specific maximum length within the connected LAN (Ethernet, token ring, . . .) or within a WAN (PPP over ISDN, ATM). The previous chapters introduced some protocols that also belong to the data-link layer (SLIP, PPP, ATM, Bluetooth, etc.). All adapters and protocols on this layer have the common property that they represent only *one* communication link between two IP routers (i.e., they don't support Internet routing).

- The *Address Resolution Protocol* (*ARP*) also resides on the data-link layer. Notice that there are contradictory opinions in the literature. ARP is used to map globally valid IP addresses to locally valid MAC addresses. ARP is actually not limited to IP addresses or specific physical addresses; it was designed for general use. ARP uses the broadcast capability of local area networks to find addresses. Chapter 15 describes this protocol in detail.

- The *Internet Protocol* (*IP*) forms the core of the entire architecture, because it allows all IP-enabled computers in the interconnected networks to communicate. Each computer in the Internet has to support the Internet Protocol. IP offers unreliable transport of data packets. IP uses information from routing protocols (OSPF, BGP, etc.) to forward packets to their receivers.

- The *Internet Control Message Protocol* (*ICMP*) has to be present in each IP-enabled computer; it handles the transport of error messages of the Internet Protocol. For example, ICMP sends a message back to the sender of a packet if the packet cannot

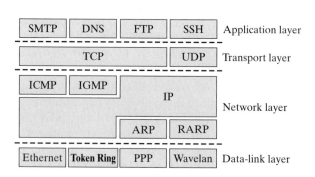

FIGURE 13–1
The protocols of the TCP/IP protocol stack.

be forwarded because routing information is missing or faulty. Section 14.4 deals with ICMP and its implementation in Linux.

■ The *Internet Group Management Protocol* (*IGMP*) is responsible for managing multicast groups in local area networks. Multicast provides for efficient sending of data to a specific group of computers. IGMP allows the computers of a LAN to inform its router that they want to receive data for a certain group in the future. Chapter 17 discusses multicast in the Internet.

■ The *Transmission Control Protocol* (*TCP*) is a reliable, connection-oriented and byte-stream-oriented transport-layer protocol. TCP is primarily responsible for providing a secured data transport between two applications over the unreliable service of the IP protocol. TCP is the most frequently used transport protocol in the Internet. It has a large functionality, and so its implementation is extensive. Chapter 24 discusses the TCP.

■ The *User Datagram Protocol* (*UDP*) is a very simple transport protocol, providing connectionless and unreliable transport of data packets between applications in the Internet. In this context, unreliable does not mean that the data could arrive corrupted at the destination computer. It means that UDP does not offer any protocol mechanisms to guarantee that the data will arrive at the destination at all. When data arrives at the destination computer, than it can only be checked for correctness.

As compared with TCP, UDP has the benefit that it has very little functionality and so can easily be extended. Many applications that normally transmit only small amounts of data (e.g., client/server applications) use UDP as their preferred transport protocol. Establishing a connection and reliable data transmission would be more costly than the retransmission of faulty or missing data.

■ The *application layer* accommodates various standardized application protocols, which form the basis of a large number of applications:

▷ The *HyperText Transfer Protocol* (*HTTP*) is currently the protocol most frequently used in the Internet application layer. It allows you to exchange data in the World Wide Web—say, by loading Web sites into your Web browser (Netscape, Mozilla, Lynx, etc.). The unprecedented success of the World Wide Web has led to the enormous proliferation of the Internet and its revolutionary growth.

▷ *TELNET* is the protocol for virtual terminals. It is used to access a computer connected to the network in the form of a terminal session. Its unsecured transmission of passwords and data has caused TELNET to be increasingly replaced by the SSH (Secure Socket Shell) protocol.

▷ The *File Transfer Protocol* (*FTP*) can be used to transport files from a local computer to another computer and vice versa. Like TELNET, its most important drawback is that passwords are transmitted in cleartext. FTP has increasingly been replaced by *Secure Copy* (*SCP*).

▷ The *Simple Mail Transfer Protocol* (*SMTP*) is the protocol used to exchange electronic mail (e-mail) in the Internet.

- ▶ The *Domain Name Service* (*DNS*) translates DNS names, which are most commonly used and are easy for humans to remember (e.g., `www.linux-netzwerkarchitektur.de`[1]) into IP addresses. It is used mainly to convert computer names and mail-server locations into IP addresses.
- ▶ The *Network File System* (*NFS*) is used to allow several computers to access the same file system. The NFS service represents an extension of local file systems beyond network boundaries.

Such protocols of the application layer are not discussed in this book, because they are not part of the Linux kernel. Simple application programming is normally sufficient to emulate them. For example, there are many of HTTP protocol implementations in different WWW browsers and WWW servers. Chapter 27 explains how applications with network functionality can be programmed.

The following chapters describe each protocol of the TCP/IP protocol stack and how they are implemented in Linux. These chapters also discuss various extensions, which are related to the Internet Protocol suite, but normally not mentioned together with it. This includes mainly concepts and protocols for computer security (firewalls, NAT) and the support of specific guaranteed services within the Internet Protocol (Quality of Service (QoS) with *TC* or *KIDS*).

# CHAPTER 14

The Internet Protocol V4

The Internet Protocol (IP) is the central element in the TCP/IP protocol stack. It provides the basic service for all the data traffic in the Internet and other IP-based networks and was specified in RFC 791. The primary task of the Internet Protocol is to hide differences between data transmission layers and to offer a uniform presentation of different network technologies. For example, the Internet protocol can run on top of LAN technologies and SLIP (Serial Line IP) or PPP (Point-to-Point Protocol) over modem or ISDN connections. The uniform presentation of the underlying technology includes an introduction of the uniform addressing scheme (IP address family) and a mechanism to fragment large data packets, so that smaller maximum packet sizes can be transported across networks.

In general, each network technology defines a maximum size for data packets—the *Maximum Transmission Unit (MTU)*. The MTU depends on the hardware used and the transmission technology and varies between 276 bytes and 9000 bytes. The Internet layer fragments IP datagrams, which are bigger than the MTU of the network technology used, into smaller packets (*fragments*). These fragments of a datagram are then put together into the original IP datagram in the destination computer. Section 14.2.3 explains how data packets are fragmented and reassembled.

In summary, the Internet Protocol handles the following functions:

- provides an unsecured connectionless datagram service;
- defines IP datagrams as basic units for data transmission;
- defines the IP addressing scheme;
- routes and forwards IP datagrams across interconnected networks;
- verifes the lifetime of packets;
- fragments and reassembles packets; and
- uses ICMP to output errors.

14.1 PROPERTIES OF THE INTERNET PROTOCOL

The Internet Protocol was developed with the idea of maintaining communication between two systems even when some transmission sections fail. For this reason, the Internet Protocol was developed on the basis of the principle of datagram switching, to transport IP data units, rather than on that of circuit-switching, like conventional telephone network.

The following sections describe the protocol mechanisms of the Internet Protocol. Section 14.2 will then explain how IP is implemented in the Linux kernel.

14.1.1 Routing IP Packets Across Routers

Figure 14–1 shows how the Internet is structured. Rather than being one single network, the Internet is composed of many smaller local area networks, which are connected by routers. This is the reason why it is often called the *network of networks* or *global network*. Each network connected to the Internet can be different both in size and in technology. Within one network (e.g., the network of a university), it is often meaningful to build several subnetworks. These—often independent—networks and subnetworks are connected by routers and point-to-point lines.

The interconnection of single local area networks offers a way to send data from an arbitrary computer to any other computer within the internetwork. Before it sends a packet, an Internet computer checks for whether the destination computer is in the same local area network. If this is not the case, then the data packet is forwarded to the next router. If both the sender and the receiver are in the same local area network, then the packet is delivered to the receiver directly over the physical medium. In either case, the IP layer uses the service of the data-link layer to physically transport the packet (horizontal communication—see Section 3.2).

Let's assume that, in the first case, the packet has not yet arrived in the destination computer. The router checks the destination address in the IP packet header and the information in the routing table to determine how the packet should be forwarded. Next, the packet travels from one router to the next until it eventually arrives in the destination computer. Chapter 16 discusses routing in IP networks.

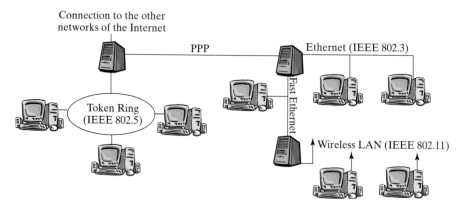

FIGURE 14–1
The structure of the global Internet.

14.1.2   The IP Packet Header

Figure 14–2 shows the format of an IP packet. The fields of the IP packet header have the properties described below.

- *Version*: This field contains the version number of the Internet Protocol used. Including the version number provides a way to use several versions of the Internet Protocol. Currently, only versions v4 and v6 are defined. In general, the two versions are not specified in the *Version* field; they are identified by their protocol identifiers on the MAC layer (0x800 for IPv4, 0x86DD for IPv6—see include/linux/if_ether.h).

- *IHL (Internet Header Length)*: This field contains the length of the packet header, because it can be longer than 20 bytes, if options are used. The length is stated in multiples of 32 bits. The smallest valid value is 5 (no options), and the highest value is 15 (corresponds to a header length of 60 bytes).

- *Codepoint*: This field was originally called *Type of Service*. Its purpose was changed to *Differentiated Services Codepoint* in RFC 2474. This field shows the forwarding behavior used [NBBB98].

- *Total length*: This value includes the entire length of the IP packet. Its 16-bit length makes the maximum size of an IP datagram 65,535 bytes. RFC 791 specifies that each IP-enabled computer should be capable of processing data packets with a size of 576 bytes. In general, however, it is possible to process packets with a bigger length. Otherwise, a packet has to be fragmented. (See Section 14.2.3.)

- *Fragment ID*: The destination computer can use this identifier, together with the sender address, to reassemble fragments of IP datagrams to reconstruct the original datagrams. All fragments of an IP datagram have the same fragment ID, which is set by the sender.

- *Flags*: An IP packet can include two flags (the third flag is currently not used): *Don't Fragment* (*DF*) and *More Fragments* (*MF*). MF is used for a fragmented packet. The DF bit means that a datagram must not be fragmented, even if this means that the packet cannot be transported any further. The MF bit shows whether more fragments follow this IP packet (i.e., the MF flag is set in all fragments of a datagram, except for the last fragment).

- *Fragment Offset*: This field specifies where in relation to the beginning of the entire datagram the present fragment has to be ordered. This information is required

IP packet format

0   3   7   15   31
Version	IHL	Codepoint		Checksum
Fragment ID	DF MF	Fragment offset
Time to Live	Protocol	Checksum
Source address
Destination address
Options and payload

FIGURE 14–2
Packet-header format of the Internet Protocol.

to reassemble the original packet from the individual fragments in the destination computer. Since this field has a size of 13 bits, a maximum number of 8192 fragments can be created from one IP datagram. All fragments, except the last fragment, have to be a multiple of 8 bytes. This is the elementary fragment unit.

■ *Time To Live (TTL)*: This is a counter used to limit the lifetime of IP packets. This field originally stated the maximum lifetime in seconds, but is used today to specify the maximum number of intermediate systems (routers). Each router on the path has to decrement this counter by at least one. If a longer buffering time is necessary, then the counter should be decremented by more. If the field has the value 0, then the packet has to be rejected, to keep a packet from wandering in the network forever.

■ *Protocol*: This field includes the number of the transport protocol to which the packet should be forwarded. Numbering of protocols was defined in [RePo94] (e.g., TCP (6), UDP (17), IDMP(1), IGMP (2)).

■ *Checksum*: This field includes the checksum over the fields of the IP packet header. The payload in the IP datagram is not checked, for efficiency reasons. In general, this check occurs within the transport protocol. The checksum has to be recomputed in each network node visited, because the IP header changes in each hop, in the TTL field. For this reason, it is important to use efficient checksums. A sender computes the 1's-complement sum of all 16-bit quantities in the header, excluding the checksum field itself, and then stores the 1's complement of the sum in the *CHECKSUM* field. A receiver computes the same 16-bit sum of values in the header, including the checksum field. If the checksum is correct, then the result is zero.

■ *Sender and destination addresses*: These fields include the 32-bit Internet addresses of the sender and the receiver. Section 15.1.5 describes the address classes of the Internet Protocol.

■ *Option and padding fields*: To keep the headers of datagrams small, IP defines a set of options that can be present, if needed. The header length is specified in 32-bit multiples; if options do not end on a 32-bit boundary, then *PADDING* that contains zero-bits is added to make the header a multiple of 32 bits. Section 14.3 describes all IP options.

14.1.3 Lifetime of an IP Data Packet

Faulty functions in the network can cause packets to circulate in the network rather than arriving at their destination address. These data packets consume valuable resources in the network, so they have to be destroyed by control mechanisms at some point in time.

The following method is used to destroy such packets: The TTL (*Time To Live*) field of the IP data header takes the number of routers (hops). This field is actually intended to specify the lifetime of a packet in seconds, but it is currently used to count the hops through the routers on the path. Each router reduces this value by 1, and the packet is rejected when the value 0 is reached. This prevents a packet that cannot be delivered from circulating forever. In addition, you can set a specific TTL value in the sender to limit the reach of a packet.

14.1.4 Addressing in the Internet

Three different addresses are used to reach a communication partner or an application in the Internet. These addresses identify a unique communication endpoint within the Internet and are often called *sockets*:

■ The *IP address* specifies a unique computer in the Internet. Each computer in an IP network has to have a unique Internet address. Section 14.1.5 explains the structure of this address format and the set of different classes.

■ The *transport protocol ID* specifies the transport protocol instance used (i.e., TCP, UDP, ICMP, etc.). The Internet Protocol uses this identifier to know which transport protocol is used.

■ The *port number* identifies a unique and specific application within the TCP and UDP transport protocols (multiplexing).

The following section discusses the first part of the sockets defined above, IP addresses and their structure. The chapters dealing with the transport layer introduce and describe the TCP and UDP protocols, which are the most important transport protocols today. These chapters also explain the meaning of port numbers.

14.1.5 IP Addresses and IP Address Classes

Each network device in the Internet or in other IP-based networks has its own unique IP address. Computers connected to several networks concurrently (*multihomed hosts*) have a separate address for each network connection. These addresses are assigned by the *Internet Assigned Numbers Authority* (*IANA*) and their national representatives (e.g., *Reseau IP Europe—RIPE*). Notice that these addresses are not assigned on an individual basis, but in blocks by so-called *network classes*. If somebody needs an IP address to connect a computer to the Internet, then he or she will obtain a network address and an entire range of addresses. For this reason, each range of network addresses is managed within those addresses themselves.

Accordingly, IP addresses are structured in a hierarchy: They are divided into a *network part* and a *computer* or *host part*. Figure 14–3 shows the classes and their different network and host parts.

The network part identifies the network to which a station is connected. All computers within a network have the same network part. The computer part identifies a specified computer within a network. If a computer is connected to more than one network, then it has a separate IP address for each network.

IP addresses are 32 bits long and are normally written in dotted decimal notation (e.g., 129.13.42.117). As was mentioned earlier, IP addresses are divided into several classes. The prefix of an IP address specifies the address class. The five classes of IP addresses are as follows:

■ *Class A*: The first bit of the address is zero (i.e., the first byte is smaller than 128). The first byte is the network number, and the last three bytes identify a computer in the network. Accordingly, there are 126 class-A networks, which can manage up to 16 million computers in one network.

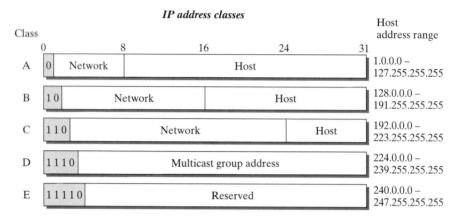

FIGURE 14–3
Address classes of the Internet Protocol.

- *Class B*: A value between 128 and 191 for the first byte (i.e., the first two bits are 10) identifies a class-B address. The first two bytes specify the network, and the last two bytes specify a computer in this network. This results in 16,382 class-B networks with up to 64,534 computers in any one network.

- *Class C*: This class uses values between 192 and 223 for the first byte (the first three bits have a value of 110). There are approximately two million class-C networks; the first three bytes are used for the network address and the last for up to 254 computers.

- *Class D*: Class-D addresses have a special meaning. They identify a group of computers that can be in different networks, rather than identifying a single computer or network adapter. Class-D addresses are also called *multicast addresses*. The first byte in a multicast address has a value in the range from 224 to 239; the first four bits are to 1110. When an application sends an IP packet to a class-D address, then the message is broadcast to all members of the addressed group. A special protocol, the *Internet Group Management Protocol* (*IGMP*), is used to manage such groups. Chapter 17 discusses IP multicast and IGMP.

- *Class E*: this last range of IP addresses, ranging from 240 to 254 in the first byte, is reserved for future use.

As mentioned earlier, IP addresses have to be unique within the Internet. For this reason, all network addresses are assigned by a central organization to ensure that all addresses are unique and visible in the Internet. However, this is not always required. Networks that do not connect to the global Internet do not need an address that is visible in the Internet. Also, it is not necessary that these addresses not be used in another private network. For this reason, address ranges were defined especially for private networks. These ranges are defined in RFC 1918. IP packets with private addresses may not be forwarded in the Internet. This means that private IP addresses can be used in an arbitrary number of nonpublic networks.

The following address ranges are reserved for use in private networks:

- The range from 10.0.0.0 to 10.255.255.254 was reserved in class A for private class-A networks.
- The range from 172.16.0.0 to 172.31.0.0 was reserved in class B for private class-B networks. This means that 16 class-B network are reserved for private use. Each of these networks can connect up to 65,534 computers.
- The range from 192.168.0.0 to 192.168.255.0, a total of 256 networks, was reserved in class C for private use. Each of these networks can connect up to 254 computers.

In addition, there are other reserved IP addresses with special meanings:

- The class-A network address 127 represents the loopback network device of a computer. IP packets to an address in the form 127.x.y.z are not output to a network adapter; they are processed locally.
- In addition to network addresses, computer addresses are also reserved for special use. The values 0 and 255 in computer addresses are reserved in all network classes.

An IP address with all bits of the computer part set to zero identifies the network itself. For example, the address 80.0.0.0 refers to the class-A network 80, and the address 128.66.0.0 refers to the class-B network 128.66.

An IP address where the computer part consists of 1-bits defines a broadcast address, which can be used to address all computers in a network.

14.2 IMPLEMENTING THE INTERNET PROTOCOL

This section explains the architecture of the IP instance in the Linux kernel. We will use the path a packet takes across the IP layer to introduce the basic properties of the Internet Protocol. We assume that this is a normal IP packet without special properties, to ensure that our explanations will be clear and easy to understand. All special functions of the Internet Protocol, such as fragmenting and reassembling, source routing, multicasting, and so on, will be described in the next chapters.

The objective of this section is to introduce the fundamental operation of the IP implementation in Linux, to be able to better understand more complex parts later on. This section also serves as an entry point into the other chapters of this book, because each packet passes the IP layer, where it can take a particular path (e.g., across a firewall or a tunnel). It is necessary to understand how the Internet Protocol is implemented in the Linux kernel to understand later chapters.

An IP packet can enter the IP instance in three different places:

- Packets arriving in a computer over a network adapter are stored in the input queue of the respective CPU, as described in Chapter 6. Once the layer-3 protocol in the data-link layer has been determined (which is ETH_PROTO_IP in this case), the packets are passed to the ip_rcv() function. The path these packets take will be described in Section 14.2.1.
- The second entry point for IP packets is at the interface to the transport protocols. These are packets used by TCP, UDP, and other protocols that use the IP protocol.

They use the `ip_queue_xmit()` function to pack a transport-layer PDU into an IP packet and send it. Other functions are available to generate IP packets at the boundary with the transport layer. These functions and the operation of `ip_queue_xmit()` will be described in Section 14.2.2.

- With the third option, the IP layer generates IP packets itself, on the Internet Protocol's initiative. These are mainly new multicast packets, new fragments of a large packet, and ICMP or IGMP packets that don't include a special payload. Such packets are created by specific methods (e.g., `icmp_send()`). (See Section 14.4.)

Once a packet (or socket buffer) has entered the IP layer, there are several options for how it can exit. We generally distinguish two different roles a computer can assume with regard to the Internet Protocol, where the first case is a special case of the second:

- *End system*: A Linux computer is normally configured as an end system—it is used as a workstation or server, assuming primarily the task of running user applications or providing application services. Also, a Web server and a network printer are nothing but end systems (with regard to the IP layer). The basic property of end systems is that they do not forward IP packets. This means that you can recognize an end system easily by the fact that it has only one network adapter. Even a system that has several network accesses can be configured as a host, if packet forwarding is disabled.

- *Router*: A router passes IP packets arriving in a network adapter to a second network adapter. This means that a router has several network adapters that forward packets between these interfaces. When packets arrive in a router, there are generally two options: they can deliver packets locally (i.e., deliver them to the transport layer) or they can forward them. The first case is identical with the procedure of packets arriving in an end system, where packets are always delivered locally. Consequently, a router can be thought of as a generalization of an end system, with the additional capability of forwarding packets. In contrast to end systems, generally no applications are started in routers, to ensure that packets can be forwarded as fast as possible.

Linux lets you enable and disable the packet-forwarding mechanism at runtime, provided that the forwarding support was integrated when the kernel was created. The directory `/proc/sys/net/ipv4/` includes a virtual file, `ip_forward`. You will see in Appendix B.3 that there is a way to change system settings from within the `proc` directory. If a 0 is written to this file, then packet forwarding is disabled. To activate IP packet forwarding, you can use the command `echo '1' > /proc/sys/net/ipv4/ip_forward`.

Figure 14–4 shows the path an IP packet takes across the Internet Protocol implementation in Linux. The gray ovals represent invoked functions, and the rectangles show the position of the netfilter hooks in the Internet Protocol.

The following sections describe different paths a packet can take across the IP implementation in the Linux kernel. We begin with incoming packets, which have to be either forwarded or delivered locally. The next section describes how packets are passed from the transport layer to IP.

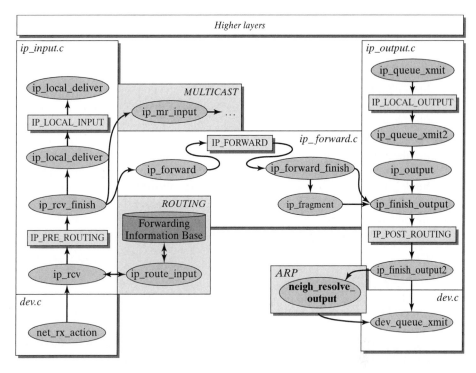

FIGURE 14–4
Architecture of the Internet Protocol implementation in Linux.

14.2.1 The Path of Incoming IP Packets

Chapter 6 introduced the path of an incoming packet up to the boundary of layer 3. Once the NET_RX tasklet has removed a packet from the input queue, netif_rx_action() chooses the appropriate layer-3 protocol. Next, the Internet Protocol is selected, and the ip_rcv() function is invoked on the basis of the identifier in the Ethernet protocol field (ETH_PROTO_IP) or from appropriate fields of other MAC transmission protocols.

ip_rcv( )	net/ipv4/ip_input.c

ip_rcv(skb, dev, pkt_type) does some work for the IP protocol. First, the function rejects packets not addressed to the local computer. For example, the promiscuous mode allows a network device to accept packets actually addressed to another computer. Such packets are filtered by the packet type (skb->pkt_type PACKET_OTHERHOST) in the lower layers.

Subsequently, the basic correctness criteria of a packet are checked:

▨ Does the packet have at least the size of an IP header?
▨ Is this IP Version 4?

- Is the checksum correct?
- Does the packet have a wrong length?

If the actual packet size does not match the information maintained in the socket buffer (skb->len), then the current packet data range is adapted by skb_trim(skb, iph->total_len). (See Section 4.1.) Now that the packet is correct, the netfilter hook NF_IP_PRE_ROUTING is invoked. Netfilter allows you to extend the procedure of various protocols by specific functions, if desired. Netfilter hooks always reside in strategic points of certain protocols and are used, for example, for firewall, QoS, and address-translation functions. These examples will be discussed in later chapters. A netfilter hook is invoked by a macro, and the function following the handling of the netfilter extension is passed to this macro in the form of a function pointer. If netfilter was not configured, then the macro ensures that there is a direct jump to this follow-up function. We can see in Figure 14–4 that the procedure continues with ip_rcv_finish(skb).

ip_rcv_finish( )   **net/ipv4/ip_input.c**

The function ip_route_input() is invoked within ip_rcv_finish(skb) to determine the route of a packet. The skb->dst pointer of the socket buffer is set to an entry in the routing cache, which stores not only the destination on the IP level, but also a pointer to an entry in the hard header cache (cache for layer-2 frame packet headers), if present. If ip_route_input() cannot find a route, then the packet is discarded.

In the next step, ip_rcv_finish() checks for whether the IP packet header includes options. If this is the case, then the options are analyzed, and an ip_options structure is created. All options set are stored in this structure in an efficient form. Section 14.3 describes how IP options are handled.

Finally in ip_rcv_finish(), the procedure of the IP protocol reaches the junction between packets addressed to the local computer and packets to be forwarded. The information about the further path of an IP packet is stored in the routing entry skb->dst. Notice that a trick often used in the Linux kernel is used here. If a switch (variable value) is used to select different functions, then we simply insert a pointer to each of these functions. This saves us an if or switch instruction for each decision of how the program should continue. In the example used here, the pointer skb->dst->input() points to the function that should be used to handle a packet further:

- ip_local_deliver() is entered in the case of unicast and multicast packets that should be delivered to the local computer.
- ip_forward() handles all unicast packets that should be forwarded.
- ip_mr_input() is used for multicast packets that should be forwarded.

We can see from the above discussion that a packet can take different paths. The following section describes how packets to be forwarded are handled (skb->dst->input = ip_forward). Subsequently, we will see how skb->dst->input = ip_local_deliver handles packets to be delivery locally.

Forwarding Packets   If a computer has several network adapters, and if packet IP forwarding is enabled (/proc/sys/net/ipv4/ip_forward 1), then packets addressed to other computers are handled by the ip_forward() function. This function does all the work necessary for forwarding a packet. The most important task—routing—was already done in ip_input(), because it is necessary to be able to discover whether the packet is to be delivered locally or has to be forwarded.

ip_forward( )	net/ipv4/ip_forward.c

The primary task of ip_forward(skb) is to process a few conditions of the Internet Protocol (e.g., a packet's lifetime) and packet options. First, packets not marked with pkt_type == PACKET_HOST are deleted. Next, the reach of the packet is checked. If the value in its TTL field is 1 (before it is decremented), then the packet is deleted. RFC 791 specifies that, if such an action occurs, an ICMP packet has to be returned to the sender to inform the latter (ICMP_TIME_EXCEEDED).

Once a redirect message has been checked, if applicable, the socket buffer is checked to see if there is sufficient memory for the headroom. This means that the function skb_cow(skb, headroom) is used to check whether there is still sufficient space for the MAC header in the output network device (out_dev->hard_header_len). If this is not the case, then skb_realloc_headroom() creates sufficient space. Subsequently, the TTL field of the IP packet is decremented by one.

When the actual packet length (including the MAC header) is known, it is checked for whether it really fits into the frame format of the new output network device. If it is too long (skb->len > mtu), and if no fragmenting is allowed because the *Don't-Fragment* bit is set in the IP header, then the packet is discarded, and the ICMP message ICMP_FRAG_NEEDED is transmitted to the sender. In any case, the packet is not fragmented yet; fragmenting is delayed. The early test for such cases prevents potential *Don't-Fragment* candidates from running through the entire IP protocol-handling process, only to be dropped eventually.

ip_forward_finish( )	net/ipv4/ip_forward.c

We can see in Figure 14–4 that the ip_forward() function is split into two parts by a netfilter hook. Once the NF_IP_FORWARD hook has been processed, the procedure continues with ip_forward_finish(). This function has actually very little functionality (unless FASTROUTE is enabled). Once the IP options, if used, have been processed in ip_forward_options(), the ip_send() function is invoked to check on whether the packet has to be fragmented and to eventually do a fragmentation, if applicable. (See Section 14.2.3.)

ip_send()	include/net/ip.h

ip_send(skb) decides whether the packet should be passed to ip_finish_output() immediately or ip_fragment() should first adapt it to the appropriate layer-2 frame size. (See Section 14.2.3.)

`ip_finish_output()`   **net/ipv4/ip_output.c**

`ip_finish_output(skb)` initiates the last tasks of the Internet Protocol. First, the skb->dev pointer is set to the output network device dev, and the layer-2 packet type is set to ETH_P_IP. Subsequently, the netfilter hook NF_IP_POST_ROUTING is processed. The exact operation of netfilter and the set of different hooking points within the Internet Protocol are described in Section 19.3. It is common for netfilter hooks to continue with the inline function `ip_finish_output2()` after their invocation.

`ip_finish_output2()`   **net/ipv4/ip_output.c**

At this point, the packet leaves the Internet Protocol, and the Address Resolution Protocol (ARP) is used, if necessary. Chapter 15 describes the Address Resolution Protocol. For now, it is sufficient to understand the following:

- If the routing entry used (skb->dst) already includes a reference to the layer-2 header cache (dst->hh), then the layer-2 packet header is copied directly into the packet-data space of the socket buffer, in front of the IP packet header. The output() function used here is dev_queue_xmit(), which is invoked if the entry in the hardware header cache is valid. dev_queue_xmit() ensures that the socket buffer is sent immediately over the network device, dev.
- If there is no entry in the *hard header cache* yet, then the corresponding address-resolution routine is invoked, which is normally the function neigh_resolve_output().

The procedure described above was optimized so that a packet can pass the router quickly without special options. However, it became clear where there are junctions to the corresponding handling routines (e.g., netfilter, multicasting, ICMP, fragmenting, or IP packet options).

Delivering Packets Locally   The previous section described the route a packet travels when it has to be forwarded. If `ip_route_input()` is the selected route, then the packet is addressed to the local computer. In this case, branching is to `ip_local_deliver()` rather than to `ip_forward()`. This section describes the path of packets to be delivered locally.

At this point, too, instead of using a conditioned `if` instruction to distinguish the two options, a pointer (skb->dst->input()) is used, which points to `ip_local_deliver()` in this case. At the end of `ip_input()`, the procedure continues with the packet's local delivery.

`ip_local_deliver()`   **net/ipv4/ip_input.c**

The first (and only) task of `ip_local_deliver(skb)` is to reassemble fragmented packets, using `ip_defrag()`. Section 14.2.3 describes in detail how packets are fragmented and defragmented. For now, it is sufficient to understand that all fragments of a packet are collected over a certain period of time, until all fragments of an IP datagram have arrived, so that they can be passed upwards as a whole.

Subsequently, it is almost mandatory to call a netfilter hook (NF_IP_LOCAL_IN) when the procedure continues with the ip_local_deliver_finish() function.

ip_local_deliver_finish()	net/ipv4/ip_input.c

The packet has now reached the end of the Internet Protocol processing. It is checked to see whether the packet is intended for a *RAW-IP* socket; otherwise, the transport protocol has to be determined for further processing (*demultiplexing*).

All transport protocols are managed in the ipprot hash table on the IP layer in Linux. At the end of the IP processing, there is now a special data structure, instead of simple query sequences and simple commands. The reason lies mainly in the nature of the Internet Protocol. Unless a packet includes special options, IP processing is very simple, and so IP is efficient and easy to implement. The complexity of IP packet options normally necessitates several more complex *programming methods*.

The protocol ID of the IP header modulo (MAX_INET_PROTOS - 1) is used to calculate the hash value in the ipprot hash table. The hash table is organized so that there are no collisions. If a new transport protocol would ever have to be integrated, then the assignment in the hash table should be checked. If the corresponding transport protocol can be found, then the appropriate handling routine (*handler*) of the protocol is invoked. The following handling routines are most common:

- tcp_v4_rcv(): Transmission Control Protocol (TCP)
- udp_rcv(): User Datagram Protocol (UDP)
- icmp_rcv(): Internet Control Message Protocol (ICMP)
- igmp_rcv(): Internet Group Management Protocol (IGMP)

If no transport protocol can be found, then the packet either is passed to a *RAW* socket (if there is one) or it is dropped and an *ICMP Destination Unreachable* message is returned to the sender.

The chapters dealing with the TCP and UDP transport protocols describe how a packet is further handled in the transport layer. Chapter 17 describes IGMP packets, and ICMP packets are discussed in Section 14.4. The following section describes the path a packet takes as it passes from the transport layer to the Internet Protocol for transmission.

14.2.2   Transport-Layer Packets

Packets created locally and passed from the transport layer to the Internet Protocol are handled in a way totally separate from the procedures introduced so far. (See Figure 14–4.) First of all, there is not just one single function available to the transport layer, but several, including ip_queue_xmit() and ip_build_and_send_pkt(). Each of these functions is specialized and optimized for a specific use.

This section considers only the ip_queue_xmit() function, because this is the one normally used for data packets; ip_build_and_send_pkt() is used for SYN or ACK packets that do not transport payload.

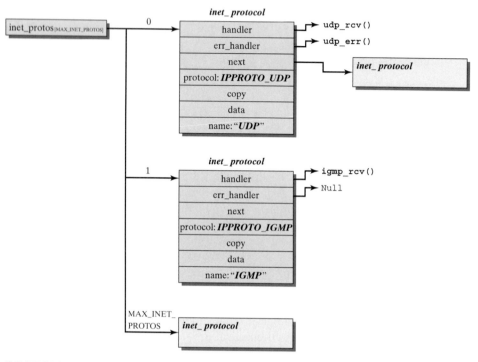

FIGURE 14–5
Hash table used to multiplex transport protocols.

`ip_queue_xmit()`	**net/ipv4/ip_output.c**

At the beginning, `ip_queue_xmit(skb)` checks for whether the socket structure `sk->dst` includes a pointer to an entry in the routing cache and, if so, whether this pointer is actually valid. The route for a packet is stored in the `skb->sk` socket structure, because all packets of a socket go to the same destination. Storing a reference means that expensive searches for routes can be avoided.

If no route is present yet (e.g., when the first packet of a socket is ready), then the `ip_route_output()` function is used to choose a route. Once this route has been entered in the routing cache, its *use counter* is incremented to ensure that the route is not inadvertently deleted as long as there is still a socket buffer referencing it.

Subsequently, the fields of the IP packet are filled (version, header length, TOS field, fragment offset, TTL, addresses, and protocol). Next, `ip_options_build()` handles options, if present, and the netfilter hook `NF_IP_LOCAL_OUTPUT` is invoked.

`ip_queue_xmit2()`	**net/ipv4/ip_output.c**

The next function, `ip_queue_xmit2(dev)` of the netfilter hook `NF_IP_LOCAL_OUTPUT`, sets the output network device as specified in the routing cache entry. Now it is necessary to check once more how much headroom is available in the socket buffer, although the buffer reservation is already complete. Also, it is necessary to learn the network device used and its MTU size. Unfortunately, it can happen that a socket buffer was created for the device dev1 (with mtu1), but the route has changed in the meantime, and the packet is sent over device dev2 with a smaller MTU. This means that, infrequently, the available headroom has to be increased. Subsequently, the packet is checked for fragmentation, and the checksum is computed (ip_send_check(iph)).

Subsequently, the packet created locally crosses the path for forwarding packets. The function pointer dst->output(), which is set during the routing process, causes the ip_output() function to be invoked, which executes the last steps in the Internet Protocol, primarily guiding the packet across the netfilter hook NF_IP_POST_ROUTING.

14.2.3 Fragmenting Packets

The Internet Protocol has to be capable of adapting the size of IP packets to the respective network type in order to be able to send IP datagrams over any type of network. Each network has a maximum packet size, which is called *Maximum Transfer Unit (MTU)*. Only packets within this size can be transported over the network. For example, if packets have to be sent over a token-ring network, they must not be larger than 4500 bytes, and 1500 bytes must not be exceeded by Ethernet packets. If the MTU of a transmission medium is smaller than the size of a packet, then the packet has to be split into smaller IP packets.

However, it is not sufficient to let the transport-layer protocols transmit smaller packets independently. The reason is that a packet can traverse several networks with a different MTU each on the way from the source host to the destination host. This means that we need a more flexible method that can create smaller packets, also in a router, on the IP layer. This method is called *fragmenting*.

Fragmenting means that the IP protocol in each IP computer (router or end system) has to be capable of splitting incoming packets, if necessary, and to transport them over a subnetwork (with a smaller MTU) all the way to the destination computer. In addition, each end system must be able to put these fragments together to rebuild the original packet. This method is called *reassembling*.

Each fragment of a split IP datagram is treated like an independent IP packet and contains a complete IP packet header. The Fragment ID field in the IP packet header can be used to identify all fragments of an IP datagram and to allocate them to their original datagram. However, the Fragment ID field alone is not a unique key to identify fragments arriving from different computers. For this reason, the following packet header fields are used additionally sender address, destination address, and protocol.

All the fragments of a datagram can take different paths to travel to the destination computer, and they may be fragmented more than once along these paths. The position of a fragment's data within the original IP datagram is marked by the Fragment Offset field. All fragments, except the last one, have the *MF (More Fragments)* bit set, which means that more fragments are to follow. Figure 14–6 shows the example of an IP datagram that has to be fragmented several times.

We will describe below how fragmenting and reassembling of IP datagrams is implemented in the Linux kernel. Remember that IP packets can be fragmented in each IP node along the path to the destination (router or end system), but can be reassembled only in the destination computer.

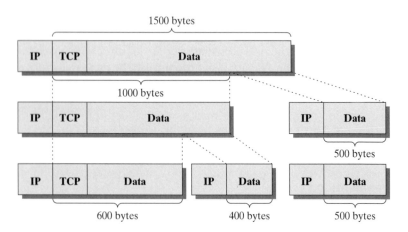

FIGURE 14–6
Fragmenting an IP datagram.

Fragmenting Large IP Datagrams

`ip_fragment()`	**net/ipv4/ip_output.c**

ip_fragment(skb, output) is responsible for fragmenting an IP datagram into smaller IP packets, if the IP datagram is too big to be transmitted over the network device. The size for the new—smaller—packets is selected so that they do not exceed the maximum frame length of the transmission medium.

First, the maximum packet size is computed, and then IP fragments are created in a while loop until the datagram has been completely divided into smaller packets. Next, alloc_skb() is used to create a new socket buffer for each new fragment. Initially, the IP packet header is copied from the original packet to the new one, and then the payload to be transported in this fragment is copied to the fragment. It should be mentioned once more that previously fragmented datagrams can be fragmented again in one or more routers later along the path. Subsequently, the new value for the Fragment Offset field has to be set in the new fragment. This field specifies the position of payload in the original IP datagram. Also, the *MF* bit has to be set, unless it is the last fragment. Before the output() function (pointer to the transmit function set in the routing process) can send the packet, the function ip_options_fragment() handles IP options, if present, and ip_send_check() computes the checksum.

Once all fragments have been created, the original packet is released by kfree_skb().

Collecting and Reassembling Packets   Fragmented IP datagrams are reassembled in the end system only. To this end, the function ip_local_deliver() passes all fragmented IP packets to ip_defrag(). The fragments are then managed in the fragment cache, until either all fragments of a datagram have arrived, so that the packet can be delivered to the local machine, or the maximum wait time for the fragments of a datagram (ipfrag_time, ~30 seconds) has expired, which means that the datagram will be discarded. The fragment cache consists of a hash table with ipq structures. Each of these ipq structures represents a fragmented IP datagram. The individual fragments of the datagram are collected in a linked list (fragments). All fragments of a datagram are ordered in the same sequence as they occur in the original packet. (See Figure 14–7.)

The parameters of the ipq structure have the following meaning:

- next and pprev are used to link ipq structures in a hash row. This means that this is a doubly linked list and a linear collision resolution in the hash table.
- The saddr, daddr, id, and protocol elements are keys for the hash function and the allocation of incoming fragments to their IP datagrams.
- last_in stores a flag that specifies whether all fragments have arrived and whether the first and the last fragments of a datagram have arrived.
- fragments is a list of linked socket buffers that stores all incoming fragments in the sequence required later to reassemble the complete datagram.
- len specifies the length of the original IP datagram, and meat specifies the number of bytes already stored in the fragment cache. When meat reaches the value of len, then all fragments of the datagram have arrived, and the fragment can be reassembled.
- lock is used to protect against parallel operations on the ipq data structure.

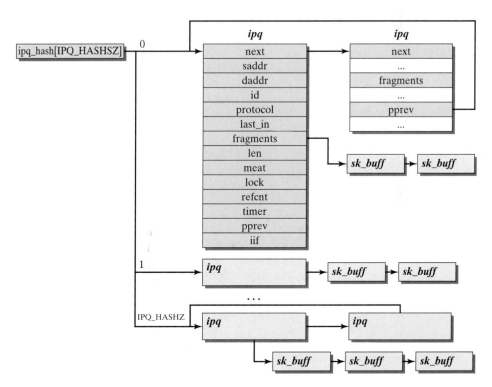

FIGURE 14–7
A fragment cache manages all incoming IP fragments.

- timer is a pointer to a `timer_list` structure. The associated timer restarts when the `IPFRAG_TIME` interval expires, and it checks for whether all fragments have arrived.
- `iif` contains an index to the network device and is used for ICMP replies.

The following functions are used to reassemble fragmented IP datagrams:

`ipq_unlink()`	**net/ipv4/fragment.c**

`ipq_unlink(qp)` removes the `ipq` entry from the fragment cache referenced by the qp pointer. The counter for arrived fragments, `ip_frag_nqueues`, is decremented by 1.

`ipq_frag_destroy()`	**net/ipv4/fragment.c**

`ip_frag_destroy(qp)` releases an `ipq` fragment list. First, `frag_kfree_skb()` releases all socket buffers of individual fragments. Subsequently, `frag_free_queue()` releases the `ipq` structure of the fragment cache.

`ip_evictor()`	**net/ipv4/ip_fragment.c**

`ip_evictor()` is invoked by `ip_defrag()` when fragmented packets use too much memory. Normally, the threshold for maximum memory in the fragment cache (`sysctl_ipfrag_high_thresh`) is 256 Kbytes. Next, all hash rows of the fragment cache are checked within this function, and entries are deleted. More specifically, `ipq` structures and their socket buffers are deleted until the bottom threshold (normally 192 Kbytes) is reached.

The two threshold values, `ipfrag_high_thresh` and `ipfrag_low_thresh`, and the maximum wait time for fragments, `ipfrag_time`, can be changed from within the proc directory (`/proc/sys/net/ipv4`).

`ip_expire()`	**net/ipv4/ip_fragment.c**

`ip_expire()` is a handling routine for the timer that starts for the fragments of an IP datagram. If this timer expires before all fragments of the packet have arrived, the entry in the fragment cache is deleted. This function does nothing, if all fragments have been received (`COMPLETE`).

If some fragments are still missing, but at least the first one is present, then an ICMP error message of the type (`ICMP_TIME_EXCEEDED/ICMP_EXC_FRAGTIME`) is sent, and then the IP datagram is discarded.

`ip_frag_create()`	**net/ipv4/ip_fragment.c**

`ip_frag_create(hash, iph)` creates a new entry in the fragment cache and uses the parameters from the IP packet header of the fragment that just arrived to initialize this entry. The new entry represents an IP datagram that could not be transmitted fully and had to be fragmented. This entry is created when the first fragment of an

IP datagram arrives and is held in the fragment cache until either the wait time for all fragments (IP_FRAG_TIME) expires or all fragments of that IP datagram have arrived.

ip_find()	net/ipv4/ip_fragment.c

ip_find(iph) searches the fragment cache for the ipq entry for an IP datagram with the iph packet header. To this end, ipqhashfn() is used to compute the hash value of this entry from the sender address, destination address, protocol ID, and fragment IP from the packet header fields. Based on these parameters, different fragmented datagrams can be distinguished, and incoming fragments can be allocated to each datagram. Collisions of several ipq structures with identical hash values are resolved linearly in a doubly linked list. (See Figure 14–7.) If ip_find() cannot find a matching entry for the iph fragment, then a new ipq entry is created in the fragment cache (ip_frag_create()).

ip_frag_queue()	net/ipv4/fragment.c

ip_frag_queue(qp, skb) orders a new fragment, as it arrives, within the queue of fragments for an IP datagram (represented by the ipq structure qp). The function checks first for whether the datagram is complete, which would mean that a new fragment is a duplicate. If this is not the case, the position (offset and end) of the fragment in the original IP datagram is computed from the Fragment Offset parameter in the IP packet header. Subsequently, the MF flag is used to check on whether this is the last fragment of a datagram (LAST_IN is set).

Subsequently, the list of received fragments (pq->fragments) is searched for the correct position, and the socket buffer is placed at this position. The meat parameter in the ipq structure of the datagram is increased by the length corresponding to the fragment just added. As mentioned earlier, the meat parameter specifies the number of bytes received for a fragmented IP datagram.

ip_frag_reasm()	net/ipv4/ip_fragment.c

This function is invoked by ip_defrag(); it reassembles all fragments of a packet (qp->len == qp->meat) arrived and treats them as a single IP datagram. First, a new socket buffer with a headroom of length qp->len is created, and the IP datagram header is initialized. Next, the IP payload of each single fragment is copied to the headroom of the new socket buffer.

ip_defrag()	net/ipv4/ip_fragment.c

The ip_defrag(skb) method is invoked in ip_local_deliver() for each IP fragment. As described in Section 14.2.1, this path of the Internet Protocol is taken only by packets to be delivered to the local machine (i.e., fragmented IP datagrams are reassembled in the destination system).

The first thing here is to check on whether there is sufficient buffer space in the fragment cache for the new fragment. If this is not the case, then ip_evictor() removes entries until the bottom threshold value, `sysctl_ipfrag_low_thresh`, is reached. Subsequently, `ip_find()` searches the fragment cache for the relevant entry. As mentioned earlier, a new `ipq` structure is created as soon as the first fragment of an IP datagram arrives.

Finally, `ip_frag_queue()` adds the new fragment to the list of present fragments. As soon as all fragments of the IP datagram have arrived, which can be checked by `pq->len == pq->meat`, reassembly of the datagram (`ip_frag_reasm()`) can start.

14.2.4 Data of the IP Instance

The primary task of an IP instance (in a router) is to forward IP packets. To this end, several network devices have to be configured for the IP instance. These network devices (*INET devices*), which are to be used by the Internet Protocol, are managed mainly by the functions stored in the file `net/ipv4/devinet.c`. We will call these network devices *IP network devices* in the further course of our discussion.

This section is aimed at briefly introducing the structure of IP network-device management. This point represents the binding member between several functions of the Internet Protocol. For example, the data structures introduced below can be used to manage IP addresses and network devices of the IP instance and active multicast groups or different IP configuration parameters (Packet forwarding permitted?, Accept redirect packets?, etc.).

The data structure `in_device` represents the starting point for IP network device management:

`struct in_device`	include/linux/inetdevice.h

An `in_device` structure is created for each network device that was configured for the Internet Protocol. This structure manages the configuration data for this IP network device. Figure 14–8 shows that the `net_device` structures of IP network devices have an `ip_ptr` parameter each, which references the pertaining `in_device` structure. There is no explicit list for IP network devices. The list is accessed with `dev_base`.

The file `net/ipv4/devinet.c` includes functions to manage IP network devices, including `inetdev_init()` to initialize an IP network device.

The structure and the elements of the `in_device` structure are as follows:

```
struct in_device
{
    struct net_device          *dev;
    atomic_t refcnt;
    rwlock_t lock;
    int dead;
    struct in_ifaddr *ifa_list; /* IP ifaddr chain */
    struct ip_mc_list *mc_list; /* IP multicast filter chain */
    unsigned long mr_v1_seen;
    struct neigh_parms *arp_parms;
    struct ipv4_devconf cnf;
};
```

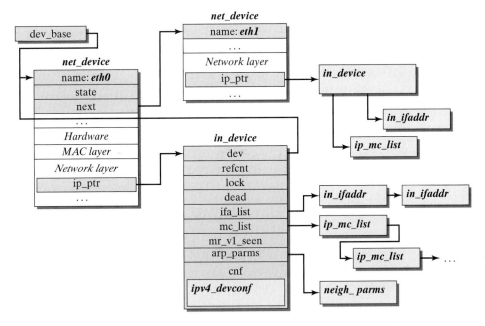

FIGURE 14–8
Data structures to manage IP network devices and their parameters.

- dev points to the net_device structure of the network device configured for the Internet Protocol.

- refcnt stores the number of references to this structure, or the number of instances currently used by this IP network device. The refcnt variable essentially is changed by the functions in_dev_get() and in_dev_put(). (Both are defined in <linux/inetdevice.h>.)

- lock is used to protect against errors caused by parallel manipulation in the in_device structure.

- dead shows whether the IP network device is still valid.

- ifa_list points to a list of in_ifaddr structures, which stores the IP addresses of this IP network device. This is a list, because Linux lets you allocate more than one IP address to a network device (*alias* function).

In addition to the IP address (ifa_address), the in_ifaddr structure stores other parameters (e.g., the subnet mask (ifa_mask), the broadcast address (ifa_address), etc.). The content of the in_ifaddr structure is as follows:

```
struct in_ifaddr
{
    struct in_ifaddr      *ifa_next;
    struct in_device      *ifa_dev;
    u32                   ifa_local;
    u32                   ifa_address;
```

```
        u32                     ifa_mask;
        u32                     ifa_broadcast;
        u32                     ifa_anycast;
        unsigned char           ifa_scope;
        unsigned char           ifa_flags;
        unsigned char           ifa_prefixlen;
        char                    ifa_label[IFNAMSIZ];
};
```

▪ mc_list is a list consisting of ip_mc_list structures. Each element in this list
  stores information for an IP multicast group to which the IP instance is currently
  subscribed, and receives it over the current network device. Section 17.4.1 describes the content of the ip_mc_list structure.

▪ mr_v1_seen is used by IGMP. (See Section 17.3.)

▪ arp_parms points to a structure of the type neigh_parms, which stores the most
  important parameters of the ARP protocol. (See Chapter 15.)

▪ cnf points to an ipv4_devconf structure, which stores important settings for the
  IP instance. ipv4_devconf is described below.

struct ipv4_devconf	include/linux/inetdevice.h

The ipc4_devconf data structure can be used to activate or deactivate various
properties of the IP instance for an IP network device. For this purpose, the proc directory /proc/sys/net/ipv4/conf includes a subdirectory for each IP network device,
from which the properties mentioned below can be set. These properties will then be
described briefly below. Appendix B discusses all proc entries for the Internet Protocol.

```
struct ipv4_devconf
{
        int       accept_redirects;
        int       send_redirects;
        int       secure_redirects;
        int       shared_media;
        int       accept_source_route;
        int       rp_filter;
        int       proxy_arp;
        int       bootp_relay;
        int       log_martians;
        int       forwarding;
        int       mc_forwarding;
        int       tag;
        int       arp_filter;
        void      *sysctl;
};
```

▪ accept_redirects accepts ICMP redirect packets.

▪ send_redirects enables the transmission of ICMP redirect packets.

- secure_redirects accepts ICMP redirect messages.
- accept_source_route accepts Source Route packets.
- rp_filter disables the sender IP address check.
- proxy_arp supports an ARP proxy.
- log_martians enables or disables the logging of "strange" addresses ("Martians"— see Section 16.2.2).
- forwarding enables this network device to forward packets.
- mc_forwarding enables multicast routing or forwarding over this IP network device.

14.2.5 Auxiliary Functions for the Internet Protocol

The functions introduced in the previous sections operate mainly in the data path of the Internet Protocol: They process incoming IP packets. In addition to these functions, there are other things to be done in the Internet Protocol that do not directly relate to socket buffers or IP packets. These auxiliary functions are introduced below.

Managing Transport Protocols   The Internet Protocol operates on the network layer and offers an unreliable datagram service for the transport layer. In general, the TCP and UDP protocols are used in the transport layer. However, a layer-based architectural model should also allow us to use our own protocols. The Linux network architecture allows you to do that. You can register and use new protocols on top of the IP layer. In connection with kernel modules, this represents a flexible and highly dynamic property of the Linux network architecture.

The Linux kernel includes two functions, inet_add_protocol() and inet_del_protocol(), which will be described below, to manage transport-layer protocols. Appendix F includes an example for a rudimentary transport protocol, which does nothing but output the length of incoming transport-layer PDUs.

inet_add_protocol()	net/ipv4/protocol.c

All protocols arranged immediately on top of the Internet Protocol are managed in a hash table, inet_protos. inet_add_protocol(prot) registers a new protocol for the transport layer and adds it to the inet_protos hash table. The required protocol information is passed in the prot structure of the type inet_protocol (as shown in Figure 14–5):

- handler() is a function pointer to the entry function of the transport protocol (handling routine), for example the tcp_v4_rcv() for TCP. The parameters passed here include the socket buffer and the length of the transport-layer PDU. Appendix F includes an example of a very simple transport protocol. All it does is output the length of a PDU.
- err_handler() is a handling routine for error cases. It is invoked only once in the current implementation, in the method icmp_unreach().

- next is used to link `inet_protocol` structures in a hash table.

- id is the protocol identifier of the registered protocol. In the future, if an IP packet with this identifier in the protocol field of the IP packet header arrives, then it is passed to the `handler()` handling routine. If several protocols with the same id are registered, then a copy of the socket buffer is passed to each of these protocols.

- The copy bit specifies whether another protocol is registered with the same protocol ID. If a protocol with the same protocol ID is already registered when you register a new protocol, then the new protocol is also added to the hash table, and the copy bit of all previous protocols with the same ID is set to one. In this case, all protocols with the same ID get a copy of the packet.

- data points to private data of the protocol, if present. However, it is not used by any of the implemented protocols (TCP, UDP, ICMP, and IGMP).

- name stores the name of the protocol in a string.

The Linux kernel currently implements four protocols on the transport layer, where only TCP and UDP are actually true transport protocols. Though ICMP and IGMP also use IP to exchange data, they are normally thought of as belonging to the network layer.

`inet_del_protocol()`	**net/ipv4/protocol.c**

`inet_del_protocol(prot)` removes the protocol, together with the passed pointer to an `inet_protocol` structure, from the hash table `inet_protos`. If there is a second protocol with the same protocol ID, then the **copy** bit of this protocol is checked and deleted, if applicable.

Useful Functions

`in_ntoa()`	**net/ipv4/utils.c**

`in_ntoa(in)` converts the IP address into the dotted decimal form, which is easier to read for humans (i.e., the 32-bit address 0x810D2A75 is converted into the string 129.13.42.117).

`in_aton()`	**net/ipv4/utils.c**

`in_aton(str)` converts the string `str` into a 32-bit IP address.

14.3   IP OPTIONS

When a packet is sent to the IP layer, then it normally includes all required information in the packet's protocol header. However, there could be times when packets require additional information in the protocol header—for example, for diagnostics purposes, or if a packet's path across the Internet is specified before it is sent. For these purposes, an Option field with variable length can be added to each IP packet header. All guidelines for these IP options are described in [Post81c].

14.3.1   Standardized IP Packet Options

Figure 14–9 shows that the IP packet options are appended to the end of an IP header. The length of the Option field is variable, and the end of a packet header has to be aligned to a 32-bit boundary, so an additional *padding field* of the appropriate length is added (and set to 0 by default). In this case, "variable" also means that the packet options can be left out, if they are not required. The Option field can take one or several packet options, where an option can be given in either of two formats:

- One single byte describes only the option type. The length of these options is always exactly one byte.
- The first byte includes the option type, and the second byte contains the length of this packet option. The following bytes include the actual data of that option.

The byte stating the length of the packet option in the second case includes merely the number of data bytes. The first two bytes are not counted. The option type in the first byte is composed as follows:

Copy Flag	Option Class	Option Number

The (1-bit) *copy flag* is required for packet fragmentation. If a packet has to be fragmented, then this bit states whether this packet option has to appear in all fragments or may be set in the first fragment only.

The *option class* is represented by 2 bits. The (5-bit) *option number* shows the length of a packet option implicitly (i.e., we can see whether the next byte also belongs to this packet option or already belongs to the next packet option). Table 14–1 lists all IP packet options defined in RFC 791, including their lengths and their defined option numbers and option classes. There are four option classes in total, but only two are currently used. Option class 0 includes packet options for control and management; option class 2 includes debugging and measurement options. The option classes 1 and 3 are reserved for future IP packet-option classes.

Version	IHL	TOS		Total Length	
Identification			Flags	Fragment Offset	
TTL		Protocol	Header Checksum		
Source Address					
Destination Address					
Options (optional)				Padding	
Data					

FIGURE 14–9
The IP packet header.

TABLE 14–1   Defined IP packet options.

Class	Number	Length	Name
0	0	–	End of Option List
0	1	–	No Operation
0	2	11	Security
0	3	var	Loose Source Routing
0	9	var	Strict Source Routing
0	7	var	Record Route
0	8	4	Stream ID
2	4	var	Internet Timestamp

We will discuss each of these IP packet options in the following sections.

End of Option List
Bit sequence:

```
?0000000
```

This packet option marks the end of a series of options; it is appended to the last packet option and must never be between any other pair of options. The *End-of-Option-List* packet option is superfluous if the end of the option list is aligned at a 32-bit boundary. (See Figure 14–9.) The question mark at the beginning of this bit sequence corresponds to the *copy flag*, which was described above. If fragmentation is necessary, then this option can be copied, inserted, or deleted, depending on the number of packet options in the fragments of an IP datagram. It then has to be inserted into a fragment—for example, if only a part of the original options has to be copied, and the end of the new option list no longer matches the 32-bit boundary.

No Operation
Bit sequence:

```
?0000001
```

No Operation can be between any two packet options, for example to let the second option begin at a 32-bit boundary. If fragmentation is necessary, then this option can be copied, inserted or deleted. Like the *End-of-Option List* option, this option can always be inserted into a fragment, if only some of the original options are copied and if a packet option must begin at a 32-bit boundary.

Security
Bit sequence:

10000010	00001011	Security
Compartments		Restrictions
Transmission Control Code		

The *Security* option is used primarily in military networks; it comprises a total of 11 bytes. The *Security* option allows end systems to send security parameters or define own (controllable) groups of communication partners, which want to exchange IP packets "in isolation" from all other traffic. The two-byte *Security* field can be used to state 16 security levels for an IP packet; of these, the original RFC 791 defines eight levels, including *Unclassified*, *Confidential*, *Restricted*, *Secret* or *Top Secret*. The other security levels are reserved for future use. As the One in the first bit (corresponding to the *Copy Flag*) of this packet option already states, this packet option has to be set in each fragment, if IP packets are fragmented.

These fields are primarily specified by the *Defense Intelligence Agency*. For this reason, the current implementation in Linux does not support the *Security* option.

Loose Source Routing
Bit sequence:

| 10000011 | Length | Pointer | Route Data |

This option is used to specify all routers an IP packet has to visit on its way across the network. In addition, it accepts data about the packet's path. The third byte includes a pointer to the address of the next router that the packet has to pass. This pointer is relative to this option—the smallest possible value is four. If the pointer points to a byte not belonging to this option according to the length byte, then the packet can be sent over an arbitrary path to the actual destination address. In contrast, if the packet has reached the address specified in the destination address field, yet the pointer still points to another valid address, then the destination address field is overwritten with this address. The pointer is incremented by the length of an IP address, 4 bytes. The consequence of this replacement strategy is that the protocol header of the IP packet maintains a constant length all the time. In contrast to the *Record Route* packet option, addresses are defined exclusively by the sender; no addresses are entered by intermediate systems.

If the packet has to be fragmented, then this packet option has to be copied to each packet fragment, because the fragments are forwarded independently of one another, which means that they can reach the receiver over different paths across the Internet.

Strict Source Routing
Bit sequence:

| 10001001 | Length | Pointer | Route Data |

The *Strict Source Routing* option differs in only one point from the *Loose Source Routing* option: The packet may pass exactly those routers specified in the Route Data list. If a packet arrives in a router not explicitly present in this list, then an ICMP message has to be generated and returned to the sender. Section 14.4 describes the *Internet Control Message Protocol* (ICMP).

As with the previous option, if fragmentation is required, then the Strict Source Routing option has to be copied in each single fragment, which means that One is in the first position of this option.

Record Route
Bit sequence:

00000111	Length	Pointer	Route Data

The *Record Route* option can be used to register the addresses of all intermediate systems an IP packet will pass on its way to the destination. The third byte includes a pointer to the field that is to accept the next address. The length of this option should never change; the sender specifies twice the available space, which is initially filled with zeros. These zeros are not treated as an *End of Option List*, because the length byte, Length, states the option's length. Each Internet node adds its address in a field specially provided for this purpose and increases the pointer by four [bytes] (corresponding to the length of an IP address). If no more space is available, then the IP packet is forwarded without storing the address. In this case, an ICMP message can be returned to the sender.

In contrast to the two previous packet options (i.e., *Loose Source Routing* and *Strict Source Routing*), this option appears only in the first fragment, if an IP packet has to be fragmented.

Stream Identifier
Bit sequence:

10001000	00000010	Stream ID

This option enables the transport of *SATNET Stream Identifiers* across the Internet. The *Stream Identifier* packet option is always 4 bytes long and has to be copied to all fragments, if fragmentation is used. However, this option currently has no practical use, and we list it here only for the sake of completeness.

Internet Timestamp
Bit sequence:

01000100	Length	Pointer	Counter	Flag
Address				
Timestamp				

The original RFC 791 includes the *Internet Timestamp* option as the only packet option of class 2 (i.e., debugging or measurement options). This option can be used to store time stamps of selected or all network nodes. A 4-bit flag determines the data to be stored here, and it can take either of the following values:

- 0—The option stores time stamps only.
- 1—The option stores all time stamps and addresses.
- 2—A router completes its timestamp only if its address is listed in this option.

Notice that the size of the *Internet Timestamp* option does not change, because the sender specifies it previously in the length field. For this reason, there is an additional (4-bit) `Counter` field, which includes the number of all routers for the time stamps of which there was no more space in the data field. The maximum length of this option is 40 bytes. The third byte points to the next four or eight bytes to be filled with an entry.

If fragmentation is required, this option appears in the first fragment only, and so the *Copy Flag* is set to 0.

14.3.2 Configuration

User Access   Each Linux user can use the `traceroute` command to track an IP packet on its way across the Internet to the destination node. This might suggest that the *Record Route* IP packet option is used in this case. Actually, this is not so; the `traceroute` command uses another method, for several reasons:

- Formerly, not all routers supported the *Record Route* packet option, which means that they wouldn't have been available for use.
- Record Route is normally intended for one-way use only—the receiver has to return an echo of the IP packet it received to the sender. This means that the recorded addresses would have to be duplicated.
- However, the main reason is lack of space: A maximum of nine IP addresses fits into the address list of the Option field. Formerly, this might have been sufficient, but today the average number of intermediate systems for a connection across the Internet is much higher.

For these reasons, `traceroute` uses the *Internet Control Message Protocol* (ICMP; see Section 14.4) and the *Time-to-Live* (TTL) field of the IP header, which stores the remaining lifetime of the packet. It sends consecutive ICMP packets with the same destination address and increments the value in the TTL field at each step. The first packet gets a lifetime of one (i.e., the first Internet node returns an ICMP message to the sender as soon as it receives the packet). The sender receives an ICMP message also from each of the next receivers, so that it can follow the path to the destination address. However, a trick has to be used at the destination address, because the receiver looks at the lifetime only if the packet is not delivered locally. For this purpose, the UDP port number is set to a meaningless value to cause the receiver to return the ICMP message *Port Unreachable*.

Notice, however, that this method works only because all IP packets from a sender normally take the same path through the Internet to reach the receiver in most cases. It was actually intended to let a user run the `traceroute` command to access the packet option *Strict Source Routing* or *Loose Source Routing*. When the first version of `traceroute` included this option, many system administrators found that it results in an excessive load on most routers. Consequently, to use these packet options today, we need a corresponding patch.

The following example uses the *Loose Source Routing* option:

```
# traceroute -g 129.13.92.254 rzstud1.rz.uni-karlsruhe.de
traceroute to rzstud1.rz.uni-karlsruhe.de (129.13.197.1), 30 hops max,
40 byte packets
1 rzasc01.rz.uni-karlsruhe.de (129.13.92.1) 20 ms 20 ms 20 ms
2 r-ascend-netz.rz.uni-karlsruhe.de (129.13.92.254) 20 ms 20 ms 20 ms
3 rzstud1.rz.uni-karlsruhe.de (129.13.197.1) 213 ms 22 ms 24 ms}
```

Because the traceroute command, which is normally installed in Linux, does not let a user access the IP packet options, another way to use it would be the ping command. ping is intended to verify that a host is reachable. For this purpose, it continually sends ICMP requests to the destination computer and expects a reply in the form of an ICMP message. Today, there are still ping implementations that allow you to use the packet options *Source Routing* and *Internet Timestamp*. For the same reasons as with traceroute, the *Internet Timestamp* option was removed from most implementations, which means that only the *Record Route* option remained. The following example shows how you can use ping with the *Record Route* packet option set. The route is output after the first request.

```
# ping -R rzstud1.rz.uni-karlsruhe.de
PING rzstud1.rz.uni-karlsruhe.de (129.13.197.1): 56 data bytes
64 bytes from 129.13.197.1: icmp_seq=0 ttl=253 time=235.977 ms
RR: isdn216-10.rz.uni-karlsruhe.de (129.13.216.10)
     rzasc01.rz.uni-karlsruhe.de (129.13.92.1)
     129.13.197.62
     rzstud1.rz.uni-karlsruhe.de (129.13.197.1)
     r-ascend-netz.rz.uni-karlsruhe.de (129.13.92.254)
     rzasc01.rz.uni-karlsruhe.de (129.13.92.1)
     isdn216-10.rz.uni-karlsruhe.de (129.13.216.10)
64 bytes from 129.13.197.1: icmp_seq=1 ttl=253 time=47.171 ms (same route)
64 bytes from 129.13.197.1: icmp_seq=2 ttl=253 time=48.728 ms (same route)
--- rzstud1.rz.uni-karlsruhe.de ping statistics ---
9 packets transmitted, 9 packets received, 0% packet loss
round-trip min/avg/max = 45.100/70.545/235.977 ms
```

If a user at the local computer has root rights, then the *verbose mode* of tcpdump lets the user additionally view the packet options of all IP packets. tcpdump monitors the data traffic at a network adapter. The following example uses tcpdump in verbose mode to monitor the previous ping example.

```
# tcpdump -v
User level filter, protocol ALL, datagram packet socket
tcpdump: listening on ippp0
15:37:56.025267 isdn216-10.rz.uni-karlsruhe.de > rzstud1.rz.uni-karlsruhe.de:
icmp: echo request (ttl 64, id 1284, optlen=40 RR{isdn216-10.rz.uni-
```

```
karlsruhe.de#0.0.0.0 0.0.0.0 0.0.0.0 0.0.0.0 0.0.0.0 0.0.0.0 0.0.0.0 0.0.0.0}
EOL)
15:37:56.261172 rzstud1.rz.uni-karlsruhe.de > isdn216-10.rz.uni-karlsruhe.de:
icmp: echo reply (ttl 253, id 28562, optlen=40 RR{isdn216-10.rz.uni-
karlsruhe.de rzasc01.rz.uni-karlsruhe.de 129.13.197.62 rzstud1.rz.uni-
karlsruhe.de r-ascend-netz.rz.uni-karlsruhe.de rzasc01.rz.uni-karlsruhe.de#
0.0.0.0 0.0.0.0 0.0.0.0} EOL)
```

Programming Access   We will use the ping program once more in another example
to show you how IP packet options can be accessed during programming. This example
uses Version 1.38. When ping starts, the first thing is to check the parameters passed. If
they include -R, then the *Echo Request* packet has to include the *Record Route* IP option. For this purpose, ping uses the setsockopt() function to inform an existing
socket about packet options.

The following example shows you how this function is invoked from within the
source code of ping:

```
if (setsockopt (s, IPPROTO_IP, IP_OPTIONS, rspace, sizeof (rspace)) < 0)
        {
             perror (_("ping: record route"));
             exit(1);
        }
```

The specified options will then be set in each packet sent over this socket in the
future. The IPPROTO_IP parameter means that the packet option to be set is an IP option. This does not necessarily mean that it is an IP option in the true sense. It could be
present in another position within the IP header (e.g., IP_TTL also belongs to the
IPPROTO_IP group). From the programming perspective, we always have to assume
that the current kernel implementation does not support the desired IP option. In this
case, setsockopt() returns the value 1 and outputs an error message. Subsequently,
an arbitrary number of packets with the packet option set are sent over this socket.

Incoming ICMP packets sent by ping are checked for their options as follows:
An option pointer that points to the first Option field in the protocol header is computed. The first option is processed, and the option pointer is incremented so that it
points to the next option. For the *Record Route* packet option, the pointer has to point
to a byte that includes the number "7". ping doesn't actually have to take care of this
value; like all other option-specific constants, it is defined in <linux/ip.h>:

```
#define IPOPT_END (0 |IPOPT_CONTROL)
#define IPOPT_NOOP (1 |IPOPT_CONTROL)
#define IPOPT_SEC (2 |IPOPT_CONTROL|IPOPT_COPY)
#define IPOPT_LSRR (3 |IPOPT_CONTROL|IPOPT_COPY)
#define IPOPT_TIMESTAMP (4 |IPOPT_MEASUREMENT)
#define IPOPT_RR (7 |IPOPT_CONTROL)
#define IPOPT_SID (8 |IPOPT_CONTROL|IPOPT_COPY)
#define IPOPT_SSRR (9 |IPOPT_CONTROL|IPOPT_COPY)
#define IPOPT_RA (20|IPOPT_CONTROL|IPOPT_COPY)
```

If one of these packet options is found, then it is output.

14.3.3 The `ip_options` Class in the Linux Kernel

This section describes all functions of the `ip_options` class implemented in the Linux kernel. If options are passed to or from functions, then this is normally done by use of the `ip_options` data type. This type is defined in `<linux/ip.h>` and includes the variables, pointers, and constants required for all packet options.

`ip_options_build()`	net/ipv4/ip_options.c

This function takes the information about IP options from the socket object and creates the options part in the IP header.

The parameters passed here include a socket buffer, the packet options, the packet destination address, the routing table, and the `is_frag` variables. The socket buffer includes a datagram with a protocol header that is not yet complete. The passed packet options are copied to the end of the protocol header. If the option *Strict Source Routing* exists, then the destination address of the packet is written to the address list of the packet option. If the packet is not a fragment, and if the *Internet Timestamp* or *Record Route* option exists, then the required data is inserted into the corresponding lists. If the packet is a fragment and one of the two options exists, then these options are replaced by *No Operation*.

`ip_options_echo()`	net/ipv4/ip_options.c

The `ip_options_echo()` routine takes the options from an IP packet received and uses them to create an echo packet (i.e., a reply to the incoming message). This function is normally used to send a reply when packets with IP options have been received—for example, to invert a *Strict Source Routing* option. The parameters passed here are a socket buffer and the destination options.

`ip_options_fragment()`	net/ipv4/ip_options.c

This function takes the fragment that was passed as socket buffer and overwrites all packet options with the *No Operation* option, with the *Copy Flag* not set. As described in Section 14.3.1, this flag is not set for the *Internet Timestamp* and *Record Route* options. The replacement by *No Operation* has the advantage that the length of the protocol header does not change.

`ip_options_compile()`	net/ipv4/ip_options.c

This function compiles the Option field at the end of the IP header. `ip_options_build()` uses data structures readily prepared for packet options, but `ip_options_compile()` has to compile all options. The parameters passed here include the packet options and the socket buffer. This function works option by option until it reaches an *End-of-Option List* or the end of the protocol header. Any *No Operation* in the option list is skipped. If an error occurs in this procedure, then an ICMP message is returned to the sender.

`ip_options_undo()`	**net/ipv4/ip_options.c**

It can be necessary to delete the last entries in the packet options *Source Routing, Record Route*, and *Internet Timestamp*. The function `ip_options_undo()` is responsible for this task. This function can follow once the `ip_options_echo()` was invoked, for example. If an *Echo Request* with the *Record Route* option is sent to the local computer, then the function `ip_options_echo()` duplicates the options set in the incoming packet. These packet options are then used to return an *Echo Reply* packet. Unless the `ip_options_undo()` function is invoked, the IP option would include two entries for the local computer. The packet options represent the only parameter passed here.

`ip_options_get()`	**net/ipv4/ip_options.c**

This function checks on whether the IP options can be accessed when `setsockopt()` is invoked. If so, then it returns 0; otherwise, it returns a negative error code (error codes are defined in the file `<include/asm/errno.h>`).

`ip_forward_options()`	**net/ipv4/ip_options.c**

If necessary, this function adds all information required about the local IP node to a packet that has to be forwarded. This information is added by the packet options *Record Route, Strict Source Route*, and *Internet Timestamp*. The only parameter passed here is the appropriate socket buffer.

`ip_options_rcv_srr()`	**net/ipv4/ip_options.c**

This function checks the IP options *Loose Source Routing* and *Strict Source Routing* in an incoming packet. For example, if the destination address in the protocol header is the local address, and if the address list has not yet been fully visited, the packet may not be delivered locally. As with the previous function, the socket buffer is the only parameter passed here.

14.3.4   IP Options in the IP Layer

Incoming Packets   There are several ways an IP packet can move across the IP layer. It can enter either from the lower or from the higher layers (i.e., from the local Internet module). Depending on whether it is intended for the local computer, the packet is passed to the next higher or next lower layer. Figure 14–10 shows this relation and the position within the packet-handling process where functions are invoked to handle IP options in the Linux kernel.

If an IP packet enters the IP layer from a lower layer, then `ip_rcv()` is the first function invoked. The packet is passed as socket buffer, and it first has to pass the *netfilters*. Netfilters have the functionality of a firewall and can do address translations. To translate addresses, `NK_HOOK()` with the `ip_rcv_finish()` parameter is invoked. Chapter 19 describes how netfilters are handled and implemented. After this process, `ip_rcv_finish()` is the function executed next. The only parameter passed to this function is the socket buffer. It finds out the packet's path and checks its protocol

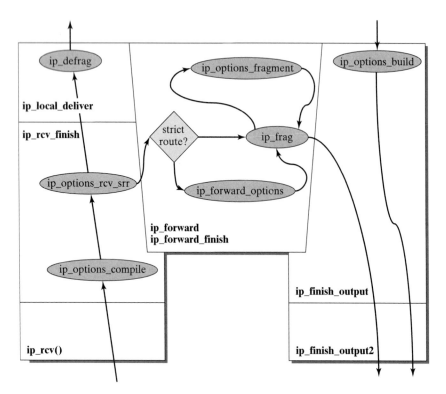

FIGURE 14–10
IP Options in the IP layer.

header. If the header length is greater than five (i.e., more than 5 * 32 bits) then the packet includes an option field that causes the function ip_options_compile() to be invoked. The packet options are separated and stored in the opt data structure. Normally, Boolean variables (e.g., opt->is_strictroute) are set at this point. Subsequently, the opt->srr pointer has to be tested. If this pointer is set to one, then the packet option *Loose Source Routing* or *Strict Source Routing* is specified, which means that the function ip_options_rcv_srr() has to be invoked.

The return value of the ip_rcv_finish() function is a pointer that points to either ip_local_deliver() or ip_forward(), depending on whether the packet has to be delivered locally or forwarded.

Local Packet Delivery   The function ip_local_deliver() is invoked if an IP packet has to be delivered to the local computer. This packet could be a fragment of a larger IP datagram, which has to be reassembled with the other fragments. This means that several things have to be checked—for example, whether all fragments have arrived, which is checked by the function ip_defrag(). Once all fragments have arrived, all options have to be removed from the first fragment to reassemble the fragments into the original datagram. The first fragment always includes all options that were copied when the datagram was fragmented. Next, the packet traverses the *netfilters* once more. The function ip_local_deliver_finish() completes a local packet delivery in the IP layer.

Forwarding Packets   The function `ip_forward()` is invoked in the event that an IP packet has to be forwarded. (See the center part of Figure 14–10.) The packet is checked again, including a test for the *Strict Source Routing* option. If this option exists, and the local address is not in the option field, then an ICMP message is returned to inform the sender accordingly. In this case, neither *Strict Source Routing* nor *Loose Source Routing* may be specified in the option field to ensure that an *ICMP Redirect* message can be returned to the sender.

A backup copy of the IP packet (including all packet options) has to be created, because the packet could be changed in the further course. The value of the TTL variable is decremented by one. If the packet is too big and the *Don't-Fragment* bit is set in the IP packet header, then the complete packet is discarded. At the end, the *netfilter* is called again, but this time with the `ip_forward_finish()` parameter.

The function `ip_forward_finish()` checks the length of each IP packet options. If the length is not null, then the function `ip_forward_options()` handles the *Record Route* and *Source Routing* options, and `ip_send()` is invoked in either case. If the packet is too big and has to be fragmented, then `ip_send()` invokes the `ip_fragment()` function. Depending on whether the *Copy Flag* is set, only some of the packet options or only the first fragment have to be copied to all fragments. This function is extremely space- and time-saving. It also means that `ip_options_fragment()` is invoked only provided that the content of the socket buffer is the first or only fragment.

The next function is `ip_finish_output()`, which completes the packet-forwarding process.

Handling Packets Created Locally   A packet created locally can take either of two paths across the IP layer:

- The function `ip_build_and_send_pkt()` is invoked. Though the passed socket buffer contains a datagram, it doesn't have a protocol header yet. In this case, packet options are passed as parameters, separately from the payload, and all pointers in the header structure are set. Depending on whether there are options, the header length, which was previously set to "5" [bytes], is corrected, and the function `ip_options_build()` is invoked, passing the socket buffer, the packet options, the destination address, and the routing table. Next, `ip_send_check()` verifies the checksum in the packet header, before the parameter `output_maybe_reroute()` invokes the *netfilters*. The IP options play no further role on the remaining path as the packet travels through the IP layer. At the end, the packet is passed to the lower layers or ARP (*Address Resolution Protocol*—see Chapter 15).

- The higher layers pass the IP packet as parameter of the function `ip_queue_xmit()` to the IP layer. Notice that the packet options are not directly passed as parameters to the function; `ip_queue_xmit()` can use a pointer referring to the socket to access them. The first step has to decide where the packet has to be sent to. If the *Source Routing* option is set, then the destination address of the packet is determined by the address specified next. This requires a check for whether the option `is_strictroute()` exists and for whether the destination address is unequal to the router registered in the local routing table. In this case, the IP packet cannot be transmitted. If the route can be determined without problem, then the next step creates the remaining protocol header, as in the first way. The packet leaves the IP layer on the same path.

14.4   INTERNET CONTROL MESSAGE PROTOCOL (ICMP)

The *Internet Control Message Protocol* (*ICMP*) is the error-report mechanism for the IP layer, which also resides in the network layer. Though ICMP is based on IP, it doesn't make IP more reliable. Packets can be lost despite the use of ICMP, and IP or ICMP won't notice that packets are lost. The only purposes of this error-report mechanism are to report errors to other computers and to respond to such reports. It is mandatory for each IP implementation to implement ICMP. The ICMP implementation is defined in the following RFC documents:

- *RFC 792* [Post81b]: This is the basic definition, describing the packet types and their uses.
- *RFC 1122* [Brad89]: Definition of the requirements on terminal equipment (hosts) connected to the Internet.
- *RFC 1812* [Bake95]: This document describes the requirements for switching computers (routers) in the Internet.

However, RFC specifications often leave much room for flexible implementation. For some functions, it is even optional whether you implement them. For this reason, ICMP implementations and even configurations of the same implementation can differ considerably.

The most popular application of ICMP is error detection or error diagnostics. In more than ninety percent of all cases, the first information transmitted by a newly installed network adapter over an IP network will probably be that of the `ping` command, which is fully based on ICMP. This allows you to check the reachability of other computers easily and without noticeable load on the network. This procedure is often done in automated form (e.g., to monitor servers). Beyond simply checking the reachability of computers, the set of different error messages allow a network administrator (or a network-analysis tool) to obtain a detailed overview of the internal state of an IP network. For example, poorly selected local routing tables or wrongly set transmit options in individual computers can be detected. And finally, it is possible to use ICMP to synchronize computer clocks within a network, in addition to other—partly outdated—functions, which will be briefly discussed in this section.

14.4.1   Functional Principle of ICMP

ICMP sends and receives special IP packets representing error or information messages. Error messages occur whenever IP packets have not reached their destinations. All other cases create information messages, which can additionally include a request for reply. Notice that the ICMP functionality becomes active within the network implementation of the Linux kernel only provided that a problem situation occurs during another data traffic or when ICMP packets arrive from another computer. As mentioned earlier,

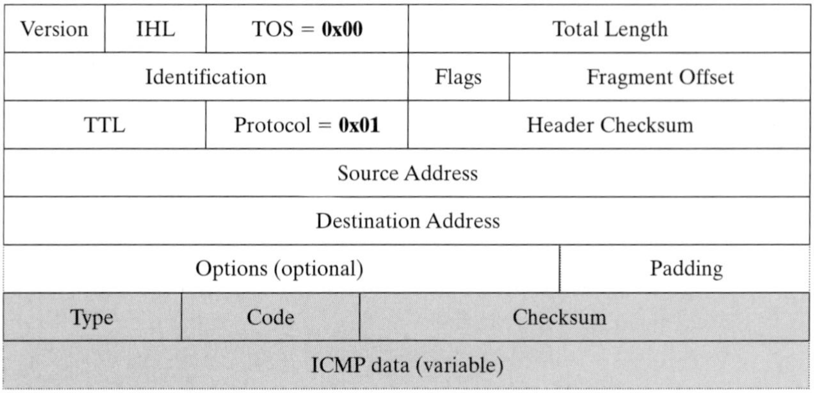

Version	IHL	TOS = **0x00**	Total Length	
Identification			Flags	Fragment Offset
TTL		Protocol = **0x01**	Header Checksum	
Source Address				
Destination Address				
Options (optional)			Padding	
Type		Code	Checksum	
ICMP data (variable)				

FIGURE 14–11
Structure of an IP packet containing an ICMP message.

ICMP transmits messages in IP packets. Figure 14–11 shows the general structure of ICMP messages (gray fields), which are transported in the payload of an IP packet. It is typical for the IP header of a packet containing an ICMP message that the *Type-of-Service* field is set to 0x00, which means that the packet is treated like a regular IP packet without priority. The protocol type in the IP header for ICMP messages is set to 0x01, as specified in RFC 790 [Post81a].

The 8-bit Type field in the ICMP part specifies the type of ICMP message. The Code field specifies the values an ICMP message can take. The original RFC 792 defines a total of eleven messages, but the current Linux implementation supports only some of them. These eleven messages are listed in Table 14–2. The 16-bit checksum extends over all fields starting from the ICMP type (i.e., over the entire part that IP treats as payload).

The following subsections describe the ICMP messages defined in RFC 791.

TABLE 14–2   ICMP packet types defined in RFC 792.

Type	Description
Destination Unreachable	The destination address cannot be reached.
Time Exceeded	A packet was discarded, because its TTL had expired.
Parameter Problem	Unknown or false options.
Source Quench	Informs the sender that IP packets were lost to overload.
Redirect	Enables path optimization.
Echo and Echo Reply	The data sent to the destination address is returned in a reply.
Timestamp and Timestamp Reply	The timestamp sent to the destination address is used to reply with the timestamp of the destination address.
Information Request und Information Reply	Request/reply used to find the network a computer connects to.

Destination Unreachable

The packet for a *Destination Unreachable* message includes the following fields:

Type–0x03	Code	Checksum
unused		
IP Header + 64 Bits of Original Data		

- ▨ Code = 0x00 (*Network Unreachable*): The network of an IP packet's receiver is not reachable. This can happen, for example, if the distance to the receiver's network is set to infinite in the routing table of a router.
- ▨ Code = 0x01 (*Host Unreachable*): The desired destination computer in the specified network cannot be reached.
- ▨ Code = 0x02 (*Protocol Unreachable*): This message can be generated if another protocol listens to the destination port specified in the TCP packet header. The message can be sent both by a router and by an end system.
- ▨ Code = 0x03 (*Port Unreachable*): The port address of the receiver specified in the TCP packet header is not reachable. The end system is "reachable" in this case, too, so both a router and an end system can generate this message.
- ▨ Code = 0x04 (*Fragmentation Needed*): This ICMP packet can be sent if an IP packet has to be fragmented in a router, but the *Don't-Fragment* flag is set in the packet header, so that the packet may not be fragmented. In this case, the router has to discard the IP packet.
- ▨ Code = 0x05 (*Source Route Failed*): If the IP packet option Source Routing is set and an error occurs, then this ICMP message is returned to the sender.

The IP header of the packet that caused the ICMP message, plus the first 64 data bits, are specified in the payload part of the ICMP message *Destination Unreachable*.

Source Quench

The packet of a *Source Quench* message is structured as follows:

Type–0x04	Code–0x00	Checksum
unused		
IP Header + 64 Bits of Original Data		

When the network load is high, it can happen that a router (or the receiver) discards IP packets because of a lack of resources (e.g., memory space or computing capacity). If this happens, then a *Source Quench* message can be transmitted to the sender. RFC 792 specifies that an ICMP implementation can generate such an ICMP message for each discarded packet. The sender should then respond by slowing down its transmission rate until no more *Source Quench* messages arrive. Subsequently, the sender can gradually increase its rate.

Instead of responding to discarded packets, routers, or end systems can send ICMP messages of the *Source Quench* type before they reach their capacity limits, to prevent the consequences of lost packets.

The only value defined for the Code field of a *Source Quench* message is 0x00. The payload part includes the IP header of the triggering IP packet and the first 64 bits of that packet's payload.

Redirect

The packet of a *Redirect* message is structured as follows:

Type–0x05	Code	Checksum
Router IP Address		
IP Header + 64 Bits of Original Data		

This ICMP message type is designed to optimize routing through the Internet. Assume that a router, R1, receives an IP packet of a sending end system, S, with receiver E. Based on a corresponding entry in the routing table of R1, this packet is forwarded to router R2. However, if R2 and S are in the same network (which can be determined based on the sender address), this route can be optimized by sending packets from S to receiver E directly to router R2 over R1, without detour. In this case, router R2 would send a *Redirect* message to end system S to announce that packets to receiver E will be sent directly to R2 in the future. Consequently, the field Router IP Address would contain the IP address of R2. The Code field would take either of the following values:

- Code = 0x00: Redirect IP packets that should be sent to the network that connects the receiver of these IP packets.
- Code = 0x01: Redirect all IP packets that should be sent to the specified receiver.
- Code = 0x02: Redirect all IP packets that should be sent to the receiver's network and have the same value in the TOS field as the IP packet that triggers the ICMP message.
- Code = 0x03: Redirect all IP packets that have the same receiver and the same TOS field as the IP packet that triggers the ICMP message.

Notice that no *Redirect* message is sent if the *Source Route* option is set in the IP packet options, even if there would be a shorter path to the receiver. The last field specifies the IP header and the first 64 data bits of the initiating packet.

Echo and Echo Reply

The packet of an *Echo* or *Echo Reply* message is structured as follows:

Type	Code–0x00	Checksum
Identifier		Sequence Number
Data . . .		

Echo and *Echo Reply* messages are normally used to verify the existence of an end system or intermediate system. To this end, an *Echo* message is sent to the desired system. The ICMP implementation in the receiver has to respond to this *Echo* request by sending an *Echo Reply* message. *Echo* and *Echo Reply* messages differ only in the Type field: 0x08 specifies an *Echo* message and 0x00 specifies an *Echo Reply* message. The Code value has to be set to 0x00 for both types. RFC 792 does not define explicit values for the other fields (i.e., Identifier, Sequence Number, and Data); therefore, the application can set these fields arbitrarily. The only thing the ICMP implementation has to ensure is that these three fields are copied from an *Echo* message to the *Echo Reply* message. The Data field can have an arbitrary length. For example, an ICMP application could use session numbers for the Identifier field and increment the sequence number for each *Echo* message it sends.

Time Exceeded

The packet of a *Time Exceeded* message is structured as follows:

Type–0x0B	Code	Checksum
unused		
IP Header + 64 Bits of Original Data		

An ICMP message of the type *Time Exceeded* is generated and returned to the sender if the lifetime of the IP packet has expired (i.e., its TTL value is 0) and the packet was discarded. There could occur either of the following two cases:

- Code = 0x00: A router sends this message if it discarded a packet because its TTL had expired.
- Code = 0x01: An end system sends a message with this code if it was unable to reassemble a fragmented IP message correctly within a certain time, because fragments were missing.

As in the *Destination Unreachable* message, the payload part in the *Time Exceeded* message includes the IP header of the packet that caused the ICMP message, plus the first 64 data bits from that packet.

Parameter Problem

The packet of a *Parameter Problem* message is structured as follows:

Type–0x0C	Code–0x00	Checksum
Pointer	unused	
IP Header + 64 Bits of Original Data		

If an error due to an invalid parameter in the IP header occurs while an IP packet is being handled in an intermediate node or end system, then this IP packet is discarded. For example, this can happen if there is a wrong argument in the IP packet options. In this case, the router or end system can generate an ICMP message of the type *Parameter Problem* and return it to the sender of the discarded IP packet. The Code field has to be set to 0x00 in all cases, which means that the Pointer field shows an error. More specifically, the pointer points to the octet in the original IP packet header where the problem occurred while the packet was being processed. For example, the value Pointer=0x01 means that the version number (i.e., the first field in the IP packet header; see Figure 14–11) is faulty.

The IP packet header of the discarded packet and the first 64 bits of its payload are attached to the ICMP message.

Timestamp and Timestamp Reply

The packet of an *Timestamp* or *Timestamp Reply* message is structured as follows:

Type	Code–0x00	Checksum
Identifier		Sequence Number
Originate Timestamp		
Receive Timestamp		
Transmit Timestamp		

These two ICMP message types are used to poll the current time from an intermediate or end system. The exchange is similar to the two previous message types, *Echo* and *Echo Reply*. The Type field is used to distinguish between *Timestamp* and *Timestamp Reply*: A value of 0x00 specifies a *Timestamp* message, and 0x0E denotes a *Timestamp Reply* message. The exclusive value for the Code field is 0x00. As for *Echo* and *Echo Reply*, the fields Identifier and Sequence Number are required by the sender to be able to allocate a *Timestamp Echo* message to a *Timestamp* message properly.

The payload part of these two ICMP messages consists of 32-bit timestamps. A timestamp is the time in milliseconds that has passed since midnight (GMT). The Originate Timestamp field defines the time when the transmitted ICMP message was last "touched" by the sender. Similarly, there is a Receive Timestamp specifying the time that the message arrived in the receiver. Transmit Timestamp stores the time at which the *Timestamp Reply* message was sent.

Information Request and Information Reply

The packet of an *Information Request* or *Information Reply* message is structured as follows:

Type	Code–0x00	Checksum
Identifier		Sequence Number

The way these two ICMP message types operate is similar to the *Echo* and *Echo Request* messages, except that they don't have a payload field. This message pair allows you to additionally identify the network that connects a computer. For this purpose, the value 0.0.0.0 is used as receiver address, which means that all computers in the local area network are addressed. The ICMP modules of these computers react to an *Information Request* by sending an *Information Reply*, where they state the LAN identifier instead of 0.0.0.0.

The Identifier and Sequence Number fields are used to allocate *Information Request* and *Information Reply* pairs, similarly to an *Echo* and *Echo Reply* pair. The Type field is defined as follows:

- Type = 0x0F: The message is an *Information Request*.
- Type = 0x10: The message is an *Information Reply*.

14.4.2 Configuring ICMP

The specified RFCs allow the local system administrator to control the behavior of some ICMP functions. The Linux implementation includes three cases where the sysctl() function can be used to control behavior at runtime:

- *Echo Replies*: The system manager can decide whether *Echo Replies* may be sent at all, for security reasons. This option is activated by default.
- *Echo Replies* to broadcast packets: The system manager can decide whether a reply should be sent to an *Echo Request* packet addressed to all computers in a LAN (i.e., destination address 0.0.0.0). This option is deactivated by default.
- *Monitoring illegal ICMP broadcast replies*: Faulty ICMP messages sent as a response to an IP broadcast can be ignored. (See RFC 1122 [Brad89].) This is not the case by default.

In addition, RFC 1812 [Bake95] specifies that the transmission rate of ICMP messages should be limited and that this limit should be configurable. The transmit function icmp_send() is limited accordingly, but the rate can be set only in the source code (in the xrlim_allow() function, XRLIM_BURST_FACTOR constant), which means that you have to recompile the Linux kernel.

14.4.3 ICMP in the Linux Kernel

The Linux implementation is done mainly in the file net/ipv4/icmp.c and in the associated header file include/linux/icmp.h. Each ICMP message type is defined as a constant with the type fields specified in RFC 792:

```
ICMP_ECHOREPLY = 0
ICMP_DEST_UNREACH = 3
ICMP_SOURCE_QUENCH = 4
ICMP_REDIRECT = 5
ICMP_ECHO = 8
ICMP_TIME_EXCEEDED = 11
ICMP_PARAMETERPROB = 12
ICMP_TIMESTAMP = 13
ICMP_TIMESTAMPREPLY = 14
```

```
ICMP_INFO_REQUEST = 15
ICMP_INFO_REPLY = 16
ICMP_ADDRESS = 17
ICMP_ADDRESSREPLY = 18
```

Almost all IP modules use the ICMP implementation to send ICMP messages.

`icmp_unit()`	**include/linux/icmp.h**

From the local perspective, the ICMP layer is stateless, except for a few internal statistics, but messages exchanged between two computers can include states. The ICMP socket is the only central structure included in the implementation. This socket can be reached exclusively with `root` privileges. This is the reason why, for example, the ping command requires `root` privileges. The initialization function `icmp_unit()` creates this socket.

The statistical information mentioned in the previous section is maintained in the data structure `icmp_statistics`. It includes the number of packets sent and received in total, the number of errors incurred, and the accumulated number of ICMP types.

The current contents from this statistics variable can be output from the pseudo file `/proc/net/snmp`. This file includes the meaning of the individual entries in the form of abbreviated ICMP types with leading "In" or "Out" for each packet and an additional row with values from the statistics array. The following listing is an example to show you what the contents of the `/proc/net/snmp` can look like:

```
> cat /proc/net/snmp
Ip: Forwarding DefaultTTL InReceives InHdrErrors InAddrErrors ForwDatagrams
InUnknownProtos InDiscards InDelivers OutRequests OutDiscards OutNoRoutes
ReasmTimeout ReasmReqds ReasmOKs ReasmFails FragOKs FragFails
FragCreates
Ip: 2 64 900 0 0 0 0 64 963 0 0 0 0 0 0 0 0 0
Icmp: InMsgs InErrors InDestUnreachs InTimeExcds InParmProbs InSrcQuenchs
InRedirects InEchos InEchoReps InTimestamps InTimestampReps InAddrMasks
InAddrMaskReps OutMsgs OutErrors OutDestUnreachs OutTimeExcds
OutParmProbs
OutSrcQuenchs OutRedirects OutEchos OutEchoReps OutTimestamps
OutTimestampReps OutAddrMasks OutAddrMaskReps
Icmp: 35 0 15 0 0 0 0 11 9 0 0 0 0 26 0 15 0 0 0 0 0 0 11 0 0 0 0
Tcp: RtoAlgorithm RtoMin RtoMax MaxConn ActiveOpens PassiveOpens
AttemptFails EstabResets CurrEstab InSegs OutSegs RetransSegs InErrs OutRsts
Tcp: 0 0 0 0 4 0 0 0 0 816 888 0 0 0
Udp: InDatagrams NoPorts InErrors OutDatagrams
Udp: 25 6 0 31
```

Sending ICMP Packets You can send ICMP packets from outside of the ICMP implementation in the Linux kernel—for example, from within the ping program. This case is independent of the functions discussed below and will not be further discussed here.

`icmp_send()`   **include/linux/icmp.h**

Within the Linux kernel, an ICMP message is sent by the function `icmp_send()` in all cases where the message is not a reply to an ICMP message. This function gets all data from an ICMP message as call parameters, which means that it can send any ICMP type. In addition, to generate an ICMP packet correctly, this function is responsible for limiting the transmission rate of ICMP messages (see also the configuration options discussed in Section 14.4.2) and for catching cases where no ICMP messages may be sent. In this respect, two cases are possible:

- If the IP packet that initiated an ICMP message was an ICMP error message, then a reply to this error message could cause an infinite cycle of ICMP messages.
- If an IP packet was fragmented, then an ICMP message is sent for the first fragment only to avoid loading the network unnecessarily with redundant packets.

Table 14–3 shows the cases where Linux kernel modules send ICMP messages.

Handling Incoming ICMP Packets   The central structure used to handle ICMP packets that arrive in an end system or intermediate system is a function pointer array named `icmp_pointers`. This array is responsible for flow control and includes the function handling ICMP type n in position n. The major benefit of this method, compared to using a switch-case instruction to implement the same behavior, is that each function in the array includes context information in the form of statistics variables. These statistics variables are defined in relation to the respective ICMP handling function. This means that this array specifies the auxiliary function used to handle an ICMP message. These auxiliary functions can be divided into two groups: auxiliary functions for local changes only, and auxiliary functions that also send a new ICMP packet.

The most important functions used in the ICMP implementation in Linux will be described next.

`icmp_rcv()`   **include/linux/icmp.h**

TABLE 14–3   Generating ICMP messages from within the kernel modules.

Type	Module	Reason
Time Exceeded	Forward and defragment packets	A packet was discarded because it's TTL expired.
Parameter Problem	Detect packet options	Unknown or false options
Redirect	Packet routing	Obvious potential for optimization
Destination Unreachable	All modules that send, forward, or deliver IP packets	Inability to deliver a packet

This function is responsible for processing incoming ICMP packets, including a preprocessing process that drops noncompliant packets. While the internal statistics are being updated when an ICMP message arrives, the packet is also checked for correct length. In addition, the checksum is computed over the packet header, and the ICMP type is checked for a valid number. If the user has not set options in `sysctl`, then incoming broadcast packets of the types *ICMP Echo, ICMP Timestamp, ICMP Information Request*, and *ICMP Information Reply* are discarded.

The following functions are invoked from within the `icmp_rcv()` function for incoming ICMP packets:

`icmp_reply()`	**include/linux/icmp.h**

The function `icmp_reply()` is generally used to reply to ICMP request packets. Before a reply is sent, the internal statistics variables are updated first; then the TOS field is taken from Request, and the IP addresses of the sender and the receiver are swapped. Next, the packet is returned to the sender, including the payload passed as argument (corresponding to the ICMP reply packet). `icmp_reply()` is used by two functions, `icmp_echo()` and `icmp_timestamp()`, to reply to *Echo Request* and *Timestamp Request*, respectively.

`icmp_redirect()`	**include/linux/icmp.h**

This function updates the routing table when an end system receives an ICMP message of the type *Redirect*.

`icmp_unreach()`	**include/linux/icmp.h**

This function handles three ICMP message types: *Destination Unreachable, Source Quench*, and *Time Exceeded*. After a number of tests for packet validity, this function passes the error message to the service of the next higher layer belonging to the initiating packet. Error messages as a result of ICMP messages are similar to the error codes defined in Section 14.4.1. In the case of *Source Quench*, the receiving computer is expected to reduce its sending rate, which will be handled by the protocol in the transport layer above IP.

`icmp_echo()`, `icmp_timestamp()`	**include/linux/icmp.h**

A new ICMP packet has to be sent to handle ICMP messages of the types *Echo Request* and *Timestamp Request*. The basic function `icmp_reply()` is used in either case. The transmission is based on the rules discussed in Section 14.4.3. For `icmp_echo()`, only the ICMP type is changed, to `ICMP_ECHOREPLY`, then the payload part is copied from the Echo packet, and finally `icmp_reply()` returns the packet to the sender.

The function `icmp_timestamp()` responds to incoming *Timestamp* requests. Initially, it checks the length of packets previously received and finds out the current time. The payload is removed from the original ICMP packet and put into the reply packet, and the time is added to the `Receive Timestamp` and `Transmit Timestamp` fields. This means that the two time values in `Receive Timestamp` and `Transmit Timestamp` are always identical. Once the packet type has been changed to `ICMP_TIMESTAMPREPLY`, the function `icmp_reply()` returns the packet.

`icmp_address()`, `icmp_address_reply()`	**include/linux/icmp.h**

The standard actually specifies that these two functions be implemented. However, this functionality is not supported by the Linux kernel, because the designers found inconsistencies in the standards and thought that an implementation would not be meaningful at this time. When `icmp_address()` is invoked, only a kernel message is output. When a Linux computer receives an *ICMP Information Reply* packet, then it checks this packet for correct network mask (and complains by outputting a kernel message if it finds an inconsistency).

Another thing specific to the Linux implementation is that no reply is sent to packet types not discussed in this chapter.

Deviations from the Standard   Several ICMP functionalities originally specified in RFCs were not included in the ICMP implementation of Linux. The following properties are missing:

- The use of a *Source Route* specified in the IP options is not supported. If an IP packet that initiates an ICMP message is to use a specified route, then the ICMP packet would actually have to follow the same path back. This property is currently missing, but will presumably be implemented later.
- Sending *Source Quench* messages: The ICMP implementation in Linux sends no *Source Quench* packets. Today, it is considered pointless to send such packets, because they generate additional network load in an overload situation. (See RFC 1812 [Bake95].)
- *Information Request/Reply*: These packet types were originally designed for tasks that have more recently been handled by other protocols (e.g., allocating of IP addresses to booting computers without persistent memory). Currently, this problem is solved by RARP. For this reason, these packets are simply ignored. In addition, the use of these ICMP packet types was found to cause problems, because these two ICMP messages cannot be correctly applied in all cases. (See RFC 1812.) Though this functionality is still specified in this RFC, the Linux designers decided not to implement it. The only thing done is that a local error message is output when the computer receives an *Information Reply* message.

# CHAPTER 15

Address Resolution Protocol (ARP)

The conversion of addresses between different protocol layers represents an important task for unique identification of resources in a computer network. Such a conversion is required at the transition between two neighbouring layers within a reference model, because each layer uses its own address types, depending on its functionality (IP, MAC, ATM addresses, etc.). For example, the destination computer is specified in the form of an IP address if a packet is sent over the Internet Protocol. This address is valid only within the IP layer. In the data-link layer, both the service used by the Internet Protocol to transport its data and different LAN technologies (e.g., Ethernet, token ring, ATM), each with its own address formats, can be used. The network adapters of a LAN are generally identified by 48-bit addresses, so-called *MAC addresses*. A MAC address identifies a unique network adapter within a local area network.

To be able to send a packet to the IP instance in the destination computer or to the next router, the MAC address of the destination station has to be determined in the sending protocol instance. The problem is now to do a unique resolution of the mapping between a MAC address and an IP address. What we need is a mapping of network-layer addresses to MAC addresses, because the sending IP instance has to pass the MAC address of the next station in the form of interface control information (ICI) to the lower MAC instance. (See Section 3.2.1.) At the advent of the Internet, this mapping was implemented by static tables that maintained the mapping of IP addresses to MAC addresses in each computer. However, this method turned out to be inflexible as the ARPANET grew, and it meant an extremely high cost when changes were necessary. For this reason, RFC 826 introduced the *Address Resolution Protocol* (*ARP*) to convert address formats.

Though the TCP/IP protocol suite has become the leading standard for almost all computer networks, it is interesting to note that ARP was not designed specifically for mapping between IP and MAC addresses. ARP is a generic protocol that finds a mapping between ordered pairs (P, A) and arbitrary physical addresses, where P is a network-layer protocol and A is an address of this protocol P. At the time at which ARP was developed, different protocols, such as CHAOS and Decnet, had been used in the network layer. The ARP instance of a system can be extended so that the required addresses can be resolved for each of the above combinations, which means that no new protocol is necessary. The most common method to allocate addresses between different layers maps the tuple (*Internet Protocol, IP address*) to 48-bit MAC addresses.

15.1 USING THE ADDRESS RESOLUTION PROTOCOL

As mentioned above, the Address Resolution Protocol (ARP) is a decentralized protocol to resolve address mappings between layer-3 addresses and layer-2 addresses in local area networks. Figure 15–1 shows how ARP works. When computer A wants to send a packet to router R in the same LAN, then it needs the layer-2 address, in addition to the IP address, to be able to tell the data link layer which computer is supposed to get this packet. For this purpose, computer A sends an *ARP Request* to all computers connected to the LAN. This request is generally sent in a MAC broadcast message by using the MAC broadcast address (FF:FF:FF:FF:FF:FF). The intended computer can see from the destination IP address in the ARP PDU that this request is for itself, so this computer returns a reply to the requesting computer, A, including its MAC address. Computer A now learns the MAC address of R and can instruct its data-link layer to deliver the packet.

To avoid having to request the MAC address again for subsequent packets, A stores the MAC address of R in a local table—the ARP cache. (See Section 15.3.) Computer R can also extract the MAC address of A from A's request and store that in its own ARP cache. It can be seen from A's request that A and R will communicate soon, which means that the MAC address of A will be needed. In this case, we avoid one ARP request, because the mapping will have been previously stored.

15.1.1 The Structure of ARP Protocol Data Units

Figure 15–2 shows how an ARP PDU is structured; this PDU is used for the two protocol data units defined in the ARP protocol, *ARP Request* and *ARP Reply*. The only difference between these two types is in the *Operation* field.

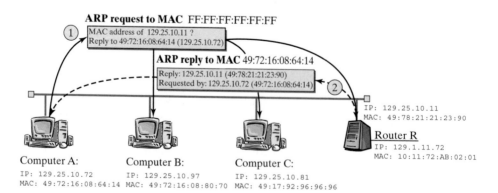

FIGURE 15–1
Example showing how ARP resolves addresses.

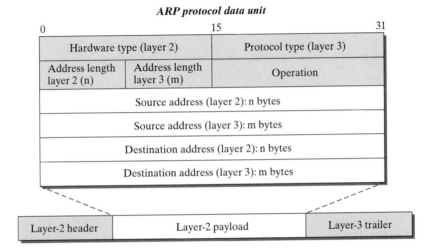

ARP protocol data unit

FIGURE 15–2
Format of the ARP Request and ARP Reply PDUs.

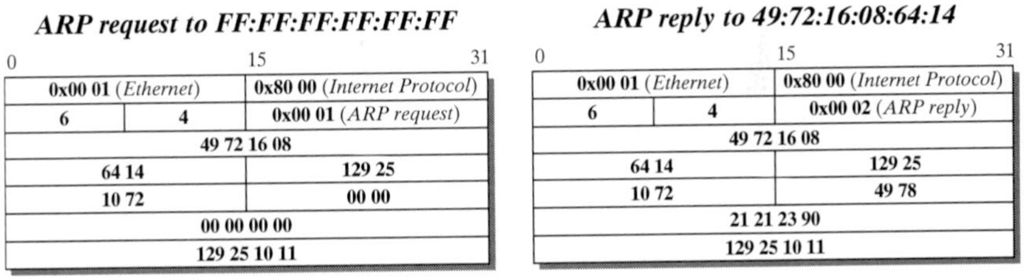

FIGURE 15–3
Example with values in the ARP Request and ARP Reply PDUs from Figure 15–1 (not considering the network byte order).

Figure 15–3 uses the above example to show how values can be assigned to the two PDUs. Computer A sends a request to router R, as shown in Figure 15–1, asking for that computer's 48-bit MAC address (say 129.25.10.11) in the local Ethernet segment.

The fields of an ARP PDU and their meanings are as follows:

- ARP packets are transported in the payload field of MAC protocols. The identification as an ARP PDU is done specifically by the MAC protocol (e.g., in the *Protocol* field for Ethernet or by an appropriate identifier in the SNAP header).
- *Hardware Type* specifies the layer-2 protocol used (e.g., 1 for an Ethernet network).
- *Protocol Type* specifies the layer-3 protocol used (e.g., 0x0800 for the Internet Protocol).
- *Layer-2 Address Length:* n specifies the length of the layer-2 address used (in bytes). This field takes the value 6 for an 48-bit MAC address. Specifying the address length enables the use of different protocols with specific address formats.

■ *Layer-3 Address Length:* m specifies the length of the layer-3 address. The field takes the value 4 for 32-bit Internet addresses.

■ The *Operation* field specifies the type of ARP PDU—1 for *ARP Request*, 2 for *ARP Reply*. In addition, the PDU types *RARP Request* (3) and *RARP Reply* (4) were defined for RARP [FMMT84]).

■ The fields *Layer-2 Sender Address* and *Layer-2 Destination Address* consist of n bytes and include the appropriate layer-2 addresses.

■ The fields *Layer-3 Sender Address* and *Layer-3 Destination Address* have the length m bytes and include the layer-3 addresses of the requesting and the receiving station.

15.1.2 Receiving an ARP Packet and Replying

As was mentioned earlier, *ARP Request* and *ARP Reply* PDUs have the same packet format; they differ only in their *Operation* fields. An *ARP Request* packet also differs from a subsequent reply by the missing layer-2 address of the destination, so that it is easy to create a reply to a request. When receiving a request packet, in which the desired station finds its layer-3 address, the following steps are completed:

■ The layer-2 address of the network adapter is inserted in the field *Layer-2 Destination Address*.

■ The two address fields for the sender and the destination are swapped.

■ The *Operation* field takes value 2 to mark the PDU as *ARP Reply*.

■ Finally, the reply packet is sent.

An ARP request includes a valid mapping between the layer-3 address and the layer-2 address of the request initiator, in addition to the layer-3 address looked for, so one entry for the initiator is created in the ARP cache when the request is received.

15.2   THE ARP COMMAND

The arp command can be used to output the ARP table (ARP cache) of a computer. It can also be used to manipulate the ARP table (e.g., to create permanent entries or delete entries).

The following options are available for the arp command:

■ *Display the ARP table:* you can use option -a when running the arp command to view the ARP table of a computer:

```
root@tux # arp -a
IP address HW type HW address
129.25.10.97 10Mbit/s Ethernet 49:72:16:08:80:70
129.25.10.72 10Mbit/s Ethernet 49:72:16:08:64:14
129.25. 10.81 10Mbit/s Ethernet 49:17:92:96:96:96
```

The first column shows the IP address of the destination computer; the second column shows the LAN category (e.g., 10-mbps Ethernet); the last column shows the layer-2 address of the network adapter.

If the word `incomplete` appears in an entry in the last column upon repeated calls, then this means that the network device specified by the entry has failed or is defective.

- *Address format:* In addition to Ethernet, ARP is also used in other broadcast-enabled LAN technologies (e.g., AX.25 amateur radio networks and token ring) for address resolution. These network technologies may use different address formats. `arp` shows the address format used in the second column. Notice that `arp` shows only the entries for Ethernet addresses, by default. To view a list of AX.25 addresses, you have to use the `-t` option with the command: `arp -a -t ax25`.
- *Deleting ARP entries:* You can use `arp` with the option `-d computer` to remove the entry of that computer. This forces a new ARP request upon the next request for the layer-2 address of the specified computer. Deleting an ARP address mapping can be useful when a computer's configuration is wrong or when the layer-2 address has changed—for example, when a network adapter has been replaced.

To avoid this case, ARP entries are automatically declared invalid after a certain period of time. This period is in the range of a few minutes, so that the replacement of a network adapter should actually not cause any problem.

- *Setting ARP entries:* It can sometimes be useful to add an entry manually to the ARP table. The option `-s computer layer-2-address` is available for such cases. It can also be used when ARP requests to a specific computer are not answered, because of faulty or missing ARP instances. The option -s can also be useful when a second computer in the same LAN identifies itself erroneously with the same IP address and replies sooner to the ARP request. The following command adds the computer `tux` having layer-2 address `49:72:16:08:64:14` to the ARP table: arp -s tux `49:72:16:08:64:14`.

In contrast to entries determined automatically in the ARP cache, entries created with the option `-s` are not removed after a certain period; they remain in the ARP cache until the computer restarts (static entry).

15.3 IMPLEMENTING THE ARP INSTANCE IN THE LINUX KERNEL

In theory, ARP would have to run an address resolution for each outgoing IP packet before transmitting it. However, this would significantly increase the required bandwidth. For this reason, address mappings are stored in a table—the so-called *ARP cache*—as the protocol learns them. We have mentioned the ARP cache several times before. This section describes how the ARP cache and the ARP instance are implemented in the Linux kernel.

Though the Address Resolution Protocol was designed for relatively generic use, to map addresses for different layers, it is not used by all layer-3 protocols. For example, the new Internet Protocol (IPv6) uses the *Neighbor Discovery* (*ND*) address resolution to map IPv6 addresses to layer-2 addresses. Though the operation of the two protocols (ARP and ND) is similar, they are actually two separate protocol instances. The Linux kernel designers wanted to utilize the similarity between the two protocols and implemented a generic support for address resolution protocols in LANs, the so-called `neighbour` management.

A `neighbour` represents a computer that is reachable over layer-2 services (i.e., directly over the LAN). Using the `neighbour` interface and the available functions, you can implement special properties of either of the two protocols (ARP and Neighbour Discovery). The following sections introduce the **neighbour** interface and discuss the ARP functions. Chapter 23 describes how Neighbor Discovery is implemented.

15.3.1   Managing Reachable Computers in the ARP Cache

As was mentioned earlier, computers that can be reached directly (over layer 2) are called *neighbor stations* in Linux. Figure 15–4 shows that they are represented by instances of the neighbour structure.

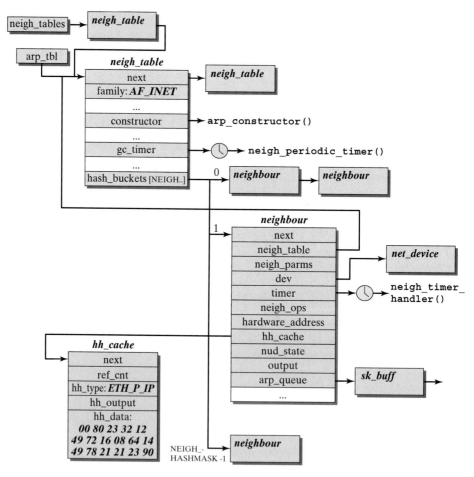

FIGURE 15–4
Structure of the ARP cache and its neighbor elements.

The set of reachable computers is managed in the ARP cache, which is organized in a hash table. The hash function `arp_hash()` can be used to map `neighbour` structures to rows in the hash table. A linear collision resolution occurs if several structures fall on the same hash row. The basic functions of the ARP hash table are handled by the *neighbour* management. This means that the ARP hash table is only an instance of the more general `neigh_table` structure.

The structures of the *neighbour* management and its linking are introduced below.

`struct neighbour`	include/net/neighbour.h

The `neighbour` structure is the representation of a computer that can be reached directly over the data-link layer. The ARP instance creates a `neighbour` structure as soon as a layer-3 protocol (normally, the Internet Protocol) asks for the layer-2 address of a computer in the LAN. This means that the ARP cache contains all reachable stations and, additionally, the addresses of stations that are currently being determined. To prevent the cache from growing endlessly, entries with layer-2 addresses that have not been requested are deleted after a certain time. The neighbour structure has the following parameters:

- `next`: Because neighbor stations are organized in hash tables, and collisions are resolved by the *chaining* strategy (linear linking), the **next** field references the next neighbor structure in a hash row.
- `tbl`: This pointer points to the `neigh_table` structure that belongs to this `neighbour` and manages the current entry.
- `parms`: The `neigh_parms` structure includes several parameters about a `neighbour` computer (e.g., a reference to the associated timer and the maximum number of probes. (See `neigh_timer_handler()` function, below.)
- `dev`: This is a pointer to the corresponding network device.
- `timer`: This is a pointer to a timer used to initiate the handling routine `neigh_timer_handler()`.
- `opts`: Neighbor options define several functions used to send packets to this `neighbour`. The functions actually used depend on the properties of the underlying medium (i.e., on the type of network device). Figure 15–5 shows the

	generic	direct	hh	broken
destructor		-	-	-
solicit	arp_solicit	-	arp_solicit	arp_solicit
error_report	arp_error_report	-	arp_error_report	arp_error_report
output	neigh_resolve_output	dev_queue_xmit	neigh_resolve_output	neigh_compat_output
connected_output	neigh_connected_output	dev_queue_xmit	neigh_resolve_output	neigh_compat_output
hh_output	dev_queue_xmit	dev_queue_xmit	dev_queue_xmit	dev_queue_xmit
queue_xmit	dev_queue_xmit	dev_queue_xmit	dev_queue_xmit	dev_queue_xmit

FIGURE 15–5
Available neighbor options.

`neigh_opts` variants. For example, the hh options are used when the network device needs an address to be resolved and supports a cache for layer-2 headers, and **direct** is used for network devices that do not need address resolution, such as point-to-point connections. The functions available in a `neigh_opts` variant are used for different tasks involved in the address-resolution process (e.g., resolve an address (`solicit()`) or send a packet to a reachable neighboring computer (`connected_output()`).

- `hardware_address`: This array stores the physical address of the neighboring computer.

- `hh`: This field refers to the cache entry for the layer-2 protocol of this `neighbour` computer. For example, an Ethernet packet header consists of the sender address, the destination address, and the `ethertype` field. It is not necessary to fill these fields every time; it is much more efficient to have them computed and readily stored, so that they need only be copied.

- `nud_state`: This parameter manages the state (i.e., valid, currently unreachable, etc.) of the neighboring station. Figure 15–5 shows all states a neighbor can possibly take. These states will be discussed in more detail in the course of this chapter.

- `output()`: This function pointer points to one of the functions in the `neigh_ops` structure. The value depends on the current state (`nud_state`) of the `neighbour` entry and the type of network device used. Figure 15–5 shows the possible combinations. The `output()` function is used to send packets to this neighboring station. If a function pointer is used, then the state of a packet does not have to be checked when it is sent. Should this state ever change, then we can simply set a new pointer.

- `arp_queue`: The ARP instance collects in this queue all packets to be sent for `neighbour` entries in the `NUD_INCOMPLETE` state (i.e., the neighboring computer currently cannot be reached). This means that they don't have to be discarded, but can be sent as soon as an address has been successfully resolved.

`struct neigh_table`	include/net/neighbour.h

A `neigh_table` structure manages the `neighbour` structures of an address-resolution protocol (see Figure 15–4), and several tables like this can exist in one single computer. We describe only the special case with an ARP table here. The `neigh_table` instance of the ARP protocol can be reached either over the linked list in the `neigh_table` structures or directly over the `arp_tbl` pointer.

The most important fields in a `neighbour` hash table are as follows:

- `next`: As mentioned earlier, a separate `neigh_table` instance is created for each protocol, and these instances are linearly linked. This is the purpose of the `next` pointer. The `neigh_tables` variable points to the beginning of the list.

- `family`: This field stores the address family of *neighbour* entries. The ARP cache contains IP addresses, so this field takes the value `AF_INET`.

- `constructor()`: This function pointer is used to generate a new `neighbour` entry. Depending on the protocol instance, different tasks may be required to generate such an entry. This is the reason why each protocol should have a special constructor. In the `arp_tbl` structure, this pointer references the function `arp_constructor()`, which will be described later.

- `gc_timer`: A *garbage collection* (GC) timer is created for each `neigh_table` cache. This timer checks the state of each entry and updates these states periodically. The handling routine used by this timer is `neigh_periodic_timer()`.
- `hash_buckets[NEIGH_HASHMASK+1]`: This table includes the pointers to the hash rows that link the `neighbour` entries linearly. The `arp_hash()` function is used to compute hash values.
- `phash_buckets[PNEIGH_HASHMASK+1]`: This second hash table manages the neighbour structures entered when the computer is used as an ARP proxy.

`struct neigh_ops`	include/net/neighbour.h

The `ops` field of each `neighbour` structure includes a pointer to a `neigh_ops` structure. The available options define different types of neighbors and include several functions belonging to a `neighbour` type (`connected_output()`, `hh_output()`, etc.). For example, the functions needed to send packets to a neighboring computer are defined in the `neighbour` options. The following four types are available for entries in the ARP cache: `generic`, `direct`, `hh`, and `broken`.

The respective functions of these types are shown in Figure 15–5. Depending on the type of network device used, the `ops` fields for new `neighbour` structures in the `arp_constructor()` function are set to one of the following four options:

- `arp_direct_ops()` is used when the existing network device does not include hardware headers (`dev->hard_header == NULL`). These stations are directly reachable, and no layer-2 packet header is required (e.g., for PPP).
- `arp_broken_ops()` is reserved for special network devices (ROSE, AX25, and NETROM).
- `arp_hh_ops()` is set when the network device used has a cache for layer-2 packet headers (`dev->hard_header_cache`). In this case, the `ops` field is set to `arp_hh_ops`.
- `arp_generic_ops()` is used when none of the above cases exists.

The `output()` functions of the `neigh_ops` structure are particularly important. Each neighbour structure includes an `output()` pointer that points to a function used to send data packets to a neighboring station. For ARP cache entries in the `NUD_REACHABLE`, `NUD_PERMANENT`, or `NUD_NOARP` state, the `output()` pointer references the function `connected_output()` of the `neigh_ops` structure; it is the fastest of all. `connected_output()` assumes that the neighboring computer is reachable, because these three states mean either that the reachability was confirmed recently or that no confirmation is required (permanent entry or point-to-point).

For `neighbour` stations in other states, the `output()` pointer references the `output()` function, which is slower and more careful. Direct reachability is doubted, so an initial attempt is made to obtain a confirmation of the neighboring computer's reachability (*probe*).

The relevant handling routine is the function `neigh_periodic_timer()`. It visits each entry in the cache and does one of the following actions, depending on the entry's state:

- NUD_PERMANENT: This is a permanent entry; nothing in its state has to be changed.

- IN_TIMER: An attempt is currently being made to reach the specified computer by sending an ARP request packet. This also means that the timer of the neighbour entry is set, and the handling routine `neigh_timer_handler()` will run soon. In this case, the entry's state is updated at the same time, so that `neigh_periodic_timer()` changes nothing in the state of this entry.

- NUD_FAILED: If a neighbour entry is in the NUD_FAILED state, or if the time `neigh->ops->staletime` has expired, the computer is considered no longer reachable, and `neigh_release()` deletes this entry from the ARP cache.

- NUD_REACHABLE: If an entry is marked as reachable, but `neigh->ops->reachable_time` jiffies have already passed since the last acknowledgment, then it is classified as old (NUD_STALE), and `neigh_suspect()` (described earlier) attempts to update this entry.

The function `neigh_periodic_timer()` runs as an independent tasklet in multiprocessor systems.

Creating and Managing neighbour Instances

`neigh_create()`	**net/core/neighbour.c**

This function is responsible for creating a new neighbour entry and entering it in the respective neighbour cache. `neigh_create()` is normally invoked by the `arp_bind_neighbour()` function when `neigh_lookup()` was unsuccessful at finding the ARP entry of the interested computer. Accordingly, it creates a new entry.

To create a new neighbour entry, the function first initializes a neighbour structure in the appropriate neighbour instance (`neigh_alloc()`). If a constructor was defined for the entries in this table, then it is invoked now.

Before it adds a neighbour to the table, the function first checks for whether such an entry already exists. If not, then the entry is added as the first element of the hash row that references pkey. A new entry is added at the beginning of the hash row, because the probability is high that it will be accessed next. The return value is a pointer to the new entry in the ARP cache.

`neigh_alloc()`	**net/core/neighbour.c**

`neigh_alloc(tbl)` creates a new neighbour structure for a specific neighbour table (tbl). This table is specified additionally, because it includes some information required for the new entry. In addition, before the neighbour structure is created, the function first checks on whether the current table is full. `tbl->gc_thresh3` is the absolute upper limit of the table. This limit must not be exceeded. gc_thresh2 is a threshold value that should be exceeded only briefly. The garbage collector allows you to exceed this limit for a maximum of five seconds. When this time expires, it runs a garbage collection. The following query tests for these two conditions:

```
if (tbl->entries > tbl->gc_thresh3 ||
        (tbl->entries > tbl->gc_thresh2 && now - tbl->last_flush > 5*HZ)).
```

If this is the case, then `neigh_forced_gc()` runs a garbage collection and checks for whether sufficient space was freed in the table. If the space freed is insufficient, the function returns `NULL` and doesn't create a new `neighbour` structure.

If the table can accommodate the new entry, a new `neighbour` structure is taken from the memory cache `tbl->kmem_cachep` and added to the table. The state of the new entry is set to `NUD_NONE`, and a pointer to the new `neighbour` structure is returned.

`neigh_forced_gc()`	**net/core/neighbour.c**

If a `neighbour` table is full (see `neigh_alloc()`), the garbage collector runs `neigh_force_gc()` immediately. This function is invoked by `neigh_alloc()` to free memory space for new `neighbour` structures. Entries that meet the following conditions are deleted from the cache:

- There is no longer any reference to the structure (`n->refcnt == 1`).
- The `neighbour` is not permanent (`n->nud_state != NUD_PERMANENT`).
- For an empty `NUD_INCOMPLETE` entry, the structure has to have been in the cache for at least `retrans_time` to avoid unnecessary duplication of request packets: (`n->nud_state != NUD_INCOMPLETE || jiffies - n->used >n->parms->retrans_time`).

The number of deleted entries is output as soon as this function has finished checking all `neighbour` entries.

`arp_constructor()`	**net/ipv4/arp.c**

Once `neigh_create()` has invoked the `neigh_alloc()` function to initialize a new `neighbour` structure, it invokes the appropriate constructor function for the specified `neigh_table`—for example, the `arp_constructor()` method for the ARP cache.

In the first step, `arp_constructor()` checks for whether the network device used requires the ARP protocol. If this is not the case, then the state of this entry is set to `NUD_NOARP`. Next, it checks for whether the `hard_header_cache` includes an entry for this network device. If so, then the `neigh_ops` field of this `neighbour` structure is set to `arp_hh_ops`. Otherwise, this `neighbour` entry uses the methods of the `arp_generic_ops` options. Finally, when the entry has reached the `NUD_VALID` state, the `connected_output()` function can be used to communicate with the neighbouring computer. Otherwise, the normal `output()` function will be used again.

`neigh_table_init()`	**net/core/neighbour.c**

`neigh_table_init()` takes the following steps to initialize a new `neigh_table` structure:

- It obtains memory for the `neighbour` cache (`tbl->kmem_cachep` = `kmem_cache_create()`).
- It initializes a timer (`tbl->gc_timer()`) and sets the expiry time to `now` + `tbl->gc_interval` + `tbl->reachable_time`. This timer calls `neigh_periodic_timer()` periodically.
- It inserts the new table into a singly linked list, `neigh_tables`.

`arp_hash()`	**net/ipv4/arp.c**

The `arp_tabl()` function uses this function as a method for computing the hash function. The hash value is computed on the basis of the IP address (`primary_key`), using modulo NEIGH_HASHMASK (ARP table size).

CHAPTER 16

IP Routing

16.1 INTRODUCTION

One of the most important functions of the IP layer (the network layer of the TCP/IP protocol architecture) is to forward packets between communicating end systems across a number of intermediate systems. (See Figure 16–1.) The determination of the route that packets will take across the Internet and the forwarding of packets towards their destination is called *routing*.

16.1.1 Networks and Routers

As was mentioned in Chapter 14, the Internet represents a network of networks. The physical subnetworks built by use of different layer-2 transmission technologies, such as Ethernet, can include a different number of nodes each—for example just two nodes connected over a point-to-point link. The IP layer interconnects these subnetworks to form a global network having millions of nodes.

Special nodes, which are integrated in all subnetworks that are connected in one place, are used to link these subnetworks; these nodes are called *routers*. Figure 16–2 shows an example with five local area networks, connected through three routers. Router A also connects the network to the rest of the Internet. The network layer abstracts from

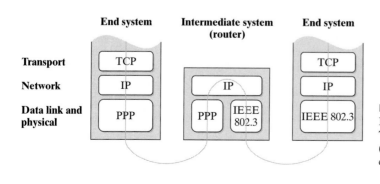

FIGURE 16–1
Routing within the IP layer in the TCP/IP protocol architecture (protocols in the other layers are examples).

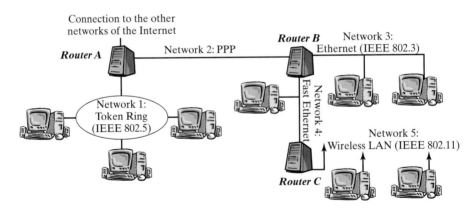

FIGURE 16–2
Routers interconnect networks.

lower layers, so it is irrelevant for the communication implemented over IP that the end systems are connected to different LAN types.

Routers are used both to link local area networks and to connect local area networks to the Internet. In addition, networks in the "core" of the Internet, which normally have a much larger geographic reach, are interconnected and linked to access networks through routers, or even built of direct links between routers ("two-node networks").

Routers are often especially designed for this purpose—so-called "dedicated routing devices." However, the Linux kernel also offers the required functionality to let you use a Linux system as a router.

16.1.2 Forwarding and Routing

Routers forward IP packets from one physical network to another, where the second network is normally "closer" to the destination network (not necessarily in the sense of geographic distance, but rather from a network-topology view) than the first network. To decide in what direction each packet has to be forwarded, the router requires a certain amount of information about the Internet topology, which it stores locally.

This topological knowledge—also called *forwarding information* in the rest of this course—can be managed manually for small networks like the example in Figure 16–2, because there is little of it and it changes only if the LAN topology changes. For example, all router B actually needs to know is the end systems in networks 3, 4, and 5. It can send all packets not addressed to end systems in these networks globally towards router A, because the "rest of the Internet" is behind router A.

In the core area of the Internet, the situation is not that simple. Rather than a small LAN, there is a large area of the entire Internet behind a network interface of a router. The knowledge required to be able to forward IP packets with arbitrary addresses in the correct direction is much more extensive. In addition, it has to be adapted continually: when new paths are added, when old ones fail or are overloaded, and when the network topology in remote places changes. For these reasons, a network the size of the global Internet requires automatic methods to continually update the topology information and determine suitable routes.

These methods to determine forwarding information in each router are also commonly called "routing." This means that we can identify two different functions that, together, form the entire IP routing mechanism, and which have to be clearly distinguished:

- *Forwarding* of IP packets in routers, which is based on given forwarding information. A router has to look up a database and make a decision for each packet that passes through this router on its way through the Internet.
- *Routing*: determining the best routes over which to transport each packet between networks, and deriving forwarding information from information about topologies and states exchanged regularly between routers within the entire network.

Forwarding is implemented in the Linux kernel, because it is a task of the IP layer. In contrast, routing is handled on higher layers: The *routing protocols* used to distribute information about network topologies and states normally build on top of transport-layer protocols, and the pertinent programs (*routing daemons*) are user-space processes running in Linux systems.

The interface between the two parts is built by a database, in which a routing daemon stores its forwarding information, and which the IP layer uses as a basis for its decisions when packets have to be forwarded.

As mentioned earlier, forwarding information in small networks at the "outskirts" of the Internet is rather static and so can be managed manually—you don't necessarily have to use a routing daemon. In this case, the system administrator can use tools like those discussed in Section 16.2.3 to add forwarding information manually to the database. This method is called *static routing*, in contrast to *dynamic routing*, which is based on routing protocols.

Routing is not done in the Linux kernel, so it is not discussed in detail in this book. Instead, we refer interested readers to general books about internetworking (e.g., [Come00]). This chapter focuses on forwarding in the IP layer and the forwarding-information database, which is also implemented in the Linux kernel.

16.1.3 IP Addresses

To be able to send packets to arbitrary end systems in the Internet, we need a means of unique identification of end systems. We know from a previous section that this is accomplished by using IP addresses, which are 32 bits in length and normally are represented by four single-byte values in dotted decimal notation for IP Version 4.

Network Addresses and End-System Identifiers   In addition to identifying network nodes, IP addresses have another important function involved in the finding of nodes. In fact, if IP addresses were randomly distributed (but unique) values, they could still serve as identifiers, but it would be hard to forward packets to a specific destination, because each router would have to know the forwarding direction for each possible destination IP address in the Internet. Considering the enormous number of end systems connected to the Internet, this would obviously be very expensive with regard to memory requirement and search time.

To allow for the forwarding direction to be determined efficiently, IP addresses are structured hierarchically, and consist of two different parts: a *network address* and an *end-system identifier*. The network address is identical for all end systems in one subnetwork; the end-system identifier distinguishes end systems in a specific subnetwork. During forwarding of packets, the end-system identifier can be totally ignored until the packet arrives in the correct subnetwork. This means that routers do not need to know end-system identifiers; in this way, the division of IP addresses into two parts dramatically reduces the amount of information routers have to store.

Because it always forms the beginning of an IP address, the network-address part of an IP address is also called *network prefix*.

Address Classes and Classless Addressing   The next question we have to answer is about the sizes of the network part and the end-system identifier part in an IP address. Three different variants were defined when addressing in the Internet was specified [Post81c]: The address classes A, B, and C, having 7, 14, and 21 bits for the network part and 24, 16, and 8 bits for the end-system identifier. The class an address belongs to is determined by the first (leftmost) bits of the address. Figure 16–3, which was also used in Chapter 14, illustrates this scheme. We will not go into detail about the two additional classes, D and E, which are reserved for special purposes, or into other reserved network prefixes and end-system identifiers again at this point; see Section 14.1.5 for this.

This addressing scheme was originally designed by assuming that each physical network could actually have a network identifier from one of the three classes mentioned above (depending on the size of the physical network). However, it was soon observed that this approach would quickly exhaust all available network prefixes. In addition, the existing classes proved often to be inappropriate: A class-A network could contain almost 2^{24} or 16777216 end systems, a number that even the largest organizations would hardly need, apart from the fact that no known physical network technology can handle that number of end systems. In contrast, class-C networks are much more numerous, but cannot hold more than 254 end systems, which is not enough in many cases.

These limitations motivated the development of technologies to better utilize the existing address space. The basic idea was to have the boundary between the network prefix and the end-system identifier at an arbitrary bit position, instead of only at the three positions dictated by the A, B, and C address classes.

■   For example, a class-A network can be divided in two networks with half the size each by using the first bit of the end-system identifier for division: All end systems with a zero at this position fall into one network, and all systems with a one

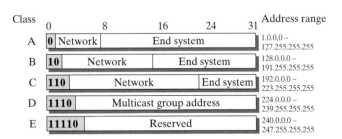

FIGURE 16–3

IP address classes with different division of network and end-system parts.

fall into the other network. This means that the network prefix has become longer by one bit inside of the new subnetworks, from the end systems' view.

This new division of addresses is totally transparent to the outside; it plays no role for routing outside the networks directly concerned: Only the router that connects the two new networks to the rest of the world has to know and consider this new division. This scheme basically allows us to divide an address space several times. The length of the valid network prefix grows then in line with the depth of the hierarchy formed by this scheme.

■ Similarly, when working in the opposite direction, we could group a block of class-C addresses into a larger address space—for example, if they belong to a single organization (e.g., an Internet Service Provider). This corresponds to shortening the network prefix, forming a larger address space, which can be divided again, if necessary.

In this case, it is not necessarily meaningful to have the new division transparent to the outside, because it would require many unnecessary routing entries. For example, if an organization had a block of 256 class-C addresses instead of one single class-B address, then 256 routing entries instead of a single one would have to be published globally.

Today, the Internet uses *Classless Inter-Domain Routing (CIDR)* [ReLi93, FLYV93], which virtually ignores the "old" class division of IP addresses: Network prefixes can have an arbitrary length. However, the information about the actual length of the network identifier of a specific network can no longer be seen from the first address bits, in contrast with the method seen in the classful scheme. Consequently, this information has to be passed on and stored with each network address. There are two common notations:

■ In the first notation, the number of bits belonging to the network prefix is denoted in decimal form, with a slash separating it from the address. For example, 192.168.152.0/21 denotes a network with its prefix consisting of the first 21 bits of the IP address 192.168.152.0.

■ The second notation denotes a bit mask in addition to the IP address; the bit mask has the same length as the IP address. It is called a *network mask* and has all bits corresponding to the positions of the network prefix in the IP address set to one. The network mentioned above would look as follows in this notation: 192.168.152.0/255.255.248.0.

Router Addresses   Routers have their own IP addresses, as do all network nodes in TCP/IP networks. Because an IP address also identifies the network it belongs to, as we know from the previous sections, and because a router has to be connected to more than one network to be able to mediate between networks, it is obvious that a router has more than one IP address. More precisely, each network interface in a router has its own IP address.

Figure 16–4 shows the sample networks from Figure 16–2 again to illustrate this concept, denoting IP addresses for all end systems and all network interfaces of each router.

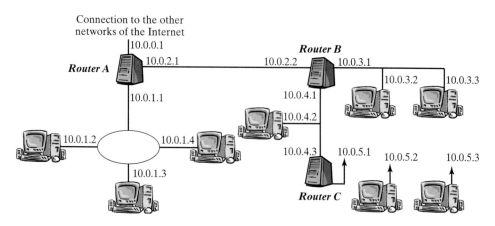

FIGURE 16–4
Assigning IP addresses to end systems and network interfaces in routers (example).

16.1.4 Forwarding Procedure

For a router, an IP packet received over a network interface falls into one of three categories, depending on its destination address:

- *The packet is addressed to the router*: In this case, the packet is not forwarded, but passed to a protocol instance of the transport layer in the router.
- *The packet is addressed to an end system in a neighboring network:* Packets addressed to an end system in a network that is connected directly to the router over a network interface can be forwarded directly to this end system. When the packet is passed to the data-link layer, the physical address of the destination system, which might previously have been discovered by the ARP protocol, is used.
- *The packet is addressed to an end system in a remote network*: If the destination system is not in a neighboring network, then the packet has to be forwarded over an additional router. This router is identified from the forwarding information, and its physical address is used as destination towards the physical layer.

The first case is characterized by the fact that the IP destination address belongs to an internal network interface. The second case can be detected by AND-combining the destination address with the network masks of neighboring networks. If the result of this operation matches the network prefix of the respective network, then the destination system is in this network. The third case applies when none of the two previous conditions is true.

In practice, the second case can be conveniently covered by the mechanism used to identify the next router in the third case, and "rule-based routing" is implemented in the recent kernel versions of Linux, so that the first case is also handled in this way. (See Section 16.1.6.)

The exact procedure involved in identifying the next router for the third case is strongly linked to the data structure used to store the forwarding information in the router. This data structure will be discussed in the next section.

Routing Table   The structure of forwarding information can be thought of as a table, where each row describes a specific address range, which is defined by a network prefix. This *routing table* specifies the network interface or the next router to be used for forwarding of packets having their destinations in the specified address range.

Figure 16–5 uses an example to show what a routing table for router B from Figure 16–4 could look like. We use designations common in Linux to name network interfaces. In practice, routing tables often include additional information in each row (e.g., describing the quality or the cost of a path, which help in selecting one of several routes to the same destination).

The example shows clearly how the second and third cases from the previous section can be distinguished: If the routing table includes an entry for a next router, then the packet has to be forwarded to that router. Otherwise, it can be sent over the specified network interface directly to the destination system.

An entry in a routing table is also called a *route* in the following discussion, to simplify matters.

Longest Prefix   Denoting a network address and a network mask means that the network prefixes entered in a routing table can have an arbitrary length. They don't even have to describe a single network that actually exists, but can instead group several networks in neighboring address spaces to reduce the size of the routing table. The most extreme example for this is an entry having its prefix length zero or its network mask 0.0.0.0. Such an entry represents *all* destination networks and is actually valid. It supplies a *default route*—the route packets should take when no specific entry exists for their destination address.

Naturally, a clear regulation has to be found for conflicting cases where several matching prefixes exist for one destination address. For example, such a conflict happens when the routing table includes a default route and additional entries. The problem is solved by selecting the entry with the longest prefix from all entries with matching prefixes. This means that more specific information in the routing table has priority over less specific information.

16.1.5 Routing Cache

The search for an entry with the longest matching prefix is the most time-critical operation in the forwarding procedure: It is used frequently, so its implementation should be efficient.

Destination	Network Mask	Router	Interface
10.0.3.0	255.255.255.0	—	eth0
10.0.4.0	255.255.255.0	—	eth1
10.0.5.0	255.255.255.0	10.0.4.3	eth1
10.0.2.0	255.255.255.0	—	ppp0
0.0.0.0	0.0.0.0	10.0.2.1	ppp0

FIGURE 16–5
Simple routing table for router B in Figure 16–4.

In Linux, all routing-table entries are sorted by prefix length, and the table is searched successively by descending prefix length. This method is not always efficient, especially when the table includes many different prefixes.

Rather than using different data structures to speed up the search process, Linux uses a *routing cache* to reduce the number of search processes. This cache stores the table entries used last and uses a hashing method that operates on the source address and destination address of packets to be forwarded, for accessing entries very fast. The routing table has to be consulted only for new address combinations not yet stored in the routing cache.

This method represents a good solution for end systems with a relatively limited number of concurrent communication partners; it is probably less suitable in the core area of the Internet.

16.1.6 Rule-based Routing

One routing particularity in Linux Version 2.4 and higher is that it lets you use several routing tables, instead of a single one. An additional set of rules is then used to select which table should be used for what packets. This method is called *rule-based routing* or *policy routing* and allows you to include other criteria (e.g., the source address) in the routing decision, in addition to the destination address, whereas routing decisions taken from one single routing table are always based only on the destination address and the destination-network prefix specified in that one table.

Rules   Each rule has a selector and a type. The selector chooses the packets to which the rule can be applied, and the type determines what should happen with a packet when the selector matches (e.g., that a specific routing table should be used or that a packet should be dropped). These rules are applied by priority values in ascending order. A unique priority value has to be assigned to each rule when it is defined. If a suitable route is found based on a rule, then the process is aborted, and the packet is forwarded. Otherwise, the process continues with the next rule.

The selector can contain the source address, the destination address, and the network interface at which the packet to be forwarded arrived. In addition, you can use the TOS field (which has more recently been called *codepoint*—see Section 14.1.2) or the iptables marking (see Section 19.3.5), which is called fwmark in the following discussion. Indirectly, the latter option lets you use additional packet properties (e.g., transport-protocol ports) for selection. All fields not explicitly stated in the selector are always considered to match.

There are five types of rules: unicast, blackhole, unreachable, prohibit, and nat. The "normal case" is the unicast type: A specific routing table stated in the rule is searched for a route. The blackhole, unreachable, and prohibit types cause the packet to be discarded when the rule is applied. They differ only in the type of feedback to the sender: blackhole creates no feedback, unreachable reports that the destination network is unreachable, and prohibit reports that the communication is not permitted. The last rule type, nat, can be used for static network-address translation (NAT). It is designed for special routing applications and not for the purpose of using one single IP address for several computers. This mechanism would be unsuitable for this purpose, because it is stateless. We will see in Chapter 21 that the masquerading mechanism of `iptables` is suitable for such cases. The `nat` routing rules are discussed in more detail in the work of Alexey Kuznetsov [Kuzn99].

Default Settings By default, the Linux kernel specifies three rules of the unicast type, with a selector each matching all packets. The priorities and identifiers for routing tables used for each type are defined as follows:

Priority	Table Name	Table Number
0	`local`	255
32766	`main`	254
32767	`default`	253

The three routing tables, `local`, `main`, and `default`, which are searched according to the above rules in this order for matching routes, are also created automatically. The latter two are initially empty, and the system administrator has to add entries (or use suitable scripts to fill them with entries) when the system boots. The `main` table is intended for "normal" routing entries; the `default` table is suitable for lower-priority backup solutions. The rules belonging to the `main` and `default` tables can also be deleted or modified.

In contrast to the second and third rules, the first rule is fixed, and the associated routing table is managed by the kernel itself. This table includes entries describing the addresses of local network interfaces. This realizes a very elegant approach to the categorizing of incoming packets, which was mentioned at the beginning of Section 16.1.4: Using just one procedure for all incoming packets, consult the set of rules and then the associated routing tables for each packet; if an entry is found in the `local` table, the packet is delivered locally—otherwise, it has to be forwarded.

Notice that only two tables, `local` and `main`, are searched in this order when rule-based routing is disabled in the kernel configuration.

16.2 CONFIGURATION

This section describes the options available to configure routing in Linux. First, this concerns the kernel configuration, which is used, for example, to determine whether advanced features, such as rule-based routing, should be integrated into the kernel. The options available for this configuration are described in Section 16.2.1. Second, you can also modify some routing parameters while the system is running. The setting options available for this in the `proc` file system are discussed in Section 16.2.2. Third, you have to add entries to routing tables and rule lists. The `ip` command, which is described in Section 16.2.3, is a good tool to manage such entries.

16.2.1 Configuring the Kernel

Some routing options can be set when you configure the Linux kernel, before it is compiled. All of them are in the networking options section and will be described briefly in this section below. In addition to the name of the preprocessor constant, which is defined when an option is activated, the label shown in the kernel configurator is given in double quotes. A prerequisite to being able to activate some of these options is that CONFIG_INET ("TCP/IP networking") should be enabled; without that, routing makes no sense, anyway.

▇ CONFIG_NETLINK   "Kernel/User netlink socket"

Rather than directly influencing the routing mechanism, this option activates the bidirectional netlink interface between the kernel and the user-address space, which is implemented with datagram sockets of the new protocol family, PF_NETLINK, and can be used to communicate with different kernel areas. The respective area is selected by an identifier, which is given instead of a protocol when you open the socket. Section 26.3.3 describes more details.

In connection with routing, the NETLINK_ROUTE "protocol identifier" is important, and it can be used by activating the following option. This option is available only provided that CONFIG_NETLINK is active:

▶ CONFIG_RTNETLINK   "Routing messages"

Routing rules and routing tables can be modified by using sockets of the PF_NETLINK protocol family and the NETLINK_ROUTE "protocol." This interface, which will also be called *RT netlink interface* below, is used in the ip configuration tool described in Section 16.2.3. Besides, by reading an RT netlink socket, you can "eavesdrop" on changes made to routing tables by other processes.

▇ CONFIG_IP_ADVANCED_ROUTER   "IP: advanced router"

This option has no direct effect; it represents a switch that allows you to select a number of additional options can be used to obtain much more control over the routing procedure. The options CONFIG_NETLINK and CONFIG_RTNETLINK are activated automatically when you select CONFIG_IP_ADVANCED_ROUTER.

▶ CONFIG_IP_MULTIPLE_TABLES   "IP: policy routing"

This option links the file fib_rules.o into the kernel and enables the rule-based routing described in Section 16.1.6. If this option is disabled, then the kernel creates only two routing tables, local and main, and searches them in this order.

The following additional options are available in connection with rule-based routing:

• CONFIG_IP_ROUTE_FWMARK   "IP: use netfilter MARK value as routing key"

This option allows you to include the fwmark, which can be added to certain packets by using packet filter rules (see Section 19.3.5), in the forwarding decision (i.e., you can specify different routes for packets with different packet filter marks). For example, you can make the route selection indirectly dependent on transport-protocol attributes (e.g., ports). CONFIG_NETFILTER ("network packet filtering") has to be active to be able to select CONFIG_IP_ROUTE_FWMARK.

- CONFIG_IP_ROUTE_NAT   "IP: fast network address translation"

When this option is active, you can use special routing entries to translate addresses (*Network Address Translation—NAT*). This functionality complements the NAT rules mentioned in Section 16.1.6; see [Kuzn99] for a description of how you can configure this rarely used option.

Activating CONFIG_IP_ROUTE_NAT causes ip_nat_dumb.o to be linked into the kernel.

▶ CONFIG_IP_ROUTE_MULTIPATH   "IP: equal cost multipath"

If the routing table includes several equal-ranking entries to a specific destination, then Linux traditionally selects the first. This behavior cannot be used meaningfully, because the order in which the entries are found cannot be seen or influenced from outside of the kernel. You can use the option CONFIG_IP_ROUTE_MULTIPATH to enable special entries that specify several equal routes, and then have one of these routes selected randomly.

▶ CONFIG_IP_ROUTE_TOS   "IP: use TOS value as routing key"

When enabled, this option causes the value of the Differentiated Services Codepoint field from the IP packet header to be included in the routing decision. (This field was formerly called Type of Service, which is the reason it is still referred to as the TOS field in the kernel and in this chapter.) You can assign values for this field in routing-table entries, which means that these entries will be used only for packets with matching values in the TOS field.

▶ CONFIG_IP_ROUTE_VERBOSE   "IP: verbose route monitoring"

If this option is enabled, then messages are written to the system log when certain error situations occur during the routing process—normally ones caused by attacks or faulty configurations.

▶ CONFIG_IP_ROUTE_LARGE_TABLES   "IP: large routing tables"

The hash tables used to manage routing table entries normally have a fixed size. The size of these tables is increased automatically when CONFIG_IP_ROUTE_LARGE_TABLES is activated, so that the access speed doesn't drop when they include many entries.

▪ CONFIG_IP_MROUTE   "IP: multicast routing"

This option activates multicast routing and links the ipmr.o file into the kernel. Multicast routing is discussed in Chapter 17.

▨ CONFIG_WAN_ROUTER   "WAN router"

This option has no effect on the routing procedure. It includes the general management functionality for special network interfaces used to build *Wide Area Networks
(WANs)*. This special hardware allows you to use a Linux computer as WAN router.

▨ CONFIG_NET_FASTROUTE   "Fast switching"

If the input and output interfaces of a forwarded packet are different, then you
can accelerate the copying process required in some cases by special hardware
support directly from network card to network card. CONFIG_NET_FASTROUTE
has to be enabled to be able to use this option. The only effect on the routing procedure is that a mark is set in situations suitable for fast copying. This can be handled by the drivers of network cards, if the required hardware is available.

▨ CONFIG_NET_SCHED   "QoS and/or fair queuing"

This option allows you to activate the options for traffic control, described in
Chapter 18. We include this option here only because routing rules and routing-
table entries can be used to classify packets. Notice that this requires the suboption CONFIG_NET_CLS ("Packet classifier API") and its suboption
CONFIG_NET_CLS_ROUTE4 to be activated. As a consequence, the symbol
CONFIG_NET_CLS_ROUTE is defined additionally. This symbol can be configured
nowhere else, and it causes the data structures for routing rules and routing-table
entries to be extended by an element required for classification.

16.2.2 Files in the proc File System

Some entries in the proc directory tree can be used to probe and manipulate data
structures and routing properties. You find such entries in two different directories,
/proc/net and /proc/sys/net/ipv4.

The /proc/net Directory   The /proc/net directory includes files that reflect extensive routing-related data structures in the kernel, namely the routing table main in
route and the routing cache in rt_cache. In rt_acct, you might additionally be able
to read statistics about the number of packets or bytes that used a specific route except
that it is not yet used and so this file is always empty. All files mentioned here have
read access only.

The /proc/sys/net/ipv4 Directory   The entries underneath /proc/sys are created by a relatively new uniform mechanism. Each of them describes a configurable parameter of the kernel. They can be probed and modified—either by reading from or
writing to a file, or by using the system call _sysctl() and the sysctl command. Entries for parameters of the IPv4 implementation, some of which are related to routing,
are located underneath /proc/sys/net/ipv4:

▨ ip_forward: This entry represents a switch for the forwarding functionality; the
system acts as a router whenever this entry is set to one. If it is set to zero, then all
packets received and not addressed to the local system are discarded.

■ `route` subdirectory: The files in the `route` subdirectory reflect numeric or Boolean values, with one exception; they are used by the kernel to manage the routing cache, amongst others. The directory entries and their variables in the kernel normally have the same names, with an `ip_rt_` prefix for the variables. The exact meanings of these entries will not be discussed here, apart from the one single exception: Writing to the flush entry causes the routing cache to be deleted.

■ `conf/device` subdirectories: `/proc/sys/net/ipv4/conf` includes a number of subdirectories—namely, one for each registered network interface (`lo`, `eth0`, ...), one named `default`, and one named `all`. All directories include the same entries, which refer to the interface with the same name. In addition, the entries in the all directory are global for all interfaces, and the entries in the `default` directory represent default values for any interfaces registered in the future. The following entries are of interest for the routing mechanism:

▶ `forwarding`: Like the entry in `/proc/sys/net/ipv4/ip_forward`, the entry in forwarding represents a switch for the forwarding mechanism. The entry in the `all` directory even reflects exactly the same value. The entries in the interface directories apply only to the forwarding of packets that arrived via specific interfaces. Each time that the switch value (except the `default` value) is changed, the routing cache is automatically deleted. The `all` value (and accordingly also the value in `/proc/sys/net/ipv4/ip_forward`) has particular semantics: When it is written, then all interface entries and the `default` entry are automatically set to the same new value.

▶ `log_martians`: If the `all` entry or the entry of an interface is set to 1, then so-called "Martians"—illegal address values (e.g., values that are incorrect with respect to the configuration of the interface that received this packet)—are shown in the system log.

▶ `rp_filter`: If the `all` entry and the entry of an interface are active, then packets arriving over this interface are subject to *Reverse-Path Filtering*, which means that a check tests whether a packet with exchanged source and destination addresses, according to the routing tables, would be sent over the interface which actually received this packet. If this test fails, then the packet is discarded. Reverse-Path Filtering is a sensible security measure against packets with forged (or spoofed) source address. However, it can sometimes be useful to use different interfaces for different directions intentionally, so this measure can cause problems and therefore is allowed to be disabled.

16.2.3 Configuration on System Level

Before a Linux system can send IP packets, or act as a router and forward IP packets for other systems, we have to add appropriate entries to routing tables. Unless we are using a routing daemon for automatic routing based on a routing protocol, a capability hardly needed at the "outskirts" of the Internet, the system administrator has to either add static entries manually or use scripts upon system start or when new interfaces are added (e.g., when a PPP connection is established).

tasks; they will be described in Section 16.3.4. These functions are also called "forwarding functions" in the following discussion.

▓ Routing rules and routing tables together form the so-called *forwarding-information base* (*FIB*). Whenever necessary, forwarding functions query the forwarding-information base; this action is also called a *forwarding query* or *FIB request* in the following discussion. An FIB request is initiated by calling the `fib_lookup()` function. The implementation of routing rules is strongly encapsulated within the FIB, so routing rules and routing tables will be discussed separately in Sections 16.3.1 and 16.3.2.

▓ Because consulting the FIB for each single IP packet received or sent would require too much time, there is an additional *routing cache* that stores the table entries used the most recently and allows fast access to these entries. Section 16.3.3 describes how this routing cache is implemented.

16.3.1 Routing Rules

As we described in Section 16.1.6, rule-based routing uses a set of rules to decide which routing tables should be searched in which sequence for a suitable entry to forward a packet and whether the packet may be forwarded at all. The rules are processed successively by ascending priority value until a decision can be made.

The entire implementation of the rules-processing method, including the data types used, is included in the `fib_rules.c` file. The rather narrow interface is described by some function prototypes and inline functions in a common header file, `ip_fib.h`. If rule-based routing was disabled in the kernel configuration (`CONFIG_IP_MULTIPLE_TABLES` option; see Section 16.2.1), then `fib_rules.c` is not compiled. In this case, the "replacement functionality" (use of the two routing tables `local` and `main`, in this sequence) is fully handled by the inline functions in `ip_fib.h`.

Data Structures   The set of rules is represented in the kernel by a linear list of `fib_rule` structures, sorted in ascending order by priority value and hooked into the static `fib_rules` variable. Initially, this list contains three entries: the `fib_rule` structures `default_rule`, `main_rule`, and `local_rule`, which are statically defined. Figure 16–6 shows this initial state of the rules list. A read-write spinlock called `fib_rules_lock` is used to regulate access to the list.

`struct fib_rule`	**net/ipv4/fib_rule.c**

The `fib_rule` structure, to begin with, contains two management fields, a link pointer, `struct fib_rule *r_next`, and a reference counter, `atomic_t r_clntref`. The latter specifies the number of references to a specific instance of the structure. This counter is incremented by `atomic_inc()` when new rules are added, and especially when a reference to a rule is returned in a result for a forwarding request. A call to `atomic_dec_and_test()` in the interface function `fib_rule_put()`, which frees `fib_rule` instances, decrements the reference counter. The memory is actually freed when this counter reaches a value of zero. In this situation, the function additionally checks for whether the entry `int r_dead` was set to one by explicitly deleting the rule

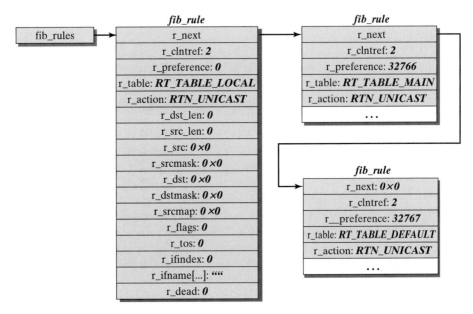

FIGURE 16–6
List with routing rules (initial state). Optional structure entries are not shown.

(by `inet_rtm_delrule()`; see further below). If this is not the case, then there must be
an implementation error, which is written to the system log for the user's attention.

Next within the structure follows some information about the described rule: the
priority value `u32 r_preference`, the `unsigned char r_table` identifier for a routing
table to be used, and the field `unsigned char r_action`, which specifies the action that
should run if the rule's selector matches the packet currently being processed. The five
rule types mentioned in Section 16.1.6 can be coded with the values `RTN_UNICAST`,
`RTN_BLACKHOLE`, `RTN_UNREACHABLE`, `RTN_PROHIBIT`, and `RTN_NAT`, which are declared in `include/linux/netlink.h`. Additional attributes for the action are the `u32`
`r_srcmap und __u32 r_tclassid` entries. The first of these two entries includes the
new source address for static address translation. The second entry is present only if the
kernel was configured with the `CONFIG_NET_CLS_ROUTE` option. (See Section 16.2.1.) It
contains a class identifier for a queuing discipline that is assigned to packets, if the routing table entry we select later does not itself contain a class identifier.

The rule's selector is represented by an address prefix and a corresponding network mask for the packet's source and destination addresses (`u32 r_src, r_src-`
`mask, r_dst, r_dstmask`), by the network interface index (`int r_ifindex`), by the
content in the TOS field (`u8 r_tos`), and additionally by the fwmark (`u32 r_fwmark`),
if activated in `CONFIG_IP_ROUTE_FWMARK`. Moreover, the structure includes the lengths
of the address prefixes (`unsigned char r_src_len, r_dst_len`) and the network interface name (`char r_ifname[IFNAMSIZ]`). These attributes are used only when rules
are inserted, deleted, and displayed at the RT netlink interface. In contrast, forwarding
decisions use only the address masks and the much faster integer index for the network
interface.

Though the u8 `r_flags` entry is accepted from the RT netlink interface, it has no meaning in rules processing.

Initialization and Internal Functions   The initialization function `fib_rules_init()`, which is invoked (from within `ip_fib_init()`, which, in turn, is invoked by `ip_rt_init()`) when the routing is initialized during system start, does not have to initialize the rules list, because its initial entries are already statically linked and anchored. However, it registers the callback function `fib_rules_export()` in the notification chain for state changes to network devices. (See Section 5.2.4.) If changes occur, `fib_rules_event()` is invoked, which branches to `fib_rules_attach()` when a new network device is registered, but to `fib_rules_detach()` when a network device is unregistered. These two functions visit all existing rules and correct the `ifindex` entry, which is meaningful for registered devices only and should otherwise be set to −1.

As was mentioned in connection with the `r_clntref` reference counter, the `fib_rule_put()` function is used to release references that point to `fib_rule` structures. This function is also declared in `ip_fib.h`, because it is invoked not only internally, but also when structures are released that were returned as replies to forwarding requests and contain a reference to the rule that led to the selection of a route from a routing table.

RT Netlink Interface   The RT netlink interface represents the only way to manage routing rules. For this purpose, the table `inet_rtnetlink_table[]` (net/ipv4/devinet.c) has pointers for the message types RTM_NEWRULE, RTM_DEL-RULE, and RTM_GETRULE that point to the functions `inet_rtm_newrule()`, `inet_rtm_delrule()`, and `inet_dump_rules()`, so that these functions are invoked to handle the corresponding RT netlink messages.

A large part of the implementation of these functions consists in converting between the data structures of RT netlink messages and the `fib_rule` structure. In addition, when new rules are added, the values entered are checked for whether or not they are valid and consistent. If a rule is added without stating a required routing table, then the function `fib_empty_table()` is invoked and searches for a table not yet used.[2] If no priority is stated, then a new rule is added to the rules list before all other rules with a nonzero priority. When rules are polled (message type RTM_GETRULE), the auxiliary function `inet_fill_rule()` is used; it appends the information of a single rule to the RT netlink reply message currently being built.

Interface to Forwarding Functions   The rules database represents the access point to the FIB virtually, because rules have to be used to identify a suitable routing table for each forwarding request. For this reason, the "central" request function, `fib_lookup()`, is also implemented in `fib_rules.c` (or in `ip_fib.h`, if rule-based routing is disabled). However, it handles only a small part of the work involved; important parts are handled by invoking functions from other FIB parts, as we will see later.

---

[2]If you invoke `ip rule` add without stating a table number, then it automatically uses the table `main`. To create an RT netlink message with unspecified table, you have to use the `table 0` option specifically with `ip rule add`.

In addition to these FIB interface functions, there are several functions that access specific elements of the fib_rule structure. This structure is not visible outside the fib_rule.c file.

- ▨ fib_rules_tclass() simply returns the queuing discipline's class identifier assigned to a rule.
- ▨ fib_rules_policy() transforms the source address as specified by a rule, if applicable.
- ▨ fib_rules_map_destination() transforms the destination address for NAT routes. (See Section 16.1.6.)

fib_lookup()	**net/ipv4/fib_rules.c**

This function, which represents the most commonly used FIB interface, returns a matching routing-table entry for a key passed as argument. The key is passed as pointer to an rt_key structure (declared in route.h). This structure contains the source and destination addresses (src and dst), the input and output network interface indices (iif and oif), the TOS value (tos), and the fwmark (?) for the packet to be forwarded, if applicable:

```
struct rt_key
{
            __u32       dst;
            __u32       src;
            int         iif;
            int         oif;
#ifdef CONFIG_IP_ROUTE_FWMARK
            __u32       fwmark;
#endif
            __u8        tos;
            __u8        scope;
};
```

The scope information (scope) can be used to limit the search range. For this, each entry in a routing table includes a scope identifier, and only entries with equal or smaller scopes are returned for a request (but smaller scopes have bigger identifiers). The following scopes are predefined:

Symbol	Value	Scope
RT_SCOPE_UNIVERSE	0	any destination
RT_SCOPE_LINK	253	destination in the same physical network
RT_SCOPE_HOST	254	destination in the local system
RT_SCOPE_NOWHERE	255	destination does not exist

To handle a request, the rules list is visited in the order of ascending priority value, and the action corresponding to the rule type runs for each rule with a selector that matches the key passed. Rules of the types `unreachable, blackhole`, and `prohibit` cause the function to be aborted and to return an appropriate error value. For `unicast` and `nat` rules, the routing table identified by the `r_table` entry of the rule is consulted.

Section 16.3.2 discusses the data structures used to represent routing tables and how these structures are searched. The interface for this is the function pointer `tb_lookup()` in the `fib_table` structure representing the root of a routing table. If a table search is successful, then the result supplied by `tb_lookup()` is returned; otherwise, `fib_lookup()` continues with the next rule.

`fib_select_default()`	`net/ipv4/fib_rules.c`

This function serves to select a route from several default routes; it is invoked whenever a previous FIB request returns a routing-table entry with a network prefix of length `null`. It obtains the request key and the request result as parameters. The default route is actually selected by the function pointer `tb_select_default()`, which is included in the `fib_table` structure.

16.3.2 Routing Tables

In the Linux kernel, routing tables are represented by rather complex data structures, which manage entries by using a number of hash tables for different prefix lengths.

Data Structures   A `fib_table` structure forms the basis for a routing table. This structure includes a pointer to an `fn_zone` structure for each potential prefix length (0 to 32 bits). All routing table entries with the same prefix length are allocated to a specific `fn_zone` structure. The `fn_zone` structure uses an additional hash table to store the individual entries, each represented by a `fib_node` structure. The hash function used for this purpose also uses the entry's network prefix. If several routing-table entries have the same hash value, then the corresponding `fib_node` structures are linked in a linear list. Ultimately, the actual data of an entry is not in the `fib_node` structure itself, but in a `fib_info` structure referenced in the former structure.

There are up to 255 different routing tables when rule-based routing is used. The associated `fib_table` structures are managed by using the array variable `struct fib_table * fib_tables[RT_TABLE_MAX+1]`. Their positions within the array correspond to the table numbers, which are used in routing rules to identify routing tables. Only position null is not used; at the interfaces, identifier null denotes an unspecified table and normally is mapped to the `main` table. If rule-based routing is not used, there are only two routing tables, each referenced by a global variable: `local_table` and `main_table`.

Figure 16–7 shows a possible instance of `fib_table` and `fn_zone` structures, where the routing table with number 254 (`RT_TABLE_MAIN`) includes entries with three different prefix lengths: 0 (default route), 16, and 24. The hash tables used to reference the respective routing-table entries are shown on the right-hand side of the figure. They have different sizes: For prefix length null, the hash function will always yield the same value, which is the reason why one single entry is sufficient here, while 16 entries

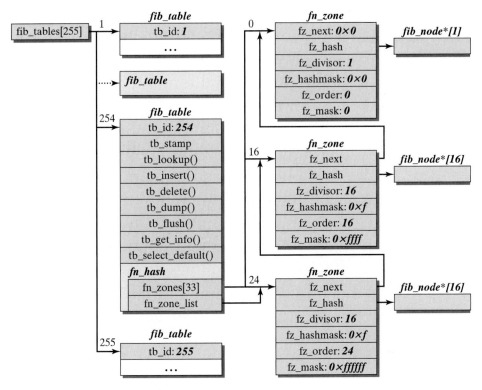

FIGURE 16–7
The fib_table structure with references to zones of different prefix lengths.

are allocated for other prefix lengths. The hash tables grow automatically when they fill up, if the option CONFIG_IP_ROUTE_LARGE_TABLES is active.

The fib_node and fib_info structures belonging to the routing-table entries are not shown in Figure 16–7, because of limited space. They are shown in Figure 16–8, which is described further along.

struct fib_table	include/net/ip_fib.h

In addition to its number, tb_id, and an unused element by the name of tb_stamp, the fib_table structure includes a number of function pointers, forming the interface to manage the entries stored in the table:

- ▨ tb_insert() and tb_delete() serve to insert and delete entries; they are used in net/ipv4/fib_frontend.c to handle RT netlink messages and ioctl() and kernel-internal calls.
- ▨ tb_dump() serves to output entries over RT netlink, and tb_get_info() serves to output entries in the /proc/net/route format.

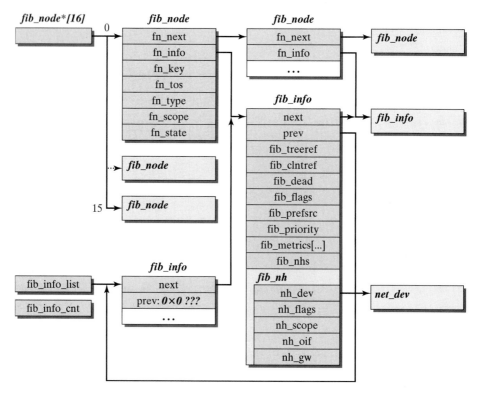

FIGURE 16–8
Hash table of a zone with fib_node and fib_info structures.

▨ tb_lookup() searches the table for an entry matching a key; it is used by the
   main query function, fib_lookup().
▨ tb_flush() frees all entries in the table that previously have been marked as
   deleted.
▨ tb_select_default() serves to select one route from several existing default
   routes.

These function pointers are set to functions in fib_hash.c, with names matching
those of the pointers, except for the prefix (fn_hash_ instead of tb_), when a new
fib_table structure is created by a call to fib_new_table() (include/net/ip_fib.h
and net/ipv4/fib_frontend.c). This initialization is accomplished by the function
fib_hash_init() (net/ipv4/fib_hash.c), invoked from within fib_new_table().
   These function pointers are the only way to access internal routing table data
structures; their implementation is fully encapsulated. The "core" structures fn_zone
and fib_node are defined exclusively in the file net/ipv4/fib_hash.c. Also, the
fn_hash structure, which is physically part of the fib_table structure, is declared
"anonymously" as unsigned char tb_data[0] in include/net/ip_fib.h; it is actually used only within net/ipv4/fib_hash.c. The fib_info structure, which includes
information about individual entries, is the only structure visible to the outside.

struct fn_zone	**net/ipv4/fib_hash.c**

An fn_zone structure manages all entries with the same prefix length by use of a hash table. The fixed prefix length is noted in the fz_order element, and fz_mask includes an appropriate network mask. The hash table consists of an array of fib_node structures, which are referenced by the fz_hash pointer. The array size is specified by fz_divisor. fz_hashmask holds a bit mask used to mask the hash value to the range permitted for indexing in the array in its last computation step.

An fn_zone structure for a specific prefix length exists only provided that entries with this prefix length actually exist. All fn_zone structures of a table are linked in a linear list in the order of descending prefix length (by using the fz_next element), which is hooked into the fn_zone_list element of the fn_hash structure at the bottom of the fib_table structure. This list forms the basis of search for an entry with the longest network prefix matching a specific destination address.

struct fib_node	**net/ipv4/fib_hash.c**

Each single entry in a routing table is represented by a fib_node structure. In its fn_key element, this structure contains the destination network prefix (with an identical length for all entries of one zone), and its fn_tos elements includes a TOS value, which is also part of the key used to search a routing table. The type and scope of an entry are coded in fn_type and fn_scope, and the fn_state element stores two flags used to manage the structure.

All additional information in a routing-table entry, which is not required for searching an entry, but represents merely part of the search results,[3] is located in the fib_info structure, which can be reached over fn_info.

struct fib_info	**include/net/ip_fib.h**

The fib_info structure represents information about the result of an FIB query, including the output interface to be used and the next hop along the route to the destination system, if necessary. This information is included in a fib_nh structure in the element fib_nh of the fib_info structure. The fib_nh element is an array to represent the situation where several equivalent routes lead to the same destination in the FIB. This array is declared with size null, and sufficient space is reserved for new entries that all stated routes can be stored. The number of these routes is then stored in the fib_nhs element of the fib_info structure.

The fib_nh structure is declared in ip_fib.h and contains the output interface to be used in the form of its index (nh_oif); as a pointer to the net_device structure (nh_dev), it also includes the IP address of the next router (nh_gw).

---

[3]Though quality information (metric) plays a role in searching, it is not explicitly used. The reason is that it already influences an entry's position in the fib_node list when the entry is inserted, so that entries with lower metric values are automatically found earlier.

The fib_info structure does not contain any backward references to its position within the routing-table data structures. Instead, the fib_next and fib_prev pointers serve to arrange all existing fib_info structures to form a doubly linked list, which is hooked into a global variable, fib_info_list. When creating a new entry, the function fib_create_info(), which is invoked by tb_insert(), first checks for whether an identical entry exists in the list. Rather than duplicating such an entry, it would merely increment the reference counter fib_clntref. This means that several fib_node structures can reference one single fib_info structure. When a fib_node is freed, then the fib_info structure is also freed, if the reference counter has reached null.

In contrast to fn_zone and fib_node, the fib_info structure becomes visible to the outside again: It is declared in include/net/ip_fib.h, and its contents are read directly in some places (e.g., in net/ipv4/route.c). All operations to manage fib_info structures that go beyond the plain reading of a data element are implemented in the file net/ipv4/fib_semantics.s, however.

Managing and Initializing Memory   The FIB implementation is initialized in ip_fib_init() (net/ipv4/fib_frontend.c). If rule-based routing is not used, then the function fib_hash_init() is invoked directly for the two tables table_local and table_main held in global variables. This function occupies memory for a fib_table structure and sets the enclosed function pointers to the fn_hash_ functions. The substructure of the type fn_hash, which contains the zone hash table, is initialized to null.

In contrast, if rule-based routing is used, routing tables are not previously initialized. The global array that references the tables is created as a memory area initialized to null when the kernel is loaded. Whenever a routing table is accessed via an element of the array, then it is checked whether the table already exists, and, if this is not the case, it is created by fib_hash_init().

The function fib_hash_init() also ensures that a slab cache (see Section 2.6.2) called "ip_fib_hash" exists. This slab cache supplies memory for fib_node structures, which are allocated in the function fn_hash_insert() to create new entries when needed.

Managing Hash Structures   The functions that access fn_zone and fib_node structures, which are used internally to manage routing-table entries by using hash tables, are collected in the file net/ipv4/fib_hash.c. They are invoked by all other FIB functions to access fn_zone and fib_node structures.

Encapsulation of these internal structures allows them to be reimplemented, if necessary, by using other data structures offering a more efficient search process, without the need to effect changes in other places.

The most important functions in net/ipv4/fib_hash.c are as follows:

- fn_rehash_zone() enlarges the hash tables, if necessary.
- fn_new_zone() creates a new fn_zone structure and sorts it into the zone list based on its prefix length.
- fn_hash_lookup() handles the main task in an FIB query: The fn_zone structures in a routing table are walked through in the sequence of descending prefix length, and the hash table is searched for an entry matching the key passed as an argument.

- ▨ fn_hash_select_default() selects one out of several default routes, considering whether the intermediate system specified as the next router is currently reachable.
- ▨ fn_hash_insert(), fn_hash_delete(), and fn_hash_dump() serve to insert, delete, and display entries over the RT netlink interface.
- ▨ fn_hash_flush() removes all fib_info structures of a zone that were previously marked as invalid.
- ▨ fn_hash_get_info() serves to display routing table entries over the proc file system.

Interfaces to the User-Address Space   From within the user-address space, you can manage routing tables both over the traditional ioctl() interface and over RT netlink.

For the RT netlink interface, the functions inet_rtm_newroute(), inet_rtm_delroute(), and inet_dump_fib() from net/ipv4/fib_frontend.c are registered in the table inet_rtnetlink_table[] in net/ipv4/devinet.c, so that they can be invoked to add, delete, or output a routing table entry and handle corresponding messages.

ioctl() system calls are handled by ip_rt_ioctl() (net/ipv4/fib_frontend.c), which is invoked in af_inet.c by the general routine that handles ioctl() calls at PF_INET sockets. (See Chapter 26.) The parameters for the call are converted into an RT netlink message by fib_convert_rtentry() and passed to inet_rtm_newroute() or inet_rtm_delroute() for further handling.

proc File System   The contents of the pseudo file /proc/net/route, which can be used to view the main routing table, are created by the function fib_get_procinfo() (net/ipv4/fib_frontend.c), which is registered by ip_fib_init(), using proc_net_create(), for this purpose. The function creates a header line and uses the function pointer tb_get_info() from the main table, which normally points to fn_hash_get_info() (ipv4/net/fib_hash.c), to output the data. There, all fib_node structures in fn_zone_list are visited, and the appropriate data is eventually output by fib_node_get_info() (net/ipv4/fib_semantics.c).

Reacting to Changes in Network Interfaces   The functions fib_inetaddr_event() and fib_netdev_event() (net/ipv4/fib_frontend.c) are registered in two notification chains for state changes to network interfaces or changes to their IP addresses when ip_fib_init() initializes the FIB.

As soon as a network device obtains an IP address or when it is reactivated after it had addresses and was deactivated previously, then fib_add_ifaddr() (invoked by fib_inetaddr_event() or fib_netdev_event()) creates entries for local and broadcast routes in the local table. When addresses are removed, these entries are deleted accordingly by fib_del_ifaddr(). In addition, during removal of addresses, all routing entries that use the removed address as their preferred source address have to be deactivated. This is handled by the function fib_sync_down() from net/ipv4/fib_semantics.c.

When deactivating or deleting a network interface (and also when the last address of an interface was removed), fib_netdev_event() invokes the function fib_disable_ip() which, in turn, uses fib_sync_down() (parametrized differently) to declare all those `fib_nh` structures, that use the interface as their forwarding-output interface as invalid. Subsequently, the routing cache is deleted, and, finally, `fib_disable_ip()` invokes `arp_ifdown()` to inform the ARP implementation that the interface disappeared.

Interfaces to the Forwarding Functions   This section describes several operations in addition to those discussed in Section 16.3.1, which are used by the functions in `net/ipv4/route.c` to access the FIB.

`fib_validate_source()`	net/ipv4/fib_frontend.c

The function `fib_validate_source()` serves to check the source addresses of IP packets within a forwarding process. This check can be implemented elegantly by an FIB query, using `fib_lookup()` for the opposite direction (i.e., with source and destination addresses swapped): If the entry found is not of the type `RTN_UNICAST` (but `RTN_LOCAL`, for example, which means that the address is assigned to a local interface), then this address is not a valid source address for an incoming packet.

If the output interface noted in an inverted FIB query matches the actual input interface, then the validation is completed successfully. This is the only acceptable result when reverse-path filtering is active.

If the actual input device does not currently have an address, then the above check is considered successful, even if the FIB query returns no result at all. If the output device found does not match the actual input device, then another FIB query is done with the actual input device specified as a fixed output device. If this query supplies either a result of the type `RTN_UNICAST` or no result at all, the check is considered to have been successful.

`fib_select_multipath()`	net/ipv4/fib_semantics.c

When a routing-table entry with several routes is used in a forwarding process, the function `fib_select_multipath()` is invoked to select one of these routes. This decision is made randomly (the `jiffies` counter is used rather than a "real" random number generator), taking weights assigned to each of these routes into account.

`ip_dev_find()`	net/ipv4/fib_frontend.c

To find the network interface that belongs to an IP address passed as parameter, `ip_dev_find()` uses the function pointer `tb_lookup()` to search the local table. The result has to be an entry of the type `RTN_LOCAL`, and a reference to the wanted `net_device` structure can be taken from the entry.

`inet_addr_type()`	net/ipv4/fib_frontend.c

`inet_addr_type()` is another function that searches the local table for a specific address, but the address type is the result looked for in this case. The semantics is slightly different and is characterized by the specific requirements of the functions that invoke `inet_addr_type()`: Formally invalid addresses are previously filtered and then yield the RTN_MULTICAST result, and an address is treated as RTN_UNICAST, even if no entry is found in the `local` table.

16.3.3 The Routing Cache

Though the FIB data structures offer relatively fast queries, the cost to run such a query for each single IP packet would be altogether excessive. For this reason, the Linux kernel has a cache, in addition to the FIB, that stores the results of the forwarding queries used most recently allowing them to be accessed quickly. Each forwarding operation first consults the routing cache, and the FIB is queried only if no matching entry exists in the cache. The result of the FIB query is then used to create a new cache entry immediately.

The routing cache is based on a relatively simple data structure. One single hash table includes the cache entries, which are linearly linked when the hash value is identical. The hash function processes the source and destination addresses for packets to be forwarded, plus their TOS values. Each cache entry contains all information required to forward a packet.

Figure 16–9 shows the hash table (left-hand side), organized as an array of `rt_hash_bucket` structures. The pointer `struct rt_hash_bucket *rt_hash_table`

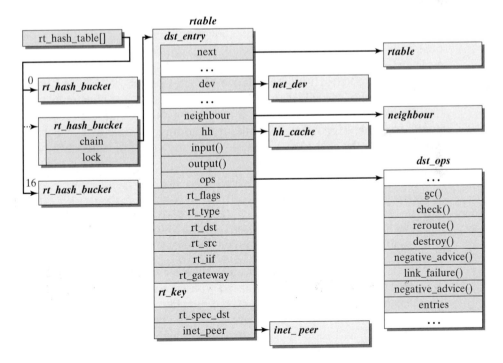

FIGURE 16–9
Data structures of the routing cache.

references this array. Within each `rt_hash_bucket` structure, the `chain` element forms the anchoring point for a list of `rtable` structures, representing the cache entries. Access to this list is controlled by the read–write spinlock `lock` in the `rt_hash_bucket` structure. The size of the hash table is defined according to the main memory size when the routing code is initialized and remains unchanged afterwards.

struct rtable	include/net/route.h

The `rtable` structure is rather extensive, and Figure 16–9 shows only an excerpt. In addition, we somewhat simplified the representation of its first element. Actually, the first element of the `rtable` structure is a `union` structure, u, which contains a `dst_entry` structure and an `rtable` pointer:

```
union {
      struct dst_entry dst;
      struct rtable *rt_next;
} u;
```

Both elements of u are used concurrently, without representing a problem, because the first element of the `dst_entry` structure is the `dst_entry` pointer `next`, and `dst_entry` structures occur only within `rtable` structures. This means that `u.dst.next` and `u.rt_next` are two different names for the same pointer; based on their types, the total object or only part of it are referenced.

The `rt_src` and `rt_dst` elements specify the source and destination addresses for IP packets handled by this entry. `rt_gateway` stores the address of the next router—or the destination address again, if no router is required. The interface identifier in `iif` can denote the output or input interface.

The `rt_key` structure integrated as element `key` is used as the key in searching the routing cache. The values stored there do not necessarily have to match those outside. For example, in searching for an entry of a packet that was created locally and should be sent now, normally no source address is specified, which means that `rt_key.src` in the cache entry is null. However, the source address to be assigned to the new packet is stored in `rt_src`.

struct dst_entry	include/net/dst.h

The `dst_entry` structure contains a large number of information elements. The most important elements are introduced below by origin and purpose:

- Some pointers refer to other data structures required when forwarding IP packets and so they are available there without additional effort—the `net_device` structure of the output interface, the `neighbour` structure to the next router or the destination system (corresponding to the `rt_gateway` element in the `rtable` structure), and the `hh_cache` structure, which includes a packet header of the data-link layer that just has to be copied.
- Function pointers to operations for further processing when receiving (`input()`) or transmitting (`output()`) an IP packet that matches the cache entry are simply

invoked at the appropriate positions within the IP protocol procedure, to result in the packet's being handled appropriately. The input() pointer in entries that can be used for incoming packets refers to ip_local_deliver() (unicast packets to be delivered locally), to ip_mr_input() (multicast packets), to ip_forward() (packets to be forwarded), or to ip_error() (forwarding impossible because destination is unreachable). The output() pointer refers to ip_output() (unicast packets) or ip_mc_output() (multicast packets).

- A reference to a dst_ops structure for IPv4 entries always points to the globally defined structure ipv4_dst_ops. It contains several function pointers, and users of routing-cache entries (e.g., TCP or ARP) can use them to supply feedback to the routing cache (e.g., about connection failures). In addition, the dst_ops structure holds a counter for occupied cache entries and stores a threshold value which, when exceeded, causes the cache garbage collection to start (as described later).

- The usage counter, __use, is incremented whenever the cache entry is used. The time of the last use is also stored in the lastuse element.

- Various parameters for transport protocols are copied from the fib_info structure.

Some functions to manage dst_entry structures are defined in the files include/net/dst.h and net/core/dst.c.

Interface to Forwarding Functions   The implementation of the routing cache is hardly encapsulated against the other program logic used for forwarding; you find both in the file net/ipv4/route.c. For example, there is no separate function that searches for a cache entry. Each search operates directly on the cache data structure in both main interface functions for IP packet processing (ip_route_input() and ip_route_output()—see Section 16.3.4). Part of the creation of new cache entries is done there as well.

Nevertheless, there are a few methods that are used by the forwarding functions, yet clearly belong to the routing cache. The most important such methods are described below.

rt_hash_code()	net/ipv4/route.c

rt_hash_code() is used to calculate the hash value from the source and destination addresses and the TOS value passed as parameters. This hash value serves as index in the hash table of the routing cache.

rt_intern_hash()	net/ipv4/route.c

The forwarding functions use the rt_intern_hash() function to insert an almost complete rtable structure into the hash table of the routing cache. New entries are always inserted in the first position in a potential collision-resolution list. If an entry with identical key exists in the list, then this entry is moved to the front, and the new entry is discarded.

In addition to inserting entries, rt_intern_hash() procures the pointer to a neighbour structure matching the next router or destination system from the rtable structure.

net/ipv4/sysctl_net_ipv4.c includes a reference to ipv4_route_table[]. This structure is embedded in the central sysctl() tree over net_table[] in net/sysctl.net.c and root_table[] in kernel/sysctl.c.

The file /proc/net/rt_cache lets you read the content of the entire routing cache. The content is formatted by the function rt_cache_get_info() from net/ipv4/route.c, which is registered using proc_net_create() when the routing is initialized in ip_rt_init().

16.3.4 The Forwarding Process

Section 14.2.1 discussed how a forwarding query is embedded into the processing of incoming IP packets: ip_rcv_finish() invokes ip_route_input() to find a dst_entry structure to determine the packet's further route. Section 14.2.2 discussed outgoing packets: their routing decision is made in ip_route_output(), which is invoked by, for example, ip_queue_xmit().

ip_route_input()	net/ipv4/route.c

The function ip_route_input() is invoked for each IP packet arriving over a network interface. The parameters are a pointer to the socket-buffer structure, the destination and source addresses, the TOS value, and a pointer to the net_device structure of the receiving network interface.[4]

First, rt_hash_code() is used on the addresses and the TOS value to compute an index in the hash table of the routing cache. If necessary, the list anchored in the chain element is walked through to find a cache entry matching addresses, input interface, TOS value, and fwmark, if present. If this search is successful, then a pointer to the entry is placed as dst in the sk_buff structure, and the task is complete.

If no matching cache entry is found, then either of the two following functions is responsible for further handling:

▪ ip_route_input_mc() is invoked if the destination address is a multicast address. Another prerequisite is that the input interface either belongs to that multicast group or has been configured for multicast routing. The packet can be discarded if this is not the case. The function ip_route_input_mc() will be discussed later in the chapter about IP multicast (Section 17.4). What is done there is similar to the procedure for local-destination addresses described below, the only difference being that the packet is always delivered to the local machine rather than causing an FIB query.

▪ ip_route_input_slow() serves to handle "normal" destination addresses and is described next.

Both functions take the same parameters as ip_route_input() itself.

---

[4]The last four parameters could, alternatively, be worked out from the first. However, because they are passed separately, knowledge about their representation in the socket-buffer structure does not have to be present in ip_route_input(). Though the socket buffer structure is still not entirely treated as an encapsulated "black box," at least only few data elements especially present for routing are accessed.

`ip_route_input_slow()`	**net/ipv4/route.c**

To begin with, an `rt_key` structure is filled with the parameters passed. However, before it is used to run an FIB query, the addresses are checked for invalid values—multicast source addresses, and addresses moving a network prefix beginning with null. Such packets are dropped, and, if verbose messages are configured with `CONFIG_IP_ROUTE_VERBOSE`, they are registered in the system log. The use of `0.0.0.0` as source and destination addresses in the sense of limited broadcast is explicitly allowed as an exception, for this is occasionally used for automatic network configuration.

Next, the FIB query is started by calling `fib_lookup()`. If no matching entry is found, then `ip_route_input_slow()` also aborts processing and returns an error code, which subsequently causes `ip_rcv_finish()` (from where `ip_route_input_slow()` was invoked) to discard the packet.

If the routing NAT mentioned in Section 16.1.6 is active, the next step transforms the source address according to the information in the routing rule used (or the destination address, if the route found is an `nat` route). However, the new addresses are added only to the `rt_key` structure; the old addresses are maintained in the call parameters of the function and are available for other operations. Once the destination address has been transformed, `fib_lookup()` has to be invoked once more to find a regular routing entry (no other transformations are permitted) to the new destination address.

Among other things, the result from the FIB query also shows whether the destination address is a local address, which means that the packet is intended for the local system. This case is handled separately in the further process.

■ *Local destination address:* A new cache entry is created once the source address has been checked by the calling of `fib_validate_source()`. The function pointer `output()` gets the `ip_rt_bug()` value, because the packet is not allowed to leave the system. Next, the `input()` pointer is set to `ip_local_deliver()`, to cause the packet to be delivered to the local machine. Because there is no next router, the `rt_gateway` element of the cache entry is set to the destination address.

Broadcast addresses, such as the `0.0.0.0` address mentioned above as source and destination or the normally limited broadcast to `255.255.255.255` are detected in the address validation at the beginning and handled identically to local destination addresses. However, `fib_validate_source()` is not called for `0.0.0.0` addresses.

■ *Nonlocal destination address:* Nonlocal destination addresses have to be handled only if the forwarding function for the input interface is enabled, so this is checked first.

If the routing-table entry found describes several output routes, then `fib_select_multipath()` is called to select one of those routes. Subsequently, the source address is checked by the function `fib_validate_source()`, which can also consider the output network interface found in this case.

`ip_forward()` and `ip_output()` are set in the new cache entry for the `input()` and `output()` function pointers. The function `rt_set_nexthop()` does the necessary assignment to `rt_gateway` and also fills in other elements of the `dst_entry` structure that are of interest for forwarded packets only.

`rt_intern_hash()` is used to integrate the `rtable` structure, which is almost complete, into the hash table of the routing cache. It also supplies the return value of `ip_route_input_slow()`, which then is complete.

`ip_route_output()`	**include/net/route.h**

According to a comment in the `route.h` header file, where it is implemented as an inline function, the function `ip_route_output()` is going to be replaced by `ip_route_output_key()`. Actually, however, it is invoked in many different positions within the network implementation as the main routing interface (e.g., by the IP transmit function `ip_queue_xmit()` [see Section 14.2.2] or by `udp_sendmsg()` [see Section 25.3.1] for packets created by UDP).

Its only function currently is to create an `rt_key` structure with the source and destination addresses, the TOS value, and the output device from the passed parameters and to subsequently invoke the function `ip_route_output_key()`, which will be described next. The last parameter is the pointer `struct rtable **rp`, which serves to return the result; it is also passed to `ip_route_output_key()`.

`ip_route_output_key()`	**net/ipv4/route.c**

The task of `ip_route_output_key()` is to determine a routing entry for the `rt_key` structure passed. The procedure is similar to that of `ip_route_input()`; the routing cache is searched for a matching entry, and the process branches to `ip_route_output_slow()` only if no such entry is found. Rather than the input interface, the output interface is used for hash computation and comparisons.

`ip_route_output_slow()`	**net/ipv4/route.c**

`ip_route_output_slow()` is invoked if no entry for the destination of a locally created IP packet exists in the routing cache. This function runs an FIB query, enters the result in the routing cache, and returns the new entry. In addition, it handles several special cases for which `fib_lookup()` alone is not sufficient.

As with `ip_route_output_key()`, the only input parameter is an `rt_key` structure. This structure initially is copied to a new structure of the same type, which can then be modified without losing the information passed. The `iif` and `scope` information is not considered; instead, the loopback device is always assumed for `iif`, and `scope` is set to either `RT_SCOPE_LINK` or `RT_SCOPE_UNIVERSE`, depending on the `RTO_ONLINK` flag in the `tos` element.

The input parameters are first checked for errors or special cases. For example, for multicast destination addresses, a route is created immediately without FIB query if a valid source address is specified, which can be used to identify a usable output device. This special handling simplifies the transmission of multicast packets (and some multicast tools that traditionally utilize this possibility continue to work). For a specified output interface, a matching source address is found, and 127.0.0.1 is used for the destination address, if none is specified.

An FIB query is started once all preparations have been completed. Notice that the process can, in some cases, continue even if this query returns a negative result. In fact, if an output interface was specified during the call, then this interface is used by simply assuming that the destination is in the adjacent network.

The query result can be used to distinguish between local and nonlocal destination addresses. The loopback device is always the output interface used for local addresses, but `fib_select_multipath()` might have to select one out of several routes, or `fib_select_default()` might have to choose from several default routes for nonlocal addresses.

Again, `ip_route_output_slow()` completes the job by filling a new `rtable` structure, where the function `rt_set_nexthop()` is used, similarly to `ip_route_input_slow()`. The `output()` function pointer is set to `ip_output()`, and the `input()` pointer is set to `ip_local_deliver()`, if the destination address is in the local system. `rt_intern_hash()` is used to add the cache entry to the hash table and also yields the return value for `ip_route_output_slow()`.

IP Multicast for Group Communication

The history of telecommunication was characterized mainly by two technologies in the past hundred years (before the Internet era began): telephony, and radio and television broadcasting. These two technologies cover two fundamentally different communication areas or needs:

■ *Individual* communication (unicast): Connections between two communication partners, where the direction of data exchange can be unidirectional (simplex) or bidirectional (duplex).

■ *Mass* communication (broadcast): One station sends data to all stations reachable over a medium, where data distribution is normally unidirectional.

After these two technologies, the Internet followed as the third communication technology, changing the telecommunication world. Though the Internet was initially designed for individual communication, the protocols and mechanisms added at the beginning of the nineties introduced a new communication form: *group* communication (multicast). Multicast makes possible an efficient data distribution to several receivers. By contrast with the mass communication of (radio) broadcasting, where data is distributed to all participants within one single transmission medium, group communication delivers data units only to those receivers explicitly interested in this data. In addition, group communication in the Internet (IP multicast) enables each Internet computer to send data directly to the members of a multicast group.

Consequently, in the designing of mechanisms and protocols, two specific tasks can be deduced for the functionality of group communication in Internet systems:

■ managing memberships in communication groups; and
■ efficient distribution of data packets to all members of a group.

The first task is solved by the Internet Group Management Protocol (IGMP), which has to be supported by each multicast-capable Internet computer. Section 17.3 introduces IGMP and its implementation in Linux systems. For the second task, we have to distinguish between end system and forwarding systems. Section 17.4 will discuss how both types are supported in Linux. As with Internet routing, group communication also separates clearly between forwarding and routing. There are different multicast routing algorithms, including the Distance Vector Multicast Routing Protocol (DVMRP), which will be introduced in Section 17.5.2 as a representative example for these algorithms, using the `mrouted` daemon.

17.1   GROUP COMMUNICATION

Before we introduce the details of IP multicast in Linux, the following sections give a brief summary of the three communication forms: *unicast, broadcast*, and *multicast.*

17.1.1   Unicast

Unicast is the classic form of communication between two partners—point to point. In the context of this book, this means that two computers communicate with each other only. When a unicast communication service is used to transmit data to several receivers, then this has to be done independently of one another in several transmit processes. This means that the cost for the data transport increases in proportion to the number of receivers, as shown in Figure 17–1.

Naturally, if there is a large number of receivers, this cost leads to an extreme load on the network, and so this technique is unsuitable for the distribution of large data volumes, such as multimedia data. Broadcast communication represents a better solution in some cases.

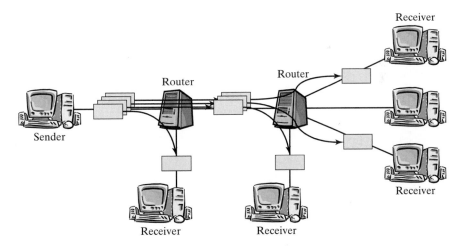

FIGURE 17–1
In unicast communication, the packet is sent to each receiver separately.

17.1.2 Broadcast

Broadcasting means that all participants in a communication network that can be reached over a specific medium receive the distributed data packets, regardless of whether they are interested in it. Examples for broadcast communication include the broadcasting of television and radio broadcasting programs, and advertisements in the mailboxes of homes.

At first sight, broadcast communication looks expensive. However, a closer look reveals that it is supported by the network technologies, especially in local area networks (LANs). In fact, each communication is a broadcast communication in local area networks, because the local network technologies (Ethernet, token ring, etc.) are broadcast media, where data packets are distributed to all stations. When a packet is received, the MAC destination address is checked to see whether the packet should be further handled by that station. This means that broadcast communication is very easy in local area networks. In fact, it is sufficient to send a packet to the network, so that all stations can receive it.

However, as with advertisements in mailboxes, not everybody will want to receive a broadcast packet they are not interested in. For this reason, though it is simple to broadcast data to a group, this approach is a burden for stations not interested in this data and reduces their performance. This holds also true for wide area network (WAN) traffic: Where point-to-point connections prevail, the benefit of the simplicity of broadcasting can easily turn into a heavy burden for the networks [Tan97].

17.1.3 Multicast

Multicast communication offers a solution to the problem described in the previous section. It enables a targeted transmission of data packets, in contrast to *n* single transmissions in unicast, yet it prevents the uncontrolled copying of data packets done in broadcast. In the Internet, this is implemented by defining groups, and each Internet

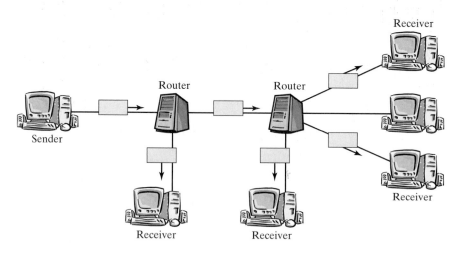

FIGURE 17–2
In multicast communication, the packets are first replicated in the network.

computer can subscribe to groups. Once a system has demonstrated its interest in participating in a multicast group, it will receive packets addressed to this group. In addition, an attempt is made to transport packets across the network so that as few network resources as possible are consumed. With multicast, data packets are not transmitted separately for each receiver. Instead, they are transmitted once and then replicated in the appropriate branching points and delivered to the receivers. (See Figure 17–2.) In contrast to broadcast, only stations that are members of that group receive data packets (with a few minor limitations, as we will see in Section 17.4.1).

In any event, IP multicast forwards data packets selectively to the subnetworks that really connect members of the corresponding multicast group. This approach reduces the network load considerably, compared to the distribution of packets in unicast and broadcast.

17.2 IP MULTICAST

IP multicast extends the unicast service of the Internet Protocol to the capability of sending IP packets to a group of Internet computers. This is realized more effectively than sending single unicast packets to the members of a group. The sender addresses the members of a group by a group address, the so-called IP multicast address. (See Section 17.2.1.) Normally, the sender doesn't know who is currently a member of a group, how many members are subscribed to a group, or where these members are located. IP multicast is one of the few implementations of the principle of group communication. Another network technology that also supports group communication is ATM. Figure 17–3 shows the IP multicast scenario in the Internet.

We basically have to distinguish between multicast communication on the MAC layer and those on the network layer (Internet Protocol). In local area networks, multicast is normally supported by the underlying technology. In this case, multicast packets are

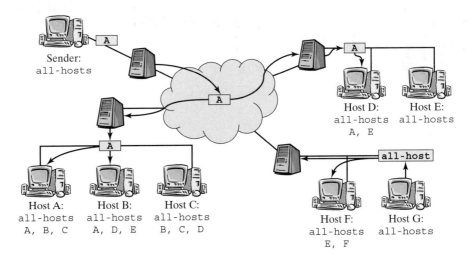

FIGURE 17–3
IP multicast scenario in the Internet.

transmitted over a broadcast-enabled network, and the connected computers use the group address to decide whether they want to receive the data. Section 17.4.1 describes in detail how multicast is supported in local area networks. In contrast, multicast communication on the IP layer (i.e., between the routers in the Internet) is much harder to implement. One of the most important functions is provided by multicast routing protocols, which organize the efficient distribution of data.

The separation between multicast in the local domain and in the routed network domain can be seen not only in how data are forwarded (data path), but also in how groups are managed. Joining and leaving groups is handled by the *Internet Group Management Protocol (IGMP)*; routers distribute their group information over multicast routing protocols. An end system tells its local multicast router only the IP address of the group it wants to join. The router will then have to find out how it can get the multicast data from the Internet. Joining and leaving of groups for computers in a local area network are handled by the *Internet Group Management Protocol*, which will be introduced in Section 17.3.

So-called *multicast distribution trees* are built to distribute multicast packets between routers across the entire network. The data packets are then distributed along these trees to the individual receivers and local area networks. These distribution trees are built by multicast routing protocols (e.g., the *Distance Vector Routing Protocol (DVMRP)* and *Multicast OSPF (MOSPF)*).

As in routing in the Internet, the control path and the data path are also separated here, as can be clearly seen in the implementation under Linux. The data path (i.e., forwarding and replicating of multicast packets) is defined by the information in the multicast routing table. The information in the routing table is procured over the control path, by the multicast routing protocols and IGMP. In addition to better structuring, another benefit of keeping the two mechanisms separate is that we can use different routing protocols. In fact, several protocols are currently available in Linux. Section 17.5.2 uses the DVMRP protocol and its implementation in the `mrouted` daemon as a representative example.

Before we take a closer look at the data and control paths of IP multicast, we will discuss important elements—multicast groups and their addresses—in the next section.

17.2.1 Addresses for Multicast Groups

The address range of the Internet Protocol (Version 4) was introduced in Section 14.1.5. (See Figure 14–3.) The classes A, B, and C are reserved for unicast communication; class E is reserved for future use. The address range of class D is reserved for multicast communication. This means that it is characterized so that the upper four bits of the 32-bit IP address begin with 1110 and take the range from 224.0.0.0 to 239.255.255.255 in the address space. The remaining 28 bits make available 2^{28} multicast groups.

One particularity of group communication is that the sender does normally not know who it is sending its packets to. The group address merely denotes a specific group and does not give information about the current members of this group. It could well be that there are no members at all in the multicast group, or that it has thousand or even millions of receivers. Each multicast-capable participant can join a group. A host that is not wanted in a group cannot be prevented from joining. The only barrier is to cipher the packet contents and to distribute the deciphering key to desired members only.

Multicast group addresses should generally be unique on a worldwide level, because nobody knows which computers join what groups. However, there is a way to limit the reach of a multicast packet, which normally is useful and is actually used by many programs. For this purpose, the *TTL* field in the IP packet is set to a specific value, which means that it will be discarded after the specified number of hops. (See also Section 17.2.3.)

Reserved Multicast Groups   In addition to user-specific multicast groups, a special range of group addresses is reserved for special applications. It is in the range between the addresses from 224.0.0.0 to 224.0.0.255 and from 239.0.0.0 to 239.255.255.255. Only some of these addresses are actually used at present. The following list shows some examples:

- *All hosts* (224.0.0.1): This group automatically includes each multicast-capable IP computer. It is also possible to leave this group. It is used, among other purposes, to determine the number of active groups within a local area network. (See Section 17.3.)
- *All routers* (244.0.0.2): Each multicast router has to belong to the *all-routers* group. It is used for multicast routing purposes.
- *DVMRP routing* (224.0.0.4): This group is used by the Distance Vector Multicast Routing Protocol (DVMRP) to exchange routing information.
- *RIP V2 routing* (224.0.0.9): This group is used by the Routing Information Protocol, Version 2, to exchange routing information.

The ping command can be used to find the computers belonging to a specific group within the local area network. For example, the command ping 224.0.0.1 shows all multicast-capable hosts. (See Figure 17–4.)

17.2.2 Configuring IP Multicast in Linux

To support IP multicast, we have to activate the option "IP: multicasting" when configuring the kernel. This integrates the IGMP protocol, and the computer is now capable of joining a multicast group and receiving its packets.

If we want our Linux computer to additionally act as multicast router, we also have to select the options "IP: multicast routing" and "IP: tunneling" (if IP tunneling is used to connect to a multicast-capable network).

```
klaus@tux # ping 224.0.0.1
PING 224.0.0.1 (224.0.0.1): 56 data bytes
64 bytes from 129.13.42.117: icmp_seq=0 ttl=255 time=0.184 ms
64 bytes from 129.13.42.28: icmp_seq=0 ttl=255 time=0.769 ms (DUP!)
64 bytes from 129.13.42.152: icmp_seq=0 ttl=255 time=1.427 ms (DUP!)
64 bytes from 129.13.42.11: icmp_seq=0 ttl=255 time=1.803 ms (DUP!)
64 bytes from 129.13.42.230: icmp_seq=0 ttl=64 time=2.111 ms (DUP!)
64 bytes from 129.13.42.64: icmp_seq=0 ttl=255 time=2.458 ms (DUP!)
```

FIGURE 17–4
Pinging all multicast-capable computers in the same LAN.

Once we have created and started the new kernel, the computer is able to receive multicast packets. To send packets to multicast groups (which capability, by the way, doesn't require multicast support in the kernel), we need a default route to be able to route multicast packets. In computers not acting as multicast routers, we normally add one route for all multicast groups—namely, to the complete 224.0.0.0 network. The command used for this purpose looks as follows, if eth0 is the computer's network card:

```
route add 224.0.0.0 netmask 240.0.0.0 dev eth0
```

In multicast routers, the routing daemon (e.g., mrouted) is responsible for setting the routes.

If the computer supports the **proc** file system, we can check the virtual file /proc/net/igmp to see the groups in which the computer is currently a member.

17.2.3 Multicast Programming

This section describes how you can integrate multicast communication into applications that you develop yourself. Berkeley sockets (see Chapter 27) are normally used to program applications with network functionality. Berkeley sockets let the programmer access network protocols to run the desired communication over these protocols. Also, socket options can be used to influence the properties of some protocols.

IP multicast is an extension of the Internet Protocol, which is the reason why the multicast options are accommodated in the options of the IP layer. Linux offers the following socket options for multicast:

- IP_MULTICAST_IF defines the network device you want to use to send multicast packets over the socket.
- IP_MULTICAST_TTL sets the *TTL* (Time To Live) value for multicast packets you send.
- IP_MULTICAST_LOOP defines whether multicast packets you send should be received over the *loopback* device.
- IP_ADD_MEMBERSHIP is used to join an IP multicast group.
- IP_DROP_MEMBERSHIP is used to leave an IP multicast group.

The socket options for IP multicast listed above will be described in the following subsections. In general, we need the following getsockopt() and setsockopt() functions to set and get socket options:

- int getsockopt(int socket, int opt_level, int opt_name, void* opt_val, int* opt_len)
- int setsockopt(int socket, int opt_level, int opt_name, const void* opt_val, int opt_len)

The two functions we use to set and get socket options have the following parameters:

- socket is the descriptor of the socket for which we change or get options. For IP multicasting, the socket has to belong to the AF_INET family. Because we can only use either UDP or Raw-IP for multicast communication, the socket will be of the type SOCK_DGRAM or SOCK_RAW.

▓ opt_level identifies the network layer that will handle the option: SOL_SOCKET (socket layer), IPPROTO_UDP (UDP), or IPPROTO_IP for the IP layer. For IP multicasting options, level should always be set to IPPROTO_IP.

▓ opt_len specifies the size of the data structure to which the opt_val pointer refers.

▓ Both getsockopt() and setsockopt() return 0 if successful, but −1 in case an error occurs.

The IP_MULTICAST_IF Socket Option   The kernel normally uses the default network device to send multicast data packets. A programmer can overwrite this behavior and define a specific output network device. The network device is identified by its IP address (if_addr):

```
struct in_addr if_addr;
setsockopt(socket, IPPROTO_IP, IP_MULTICAST_IF, &if_addr, sizeof(if_addr));
```

From now on, the entire multicast traffic created in this socket is transported over the specified network device. To undo this behavior (i.e., to use the network device selected by the system administrator again), we have only to call setsockopt() once more and set the device address to INADDR_ANY.

The IP_MULTICAST_TTL Socket Option   In the multicasting context, the TTL (Time To Live) field in the IP packet header has a dual meaning. First, it controls the lifetime of a packet, to keep the packet from traveling infinitely across the network. Each router decrements the TTL value by one and eventually discards it.

Second, the TTL field has the meaning of a threshold value. We have to avoid multicast packets from being routed out of the local area network or routing range. Otherwise, parts of the Internet could be loaded with undesired multicast packets. This is why we split the potential reach of a multicast packet into different zones. These zones are controlled by the *TTL* value specified in the packets. If a multicast packet exceeds a zone, it has to have a sufficient residual *lifetime* to overcome this hurdle.

▓ 0: limits the reach to the local system. The packet is not output on a physical network device.

▓ 1: The packet can spread only within the subnetwork. It is not forwarded by any router.

▓ <32: Local domain, organization, or department.

▓ <64: Region, country, national corporate intranet.

▓ <128: Continent.

▓ <255: Worldwide.

If a router's threshold value is larger than or equal to the TTL value of a multicast packet, then this packet is discarded. The default value of the TTL field in a multicast packet is one. This means that an application programmer has to set the TTL value explicitly to make it possible for a multicast packet to be transported beyond the local subnetwork. Notice that the TTL value of nonmulticast packets is larger than one for IP. The socket option IP_MULTICAST_TTL can be used to change the default value:

```
int ttl = NEW_TTL;
setsockopt(socket, IPPROTO_IP, IP_MULTICAST_TTL, &ttl, sizeof(ttl));
```

The IP_MULTICAST_LOOP Socket Option   There is a special network device, called the *loopback* device, to enable applications in the local computer to communicate. This device works at minimal cost and behaves like a physical network device. This is the reason it is often used to test network applications locally or to design them so that there will be no difference between situations where the communication partner is reachable locally or remotely over the network. One example is the X-Windows system. The loopback device in Linux is denoted lo and has the reserved IP address 127.0.0.1.

The socket option IP_MULTICAST_LOOP can now be used to define whether multicast packets to be sent should be replicated over the loopback device to local sockets. For example, this could be useful for the video part in a videoconference, so that the users can receive their own images for control purposes. In contrast, this is not desirable for audio data, because it would cause interferences.

When setting the IP_MULTICAST_LOOP, we have to make sure that opt_val is a pointer to a variable specifying the Boolean value for enabled (1) or disabled (0). For example, the compiler would not accept the following call:

```
setsockopt(socket, IPPROTO_IP, IP_MULTICAST_LOOP, 0, 1)
```

The correct call looks like this:

```
int loop = 1;
setsockopt(socket, IPPROTO_IP, IP_MULTICAST_LOOP, &loop, sizeof(loop));
```

The IP_ADD_MEMBERSHIP Socket Option   The socket option (IP_ADD_MEMBERSHIP) is available on application level to join an IP multicast group. In the kernel, the call results in the function ip_mc_join_group(). The kernel is instructed to use IGMP, unless it is already used, to join the desired group, and to forward the data to the application. Notice that more than one application in one single computer can be members of a group.

For example, the code sequence to join group 233.25.10.72 looks like this:

```
/* struct ip_mreq {
 *      struct in_addr imr_multiaddr;    // multicast group to join
 *      struct in_addr imr_interface;    // interface to join on */
struct ip_mreq imr;

imr.imr_multiaddr.s_addr = inet_addr("233.25.10.72");
imr.imr_interface.s_addr = htonl("129.13.42.110");

setsockopt(socket, IPPROTO_IP, IP_ADD_MEMBERSHIP, (void *) &imr,
            sizeof(struct ip_mreq));
```

The IP_LEAVE_MEMBERSHIP Socket Option   This option is invoked to denote that a socket or application is no longer interested in receiving data from that multicast group. Internally, the option is implemented by `ip_mc_leave_group()`. However, this does not automatically mean that the computer won't receive any more packets for the multicast group. The computer's membership in the group is terminated only when no application is any longer interested in the group. Packets for groups that the computer is no longer interested in are simply ignored by the kernel.

The computer in the above example could leave the group as follows:

```
setsockopt(socket, IPPROTO_IP, IP_DROP_MEMBERSHIP, &imr, sizeof(imr));
```

17.3   INTERNET GROUP MANAGEMENT PROTOCOL (IGMP)

The *Internet Group Management Protocol (IGMP)* is used to manage group memberships in local area networks. A multicast router should know all groups having members in the local area network. Accordingly, the Multicast Routing Protocol subscribes packets for these groups. The router does not have to know exactly who in the local area network belongs to a group. It is sufficient for the router to know that there is at least one receiver. The reason is that, when the router transports a packet to the local area network, all stations subscribed to this group receive it automatically.

To avoid unnecessary data transmissions, the router checks periodically for multicast groups that are still desired. For this purpose, it sends a *membership query* to all local computers (i.e., to the *all-hosts* group) within a specific time interval (approximately every two minutes). Each computer currently interested in a group should then return a reply for each of its groups to the router. As was mentioned earlier, the router is not interested in knowing who exactly is a member of a group; it is interested only in knowing whether there is at least one member in the LAN. For this reason, and to prevent all computers from replying at the same time, each computer specifies a random delay time, and it will reply when this time expires. The first computer to reply sends its message to the router *and* to all other local computers of the specified group. Cleverly, it uses the multicast group address for this message. This means that the other computers learn that the router has been informed, so that they don't have to reply. The router has to continue forwarding data for this group from the Internet to the local area network.

Naturally, if a computer wants to join a group, it does not have to wait for a membership query; it can inform the router immediately about the group it wants to join. Section 17.3.3 describes how exactly the IGMP protocol works.

In addition to the tasks discussed above, IGMP is used for other things. The following list summarizes everything the IGMP is used for:

- Query a multicast router for groups desired in a LAN.
- Join and leave a multicast group.
- Exchange membership information with neighboring or higher-layer multicast routers.

17.3.1 Formatting and Transporting IGMP Packets

IGMP messages are transported in the payload field of IP packets, and the number 2 in the Protocol field of the IP packet header identifies them as IGMP messages. They are always sent with the TTL value one, which means that they cannot leave the area of a subnetwork and so means that IGMP manages group memberships only within a subnetwork. To distribute this information beyond these limits, we have to use multicast routing protocols.

Figure 17–5 shows the format of IGMP packets; it includes the following fields:

- *Version*: Number of the IGMP version used.
- *Type*: Type of the IGMP message.
- *Max. Response Time*: This field is used differently, depending on the IGMP version. (See Section 17.3.2.)
- *Checksum*: Checksum of the IGMP message.

The information in an IGMP packet is managed internally by the `igmphdr` structure in the Linux kernel. Consequently, it corresponds to an IGMP packet, also shown in Figure 17–5.

17.3.2 Different Versions

The Internet Group Management Protocol comes in three different versions: *IGMPv0*, *IGMPv1*, and *IGMPv2*. The first version (IGMPv0) is outdated [Deer86] and no longer used, so we won't discuss it here.

The successor version (IGMPv1) is specified in RFC 1112 and fully implemented in the Linux kernel. This version defines two protocol messages, which can be distinguished by the contents of the Type field:

- 0×11: A multicast router directs a query (`IGMP_HOST_MEMBERSHIP_QUERY`) for desired multicast groups to all computers in the LAN.
- 0×12: There is a reply to such a query (`IGMP_HOST_MEMBERSHIP_REPORT`).

The field *Max. Response Time* is set to null in this IGMP version when a packet is sent, and it is ignored by the receiver.

Version 2 of the Internet Group Management Protocol was specified in [Fenn97]. In this version, the field *Type* can take any of four values, and the field *Max. Response Time* plays a more important role.

FIGURE 17–5
The IGMP packet format and its representation in the Linux kernel.

- 0×11: Query sent by a router (IGMP_HOST_MEMBERSHIP_QUERY)
- 0×12: Reply sent by an end system (IGMP_HOST_MEMBERSHIP_REPORT)
- 0×16: Reply of type 2 (IGMP_HOST_NEW_MEMBERSHIP_REPORT)
- 0×17: Request to leave a group (IGMP_HOST_LEAVE_MESSAGE)

The value in the field *Max. Response Time* is specified in tenth-second units. It specifies an interval within which a computer may not send a reply. Once this interval has expired, a reply is sent after a random time.

17.3.3 Operation of the IGMP Protocol

Now that we explained how an IGMP message is structured and how it is transmitted, this section will discuss group management, including the differences between IGMPv1 and IGMPv2.

Multicast routers send group membership queries (IGMP_HOST_MEMBERSHIP_QUERY) to the *all-hosts* group members with group address 224.0.0.1 periodically, at an interval of a few minutes (125 seconds is recommended). Each multicast-capable computer is a member of this group, so all multicast systems receive these queries. (See Figure 17–6.)

Notice that, in these queries, the router sets the TTL value to 1 to ensure that its query packets travel only within the local area network. Next, each computer belonging to one or more multicast groups starts a timer with a random value for each group. (See Figure 17–7.)

Next, as soon as the timer for one of these groups in one computer expires, this computer sends a report (IGMP_HOST_MEMBERSHIP_REPORT) addressed to the multicast group. In addition, the value of the TTL field is set to one in this case. All members of the group receive this report and stop their timers. The effect is that only one computer sends a report, and thus a flood of reports is prevented. The router also receives the report. This reply is sufficient for the router to learn that at least one computer interested in receiving group data is in its local area network. Consequently, the router will subscribe packets of this group via the multicast routing protocol and forward them in the LAN.

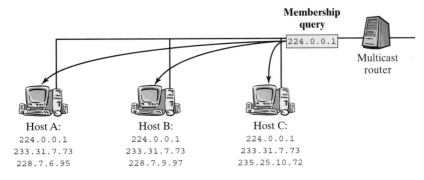

Host A:
224.0.0.1
233.31.7.73
228.7.6.95

Host B:
224.0.0.1
233.31.7.73
228.7.9.97

Host C:
224.0.0.1
233.31.7.73
235.25.10.72

FIGURE 17–6
A multicast router sends a membership query to all multicast computers in the local area network (224.0.0.1).

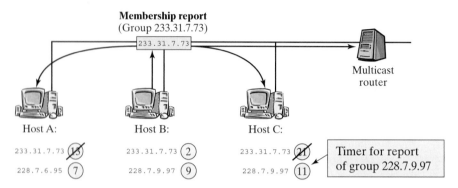

FIGURE 17–7

Membership report of a group by the participant with the smallest timer value in that group.

If the router does not receive reports for a specific group over a certain period of time, it assumes that there are no more interested computers, and deletes this group from its list. If a computer wants to join a group, it can explicitly request this in IGMPv2 by sending a *New Membership Report* packet. In older protocols, the computer may have had to wait a few minutes until the router sends a query message.

When IGMPv2 routers send their queries, they write a specific value to the *Max Resp Time* field. A value larger than null tells the computers that this is an IGMPv2 router. This means that IGMPv2 computers can send version-2 reports (IGMP_HOST_NEW_MEMBERSHIP_REPORT).

In addition, IGMPv2-enabled computers can leave a specific group by sending an IGMP_HOST_LEAVE_MESSAGE to the *all-routers* group. The group to be left is identified in the group address field. Early notification of a station to leave a group can help to reduce the load in the local area network. However, each group member's request to leave a group are sent to the local area network not when it is no longer interested in this data, but only if the group member was the *reporter*—the computer that originally sent the membership report for that group. This approach avoids a large number of *Leave* packets. If the reporter was the only group member, then the router can stop delivering packets of this group in any event. If there are members other than the reporter in the local area network, then these members can react to a *Leave* message immediately by sending a report to the router telling it that there is still an interest in this data.

A conflict can arise if there is more than one multicast-capable router in one local area network. In such a situation, two routers could transport redundant multicast packets to the LAN. The question is: Who decides which router will serve which group? The problem is solved by a simple mechanism known from other protocols: The router with the smallest IP address assumes the role of a *coordinator*. The other routers just listen to the traffic until the coordinator fails. In this case, the router with the next smaller address assumes the role of the multicast router. A good indicator that a multicast router has failed occurs when no more group queries arrive.

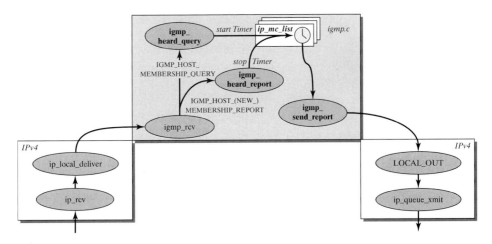

FIGURE 17–8
Implementing IGMP in the Linux kernel.

17.3.4   Implementing IGMP

This section describes how the Internet Group Management Protocol (IGMP) is implemented in the Linux kernel. Among other things, we will explain how entries for multicast groups are stored and how an IGMP query is handled in the kernel.

    We saw how a packet is handled in the Linux kernel in Figure 14–4, and we learned that a packet can travel over different paths. The processing of IGMP packets begins at the multiplex point of IP: the point where the mechanism branches to the handling routine of the respective layer-4 protocol. The further path that an IGMP packet takes (see Figure 17–8) will be explained in the section that describes the `igmp_rcv()` function.

`igmp_rcv()`	**net/ipv4/igmp.c**

    The starting point of the IP multicast control path is in `igmp_rcv()`. Once an IGMP packet has passed the lower layers and arrived in the IP layer, its protocol type is checked and the appropriate protocol-handling routine is invoked. For IGMP messages (protocol identifier 2), this is the function `igmp_rcv(skb, len)`. The function involves the following steps:

```
int igmp_rcv(struct sk_buff *skb, unsigned short len)
{
        struct igmphdr *ih = skb->h.igmph;

        switch (ih->type) {
                case IGMP_HOST_MEMBERSHIP_QUERY:                 //0x11
                        igmp_heard_query(in_dev, ih->code, ih->group);
                        break;
                case IGMP_HOST_MEMBERSHIP_REPORT:               //0x12
                case IGMP_HOST_NEW_MEMBERSHIP_REPORT:           //0x16
```

```
                igmp_heard_report(in_dev, ih->group);
                break;
        case IGMP_HOST_LEAVE_MESSAGE:                            //0x17
                break;
                ...
}
```

In this function, the type of the IGMP packet is extracted, and, once the IGMP packet has been checked for correctness, the function branches to the corresponding routine. If the message type is IGMP_HOST_LEAVE_MESSAGE, then the packet is ignored in a simple computer. For queries arriving from a router, further handling of the message is started by igmp_heard_query(). If the message is a report from another system, then it is handled by igmp_heard_report(). All other packet types are ignored.

igmp_heard_query()	net/ipv4/igmp.c

The function igmp_heard_query is invoked for IGMP queries arriving from a router (IGMP_HOST_MEMBERSHIP_QUERY). In this case, the function walks through the list of all active IP multicast groups to which the computer with the network card that received the query belongs. This list is managed in the structure dev->ip_ptr->in_device->mc_list. Next, igmp_mod_timer is used to start a timer or update a running timer for every group except the *all-hosts* group.

Notice that each computer belongs to the *all-hosts* group and that no timer is started for this group, for performance reasons. The requesting router assumes that, in addition to itself, at least one active multicast computer is connected to each local area network.

igmp_heard_report()	net/ipv4/igmp.c

If another computer responds to a query, it directs its reply to the appropriate group, and all other members of this group will receive this reply. The IGMP message type is either IGMP_HOST_MEMBERSHIP_REPORT or IGMP_HOST_NEW_MEMBERSHIP_REPORT, depending on the version used to send the message. As a response to an incoming query report, each other computer in the local area network can stop its timer for the group concerned. In the Linux kernel, this task is handled by igmp_heard_report. For this purpose, the list of active multicast groups of the network device that received the report is walked through. This list is managed in the structure dev->ip_ptr->in_device->mc_list. The timer of this group is stopped (igmp_stop_timer()), and the variable reporter records that this computer has not replied for this group (reporter = 0;).

igmp_send_report()	net/ipv4/igmp.c

Once a query message has been sent, a timer is started for each multicast group in each computer. The computer with the timer expiring first sends a query report. This is done by the function igmp_send_report, which was started by the timer handler (`igmp_timer_expire()`) for this group (`timer` in the `ip_mc_list` structure). In addition, the variable `reporter` in the function `igmp_timer_expire()` remembers that this station replied to the query. This information may be required later to tell the router that the computer wants to leave that group.

However, `igmp_send_report()` serves not only to send *query reports*; it can also be used to generate packets to announce that a computer wants to leave a group (*leave messages*). The actions required are identical in both cases; only the destination address and the IGMP message type are different. In case of a report, the packet is sent to the corresponding group; in the case of a leave message, all multicast routers in the LAN (*all-routers*) are addressed. Notice that the value of the TTL field has to be set to 1 to ensure that the response will spread only within the LAN. Next, the IP packet is built, and the IGMP fields are set accordingly. Finally, the packet is shipped out over the LOCAL_OUT hook.

`ip_check_mc()`	**net/ipv4/igmp.c**

`ip_check_mc(in_dev, mc_addr)` is actually not part of the IGMP protocol; it is used for IP routing. More specifically, `ip_check_mc()` checks on whether the local computer is currently a member of the multicast group `mc_addr`. For this purpose, the list of active groups of the network device's IP instance (`mc_list` in the `in_device` structure) is checked and compared against the group address passed. If a match is found, then one is returned; otherwise, **null** is returned.

`ip_check_mc()` is also used in the function `ip_route_input()` to learn whether the packet should be delivered locally. If this is the case (as is always true for multicast routers), then the packet is passed to `ip_route_input_mc()`. If the computer does not act as a multicast router, and if the packet does not belong to any group of the input network device, then it will be discarded. This actually means that rather few packets are discarded, because most undesired multicast packets are normally filtered out by the hardware filter in the network card. (See Section 17.4.1.)

17.4   MULTICAST DATA PATH IN THE LINUX KERNEL

This section describes how multicast data packets are processed in the Linux kernel. To get a good insight into matters, we will first explain the path a multicast packet takes across the kernel, then discuss different aspects of the data path. We will begin on the MAC layer, to see how multicasting is supported in local area networks and to introduce the following IP multicast concepts:

- virtual network devices,
- multicast routing tables, and
- replicating of data packets.

As we introduce the implementation, we will emphasize differences between multicast-capable end systems and multicast routers.

17.4.1 Multicast Support on the MAC Layer

In general, IEEE-802.x LANs are broadcast-enabled: each data packet is sent to each participant. Each network adapter looks at the MAC destination address to decide whether it will accept and process a packet. This process normally is handled by the network adapter and doesn't interfere with the central processor's work. The central processor is stopped by an interrupt only when the adapter decides that a packet has to be forwarded to the higher layers. This means that the filtering of packets in the network adapter take load off the CPU and ensures that it will receive only packets that are actually addressed to the local computer.

Filtering undesired MAC frames works well in the case of unicast packets, because each adapter should know its MAC address. However, how can the card know whether the computer is interested in the data of a group when a multicast packet arrives? In case of doubt, the adapter accepts the packet and passes it on to the higher-layer protocols, which should know all subscribed groups. The next question is whether multicast packets use the MAC address at all. The MAC format supports group addresses, but how are they structured?

There is a clever solution for IP multicast groups to solve the problems described above. On the one hand, this solution prevents broadcasting of multicast packets; on the other hand, it concurrently filters IP groups on the MAC layer. The method, described here, is simple, and it relieves the central processing unit from too many unnecessary interrupts.

IP multicast packets are packed in MAC frames before they are sent to the local area network, and they contain a MAC group address. The MAC address is selected so that it gives a clue about which multicast group the packet could belong to. Figure 17–9 shows how this address is structured; it contains the following elements:

■ The first 25 bits of the MAC address identify the group address for IP multicast. The first byte (0x01) shows that the address is a group MAC address, where the

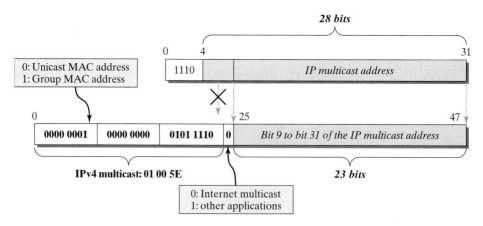

FIGURE 17–9
Mapping an IP multicast group address to an IEEE-802 MAC address.

last bit is decisive. Notice that the address shown in Figure 17–9 is represented in the network byte order.

The next 17 bits (0x005E) state that the MAC packet carries an IP multicast packet. The identifier here would be different for other layer-3 protocols.

▪ The last 23 bits carry the last 23 bits of the IP multicast address.

We can easily see that this is not a reversible mapping between an IP multicast address and a MAC address. For each multicast MAC address, there are $2^5 = 32$ possible IP multicast groups matching this MAC address. This means that the network adapters cannot filter exactly. Instead, they pass all matching multicast groups to IP. In any event, this filtering takes a lot of load off the central processing unit, because only multicast packets actually subscribed are normally delivered to IP.

We still have to answer one question: How can the network adapter know to which groups IP subscribed? To solve this problem, each network adapter manages a list with multicast group addresses that should be received on this adapter. If the network adapter can support hardware filtering of multicast packets from the technical perspective, then a driver method transfers this list to the adapter (`set_multicast_list()`). The adapter can then filter without disturbing the central processing unit.

The active multicast groups of a network device's IP instance are maintained in the `mc_list` of the `in_device` structure. When an application joins an IP multicast group, the IP group address and some other information are recorded in this list. In addition, `ip_eth_mc_map()` computes the appropriate MAC group address (for Ethernet networks) and adds it to the list `dev->mc_list`. Once `set_multicast_list()` has updated the card, the network adapter should be able to receive packets for this group. Figure 17–10 shows schematically how groups are managed in the IP instance and in the network device.

`struct ip_mc_list`	include/linux/igmp.h

▪ `multiaddr` is the multicast address of the subscribed group.

▪ `interface` points to the `net_device` structure of the network adapter.

▪ `next` points to the next entry in the list.

▪ `timer` is a timer used by IGMP to delay membership reports.

▪ `tm_running` shows whether or not the timer is currently active.

▪ `reporter` contains the value 1, if this computer sent the last membership report for this group to the multicast router. If another computer was faster, then `reporter` is set to 0. This information is required to send `leave` messages, which are transmitted exclusively by the reporter.

▪ `users` counts the number of sockets that subscribed this group. During closing of one of these sockets, a `leave` message is sent over IGMPv2 only when no more users exist.

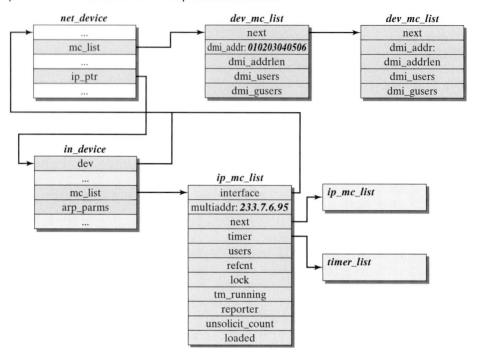

FIGURE 17–10
Managing multicast groups or addresses in an IP instance and in a network device.

`dev->mc_list`	include/linux/netdevice.h

▤ `next` points to the next entry in the list.

▤ `dmi_addr[MAX_ADDR_LEN]`: This is the layer-2 address of the group the packets of which should be received.

▤ `dmi_addrlen` specifies the length of the layer-2 address in `dmi_addr`.

17.4.2 Multicast Data Path in the Internet Protocol

Now that we have described how multicasting is supported on the MAC layer, this section explains how IP multicast packets are processed in the Linux implementation of the Internet Protocol. We will first look at end systems and multicast routers.

However, before we discuss the details of the processes involved, we want to introduce two important components of the multicast implementation: virtual network devices, which abstract from the two possible transmission types for multicast packets (i.e., LAN adapter card or IP tunnel), and the multicast routing table (multicast forwarding cache).

Virtual Network Devices   Multicast packets can be received and sent in either of two different ways: either directly over the network adapter in a LAN, or packed inside a second unicast IP packet and transported through a *tunnel*. To prevent having to distinguish these two cases in the entire multicast implementation, an abstraction—the so-called *virtual network device* or virtual interface (VIF)—was introduced for both types.

`struct vif_device`	**include/linux/mroute.h**

In the Linux kernel, virtual network devices are represented by the `vif_device` structure. A *virtual interface* describes either a physical network device of the type `net_device` or an IP-IP tunnel. A flag is used to distinguish these two methods.

```
struct vif_device {
        struct net_device *dev;             /* Device we are using */
        unsigned long      bytes_in,bytes_out;
        unsigned long      pkt_in,pkt_out;  /* Statistics */
        unsigned long      rate_limit;      /* Traffic shaping (NI) */
        unsigned char      threshold;       /* TTL threshold */
        unsigned short     flags;           /* Control flags */
        __u32              local,remote;    /* Addresses(remote for
                                                tunnels)*/
        int                link;            /* Physical interface index */
};
```

- ▨ `dev`: a pointer to the network device (`net_device`), which may be used
- ▨ `bytes_in`, `bytes_out`: statistical information about the transported bytes
- ▨ `pkt_in`, `pkt_out`: number of packets handled
- ▨ `threshold`: threshold value for packets that should be sent over this virtual network device (as in Section 17.2.3)
- ▨ `flags`: Flags to specify, for example, whether the VIF represents a tunnel (`VIFF_TUNNEL`).
- ▨ `local` and `remote`: either (a) the IP addresses of the tunnel starting point and the tunnel end point, or (b) the IP address of the network device
- ▨ `link`: Index of the physical network device.

Figure 17–11 shows how the `vif_device` structure is structured and embedded in its environment. Virtual network devices are stored in the table (array) `vif_table`. It can maintain a maximum of `MAXVIFS` entries for each computer. The maximum number is 32, and this number cannot be increased in current personal computers, to fit the variable `vifc_map` (`net/ipv4/ipmr.c`). Each bit of `vifc_map` marks whether the virtual network device with the index corresponding to the bit index had already been created. The maximum number, 32 VIFs for a 32-bit architecture, results from the data type, `unsigned long`, of this variable. Consequently, this number can be limited (but not extended) by `MAXVIFS`. This limitation results in the fact that a multicast router can be directly connected to a maximum of `MAXVIFS` other multicast routers.

Each entry in the array represents either a physical network device or a tunnel. The entries are set and removed by the multicast routing daemon (e.g., `mrouted`) by use of the socket options `MRT_ADD_VIF` and `MRT_DEL_VIF`. The parameters of the `vif_device` structure are passed in a `vifctl` structure (VIF control). Section 17.5.2 discusses how virtual network devices are configured.

Multicast Forwarding Cache   The multicast forwarding cache (MFC) is the central structure used to store information about how often incoming multicast packets have to

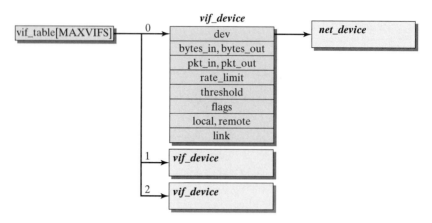

FIGURE 17–11
The vif_table of a virtual network device.

be replicated and where they have to be forwarded to. This means that the MFC implements the multicast routing table. The MFC is built in the form of a hash table, as we can easily see from the `mfc_cache` structure. All entries with the same hash value are linearly linked with the respective cache rows (singly linked list). All cache rows are grouped in the field `mfc_cache_array` to form an MFC hash table with a size specified by `MFC_LINES` (`include/linux/mroute.h`). By standard, the multicast forwarding cache comprises 64 rows or lines. Figure 17–12 shows schematically how the MFC is structured.

When additional routes should be found for an incoming multicast packet, then the multicast forwarding cache has to be searched for a matching entry. To find a matching entry, `mfc_hash` is initially used to determine the correct cache line. The input network device and the multicast group address are used as parameters. Next, the linked list in the cache line is processed until a matching entry is found. The entries in the MFC are of the `mfc_cache` data type.

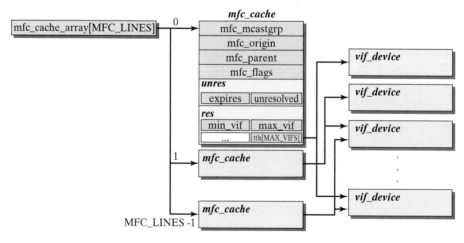

FIGURE 17–12
Structure of the multicast forwarding cache (`mfc_cache`).

The `ttls` field includes information about virtual network devices that can be used to forward the packet. A TTL entry smaller than 255 means that the virtual network device with an index identical to the index in the `ttls` array should forward these packets. The `ttls` array is processed sequentially. To optimize this process, `minvif` and `maxvif` store the minimum and maximum VIF indexes that should receive the packet.

struct mfc_cache	include/linux/include/mroute.h

```
struct mfc_cache
{
        struct    mfc_cache *next;           /* Next entry on cache line
                                                */
        __u32     mfc_mcastgrp;              /* Group, entry belongs to
                                                */
        __u32     mfc_origin;               /* Source of packet */
        vifi_t    mfc_parent;               /* Source interface */
        int       mfc_flags;                /* Flags on line */

        union
        {
                struct
                {
                        unsigned long expires;
                        struct sk_buff_head unresolved; /* Unres. buffers */
                } unres;
                struct
                {
                        unsigned long last_assert;
                        int minvif, maxvif;
                        unsigned long bytes;
                        unsigned long pkt;
                        unsigned long wrong_if;
                        unsigned char ttls[MAXVIFS];  /* TTL thresholds */
                } res;
        } mfc_un;
};
```

- next points to the next entry in the multicast forwarding cache. The cache lines are organized in singly linked lists. A NULL pointer in this field marks the end of a cache line.
- mfc_mcastgrp and mfc_origin together form the key for an entry in the multicast forwarding cache. mfc_origin is the IP address of the sending computer, and mfc_mcastgrp specifies the multicast group for a multicast packet, the route of which is represented by this entry.
- mfc_parent is the index of the virtual network device in the vif_table, over which packets of this MFC entry should arrive.
- The mfc_un structure is a *union* structure: It is either an unres structure or a res structure. The two structures are defined per union, because either one structure or the other is required, but never both.

▨ unres is used for entries in the multicast forwarding cache when the multicast
routing daemon has not yet finalized the routing selection. The entry for the
mfc_cache structure is created in the MFC as soon as a packet for it arrives.

 ▷ unresolved is a queue for socket buffers that store packets for this routing
 entry until the multicast routing daemon has selected a route.

 ▷ expires specifies the time by which the daemon should have selected a route.

▨ res is used in the mfc_un union when the multicast routing daemon has specified
the routes for this entry.

 ▷ minvif and maxvif are indexes to elements in the ttls list of the MFC entry.
 They limit the range currently used by virtual network devices, which are used to
 send packets of this MFC entry. Stating this indexes saves computing time required to duplicate multicast packets. The maxvif index is limited by the MAXVIFS
 constant.

 ▷ ttls[MAXVIFS] is an array with MAXVIFS entries, where each entry specifies
 whether a packet should be forwarded over the virtual network device in the
 vif_table list with the corresponding index. This is the case when a value less
 than 255 exists. The value 0 cannot occur, because it is mapped to the value 255
 when the table is built. However, an entry less than 255 is not sufficient to forward a packet; the TTL value of a packet has to be at least equal to the TTL
 value in the ttls array. This is the method used to create the threshold value
 for multicast packets described in Section 17.2.3.

Paths of a Multicast Packet Through the Linux Kernel   Figure 17–13 shows the paths a
multicast packet can take to travel through the Linux kernel. Like any other IP packet,

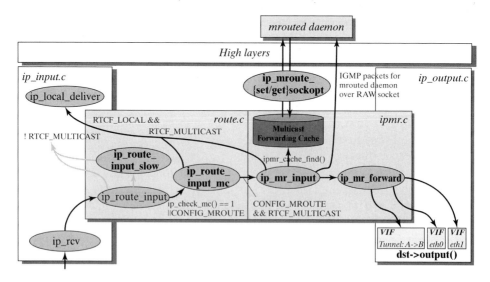

FIGURE 17–13
Overview of how a multicast packet can travel through the Linux kernel.

a multicast packet is received by `ip_rcv()`. The routing cache is normally asked for further packet-forwarding instructions in `ip_route_input()` (see Chapter 16), and multicast packets are no exception. In the case of an end system, `ip_check_mc()` checks on whether the multicast group is required in the computer at all. This means that all undesired multicast packets (i.e., packets passed upwards by the network card, either because of an unclear mapping of IP multicast addresses to MAC addresses, or because of an adapter without hardware filter, or by the promiscuous mode) are discarded. If a socket desires a packet, then the flag `RTCF_LOCAL` is attached to the packet at this point. In general, the flag `RTCF_MULTICAST` is also set in multicast packets.

If the packet is accepted (i.e., if the group is desired or the station is a multicast router, which accepts all packets), then the multicast packet continues its path in `ip_route_input_mc()`, where paths go in different directions, depending on whether the station is an end system or a multicast router. In end systems, *local* packets are passed to the function `ip_local_deliver()`, which forwards them to the application layer.

In multicast routers, all packets (including local packets) are first handled by `ip_mr_input()`. The most important task of this function is to use `ipmr_cache_find()` to find the entry in the MFC. Local packets are passed to `ip_local_deliver()`, and packets with other destinations are transported to `ip_mr_forward()`, where they will eventually be replicated. The details of each of these functions are described next.

`ip_route_input_mc()`	**net/ipv4/route.c**

`ip_route_input()` invokes `ip_route_input_mc(skb, daddr, saddr, tos, dev, our)` if the incoming packet is a multicast packet. First, the function checks the source and destination addresses (`saddr, daddr`) and returns an error, if present. Also, packets originating from the same computer should not arrive over this input routine for several reasons, including protection against spoofing. Once the sender address has been checked in the forwarding information base, memory space is allocated for a new entry in the routing cache. The route is entered in the cache, and the flag `RTCF_MULTICAST` is added. Subsequently, the packet is handled in `ip_local_deliver()` (for end systems) or `ip_mr_input()` (for multicast routers), and the computed hash value is returned.

`ip_mr_input()`	**net/ipv4/ipmr.c**

`ip_rcv_finish()` invokes `ip_mr_input(skb)` by use of the function pointer `dst->input()`, which is set to `ip_mr_input()` in `ip_route_input_mc()`, if the computer was configured as a multicast router. The first thing to be checked is whether the packet is an IGMP packet for the multicast routing daemon. If so, the packet is delivered to this daemon over the *raw* socket. Subsequently, the function `ipmr_cache_find` searches the multicast forwarding cache for a matching entry for the `skb` packet. If no matching entry can be found, then a local packet (`RTCF_LOCAL`) is passed to `ip_local_deliver()`, and packets that have to be forwarded are added to the queue for incomplete routing entries (`unresolved` queue in the `mfc_cache` structure). As soon as the routing daemon has determined the route, these packets are forwarded by `ip_mr_forward()`.

If a valid entry was found in the multicast forwarding cache, then `ip_mr_input()` passes a pointer to this routing entry to the function `ip_mr_forward`, which duplicates and forwards the packet. Finally, packets marked local (RTCF_LOCAL) are passed upwards by ip_local_deliver.

| ip_mr_forward()   net/ipv4/ipmr.c |

ipmr_cache_find(origin,mcastgrp) searches the multicast forwarding cache (see above) for a specific entry. The source address of the packet and the multicast group address together are used as search key. An MFC entry found includes all virtual network devices (VIFs), which should be used to forward packets. The result is returned in an mfc_cache structure (see above).

| ip_mr_forward()   net/ipv4/ipmr.c |

ip_mr_input(skb, mfc, local) obtains the mfc pointer from ip_mr_input(), which points to the entry of the skb packet in the multicast forwarding cache and then duplicates the packet for each virtual network device that should be used to forward duplicates:

```
for (ct = cache->mfc_un.res.maxvif-1; ct >= cache->mfc_un.res.minvif; ct-)
{
        if (skb->nh.iph->ttl > cache->mfc_un.res.ttls[ct])
        {
                if (psend !=-1)
                        ipmr_queue_xmit(skb, cache, psend, 0);
                psend=ct;
        }
}
```

The actual replication of multicast packets is done in the for loop, which checks all array entries in the ttls field of the mfc structure from maxvif-1 to minvif. However, the copies of socket buffers are not directly created by ip_mr_forward(). They are created later by the function ipmr_queue_xmit(), which is invoked if the multicast packet has sufficient lifetime (TTL) left to be sent over the current virtual network device. It passes the entire MFC structure and an index to each VIF that should receive the packet to ipmr_queue_xmit for each VIF.

Before a packet is replicated, ip_mr_forward() checks on whether the packet has arrived in the expected network device and on whether it was discarded, if applicable. One reason for this check will be discussed in Section 17.5.3. A conflict situation can occur if a computer acts as multicast router and runs multicast applications at the same time. If multicast packets are transported across the loopback network device, then the input network device can deviate from the default multicast route for these packets, and these packets will be discarded.

| ipmr_queue_xmit()   net/ipv4/ipmr.c |

ip_mr_forward invokes ipmr_queue_xmit(skb, mfc, vifi, last) to transmit the multicast packet skb. If the packet is not exclusively available (for example, because there are several references to the packet payload (`cloned`)), or if the packet is not the last of all of its replicates, then a clone of the socket buffer is created. In addition, a decision has to be made for the packet as to whether it should be transported through a tunnel or through a regular network device. In either case, `ip_route_output` with the respective parameters is invoked. For a tunneled packet, the variables `local` and `remote` from the pertaining VIF structure are passed; otherwise, the destination IP address from the socket buffer's structure is sufficient. In both cases, the variable `link` from the VIF structure passes an index to the relevant physical network device. Subsequently, the netfilter hook `NF_IP_FORWARD` is invoked. If it does not have to be fragmented, the packet is sent over the function pointer `dst-> output()`; otherwise it is sent over `ip_fragment(skb, dst->output)`.

17.5   MULTICASTING IN TODAY'S INTERNET

Multicasting was a thing unheard of at the advent of the Internet, and neither group addresses nor protocols to manage groups or multicast routing were available. In fact, the most important prerequisites to implementing an efficient group communication service were missing. The Internet was a pure unicast network.

Several proposals in this field were made [Deer91] when the Internet community had started to think that such a service was necessary, at the beginning of the nineties. Eventually, IP multicast was born when the Internet Group Management Protocol and the address class D were standardized. In addition, multicast routing protocols were proposed, so that nothing was actually impeding the introducing of the new communication form. However, though the Internet had evolved into an enormous global network during the last twenty years, it was still a unicast network, and gradually each system connected to the Internet would have had to be extended to IP multicast support. This change would certainly have taken several years to complete. In addition, the new technology had not yet been tested extensively. Consequently, a decision was made to build a multicast test network within the unicast Internet, the so-called *MBone* (Multicast Backbone On the Internet), rather than converting to multicast from scratch.

17.5.1   The Multicast Backbone (MBone)

The Internet Engineering Task Force (IETF) ran a pilot transmission session to officially introduce MBone in March 1992. Since then, more than 10,000 subnetworks have been connected to this network worldwide. MBone enables the connected multicast-enhanced subnetworks to run IP multicasting over the existing Internet, even though the Internet itself is not multicast capable.

The solution offered by MBone is relatively simple: It builds a virtual multicast network over the conventional Internet, which understands only unicasting, and connected systems communicate over multicast-capable routers (multicast routers). As soon as there is a nonmulticast network between them, multicast routers bridge this situation by a so-called IP-in-IP tunnel. This tunnel consists of a unicast connection used to transport multicast traffic. For this purpose, the multicast router packs a multicast packet into another IP packet at the beginning of the tunnel and sends it as a normal unicast IP packet over the network to the tunnel output. The multicast router at that end of the tunnel removes the outer unicast packet and sends the multicast packet to the multicast-capable network.

This method led to the formation of many multicast-capable islands interconnected by tunnels over the conventional Internet. Figure 17–14 shows an example for the basic MBone architecture. Technically, MBone is a virtual overlay network on top of the Internet. Similar overlay networks have been built to study other Internet technologies, including 6Bone (Six-Bone) for IPv6 and QBone to study quality of service (QoS) mechanisms.

17.5.2 Accessing MBone Over the mrouted Daemon

The mrouted daemon is a tool you can use to connect to MBone. It enables you to build tunnels to other MBone nodes and ensure connectivity. In addition, this daemon enables multicast routing for multicast packets within or at the boundaries of a multicast network. The standard implementation of mrouted in UNIX uses the *Distant Vector Multicast Routing Protocol* (*DVMRP*; see Section 17.5.3).

Like all daemons, mrouted operates in the user-address space and can be started and stopped at system runtime. It communicates with the kernel over specific interfaces, which will be introduced in the course of this chapter. The mrouted daemon can be exchanged at runtime, so we can implement different routing algorithms. The mrouted daemon is not the only multicast routing daemon for Linux, but it is the most popular and the most frequently used today.

How mrouted Operates Multicast packet forwarding is separate from selecting of forwarding routes; the kernel is responsible for forwarding, and the routing daemon determines the routes. Again, this shows a known principle, the separating of the data path from the control path. To determine routes, the mrouted daemon obtains information about all incoming multicast packets, including their destination and origin. Using this information, it computes the multicast routing tables and passes them to the kernel over a specific interface. This means that the daemon tells the kernel how it should forward packets from a specific sender to a specific group. The paths or routes for multicast packets are stated in the form of virtual network devices, which were introduced in Section 17.4.2.

Interface Between the Multicast Routing Daemon and the Kernel The mrouted daemon communicates with the Linux kernel over a special socket. The kernel obtains routing information for multicast packets by setsockopt() calls over a raw socket. mrouted uses the IPPROTO_IGMP protocol to open this socket a head of time. Within the kernel, a reference to the socket used by mrouted to communicate with the kernel

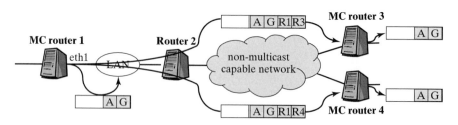

FIGURE 17–14
MBone consists of multicast islands connected by tunnels.

is stored in the variable mroute_socket. If mroute_socket contains the value NULL, then no instance of the mrouted daemon is running yet; otherwise, an instance is already active, and the socket is denied. This allows you to check for whether an attempt is made to create a second instance of the daemon and to ensure that the commands to manipulate multicast routing information in the kernel originate from the correct mrouted socket.

The options available to change the multicast routing table are handled by the function ip_mroute_setsockopt() (defined in net/ipv4/ipmr.c). MRT_INIT has to be the first option or the first command we send to the socket. All other commands (MRT_DONE, MRT_ADD_VIF, MRT_DEL_VIF, MRT_ADD_MFC, MRT_DEL_MFC, and MRT_ASSERT) are ignored; they return the result -EACCESS if the socket was not previously reserved by MRT_INIT.

The following subsections describe the most important functions and structures available in the Linux kernel for tasks handled by the multicast routing daemon. These functions and structures are declared primarily in the file net/ipv4/mroute.c. Subsequently, we use a few examples to show how the daemon and the kernel exchange data by use of ioctl() commands and socket options.

Kernel Functions Used by mrouted

`ip_mroute_setsockopt()`	**net/ipv4/ipmr.c**

ip_mroute_setsockopt(sk,opt_name,opt_val,opt_len) accepts commands from the mrouted daemon and processes them, including, for example, the creating and deleting of virtual network devices (VIFs) and entries in the multicast routing table (MFC). ip_mroute_setsockopt() is invoked by ip_setsockopt() in net/ipv4/ip_sockglue.c, because these are socket options.

In addition to the sk socket and the actual command, opt_name, this function can accept other parameters, including additional information (opt_val), if required for the command, and the length of this information (opt_len). In summary, this function can accept the following commands and additional information:

- MRT_INIT: This command sets the variable mroute_socket. It takes the value unequal NULL by default, and it returns an -EADDRINUSE error if another instance of mrouted (or another multicast routing daemon) is already running. Otherwise, mroute_socket obtains a pointer to the socket used to send MRT_INIT. This command has to be the first command for mrouted, because all other commands check on whether they originate from the socket specified in mroute_socket. If an error occurs, then -EACCESS is returned, and the command is not executed.

  Before we can use a socket, we have to run the protocol option IPPROTO_IGMP to create the socket. Otherwise, an -ENOPNOTSUPP error is returned. opt_val has to point to an integer value with the value one; otherwise, the result will again be an error (this time, -ENOPROTOOPT).

- MRT_ADD_VIF: This command instructs the kernel to create a new virtual network device (VIF). The additional information this command takes is a pointer to a `vifctl` structure (see Section 17.5.2) in `opt_val`, which is passed to the kernel because it includes all parameters required. These parameters include an index of the virtual network device, the address of the physical network device, and tunnel information. Another important thing is the flag that states whether this virtual network device is a tunnel (`VIFF_TUNNEL`). If this is the case, then the kernel uses the function `ipmr_new_tunnel()` to create a new tunnel. Otherwise, `ip_dev_find()` is used to search for the corresponding network device. If `MRT_ADD_VIF` is sent before `MRT_INIT` initialized the socket, then `-EACCESS` is returned. This is also the case when `MRT_ADD_VIF` was invoked by another socket.

Other errors that can potentially occur are `-EINVAL`, `-EFAULT`, `-ENFILE`, and `-EADDRINUSE`—if `opt_val` is an invalid structure, if the structure cannot be copied from the user address space, if the VIF index is outside the valid range, or if the virtual network device already exists, respectively.

In the creating of a new virtual network device, a new `vif_device` structure is added to its list (`vif_table`), and the information relevant for this entry is taken from the `vifctl` structure.

- `MRT_DEL_VIF`: This command is used to remove the entry for a virtual network device from the list of virtual network devices (`vif_table`). The parameters used here are identical to those used in `MRT_ADD_VIF`. However, only the VIF index is evaluated.

- `MRT_ADD_MFC`: This command instructs the kernel to add a new entry in its multicast routing table (multicast forwarding cache) or, if an entry matching the specified search key exists, to update this entry. For this purpose, an `mfcctl` structure (see below) is additionally passed in `opt_val`. Once the validity check of the structure (error: `-EINVAL`) has been completed, `ipmr_cache_find()` (see below) checks the MFC cache to see whether a corresponding entry exists. If this is the case, then this entry is adapted to the new values; otherwise, a new entry is created. When a new cache entry is created, an `mfc_cache` structure is allocated at the same time, and all relevant information is taken from the `mfcctl` structure and transmitted. In this case, the entries in the field `mfc_ttls` having the value **null** are mapped to 255. The reason is that the validation process need only test whether the value is smaller than 255 to see whether a packet is to be routed to a VIF.

- `MRT_DEL_MFC`: This command instructs the kernel to remove an entry from the MFC. The kernel uses the function `ipmr_mfc_delete()` to delete an entry from the MFC.

`ip_mroute_getsockopt()`	**net/ipv4/ipmr.c**

The function `ip_mroute_getsockopt(sk,opt_name,opt_val,opt_len)` normally is used to poll the version number (0x0305). For this purpose, `MRT_VERSION` should be specified in `ip_getsockopt()`. `net/ipv4/ip_sockglue.c` invokes `opt_val`. `ip_mroute_getsockopt()`. We can use `ioctl()` queries to poll additional status information for multicast forwarding.

`ipmr_ioctl()`	**net/ipv4/ipmr.c**

`ipmr_ioctl(sk,cmd,arg)` can be used to poll various status information. If `cmd` has the value SIOCGETVIFCNT, then a pointer to a `sioc_vif_req` structure (see below) in `arg` is expected. It includes the index to the virtual network device for which information is to be queried (e.g., how many packets and what data volumes have been received and sent over this device). The result is added to the passed `sioc_vif_req` structure.

If `cmd` is equal SIOCGETSGCNT, then a pointer to a `sioc_sg_req` structure in `arg` is expected. The corresponding information about the matching entry in the multicast forwarding cache is determined.

`ipmr_ioctl()` is entered in `inet_create()` (in `net/ipv4/af_inet.c`) as `ioctl()` handling routing in the `proto` structure for *raw* sockets.

`ip_mr_init()`	**net/ipv4/ipmr.c**

`ip_mr_init(void)` initializes the multicast routing functions in the kernel; it is invoked when `inet_proto_init()` (in `net/ipv4/af_inet.c`) starts.

`ipmr_get_route()`	**net/ipv4/ipmr.c**

`ipmr_get_route(skm,rtm,nowait)` determines the route for a packet from a specific source for a specific group. This function is used for informative purposes only. The result is packed into a packet to send it to other routers (e.g., so that these routers can exchange routing information). The route for the actual routing of multicast packets is specified directly in `ip_mr_forward()`.

`ipmr_cache_find()`	**net/ipv4/ipmr.c**

`ipmr_cache_find(origin,mcastgrp)` searches the multicast forwarding cache (see Section 17.4.2) for a specific entry. The packet's source address and the multicast group address serve as search keys. If an MFC entry is found, it includes all virtual network devices (VIFs) that can be used to forward the packet. The result is returned in the form of a pointer to an `mfc_cache` structure.

`ipmr_new_tunnel()`	**net/ipv4/ipmr.c**

`ipmr_new_tunnel(v)` is responsible for creating a new tunnel. All information required toward this end is passed, together with the `vifctl` structure (`v`). The function gets the tunnel network device, `tun10`, and tries to create a tunnel to the destination specified in `v`. If it is successful, then this *new* virtual network device is returned; otherwise an error message (`null`) is returned.

`ipmr_cache_unresolved()`	**net/ipv4/ipmr.c**

`ipmr_cache_unresolved(cache,vifi,skb)` is invoked by `ip_mr_input()` and `ipmr_get_route()`, if a specific entry was polled from the multicast forwarding cache, and if this entry either does not exist or has not been filled yet, though it was requested by `mrouted`. `ipmr_cache_unresolved` creates a new entry in the multicast forwarding cache and sets its status to `MFC_QUEUED`, which means that the route specified in this entry has not yet been entered by `mrouted`.

Subsequently, the timer is activated, and `ipmr_cache_report` is invoked to ask `mrouted` for the required route. The timer causes the entry to be deleted from the cache at a certain time, if `mrouted` cannot determine the route before this time.

`ipmr_cache_report()`	**net/ipv4/ipmr.c**

`ipmr_cache_report(pkt,vifi,assert)` asks `mrouted` to create an entry in the multicast forwarding cache (MFC) for a specific packet—its origin and multicast group—to determine the route. For this purpose, a packet is created, and `sock_queue_rcv_skb()` is used to send it to `mrouted`.

`ipmr_cache_timer()`	**net/ipv4/ipmr.c**

`ipmr_cache_timer(data)` deletes an entry from the MFC, if the `mrouted` daemon was requested to determine the route, and if it was unable to do this within a specific time. `ipmr_cache_timer()` is the timer-handling routine for `mfc_timer` defined in the `mfc_cache` structure.

`ipmr_cache_alloc()`	**net/ipv4/ipmr.c**

`ipmr_cache_alloc(priority)` creates a new `mfc_cache` structure and adds a few initial values, including the timer data and handling routine and information stating that the route does not exist yet. `ipmr_cache_alloc()` does *not* write the created structure to the multicast forwarding cache; `ipmr_cache_insert()` has to be invoked separately for that purpose.

`ipmr_mfc_modify()`	**net/ipv4/ipmr.c**

`ipmr_mfc_modify(action,mfc)` is invoked when the `mrouted` daemon uses `MRT_ADD_MFC` or `MRT_DEL_MFC` to manipulate an MFC entry over `setsockopt()`. In addition to this action, the function checks for whether this is a new entry or the entry already exists and just has to be filled. If the latter is the case, and if the MFC entry is set to the `MFC_QUEUED` status, then `ipmr_cache_resolve()` is invoked to send waiting packets.

`ipmr_cache_resolve()`	**net/ipv4/ipmr.c**

`ipmr_cache_resolve(cache)` is invoked by `ipmr_mfc_modify()` when the route is set in an MFC entry and packets are waiting to be sent. The timer (see above) is deleted, and `ip_mr_forward()` sends the waiting packets.

Data Exchange Between the `mrouted` Daemon and the Kernel   This section explains the most important structures exchanged between the Linux kernel and the `mrouted` daemon. The daemon passes data to the kernel as shown below. We use the example of a query of the virtual network device and an MFC entry to better explain the procedure:

Initially, the `mrouted` daemon allocates memory space for a `sioc_vif_req` structure and writes the index of the desired virtual network device to the `vifi` field. Calling of the `ioctl()` command `SIOCGETVIFCNT` makes the appropriate part be executed in `ipmr_ioctl`. The argument for the `ioctl()` command is the address by which the daemon has created this structure. Then it is checked whether the `vifi` index points to a valid virtual network device. If this is the case, then the referenced structure is filled with the appropriate values and copied back to the user address space by `copy_to_user()`. The structure used to pass the data of a virtual network device is as follows:

struct sioc_vif_req	include/linux/mroute.h

```
sioc_vif_req {
      vifi_t               vifi;        /* Which iface */
      unsigned long        icount;      /* In packets */
      unsigned long        ocount;      /* Out packets */
      unsigned long        ibytes;      * In bytes */
      unsigned long        obytes;      /* Out bytes */
};
```

- ▩ `vifi`: This is the index of the virtual network device specified in the `vif_table`: the VIF used to request information.
- ▩ `icount`, `ocount`: This is the number of packets received or sent, respectively, over this VIF.
- ▩ `ibytes`, `obytes`: This is the sum of bytes included in the packets received or sent.

The procedure involved in querying an entry in the multicast forwarding cache is identical, except that the `sioc_sg_req` structure and the `ioctl()` command `SIOCGETSGCNT` are used:

struct sioc_sg_req	include/linux/mroute.h

```
struct sioc_sg_req
{
      struct               in_addr src;
      struct               in_addr grp;
      unsigned long        pktcnt;
      unsigned long        bytecnt;
      unsigned long        wrong_if;
};
```

The elements of the `sioc_sg_req` structure handle the following tasks:

- ▩ `src`: This is the sender address; it is part of the key for the MFC entry.
- ▩ `grp`: This is the multicast group address; it is the second part of the key for the MFC entry.

- pktcnt: This is the number of packets sent over the desired MFC entry.
- bytecnt: This is the number of bytes forwarded over the MFC entry.

Because multicast packets can be received and sent both over physical network adapters and through tunnels, we use an abstraction of virtual network devices (VIFs). The mrouted daemon passes vifctl structures to the kernel. These structures define virtual network devices, including whether a VIF is a physical network device or a tunnel. The multicast routing table of the kernel is influenced by mfcctl (*multicast forwarding cache entries*—MFCs) structures. They represent routing entries used by the kernel to learn how to forward multicast packets.

struct vifctl	include/linux/mroute.h

```
struct vifctl {
        vifi_t              vifc_vifi;          /* Index of VIF */
        unsigned char       vifc_flags;         /* VIFF_ flags */
        unsigned char       vifc_threshold;     /* ttl limit */
        unsigned int        vifc_rate_limit;    /* Rate limiter values (NI) */
        struct in_addr      vifc_lcl_addr;      /* Our address */
        struct in_addr      vifc_rmt_addr;      /* IPIP tunnel addr */
};
```

- vifc_vifi: This is the index of this virtual network device in the array vif_table, which stores all VIFs (0 - vifc_vifi < MAXVIFS).
- vifc_flags: This part can be used to set options (i.e., VIFF_TUNNEL, if you want to use a tunnel).
- vifc_lcl_addr: This is the local address of the network device. For a tunnel, this address represents the entry point into the tunnel virtually.
- vifc_rmt_addr: This part includes the destination address of the tunnel, if the VIF is a tunnel.

struct mfcctl	include/linux/mroute.h

```
struct mfcctl {
        struct in_addr      mfcc_origin;        /* Origin of mcast */
        struct in_addr      mfcc_mcastgrp;      /* Group in question */
        vifi_t              mfcc_parent;        /* Where it arrived */
        unsigned char       mfcc_ttls[MAXVIFS]; /* Where it is going */
        unsigned int        mfcc_pkt_cnt;       /* pkt count for src-grp */
        unsigned int        mfcc_byte_cnt;
        unsigned int        mfcc_wrong_if;
        int                 mfcc_expire;
};
```

- mfcc_origin: This is the packet's source address (i.e., the address of the computer that originally sent the packet).
- mfcc_mcastgrp: This identifies the multicast group that should receive the packet.

- ■ `mfcc_parent`: This identifies the VIF that received the packet.
- ■ `mfc_ttls`: This field specifies the VIFs a packet should be routed to. The field includes one entry for each potential VIF. A value of 0 or 255 means that the VIF with the corresponding index in the `vif_table` is *not* interested in the packet.

17.5.3   The DVMRP Routing Algorithm

The *Distance Vector Multicast Routing Protocol (DVMRP)* is the oldest multicast routing protocol; it was defined initially in [WaPD88] and extended later [Pusa00]. DVMRP was the multicast routing protocol used as basis to build MBone, and it has since remained the most popular multicast routing protocol. DVMRP uses a distance vector routing algorithm, which determines the shortest path to the sender. This means that it extends the principles of the RIP distance vector unicast routing protocol [Malk98] to multicasting capabilities.

DVMRP supports both physical network devices and tunnels as potential routes to forward multicast packets, mainly because these capabilities were required when MBone was introduced. This section briefly explains the approach of DVMRP, including a practical example.

How DVMRP Works   To build a distribution tree, DVMRP in its current version uses a principle called *Reverse Path Multicasting*. The shortest path to the sender is learned when a multicast router receives a multicast packet in a network adapter. If this route leads over the network device that received the packet, then it is forwarded to all neighboring multicast routers except for the interface that received the packet. Otherwise, the multicast packet is discarded, because it didn't arrive on an optimal route, which means that it is assumed that it does not originate from the direct path to the sender. More specifically, it is assumed to be a duplicate that might previously have been received. A multicast router is not able to see whether it has already received a packet or the packet is arriving for the first time. This is the reason why packets are accepted only if it can be assumed that they originate directly from the sender. This approach avoids a large number of duplicates—those created by a routing principle called flooding. Figure 17–15 shows how DVMRP works.

A unicast routing protocol is used to determine the shortest path back to the sender. In this respect, the `mrouted` daemon does not use the kernel's unicast routing table, but instead builds separate tables. The routing information stored in these tables is then exchanged between DVMRP routers in the network.

Though the Reverse Path Multicasting principle enables multicast packets to be distributed across the entire network without creating duplicates, it doesn't consider whether a specific subtree in the multicast routing tree is interested in the packets of a group. Packets are simply distributed, which means that they load the network with undesired packets. This is the reason why the method was extended to *pruning*. When the subnetwork of a router does not want to receive data for a specific multicast group, then the router can return a *prune* message to the higher-layer multicast router in the multicast routing tree. If this router doesn't have interested computers for that group, it can also send a *prune* message to a higher-level router. This method prevents an excessive number of packets from being forwarded in networks where there are no receivers. In addition, *graft* messages can be used to include a router or subnetwork in the

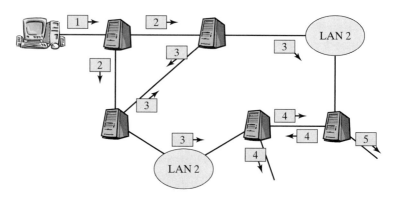

FIGURE 17–15
Schematic representation of how the Distance Vector Multicast Routing Protocol
(DVMRP) works.

distribution tree dynamically. To prevent a router from having to continually learn the
prune state for each network device and each group, it can use a timeout mechanism.
The status is discarded and the subnetwork is included in the multicast tree again as
soon as the time interval expires.

DVMRP belongs to the class of *dense-mode* routing protocols. Initial flooding
causes this method to work best in scenarios where the group members in the network
infrastructure are geographically close, so that flooding won't limit the bandwidth ex-
cessively until pruning has built the multicast routing tree. Other multicast routing protocols are Multicast-OSPF and Protocol Independent Multicast (PIM) in sparse mode
(PIM-SM) or dense mode (PIM-DM).

17.6   MULTICAST TRANSPORT PROTOCOLS

So far, we have actually discussed only unreliable and connectionless multicast transmissions based on UDP. This type of transmission is generally the most frequently used
application of multicast, mainly because it is much easier to handle. Nevertheless, there
are application cases for connection-oriented and reliable multicast communication,
and so extensive interesting research work is undertaken in this field.

Because the tasks involved in the reliable and connection-oriented transmission
of multicast data correspond mainly to the tasks of a transport protocol and these work
on top of the *IP Multicast*, a layer-3 service, the protocols developed so far are normally
called multicast transport protocols. The most important tasks of a transport protocol,
including connection management, flow control, error correction, and congestion control, are relatively complex and expensive for unicast communication, and point-to-mul-
tipoint communication adds special problems to this situation. For example, consider the
sender implosion problem, which occurs when many receivers return acknowledgements
for received data packets to the sender, overloading the sender with an enormous data
volume.

We will not discuss multicast transport protocols any further at this point, because there is currently no protocol used as a standard under Linux. We do list a few

protocols and research projects here. Some of these protocols have been implemented and evaluated. However, none of these protocols is especially suited for all multicast applications; each one has specific benefits and drawbacks.

- *Real-Time Transport Protocol (RTP)*—for real-time and multimedia applications.
- *Scalable Reliable Multicast (SRM)*—is currently used by the White Board tool.
- *Uniform Reliable Group Communication Protocol (URGC)*—supports reliable and in-order communication.
- *Muse*—an application-specific protocol for multicast news.
- *Multicast File Transfer Protocol (MFTP)*—works much like the File Transfer Protocol (*FTP*).
- *Local Group Concept (LGC)*—uses a hierarchy of local groups to prevent sender implosion.

C H A P T E R   1 8

Using Traffic Control to Support Quality of Service (QoS)

18.1   INTRODUCTION

In the Linux world, the term *traffic control* represents all the possibilities to influence incoming and outgoing network traffic in one way or another. In this context, we normally distinguish between two definitions, although it is often difficult to draw a clear line between the two:

- *Policing*: "Policing" means that data streams are monitored and that packets not admitted by a specified strategy (policy) are discarded. Within a networked computer, this can happen in two places: when it is receiving packets from the network (ingress policing) and when it is sending packets to the network.
- *Traffic shaping*: "Traffic shaping" refers to a targeted influence on mostly outgoing traffic. This includes, for example, buffering of outgoing data to stay within a specified rate, setting priorities for outgoing data streams, and marking packets for specific service classes.

The traffic-control framework developed for the Linux operating system creates a universal environment, which integrates totally different elements for policing and traffic shaping that can be interconnected. These elements can even be dynamically loaded and unloaded as a module during active operation. We describe this framework in detail below, but limit the discussion of the implementation of elements in this framework to a single example. Subsequently, we will describe configuration options in the user space.

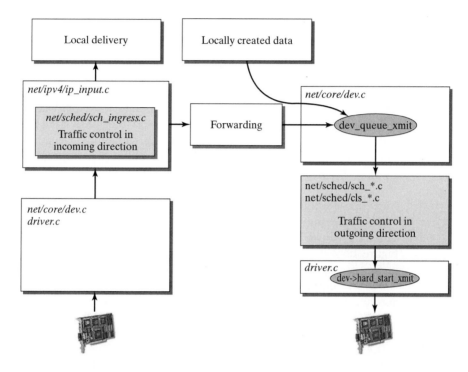

FIGURE 18–1
Traffic control in the Linux kernel.

18.2 BASIC STRUCTURE OF TRAFFIC CONTROL IN LINUX

Figure 18–1 shows where traffic control is arranged in the Linux kernel. Traffic control in the incoming direction is handled by the functions from the file `net/sch/sch_ingress.c` before incoming packets are passed to higher protocol layers or forwarded over other network cards within the kernel.

The largest part of traffic control in Linux occurs in outgoing direction. Here, we can use and interlink different elements for policing and traffic shaping.

18.3 TRAFFIC CONTROL IN THE OUTGOING DIRECTION

The traffic-control framework defines three basic elements:

- *Queuing discipline*: Each network device is allocated to a queuing discipline. In general, packets to be sent are passed to a queuing discipline and sorted within this queue by specific rules. During a search for packets ready to be sent, these packets can be removed no earlier than when the queuing discipline has marked them as ready for transmission. The algorithm used within a queuing discipline remains invisible to the outside. Examples for queuing disciplines include simple FIFO buffers and token buckets. More elaborate queuing disciplines can also manage several queues. Queuing disciplines are defined in files with names beginning with sch_ (in the net/sched directory).

■ *Classes*: Queuing disciplines can have several interfaces, and these interfaces are used to insert packets in the queue management. This allows us to distinguish packets by classes. Within one single queue discipline, we could allocate packets to different classes (e.g., to handle them with different priorities). Classes are defined within the queuing discipline (i.e., also in files with names beginning with sch_).

■ *Filters*: Filters are generally used to allocate outgoing packets to classes within a queuing discipline. Filters are defined in files with names beginning with cls_.

Much as with a construction kit, single elements can be connected, even recursively: Other queuing disciplines, with their corresponding classes and filters, can be used within one single queuing discipline.

Figure 18–2 shows an example for the resulting traffic-control tree. On the outside, we first see only the enqueue and dequeue functions of the upper queuing discipline. In this example, packets passed via the function enqueue() are checked one after another by the filter rules and allocated to the class visited by the filter for the first time. If none of the filter rules matches, then a default filter can be used to define an allocation system. Behind the classes there are other queuing disciplines. Because this is a tree, we also speak of the *parent* of a queuing discipline. For example, the queuing discipline 1:0 is a so-called outer queuing discipline and the parent of the classes 1:1 and 1:2. The queuing disciplines 2:0 and 3:0 are also called inner queuing disciplines.

Packets are removed recursively from this tree for transmission: When the dequeue() function of the outer queuing discipline is invoked, the function searches the queuing disciplines of the respective classes recursively for packets ready to be sent, depending on the type of queuing discipline.

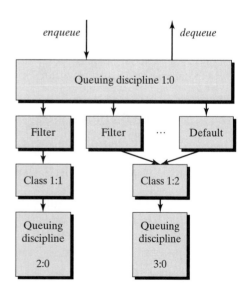

FIGURE 18–2

Example for a tree consisting of queuing disciplines, classes, and filters.

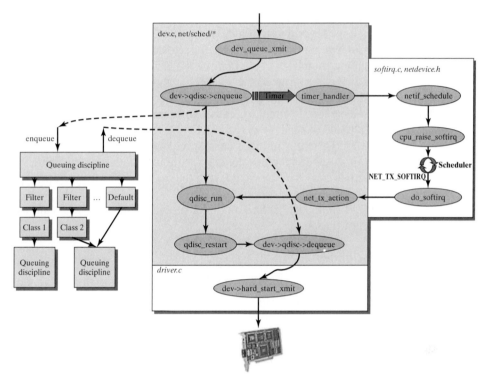

FIGURE 18–3
Inserting the traffic-control tree in the transmission process in the Linux kernel.

The path a packet takes through the kernel was described in detail in Chapter 6. Figure 18–3 shows how the traffic-control example relates to the transmission process shown in Figure 6–4. Rather than one single FIFO queue, we now insert a more extensive and configurable tree to handle transmit data streams; no other changes to the functions of the transmission process are required.

The following sections describe the interfaces of queuing disciplines, classes, and filters.

18.4   KERNEL STRUCTURES AND INTERFACES

The interfaces available for queuing disciplines and filters are mostly independent of the functionality available within an element.

18.4.1   Handles

All elements within the traffic-control tree can be addressed by 32-bit identifiers called handles. For example, the instances of the queuing disciplines discussed further below are marked with 32-bit identifiers, divided into a major number and a minor number. However, these numbers have nothing to do with the major and minor numbers for device files. These identifiers are unique for each network device, but they can occur more than once for several network devices.

In contrast, the minor number for a queue discipline is always null, except for input queuing discipline number `ffff:fff1` `TC_H_INGRESS` (in `include/linux/pkt_sched.h`) and the top queue of output queuing discipline number `ffff:ffff` `TC_H_ROOT`. Major numbers are assigned by the user and are in the range from 0x0001 to 0x7fff. If the user specifies major number 0, then the kernel allocates a major number between 0x8000 und 0xffff.

For classes, the major number corresponds to the associated queuing discipline, while the minor number specifies the class within that queuing discipline. In this case, the minor number can be in the range from 0x0 to 0xffff. Minor numbers are unique only within all classes of a queuing discipline.

`include/linux/pkt_sched.h` defines several macros you can use to mask major and minor numbers.

18.4.2 Queuing Disciplines

The functions supplied by a queuing discipline are defined in the `Qdisc_ops` structure in `include/net/pkt_sched.h`:

```
struct Qdisc_ops {
        struct Qdisc_ops         *next;
        struct Qdisc_class_ops   *cl_ops;
        char                     id[IFNAMSIZ];
        int                      priv_size;

        int                      (*enqueue)(struct sk_buff *, struct Qdisc *);
        struct sk_buff *         (*dequeue)(struct Qdisc *);
        int                      (*requeue)(struct sk_buff *, struct Qdisc *);
        int                      (*drop)(struct Qdisc *);

        int                      (*init)(struct Qdisc *, struct rtattr *arg);
        void                     (*reset)(struct Qdisc *);
        void                     (*destroy)(struct Qdisc *);
        int                      (*change)(struct Qdisc *, struct rtattr *arg);

        int                      (*dump)(struct Qdisc *, struct sk_buff *);
};
```

The first four entries are a link to a list (`struct Qdisc_ops *next;`), a reference to the class-related operations (`struct Qdisc_class_ops *cl_ops`), which will be described later. They represent an identifier (`char id [IFNAMSIZ]`) and values used internally.

The following functions are available externally:

enqueue()	include/net/pkt_sched.h

The function enqueue() is used to pass packets to a queuing discipline. The return value is null (NET_XMIT_SUCCESS, see `include/linux/netdevice.h`), if the packet is accepted by the queuing discipline. If this or another packet is discarded when ordering packets, then the return value is unequal null:

- NET_XMIT_DROP: The packet just passed was discarded.
- NET_XMIT_CN: A packet was discarded—for example, because of buffer overflow (CN stands for "congestion").
- NET_XMIT_POLICED: A packet was discarded because the policing mechanism detected violation of a rule (e.g., the admissible rate was exceeded).
- NET_XMIT_BYPASS: The passed packet was accepted, but won't leave the queuing discipline over the regular dequeue() function.

dequeue()	include/net/pkt_sched.h

When the function dequeue() is invoked, the queuing discipline returns a pointer to a packet (skb), which may be sent next. The return value **null** doesn't mean that there are no more packets waiting in the queuing discipline; it means only that there are no packets ready to be sent at the time of the call. The total number of packets waiting in a queuing discipline is stated in struct Qdisc* q->q.len. This value should be valid when a queuing discipline manages more than one queue.

requeue()	include/net/pkt_sched.h

The requeue() function puts a previously removed packet back into the queue. In contrast to enqueue(), however, the packet should be arranged at the position in the queuing discipline where it had been before, and the counter of packets running through this queuing discipline should not be increased. This function is intended for cases where a packet was removed by dequeue() to send it, but eventually it couldn't be sent, for an unexpected cause.

drop()	include/net/pkt_sched.h

This function removes a packet from the queue and discards it.

reset()	include/net/pkt_sched.h

The reset() function sets a queuing discipline back into the initial state (empty queues, reset counters, delete timers, etc.). If this queuing discipline manages other queuing disciplines, then their reset() functions will also be invoked.

init()	include/net/pkt_sched.h

The init() function is used to initialize a new, instantiated queuing discipline.

destroy()	include/net/pkt_sched.h

The destroy() function frees the resources that had been reserved during the initialization and runtime of the queuing discipline.

change()	include/net/pkt_sched.h

The change() function can be used to change parameters of a queuing discipline.

dump()	include/net/pkt_sched.h

The dump() function serves to output configuration parameters and statistics of a queuing discipline.

The central structure of each queuing discipline, which is referred to by all functions introduced so far, is the structure struct Qdisc (include/net/pkt_sched.h), printed as follows:

```
struct Qdisc {
        int                     (*enqueue)(struct sk_buff *skb, struct Qdisc
*dev);
        struct sk_buff *        (*dequeue)(struct Qdisc *dev);
        unsigned                flags;
#define TCQ_F_BUILTIN 1
#define TCQ_F_THROTTLED 2
#define TCQ_F_INGRES 4
        struct Qdisc_ops        *ops;
        struct Qdisc            *next;
        u32                     handle;
        atomic_t                refcnt;
        struct sk_buff_head q;
        struct net_device       *dev;
        struct tc_stats         stats;
        int                     (*reshape_fail)(struct sk_buff *skb, struct Qdis
c *q);

        /* This field is deprecated, but it is still used by CBQ
         * and it will live until better solution will be invented.
         */
        struct Qdisc            *__parent;
        char                    data[0];
};
```

In addition to a reference to the Qdisc_ops structure, there is a pointer to link Qdisc structures and a handle for unique marking of an instance of the structure within the kernel. For a simple queuing discipline with only one queue, the entry struct sk_buff_head q; represents the header of this queue. Each queuing discipline is always allocated to exactly one network device, which is referred to by struct net_device *dev.

The function reshape_fail() can be used to implement more complex traffic-shaping mechanisms. When an outer queue passes a packet to an inner queue, then it can happen that the packet has to be discarded—for example, when there is no buffer space available. If the outer queuing discipline implements the callback function reshape_fail(), then it can be invoked by the inner queuing discipline in this case. Subsequently, the outer queuing discipline can select a different class.

The structure `struct   tc_stats` contained in `struct    Qdisc` (`include/linux/pkt_sched.h`) serves to carry along statistics (in addition to the `q.qlen` entry described earlier for the number of packets to be ordered). The following counters exist in the structure `tc_stats`:

```
__u64  bytes:          /* Number of enqueued bytes */
__u32  packets;        /* Number of enqueued packets */
__u32  drops;          /* Packets dropped because of lack of re-
                          sources */
__u32  overlimits;     /* Number of throttle events when
                          this flow goes out of allocated bandwidth */
__u32  bps;            /* Current flow byte rate */
__u32  pps;            /* Current flow packet rate */
__u32  qlen;
__u32  backlog;
```

These statistics can have certain inaccuracies if a queuing discipline manages additional inner queuing disciplines. This is the case, for example, when a packet was dropped in an inner queuing discipline, because the number of ordered `bytes` can then deviate from the real value. If a queuing discipline has several classes, then separate statistics can be maintained for each class.

A queuing discipline can be added in either of the following two ways:

`pktsched_init()`	**net/sched/sch_api.c**

This function is used when a queuing discipline is permanently compiled in the kernel. In this case, the RT-NETLINK interface, which will be introduced later, is initialized, and the function `register_qdisc()` is invoked. Unless additional queuing disciplines were selected when the kernel was configured, only the `bfifo` and `pfifo` queuing disciplines (defined in `net/sched/sch_fifo.c`) are selected here.

`register_qdisc()`	**net/sched/sch_api.c**

This function is invoked either by the above described function, `pktsched_init()`, or by `init_module()`, if we want to include the queuing discipline as a module. Initially, this function checks for whether a queuing discipline with the same identification—`id[IFNAMSIZ]`—of the `Qdisc_ops` structure already exists. If this is not the case, then the new queuing discipline is appended to the end of the list, and the functions are allocated.

18.4.3 Classes

Classes can be thought of as logically independent elements, but they relate closely to queuing disciplines as far as the implementation is concerned. Rather than independent files that implement classes, classes are always offered by queuing disciplines. In addition, notice that the classification (i.e., allocation of packets to a class) is handled by the filters described later (packet classifiers), which are logically separate from classes.

Unique class identifiers, similarly to queuing disciplines, are used to be able to address a class within the kernel. However, there are two identifying options for classes: The `classid` of type `u32` serves primarily to identify a class by the user and the configuration tools in the user space; this option will be discussed in Section 18.7. In addition, there is an internal identification of the type `unsigned long`, which can be used for general identification of a class within the kernel. In this case, various `classids` can be mapped from the user space onto an internal identification, if other filter information play a role (e.g., specific fields of the `skb` structure).

Queuing disciplines that supply classes offer various functions, including functions to bind queues to classes and functions to change or dump a class configuration. The functions introduced below are defined in the `sch_*` files and exported over the structure `Qdisc_ops` (`include/net/pkt_sched.h`) (except for the `qdisc_graft()` function, which builds on top of the former):

`graft()`	**include/net/pkt_sched.h**

The `graft()` function serves to bind a queuing discipline to a class. The return value is the queuing discipline that was previously bound to that class.

`get()`	**include/net/pkt_sched.h**

The `get()` function maps the `classid` to the internal identification; this is its return value. If a usage counter exists within the class, then `get()` increments this counter by one.

`put()`	**include/net/pkt_sched.h**

In contrast to `get()`, the `put()` function decrements the usage counter. If this causes the usage counter to reach null, then `put()` can remove the class.

`qdisc_graft()`	**net/sched/sch_api.c**

This function is used in all cases where a new queuing discipline should be attached to the traffic-control tree. It initially checks on whether there is a `parent` or the queuing discipline itself should form the root of the traffic control tree. In the latter case, the function `dev_graft_qdisc()` from `net/sched/sch_api.c` is invoked. If a `parent` is present, then the `get()` function is invoked first to map the classid to the internal identification. Subsequently, the `graft()` function is invoked to bind the new queuing discipline to the classes. Finally, `put()` is invoked to decrement the reference counter of the old class.

`leaf()`	**include/net/pkt_sched.h**

This function returns a pointer to the queuing discipline currently bound to that class.

| change() | include/net/pkt_sched.h |

The change() function is used to change class parameters or create new classes, provided that the queuing discipline allows this.

| delete() | include/net/pkt_sched.h |

This function checks on whether the class is still referenced, and it deletes the class if this holds true.

| walk() | include/net/pkt_sched.h |

This function walks through the linked list of all the classes of a queuing discipline and, if it is implemented, invokes a callback function to fetch configuration data and statistical parameters.

| tcf_chain() | include/net/pkt_sched.h |

Figure 18–2 shows that each class is bound to at least one filter. The function tcf_chain() returns a pointer to the beginning of a linked list for the filter bound to that class.

| bind_tcf() | include/net/pkt_sched.h |

This function tells the queuing discipline that a filter is going to be bound to the class. This means that the function is similar to the get() function, but can be used in some cases where we have to run additional checks.

| unbind_tcf() | include/net/pkt_sched.h |

This function is the counterpart of the previous function, bind_tcf(), which means that it represents an extension of the put() function.

| dump_class() | include/net/pkt_sched.h |

Like the dump() function for queuing disciplines, the function dump_class() serves to output configuration parameters and statistical data for a class.

18.4.4 Filters

The class packets that passed by the enqueue() function in a queuing discipline belong to is decided by filters.

To make this decision, a filter uses the `classify()` function. This function and other filter functions, which will be described below, are exported over the `tcf_proto_ops` (`include/net/pkt_cls.h`) structure:

`classify()`	**include/net/pkt_cls.h**

This function classifies a packet (i.e., the filter checks for whether there is a filtering rule that could be applied to the packet). The following return values are possible (as for `include/linux/pkt_cls.h`):

- `TC_POLICE_OK`: The packet was accepted by the filter.
- `TC_POLICE_RECLASSIFY`: The packet violates agreed parameters (e.g., a maximum rate) and should be allocated to a different class. However, the packet is not dropped yet, to enable the queuing discipline to transport the packet over a different class.
- `TC_POLICE_SHOT`: The packet was accepted by the filter, but the filter dropped it, because it violated agreed parameters.
- `TC_POLICE_UNSPEC`: The rule applied by the filter doesn't match the packet, and it should be passed to the next filter or filter element.

In addition, the `classify()` function in the structure `tcf_result` (`include/net/pkt_cls.h`) returns the `classid` and, if present, the internal identification of the pertaining class. The internal identification can then simply be made available, if a separate instance of the filter exists for each class. If the internal identification is not written to the result structure, then the `classid` has to be mapped to the internal identification in the queuing discipline (normally by use of a linear search). In some cases, the filter can be informed about the internal identification while binding to a class, so that no mapping cost occurs.

`init()`	**include/net/pkt_cls.h**

This function initializes a filter.

`destroy()`	**include/net/pkt_cls.h**

The `destroy()` function removes a filter. To remove bindings to a class, it will have to invoke `unbind_tcf()`.

`get()`	**include/net/pkt_cls.h**

Again, the `get()` function is used to map identifiers—in this case, to map a handle of a filter element to an internal filter identification.

`put()`	**include/net/pkt_cls.h**

The `put()` function is invoked to unreference a filter.

change()	include/net/pkt_cls.h

This function serves to configure a new filter or change the configuration of an existing filter. bind_tcf() is used to bind new filters to classes.

delete()	include/net/pkt_cls.h

In contrast to the destroy() function, this function is used to delete one single element of a filter. The difference between a filter and a filter element will be discussed later.

walk()	include/net/pkt_cls.h

As with classes, the walk() function walks through all elements and invokes call-back functions to get configuration data and statistical parameters.

dump()	include/net/pkt_cls.h

The dump() function serves to output configuration parameters and statistical data of a filter or filter elements.

Next, when a packet is passed to a queuing discipline with several classes, then the latter invokes the function tc_classify() from include/net/pkt_cls.h. This function checks on whether the filter accepts the protocol specified in skb->protocol and then invokes the filter's classify() function. The return values are identical to those of the classify() function.

The central structure of filters within Linux traffic control is struct tcf_proto in include/net/pkt_cls.h. The entry struct tcf_proto *next can be used to link several filters to a list. In addition, there are entries for the accepted protocol, for the classid of the appropriate class, and for a priority. The priority can be used to order filters that can be applied to the same protocol. For this purpose, the filters are walked through from prio variables with small values towards larger values, and a packet is allocated to the filter with rules matching first.

In addition, a filter can be split internally into filter elements, and handles of the type u32 are allocated to these internal elements. How filters are split and managed (i.e., in linear lists or in more efficient data structures such as hash tables) depends on the implementation.

As in queuing disciplines, there are two functions available to add new filters. The function tc_filter_init() (net/sched/cls_api.c) is used when a filter is permanently compiled in the kernel. From within this function, the function register_tcf_proto_ops() (net/sched/cls_api.c) is invoked, including the case where we want to embed the filter as a module. This function initially checks for whether a filter of the same type (kind element in the tcf_proto_ops structure) already exists. If this is not the case, then the new filter is appended to the end of the filter list, and functions are allocated.

18.5 INGRESS POLICING

The file net/sched/sch_ingress.c implements a queuing discipline designed for ingress policing. Its structure is similar to that of other queuing disciplines, and the exported functions are similar to the functions described in the previous section.

However, rather than buffering packets, this queuing discipline classifies packets to decide whether a packet will be accepted or discarded. This means that the queuing discipline actually assumes a firewall or Netfilter functionality. This functionality also reflects in the return values of the enqueue() function, which are converted to Netfilter return values, as shown in the following excerpt from the function ingress_enqueue() (net/sched/sch_ingress.c):

```
case TC_POLICE_SHOT:
     result = NF_DROP;
     break;
case TC_POLICE_RECLASSIFY: /* DSCP remarking here ? */
case TC_POLICE_OK:
case TC_POLICE_UNSPEC:
default:
     result = NF_ACCEPT;
     break;
```

First, the function register_qdisc() registers the functions of the queuing discipline with the network device. Subsequently, the function nf_register_hook() hooks them into the hook NF_IP_PRE_ROUTING.

Next, additional filters can be appended to this particular queuing discipline. These filters can access functions from net/sched/police.c to check on whether a data stream complies with a token bucket.

18.6 IMPLEMENTING A QUEUING DISCIPLINE

This section describes how we can implement a queuing discipline. We will use the token-bucket filter as an example, because it represents a fundamental element of many traffic-shaping approaches.

18.6.1 The Token-Bucket Filter

A token-bucket filter is used to control and limit the rate and burst (when a specified data rate is briefly exceeded) of data streams. Figure 18–4 illustrates the basic idea of a token bucket. In this model, the determining parameters are the rate, R, at which a token bucket is filled with tokens, and the maximum number of tokens, B, this token bucket can hold. Each token represents a byte that may be sent. Subsequently, the token bucket declares a packet to comply with the rate and burst parameters, if the number of tokens in the token bucket corresponds at least to the length of the packet in bytes.

If a packet is compliant, it may be sent. Subsequently, the number of tokens in the token bucket is reduced by a number corresponding to the packet length. If a

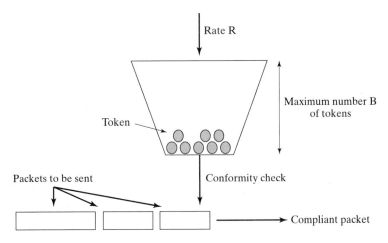

FIGURE 18–4
Model of a token bucket.

noncompliant packet is deleted immediately, then the token bucket runs a traffic-policing process. In contrast, if the packet is held back until sufficient tokens have accumulated in the token bucket, we talk of traffic shaping.

A real-world implementation will realize this model differently, so that the computing cost is less, though the result is the same. It would not make sense to increment a counter representing the number of tokens several times per second, even when there is no packet to send. Instead, computations are made only provided that a packet is ready to be sent and waiting at the input of the token bucket. In this case, we can compute how many tokens have to be present in the token bucket at that point in time. To do this computation, we need to know when the last packet was sent and what the filling level of the token bucket was after that. The current number of available tokens is calculated from the sum of tokens available after the last transmission, plus the tokens arrived in the meantime (i.e., plus the interval, multiplied by the rate, R). Notice that the number of available tokens can never be larger than B. If the number of tokens computed in this way corresponds to at least the length of the waiting packet, then this packet may be sent. Otherwise, instead of sending the packet, a timer is started. This timer expires when more packets can be sent as a sufficient number of tokens has arrived. The timer has to be initialized to an appropriate interval, which can be easily calculated from the number of tokens still missing and the rate, R, at which the bucket is filled with more tokens.

Such a token-bucket filter is implemented within the traffic-control framework in the file `net/sched/sch_tbf.c`. However, this is an extension (i.e., a dual token bucket). More specifically, two token buckets are arranged back to back, in a frequently used arrangement, to guarantee a mean rate and limit bursts. The first token bucket is set to a rate, R, corresponding to the desired mean data rate, and the second token bucket is set to the peak rate and a significantly smaller number of tokens, B. However, B corresponds at least to the maximum size of one maximum transmission unit (MTU).

To be able to store states between single transmit processes, the token-bucket implementation uses the `tbf_sched_data` structure:

```
struct tbf_sched_data{
/*Parameters*/
u32          limit;          /*Maximal length of backlog: bytes*/
u32          buffer;         /*Token Bucket depth/rate: MUST Be >= MTU/B */
u32          mtu;
u32          max_size;
struct qdisc_rate_table *R_tab;
struct qdisc_rate_table *P_tab;
/* Variables */
long         tokens;         /* Current number of B tokens */
long         ptokens;        /* Current number of P tokens */
psched_time_t t_c;          /* Time check-point */
struct timer_list wd_timer; /*Watchdog timer */
};
```

The `limit` field specifies the number of bytes in the queue used to buffer packets that cannot be sent immediately. The `buffer` field shows that the byte-to-rate ratio (i.e., times) is used rather than bytes and rates for computations in most places within the implementation. This means that a packet with a specific length takes some transmit time from the token bucket, the available transmit time of which is calculated from the current number of tokens to the rate R ratio. The variables `tokens` and `ptokens` store the number of tokens in the respective token bucket. The time at which the last packet was transmitted is written to the `t_c` entry, and the `wd_timer` field is needed when a timer has to be started for a packet's delayed transmission. Two pointers, `R_tab` and `P_tab`, point to the structure `qdisc_rate_table`, which stores the allocations of packet lengths to transmit times to avoid divisions during each transmission process. This table is created by the function `qdisc_get_rtab()` when `tbf_change()` (net/sched/sch_tbf.c) initializes the token-bucket filter. However, the actual computation is done in the user space by use of the `tc_calc_rtable()` function in `iproute2/tc/tc_core.c`.

We will now introduce and explain additional functions of the token-bucket filter.

`tbf_init()`	**net/sched/sch_tbf.c**

Initialization of the token bucket means merely that the start time has to be defined to initialize the timer. The macro `PSCHED_GET_TIME` (include/net/pkt_sched.h) is used to establish the start time. This macro accesses the TSC register described in Chapter 2, if it is present. A structure containing a pointer to private data and a pointer to the `tbf_watchdog()` function are passed to the timer. The `tbf_watchdog()` function has to be invoked when the timer expires.

`tbf_enqueue()`	**netsched/sch_tbf.c**

This function serves to accept packets and to append them to the end of the queue. Also, a number of statistics are updated, and error cases are handled.

`tbf_dequeue()`	**netsched/sch_tbf.c**

This function handles the actual traffic-shaping work. First, PSCHED_GET_TIME(now) is used to learn the current time. Subsequently, the number of available tokens is computed from the old value (q->ptokens or q->tokens) and the time elapsed. Next, qdisc_rate_table is used to compute the number of tokens required by the packet, and the difference between existing and required tokens is calculated. However, notice that a token stands for an interval rather than for a byte. If the number of tokens in both token buckets is sufficient, then tbf_dequeue() returns the top skb from the queue; otherwise, a timer is started. The inaccuracies of the standard Linux timers, described in Chapter 2, can cause a value of null to result from the conversion of the interval into jiffies. In this case, a minimum delay of one jiffie is selected, to ensure that a packet is never sent too early.

`tbf_watchdog()`	**netsched/sch_tbf.c**

The tbf_watchdog function is invoked when the timer for a packet expires. Within this function, only the netif_schedule() function is invoked, which eventually invokes the function dev->qdisc->dequeue() once computing time has been allocated, as shown in Figure 18–3. In the simplest case, this happens without multiple queues in the traffic-control tree tbf_dequeue().

18.7 CONFIGURATION

This section describes how the traffic-control elements are configured from within the user space. To configure traffic-control elements, the tc tools are used. This toolset is a command-line configuration program (available in [Kuzn01] as part of the iproute2 package). In addition, the RT netlink interface is used to pass configuration information to the kernel.

18.7.1 The RT Netlink Interface

The RT netlink interface is fully described in Chapter 26. For the purposes of this section, it is sufficient to know that the RT netlink interface is used to pass a pointer to the rtattr (in include/linux/rtnetlink.h) structure to the init() or change() functions of the traffic-control framework. The function rtattr_parse (net/core/rtnetlink.c) can be used to structure the data passed, and various macros, including RTA_PAYLOAD und RTA_DATA (include/linux/rtnetlink.h), can be used to print this information. The tcmsg (include/linux/rtnetlink.h) structure defines traffic-control messages that can be sent over the RT netlink interface from within the user space.

18.7.2 The User Interface

The tc program provides a command-line user interface to configure the Linux traffic control. This tool is available from [Kuzn01].

The tc tool enables you to set up and configure all elements of the traffic-control framework discussed here, such as queuing disciplines, filters, and classes. To be able to use the Differentiated Services support in Linux, we first have to set the entry TC_CONFIG_DIFFSERV=y in the Config file in the iproutes/tc directory. If the kernel version and the version of your tc tool match, then calling make in the same directory should enable you to compile successfully.

Depending on the element we want to configure, we now have to select the appropriate element, together with additional options:

```
Usage: tc [ OPTIONS ] OBJECT { COMMAND | help } where OBJECT :=
{ qdisc | class | filter }
        OPTIONS := { -s[tatistics] | -d[etails] | -r[aw] | -b[atch] file }
```

A detailed description of all additional options would go beyond the scope and volume of this book. You can use the help command (e.g., tc qdisc add tbf help) to easily obtain information. In addition, you can find an overview of ongoing work in the field of more comfortable user interfaces in [Alme01].

C H A P T E R   1 9

Packet Filters and Firewalls

19.1   INTRODUCTION

Each network packet handled by a Linux computer passes a number of distinctive points within the network implementation on its way through the Linux kernel before it either is delivered to a local process or leaves the computer for further routing. Direct access to the packet stream in the kernel opens up a large number of ways to manipulate packets, which are also suitable for implementing a security strategy in the network. For example, functions were built into the routing code early in the course of the Linux development. These functions allow the system administrator to influence how packets are handled, depending on their source and destination addresses. In addition to the pure filtering function, which lets you drop certain packets completely, this also includes more complex manipulations, including address-conversion mechanisms (*Network Address Translation—NAT*) or the support of transparent proxies. After its introduction in the form of `ipfwadm` in Linux Version 1.2, this packet-filter code later underwent two complete revisions to ensure better manageability, extension of the control options, and better integration of additional functionality (e.g., NAT). This chapter discusses the differences between the packet-filter architecture of the current Linux Version 2.4 and that of the previous Linux Version 2.2.

19.1.1   The Functional Principle of a Firewall

In its original meaning, the term *firewall* denotes a fire-resistant wall constructed to prevent the spread of fire. In connection with computer networks, a firewall is a protection mechanism used in a specific and exactly limited network (e.g., a corporate intranet) at a transition point from a neighboring network (generally to the Internet) to protect the intranet against dangers from the outside.

A firewall consists normally of two types of components:

▪ *Packet filters* are normally implemented in routers and monitor the entire network traffic flowing through these routers. These routers use a well-defined set of

383

rules (e.g., address information contained in a packet header) to decide which packets can pass and which will be dropped.

In the case of IP networks, packet-filter rules normally refer at least to the IP source and destination addresses, the transport protocol (TCP or UDP), the TCP or UDP source and destination ports, and some TCP flags (for TCP; particularly the SYN flag, which can be used to see whether a packet is a connection-establishment request).

■ *Application gateways* or *proxies* (e.g., mail relays and HTTP proxies) act as mediators between the communicating application processes and can implement fine-grained, application-specific access control.

A complete firewall configuration (see Figure 19–1) normally consists of an inner router with packet-filtering functionality, which forms the transition to the network to be protected; an outer router with packet-filtering functionality, which forms the transition to the external network; and a number of application gateways located in an independent local area network between these routers. This network within the firewall is normally called a *demilitarized zone* (*DMZ*) or *screened subnet*. If gateways are available for all required application protocols, then the packet filters can be configured so that no packets are forwarded directly between the internal and the external networks. Instead, exclusive communication is between the internal network and the DMZ and between the external network and the DMZ.

In the most frequent case, that in which the network to be protected has only this single connection to the Internet and so represents an edge network from the topological view, the most fundamental firewall functionality is to limit packet forwarding to packets with topologically correct addresses. This means that only packets with a source address outside of the network and a destination address within the network are permitted into the network (so-called *ingress filtering*). In opposite direction, for a packet to be able to leave the network, the packet's source address has to be within the network and its destination address has to be outside the network (*egress filtering*). If all edge networks would strictly implement this functionality, this would effectively

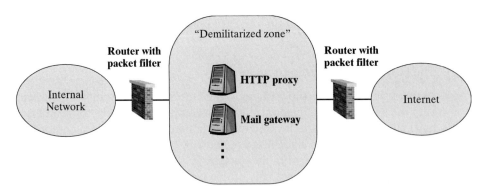

FIGURE 19–1
Structure of a firewall.

protect computers against attacks where hackers use falsified source addresses to hide their origin. This is the reason why the IETF explicitly recommends this approach in RFC 2827 [FeSe00].

Because the number of available IP addresses is extremely limited in IP Version 4, many firewalls in networks implement the *Network Address Translation* (*NAT*) mechanism. In this case, the internal network uses private addresses not visible from the outside. Chapter 21 discusses the NAT implementation in Linux 2.4.

19.1.2   Protocol-specific Particularities: TCP, FTP, and others

In practice, it often is insufficient to filter individual packets exclusively by addresses, protocol numbers, and port numbers. For example, the connection-oriented TCP transport protocol groups many IP packets to a logical connection. If we want to implement address translation (NAT), these packets have to be seen as a group, of course, and they have to be handled equally. The connection-tracking mechanism discussed in Chapter 20 is responsible for this task.

Special treatment of some packets is not only important for NAT, but it is also important for a pure filter functionality. For example, it often is desirable to permit only outgoing connections on specific TCP ports. To achieve this, we can utilize the fact that the SYN flag is set and the ACK flag is cleared in the TCP header of the first packet only in a TCP connection (connection-establishment request). To block TCP connections incoming on a specific port, all we have to do is to filter out all incoming packets that have the SYN flag set and the ACK flag cleared in their headers.

More serious problems arise in connection with some application protocols that use dynamically assigned port numbers. One of the best known examples is the *File Transfer Protocol* (*FTP*). In FTP, the client initially establishes a control connection to TCP port 21 in the server, and then uses this connection to transmit FTP commands and replies. As soon as a file has to be transmitted or a directory has to be displayed, FTP opens an additional data connection in the "reverse direction": from TCP port 20 in the server to a dynamically selected client port, where the client-side port number is sent over the control connection.

For a firewall that wants to permit outgoing FTP sessions only, either it would have to accept all incoming connections originating from TCP port 20 or a *stateful filter* would have to be installed to eavesdrop on and analyze all commands and replies from the FTP control connection and then permit only selected incoming FTP data connections. The first method is not optimal from the security perspective, and the second method causes considerable additional cost.

However, to solve these problems for the FTP protocol, there is an additional method that prevents firewall problems by selecting the "passive" mode of operation. Unfortunately, this operation mode, which establishes data connections from a client to a server, is not supported in all FTP implementations. The problem is even more difficult when filtering is used for some other protocols (e.g., the H.323 multimedia conference protocol, which is used in many applications, including the popular Microsoft NetMeeting; a number of control and data connections with dynamically assigned TCP and UDP port numbers belong to one single H.323 session, so that a stateful filter would become very complex).

Independent of the application protocol, we cannot use stateful filters when the control connections are encrypted. In this case, the only feasible method is to employ specially adapted client and server software that uses an appropriate protocol, such as SOCKS [LGLK⁺96], to let the firewall dynamically and selectively permit traffic on specific ports.

19.1.3 Quality Criteria for Packet-Filter Implementations

To be able to evaluate the quality of a packet-filter architecture, [ChBe94] formulates the following criteria:

1. Filtering is done both for incoming and for outgoing packets.
2. There is an option to distinguish connection-establishment requests from other packets within one single connection.
3. Filter options for protocols other than IP, TCP, and UDP either are available or can be added easily.
4. There are filter options for arbitrary bit patterns within packets.
5. There are filter options for routing information at both the input and the output.
6. There is an option to reject data packets, if the destination address of these packets was changed by source routing.
7. The set of rules is clearly represented, and there is an option to control the sequence in which rules are applied to a packet.
8. Dropped data packets can be logged.

We will see in our discussion in the following sections that the new netfilter architecture of Linux Version 2.4 meets all those criteria.

19.1.4 Limits of the Firewall Principle

Though a properly configured firewall is an important component for protecting a network, we have to understand that a firewall can never be a panacea. All packet filters operate on the basis of information contained in the protocol headers of incoming data packets. This information can be tampered with easily. For example, an adapted TCP/IP implementation makes it very easy for an intruder to send IP packets whose source address in the IP header is not the address of the actual sender (so-called *IP spoofing*).

To achieve tamper-proof identification of a packet's origin as a prerequisite for effective filtering of incoming data traffic, it is recommended that one use cryptographic mechanisms (e.g., the IP security architecture of IPsec). In Linux, we can use FreeS/WAN, which is an IPsec implementation.

19.2   THE IPCHAINS ARCHITECTURE OF LINUX 2.2

ipchains is a packet-filtering architecture consisting of an infrastructure in the Linux kernel and a user-space program to manage rules lists, like all packet-filtering architectures currently implemented in Linux. In Linux 2.2, this product is called ipchains.

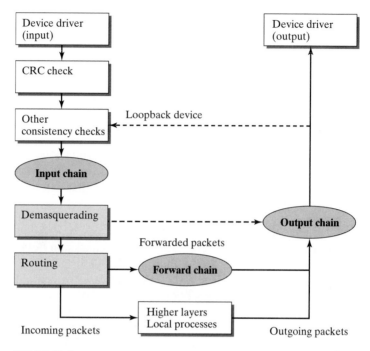

FIGURE 19–2
The packet-filtering architecture in Linux 2.2 (ipchains).

(See Figure 19–2.) Section 19.2.1 will discuss its invocation syntax and how we can define rules.

The filtering mechanisms implemented in Linux kernel Version 2.2 divide all data packets into the following three classes, depending on their source and destination addresses:

1. incoming packets—those addressed to the local computer;
2. packets to be forwarded and leaving the local computer over a different network interface based on a routing decision;
3. outgoing packets created in the local computer.

For each of these classes, the network stack of the respective protocol includes a prominent position, and each packet of the corresponding class has to pass it. In each of these positions, there is a *hook*, where a linked rules list (*chain*) is hooked, hence the name ipchains.

According to the packet class they are allocated to, the rules lists are called *input chain, forward chain*, and *output chain*. These chains are organized so that they are processed sequentially, beginning from the first defined rule. If a rule accepts an incoming packet, then this packet is handled according to the branch destination defined in the rule, where Linux Version 2.2 introduced the support of user-defined rules lists. This means that, in addition to the linear processing of rules lists, we can also implement branching. Other possible branch destinations are the following:

- ACCEPT—completes processing of the rules list and releases the packet for further handling.
- DENY—drops the packet.
- REJECT—discards the packet and returns an ICMP message of the "destination unreachable" type to the sender.
- REDIRECT—(an item new with Linux 2.2) makes sense only for the input chain and directs the packet to another local port. This is useful, for example, to implement transparent proxies, where all HTTP requests are redirected from port 80 to the port of a local HTTP proxy.

This means that, if a TCP/IP packet is addressed to the local computer, then it first has to undergo the usual verifications of the checksum field and the packet length before it arrives in the input chain, where it is handled according to this rule list.

Packets belonging to the second class (addressed to computers in a different network) visit all three rules chains hooked into the kernel in ipchains. As mentioned above, they first arrive in the input chain. The destination address is not in the local computer, so the packet is passed to the forward chain. Before this step, the packet is checked to see whether it is a packet masked by NAT. If this is the case, the packet is first unmasked and then passed directly to the output chain, bypassing the forward chain. If the forward chain accepts the packet, then a final step checks it in the output chain, before it leaves the router. Outgoing packets created in the local computer are handled exclusively by the output chain.

Each rules list has options to log the network traffic it handles. The counters of these functions have been 64 bits wide since Linux Version 2.2; this much finer granularity, as compared with that of the 32-bit predecessor versions, prevents overflow. In addition to the core functionality covered by ipchains, the packet-filtering architecture of Linux 2.2 uses additional modules to support more complex protocols, including active FTP (see Section 19.2.1), RealAudio or CUSeeMe, which are controlled over additional management tools (e.g., ipmasqadm). The entire core functionality is managed in the ipchains program, which is described in more detail below.

19.2.1 The ipchains Rule Syntax

This section describes the ipchains program, which is used to manage rules lists.

The basic structure of a rule definition is given by the following form: ipchains -<operation> <chain> <criterion> -j <branch destination>. Table 19–1 shows command-line options of ipchains and iptables, before we describe the options in detail.

- *Operation*: We can use one of the keywords listed in Table 19–1 to specify how we want the existing rules list to be manipulated. We use APPEND to build a list, which means that the new rule we just defined is appended to the end of a list. To generate a user-defined rules list, we use NEW. User-defined rules lists behave like subfunctions of the respective lists. This means that, when they are reached, they

TABLE 19–1   Command-line options of ipchains and iptables

Option	ipchains	iptables
Standard rules lists:		
	input	INPUT
	output	OUTPUT
	forward	FORWARD
Branch destinations:		
Accept packet	-j ACCEPT	-j ACCEPT
Drop packet	-j DENY	-j DROP
Reject packet	-j REJECT	-j REJECT
Convert/mask address	-j MASQ	-j MASQUERADE
Redirect to other port	-j REDIRECT	-j <Port>
Return from rules list	-j RETURN	-j RETURN
Log packet (*log*)	-j <branch destination>	-j LOG
	-l	
Criteria for filter rules:		
IP source address (*source*)	-s [!] <address>	-s [!] <address>
IP destination address (*destination*)	-d [!] <address>	-d [!] <address>
Source address and source port	-s [!] <address>	-s [!] <address>
	[!] <port>	—sport [!] <port>
Destination address and destination port	-d [!] <address>	-d [!] <address>
	[!] <port>	-dport [!] <port>
Transport protocol	-p <protocol>	-p <protocol>
Network device (*interface*)	-i [!] <device>	-i [!] <device>
TCP-SYN flag set	[!] -y	[!] -y
Fragments (consecutive packets)	[!] -f	[!] -f

are evaluated with regard to the current packet and then this packet is returned to the calling rules list, if none of the other rules applies to the packet.

- *Chain*: This is the rules list (input, output, forward, or a user-defined list) that the operation should run on.

- *Criterion*: This is the most complex part of the definition; it specifies packets that this rule should be applied on. First, the protocol (-p <protocol>) and ranges for the source and destination addresses (-s <address(es)> and -d <address(es)>, respectively) are defined.

In addition, we can limit the validity range for the TCP and UDP protocols to specific port numbers (-s <address(es)> <port(s)> and -d <address(es)> <port(s)>, respectively).

The criterion -i <interface> can be used to select only packets that arrive at or leave from a specific interface.

For the TCP protocol, we can use -y to specify that only packets with the SYN flag set and the ACK flag cleared should be considered. (See Section 19.1.2.)

We can use -f to specify that the rule should apply only to the second and all consecutive fragments of a fragmented IP packet. This criterion can be thought of as a simpler predecessor of the netfilter introduced in Chapter 20, which implements stateful connection tracking. Only the first fragment includes the transport protocol header, so we cannot specify port numbers together with this criterion.

All criteria can be negated by a leading exclamation sign— -s ! 127.0.0.1 would select all packets with a source address unequal 127.0.0.1.

- *Branch destination*: This parameter specifies what should happen to packets subject to these rules. ACCEPT lets these packet pass; DENY discards the packets silently; REJECT returns an ICMP error message of the type "Destination Unreachable" to the sender before it drops them. The branch destination RETURN is used for a conditioned return from a rules chain. This is particularly interesting during handling of user-defined rules lists, because it allows us to return to the calling rules lists.

Packets can be logged by the syslog mechanism by stating -l (log), in addition to one of the above branch destinations. This allows us, for example, to better detect and trace attempts of attacks (which means that one of the criteria described in Section 19.1.3 is met) or to monitor the traffic volume at a specific network interface.

19.2.2 Drawbacks of the ipchains Architecture

Design flaws were observed soon after the introduction of ipchains in Linux 2.2. The most important problems are as follows:

- ipchains had no uniform programming interface that would have enabled us to embed new rules lists into the kernel without having to consider network implementation details. For this reason, adding new rules lists was tiresome and extremely error-prone.
- In contrast, the netfilter architecture supplies a framework that minimizes direct interventions in the network code and allows us to append additional code in the form of modules for *packet mangling* into the kernel by using the regular interface.
- The integration of code for transparent proxies was expensive in ipchains and was connected to many interventions in the Linux kernel.
- In ipchains, rules were necessarily bound to a network address in general, which made the creation of rule sets much too complicated, because the address was the only way to distinguish packets generated locally from packets to be forwarded.
- ipchains implemented "masquerading" (a simple NAT variant) and the packet filter code in one piece, which made the code harder to read and unnecessarily complex.

19.3 THE NETFILTER ARCHITECTURE OF LINUX 2.4

Linux Version 2.4 divides the packet-filtering functionality into two large blocks: The so-called *netfilter hooks* offer a comfortable way to catch and manipulate processed IP packets at different positions on their way through the Linux kernel. Building on this background, the iptables module implements three rules lists to filter incoming, forwarded, and outgoing IP packets. These lists correspond roughly to the rules lists used by ipchains. In addition, similar modules are available for other network protocols (e.g., ip6tables for IP Version 6).

19.3.1 Netfilter Hooks in the Linux Kernel

As was mentioned briefly in Section 19.2.2, the netfilter architecture includes a uniform interface, reducing the cost involved to implement new functions. It is called *netfilter hook*, which means that it provides a hook for packet-filter code. This section discusses the components of this architecture and its implementation in the Linux kernel. Actually, this section supplies brief instructions to facilitate your writing your own netfilter modules.

Netfilter modules can be loaded into the Linux kernel at runtime, so we need hooks in the actual routing code to enable dynamic hooking of functions. An integer identifier is allocated to each of these netfilter hooks. The identifiers of all hooks for each supported protocol are defined in the protocol-specific header file (<linux/netfilter_ipv4.h> or <linux/netfilter_ipv6.h>). The following five hooks are defined for IP Version 4 in <linux/netfilter_ipv4.h>:

- NF_IP_PRE_ROUTING (0): Incoming packets pass this hook in the ip_rcv() function (see Section 14.2.1) before they are processed by the routing code. Prior to that, only a few simple consistency checks with regard to the version, length, and checksum fields in the IP header are done.

  Meaningful opportunities to use this hook result whenever incoming packets should be caught before they are processed—for example, to detect certain types of denial-of-service attacks that operate on poorly built IP packets, or for address-translation mechanisms (NAT), or for accounting functions (counting of incoming packets).

- NF_IP_LOCAL_IN (1): All incoming packets addressed to the local computer pass this hook in the function ip_local_deliver(). At this point, the iptables module hooks the INPUT rules list into place to filter incoming data packets. This corresponds to the input rules list in ipchains.

- NF_IP_FORWARD (2): All incoming packets not addressed to the local computer pass this hook in the function ip_forward()—that is, packets to be forwarded and leaving the computer over a different network interface.

  This includes any packet the address of which was modified by NAT. At this point, the iptables module hooks the FORWARD rules list into place to filter forwarded data packets. This corresponds to the forward rules list in ipchains.

- NF_IP_LOCAL_OUT (3): All outgoing packets created in the local computer pass this hook in the function ip_build_and_send_pkt(). At this point, the iptables module hooks the OUTPUT rules list into place to filter outgoing data packets. This corresponds to the output rules list in ipchains.

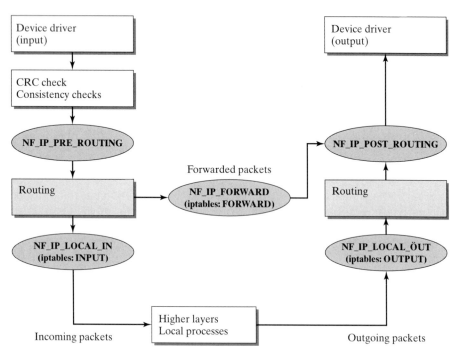

FIGURE 19–3
The packet filtering architecture of Linux 2.4 (netfilter).

■ NF_IP_POST_ROUTING (4): This hook in the `ip_finish_output()` function represents the last chance to access all outgoing (forwarded or locally created) packets before they leave the computer over a network device. Like the NF_IP_PRE_ROUTING hook, this is a good place to integrate accounting functions.

Figure 19–3 shows data packets traveling through different hooks.

NF_HOOK()	include/linux/netfilter.h

Calling the NF_HOOK macro causes the routing code to process the filter functions hooked into a netfilter hook. This macro is defined in `<linux/netfilter.h>` as follows:

```
#define NF_HOOK(pf, hook, skb, indev, outdev, okfn)              \
(list_empty(&nf_hooks[(pf)][(hook)])                             \
    ? (okfn)(skb)                                                \
    : nf_hook_slow((pf), (hook), (skb), (indev), (outdev), (okfn)))
```

The following fragment from net/ipv4/ip_output.c (at the end of the ip_build_and_send_pkt() function) serves as an example to see how we can use the NF_HOOK macro:
```
/* Send it out. */
return NF_HOOK(PF_INET, NF_IP_LOCAL_OUT, skb, NULL, rt->u.dst.dev,
               output_maybe_reroute);
```

In this example, rather than calling the function output_maybe_reroute() immediately, the packet-filtering functions registered with the hook NF_IP_LOCAL_OUT are processed first to send an IP packet. The values that filter functions can return are defined in <linux/netfilter.h>. If all functions return the value NF_ACCEPT, then the "okay" function okfn() at this hook (i.e., output_maybe_reroute() in this case) is invoked. If, however one of the filter functions returns NF_DROP, then the packet is dropped, and okfn() is not invoked.

More specifically, the NF_HOOK macro has the following arguments:

- pf (*protocol family*): This is the identifier of the protocol family: PF_INET for IP Version 4, PF_INET6 for IP Version 6.
- hook: This is the hook identifier. All valid identifiers for each protocol family are defined in a header file (e.g., <linux/netfilter_ipv4.h>).
- skb: This is a pointer to the sk_buff structure with the packet to be handled.
- indev (*input device*): This is a pointer to the net_device structure of the network device that received the packet. It is set to NULL in the above example, because the packet is an outgoing packet.
- outdev (*output device*): This is a pointer to the net_device structure of the network device that should be used by the packet to leave the local computer. In the above example, the device used has to be determined first by use of the routing table (rt).
- okfn() (*okay function*): This function is invoked when all filter functions registered with this hook returned NF_ACCEPT, thereby okaying the packet's transit.

19.3.2 Registering and Unregistering Packet-Filter Functions

The packet-filter functions that are actually hooked into the netfilter hooks are so-called *hook functions* of the type nf_hookfn. The signature of a hook function is defined in <linux/netfilter.h> as follows:

```
typedef unsigned int nf_hookfn(unsigned int hooknum,
                               struct sk_buff **skb,
                               const struct net_device *in,
                               const struct net_device *out,
                               int (*okfn)(struct sk_buff *));
```

The parameters (except for the protocol family identifier) correspond exactly to those of the NF_HOOK macro (see Section 19.3.1), and they are passed by this macro to the packet-filter functions. [Russ00d] includes a simple example showing how a packet-filter function is implemented, with detailed explanations.

The return value of a packet-filter function specifies what should happen to the packet. It is of the type unsigned int and can take any of the following values, defined in <linux/netfilter.h>:

- NF_DROP (0): The active rules list processing is stopped, and the packet is dropped.
- NF_ACCEPT (1): The packet is passed to the next packet filter function in the rules list. Once the end of the list has been reached, the packet is released by okfn() for further processing.

- NF_STOLEN (2): The packet filter function withholds the packet for further processing, so that the active rules list processing is stopped. In contrast to NF_DROP, however, the packet does not have to be explicitly dropped.
- NF_QUEUE (3): The function nf_queue() (net/core/netfilter.c) puts the packet in a queue from which it can be removed and processed (e.g., by a user space program). Subsequently, nf_reinject() has to be invoked to return the packet to the Linux kernel for further processing by netfilter.
- NF_REPEAT (4): In contrast to NF_ACCEPT, rather than a continuation of processing at the next packet-filter function, the current filter function is invoked again.

nf_register_hook(), nf_unregister_hook()	**net/core/netfilter.c**

This function registers or unregisters a packet-filter function with the Linux kernel. The parameter passed is a nf_hook_ops structure, which includes all information required.

struct nf_hook_ops	**linux/netfilter.h**

To register a new packet-filter function with the Linux kernel, we first have to initialize a structure of the type nf_hook_ops with all of the management information required:

```
struct nf_hook_ops
{
        struct list_head list;

        /* User fills in from here down. */
        nf_hookfn *hook;
        int pf;
        int hooknum;
        /* Hooks are ordered in ascending priority. */
        int priority;
};
```

The fields of this structure have the following meaning:

- list: The nf_hook_ops structures are maintained in a linked list within the Linux kernel.
- hook(): This is a pointer to the actual packet-filter function of the type nf_hookfn.
- pf, hooknum: The protocol family identifier (e.g., PF_INET or PF_INET6) and the hook identifier (e.g., NF_IP_INPUT) are used to determine the hook for this packet-filter function.
- priority: Packet-filter functions within the rules list of a hook are sorted by the priority field in ascending order, so that they will be invoked in this order

when a packet transits. Priority values are defined as follows, e.g., in `<linux/netfilter_ipv4.h>`:

```
enum nf_ip_hook_priorities {
        NF_IP_PRI_FIRST = INT_MIN,
        NF_IP_PRI_CONNTRACK = -200,
        NF_IP_PRI_MANGLE = -150,
        NF_IP_PRI_NAT_DST = -100,
        NF_IP_PRI_FILTER = 0,
        NF_IP_PRI_NAT_SRC = 100,
        NF_IP_PRI_LAST = INT_MAX,
};
```

19.3.3   Comparing `iptables` and `ipchains`

The most important differences between netfilter and the old `ipchains` architecture are doubtless that the flaws mentioned in Section 19.2.2 were removed: New packet-filter functions can easily be integrated into the Linux kernel by use of the programming interface introduced in Section 19.3.2. In addition, more complex functions, such as the support of transparent proxies or of address-translation mechanisms (NAT), are now implemented as independent modules with clearly defined interfaces. The changes to the existing network code to integrate a new hook for packet-filter functions are limited to one single call of the NF_HOOK macro in the netfilter architecture. (See Section 19.3.1.)

Moreover, the netfilter architecture changed the path different packet streams take across the kernel. In contrast to `ipchains`, `iptables` now handles each packet based on exactly one of the three rules lists used: INPUT, FORWARD, or OUTPUT. The routing decision is made early, before the transit through the INPUT or FORWARD hook, so that forwarded packets do not have to traverse all three hooks. (See Figure 19.3.) In `ipchains` (Figure 19.2), all packets had to traverse the input list before a routing decision was made; given this decision, packets were then redirected to a local process or to the forward list. This modification simplifies the rules-lists handling, because no undesired dependencies between them can occur, and it reduces the processing cost in the kernel, so that packets are handled faster.

And, finally, there was a slight change to the syntax of the iptables command-line tool used to manage rules lists, compared to the older `ipchains`. Table 19.1 gives an overview of the most important changes. Most options and parameters are identical. However, `iptables` rules lists use uppercase letters; also, DENY was renamed in DROP, and MASQ replaces the former MASQUERADE.

19.3.4   The `iptables` Command-line Tool

The `ipchains` management tool is a direct counterpart of the `iptables` program used in netfilter. This tool can be used to manipulate the rule sets in different tables and the associated rules lists. We saw in Table 19–1 that the invocation syntax of `ipchains` and `iptables` is similar in many aspects, because the netfilter architecture uses some of the same concepts, such as linked rules lists.

One of the most important differences is the name-giving introduction of several filter tables, reflecting the modular structure of the netfilter architecture. This modular structure includes NAT and other packet-manipulating functions, in addition to the pure filter functions. This is considered in the invocation syntax by introducing a new parameter, -t <table>, which expresses the reference of a rule definition to a table associated with a specific module. Accordingly, this changes the basic structure of an invocation to

```
iptables -t <table> -<operation> <chain> -j <branch destination> <criterion>.
```

This new form extends iptables, so that users don't have to use different management tools (e.g., ipmasqadm) to address additional functions and protocols.

The following program segment shows a simple configuration for a communication server that can be used by a network with the private address space 192.168.1.0-192.168.1.255 [RMKG + 96] to access the Internet; it obtains a dynamic IP address from the Internet provider:

```
#!/bin/bash

## enable IP forwarding
echo 1 >/proc/sys/net/ipv4/ip_forward
## insert connection-tracking modules (not needed if built into kernel).
if [ ! -e /proc/net/ip_conntrack ] ; then
                insmod ip_tables
                insmod ip_conntrack
                insmod ip_conntrack_ftp
                insmod iptable_nat
                insmod ipt_MASQUERADE
                insmod ipt_LOG
fi

iptables -F ## clean up before calling new ruleset
iptables -A FORWARD -m unclean -j DROP
## enable routing (source and destination)
iptables -A FORWARD -s 192.168.1.0/24 -j ACCEPT
iptables -A FORWARD -d 192.168.1.0/24 -j ACCEPT
## do NAT for all outbound connections
iptables -t nat -A POSTROUTING -d ! 192.168.1.0/24 -j MASQUERADE
```

The echo command at the beginning activates the forwarding of IP packets in the Linux kernel.

The if branch following next loads the kernel modules required, unless they were already loaded. ip_tables and ip_conntrack are the basic modules of the netfilter architecture for IP Version 4. The iptable_nat and ipt_MASQUERADE modules enable masquerading (a simple sort of NAT).

When iptables -F is invoked, all existing rules are deleted, to prevent a rule from being loaded twice.

The rule -m unclean -j DROP causes all packets with faulty IP headers (e.g., like those in a teardrop attack) to be dropped.

The next two rules enable access to addresses in any other IP network from the internal network (-s 192.168.1.0/24) and let packets from this network through to internal computers (-d 192.162.1.0/24).

The last rule activates the masquerading process, if the destination computer is not in the internal network.

19.3.5   The Netfilter Standard Modules

With the new netfilter architecture, we now have both the standard functionality and extensions (e.g., NAT) in the form of kernel modules. This section introduces some important netfilter modules:

■ *Stateful connection tracking*: The ip_conntrack.o module, which includes additional protocol-specific helper modules (e.g., ip_conntrack_ftp.o), allows us to assign specific states to the packets of a TCP connection, where four different states are available:

▶ NEW: The connection is currently being established, and no reply packet has yet been received for the first packet of this connection.

▶ ESTABLISHED: The packets belong to an existing TCP connection.

▶ RELATED: The packets are in relation to an existing connection, but not an integral part of that connection.

▶ INVALID: All packets that cannot be classified (packets that cannot be assigned to any named connection and that do not initiate connection establishments) fall into this category.

In addition, the connection-tracking module lets you limit the packet quantities directed over a network interface. This can be used to prevent denial-of-service attacks, where an intruder tries to flood the network with IP packets. For example, an exceptionally fast increase of the packet traffic can be intercepted as follows:

```
iptables -A INVALID-DROP -m limit -limit 5/hour --limit-burst 3 --limit
LOG
```

Chapter 20 discusses the connection-tracking functionality in detail.

■ *Address translation (NAT)*: The new implementation of the NAT functionality (iptable_nat.o module, including protocol-specific helper modules, such as ip_nat_ftp.o) is much better performing than the "masquerading" of Linux 2.2. It is addressed from the nat table and implements various operating modes for address translation. The following four operating modes are currently available:

▶ *Source NAT* changes the source address of an incoming packet before it is forwarded. This function is addressed by the SNAT option in iptables. This mode lets computers access Internet services from a network with private IP addresses, where the actual source address is hidden from the outside and replaced by the address of the firewall computer. A typical rule definition for source NAT is as follows:

```
iptables -t nat -A POSTROUTING -j SNAT --to-source <firewall address>
```

▶ The second operating mode is a special version of source NAT, one especially used in communication servers for *masquerading*. It is designed for interplay with dynamically allocated IP addresses. For this reason, all old connection data yielded by the connection-tracking module is dropped whenever the connection is interrupted. A typical rule definition looks like this:

```
iptables -t nat -A POSTROUTING -j MASQUERADE -o ppp0
```

This definition causes the source address of all packets leaving the router over the first PPP interface to be set to the address of this interface.

▶ The *destination NAT* functionality is new in netfilter. It can be used to redirect packets to a different destination address exactly in line with the source NAT. For this purpose, the destination address in the IP header has to be changed before the packet passes the router, so that destination NAT is hooked in the netfilter hook NF_IP_PRE_ROUTING.

For example, destination NAT can be used to implement transparent proxies. The following rule definition directs all HTTP packets (TCP port 80) arriving over the second Ethernet interface to port 8080 of the HTTP proxy with address 192.168.1.2:

```
iptables -t nat -A PREROUTING -j DNAT \
    --to-destination 192.168.1.2:8080 -p tcp --dport 80 -i eth1
```

A special case of the destination NAT functionality is the REDIRECT branch destination. It redirects packets to a specific port in the local computer, so that transparent proxies can be easily included, if present in the local computer:

```
iptables -t nat -A PREROUTING -j REDIRECT \
    --to-port 8080 -i eth1 -p tcp --dport 80
```

▨ *Other possibilities for manipulating packets:*

Additional options that manipulate packets are available in the mangle tables. For example, we could mark specific packets to recognize them within the scope of a security concept or allocate packets to a specific queue in connection with the ip_queue.o module. For this purpose, we use the MARK branch destination. For example, the following call marks all TCP packets with the value 0x0a:

```
iptables -t mangle -A PREROUTING -j MARK --set-mark 0x0a -p
```

If packets are treated differently in the network, depending on the TOS or DS field (*type of service / differentiated services*) in the IP header, then this field can be changed by use of the TOS option, for example, to handle SSH packets in a special way:

```
iptables -t mangle -A PREROUTING -j TOS --set-tos 0x10
    -p tcp --dport ssh
```

▨ *Compatibility modules for* ipchains *and* ipfwadm:

The ipchains.o and ipfwadm.o compatibility modules ensure a soft transition from old Linux versions to Linux 2.4, because the old configuration files and scripts for ipchains (Linux 2.2) and ipfwadm (Linux 2.0) can be reused during a transition period. Because they exist solely for compatibility reasons, they will not be further developed in the future.

CHAPTER 20

Connection Tracking

20.1 INTRODUCTION

This chapter discusses the *connection-tracking* module, which forms the basis for extended packet-filter functions, particularly for network address translation (NAT—see Chapter 21) in Linux 2.4.

The connection-tracking module manages individual connections (particularly TCP connections, but also UDP associations) and serves to allocate incoming, outgoing, and forwarded IP packets to existing connections. A new connection entry is generated as soon as the connection-tracking module registers a connection-establishment packet. From then on, each packet belonging to this connection is uniquely assigned to this connection. For example, this enables the NAT implementation to figure out exactly whether an incoming packet needs a free IP address and port number or one of the addresses and port numbers previously assigned can be used. The connection is deleted after a certain period of time has elapsed without traffic (timeout), which depends on the transport protocol used (i.e., TCP, UDP, or ICMP). Subsequently, the NAT module can reuse the address and port number that have become available.

The connection-tracking module is not limited to transport protocols; it can basically also support complex application protocols. For example, a stateful filter and an address-translation mechanism for active FTP (see Section 19.1.2) can be implemented. For this purpose, the connection-tracking module has to be able to associate newly established data connections with an existing control connection.

20.1.1 Using the Connection-Tracking Module

Two functions can be invoked to access connection entries: `ip_conntrack_get()` and `ip_conntrack_put()`. The `ip_conntrack_get()` function returns a connection entry for an IP packet passed as an `sk_buff` structure and automatically increments the reference counter for this connection. The `ip_conntrack_put()` function informs the connection-tracking module that the previously requested connection is no longer needed and decrements the reference counter.

To find a connection entry, we can use a so-called *tuple* (see Section 20.2.2) instead of an sk_buff structure with a complete IP packet. Such a tuple contains only the source and destination addresses and additional protocol information. The ip_conntrack_find_get() is used for this purpose.

20.2 IMPLEMENTATION

The module interface of the connection-tracking module is located in the file net/ipv4/netfilter/ip_conntrack_standalone.c. The file net/ipv4/netfilter/ip_conntrack_core.c contains the actual connection-tracking functionality.

20.2.1 Basic Structure

The connection-tracking module hooks itself into the netfilter hooks NF_IP_PRE_ROUTING and NF_IP_LOCAL_OUT (see Section 19.3.1 and Figure 20–1) with very high priority (the NF_IP_PRI_CONNTRACK is set to −200 in <linux/netfilter_ipv4.h>). This means that each incoming packet is first passed to the connection-tracking module. Subsequently, other modules also hooked into these hooks, but with lower priority, get their turns.

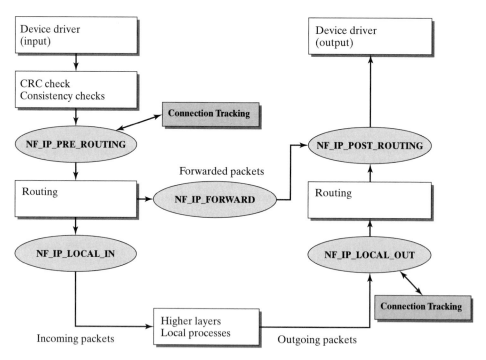

FIGURE 20–1
Netfilter hooks used by the connection-tracking module.

20.2.2 Connection Entries

struct ip_conntrack	linux/netfilter_ipv4/ip_conntrack.h

A connection entry is represented in the Linux kernel by an ip_conntrack structure, consisting of the following fields:

- A structure of the type nf_conntrack (defined in <linux/skbuff.h>), which includes a reference counter (use) that counts the number of open references to this connection entry.
- Two tuples for forward and reverse direction (tuplehash[0], tuplehash[1]), consisting of address and protocol information, which can be used to reference this entry.
- A status field (status), containing a bit vector with the following bits:

  - IPS_EXPECTED: The connection was expected.
  - IPS_SEEN_REPLY: Packets have already occurred in both directions.
  - IPS_ASSURED: The connection entry should never be deleted prematurely, not even when the timeout expires.

- A pointer (timeout) to a function that is invoked as soon as the timeout of this connection expires (i.e., when this connection has not been used over a lengthy period of time).
- A data structure of the type ip_conntrack_expect, which can be used to allocate expected connections (e.g., FTP data connections after a command was sent over the control connection) to existing connections (in this case to the control connection).
- Several structures of the type nf_ct_info, each belonging to a specific state. A pointer to the entry that matches an IP packet is entered in the nfct field of the pertaining sk_buff structure. The enumeration type ip_conntrack_info (defined in <linux/netfilter_ipv4/ip_conntrack.h>), which can take any of the following values, is used as index in the table that contains the nf_ct_info structures:

  - IP_CT_ESTABLISHED: The packet belongs to a fully established connection.
  - IP_CT_RELATED: The packet belongs to a new connection, which, however, refers to an existing connection (i.e., an expected connection).
  - IP_CT_NEW: The packet belongs to a new connection.
  - IP_CT_IS_REPLY: The packet belongs to the reverse direction of a connection.

- A pointer to an optional *helper* module to extend the connection-tracking functionality. (See Section 20.2.4.)

struct ip_conntrack_tuple_hash	linux/netfilter_ipv4/ip_conntrack_tuple.h

Connection entries are managed in a hash table, where a linked list is used to resolve collisions. An entry in this hash table is of the type `ip_conntrack_tuple_hash` and contains a reverse pointer to the `ip_conntrack` structure of that connection, in addition to the actual address information (tuple) (i.e., source and destination addresses) and protocol-specific information (e.g., port numbers). As is shown in Figure 20–2, this pointer is required to access the connection status or to check for whether the entry represents a tuple for the forward or reverse direction of a connection.

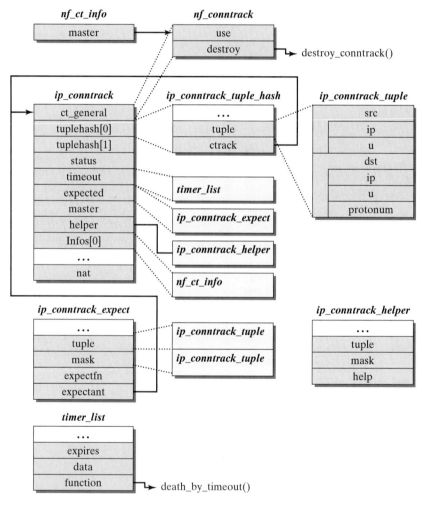

FIGURE 20–2
Data structures of the connection-tracking module.

| `struct ip_conntrack_tuple` | **linux/netfilter_ipv4/ip_conntrack_tuple.h** |

An `ip_conntrack_tuple` is divided into a manipulable part, for the source address and perhaps the source port (`ip_conntrack_manip`), and a nonmanipulable part for destination address, protocol, and perhaps destination port. This division facilitates the use of connection entries by the NAT module.

20.2.3 Transport Protocols

| `struct ip_conntrack_protocol` | **linux/netfilter_ipv4/ip_conntrack_protocol.h** |

To enable use of different transport protocols, there is a global list with these protocols (`protocol_list`). A protocol is represented by a structure of the type `ip_conntrack_protocol`. The two functions `ip_conntrack_protocol_register()` and `ip_conntrack_protocol_unregister()` are used to add a protocol to or remove one from the list of supported protocols in the form of modules at runtime. Notice that, when you delete a protocol from the list, all connections currently using this protocol are also deleted.

To support a specific protocol, such a module has to contain the following functions:

- Functions to output specific details about a connection in clear text (used by the proc file system).
- Helper functions to invert tuples (i.e., to swap source and destination addresses) and to extract a tuple from an `sk_buff` structure.
- Its own protocol-specific processing functions (e.g., functions to track the current state of the TCP protocol automaton, in the case of the TCP protocol).
- Update functions for the timeout timer to ensure that a connection entry can be deleted, if it hasn't been used over a lengthy period of time.

20.2.4 Helper Modules

| `struct ip_conntrack_helper` | **linux/netfilter_ipv4/ip_conntrack_helper.h** |

The so-called *helper modules* provide an interface to extend the connection-tracking functionality. The functions `ip_conntrack_helper_register()` and `ip_conntrack_helper_unregister()` are used to add or remove a structure of the type `ip_conntrack_helper` to or from a linked list (`helpers`). Each packet that traverses one of the connection-tracking hooks is passed to each of the registered helper modules.

This enables us to support active FTP, where the associated helper module, `ip_conntrack_ftp.o`, updates the list of expected connections as soon as it detects a GET or PUT command while listening to the control connection. This means that it can assign data connections arriving from the outside to existing control connections.

20.2.5   Global Variables

The following global variables are important for the connection-tracking functionality:

- ip_conntrack_hash, the hash tables with all connection entries—see Section 20.2.2 for details;
- expect_list, the list of expected connections. A connection is expected, for example, when a file transfer is started over an FTP control connection. This functionality is currently used by the FTP protocol only;
- protocol_list, the list of registered transport protocols. TCP, UDP, ICMP, and a generic transport protocol module with minimum functionality, which is used when no matching protocol is found, are currently implemented;
- helpers, the list of registered helper modules—see Section 20.2.4.

20.2.6   Functions

print_tuple()	net/ipv4/netfilter/ip_conntrack_standalone.c

This function is invoked by print_conntrack() and outputs a single tuple for a connection (forward and reverse directions) in text form:

```
src=129.13.65.4 dst=168.42.17.1 sport=8080 dport=80
```

print_expect()	net/ipv4/netfilter/ip_conntrack_standalone.c

This function outputs a single tuple from the list of expected connections in text form:

```
EXPECTING: proto=23 src=129.13.65.4 dst=168.42.17.1 sport=8080 dport=80
```

print_conntrack()	net/ipv4/netfilter/ip_conntrack_standalone.c

This function outputs the connection entry for an entire connection (forward and reverse directions) in text form. In addition to the two tuples, this includes their status and the states of their timeout timers.

conntrack_iterate()	net/ipv4/netfilter/ip_conntrack_standalone.c

This is a helper function used to walk through all connections; it is invoked by list_conntracks().

list_conntracks()	net/ipv4/netfilter/ip_conntrack_standalone.c

This function outputs the connection entries of all connections, both those currently active and those expected. It is required to generate an entry for the proc file system.

`init()`, `fini()`, `init_or_` `cleanup()`	**net/ipv4/netfilter/ip_conntrack_standalone.c**

The `init()` and `fini()` functions are invoked to initialize or remove the connection-tracking module, and they, in turn, invoke the function `init_or_cleanup()` with the parameter 1 (initialize) or 0 (remove).

During the initialization, the actual connection-tracking functionality is initialized first by the calling of `ip_conntrack_init()`. Subsequently, the entry in the proc file system is generated, and the functions `ip_conntrack_in()` and `ip_conntrack_local()` are hooked into the appropriate netfilter hooks. Inversely, these functions are unhooked when the module is removed, the entry is deleted from the proc file system, and, finally, the function `ip_conntrack_cleanup()` is invoked.

`ip_conntrack_init()`	**net/ipv4/netfilter/ip_conntrack_core.c**

This is the initialization routine for the actual connection-tracking functionality. It adds the three standard protocols—TCP, UDP, and ICMP—to the protocol list and initializes the `ip_conntrack_hash` hash table.

`ip_conntrack_cleanup()`	**net/ipv4/netfilter/ip_conntrack_core.c**

This function prepares for a removal of the connection-tracking module. More specifically, a locking mechanism is used to ensure that all IP packets currently handled are properly completed. Subsequently, a few reserved memory locations are released.

`hash_conntrack()`	**net/ipv4/netfilter/ip_conntrack_core.c**

This helper function computes the hash value for a data structure of the type `ip_conntrack_tuple`.

`get_tuple()`	**net/ipv4/netfilter/ip_conntrack_core.c**

This function uses the protocol data passed from an IP packet to create a matching data structure of the type `ip_conntrack_tuple`. First, the IP source and destination addresses and the transport protocol are taken, and then the `pkt_to_tuple` function of the matching transport protocol module is invoked.

`invert_tuple()`, `invert_tuplepr()`	**net/ipv4/netfilter/ip_conntrack_core.c**

These functions invert an `ip_conntrack_tuple` structure by swapping the IP source and destination addresses. In addition, the function `invert_tuple()` of the matching transport protocol module is invoked—for example, to swap the source and destination ports for TCP or UDP.

For `invert_tuple()`, a pointer to the `ip_conntrack_protocol` structure of the transport protocol has to be passed as parameter; `invert_tuplepr()` determines this itself from the passed `ip_conntrack_tuple` structure.

`ip_conntrack_alter_reply()`	net/ipv4/netfilter/ip_conntrack_core.c

This function replaces the tuple in a connection entry for the reverse direction by the value passed in `newreply`.

`ip_conntrack_find_get()`	net/ipv4/netfilter/ip_conntrack_core.c

This function uses the `__ip_conntrack_find()` function to search the `ip_conntrack_hash` hash table for a connection entry matching an `ip_conntrack_tuple` structure, where the parameter `ignored_conntrack` can be used to exclude a specific connection from the search explicitly. If the entry exists, then it is returned, and the `ct_general.use` reference counter is incremented by one. Otherwise, the function returns NULL.

`ip_conntrack_get()`	net/ipv4/netfilter/ip_conntrack_core.c

This function gets the connection entry and the connection status matching a passed `sk_buff` structure. The information required are simply extracted from the `nfct` field in the `sk_buff` structure.

`ip_conntrack_put()`	net/ipv4/netfilter/ip_conntrack_core.c

This function decrements the reference counter of a connection entry by one. For this purpose, it invokes the inline function `nf_conntrack_put()` defined in `<linux/skbuff.h>`, which uses `atomic_dec_and_test()` to decrement the reference counter. If this action causes the counter to reach 0 (i.e., there are no more references to this connection), then the function pointer `destroy()` is invoked to delete this connection entry. This pointer normally points to the function `destroy_conntrack()`.

`resolve_normal_ct()`	net/ipv4/netfilter/ip_conntrack_core.c

This function tries to find a connection entry matching a passed `sk_buff` structure or creates such an entry, if it doesn't exist. First, it uses `get_tuple()` to create a structure of the type `ip_conntrack_tuple` from the packet's protocol data. Next, `ip_conntrack_find_get()` is used to find a matching connection entry. If no matching tuple is found, then `init_conntrack()` is invoked to create a new connection entry. Finally, the connection entry status is determined, and this status is used to set the `nfct` field of the passed `sk_buff` structure.

`init_conntrack()`	**net/ipv4/netfilter/ip_conntrack_core.c**

This function creates a new connection entry. First, it creates a structure of the type `ip_conntrack`. This structure consists of the passed tuple for the forward direction and its inversion (created by `invert_tuple`) for the reverse direction. Next, `atomic_set()` sets the reference counter `ct_general.use` to value 1. The only reference that exists initially is owned by the timeout timer, which is also initialized, and its timeout function pointer is set to the function `death_by_timeout()`. Previously, the relevant protocol module was initialized by calling its `new()` function. The function pointer `ct_general.destroy()`, which is invoked to delete a connection entry, is set to the function `destroy_conntrack()`. In addition, a helper is entered, if one was registered for the protocol used.

As soon as all data structures have been initialized, the next step checks on whether the connection to be entered was expected (i.e., whether it exists in the `expect_list`). If so, it is deleted from this list and set to the `IPS_EXPECTED` status.

`ip_conntrack_in()`	**net/ipv4/netfilter/ip_conntrack_core.c**

This function is hooked into the netfilter hook `NF_IP_PRE_ROUTING`; it is invoked for each packet arriving from the outside. It is also used by `ip_conntrack_local()`, because the only difference is in how fragmented IP packets are handled.

IP packets have to be defragmented before they can be assigned to a connection; fragments that have already arrived are collected by the function `ip_ct_gather_frags()`, which, in turn, uses the `ip_defrag()` function. When the last fragment of a fragmented packet is received, or if the packet was not fragmented, then an attempt is made to assign the packet to a connection.

First, `find_proto()` is used to determine the connection-tracking module for the transport protocol used. Next, the packet is checked to see whether it is an ICMP packet. If so, it is first passed to the function `icmp_error_track()`. If successful, this function returns one, and the packet is accepted by returning `NF_ACCEPT`.

In contrast, if `icmp_error_track()` returns `null`, the packet is further handled like any other packet. `resolve_normal_ct()` chooses the correct connection entry (or creates one, if none exists). Subsequently, the `packet()` function of the associated transport protocol module is invoked, and then the `help()` functions of all registered helper modules are invoked. If one of these functions fails, then `nf_conntrack_put()` releases this connection entry.

`ip_conntrack_local()`	**net/ipv4/netfilter/ip_conntrack_standalone.c**

This function is hooked into the netfilter hook `NF_IP_LOCAL_OUT`; accordingly, it is invoked for each IP packet originating from a local process. The only difference from how incoming packets are handled in `ip_conntrack_in()` is that fragmented packets are not handled by the connection-tracking module. All other packets are simply passed to `ip_conntrack_in()`.

`icmp_error_track()`	**net/ipv4/netfilter/ip_conntrack_core.c**

This function serves to handle ICMP packets. First, some consistency checks are done with regard to the length field, the ICMP message type, and the ICMP checksum. More detailed handling is done for the following ICMP message types, each of which refers to a specific IP packet—one where the payload field in the header contains the ICMP message (described in Section 21.1.4):

```
ICMP_DEST_UNREACH
ICMP_SOURCE_QUENCH
ICMP_TIME_EXCEEDED
ICMP_PARAMETERPROB
ICMP_REDIRECT
```

`ip_conntrack_find_get()` finds a connection entry for the original packet header, which is also sent by this function, where the function `invert_tuple()` is used first, because the packet's source and destination addresses have to be swapped. If the function finds the entry, then a pointer to the appropriate `ct_info` structure is entered in the `nfct` field of the passed `sk_buff` structure.

`destroy_conntrack()`	**net/ipv4/netfilter/ip_conntrack_core.c**

Normally, this function is invoked over the function pointer `ct_general.destroy()` in the `ip_conntrack` structure to delete a connection entry. If this entry is linked to a "master" entry, then its reference counter is decremented by `nf_conntrack_put()`. Subsequently, a cleanup function hooked into the function pointer `ip_conntrack_destroyed()` is invoked, if present. Finally, `atomic_dec()` decrements the counter `ip_conntrack_count` to the number of existing connection entries.

`death_by_timeout()`	**net/ipv4/netfilter/ip_conntrack_core.c**

This function is invoked as soon as the timeout timer for a connection expires. Initially, `clean_from_lists()` (also defined in `net/ipv4/netfilter/ip_conntrack_core.c`) removes the connection entry from the list of active connections. Subsequently, `ip_conntrack_put()` decrements the reference counter. This deletes the connection, if there are no other references.

`ip_conntrack_protocol_` `register()`	**net/ipv4/netfilter/ip_conntrack_standalone.c**

This function registers a module for a transport protocol. The protocol is added to the `protocol_list`, if it is not yet present.

| `ip_conntrack_protocol_`
`unregister()` | **net/ipv4/netfilter/ip_conntrack_standalone.c** |

This function unregisters a module for a transport protocol; it is currently (in Linux Version 2.4.8) still empty.

| `find_proto()` | **net/ipv4/netfilter/ip_conntrack_core.c** |

This function searches the `protocol_list` for a protocol and returns the appropriate entry, if successful. If the function doesn't find a matching entry, then the generic protocol is returned. First, `READ_LOCK` locks the management data of the connection-tracking module for reading, before the helper function `__find_proto()` is invoked for the actual search.

| `ip_conntrack_helper_register()` | **net/ipv4/netfilter/ip_conntrack_core.c** |

This function registers a helper module by adding it to the `helpers` list, if note is not yet present.

| `ip_conntrack_helper_unregister()` | **net/ipv4/netfilter/ip_conntrack_core.c** |

This function unregisters a helper module by deleting it from the `helpers` list. For this purpose, it searches all connection entries that point to this helper module. Subsequently, the function `unhelp()` sets the `helper` pointer for each such connection to `NULL`. If a connection occurs in the `expect_list`, then this instance is deleted.

Currently, the most important application for connection tracking—and the reason why connection tracking was initially developed—is the so-called *network address translation* (*NAT*), which will be discussed in the next chapter.

CHAPTER 21

Network Address Translation (NAT)

21.1 INTRODUCTION

The *Network Address Translation (NAT)* mechanism deals generally with the translation of IP addresses. It represents an effective way to encounter the exhaustion of free IP addresses (Version 4) in view of the explosive growth of the Internet. However, transition to IP Version 6 with its much larger address space progresses only slowly, because it was found extremely difficult to convert a decentralized network like the global Internet to a new protocol at one shot. Exactly this is where NAT comes in useful: For example, it allows all users in a local area network to access the Internet and its services, even though there is only one single official IP address available, and only private IP addresses (according to RFC 1918 [RMKG + 96]) are used within the local area network. A router accessible to the network, used by the users to connect to the global Internet, handles the required address mapping.

The NAT implementation in Linux 2.4 consists of two parts: *connection tracking*, and the actual NAT. Chapter 20 described how the connection-tracking mechanism is implemented.

21.1.1 Important Terminology

One of the most important technical terms in the NAT area is the so-called *session flow*. A session flow is a set of IP packets, exchanged between two instances and forming a unit in that they are treated equally by a NAT router. Such a session flow is directed to the direction the first packet was sent. For this reason, we speak of original and reverse directions in the following discussion. One good example is a telnet session: The corresponding TCP connection is initiated by the terminal computer, so the original direction of the relevant session flow points from the terminal to the server. TCP/UDP-based session flows can be described uniquely by an {IP source address, source port, IP destination address, destination port} tuple. Similarly, an ICMP session flow can be identified by an {IP source address, IP destination address, ICMP type, ICMP ID} tuple.

[SrHo99] describes three characteristic requirements that should be met by all NAT variants:

- transparent address allocation;
- transparent routing; and
- correct handling of ICMP packets.

The following sections explain each of these requirements and what they mean.

21.1.2   Transparent Address Allocation

Because we can use NAT to connect networks with different address spaces, these addresses from the respective address spaces have to be allocated among them. This allocation can be either static or dynamic. If we use static allocation, the allocations are maintained during the entire operation of a NAT router. Static allocations simplify the address translation, because no state information about specific session flows has to be maintained. In dynamic allocation, the allocation is specified at the time that a session flow is opened. This allocation remains valid until the session is terminated. In some cases, the allocation rule can be extended beyond the IP addresses to include the transport protocol ports. (See Section 21.1.6.) In any event, address allocation should be transparent: The mechanisms should be hidden from the applications in end systems.

21.1.3   Transparent Routing

We use the term "transparent routing" in the following discussion to distinguish the routing functionality of a NAT router from the functionality of a normal router. Transparent routing differs from normal routing in that packets are forwarded between two different address spaces by changing the address information in IP packets and routing to match these modified addresses.

Transparent routing can be divided into three phases: address binding, address translation, and releasing of the address binding.

- *Address binding*: This phase permanently binds two addresses from the two address spaces to be bound. This should not be confused with the address allocation mentioned above—the address allocation only determines valid bindings. These bindings will then actually exist only after the address binding. In connections with static address allocation, address binding is also static, but dynamic binding occurs at the beginning of a session flow and is released as soon as this session ends. If we want to map internal network addresses to global, external addresses, then we should bind each additional session flow originating from the same end system to the same address.

- *Address translation*: Once an address has been bound, each IP packet of that session flow has to be manipulated. This manipulation can be limited to the IP addresses, but it could also extend to TCP/UDP ports. (See Section 21.1.6.) Notice that the checksum in the IP header, or in the UDP/TCP header, has to be recomputed.

■ *Releasing address binding*: An address binding has to be released as soon as the last associated session flow ends, if we use dynamic binding, to ensure that the external address can be reused. In contrast, the binding is maintained if we use static binding.

21.1.4 Correct Handling of ICMP Packets

ICMP error messages normally require special handling (except for ICMP Redirect messages), because the payload (PDU) of these messages includes the header of the IP packet that caused the error. To achieve total transparency, this inner packet header has to be properly manipulated.

21.1.5 Differences from Masquerading in Linux 2.2

A simple NAT implementation, called "masquerading," had been an integral part of the Linux kernel (Linux 2.0 and 2.2). Later, the NAT functionality was moved to an external module in the course of converting to the netfilter architecture. The NAT support was heavily extended, so that now masquerading represents only a special case of the general address-translation functionality.

In contrast to the old masquerading, we now have a way to map more than one public IP address to the internal network. In addition, we can map a public IP address to several internal computers to implement *load sharing*.

The problems of the old masquerading included a close involvement of the packet-filter code, which meant extremely complex rule sets in firewall computers. This problem becomes clear from looking at the different hooks for "IP chains" (see Section 19.2): In the *input chain*, a packet arriving from the outside appears to be intended for the firewall itself; in the *forward chain*, the previously unmasked packet is not recognized, because its destination address has changed; and, finally, in the *output chain*, the packet appears to originate from the firewall itself.

In Linux 2.4, the NAT functionality was divided into two main parts: connection tracking, and actual translation. The connection-tracking module manages connections in the transport and application layers; the NAT module actually translates addresses. Both modules can be loaded into the Linux kernel at runtime, to strongly improve maintainability.

21.1.6 NAT Variants

We will be using the sample topology shown in Figure 21–1 in the following discussion to better understand the different NAT flavors and their main differences. The local class-C network with two end systems, A and B, uses the private address space 192.168.1.0–192.168.1.255; it connects to the Internet over a NAT router. This NAT router has the internal network address 192.168.1.254 and a reserve of global addresses, which can be mapped to the internal addresses (it could also consist of one single address—199.10.42.1 in this example). A server with the address 100.1.1.1 is the communication partner of end systems A and B in this example.

■ *Traditional NAT*: Traditional NAT is generally used (1) to connect a local area network using private addresses, as specified in RFC 1918, to an external network and (2) to allow the internal end systems to access the external network transparently. Traditional NAT is unidirectional: An address can be bound in one direction only

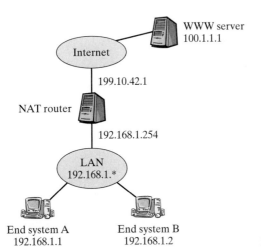

End system A   End system B   FIGURE 21–1
192.168.1.1   192.168.1.2   Example of a network using NAT.

(normally, when a session flow is established from the internal network towards the external network). In addition, you can translate either the source address (*source NAT*) or the destination address (*destination NAT*) of a session flow, but never both addresses at the same time.

▶ *Basic NAT*: This NAT variant is used to map internal IP address to one or several external IP addresses. To understand it better, let's assume that there is a (dynamic) allocation between the end system A (internal address 192.168.1.1) and a global address from the address space reserved for NAT (e.g., 199.10.42.1 in the sample network of Figure 21–1). Let's further assume that a WWW browser in end system A establishes a TCP connection from its port 1200 to port 80 in the WWW server 100.1.1.1. The NAT router binds the internal address 192.168.1.1 to the global address 199.10.42.1 for this session flow. However, this binding is valid for this single session flow only, and a new binding (to the same address) has to be done for each additional, secondary session flow.

▶ *Network Address and Port Translation (NAPT)*: This NAT variant represents an extension of Basic NAT. NAPT can translate IP addresses and additionally TCP or UDP port numbers. It is used to map various session flows from different internal end systems to one global IP address. (If only one single global address is available, then this corresponds to the "masquerading" of Linux 2.2.) This means that, in our above example, we could establish a TCP connection from port 1200 of end system B to the same port 80 of the same server by translating port number 1200 (e.g., into 1201) in addition to the IP address. In this case, we would obtain the following bindings:

- 192.168.1.1:1200 → 199.10.42.1:1200
- 192.168.1.2:1200 → 199.10.42.1:1201

Notice that, for mapping of source port numbers, port numbers from the privileged range (ports 1-1023) are mapped again to the privileged range. For transforming of the destination address, the ports should not be changed at all.

▷ *Bidirectional NAT and Twice NAT*: These two NAT variants are listed here only for the sake of completeness. In contrast to traditional NAT, bidirectional NAT lets you bind addresses during the establishment of session flows in both directions. Twice NAT removes the limitation of traditional NAT that we can transform either only the destination address or only the source address, but never both.

21.1.7   Problems

One general problem in address translation is application-layer protocols, where applications exchange address information. One good example is the File Transfer Protocol (FTP—see [Stev94a]). If an FTP client accesses an FTP server, then TCP first establishes a control connection to exchange FTP commands, such as GET or PUT. Now, if it wants to obtain data from the server, the client uses the PORT command to send an IP address and a port number. The client opens this port passively (see Chapter 27) and waits for the data connection, which is established by the server to the address it obtained earlier, to transmit payload.

The problems arising in the above case are similar to those known from packet filters. (See Section 19.1.2.) One major problem is that, if there is a NAT router somewhere between the client and the server, this router maps the client's source IP address transparently to another address, whereas the client sends its internal address in the PORT command, and this address is invalid from the server's view. To ensure that the PORT command can operate correctly, the NAT router has to also translate the address transported in the PORT command; it has to be able to intervene in the FTP protocol on the application layer.

Another major problem occurs in NAPT and relates to IP packet fragmenting. When IP packets are fragmented, only the first fragment contains the transport-protocol header with the port numbers of the source and the destination; but NAPT relies on this information when mapping addresses, so this means that the other fragments of the same packet cannot be handled properly. Consequently, we have to ensure that fragmented packets are reassembled before an attempt is made to translate addresses.

21.2   CONFIGURING NAT IN LINUX

The `iptable _nat.o` module implements the unidirectional NAPT variant described in Section 21.1.6. Like the Twice NAT variant, it can change the source and destination addresses of a session flow simultaneously.

To intercept and process packets, NAT uses the infrastructure supplied by the netfilter architecture. (See Section 19.3.1.) Figure 21–2 shows that it hooks itself into the netfilter hooks NF_IP_PRE_ROUTING, NF_IP_POST_ROUTING, and NF_IP_LOCAL_OUT for this purpose. The NAT module is invoked as soon as a packet traverses the appropriate hook, and a pointer to the `sk_buff` structure is passed, together with the packet. For configuration purposes, it is important that the source address be translated at the NF_IP_POST_ROUTING hook while the destination address is being translated in one of the other two hooks.

The first, preliminary versions of the new netfilter architecture allowed you to configure NAT by using an independent tool called `ipnatctl`. More recently, this

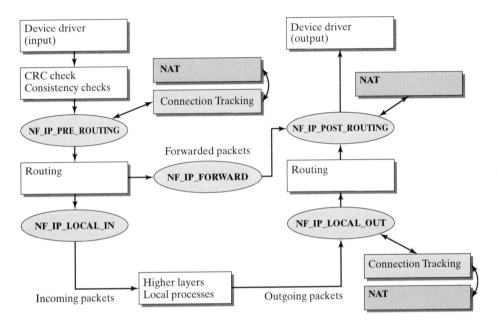

FIGURE 21–2
Netfilter hooks used by the NAT module.

functionality was fully integrated in the iptables tool. iptables can be used to specify rules that control the behavior of the NAT module. As was described in Section 19.2.1, a rule consists of a set of criteria to select session flows (*matching rule*) and a second part specifying how a session flow should be transformed (*binding type* or *mapping type*).

Criteria identical to packet-filter rules are available to select session flows: the IP source and destination addresses, the transport protocol, the port numbers, and the protocol-specific flags. The second part of a NAT rule defines how a session flow should be transformed. To this end, there are additional branch destinations, which are valid in the nat table only. We can use -j SNAT to activate the translation of the source address (*source NAT*) and -j DNAT to translate the destination address (*destination NAT*). In addition, we have to use --to-source or --to-destination to specify a range of IP addresses and port numbers, if present, for the address-translation process.

The selection criteria of the source NAT rule are applied to the original packet-address information in the event that both a source NAT and a destination NAT rule apply to the packet, though the destination address has already been changed by the destination NAT at that point. There are additional branch destinations (e.g., -j MAS-QUERADE for masquerading in the Linux 2.2 style) for special cases.

In the example discussed in Section 21.1.6, where source NAT is used to map the internal addresses from the private address range 192.168.1.0–192.168.1.255 to the global address 199.10.42.1, the corresponding iptables invocation would have the following form:

```
iptables -t nat -A POSTROUTING -s 192.168.1.0/24 \
         -j SNAT --to-source 199.10.42.1
```

21.3 IMPLEMENTING THE NAT MODULE

This section first introduces important data structures to manage session flows, allocations, and address bindings. Subsequently, it will explain the functions used to establish and tear down address bindings, to actually translate addresses, and to handle ICMP error messages.

21.3.1 Important Data Structures

All session flows are completely managed by the connection-tracking module described in Chapter 20. A structure of the type ip_conntrack is stored for each session flow. (See Section 20.2.2.) This structure includes two data structures of the type ip_conntrack_tuple_hash, representing the forward and reverse directions of a session flow. If a session flow is translated by the NAT module, then the ip_conntrack_tuple_hash structure for the reverse direction is adapted so that reply packets can be allocated to it properly.

In the example discussed in Section 21.1.6, where the internal address 192.168.1.1 is translated into the global address 199.10.42.1, a connection from port 1200 to port 80 in the WWW server 100.1.1.1 would be represented by the following entries:

- Forward: 192.168.1.1:1200 → 100.1.1.1:80
- Reverse: 100.1.1.1:80 → 199.10.42.1:1200

The connection-tracking module stores a pointer to the relevant data structure of the type ip_conntrack in the sk_buff of each packet. If the NAT module wants to allocate an IP packet to a session flow, it invokes its own ip_conntrack_get() function, which returns the matching ip_conntrack structure.

`struct ip_nat_expect`	**linux/netfilter_ipv4/ip_nat_rule.h**

The NAT module has an ordered list, nat_expect_list, with data structures of the type ip_nat_expect, to enable protocol-specific NAT modules (e.g., for FTP—see Section 21.1.7) to decide when a new session flow was expected, so that it requires special handling. Each of these structures consists essentially of a pointer to a function that actually makes that decision:

```
struct ip_nat_expect
{
struct list_head list;

      /* Returns 1 (and sets verdict) if it has setup NAT for this
         connection */
      int (*expect)(struct sk_buff **pskb,
                    unsigned int hooknum,
                    struct ip_conntrack *ct,
                    struct ip_nat_info *info,
                    struct ip_conntrack *master,
                    struct ip_nat_info *masterinfo,
                    unsigned int *verdict);
};
```

struct ip_nat_multi_range	linux/netfilter_ipv4/ip_nat.h

The `ip_nat_multi_range` structure is used mainly to specify the set of addresses available for address translation. It contains one or several structures of the type `ip_nat_range`, each specifying a continuous IP address range, and a `rangesize` field that takes the number of contained `ip_nat_range` structures:

```
struct ip_nat_multi_range
{
        unsigned int rangesize;

        /* hangs off end. */
        struct ip_nat_range range[1];
};
```

struct ip_nat_range	linux/netfilter_ipv4/ip_nat.h

The `ip_nat_range` structure serves to represent a continuous IP address range; the range boundaries are specified in the `min_ip` and `max_ip` fields:

```
/* Single range specification. */
struct ip_nat_range
{
                /* Set to OR of flags above. */
                unsigned int flags;

                /* Inclusive: network order. */
                u_int32_t min_ip, max_ip;

                /* Inclusive: network order */
                union ip_conntrack_manip_proto min, max;
};
```

If the flags bit vector contains the value `IP_NAT_RANGE_PROTO_SPECIFIED`, then the `min` and `max` fields additionally specify a protocol-specific address range: a port-number range for TCP and UDP, a value range from the ICMP ID field for ICMP.

NAT fully relies on the means offered by the netfilter architecture to manage the selection rules needed to specify packets requiring an address translation. For this purpose, two new branch destinations, SNAT and DNAT, are defined with the functions `ipt_snat_target()` and `ipt_dnat_target()`, which do the actual address-translation work. A multipurpose parameter, `targinfo`, is used to pass the address range available for translation to these functions in the form of an `ip_nat_multi_range` structure.

struct ip_nat_info	linux/netfilter_ipv4/ip_nat.h

As was explained in Chapter 20, the connection-tracking module creates a data structure of the type `ip_conntrack` for each session flow, to store all relevant information. If the NAT functionality was activated in the Linux kernel (`CONFIG_IP_NAT_NEEDED`), then this structure additionally contains a nat substructure, and the info field of that sub-structure contains a structure of the type ip_nat_info:

```
struct ip_conntrack
{
...
#ifdef CONFIG_IP_NF_NAT_NEEDED
        struct {
                struct ip_nat_info info;
...
        } nat;
#endif /* CONFIG_IP_NF_NAT_NEEDED */
};
```

The ip_nat_info structure stores the address bindings of a session flow:

```
struct ip_nat_info
{
        /* Set to zero when conntrack created: bitmask of maniptypes */
        int initialized;

        unsigned int num_manips;

        /* Manipulations to be done on this conntrack. */
        struct ip_nat_info_manip manips[IP_NAT_MAX_MANIPS];

        /* The mapping type which created us (NULL for null mapping). */
        const struct ip_nat_mapping_type *mtype;

        struct ip_nat_hash bysource, byipsproto;

        /* Helper (NULL if none). */
        struct ip_nat_helper *helper;
};
```

The initialized bit vector specifies whether the address binding for the source address (bit 0) or the destination address (bit 1), or both, was initialized.

The num_manips field specifies the number of executable manipulations stored in the manips vector. Manipulations are counted separately at different hooks and for different directions. Each of these manipulations is represented by a structure of the type ip_nat_info_manip.

The bysource and byipsproto fields include hash values used to sort the structure in the two hash tables described below, and helper is a pointer to an optional helper module. (See Section 21.4.2.)

struct ip_nat_info_manip	linux/netfilter_ipv4/ip_nat.h

```
struct ip_nat_info_manip
{
        /* The direction. */
        u_int8_t direction;

        /* Which hook the manipulation happens on. */
        u_int8_t hooknum;
```

```
/* The manipulation type. */
u_int8_t maniptype;

/* Manipulations to occur at each conntrack in this dirn. */
struct ip_conntrack_manip manip;
};
```

The `ip_nat_info_manip` structure represents a manipulation or address binding. It contains the direction (`IP_CT_DIR_ORIGINAL` for the forward direction, `IP_CT_DIR_REPLY` for the reverse direction), the netfilter hook number, and the address translation type (`IP_NAT_MANIP_SRC` for source NAT, `IP_NAT_MANIP_DST` for destination NAT), and its `ip_conntrack_manip` structure includes the IP address and port number to which the former address should be mapped.

To manage address bindings, the NAT module uses two hash tables, `bysource` and `byipsproto`, where collisions are resolved by linear lists. The `byipsproto` table is used to account for mappings done, to ensure that no two mappings to the same IP address exist. The keys are the transport protocol number and the IP source and destination addresses of the session flow after the address translation.

The keys for the `bysource` table are the transport protocol, the IP source address, and the source port before the address translation. This table is used by the `find_appropriate_src()` function to detect existing session flows. (See Section 21.3.4.)

21.3.2   Initializing and Uninitializing the NAT Module

The two functions `init()` and `fini()` are used to initialize and uninitialize the NAT module. In turn, these two functions invoke the `init_or_cleanup()` function with parameter 1 (initialize) or 0 (uninitialize).

`init_or_cleanup()`	net/ipv4/netfilter/ip_nat_standalone.c

The `init_or_cleanup()` function serves to initialize or uninitialize the NAT module, depending on the value of the init parameter.

To initialize the NAT module, the `ip_nat_rule_init()` function (from `net/ipv4/netfilter/ip_nat_rule.c`) is invoked first. This function uses `ipt_register_table()` to create the new netfilter table, `nat`. Subsequently, it uses `ipt_register_target()` to register the new branch destinations, SNAT and DNAT, with the handling functions `ipt_snat_target()` and `ipt_dnat_target()`. Next, the `ip_nat_init()` function (from `net/ipv4/netfilter/ip_nat_core.c`) initializes the standard protocols—TCP, UDP, and ICMP—and the two hash tables—`bysource` and `byipsproto`. Finally, the functions `ip_nat_fn()`, `ip_nat_local_fn()`, and `ip_nat_out()` are registered with the appropriate hooks, and the usage counter of the connection-tracking module is incremented.

To uninitialize the NAT module, the cleanup work is done in reverse order: First, the usage counter of the connection tracking module is decremented; then, the NAT functions are removed from the hooks; next, `ip_nat_cleanup()` deletes the hash tables and the transport protocol modules; and, finally, `ip_nat_rule_cleanup()` releases the NAT branch destinations and the NAT table.

21.3.3 How an IP Packet Travels Through the NAT Module

An IP packet that traverses the system is handed over to the NAT module twice:

- When it enters the system at the netfilter hook NF_IP_PRE_ROUTING. At this point, the packet is handled by the ip_nat_fn() function.
- Once it has been created by a local process—at the netfilter hook NF_IP_LOCAL_OUT. Notice that fragmented packets slip past NAT, and ip_nat_fn() is invoked for all other packets.
- At netfilter hook NF_IP_POST_ROUTING, when the packet leaves the system. The appropriate function is ip_nat_out(); it first reassembles fragmented packets, if present, and then invokes ip_nat_fn(). As was described in Section 20.2.6, although fragmented packets are reassembled by the connection-tracking module (ip_conntrack_in() function), these packets might have been fragmented again by the routing code in the meantime.

---

ip_nat_fn()	net/ipv4/netfilter/ip_nat_standalone.c

This function is invoked for each packet (not only for packets subject to address translation). The parameters it takes include the number of the netfilter hook where it was invoked and a pointer to an sk_buff structure, together with the packet.

First, the HOOK2MANIP macro is used to select the NAT variant to be used from the hook number. At netfilter hook NF_IP_POST_ROUTING, the source address (IP_NAT_MANIP_SRC) should be changed; otherwise, the destination address (IP_NAT_MANIP_DST) has to be changed. Subsequently, the ip_conntrack_get() function is invoked from the connection-tracking module to discover the associated connection entry and its state. The further approach differs, depending on this state:

- *Expected connection* (IP_CT_RELATED): If the packet is an ICMP message, then the function icmp_reply_translation() is invoked, which does the actual address translation. Otherwise, the packet is handled exactly as in the IP_CT_NEW case.
- *New connection* (IP_CT_NEW): The ip_nat_info structure in the connection entry is checked to see whether the address allocation has already been initialized. (This can happen, for example, when a connection establishment packet is retransmitted after a timeout.) If this is not the case, then the function ip_nat_rule_find() initiates the nat netfilter table processing. If the new connection requires address translation, netfilter invokes one of the branch destination functions, ipt_snat_target() or ipt_dnat_target(), to initialize a new address binding. Finally, place_in_hashes() adds the new address to the two hash tables, byipsproto and bysource.
- *Other cases*: No new address binding has to be created in any other case. Instead, only the ip_nat_info structure is read from the connection entry, to see whether any address binding applies.

Finally, the last step invokes do_bindings (see Section 21.3.5), which handles the actual address translation; the return value (normally NF_ACCEPT) is passed to the calling function.

21.3.4   Initializing an Address-Binding Process

`ipt_snat_target()`, `ip_dnat_target()`	**net/ipv4/netfilter/ip_nat_rule.c**

The `ipt_snat_target()` and `ipt_dnat_target()` functions are registered branch destinations for the netfilter table, nat. This table is processed only if the first packet of a new session flow was registered in `ipt_nat_fn()`. The table uses its rules list to identify session flows subject to source NAT or destination NAT.

Initially, either of the two functions uses `ip_conntrack_get()` to find the corresponding connection entry of the connection-tracking module and then invokes the `ip_nat_setup_info()` function to do a new address binding. The result of this invocation, the address information of the newly assigned binding, is passed to the calling function.

`ip_nat_setup_info()`	**net/ipv4/netfilter/ip_nat_core.c**

This function is invoked by the handling functions for the SNAT and DNAT branch destinations and does essentially three things:

- When the `get_unique_tuple()` (see below) is invoked, it searches for a free address available to do the address translation. If no free address is available, then the value NF_DROP is returned and the packet is dropped.

  To take other address translations into account, the entry for the reverse direction inverted by `invert_tuplepr()` is used as the basis rather than the connection-tracking address entry for the forward direction of the session flow, because the reverse direction entry already includes the translated addresses, in contrast to the forward direction.

- Invoking the `ip_conntrack_alter_reply()` function causes the reverse direction of a connection entry to be altered so that reply packets can be allocated properly to the correct connection, despite its translated address.
- Finally, the new address binding is added to the substructure of the `ip_nat_info` connection entry. The mapping rules (e.g., transformation of source address and source port) result from comparing the original `ip_conntrack_tuple` structure with the new structure, supplied by `get_unique_tuple`.

`get_unique_tuple()`	**net/ipv4/netfilter/ip_nat_core.c**

This function is invoked by `ip_nat_setup_info()` to search for a free address within a specified address range (represented by a structure of the type `ip_nat_multi_range`).

If the function is invoked at the NF_IP_POST_ROUTING hook (i.e., to map the source address), then invoking the function `find_appropriate_src()` checks for whether an address binding exists for the source address (IP address, protocol number, and protocol-specific part) in the `bysource` hash table for that packet. If this binding is within the specified address range, it is returned as a new address entry.

In all other cases, the combination of IP address and protocol number least used within the specified address range is determined by the function `find_best_ips_proto_fast()`. This function iterates over all possible IP addresses in the address range and uses the `byipsproto` hash table to check the number of bindings existing at this IP address. If it finds an appropriate IP address, it lets the function `ip_nat_used_tuple()` check on whether this address is unique and, if the `IP_NAT_RANGE_PROTO_SPECIFIED` flag is set, whether the protocol-specific part is within the address range (with the help of the protocol-specific function, `proto->in_range`). If this is the case, then the tuple is returned. If this is not the case, both the new address and the address range are passed to the protocol-specific function, `proto->unique_tuple()`. Now, this function attempts to vary the protocol-specific part (e.g., TCP port number or ICMP ID) to find a unique combination. If this attempt is unsuccessful, the function uses `find_best_ips_proto_fast()` to select the next best IP address, and the checking process starts over again. Eventually, if no combination can be found, value 1 is returned, and the packet is dropped.

21.3.5 The Actual Address Translation

`do_bindings()`	net/ipv4/netfilter/ip_nat_core.c

This function applies the address bindings specified in the `ip_nat_info` structure to a packet. To this end, it searches the `info->manips` list for all bindings that belong to the matching direction and the matching hook. Next, it invokes the `manip_pkt` function to do the appropriate transformations. This function transforms the IP addresses, recalculates the checksum in the IP header, and invokes the `proto->manip_pkt()` function for the protocol-specific part, which does the actual translation and computes checksums, if present.

Finally, `do_bindings()` invokes a helper module, if present (e.g., for correct FTP handling—see Section 21.1.7).

21.4   INTERFACES TO EXTEND THE NAT MODULE

The NAT module offers various extension options. These extensions are actually independent modules that can use the registration functions of the NAT module to register and unregister themselves. The following extensions are possible:

- *Transport protocols* (e.g., TCP): To use a new protocol, we have to write two extension modules—one for connection tracking and one for NAT.
- *Helper modules* (helpers): To be able to handle application protocols, such as FTP (see Section 21.1.7), properly, we can register helper modules. Again, this requires one helper each for connection tracking and NAT.
- *Configuration-tool extensions*: In addition, the `iptables` configuration tool has to be extended by the corresponding command-line parameters for each new protocol and each new helper module. We will not discuss this issue any further.

21.4.1 Transport Protocols

The functions `ip_nat_protocol_register()` and `ip_nat_protocol_unregister()` can be used to register a new transport protocol or to unregister an existing protocol. When registering a new protocol, we have to pass a pointer to a structure of the type `ip_nat_protocol` as a parameter.

`struct_ip_nat_protocol`	**linux/netfilter_ipv4/ip_nat_protocol.h**

```
struct_ip_nat_protocol
{
        struct list_head list;

        /* Protocol name */
        const char *name;

        /* Protocol number. */
        unsigned int protonum;

        /* Do a packet translation according to the ip_nat_proto_manip
        * and manip type. */
        void (*manip_pkt)(struct iphdr *iph, size_t len,
                const struct ip_conntrack_manip *manip,
                enum ip_nat_manip_type maniptype);
        /* Is the manipable part of the tuple between min and max incl? */
        int (*in_range)(const struct ip_conntrack_tuple *tuple,
                enum ip_nat_manip_type maniptype,
                const union ip_conntrack_manip_proto *min,
                const union ip_conntrack_manip_proto *max);


        /* Alter the per-proto part of the tuple (depending on
        maniptype), to give a unique tuple in the given range if
        possible; return false if not. Per-protocol part of tuple
        is initialized to the incoming packet. */
        int (*unique_tuple)(struct ip_conntrack_tuple *tuple,
                const struct ip_nat_range *range,
                enum ip_nat_manip_type maniptype,
                const struct ip_conntrack *conntrack);
        unsigned int (*print)(char *buffer,
                const struct ip_conntrack_tuple *match,
                const struct ip_conntrack_tuple *mask);

        unsigned int (*print_range)(char *buffer,
                const struct ip_nat_range *range);
};
```

The list header required to manage the protocol list contains pointers to predecessors and successors and is initially set to {NULL,NULL}.

name is a character string containing the name of the protocol.

protonum is the protocol number that will be entered in the IP header. A list of protocol numbers is normally available in the /etc/protocols file.

manip_pkt is a pointer to a function invoked by the manip_pkt function of the NAT module to manipulate the protocol-specific part of a packet according to the manip parameter. (See Section 21.3.5.)

in_range is a pointer to a function that checks for whether the protocol-specific part of an address (e.g., the TCP port) is within the specified interval [min,max]. Whether the source or destination address will have to be checked is specified of the value of the maniptype parameter (IP_NAT_MANIP_SRC or IP_NAT_MANIP_DST). The function returns value 1 if the condition is met, otherwise 0.

unique_tuple is a pointer to the module's "core function." It is invoked within get_unique_tuple() (see Section 21.3.4) to obtain a unique address by altering the protocol-specific part. The value of the manip type shows whether the source or destination address should change; the respective protocol-specific part of tuple is set to the value of the original tuple.

The protocol-specific part generally is altered according to a simple scheme (e.g., by incrementing the port number for TCP). Subsequently, the function ip_nat_used_tuple() is used to see whether the new address is still free. If so, then the function returns 1; otherwise, it has to return the value 0. If the flag IP_NAT_RANGE_PROTO_SPECIFIED is set, then range also contains information about the range in which the protocol-specific part of the tuple should be. Naturally, this information has to be taken into account.

The two function pointers, print() and print_range(), are invoked when the protocol-specific information in match and mask or range should be output in text form. This informative text should be written to the buffer passed, and the number of output characters should be returned. For example, TCP would invoke this function to output the port numbers.

21.4.2 Helper Modules

A *helper* is a function invoked by the NAT module from within the do_bindings() function, once an address binding has been added (see Section 21.3.5). This allows us to verify the payload of a packet and to modify address transmitted in that packet—for example, to detect PORT commands over an FTP control connection. (See Section 21.1.7.) A helper module is registered by ip_nat_helper_register(), and the only parameter it takes is a data structure of the type ip_nat_helper.

struct ip_nat_helper	linux/netfilter_ipv4/ip_nat_helper.h

```
struct ip_nat_helper
{
        /* Internal use */
        struct list_head list;

        /* Mask of things we will help: vs. tuple from server */
```

```
        struct ip_conntrack_tuple tuple;
        struct ip_conntrack_tuple mask;

        /* Helper function: returns verdict */
        unsigned int (*help)(struct ip_conntrack *ct,
              struct ip_nat_info *info,
              enum ip_conntrack_info ctinfo,
              unsigned int hooknum,
              struct sk_buff **pskb);

        const char *name;
};
```

help is a pointer to the main function of the helper module, which is invoked by do_bindings(), as was mentioned previously.

Extending the Linux Network Architecture Functionality— KIDS

This chapter deals with the introduction of new, dynamically extendable functionalities in the Linux network architecture or in the Linux kernel. We will first show the usual approach to manage dynamically extendable functionalities and the operations generally involved in this approach.

Subsequently, we will use Linux KIDS, the implementation of a construction system to support network services, to show how a dynamically extendable functionality can be managed. Another interesting aspect of Linux KIDS is how its object-oriented concept is implemented in the Linux kernel, considering that the Linux kernel was not designed with object orientation in mind.

In addition, we will explain how the KIDS components can be embedded into the processes of protocol instances over existing interfaces, which means that you can use the functionality of Linux KIDS without having to change the kernel source code. Finally, this chapter describes how you can use a character-oriented device to configure the KIDS construction system, allowing you to easily configure this functionality in the kernel.

22.1 MANAGING DYNAMICALLY EXTENDABLE FUNCTIONALITIES

The Linux network architecture is continually extended by new functions and protocol instances. In most cases, such an extension can even be dynamic (i.e., at runtime), as we saw in earlier chapters: network-layer protocols (Section 6.3), transport-layer protocols (Section 14.2.5), and packet filters (Section 19.3).

All we need to implement such a dynamic extendibility are an appropriate interface and structures that manage the registered functionality. Functions like register_*functionality*() and unregister_*functionality*() can be used to register new functionalities with the kernel or remove existing functionalities.

These registering and unregistering functions execute all initialization or cleanup steps required. For example, when removing a functionality, we have to ensure that it is no longer used in any other location of the kernel. This means that it has to use a reference counter (*use counter*) and check this counter (`use_counter == 0?`) before unregistering a functionality.

The following operations are some of those normally executed in the registration function of an interface and undone, accordingly, in the unregistering functions:

- storing the new functionality of its management structure in a list, hash table, or another data structure;
- reserving memory for the required data structures or procuring other resources (IRQ, DMA, timer, etc.);
- incrementing reference counters;
- creating entries in the proc directory;
- using `printk()` to output status messages.

A new functionality (e.g., a new network-layer protocol or a new network device) normally takes many parameters. It would be difficult the pass all of these parameters individually in the registration function, mainly because they are required while the functionality is being used, which is normally outside the registration function. For this reason, a structure to manage the functionality is normally created. When registering a new functionality, this structure can be entered in a list, hash table, or similar management structures. This method ensures that we can access these functionalities and their parameters after the registration. Earlier chapters introduced a large number of such management structures, including the `net_device` structure for network devices and the `packet_type` structure for network-layer protocols.

Such a management structure is filled with the parameters required before it is registered. Subsequently, a pointer to this management structure is passed to the registration function. The elements of these management structures assume two different tasks:

- *Configuration data* is set before a functionality is registered and passed as (configuration) parameter within the structure. In the `packet_type` structure (Chapter 6), for example, these parameters include the `type` and `func` variables.
- *Runtime variables* are not explicitly set before a functionality is registered. They are needed later when the functionality is used (e.g., `next` to link structures, or a use counter to count references).

After a registration, of course, we can also use configuration variables as runtime variables, if the initial value is no longer needed.

After this brief overview of the principles of how to manage functionalities registered dynamically, the sections following discuss how the KIDS framework is implemented in the Linux kernel 2.4 (Linux KIDS). This framework relies heavily on the concept of dynamically extendable functionalities, as shown in our Linux KIDS example further below. Another interesting point is that the components and their instances are based on the object-oriented concept, and this approach could probably be adopted for other software projects in the Linux kernel. The next section begins with an introduction of its basics to better understand how the KIDS construction system works.

22.2   STRUCTURE OF THE KIDS CONSTRUCTION SYSTEM

KIDS stands for *Karlsruhe Implementation architecture of Differentiated Services* and was developed for the design, evaluation, and use of quality-of-service (QoS) mechanisms in networks [Wehr01b]. KIDS is an abstract model describing the structure and interaction of quality-of-service mechanisms, and it allows you to define individual QoS behavior in a flexible way. The KIDS framework was implemented on various platforms, including Linux (kernel Version 2.4) and the OMNeT++ simulation tool. Though Linux already supports some QoS features (see Chapter 18), KIDS introduces several important benefits, as we will see in the further course of this chapter. The next two sections will introduce the general structure of the KIDS framework; however, we will leave out a few details to keep things short—see [Wehr01a] for details.

22.2.1   Elementary QoS Components

KIDS was designed to create a flexible, extendable, and modular framework for implementing individual QoS mechanisms. It is based on the use of components that implement the elementary QoS mechanisms, and so it is easy to combine them to more complex QoS mechanisms. Simple combination of components and ensuring all potential degrees of freedom and easy extendability were the most important factors in the design of the KIDS framework.

KIDS can be thought of as a construction kit, similarly to the popular Lego system, consisting of components that have different interfaces. Components with similar interfaces can be connected (almost arbitrarily) to form complex constructions (in this case QoS mechanisms).

We can distinguish two different interfaces in the components of the KIDS framework (as seen in Figure 22–1):

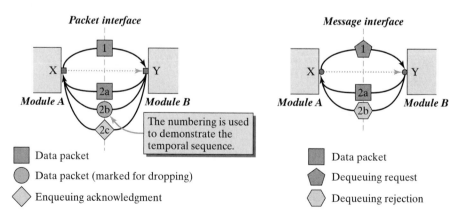

FIGURE 22–1
Interactions at the interfaces between two KIDS components.

■ At a *packet interface* (□), a component, *A*, uses packet output *X* to pass a data packet it received at its input to the successor component, *B*. By convention, a KIDS component has but a single input.

■ At a *message interface* (○), component *A* uses message output *X* to pass a message to component *B*, requesting the latter for a packet.

By using these two interface types, we can distinguish five component classes, as shown in Figure 22–2. Each QoS mechanism can be assigned to one of these classes:

■ *Operative components* (BHVR) operate on packets: They receive a packet and operate their algorithm on this packet. The algorithm implemented in a component either changes the packet (active operative component) or studies its output to forward the packet (passive operative component).

Examples: Token Bucket, Shaper, Marker, Dropper, Classifier, Random Early Detection (RED).

■ *Queue components* (QUEUE) are data structures used by components to enqueue or dequeue packets.

Examples: FIFO Queue, Earliest-Deadline-First-Queue.

■ *Enqueuing components* (ENQ_BHVR) enqueue packets in queues based on special methods, which is the reason why they have no outputs.

Examples: Head-Enqueue, Tail-Enqueue, EDF-Enqueue.

■ *Dequeuing components* (DEQ_BHVR) dequeue packets from a queue based on a special method. They receive a dequeue request on their message input and subsequently try to dequeue a packet from the queue. If successful, the packet is transported from the packet output; otherwise, a negative message is returned.

Examples: Head-Dequeue, Tail-Dequeue.

■ *Strategic components* (DEQ_DISC) implement special strategies that can be combined in a flexible way to serve queues. This means that they decide on the route for dequeue requests to dequeue components, which eventually serve the queue.

Examples: Priority Queuing, Weighted Fair Queuing, Round Robin.

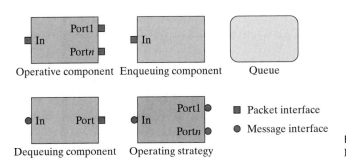

Operative component   Enqueuing component   Queue

Dequeuing component   Operating strategy

■ Packet interface
● Message interface

FIGURE 22–2
Five different KIDS component classes.

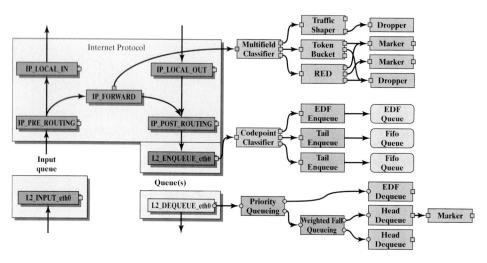

FIGURE 22–3
Example of a KIDS configuration.

By observing relatively simple rules to link components (see [Wehr01a]), we can design complex configurations. Figure 22–3 shows an example for such a configuration; it implements a router that distinguishes three service classes.

22.2.2 Hooks

QoS mechanisms extend the behavior of a protocol instance to enable us to handle packets in a differentiated way and obtain different qualities of service. Though the five component classes of the KIDS framework supply a construction system for flexible linking of QoS components to combine QoS mechanisms, we still don't know how a newly designed QoS mechanism can be integrated into the process of a conventional protocol instance. One of the most important factors is to select a location for the extension of a protocol instance, because we achieve a different set of packets, depending on these locations.

KIDS implements the concept of hooking points—*hooks*, for short—representing a defined extension of existing protocol instances to bind components of the KIDS framework. Figure 22–3 shows five strategic positions in the IP protocol and three in the data link layer, where hooks were integrated to subsequently hook in KIDS components at those points. Section 22.3.4 describes how these hooks were implemented on the basis of different interfaces in the Linux network architecture.

We define three types of hooks:

- *Packet hooks* are used at positions where a packet normally passes without differentiated handling (e.g., IP_FORWARD is passed by all packets to be forwarded).
- *Enqueuing and Dequeuing hooks* are used at positions where we would normally use a FIFO queue (e.g., the output queues of network devices on the data-link layer).

22.3   USING THE KIDS EXAMPLE TO EXTEND THE LINUX NETWORK ARCHITECTURE

Now that we have given a brief overview of the elements in the KIDS framework, this section will discuss its implementation in the Linux kernel as an example of how the functionality of the Linux network architecture can be extended. We focus our discussion on the design and management of the components: how and why they were designed, and how they are introduced to the kernel at runtime. In addition, we will see how hooks are implemented on the basis of different existing kernel interfaces, which means that we don't have to change the kernel to be able to use KIDS. Finally, we use the `kidsd` daemon as an example to show how components and hooks are configured and how they interact between the kernel and the user level.

22.3.1   Components and Their Instances

The KIDS framework offers different types of components that can be used to implement different QoS mechanisms (e.g., token buckets—see Section 18.6.1). A component can occur more than once within a component chain, and each of these occurrences can have different parameters. This means that we should be able to create an arbitrary number of instances from a component, but still try to keep the memory required by these instances low. This principle reminds us strongly of the object-orientation concept that lets you create an arbitrary number of object instances from a class. Although all of these classes exist independently, they have the same behavior, because they use the same methods.

This means that the component concept of Linux KIDS has an object-oriented character, though it was written in C, a programming language that doesn't support object orientation. The component concept of Linux KIDS consists of the following two parts:

- *Components* are QoS mechanisms implementing a specific behavior. They are managed in the `bhvr_type` structure of Linux KIDS. This structure contains all properties of a component (e.g., its behavior in the form of pointers to corresponding methods—shown below). These methods are used by several instances of that component concurrently, so they have to be *reentrant*. Components correspond to the principle of classes in the object-oriented model.
- *Component instances* are created when we need an instance of a component. To this end, we create a data structure of the type `bhvr`. It stores all information about this component instance—mainly, its individual parameter configuration. The instance should have the component's behavior, so reference is made to the information stored in the `bhvr_type` structure of the component. Component instances correspond to objects (or object instances) in the object-oriented model.

The following discussion introduces how these two structures are built and what the parameters mean. Subsequently, we will see how components can be registered or unregistered dynamically.

`struct bhvr_type`	**kids/kids_bhvr.h**

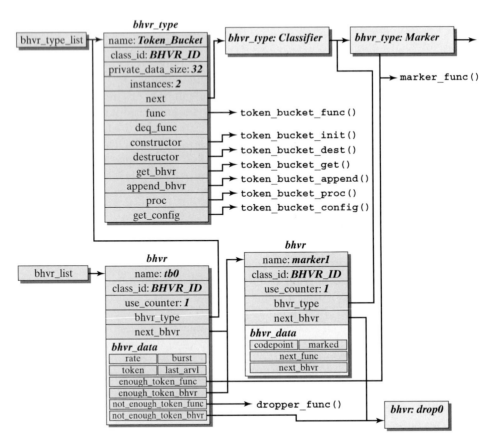

FIGURE 22–4

The bhvr_type and bhvr structures manage components and their instances.

Figure 22–4 shows how components and their instances interact. The bhvr_type structure of the token bucket stores general component information.

```
struct bhvr_type
{
    char                name[STRLEN];
    unsigned int        bhvr_class_id;
    unsigned long       private_data_size;
    unsigned int        instances;
    struct bhvr_type    *next;
    int                 (*func)(struct bhvr *, struct sk_buff *);
    struct sk_buff*     (*deq_func)(struct bhvr *);
    int                 (*constructor)(struct bhvr *bhvr, char * data, int flag);
    int                 (*destructor)(struct bhvr *bhvr);
    struct bhvr*        (*get_bhvr)(struct bhvr *bhvr, char * port);
```

```
int                    (*append_bhvr)(struct bhvr *new_bhvr, struct bhvr
                           *old_bhvr, char *port);
int                    (*proc)(struct bhvr *bhvr, char *ptr, int layer);
int                    (*get_config)(struct bhvr *bhvr, char *ptr);
};
```

The fields have the following meaning:

▪ name is the name of the component (e.g., Token_Bucket).

▪ bhvr_class_id contains the component's class. (see Section 22.2.1.) Possible values are BHVR_ID, ENQ_BHVR_ID, DEQ_BHVR_ID, DEQ_DISC_ID, and QUEUE_ID.

▪ private_data_size specifies the size of the private data structure used in the bhvr structure for each instance of a component. Preferably, a separate private structure should be defined here (e.g., tb_data—see below), and a sizeof instruction to specify the size of this structure should be inserted in this position.

▪ instances manages the number of instances created from a component. This variable is managed by Linux KIDS. It should show a value of 0 when a component is removed from the kernel.

▪ next is also used internally, namely to link bhvr_type structures in the bhvr_type_list. (See Figure 22–4.)

The following elements of the bhvr_type structure are function pointers that specify the behavior of a component and are used to managing it.

▪ func(bhvr, skb) refers to a function that is invoked when a packet (or a socket buffer, skb) is passed to an instance (bhvr) of this component. It implements the functionality of this component type. A socket buffer is passed when func() is invoked. This means that this function corresponds to the implementation of a packet interface and is used only for operative components and enqueuing components. Section 22.3.5 uses an example introducing the func() method of the Token-Bucket component.

The bhvr parameter contains a pointer to the bhvr structure of the component instance, which is passed to the socket buffer, skb, when the func() function is invoked. Because the func() method is used for all instances of the Token_Bucket component, the pointer to the instance-specific information also has to be passed. Otherwise, it would be impossible to see which instances, with what parameter or variable assignments, is meant.

▪ deq_func(bhvr) is used for dequeuing and strategic components. It corresponds to the implementation of a message interface and is invoked when a packet is requested from an instance (bhvr) of this component. A component implements only one of two functions, either func() or deq_func(), depending on whether its input has a packet interface or a message interface.

▪ constructor(bhvr, data, flag) is invoked when a bhvr instance of this component is initialized or when its configuration changed. This method takes the character-string data with the component's private data to be configured as parameters. The `flag` parameter shows whether this is the first initialization of this instance (INIT_BHVR) or it is a change to its parameters at runtime, where only the information passed should be altered.

- `destructor(bhvr)` is invoked to destroy the `bhvr` instance of the component. All cleanup work required (e.g., free memory or deactivate timer) should be done at this point.

- `get_bhvr(bhvr, port)` is invoked by KIDS to obtain a pointer to the `bhvr` structure of the component instance appended to the output, `port`. The number and names of a component's outputs are individual, so we have to implement a component-specific function.

- `append_bhvr(new_bhvr, old_bhvr, port)` connects the `new_bhvr` component instance to the output, `port`, of the existing component instance, `old_bhvr`. Again, we have to implement separate functions for the individual outputs of a component.

- `proc(bhvr, ptr, layer)` creates information about the `bhvr` component instance. This information can be output from `proc` files. The `layer` parameter specifies the distance from the component instance to the hook; this is required for indenting within the output. The `ptr` pointer specifies the buffer space this output should be written to. (See Section 2.8.)

- `get_config(bhvr, ptr)` is invoked by KIDS to write the configuration of the `bhvr` component instance to the `ptr` buffer space, based on the KIDS configuration syntax (see Section 22.3.6).

struct bhvr	kids/kids_bhvr.h

Each of the `bhvr` structures representing the specific instances of a component manages the information of a component instance (e.g., name on number of references). The `bhvr` data structure is built as follows:

```
struct bhvr
{
        char                    name[STRLEN];
        unsigned int            use_counter;
        struct bhvr             *next_bhvr;
        struct bhvr_type        *bhvr_type;
        char                    bhvr_data[0];
};
```

The fields have the following meaning:

- name: The name of this instance (e.g., `tb0` or `marker1`);

- `use_counter` specifies the number of direct predecessors of this component instance—the number of references to this `bhvr` structure.

- `next_bhvr` is used to link the individual `bhvr` data structures in the `bhvr_list`. This list is managed by KIDS and used to search for a component by its name (`get_bhvr_by_name()`).

- bhvr_type points to the relevant bhvr_type structure, representing the type of this component instance. This means that this pointer specifies the behavior of the component instance, which is registered in the bhvr_type structure.

- bhvr_data is a placeholder for the private information of this component instance (as is shown later). No type can be specified, because the structure of each component's information is individual. A *type cast* is required before each access—for example,

```
struct tb_data *data = (struct tb_data *) &(tb_bhvr->bhvr_data);}
```

The private information space is directly adjacent to the bhvr structure. The length of private information is taken into account for reserving the memory of the bhvr structure. As was mentioned earlier, it is managed in the bhvr_type structure.

Using the Token-Bucket Component as an Example for a Private Data Structure   The data structure containing private information (bhvr_data) is of particular importance. Its structure depends on the respective component, because it stores that component's parameters and runtime variables. Because all instances of a component have the same variables, though with different assignments, this data structure is stored in the instances (i.e., in the bhvr structures), and its length (which is identical for all instances of a component) is stored in the bhvr_type structure.

This tells us clearly that all information concerning the state or configuration of a special component instance is managed in the instance itself in the private data structure of the bhvr structure.

The following example represents the private data structure of the Token_Bucket component:

```
struct tb_data
{
    unsigned int    rate, bucket_size;
    unsigned long   token, packets_arvd, packets_in, packets_out;
    CPU_STAMP       last_arvl, cycles_per_byte;
    struct bhvr     *enough_token_bhvr;
    struct bhvr     *not_enough_token_bhvr;
    int             (*enough_token_func)(struct bhvr *, struct sk_buff *);
    int             (*not_enough_token_func)(struct bhvr *, struct sk_buff *);
};
```

The meaning of each of the variables in such a private data structure can be divided into three groups:

- The parameter and runtime variables of a component are individual in that the component implements a special algorithm. This is the reason why they are managed in a private data structure of the component, which exists separately in each of that component's instances. Examples for parameter and runtime variables include the rate and bucket_size variables in the Token-Bucket component.

▓ In addition, private information manages the following two elements for *each component output*, because the number of outputs is also individual to the respective component and so it cannot be accommodated in the bhvr_type structure:

▶ The first element is a *function pointer* to the func() function (for a packet interface) or deq_func() (for a message interface) in the subsequent component instance. This means that a component instance stores a reference to the handling routine for the component instance appended to this output.

▶ The second element is a *reference* to the bhvr_structure of the subsequent component instance at this output. This pointer is used eventually to link the component instances.

The reference to the handling routine of the subsequent component instance is actually not required, because it can be identified over the bhvr_type pointer from the corresponding structure of the successor. However, this double unreferencing method is saved at the cost of an additional pointer, for performance reasons. If no component instance is appended to an output, then the two variables take the value NULL, and a packet to be forwarded is recursively returned to the hook. (See Section 22.3.5.)

22.3.2 Registering and Managing Components

Before we can use Linux KIDS to implement the desired QoS mechanisms, we have to tell the kernel which components are currently available. To this end, Linux KIDS maintains a list, bhvr_type_list, to manage all registered components. This list is based on simple linking of the respective bhvr_type data structures that store the entire information about components. (see Figure 22–4.) Linking of the data structures into a list corresponds to the normal approach to manage functionalities in the Linux kernel. (see Section 22.1.)

We can use the function register_bhvr_type(bhvr_type) to register a component represented by a bhvr_type structure. (See Figure 22–5.) More specifically, the bhvr_type structure is entered in the bhvr_type_list. (See Figure 22–4.) From then on, this component is known in the kernel, and we can create instances of that component. To remove a component from the list, we can invoke unregister_bhvr_type(bhvr_type). Of course, we have to ensure that there are no instances of the component left before we remove it, which is the reason why the instances variable has to be checked first.

In addition to the list of component categories, Linux KIDS has two other elements that can be used to register or unregister functionalities dynamically. To prevent this chapter from getting too long, we will discuss these two elements only briefly. They are managed similarly to the previous elements:

▓ *Hooks* are represented by the hook data structure; they are registered by register_hook(hook) and unregistered by unregister_hook(hook). If a protocol instance wants to supply a hook, it simulates a packet interface or message interface,

```
struct bhvr_type token_bucket_element = {
    "Token_Bucket",                     /* name                 */
    BHVR_ID,                            /* class                */
    sizeof(struct token_bucket_data),   /* private data size    */
    0,                                  /* instances            */
    NULL,                               /* next                 */
    token_bucket_func,                  /* packet interface     */
    NULL,                               /* message interface    */
    token_bucket_init,                  /* constructor          */
    NULL,                               /* destructor           */
    token_bucket_get,                   /* get bhvr of a port   */
    token_bucket_append,                /* append bhvr on a port */
    token_bucket_proc,                  /* proc output routine  */
    token_bucket_config                 /* get config of a bhvr */
};


int init_module(void) {
    register_bhvr_type(&token_bucket_element);
}


void cleanup_module(void) {
    unregister_bhvr_type(&token_bucket_element);
}
```

FIGURE 22–5

builds an appropriate hook data structure, and registers the hook. Subsequently, components can be appended to this hook. The files `kids/layer2_hooks.c` and `kids/nf_hooks.c` include examples for hooks based on the TC or netfilter interface.

▪ Different *queue categories* are managed by the `kids_queue_type` data structure; we can use `register_queue_type()` to register or `unregister_queue_type()` to unregister them. An instance of a queue variant is represented by a `kids_queue` structure. The management of queues is almost identical to that of component categories, but components and queues are different, so it was found necessary to manage them separately.

22.3.3 Managing Component Instances

The previous section described how we can register and manage components in Linux KIDS; this section discusses how we can manage instances of components—how component instances are created, deleted, and linked. A special syntax was developed to keep the managing of the QoS mechanisms as simple as possible. Section 22.3.6 will introduce this syntax. A character-oriented device, `/dev/kids`, is used to pass configuration commands to Linux KIDS and to invoke one of the methods introduced below.

`create_bhvr()`   **kids/kids_bhvr.c** create_bhvr(type, name, data, id) creates an instance of the type component designated by name. For creating this instance, that component has to be present in the list of registered components (bhvr_type_list).

Initially, storage space is reserved for the data of the new component instance. This memory space consists of a bhvr structure that is identical for all components and a private data structure that is individual to each component. Subsequently, the bhvr structure is initialized, and the constructor of the component occupying this private data with this component's configuration parameters is invoked. These configuration parameters were extracted from the CREATE command and passed in the data character string. Once it has been created, the component is no longer connected to any other component. Finally, it is added to the bhvr_list.

remove_bhvr()	kids/kids_bhvr.c

remove_bhvr(name, force) deletes the component instance designated by name and removes it from the bhvr_list. force can be specified to state that the use_counter of that instance should be ignored, as normally should not be the case, because there could still be references to this data structure. Before the data structure is released, the component's destructor is invoked to free resources, if present.

change_bhvr()	kids/kids_bhvr.c

change_bhvr(name, data) can be used to alter the private data of a component instance at runtime. All that happens here, however, is that the data character string holding the information to be changed invokes the constructor. The INIT_BHVR flag is not set; thus, the constructor knows that only the parameters specified have to be altered. Otherwise, the entire component instance would be reset.

22.3.4 Implementing Hooks

Hooks are extensions of existing protocol instances allowing us to easily embed QoS components based on the rules of the KIDS framework [Wehr01a]. One of the most important factors is the position we want to extend by a hook—and thus by QoS mechanisms—within the process of a protocol instance. The reason is that we can always address a certain number of packets at specific positions (e.g., all packets to be forwarded, at the IP_FORWARD hook, or all packets of the IP instance to be delivered locally, at the IP_LOCAL_DELIVER hook).

Thanks to its set of different interfaces, the Linux network architecture offers an inherent way to extend a protocol instance by a functionality. These interfaces have been utilized in the KIDS framework, and so the hooks shown in Figure 22–3 could be implemented without the need to change the source code of the Linux kernel. The hooks for the IP instance are based on the netfilter interface (see Section 19.3); the data-link layer hooks are based on the Traffic Control interface.

The following example represents the netfilter handling method of the IP_FORWARD hook. It merely checks for whether a component instance is appended and invokes that instance, if present:

```
unsigned int ip_forward_hook_fn(unsigned int hooknum, struct sk_buff **skb, ...)
{
    if (ip_forward_hook && ip_forward_hook->bhvr && ip_forward_hook->func)
            return ip_forward_hook->func(ip_forward_hook->bhvr, skb[0]);
    else
            return NF_ACCEPT;
};
```

Additional hooks can be integrated easily, even at runtime. To integrate a hook, we have to store the information required about the hook in a hook data structure and use the register_hook() method to register it. The protocol instance we want to extend is then simply extended by a function call, structured similarly to the above example with the IP_FORWARD hook. You can find additional information about the concept of hooks in [Wehr01a].

22.3.5   How a Component Works

Once we have registered all components of the KIDS framework with the kernel and created a component chain and appended it to a hook, we need a description of how such a component should operate. The following example uses a packet in the Token_Bucket component to describe how this component operates:

token_bucket_func()	kids/std_bhvr.c

```
int token_bucket_func(struct bhvr *tb_bhvr, struct sk_buff *skb)
{
    struct tb_data  *data = (struct tb_data *) &(tb_bhvr->bhvr_data);
    CPU_STAMP       now;

    data->packets_arvd++;
    TAKE_TIME(now);
     /* calcs the tokens, that are produced since the last packet arrival */
    (unsigned long) data->token += (((unsigned long) (now - data->last_arvl)) /
                                    (unsigned long) data->cycles_per_byte);

    /* check, if the bucket is overflood */
    if (data->token > data->bucket_size)
        data->token = data->bucket_size;
    data->last_arvl = now;

    /* check, if there are enough tokens to send the packet */
    if (data->token < skb->len)
```

```
{   /* not enough tokens -> out of profile */
    data->packets_out++;
    /* forward the packet to the next behavior (out-of-profile) */
    if ((data->not_enough_token_bhvr) && (data->not_enough_token_func))
       return data->not_enough_token_func(data->not_enough_token_bhvr, skb);
}
else
{   /* enough tokens -> in profile */
    data->token -= skb->len;
    data->packets_in++;
    /* forward the packet to the next behavior (in-profile) */
    if ((data->enough_token_bhvr ) && (data->enough_token_func))
       return data->enough_token_func(data->enough_token_bhvr, skb);
}
return KIDS_ACCEPT; /* Do not discard packet, when no behavior is attached */
}
```

The Token_Bucket component belongs to the operative component class, which means that it has a packet input and up to *n* packet outputs. In this example, these are the Conform and Non_Conform outputs.

When an instance of the Token_Bucket component receives a packet, the corresponding func() handling routine is invoked, as shown in the example. The parameters it gets include the socket buffer, skb, and a pointer to the data in the component instance (bhvr). At the very beginning, a pointer to the instance's private data is set from within this pointer, which requires a *type cast*. Since the function has to be fully reentrant, it must operate only on its own private data or local variables.

Subsequently, computations according to the token bucket algorithm (see Section 18.6.1) are done, and statistic variables are updated. The result from these computations determines the output that should be used to forward the socket buffer (i.e., the kind of handling to follow). If no instance is appended to the corresponding output, the function returns the KIDS_ACCEPT result, which means that the packet was processed and should now be forwarded to the hook. The counterpart is KIDS_DROP; it tells the hook that it should drop the socket buffer.

However, if a component instance follows at the desired output (data->..._bhvr != NULL), then that instance's handling routine is invoked (data->..._func()), and a pointer to the data of the subsequent instance is passed to this handling routine, in addition to the socket buffer. The return value of the subsequent component instance is used immediately for the return value of the token-bucket component.[1]

Linux KIDS handles packets in component chains via these nested function calls. Figure 22–6 shows this once more schematically. A description of the enqueuing and dequeuing hooks would go beyond the scope and volume of this chapter. We refer our readers to [Wehr01a].

---

[1] Of course, as an alternative, the token bucket could evaluate the call's result, however, this is not implemented yet. In the case of a packet marked to be dropped (KIDS_DROP), for example, it could put the tokens used by this packet back into the bucket.

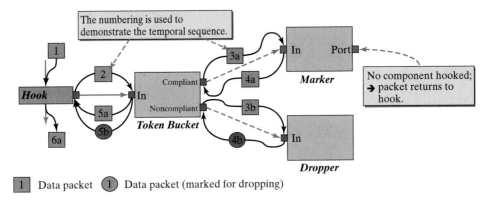

FIGURE 22–6
Component instances interacting at a packet hook.

22.3.6 Configuring KIDS Components

This section briefly introduces how component chains are configured in Linux KIDS. The first question we have to answer is how configuration information gets from the user to the appropriate positions in the kernel. Various methods are available, including new system calls and special socket interfaces. Linux KIDS uses a different and very simple method, one based on a character-oriented device. (See Section 2.5.)

First, we create a character-oriented device, /dev/kids. On the user level, this device is explained in [RuCo01].

To configure Linux KIDS, we use the following commands, which can either be written directly into /dev/kids or sent to the KIDS daemon, kidsd, over a TCP connection. This daemon will then pass our commands on to the kernel.

- CREATE *bhvr_class bhvr_type bhvr_name* DATA *private data** END

  creates an instance of the *bhvr_type* component (e.g., Token_Bucket) and initializes this instance with the private data specified in the command. Possible component classes (*bhvr_class*) include BHVR, QUEUE, ENQ_BHVR, DEQ_BHVR, and DEQ_DISC—for example,

  CREATE BHVR Token_Bucket tb1 DATA Rate 64000 Bucket_Size 5000 END

- REMOVE *bhvr_class bhvr_name* END

  removes the specified component, if it has no successors.

- CHANGE *bhvr_class bhvr_name* DATA *private data* END

  changes the specified data of the component instance, *bhvr_name*. This command changes nothing to the existing structure; it merely accesses the private data of the specified instance.

- CONNECT *bhvr_class* *bhvr_name* TO *bhvr_class* *bhvr_name* port | HOOK *hook_name* END

  connects the input of the *bhvr_name* instance to the output, *port*, of the specified instance following next, or to the specified hook, *hook_name*. One single instance can be connected to several outputs or hooks. However, only one single component instance can be appended to each output or hook.

- DISCONNECT *bhvr_class* *bhvr_name* port END

  deletes the connection on the specified output. The REMOVE command can delete a component instance only provided that all links have been deleted.

IPv6—Internet Protocol Version 6

23.1 INTRODUCTION

Several years have passed since RFC 791 for IPv4 was published. During this time, the requirements on the IP version used in the Internet have changed considerably. For example, the address space for 32-bit IPv4 addresses is almost depleted, in particularly because each mobile device, or even each household device, is expected to get its own IP address. In addition, the transmission technologies in fixed networks have so matured that packet errors have virtually been eradicated. These facts were motivation for further development beyond IPv4 to the protocol for the future Internet, resulting in IPv6. Since 1998, several standards have been introduced for IPv6, and the bases for these standards are the following RFCs:

- RFC 2460 [HiDe98a] specifies IPv6.
- RFC 2373 [HiDe98b] describes the architecture for IPv6 addressing.

23.2 IPv6 FEATURES

The new IP version was improved in many important points, but this protocol has been used in the real world only to a limited extent. One of the reasons is that existing applications cannot run directly on top of IPv6. The most important changes from IPv4 are the following:

- *Extended address size*: Instead of 32 bits, each IPv6 address contains 128 bits, enabling several hierarchical levels and addressing a much larger number of nodes. In addition, the IPv6 address of each node can be configured automatically. The support of multicast routing has been improved. Moreover, a new address type, the *anycast address*, was defined, which allows you to send a packet to an arbitrary node from within a group.

- *Simplified header format*: Some of the IPv4 packet-header fields are no longer supported, or are now optional, to reduce the cost involved in processing IPv6 packets.
- *Extension headers*: The way IPv6 encodes information is completely different from that in IPv4, enabling more efficient forwarding, less strict limitations with regard to the length of options, and more flexibility for new, future packet options.
- *Flow labeling*: IPv6 is able to mark packets that belong to a specific stream. This allows the sender to request special handling of these packets, enabling a much better support of service qualities, such as priority handling or real-time services.
- *Authentication and data protection*: IPv6 specifies extensions to support authentication, integrity, and confidentiality of data.

23.2.1 Addressing

The address space, extended from 2^{32} (IPv4) to 2^{128} (IPv6) addresses, requires a new address notation. The preferred and abbreviated notation is the hexadecimal notation (e.g., `FEDC:BA98:7654:3210:FEDC:BA98:7654:3120`). Each group (i.e., one block between two colons, or between the beginning/end and a colon) represents 16 bits. Leading zeros can be omitted, so one group can consist of one to four hexadecimal numbers. In addition, it is assumed that many consecutive blocks consist of zeros, so a compressed notation was introduced: Each address may contain at most one occurrence of two consecutive colons. In between, as many zeros as necessary are used to reach the full length of an address. The following examples show this notation (the meaning of each of these addresses will be discussed further below):

- A "loopback" address:

    `::1 or 0:0:0:0:0:0:0:1 = 0000:0000:0000:0000:0000:0000:0000:0001`

- A normal address:

    `F83:5::12 or F83:5:0:0:0:0:0:12`
    `= 0F83:0005:0000:0000:0000:0000:0000:0012`

Alternatively, addresses can be represented in mixed form, composed of the new hexadecimal notation and the decimal IPv4 notation. The format is then `x:x:x:x:x:x:d.d.d.d`, where x represents the hexadecimal groups of IPv6 and d stands for the decimal IPv4 convention. One example would be `0:0:0:0:0:FFFF:129.13.64.5` (or `::FFFF:129.13.64.5` in the abbreviated form). How useful this is becomes obvious if you think of embedding IPv4 in IPv6.

As does IPv4, IPv6 supports unicast and multicast addresses. A new form of communication introduced in IPv6 is *anycast*. Anycast is a mixture of unicast and multicast: A packet is sent to *one* computer in a multicast group, where the network itself decides which computer this is. The "broadcast" address of IPv4 (`255.255.255.255`) doesn't exist in IPv6. This functionality, which was used mainly by ARP (*Address Resolution Protocol*) to resolve IP addresses, is achieved by use of multicast addresses in IPv6.

ARP is no longer supported in IPv6. It was replaced by *Neighbor Discovery*, which was integrated into ICMPv6.

The structuring of the IPv6 address space is implemented by *prefixes*. A prefix is a sort of logical interconnection of a network, similarly to the subnetworks known from IPv4. A prefix virtually groups all IPv6 nodes with addresses beginning in the same way. For example, almost all IPv4 addresses of the Karlsruhe University begin with 129.13, using the notation 129.13.0.0/16. Subnetworks in IPv6 are denoted accordingly. The number of leading bits denoting the network are written after the complete IPv6 address and a slash. For example, the University of Münster, Germany, has the 6bone prefix 3FFE:400:10::/48. Normally, the bits in an address not belonging to the prefix are set to null; however, stating a complete address denotes the IPv6 address of a computer connected to the subnetwork specified by the prefix. In this representation, it is important to note that the compressed notation is also extended to 128 bits, rather than to the prefix length. This means that 3::16/64 is the subnetwork with prefix 0003:0000:0000:0000 and not prefix 0003:0000:0000:0016.

We can basically distinguish between multicast addresses and "other" addresses. Multicast addresses begin with eight ones (= FF:). All other addresses are unicast or anycast addresses, and which of the two is the case cannot be told from the address itself. The lower 64 bits of all (nonmulticast) addresses not beginning with the bit string 000 must have an interface identifier corresponding to the *EUI-64 format*; for Ethernet, this would be the MAC address of the network card.

Like IPv4, IPv6 uses special addresses required for specific purposes:

■ *Unspecified* (:: = 0:0:0:0:0:0:0:0)

This address, entirely consisting of zeros, does not stand for a real address, but for the absence of it. It must be selected only for source addresses and is used, for example, to configure the address of a computer automatically.

■ *Loopback* (::1)

Similarly, the loopback address does not stand for an actual network address either; it is used by a computer to send packets to itself. For this reason, it is inadmissible to send packets with the source or destination address set to ::1 to other computers. In addition, it would not be meaningful to use this address for a network interface. IPv6-capable routers have to drop such packets.

■ IPv4-compatible addresses (::d.d.d.d)

To be able to dynamically tunnel IPv6 packets over an existing IPv4 infrastructure, special IPv4-compatible IPv6 unicast addresses are assigned to the computers involved. These IPv6 addresses contain the IPv4 address in the lower 32 bits of their address; the remaining bits are set to null.

■ Embedded IPv4 addresses (::FFFF:d.d.d.d)

On the IPv6 side, an embedded IPv4 address is assigned to all computers actually supporting IPv4 only, so that these computers can be addressed by IPv6 computers. This addressing type is also called *IPv4 mapped IPv6 Address*; it consists of 80 zeros, 16 ones, and finally the 32-bit IPv4 address.

■ Local addresses (FE80::x:x:x:x, FEA0::x:x:x:x)

▶ *Link-local addresses* (FE80::x:x:x:x)

A link-local address is uniquely allocated to an interface directly connected to the network. Its prefix is FE80::/64, and the remaining bits hold an EUI-64-compliant address. The link-local address can be used exclusively for this interface and in the connected network. It serves primarily for automatic address configuration, for neighbor discovery, and for networks without routers.

▶ *Site-local addresses* (FEA0::x:x:x:x)

Site-local addresses are designed for networks that do not require a global prefix, which means that they are not reachable from the outside. The format for these addresses has an EUI-64-compliant address in the lower 64 bits, and a 16-bit wide subnetwork number between the prefix, FEA0::, and the EUI-64-compliant address. Routers may not transport packets with local source or destination addresses beyond the corresponding network.

23.2.2 IPv6 Packet Header

The IPv6 packet header includes 40 bytes in total, as shown in Figure 23–1. It is interesting that an IPv6 packet header fewer less fields than a comparable IPv4 packet header, which includes twelve fields in its 20 bytes, excluding packet options. The slimmer packet header in IPv6 reduces the cost involved in handling IPv6 packets in routers.

The Version field defines the version of the IP protocol used; it is set to Version = 0x06 for IPv6. The TOS (Type Of Service) field known from IPv4 is called Traffic Class in IPv6. It is used to identify different classes or priorities of IPv6 packets and is set to

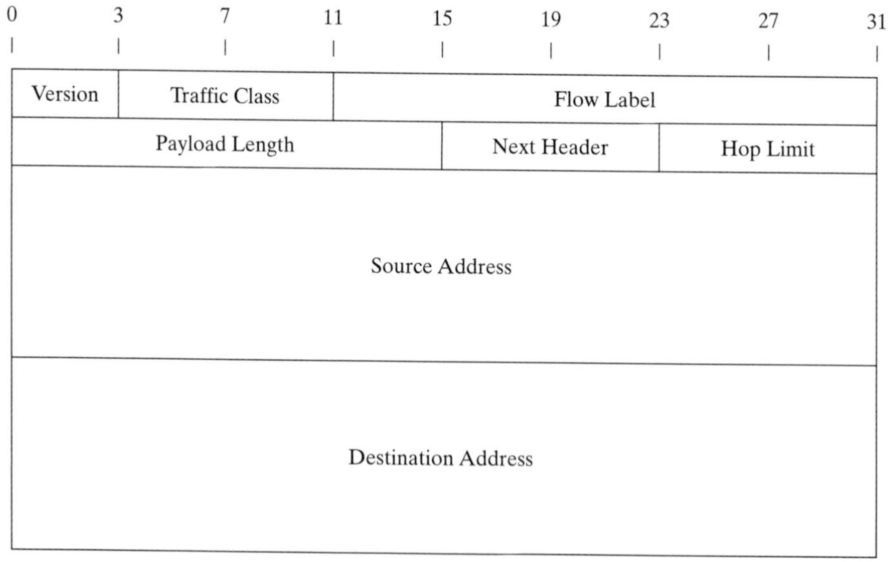

FIGURE 23–1
The IPv6 packet header.

0x00 by default. The semantics of this field corresponds to the TOS field: *codepoints* in the Differentiated Services architecture are equally mapped to the TOS and the Traffic Class fields. The Flow Label field can be used to mark a related stream of IPv6 packets. These packets are then treated accordingly in the routers on their way to the receiver. This means that we can support QoS for individual packet streams (e.g., to support real-time services in a network). RFC 2460 does not specify the semantics of this field in detail. The Payload Length field is 16 bits wide and specifies the length of a packet (in bytes), excluding the packet header. It takes packet-header extensions into account, if present. The Next Header field specifies the type of "data" following after the IPv6 packet header: This can be either a packet-header extension (see next section) or pure payload specified by the higher-layer transport protocol (e.g., TCP). In this case, the values of the Protocol field known from IPv4 are used. (See RFC 1700 [RePo94].) The TTL (Time To Live) field in the IPv4 packet header corresponds to the Hop Limit field in IPv6, which serves a similar purpose: Each IPv6 router decrements the Hop Limit field. Once it has reached the value 0, the IPv6 packet is dropped, and an ICMPv6 error message is returned to the sender. Finally, the IPv6 packet header includes two 128-bit fields for the sender (Source Address) and receiver (Destination Address) addresses.

23.2.3 Packet-Header Extensions

IPv6 encodes optional information of the Internet layer in separate packet-header extensions, placed between the IPv6 packet header and the payload. The set of different packet-header extensions used is designated by different Next-Header values.

An IPv6 packet can have several extension headers, each determined by the Next Header field of the previous packet header or the previous packet-header extension. This is the reason why this field exists in each packet-header extension. Figure 23–2 shows how packet-header extensions are used. The length of each packet-header extension has to be a multiple of 8 bytes.

Packet-header extensions are processed in the sequence of their occurrence and only in the destination host, except for the *Hop-by-Hop* packet-header extension. For this reason, the *Hop-by-Hop* packet-header extension must be at the first position, if present. A full IPv6 implementation has to include the following packet-header extensions: *Hop-by-Hop Options, Destination Options, Routing, Fragment, Authentication Header*, and *Encapsulating Security Payload*. Except for the last two, all of these packet-header extensions will be discussed below.

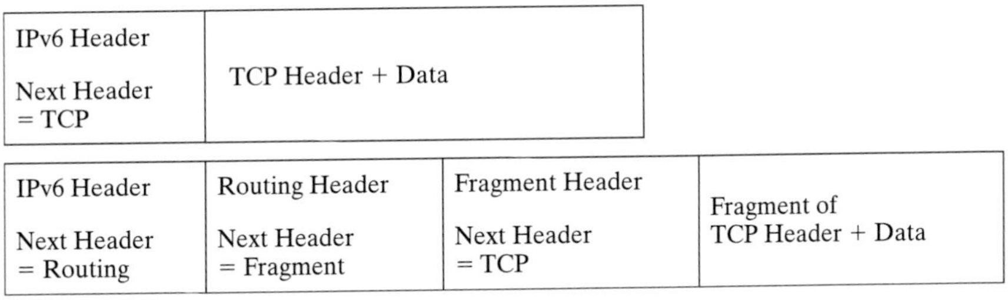

IPv6 Header Next Header = TCP	TCP Header + Data		
IPv6 Header Next Header = Routing	Routing Header Next Header = Fragment	Fragment Header Next Header = TCP	Fragment of TCP Header + Data

FIGURE 23–2
Examples of using IPv6 packet-header extensions.

Hop-by-Hop Options and Destination Options   The *Hop-by-Hop Options* and
Destination Options packet-header extensions hold optional information relevant for
the nodes on the way to the receiver. The *Hop-by-Hop Options* are processed in each
IPv6 router along the delivery path; the *Destination Options* are processed in the receiver of an IPv6 packet. Both header extensions have the same format; they differ
only in the Next Header field of the previous packet-header extension. The following
values are defined for this Next Header field:

- Hop-by-Hop Options: 0x00
- Destination Options: 0x3C

Both packet-header extensions have the following format:

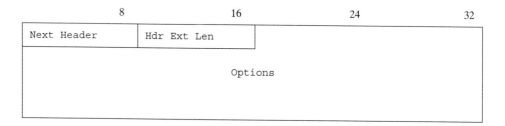

The length of these packet header extensions can be variable, so Hdr Ext Len specifies the length of a packet-header extension, in 8-byte blocks (excluding the first 8 bytes).
The Options block includes one or several encoded option(s). The original specification
of IPv6 (RFC 2460) defines two options used essentially for data *padding* to align subsequent packet-header extensions accordingly. One of these options, PAD1, corresponds to
a sequence of eight zeros (i.e., 0x00); the second option (PADN) pads to an arbitrary
length (in bytes) and is composed of three : 0x01 to designate PADN, the length of
padded data (1 byte; includes the length without the first two bytes), and the subsequent
"padding data."

Routing   The *Routing* packet-header extension is used to specify a number of nodes
(routers) that a packet has to visit along the way to its final destination. This corresponds to the *Source Routing* option in IPv4. The *Routing* packet header extension is
identified by the Next Header value 0×2B (in the previous packet-header extension)
and has the following format:

	8	16	24	32
Next Header	Hdr Ext Len	Routing Type	Segments Left
Type-Specific Data				

Again, the Hdr Ext Len field specifies the length of this packet-header extension in 8-byte blocks, excluding the first 8 bytes. Routing Type specifies the variant of the Routing packet-header extension. RFC 2460 standardizes only *Loose Source Routing* (known from IPv4) to Routing Type = 0×00. The Segments Left parameter holds the number of explicitly defined nodes a packet still has to visit. The last field holds type-specific information: the addresses of nodes left along the path (in addition to four reserved bytes, in the case of *Loose Source Routing*).

How an IPv6 packet that includes the Routing packet-header extension is forwarded can best be explained by a simple practical example. Assume that an IPv6 packet should be transported from the sender, S, over nodes R1 and R2 to the receiver, R. These nodes are addressed directly in the IPv6 packet header, and the Routing packet-header extension specifies the previous and subsequent destinations, including the end system. Each addressed node replaces the IPv6 receiver address by an entry for the next hop, and then replaces this entry by its IPv6 address. In this example, the IPv6 packet would be composed as follows in the respective stations:

- *Node S*: Source = S, Destination = R1, Segments Left = 2, Address[1] = R2, Address[2] = R.
- *Node R1*: Source = S, Destination = R2, Segments Left = 1, Address[1] = R1, Address[2] = R.
- *Node R2*: Source = S, Destination = R, Segments Left = 0, Address[1] = R1, Address[2] = R2.
- *Node R*: Source = S, Destination = R, Segments Left = 0, Address[1] = R1, Address[2] = R2.

Fragment   The *Fragment* packet-header extension is required for sending an IPv6 packet to a receiver when its size is larger than the maximum packet size (*Maximum Transfer Unit—MTU*) of a connection on the route used. In contrast to IPv4, an IPv6 packet is fragmented by the sender only, never in the routers it traverses along the way. The *Fragment* packet-header extension is specified by the Next Header value 0x2C and looks like this:

8	16	29	31	32
Next Header	Reserved	Fragment Offset	Res	M
Identification				

Each of the two reserved fields has to be initialized to null. The 13-bit Fragment Offset specifies the offset (in 8-byte units) of the data following this packet-header extension in relation to the fragmentable part of the original packet. The M bit specifies whether more fragments are to follow (M = 1) or this is the last fragment of an IPv6 packet (M = 0). This corresponds to the segmenting and reassembling in IPv4. The Identification field identifies packets belonging together by a unique number. This number must be assigned only once for each sender/receiver relationship during a packet's lifetime, to avoid confusion with other fragmented IPv6 packets. The details are left to the implementation.

A simple example will help us better understand how fragmenting in IPv6 works. Assume that an IPv6 packet consists of a nonfragmentable part and a fragmentable part. The nonfragmentable part includes the IPv6 packet header and all packet-header extensions that will have to be processed by each node along the route (i.e., all extensions but the Routing header extension). The fragmentable part of this IPv6 packet is decomposed into fragments. Each of these fragments, except the last fragment (bit M = 0), is a multiple of 8 bytes. The resulting fragments will then look like this:

IPv6 Header + Hdr Ext	Fragment Header	First Fragment

IPv6 Header + Hdr Ext	Fragment Header	Second Fragment

...

IPv6 Header + Hdr Ext	Fragment Header	Last Fragment

Sequence of Packet-Header Extensions   In general, an IPv6-capable node has to be able to process packet-header extensions in any arbitrary sequence, even in case of multiple occurrence. One exception is the packet-header extension of the type *Hop-by-Hop Options*. However, RFC 2460 recommends the following sequence:

1. IPv6 packet header
2. *Hop-by-Hop Options*
3. *Routing* packet header extension
4. *Fragment* packet header extension
5. *Destination Options*
6. *Authentication Header*
7. *Encapsulating Security Payload*
8. Payload/packet headers of higher layers.

In addition, the standard requires that none of the packet-header extensions, except *Destination Options*, occur more than once. The last two packet-header extensions, *Authentication Header* and *Encapsulating Security Payload Header*, are also packet-header extensions, but they serve for seamless integration of IPSec in IPv6. For this reason, we will not discuss them any further here. A detailed description of IPSec is included in the following standardized RFCs:

- RFC 2401: Architecture of IPSec
- RFC 2402: Authentication Header
- RFC 2406: Encapsulating Security Payload

23.3   IPv6 IMPLEMENTATION

The implementation of IPv6 in the Linux kernel is in the net/ipv6 directory and in the header file <include/net/ipv6.h>. The code of IPv4 formed the basis for the

IPv6 implementation, so that most things are similar. As in IPv4, packets can reach the IPv6 layer in either of three possible ways. Figure 23–3 shows how a packet travels across the Linux kernel. Packets received by the network card are passed by the function `ipv6_rcv(sbk, dev, pt)` to the data-link layer, and `ip6_xmit(skb)` sends packets created by higher layers or protocols (e.g., UDP or TCP). Finally, special commands, such as `icmpv6_send()`, can be used to create IPv6 packets in the IP layer.

23.3.1 Incoming Packets

`ipv6_rcv()`	**include/net/ipv6.h**
`ip6_rcv_finish()`	**net/ipv6/ip6_input.c**

The `ipv6_rcv()` function accepts IPv6 packets incoming from the lower layer. If an incoming packet is addressed to a different computer, it is dropped immediately by `ipv6_rcv()`. If an IPv6 packet is addressed to the local computer, then the first things

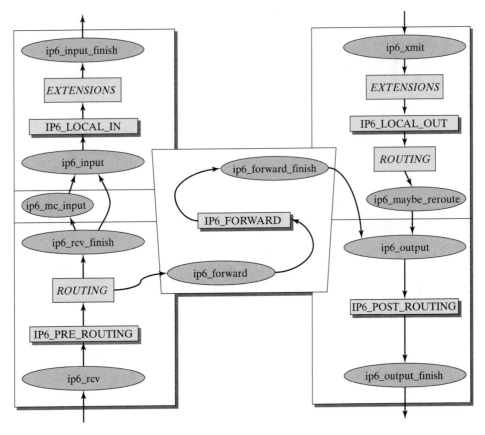

FIGURE 23–3
IPv6 implementation in the Linux kernel.

to do are to check the IPv6 packet header and the packet length and to use the
`skb_trim()` function to correct things, if necessary. If a packet-header extension of the
type *Hop-by-Hop Options* follows next, this extension is processed by the function
`ipv6_parse_hopopts()`. Subsequently, the NETFILTER call NF_IP6_PRE_ROUTING
passes the IPv6 packet to the `ip6_rcv_finish()` function, which invokes one of these
three functions: `ip6_input()`, `ip6_mc_input()`, `ip6_forward()`.

23.3.2 Forwarding Packets

`ip6_forward()`	**include/net/ipv6.h**

`ip6_forward_finish()`	**net/ipv6/ip6_output.c**

The `ip6_rcv_finish()` function invokes `ip6_forward()` when an IPv6 packet has to
be forwarded. The latter checks first to see whether forwarding is enabled; otherwise,
the packet could simply get dropped. Subsequently, the packet's lifetime is checked,
and, if the value in the Hop Limit field is smaller than or equal to one, the packet is actually dropped, and an ICMPv6 message is sent to the corresponding node. If the IPv6
packet is not explicitly sent over this computer on its way to the destination, (which
means that the address of the local node is in the *Routing* packet-header extension),
and if the packet would leave the computer over the same interface on which it arrived
in the local node, then an ICMPv6 message of the type *Redirect* is returned to the
sender. IPv6 packets with a *Link-Local, Multicast* or *Loopback* source address will also
be dropped. The final check is to see whether the length of the new MTU is exceeded
and, if so, to send an ICMPV6_PKT_TOOBIG message to the sender. Finally, the NETFIL-
TER call NF_IP6_FORWARD passes the IPv6 packet to the `ip6_forward_finish()`
function, which, in turn, invokes `ip6_output()`.

23.3.3 Packets Delivered Locally

`ip6_xmit()`	**include/net/ipv6.h**

`ip6_output()`	**include/net/ipv6.h**

`ip6_output_finish()`	**net/ipv6/ip6_output.c**

Packets that have to be delivered locally are taken by the `ip6_rcv_finish()` function
and passed either to `ip6_mc_input()` or directly to `ip6_input()`. However,
`ip6_mc_input()` merely checks to find out whether the multicast packet is addressed
to this computer and, if so, passes it to `ip6_input()`. In turn, `ip6_input()` invokes the
`ip6_input_finish()` function over a NF_IP6_LOCAL_IN netfilter call and assumes
further processing. Initially, `ip6_input_finish()` checks to see whether the next packet-header extension is of the type *Hop-by-Hop Options*; if this is true, this extension will

be skipped. If the next header extension is either a TCP header or a UDP header, then all further packet-header extensions are processed by the ip6_parse_extheaders() function. Figure 23–3 shows this process in the Extensions box. If the IPv6 packet is not for a RAW IPv6 socket, then the next step determines the transport protocol. Similarly to IPv4, the IPv6 implementation uses a hash function over the maximum number of protocols (MAX_INET_PROTOS - 1). Subsequently, the IPv6 packet is passed to the function in charge, which processes the payload. If no transport protocol was identified, the IPv6 packet is passed to the matching RAW IPv6 socket (if present); otherwise, the packet will be dropped and an ICMPV6_UNK_NEXTHDR message returned to the sender.

23.3.4 Transport-Layer Packets

ip6_xmit()	include/net/ipv6.h
ip6_output()	include/net/ipv6.h
ip6_output_finish()	net/ipv6/ip6_output.c

Packets created by the transport layer can be sent via several different functions; one example is the function ip6_xmit(). This function accepts a packet—for example, from the TCPv6 implementation—and then uses the function skb_realloc_headroom() to first create free storage before the packet arrives, if the available storage is too small. Subsequently, the individual parameters for the IPv6 packet header are set, and the packet is passed to the function ip6_maybe_reroute() via the NETFILTER call NF_IP6_LOCAL_OUT, if it does not exceed the MTU. The function ip6_maybe_reroute(), in turn, ensures that an alternative route is found, if an entry in the routing table is no longer up to date. Next, ip6_maybe_reroute() passes the packet to the function ip6_output(), which filters multicast packets again before it sends the packet. Via the NETFILTER call NF_IP6_POST_ROUTING, the IPv6 packet eventually reaches ip6_output_finish(). This latter function uses Neighbour Discovery to figure out the further route for the IPv6 packet and then passes the packet to the transmit functions of the lower layer, from which the IPv6 packet leaves the local computer.

Layer IV—Transport Layer

CHAPTER 24

Transmission Control Protocol (TCP)

The *Transmission Control Protocol* (*TCP*) offers a reliable, byte-oriented, connection-oriented transport service, in contrast to the unreliable datagram service used by the Internet Protocol (IP). Providing these abilities makes the TCP transport protocol very complex. A large number of protocol mechanisms are required to achieve the expected service. This chapter introduces these protocol mechanisms and describes how they were implemented in the Linux kernel.

The TCP protocol belongs to the transport layer and can be used as an alternative to the *User Datagram Protocol* (*UDP*), which offers a connectionless transport service. (See Chapter 25.) The transport layer is immediately below the application layer. Consumers using the service of the protocol are applications, and they reach the services of the TCP protocol instance over the socket interface introduced in Chapters 26 and 27. To implement the transport service, the TCP layer uses the *Internet Protocol* (*IP*). It provides an unreliable, connectionless datagram service, as described in Chapter 14.

24.1 OVERVIEW

The protocol units that exchange TCP instances in this way are called *segments*, and the protocol units of the IP protocol instances are called *IP packets* or *datagrams*.

24.1.1 Requirements on TCP

The TCP protocol was developed in the beginning of the eighties to run on top of the IP protocol and provide a byte-oriented, reliable, connection-oriented transport service. The requirements on such a protocol are as follows [Pete00]:

- to guarantee transmission of byte streams;
- to maintain the transmission order when delivering byte streams;

▨ to deliver not more than one single copy of each data unit passed for transmission;

▨ to transport data for an arbitrary length;

▨ to support synchronization between sender and receiver;

▨ to support flow control at the receiver's end; and

▨ to support several application processes in one system.

To meet these requirements, the TCP protocol provides a reliable, connection-oriented, byte-oriented full-duplex transport service allowing two applications to set up a connection, to send data in both directions reliably, and to finally close this connection. Each TCP connection is set up and terminated gracefully, and all data are delivered before a connection is torn down, provided that the IP protocol behaves in a service-compliant way. From an application's view, the TCP service can be divided into the following properties [Pete00, Come00]:

▨ *Connection orientation*: TCP provides connection-oriented service where an application must first request a connection to a destination and then use the connection to transfer data.

▨ *Peer-to-peer communication*: Each TCP connection has exactly two endpoints.

▨ *Complete reliability*: TCP guarantees that the data sent across a connection will be delivered exactly as sent, with no data missing or out of order.

▨ *Full-duplex communication*: A TCP connection allows data to flow in either direction and allows either application program to send data at any time. TCP can buffer outgoing and incoming data in both directions, making it possible for an application to send data and then to continue computation while the data is being transferred.

▨ *Byte-stream interface*: We say that TCP provides a stream interface in which an application sends a continuous sequence of octets across a connection. That is, TCP does not provide a notion of records, and does not guarantee that data will be delivered to the receiving application in pieces of the same size in which it was transferred by the sending application.

▨ *Reliable connection startup*: TCP requires that, when two applications create a connection, both must agree to the new connection; duplicate packets used in previous connections will not appear to be valid responses or otherwise interfere with the new connection.

▨ *Graceful connection shutdown*: An application program can open a connection, send arbitrary amounts of data, and then request that the connection be shut down. TCP guarantees to deliver all the data reliably before closing the connection.

24.1.2 The TCP Packet Format

Figure 24–1 shows how a TCP segment is structured. TCP groups data from higher layers and adds a header, as will be described below:

▨ The 16-bit SOURCE PORT (SRC PORT) field identifies a process in the sending end system.

Source Port	Destination Port		
Sequence Number			
Acknowledgement Number			
Length	Reserved	Control Flags	Window Size
Checksum			Urgent Pointer
Options (optional)			
Data (optional)			

FIGURE 24–1
The TCP segment format.

- The 16-bit DESTINATION PORT (DEST PORT) field identifies a process in the end system of the communication partner.
- The 32-bit SEQUENCE NUMBER (SEQ) field identifies the sequence number of the first data byte in this segment.
- The 32-bit ACKNOWLEDGEMENT NUMBER (ACK) field means that, if the ACK control bit is set, then this value includes the next sequence number expected by the sender.
- The DATA OFFSET field is 4 bits wide and specifies the number of 32-bit words in the TCP data header. This field is required, because the Options field has a variable size.
- RESERVED (6 bits) is reserved for future use and has to be set to null.
- CONTROL FLAGS are divided into the following flags:

  - URG (Urgent Pointer) points to important data that have to be forwarded immediately.
  - SYN is used to establish connections. SYN = 1 denotes a connection request.
  - ACK shows that the ACKNOWLEDGEMENT NUMBER field includes relevant data.
  - RST can request a connection to be reset. RST = 1 denotes a request to reset a connection.
  - PSH means that, if this bit is set, the TCP instance must immediately pass the data received to the higher layers.
  - FIN means that, if this bit is set, the connection is to be torn down.

- The 16-bit WINDOW (WNDW) field specifies how much additional buffer space is available for more data.
- The 16-bit CHECKSUM field contains a checksum that covers the TCP segment header and the data. As in UDP, a pseudo header is computed. (See Chapter 25.)
- The 16-bit URGENT POINTER (URGPTR) field points to the last byte of important data.
- The OPTIONS field is variable and can contain, for example, the maximum segment size.

24.2   IMPLEMENTING THE TCP PROTOCOL INSTANCE

The protocol instance of the Transmission Control Protocol is one of the most complex parts in the Linux network architecture. The protocol uses a large number of algorithms and features that require extensive mechanisms to implement them. This section explains how these mechanisms are implemented and how they interact in the TCP implementation.

First, we will have a look at "normal" receive and transmit processes in the TCP instance, where we will leave out many details. Too much detail would make it difficult at this point to understand the entire process in the TCP instance and the features of each of the TCP algorithms.

Section 24.3 discusses connection management—how TCP connections are established and torn down; Section 24.4 discusses each of the algorithms used to exchange data (e.g., congestion control and window scaling). Finally, Section 24.5 will introduce the tasks of the TCP protocol instance and how its timers are managed.

The TCP protocol instance is extremely complex. It consists of a large number of functions, inline functions, structures, and macros. In addition, the large number of algorithms used within the TCP protocol makes its description rather difficult. For this reason, we will begin with a general overview of the process involved when receiving, and then when sending, a TCP segment. A detailed discussion of the large number of algorithms used in TCP will follow in Section 24.4. In addition, this section assumes that data is exchanged over an existing connection. The complex management of TCP connections is dealt with in Section 24.3.

24.2.1   Handling Incoming TCP Segments

The transport protocol for an incoming packet is selected early, by the time it is needed in the IP layer, to be able to pass the packet to the appropriate protocol-handling routine in the transport layer. (See Section 14.2.5.) In the TCP instance, this task is handled by the `tcp_v4_rcv()` function (`net/ipv4/tcp_ipv4.c`).

Figure 24–2 shows how packets are processed in the TCP instance, and Figure 24–3 gives an overview of what happens when the TCP instance receives a segment.

`tcp_v4_rcv()`	`net/ipv4/tcp_ipv4.c`

`tcp_v4_rcv(skb, len)` checks for whether the packet in the form of the socket buffer, `skb`, is really addressed to this computer (`skb->pkt_type == PACKET_HOST`). If so, then the IP packet header is removed, and the protocol processing continues; otherwise, the socket buffer is dropped.

`tcp_v4_lookup()` searches the hash table of the active socket for the socket or sock structure. The IP addresses and the ports of the two communication partners and the network device index, `skb->dst->rt_iif` at which this segment arrived are the parameters used. If a socket with these addresses and ports can be found, the `tcp_v4_do_rcv()` function continues with an appropriate handling routine, depending on the connection state. If no socket can be found, then `tcp_send_reset()` sends a RESET segment.

`tcp_v4_do_rcv()`	`net/ipv4/tcp_ipv4.c`

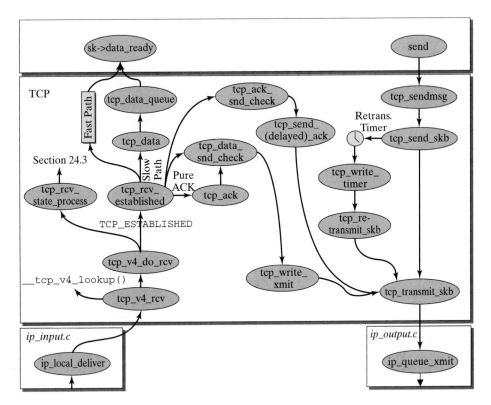

FIGURE 24–2
Partial representation of how packets are handled in the TCP instance.

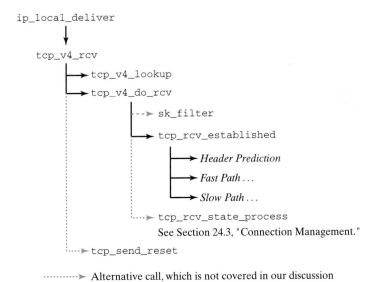

FIGURE 24–3
Overview of the process for receiving a segment in the TCP instance.

First, if socket filters are activated, the `sk_filter()` function checks the socket buffer. If the result is negative, the packet is dropped. Otherwise, the process continues with either of the following functions, depending on the TCP connection state (`sk->state`):

- TCP_ESTABLISHED: With a connection established, the socket buffer is further processed in `tcp_rcv_established()` (as is shown later).
- If the socket is in one of the *other states*, the function `tcp_rcv_state_process()` processes the socket buffer. This function is described in Section 24.3.

The latter cases—how all packets not arriving in the TCP_ESTABLISHED are handled—are introduced in Section 24.3. This section will explain how the TCP *finite state machine* was implemented. As we can already see at this point, the implementation of the TCP instance in the Linux kernel deviates from the usual concept of such an implementation. In educational operating systems, the state machine would probably be implemented with a central `case` statement to branch, depending on the state. However, real-world systems often prefer a "fast" over an "elegant" implementation for performance reasons.

At this point, let's return to the `tcp_rcv_established()` function and how it handles packets as they arrive. Receiving packets over an established connection is the most common case, but we will not discuss it in detail for lack of space. The TCP protocol has a large number of algorithms, which are discussed in Section 24.4 rather than in this section. This approach allows us to concentrate on the path a packet takes through the TCP instance without having to discuss each algorithm. Section 24.4 describes the features of these algorithms and how they were implemented.

`tcp_rcv_established()`	**net/ipv4/tcp_input.c**

`tcp_rcv_established(sk, skb, th, len)` handles TCP packets incoming over an established connection (i.e., in the data-exchange phase (TCP_ESTABLISHED)). Once again, this function is a good example of the intended objective: to achieve efficient protocol handling. In fact, `tcp_rcv_established()` distinguishes between two paths for packet-handling purposes:

- *Fast Path* is used to handled the ideal case of an incoming packet. The most common cases occurring in a normal TCP connection should be detected as fast as possible and processed optimally, without having to test for marginal cases, which normally won't occur in this situation.
- *Slow Path* is used for all packets not corresponding to the ideal case and requiring some special handling. For example, if a packet had to be manipulated to deal with a transmission error, or if it is a retransmitted packet, it is processed in Slow Path by appropriate error-correction mechanisms.

Fast Path and Slow Path are not distinguished specifically in the Linux kernel. It fact, this differentiation was proposed by Van Jacobson [Jaco90a] at the beginning of the nineties, and it was implemented in BSD UNIX in a similar form. A study in [Stev94b] showed that Fast Path was applied in from 97% to 100% of all packets incoming over a

TCP connection within a local area network and in from 83% to 99% of all cases in a WAN connection. Though these results are not necessarily representative and depend on the actual load of the networks, they show that it appears useful to differentiate between Slow Path and Fast Path.

Packets are processed in Fast Path in the following two situations:

- The segment received is a pure ACK segment for the data sent last (no *duplicate ACK*).
- The segment received includes data expected next, so that they are consecutive with the data received until then.

Fast Path is not accessed in the following situations (and so a detailed protocol-handling process is performed in Slow Path):

- *Unexpected TCP flags*: The process continues in Slow Path if a SYN, URG, FIN, or RST flag is set. These cases are detected by the *Header Prediction* described later.
- If the sequence number of an incoming segment does not correspond to the sequence number expected next (tp->rcv_nxt), then the segment is either a retransmitted segment or an out-of-order segment.
- *Both communication partners exchange data*: Fast Path cannot be used except in situations where the relevant TCP instance either only sends or only receives (i.e., where either the sequence number or the acknowledgement number remains constant).
- The current TCP instance sent a *Zero Window* (i.e., no transmit credit can currently be granted to the communication partner).
- *Unexpected TCP options* are processed in Slow Path. The Timestamp option is the only option that can be handled in Fast Path.

To make the differentiation between Fast Path and Slow Path worthwhile, Fast Path has to be detected quickly and reliably. Most of the cases mentioned above can be detected by the so-called *Header Prediction*, which uses a simple comparative operation on the Header Length, Flags, and Window Size fields and a predicted value to decide whether the Fast Path can be used:

```
/* pred_flags is 0xS?10 << 16 + snd_wnd
 * if header_prediction is to be made
 * 'S' will always be tp->tcp_header_len >> 2
 * '?' will be 0 for the fast path, otherwise pred_flags is 0 to
 *       turn it off (when there are holes in the receive space
 *       for instance), PSH flag is ignored.
 */

if ((tcp_flag_word(th) & TCP_HP_BITS) == tp->pred_flags &&
        TCP_SKB_CB(skb)->seq == tp->rcv_nxt)
{ (...FAST PATH...) }
else
{ (...SLOW PATH...) }
```

The comparative value (tp->pred_flags) is computed in the tcp_fast_path_on() function in advance, which means that it activates processing over the Fast Path (if the packets meet the preconditions):

```
static __inline__ void __tcp_fast_path_on(struct tcp_opt *tp, u32 snd_wnd)
{
        tp->pred_flags = htonl((tp->tcp_header_len << 26) |
                               ntohl(TCP_FLAG_ACK) |
                               snd_wnd);
}
static __inline__ void tcp_fast_path_on(struct tcp_opt *tp)
{
        __tcp_fast_path_on(tp, tp->snd_wnd>>tp->snd_wscale);
}
```

Should it ever happen that the TCP connection gets into a situation where Fast Path cannot be used, then the problem is solved by simply writing a null to the comparative operator of the Header Prediction—for example, much like what is done when sending a Zero Window in tcp_select_window().

Fast Path   Once an incoming segment has successfully passed the Header Prediction, its processing in the Fast Path begins, where the following operations are done:

- The sequence number is checked to filter out-of-order packets (TCP_SKB_CB(skb)->seq == tp->rcv_nxt).
- The Timestamp option is checked, but only by evaluating the length of the packet header. All other options fail the Header Prediction, which means that a simple check of the packet-header length is sufficient. Subsequently, the Timestamp values, TSval and TSecr, are read directly. (See Section 24.4.1.) If the subsequent PAWS check fails, then the process continues in Slow Path; otherwise, the segment is all right. If the condition to update the tp->ts_recent timestamp is met, it is accepted by tcp_store_ts_recent().
- Subsequently, the packet-header length is compared with the segment length to distinguish pure acknowledgement packets from payload packets, and segments that are too short are dropped.

  ▷ *ACK segment*: The acknowledgement number, if present, in a packet that contains no payload is processed in tcp_ack. Subsequently, __kfree_skb() releases the socket buffer, which completes the process of handling this segment. Finally, tcp_data_snd_check() checks for whether local packets can be sent.
  ▷ *Data segment*: In this case, the segment contains the data expected next (was previously checked).

  At this point, the only thing tested is whether the payload can be copied directly into the user-address space:

    • If the payload can be copied directly into the user-address space, then the statistics of this connection are updated, the relevant process is informed, the payload is copied into the receive memory of the process, the TCP packet header is removed, and, finally, the variable with the sequence number expected next is updated.

- If the payload cannot be directly copied into the user-address space, then the availability of buffer memory in the socket is checked, statistical information is updated, the TCP packet header is removed, the packet is added to the end of the socket's receive queue, and, finally, the sequence number expected next is set.

▶ All management tasks arising from the receipt of a payload segment are completed in the `tcp_event_data_rcv()` function.

▶ If the segment's acknowledgement number confirms data not yet acknowledged, then the actions required are done in `tcp_ack()`. Subsequently, `tcp_data_snd_check()` initiates the transmission of waiting data that may be sent now that the acknowledgement was received.

▶ Finally, the process checks whether an acknowledgement has to be sent as response to the receipt of this segment, in the form of either *Delayed ACK* or *Quick ACK*.

Slow Path   A packet is processed in Slow Path if the prerequisites for Fast Path are not met or the Header Prediction fails. Slow Path processing considers all possibilities of a segment received over an established connection. The following operations are done consecutively:

▨ The checksum is verified.

▨ The Timestamp option is checked in `tcp_fast_parse_options()`, and the PAWS check works out whether the packet has to be dropped (`tcp_paws_discard()`).

▨ Using the sequence number, `tcp_sequence()` checks for whether the packet arrived out of order (OfO). If it is an OfO packet, then the *QuickAck* mode is activated to send acknowledgements as fast as possible.

▨ If the RST flag is set, `tcp_reset()` resets the connection (changes connection state and deactivates timer), and the socket buffer is freed.

▨ If the TCP packet header contains a Timestamp option, then `tcp_replace_ts_recent()` updates the *recent timestamp* stored locally.

▨ If the SYN flag is set to signal an error case in an established connection, then `tcp_reset()` resets the connection.

▨ If the ACK flag is set, the `tcp_ack()` function processes the acknowledgement.

▨ If the URG flag denotes that the packet contains priority data, then this data is processed in `tcp_urg()`.

▨ `tcp_data()` and `tcp_data_queue()` process the payload. Among other things, this includes a check for sufficient space in the receive buffer and insertion of the socket buffer into the receive queue or the out-of-order queue.

▨ Finally, two methods, `tcp_data_snd_check()` and `tcp_ack_snd_check()`, are invoked to check on whether data or acknowledgements waiting can be sent.

These actions complete the process of handling a received TCP segment. This section is only an overview of the rough process involved in handling incoming segments. At some point, we mentioned functions invoked in Fast Path or Slow Path, but we didn't explain them in detail. For this reason, we will briefly describe these functions in the following subsection.

Helper Functions to Handle Incoming TCP Segments

`tcp_ack()`	net/ipv4/tcp_input.c

`tcp_ack(sk, th, ack_seq, ack, len)` handles all tasks involved in receiving an acknowledgement packet or a data packet with valid ACK number (*piggybacking*):

- Adapt the receive window (`tcp_ack_update_window()`).
- Delete acknowledged packets from the *retransmission* queue (`tcp_clean_rtx_queue()`).
- Check for *Zero Window Probing* acknowledgement.
- Adapt the congestion window (`tcp_may_raise_cwnd()`).
- Update the packet round-trip time (*RTT*) and the timeout for packet retransmissions (*Retransmission TimeOut—RTO*).
- Retransmit packets and update the retransmission timer.
- Activate the Fast Retransmit mode, if necessary.

`tcp_event_data_recv()`	net/ipv4/tcp_input.c

`tcp_event_data_recv(tp, skb)` handles all management work required for receiving of payload. This includes updating the maximum segment size, the timestamp, and the timer for delayed acknowledgements (*Acknowledgement Timeout—ATO*).

`tcp_data_snd_check()`	net/ipv4/tcp_input.c

`tcp_data_snd_check(sk)` checks on whether data is ready and waiting in the transmit queue, and it starts the transmission, if permitted by the transmit window of the sliding-window mechanism and the congestion-control window. The actual transmission is initiated by `tcp_write_xmit()`:

```
static __inline__ void tcp_data_snd_check(struct sock *sk) {
    struct sk_buff *skb = sk->tp_pinfo.af_tcp.send_head;
    struct tcp_opt *tp = &(sk->tp_pinfo.af_tcp);

    if (skb != NULL)
    {
    if (after(TCP_SKB_CB(skb)->end_seq, tp->snd_una + tp->snd_wnd) ||
            tcp_packets_in_flight(tp) >= tp->snd_cwnd ||
            tcp_write_xmit(sk))
                    tcp_check_probe_timer(sk, tp);
    }
    tcp_check_space(sk);
}
```

tcp_ack_snd_check()	net/ipv4/tcp_input.c

`tcp_ack_snd_check(sk, ofo_possible)` checks for various cases where acknowledgements can be sent. Also, it checks the type of acknowledgement (i.e., whether it should be quick or delayed):

```
static __inline__ void tcp_ack_snd_check(struct sock *sk) {
    struct tcp_opt *tp = &(sk->tp_pinfo.af_tcp);
    if (!tcp_ack_scheduled(tp)) {
            /* We sent a data segment already. */
            return;
    }
                /* More than one full frame received... */
    if ((((tp->rcv_nxt - tp->rcv_wup) > tp->ack.rcv_mss
                /* ... and right edge of window advances far enough.
                 * (tcp_recvmsg() will send ACK otherwise). Or...*/
            && __tcp_select_window(sk) >= tp->rcv_wnd) ||
                /* We ACK each frame or... */
            tcp_in_quickack_mode(tp) ||
                /* We have out of order data. */
            (skb_peek(&tp->out_of_order_queue) != NULL)
    {
            tcp_send_ack(sk); /* Then ack it now */
    }else
    {
            tcp_send_delayed_ack(sk); /* Else, send delayed ack. */
    }
}
```

tcp_fast_parse_options()	net/ipv4/tcp_input.c

`tcp_fast_parse_options(sk, th, tp)` handles the Timestamp option in the TCP packet header. (See Section 24.4.1.) `tcp_parse_options()` is invoked if the packet header contains several options.

Handling Incoming Packets in Other States

tcp_rcv_state_process()	net/ipv4/tcp_input.c

The `tcp_rcv_state_process()` function processes incoming segments when the TCP connection is not in the ESTABLISHED state. It mainly handles state transitions and management work for the connection. The detailed process is described in Section 24.3.

24.2.2 Sending TCP Segments

This section describes how payload is sent over a TCP instance (i.e., how TCP segments containing payload are transmitted). The transmission of acknowledgements (ACKs) is initiated by incoming TCP segments or by the *Delayed ACK* timer. (See Sections 24.2.1 and 24.5.)

A TCP instance uses the send() system call to send payload. The send() system call causes the tcp_sendmsg() function to be invoked. This function is present as a handling routine for this system call in the tcp_prot structure (net/ipv4/tcp_ipv4.c). Figure 24–4 shows the invocation hierarchy during the process of sending payload over the TCP instance.

`tcp_sendmsg()`	**net/ipv4/tcp.c**

tcp_sendmsg(sock, msg, size) copies payload from the user-address space into the kernel and starts sending this data in the form of TCP segments. Before it starts sending, however, it checks on whether the connection has already been established and on whether it is in the TCP_ESTABLISHED state. If no connection has been established yet, the system call waits in wait_for_tcp_connect() for a connection.

The next step computes the maximum segment size (tcp_current_mss) and starts copying the data from the user-address space. First, it checks for whether a "half empty" segment is present at the end of the socket's transmit queue (tp->write_queue), which could be used to pack data. Subsequently, or if no small segment was available, tcp_alloc_skb() creates new socket buffers. The data to be sent is copied from the user-address space into the socket buffers, and tcp_send_skb() is invoked to order data within the socket's transmit queue.

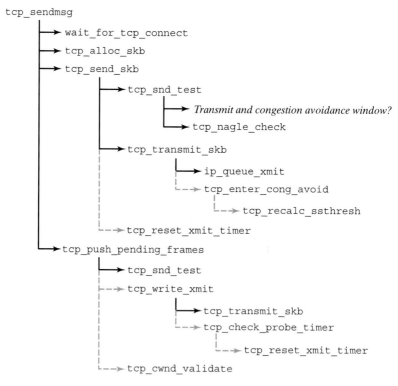

FIGURE 24–4
Sending payload in the TCP protocol instance.

Finally, the __tcp_push_pending_frames() routine takes TCP segments from the socket transmit queue (tp->write_queue) and starts sending them.

tcp_send_skb()	net/ipv4/tcp_output.c

tcp_send_skb(sk, skb, force_queue, cur_mss) adds the socket buffer, skb, to the socket transmit queue (sk->write_queue) and decides whether transmission can be started or it has to wait in the queue. It uses the tcp_snd_test() routine to make this decision. If the result is negative, the socket buffer remains in the transmit queue.

If the result is positive, it starts sending the present segment, that is, it uses the tcp_transmit_skb() function to complete the TCP packet header and pass the segment to the IP instance. As shown in Figure 24–2, the latter function is also used in other places within the TCP instance for this purpose.

The timer for automatic retransmission is started automatically in tcp_reset_xmit_timer(), if the transmit process was successful. This timer is initiated if no acknowledgement for this packet arrived after a specific time.

tcp_snd_test()	include/net/tcp.h

tcp_snd_test(tp, skb, cur_mss, nonagle)() is an inline method that checks on whether the TCP segment, skb, may be sent at the time of invocation. It verifies the criteria specified in RFC 1122 to ensure standard-compliant behavior and, mainly, that there is sufficient space in the transmit and congestion-control windows and what the Nagle algorithm says with regard to sending this packet. The behavior of the participating algorithms is described in Section 24.4.

```
/* This checks if the data bearing packet SKB (usually tp->send_head)
 * should be put on the wire right now.
 */
static __inline__ int tcp_snd_test(struct tcp_opt *tp, struct sk_buff *skb,
                        unsigned cur_mss, int nonagle)
{       /*      RFC 1122 - Section 4.2.3.4:
         *      We must queue if
         *      a) The right edge of this frame exceeds the window
         *      b) There are packets in flight and we have a small segment
         *         [SWS avoidance and Nagle algorithm]
         *         (part of SWS is done on packetization)
         *         Minshall version sounds: there are no _small_
         *         segments in flight. (tcp_nagle_check)
         *      c) We have too many packets 'in flight'
         *
         *      Don't use the nagle rule for urgent data (or
         *      for the final FIN -DaveM).
         */
return ((nonagle==1 || tp->urg_mode
        || !tcp_nagle_check(tp, skb, cur_mss, nonagle)) &&
        ((tcp_packets_in_flight(tp) < tp->snd_cwnd) ||
        (TCP_SKB_CB(skb)->flags & TCPCB_FLAG_FIN)) &&
        !after(TCP_SKB_CB(skb)->end_seq, tp->snd_una + tp->snd_wnd));
}
```

`tcp_transmit_skb()`	**include/linux/tcp_output.c**

`tcp_transmit_skb(sk, skb)` is responsible for completing the TCP segment in the socket buffer, `skb`, and for subsequently sending it over the Internet Protocol. To this end, it first fills the TCP packet header with the appropriate values from the opt structure—for example, much like an explicit transmit credit specified by `tcp_select_window()`. `tcp_syn_build_options()` registers the TCP options for SYN packets, and `tcp_build_and_update_options()` registers the options for all other packets.

Subsequently, all actions required to send a payload-carrying segment or a segment with its ACK flag set are executed:

- If the ACK flag is set, the number of permitted Quick ACK packets is decremented in the `tcp_event_ack_sent()` method (provided that the connection is in the Quick ACK mode). Subsequently, the timer for delayed ACKs is stopped, because the next step sends an acknowledgement.

- If the segment to be sent carries payload, we first have to check for whether an interval corresponding to the retransmission timeout has elapsed since the last data segment (stored in `tp->lsntime`) was sent. If this is the case, then the congestion window, `snd_cwnd`, is set to the minimum value (`tcp_cwnd_restart`), as specified in RFC 2861.

Subsequently, the function pointer `tp->af_specific->queue_xmit()`, which references the corresponding transmit function—depending on the Internet Protocol version (e.g., `ip_queue_xmit()` for IPv4)—passes the socket buffer to the IP layer for transmission.

Finally, the `tcp_enter_cwr()` method adapts the threshold value for the slow-start algorithm. This completes the transmit process for the TCP segment within the TCP instance, unless no acknowledgement arrives for this packet during the retransmission timeout, so that it would have to be retransmitted; see details in Section 24.5.

`tcp_push_pending_frames()`	**include/net/tcp.h**

`tcp_push_pending_frames` checks for whether there are segments ready for transmission that couldn't be sent during the regular transmission attempt. If this is the case, then `tcp_write_xmit()` initiates the transmission of these segments, if the `tcp_snd_test()` function agrees:

```
struct sk_buff *skb = tp->send_head;

if (skb)
{
if (!tcp_skb_is_last(sk, skb))
        nonagle = 1;
if (!tcp_snd_test(tp, skb, cur_mss, nonagle) ||
        tcp_write_xmit(sk))
```

```
            tcp_check_probe_timer(sk, tp);
}
tcp_cwnd_validate(sk, tp);
```

tcp_write_xmit()	net/ipv4/tcp_output.c

`tcp_write_xmit(sk)` continues to send segments from the transmit queue of the socket, `sk`, as long as it is allowed to do so by `tcp_snd_test()`. It checks for whether the conditions of TCP algorithms (e.g., slow-start method and congestion-control algorithm) are maintained. Data segments can also be fragmented (`tcp_fragment()`) before the maximum segment size is exceeded. `tcp_transmit_skb()` handles the final completion of the TCP packet and passes it to the Internet Protocol.

tcp_retransmit_skb()	include/linux/tcp_output.c

`tcp_retransmit_skb(sk, skb)` retransmits a TCP segment. The segment may have to be fragmented (`tcp_fragment()`), or it might be joined with the next segment (`tcp_retrans_try_collapse()`).

tcp_send_ack()	include/linux/tcp_output.c

`tcp_send_ack(sk)` is responsible for building and sending ACK packets. For this purpose, it requests a socket buffer and assigns the corresponding values to this buffer. Subsequently, it uses `tcp_transmit_skb()` to send an ACK segment.

24.2.3 Data Structures of the TCP Instance

struct tcp_opt	include/net/sock.h

The `tcp_opt` structure contains all variables of the TCP algorithms for a TCP connection. The names of these variables were adopted from RFCs 793 and 1122 for the sake of better understanding (except for uppercase and lowercase). This facilitates reading the source text and comparing with the TCP standard.

The `tcp_opt` structure is very complex, which shouldn't come as a surprise considering the complexity of the TCP protocol and the large number of its algorithms. A detailed description of the `tcp_opt` structure would go beyond the scope and volume of this chapter, especially because they are well documented and because the variable names correspond to the TCP standard. Nevertheless, we will list the variables and their tasks, to facilitate quick references when reading the following sections.

Among other things, the `tcp_opt` structure consists of variables for the following algorithms or protocol mechanisms:

- sequence and acknowledgement numbers;
- flow-control information;
- packet round-trip time;

■ congestion control and congestion handling;

■ timers;

■ TCP options in the packet header; and

■ automatic and selective packet retransmission.

```
struct tcp_opt
{
  int  tcp_header_len;    /* Bytes of tcp header to send              */

  /* Header prediction flags * 0x5?10 << 16 + snd_wnd in net byte order  */
  __u32 pred_flags;

  __u32 rcv_nxt;          /* What we want to receive next             */
  __u32 snd_nxt;          /* Next sequence we send                    */
  __u32 snd_una;          /* First byte we want an ack for            */
  __u32 snd_sml;          /* Last byte of most recently xmitted small packet */
  __u32 rcv_tstamp;       /* timestamp of last received ACK (for keepalives) */
  __u32 lsndtime;         /* timestamp of last sent data packet (for restart
                                       window)                        */

  /* Delayed ACK control data */
  struct
  {
      __u8 pending;           /* ACK is pending                       */
      __u8 quick;             /* Scheduled number of quick acks       */
      __u8 pingpong;          /* The session is interactive           */
      __u8 blocked;           /* Delayed ACK was blocked by socket lock */
      __u32 ato;              /* Predicted tick of soft clock         */
      unsigned long timeout;  /* Currently scheduled timeout          */
      __u32 lrcvtime;         /* timestamp of last received data packet */
      __u16 last_seg_size;    /* Size of last incoming segment        */
      __u16 rcv_mss;          /* MSS used for delayed ACK decisions   */
  } ack;
  __u32 snd_wl1;          /* Sequence for window update               */
  __u32 snd_wnd;          /* The window we expect to receive          */
  __u32 max_window;       /* Maximal window ever seen from peer       */
  __u32 pmtu_cookie;      /* Last pmtu seen by socket */
  __u16 mss_cache;        /* Cached effective mss, not including SACKS */
  __u16 mss_clamp;        /* Maximal mss, negotiated at connection setup */
  __u16 ext_header_len;   /* Network protocol overhead (IP/IPv6 options) */
  __u8 ca_state;          /* State of fast-retransmit machine         */
  __u8 retransmits;       /* Number of unrecovered RTO timeouts.      */
  __u8 reordering;        /* Packet reordering metric. */
  __u8 queue_shrunk;      /* Write queue has been shrunk recently.    */
  __u8 defer_accept;      /* User waits for some data after accept     */

  /* RTT measurement */
  __u8 backoff;           /* backoff                                  */
```

```
    __u32 srtt;                     /* smoothed round trip time << 3      */
    __u32 mdev;                     /* medium deviation                   */
    __u32 mdev_max;                 /* maximal mdev for the last rtt period */
    __u32 rttvar;                   /* smoothed mdev_max                  */
    __u32 rtt_seq;                  /* sequence number to update rttvar   */
    __u32 rto;                      /* retransmit timeout                 */
    __u32 packets_out;              /* Packets which are "in flight"      */
    __u32 left_out;                 /* Packets which leaved network       */
    __u32 retrans_out;              /* Retransmitted packets out */

/* Slow start and congestion control (see also Nagle and Karn & Part.) */
    __u32 snd_ssthresh;             /* Slow start size threshold          */
    __u32 snd_cwnd;                 /* Sending congestion window          */
    __u16 snd_cwnd_cnt;             /* Linear increase counter            */
    __u16 snd_cwnd_clamp;           /* Do not allow snd_cwnd to grow above this */
    __u32 snd_cwnd_used;
    __u32 snd_cwnd_stamp;

/* Two commonly used timers in both sender and receiver paths.          */
    unsigned long        timeout;
    struct timer_list    retransmit_timer;  /* Resend (no ack)           */
    struct timer_list    delack_timer;      /* Ack delay                 */
    struct sk_buff_head out_of_order_queue;         /* Out of order segments go
                                                       here */
    struct tcp_func *af_specific;   /* AF_INET{4,6} specific operations  */
    struct sk_buff  *send_head;     /* Front of stuff to transmit        */
    __u32 rcv_wnd;                  /* Current receiver window           */
    __u32 rcv_wup;                  /* rcv_nxt on last window update sent */
    __u32 write_seq;                /* Tail(+1) of data held in tcp send buffer */
    __u32 pushed_seq;               /* Last pushed seq, required to talk to windows */
    __u32 copied_seq;               /* Head of yet unread data           */
/* Options received (usually on last packet, some only on SYN packets)  */
    char        tstamp_ok,          /* TIMESTAMP seen on SYN packet      */
                wscale_ok,          /* Wscale seen on SYN packet         */
                sack_ok;            /* SACK seen on SYN packet           */
    char        saw_tstamp;         /* Saw TIMESTAMP on last packet      */
    __u8        snd_wscale;         /* Window scaling received from sender */
    __u8        rcv_wscale;         /* Window scaling to send to receiver */
    __u8        nonagle;            /* Disable Nagle algorithm?          */
    __u8        keepalive_probes;   /* num of allowed keep alive probes  */

/* PAWS/RTTM data */
    __u32       rcv_tsval;          /* Time stamp value                  */
    __u32       rcv_tsecr;          /* Time stamp echo reply             */
    __u32       ts_recent;          /* Time stamp to echo next           */
    long        ts_recent_stamp;    /* Time we stored ts_recent (for aging) */

/* SACKs data */
    __u16       user_mss;           /* mss requested by user in ioctl    */
```

```
__u8        dsack;          /* D-SACK is scheduled                  */
__u8        eff_sacks;          /* Size of SACK array to send with next packet */
struct tcp_sack_block duplicate_sack[1]; /* D-SACK block           */
struct tcp_sack_block selective_acks[4]; /* The SACKS themselves   */

__u32       window_clamp;   /* Maximal window to advertise          */
__u32       rcv_ssthresh;   /* Current window clamp                 */
__u8        probes_out;     /* unanswered 0 window probes           */
__u8        num_sacks;      /* Number of SACK blocks                */
__u16       advmss;         /* Advertised MSS                       */
__u8        syn_retries;    /* num of allowed syn retries           */
__u8        ecn_flags;      /* ECN status bits.                     */
__u16       prior_ssthresh; /* ssthresh saved at recovery start     */
__u32       ost_out;        /* Lost packets                         */
__u32       sacked_out;     /* SACK'd packets                       */
__u32       fackets_out;    /* FACK'd packets                       */
__u32       high_seq;       /* snd_nxt at onset of congestion       */
__u32       retrans_stamp;  /* Timestamp of the last retransmit, also used in
                               SYN-SENT to remember stamp of the first SYN */
__u32       undo_marker;    /* tracking retrans started here.       */
int  undo_retrans;   /* number of undoable retransmissions.         */
__u32    syn_seq;    /* Seq of received SYN.                         */
__u32    fin_seq;    /* Seq of received FIN.                         */
__u32    urg_seq;    /* Seq of received urgent pointer              */
__u16    urg_data;   /* Saved octet of OOB data and control flags   */
__u8     pending;    /* Scheduled timer event                       */
__u8     urg_mode;   /* In urgent mode                              */
__u32    snd_up;     /* Urgent pointer                              */
    /* The syn_wait_lock is necessary only to avoid tcp_get_info having
     * to grab the main lock sock while browsing the listening hash
     * (otherwise it's deadlock prone).                             */
rwlock_t                syn_wait_lock;
struct tcp_listen_opt   *listen_opt;
    /* FIFO of established children */
struct open_request     *accept_queue;
struct open_request     *accept_queue_tail;
int          write_pending;         /* A write to socket waits to start. */
unsigned int keepalive_time;        /* time before keep alive takes place */
unsigned int keepalive_intvl;       /* interval between keep alive probes */
int          linger2;
};
```

struct tcp_skb_cb	include/net/tcp.h

```
struct tcp_skb_cb {
    ...
        __u32        seq;               /* Starting sequence number*/
```

```
        __u32           end_seq;        /* SEQ + FIN + SYN + datalen*/
        __u32           when;           /* used to compute rtt's*/
        __u8            flags;          /* TCP header flags*/

        #define TCPCB_FLAG_FIN          0x01
        #define TCPCB_FLAG_SYN          0x02
        #define TCPCB_FLAG_RST          0x04
        #define TCPCB_FLAG_PSH          0x08
        #define TCPCB_FLAG_ACK          0x10
        #define TCPCB_FLAG_URG          0x20
        #define TCPCB_FLAG_ECE          0x40
        #define TCPCB_FLAG_CWR          0x80

        __u8            sacked;         /* State flags for SACK/FACK*/
        #define TCPCB_SACKED_ACKED      0x01 /* SKB ACK'd by a SACK
                                             block*/
        #define TCPCB_SACKED_RETRANS    0x02 /* SKB retransmitted*/

        __u16           urg_ptr;        /* Valid w/URG flags is set*/
        __u32           ack_seq;        /* Sequence number ACK'd*/
};
```

The preceding structure represents the control block of a packet. This type of structure is included in each packet.

struct tcphdr	include/linux/tcp.h

```
struct tcphdr {
        __u16           source;
        __u16           dest;
        __u32           seq;
        __u32           ack_seq;
#if defined(__LITTLE_ENDIAN_BITFIELD)
        __u16           res1:4, doff:4, fin:1, syn:1, rst:1,
                        psh:1, ack:1, urg:1, ece:1, cwr:1;
#elif defined(__BIG_ENDIAN_BITFIELD)
        __u16           doff:4, res1:4, cwr:1, ece:1, urg:1,
                        ack:1, psh:1, rst:1, syn:1, fin:1;
#else
#error "Adjust your <asm/byteorder.h> defines"
#endif
        __u16           window;
        __u16           check;
        __u16           urg_ptr;
};
```

Section 24.1.2 introduced the protocol header. The tcphdr structure maps this header, depending on the memory sequence.

24.3   CONNECTION MANAGEMENT

Being a connection-oriented protocol that supports a number of additional mechanisms, such as packet transmission in the correct order or urgent data, the TCP protocol is extremely complex. The protocol machine shown in Figure 24–5 is characterized by a total of twelve states. This complexity calls for extensive management of the current state of active connections.

24.3.1   The TCP State Machine

A TCP connection's state is stored in the `state` field of the associated `sock` structure. The response to the receipt of packets is different, depending on the state, so this state has to be polled for each incoming packet. There are three phases: the connection-establishment

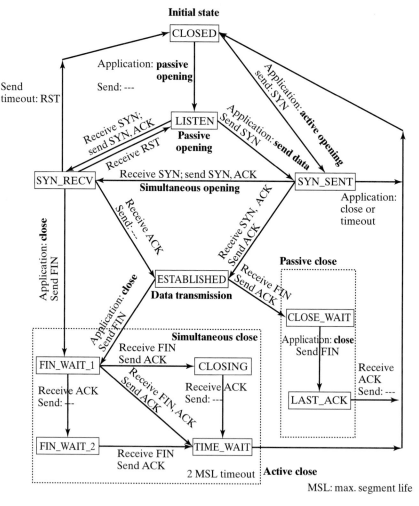

FIGURE 24–5
The TCP state automaton.

phase, the data-transmission phase, and the connection-teardown phase. Section 24.4 describes the protocol mechanisms of the data-transmission phase in detail. This section discusses the connection-establishment and connection-teardown phases.

As shown in Section 24.2, `tcp_rcv_state_process()` (net/ipv4/tcp_input.c) is the most important function for connection management, as long as the connection has not yet been established. Packets in the TIME_WAIT state are the only packets handled earlier in the `tcp_v4_rcv()` function.

`tcp_rcv_state_process()`	net/ipv4/tcp_input.c

The `tcp_rcv_state_process()` function handles mainly state transitions and the management work for the connection. Depending on the connection state, there are different actions when a packet is received:

- In the CLOSED state: The packet is dropped.
- In the LISTEN state: If ACK or SYN flags are set, then the connection establishment is registered, and data is ignored.
- In the SYN_SENT state: `tcp_rcv_synsent_state_process()` checks for correct connection establishment, and the connection is moved to the ESTABLISHED state. If this fails, then the remaining flags are processed.
- If the PAWS check finds an error, then a DUPACK is returned, and the function is exited.
- Subsequently, the sequence number is checked, and if a packet arrived out of order, then a DUPACK is returned and the packet is dropped.
- If the RST flag is active, the connection is reset and the packet is dropped.
- If a timestamp is present in the segment header, the recent timestamp stored locally is updated.
- If the SYN flag is set, but invalid due to the sequence number, the connection is reset and the packet is dropped.
- If the ACK flag is active, the next action is different, depending on the state:

  - In the SYN_RCVD state: The connection state changes to ESTABLISHED, and the acknowledgement is processed.
  - In the FIN_WAIT_1 state: The connection state changes to FIN-WAIT2 and the TIMEWAIT timer is set.
  - In the CLOSING state: Transition to the TIMEWAIT state occurs, if the packet is not out of order.
  - In the LAST_ACK state: The socket is reset, and the state changes to the CLOSED state, if the packet is not out of order.

- If the URG flag is active, then the urgent data is processed (by the `tcp_urg()` function).
- If the packet contains payload, then this data is processed or dropped, or an RST packet is sent, depending on the connection state.
- The packet is deleted in all other cases.

24.3.2 Establishing a Connection

A connection to the partner instance has to be established before a TCP instance can send payload. A connection is established on the basis of the so-called *three-way handshake* to reduce the probability of establishing a wrong connection. This could happen, for example, if a connection is established more than once, because of timeouts, or when a connection is established between two TCP protocol instances before an existing connection is reset.

To begin establishing a connection, both TCP protocol instances define an initial value for the sequence number (Initial Sequence Number—ISN). These initial values are exchanged and acknowledged between the participating TCP protocol instances in the three-way handshake.

The connection diagram shown in Figure 24–5 has the following states for the connection establishment phase:

- LISTEN: After passive opening, the local TCP waits for a SYN as a request to establish a connection.
- SYN_SENT: After sending a SYN, the local TCP waits for a connection establishment by the TCP instance of the communication partner.
- SYN_RECV: The local TCP waits for an acknowledgement that the connection has been established (ACK to SYN).
- ESTABLISHED: The connection is established, and the two communicating partners can exchange data; the connection-establishment phase was exited.

The most interesting functions during the establishment of a connection are those to initialize the sock structure, to set options before transmitting data, and to request a connection.

`tcp_v4_init_sock()`	**net/ipv4/tcp_ipv4.c**

This function runs various initialization actions: initialize queues and timers, initialize variables for slow start and maximum segment size, and set the appropriate state (TCP_CLOSE) and the pointer for PF_INET-specific routines.

`tcp_setsockopt()`	**net/ipv4/tcp.c**

This function sets the options selected by the service consumer for the TCP protocol: TCP_MAXSEG, TCP_NODELAY, TCP_CORK, TCP_KEEPIDLE, TCP_KEEPINTVL, TCP_KEEPCNT, TCP_SYNCNT, TCP_LINGER2, TCP_DEFER_ACCEPT, and TCP_WINDOW_CLAMP. The following options are important for the throughput of the TCP protocol:

- TCP_MAXSEG: This option specifies the maximum segment length stored in the user_mss variable of the tcp_opt data structure.
- TCP_NODELAY: This option deactivates the load-control function by setting a suitable value for the nonagle variable in the tcp_opt data structure. (See Section 24.4.3.)

`tcp_connect()`	**net/ipv4/tcp_output.c**

This function initializes an outgoing connection: It reserves memory for the data unit headers in the `sk_buff` structures, initializes the sliding-window variables, sets the maximum segment length (taking the service consumer options into account), sets the TCP header (including the SYN flag), sets the appropriate TCP state, initializes the timers and control variables for retransmission, and finally passes a copy of the initialized segment to the `tcp_transmit_skb()` routine to send and, subsequently, set the timer for retransmission of the connection-establishment segment.

Transition from CLOSED to SYN_SENT To establish the connection, the client sends a packet with the SYN flag set, and then changes from the CLOSED state to the SYN_SENT state. This happens in the `tcp_connect()` method, which is invoked by `tcp_v4_connect()` (see Figure 24–6). The `tcp_v4_connect()` function is invoked when the client application calls `connect()` at the socket interface.

    `tcp_connect()` (`net/ipv4/tcp_output.c`) changes the state to SYN_SENT: `tcp_set_state(sk, TCP_SYN_SENT);`.

Transition from LISTEN to SYN_RECV The LISTEN state is assumed by the server's TCP when the server application activates the `listen()` invocation at the socket interface. When the TCP in the server receives the SYN character in the LISTEN state, it changes to the SYN_RECV state. This happens in the `tcp_create_openreq_child()()` function with the `newsk->state = TCP_SYN_RECV;` assignment. The left path in Figure 24–7 shows how this method is invoked. Subsequently, the `tcp_rcv_state_process()` function assumes

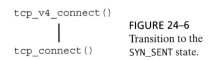

FIGURE 24–6
Transition to the
SYN_SENT state.

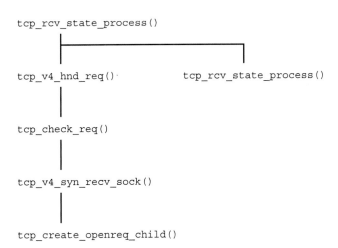

FIGURE 24–7
Transition from LISTEN to the
SYN_RECEIVED and ESTABLISHED states.

further handling. This function uses the function pointer `tcp->af_specific->conn_re-quest()` to invoke the `tcp_v4_conn_request()` function (net/ipv4/tcp_ipv4.c), which specifies the initial sequence number. Finally, the `tcp_v4_send_synack()` function is used to send a reply with the SYN and ACK flags set.

Transition from SYN_SENT to ESTABLISHED   After it has received a packet with the SYN and ACK flags set, the client TCP sends an ACK to the server and changes from the SYN_SENT state into the ESTABLISHED state.

`tcp_rcv_synsent_state_process()`	net/ipv4/tcp_input.c

The appropriate part of this function checks on whether the ACK and SYN flags were set and then returns a packet with the ACK flag set. The TCP changes into the ESTABLISHED state:

```
if (th->ack) {
          (...)
          if (!th->syn)
                  goto discard;
          (...)
          tcp_set_state(sk, TCP_ESTABLISHED);
          (...)
          tcp_schedule_ack(tp);
          (...)
}
```

Transition from SYN_SENT to SYN_RECEIVED   If the client TCP is in SYN_SENT state and receives only one packet with the SYN flag set, it returns a packet with the SYN and ACK flags set to the server and changes into the SYN_RECEIVED state. This happens when both TCP protocol instances start establishing a connection simultaneously.

`tcp_rcv_synsent_state_process()`	net/ipv4/tcp_input.c

TCP changes into the SYN_RECEIVED state:

```
if (th->syn) {
          tcp_set_state(sk, TCP_SYN_RECV);
          (...)
          tcp_send_synack(sk);
          (...)
}
```

Transition from SYN_RECEIVED to ESTABLISHED   From the SYN_RECEIVED state, the server switches to the ESTABLISHED state as soon as it receives an ACK character (ACK to SYN).

`tcp_rcv_state_process()`	**net/ipv4/tcp_input.c**

TCP changes into the ESTABLISHED state:

```
if (th->ack) {
            switch(sk->state) {
            case TCP_SYN_RECV:
                (...)
                tcp_set_state(sk, TCP_ESTABLISHED);
            }
}
```

Now the connection is established and the communication partners can exchange data.

24.3.3 Tearing Down a Connection

A connection between two communicating partners can be terminated in either of two different ways: graceful close and abort.

- *Graceful close*: The higher-layer protocols of both computers start tearing down the connection either simultaneously or consecutively. TCP monitors this process and ensures that the connection is not disestablished unless all data has finally been transmitted.
- *Abort*: A higher-layer protocol forces the establishment to be torn down. In this case, the process of tearing down a connection is not monitored, and so data can be lost.

The state-transition diagram includes the following states for the connection-closing phase:

- *FINWait 1*: The local TCP initiated the connection teardown process and is waiting for a FIN or ACK to the FIN sent by the remote TCP.
- *FINWait 2*: The local TCP received an ACK to the FIN sent by the remote TCP and is now waiting for the connection to be closed by the remote TCP (FIN).
- *Closing*: Once a FIN has been sent and received, the local TCP waits for the final ACK.
- *TimeWait*: Once it has received the connection-closing ACK from the remote TCP, the local TCP has to wait until it is sure that the remote TCP has received the final ACK.
- *CloseWait*: A request to close the connection (FIN) has been received.
- *Last ACK*: Having sent a FIN to acknowledge the connection teardown, the local TCP is now waiting for the final ACK.
- *Closed*: The connection was closed.

Transition from ESTABLISHED to FIN_WAIT_1 Like the connection-establishment phase, the connection-teardown phase also uses a kind of three-way handshake. In this case, it is assumed that both communication partners are in the ESTABLISHED state. Specifically, a computer, A, initiates the connection closing by sending a packet with the FIN flag set to computer B and then switches to the FIN_WAIT_1 state. (See Figure 24–8.)

```
tcp_close()
    |
tcp_close_state()
```

FIGURE 24–8
Transition from
FIN_WAIT_1 to LAST_ACK.

tcp_close_state()   **net/ipv4/tcp.c**

This function switches the TCP to the next state, FIN_WAIT_1:

```
/* ns: next state (FIN wait 1) */ tcp_set_state(sk, ns);
```

Transition from ESTABLISHED to CLOSE_WAIT   When computer B receives the packet with the FIN flag set, it sends an ACK character to computer A and switches from the ESTABLISHED state into the CLOSE_WAIT state. (See left path in Figure 24–9.)

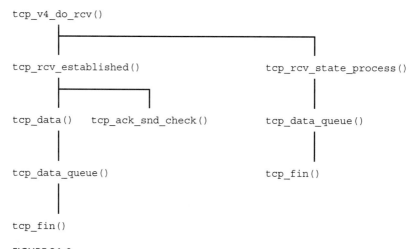

FIGURE 24–9
Transition from CLOSE_WAIT to FIN_WAIT_2 to TIME_WAIT and finally to CLOSING.

tcp_fin()   **net/ipv4/tcp_input.c**

This function is invoked if the FIN flag is set in the packet received, and TCP is switched to the CLOSE_WAIT state:

```
switch(sk->state) {
        case TCP_SYN_RECV:
        case TCP_ESTABLISHED:
            /* Move to CLOSE_WAIT */
            tcp_set_state(sk, TCP_CLOSE_WAIT);
```

```
                     if (th->rst)
                             sk->shutdown = SHUTDOWN_MASK;
                     break;
              (...)
}
```
`tcp_ack_snd_check()` (`net/ipv4/tcp_input.c`) sends a packet with the ACK flag set: `tcp_send_ack(sk);`.

Transition from CLOSE_WAIT to LAST_ACK   While in the CLOSE_WAIT state, TCP tries to pass all data from the receive buffer to the higher-layer protocol as quickly as possible. TCP sends a FIN character to the TCP in computer A only if the local application in computer B has no more data to send. This confirms the connection teardown process, and the TCP in computer B switches to the LAST_ACK state. (See Figure 24–8.)

`tcp_close_state()`	`net/ipv4/tcp.c`

TCP switches to the LAST_ACK state as follows:

```
/* ns: next state (Last ACK) */ tcp_set_state(sk, ns);
```

For the TCP in the FIN_WAIT_1 state in computer A, there are different ways to tear down the connection, depending on how computer B responds.

Transition from FIN_WAIT_1 to FIN_WAIT_2   When the user at computer B sends data ready for transmission, after the FIN character was received, then computer B acknowledges the FIN character by sending an ACK character. Subsequently, it will send the FIN character after all data has been sent. In this case, the TCP in computer A switches to the FIN_WAIT_2 state once it has received the ACK character. (See right-hand path in Figure 2–49.)

`tcp_rcv_state_process()`	`net/ipv4/tcp_input.c`

This switches TCP into the FIN_WAIT_2 state:

```
if (th->ack) {
      switch(sk->state) {
             (...)
             case TCP_FIN_WAIT1:
                    (...)
                    tcp_set_state(sk, TCP_FIN_WAIT2);
                    (...)
             (...)
      }
}
```

Transition from FIN_WAIT_2 to TIME_WAIT   As soon as the TCP in the FIN_WAIT_2 state in computer A receives a FIN character from computer B, it sends an ACK and switches into the TIME_WAIT state (right-hand path in Figure 24–9).

`tcp_fin()`	**net/ipv4/tcp_input.c**

```
switch(sk->state) {
    (...)
    case TCP_FIN_WAIT2:
        /* Received a FIN - send ACK and enter TIME_WAIT */
        tcp_send_ack(sk);
        tcp_time_wait(sk, TCP_TIME_WAIT, 0);
        break;
    (...)
}
```

Transition from FIN_WAIT_1 to TIME_WAIT   When computer A in the FIN_WAIT_1 state receives an ACK and a FIN character as a response to its FIN character, then it sends an ACK to acknowledge the connection-closing process, then switches to the FIN_WAIT_2 state:

`tcp_rcv_state_process()`	**net/ipv4/tcp_input.c**

This function causes TCP to switch into the FIN_WAIT_2 state. If the FIN flag was set, then the transition from FIN_WAIT_2 to TIME_WAIT described above is initiated:

```
switch(sk->state) {
    (...)
    case TCP_FIN_WAIT1:
        (...)
        tcp_set_state(sk, TCP_FIN_WAIT2);
        (...)
        sk->state_change(sk);
    (...)
}
```

Immediately afterwards, the function `tcp_rcv_state_process()` uses `tcp_data_queue()` to invoke the `tcp_fin()` function, if a FIN was set additionally. (See Figure 24–9.) Next, an ACK is sent from within the `tcp_fin()` function, and the state is moved to TIME_WAIT:

```
switch(sk->state) {
    (...)
    case TCP_FIN_WAIT2:
        /* Received a FIN -- send ACK and enter TIME_WAIT. */
        tcp_send_ack(sk);
        tcp_time_wait(sk, TCP_TIME_WAIT, 0);
        break;
    (...)
}
```

Transition from the FIN_WAIT_1 State to CLOSING   If computer A in the FIN_WAIT_1 state initially receives a FIN character, then it switches into the CLOSING state. (See Figure 24–9.)

| `tcp_fin()` | **net/ipv4/tcp_input.c** |

This function switches the TCP into the CLOSING state and sends a packet with the ACK flag set:

```
switch(sk->state) {
    (...)
    case TCP_FIN_WAIT1:
        tcp_send_ack(sk);
        tcp_set_state(sk, TCP_CLOSING);
    (...)
}
```

Transition from CLOSING to TIME_WAIT   While in the CLOSING state, TCP waits until it receives an ACK character. Subsequently, it switches into the TIME_WAIT state. (See Figure 24–9.)

| `tcp_rcv_state_process()` | **net/ipv4/tcp_input.c** |

```
if (th->ack) {
    switch(sk->state) {
        (...)
        case TCP_CLOSING:
            (...)
            tcp_time_wait(sk, TCP_TIME_WAIT, 0
            (...)
        (...)
    }
}
```

The TIME_WAIT State   The three different ways to tear down a connection all converge in the TIME_WAIT state. Computer A has to wait a specific period of time (twice the maximum segment lifecycle) before the connection is finally closed.

Additional functions are required to handle the TIME_WAIT state, and the special cases that can occur in this state, correctly.

| `_tcp_time_wait()` | **net/ipv4/tcp_minisocks.c** |

This function activates the TIME_WAIT state by initializing the `tcp_tw_bucket` structure and entering it in a hash table. As described earlier, this function is invoked by `tcp_fin()` when a connection changes to the TIME_WAIT state.

| `_tcp_tw_hashdance()` | **net/ipv4/tcp_minisocks.c** |

This function is a helper function of the `tcp_time_wait` function. It adds the `tcp_tw_bucket` structure to a hash table.

`tcp_timewait_kill()`	**net/ipv4/tcp_minisocks.c**

This function deletes a connection, or its representation in the form of a `tcp_tw_bucket` structure, from the hash table for `established` connections.

The receipt of packets for a connection currently in the TIME_WAIT state is separated in the function `tcp_v4_do_rcv()` and taken over by the function `tcp_timewait_state_process()` for further handling.

`tcp_timewait_state_process()`	**net/ipv4/tcp_minisocks.c**

This function processes a packet in the TIME_WAIT state, a state in which packets can be received only under specific conditions. Specifically, in relation to the `tcp_v4_rcv()` function, the following three cases are handled: receiving of a SYN packet, of a SYN-ACK packet, and of an RST packet. The connection is reestablished when an SYN packet arrives under certain conditions. Also, an ACK is sent as a response to a SYN-ACK packet under certain conditions. In contrast, an RST packet is normally sent as a response to an RST packet.

24.4   PROTOCOL MECHANISMS FOR DATA EXCHANGE

The following subsections introduce several protocol mechanisms of the TCP protocol. However, the TCP protocol uses a large number of algorithms; a detailed description of all of these mechanisms would go beyond the scope and volume of this chapter, but we will discuss selected parts of the TCP instance here.

To begin with, Section 24.4.1 will discuss flow control by use of the sliding-window method. In addition to flow control, we will have a look at the methods for window scaling, zero-window probing, and the PAWS mechanism, including the timestamp option. Subsequently, Section 24.4.2 will discuss methods for detection, handling, and avoidance of congestions: slow-start, congestion-avoidance, fast-retransmit, and fast-recovery methods. Finally, Section 24.4.3 covers methods for load avoidance, concentrating on the Nagle algorithm and the transmission of delayed acknowledgements.

The different timers used by a TCP instance and their management will be discussed in Section 24.5.

24.4.1   Flow Control

The TCP protocol uses flow control to regulate the data flow—the data volume exchanged between a sender and a receiver—on a per-time-unit basis.[1] Flow control limits the number of bytes sent in one communication direction to prevent buffer overflows in

---

[1]This section considers flow control in only one direction of a TCP connection and treats the two TCP instances as a sender and a receiver. In bidirectional data exchange, the flow is controlled separately for each direction, where each instance assumes both the role of a sender and the role of a receiver.

the receiving TCP instance and to meet the service consumer requirements. Reasons to limit the data flow by the receiving TCP instance include the following:

- The computing performance of the sending TCP instance can be higher than that of the receiving instance. This means that the sender creates segments faster than the receiving TCP instance can process them. In such a situation, the receive buffer at the receiver's end over flows, causing segments to be discarded.
- An application removes data from the socket receive buffer at specific intervals, which means that this buffer empties only occasionally. Examples include applications that output multimedia contents, receiving contents faster than their playback rate.

Consequently, flow control can be used to prevent the receive buffer of a receiving TCP instance from overflowing, which would cause additional incoming packets to be dropped. To implement flow control, the TCP protocol uses the *sliding-window mechanism*. This mechanism is based on the assignment of *explicit transmit credits* by the receiver [Pete00]. We will introduce it in the following section.

The Sliding-Window Mechanism The sliding-window protocol mechanism is used commonly in transport protocols or connection-oriented protocols, because it provides for three important tasks:

- The original order of a set of data segmented and sent in several packets can be restored in the receiver.
- Missing or duplicate packets can be identified by ordering of packets. Together with additional packet-retransmission methods, this enables us to guarantee reliable data transport.
- The data flow between two TCP instances can be controlled by assigning transmit credits. Specifically, it is distinguished between a fixed credit quantity (e.g., in HDLC) and explicit credit assignment (e.g., in TCP).

The following elements are added to the protocol header (using the TCP protocol as our example) to handle these tasks:

- All data is numbered consecutively by *sequence numbers*. The sequence numbers of the first payload byte in a data packet is carried in the packet header and denotes the sequence number of this segment. The tp->snd_nxt variable in the tcp_opt structure stores the sequence number of the packet to be sent next.
- Together with each segment, a TCP instance informs its communication partner about the number of bytes it can still receive in the *Window* field of the packet header. This is an explicit transmit credit granted to the partner. When a segment is sent, this value is specified by the tcp_select_window() function (described later).
- Together with each segment, the other TCP instance is informed about the sequence number up to which data has been received correctly (accumulative

acknowledgement). More specifically, this value is higher by one, because the sequence number of the data set expected next is specified, so that all data from this sequence number on are implicitly acknowledged (ACK).

Example: Figure 24–10 shows how the sliding-window mechanism is used to implement flow control [Stev94a]. This example uses a simplified version of the slow-start algorithm. The figure shows a scenario where a fast sender ships 8192 bytes to a slow receiver.

In this example, the segments 1 through 3 belong to the connection-establishment phase. In this phase, the receiver grants the sender an initial transmit credit of 4096 bytes in segment 2 (in the win field). Together with the segments 4 through 7, instance A sends 4096 bytes, exhausting its transmit credit. It may not send more segments and has to wait for an acknowledgement from instance B, which actually grants it a new transmit credit. Together with segment 8, all 4096 bytes sent are acknowledged.

However, because it has not yet been able to empty its buffer, the slow receiver does not grant transmit credit to the sender (passing a value of 0 in the win field). Later, an acknowledgement arrives at TCP instance A, together with segment 9, granting it an additional credit of 4096 bytes. Subsequently, the source instance can send its remaining data (segments 10 through 13), arriving again at the situation described above, which results in the transmission of segments 14 and 15. Segments 16 and 17 refer to the connection-teardown phase.

In order for the sender to keep control over all bytes with regard to error handling and flow control, it has to take a certain view on the data. The view of the sending

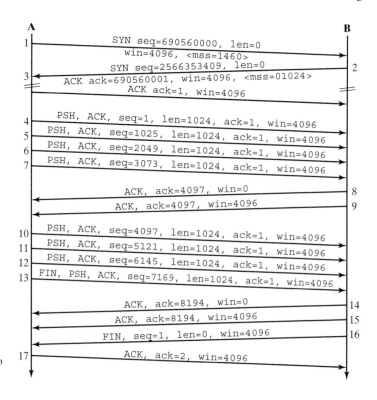

FIGURE 24–10

A fast sender transmits 8192 bytes to a slow receiver.

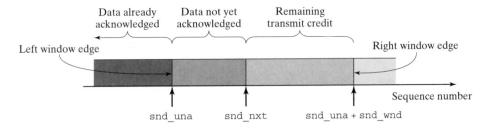

FIGURE 24–11
Byte-sequence range from the sender's view.

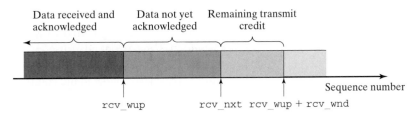

FIGURE 24–12
Byte-sequence range from the receiver's view.

TCP instance on the sliding-window mechanism is shown in Figure 24–11. The receiver's view on the sliding-window mechanism is shown in Figure 24–12.

Notice that the byte sequence range between the segment received last and the right-hand window margin corresponds to the remaining free buffer space. When the receiving TCP instance receives a segment that moves the byte-sequence number of the data byte received last to the right-hand receive window margin, then the buffer of this instance is full, and all segments arriving later cause a buffer overflow, until the right-hand window margin is moved further to the right, so that buffer capacity is available again.

Specifying the Transmit Credit The flow-control mechanism is effective in many places within a TCP instance. A detailed description of all of these situations would go beyond the scope and volume of this chapter, especially because Section 24.2 discussed several flow-control aspects. This section explains how the explicit transmit credit for a partner instance can be specified in each TCP segment sent.

`tcp_select_window()`	**net/ipv4/tcp_output.c**

```
static __inline__ u16 tcp_select_window(struct sock *sk)
{
        struct tcp_opt *tp = &(sk->tp_pinfo.af_tcp);
        u32 cur_win = tcp_receive_window(tp);
        u32 new_win = __tcp_select_window(sk);
```

```
/* Never shrink the offered window */
if(new_win < cur_win)
{
        new_win = cur_win;
}
tp->rcv_wnd = new_win;
tp->rcv_wup = tp->rcv_nxt;

/* RFC1323 scaling applied */
new_win >>= tp->rcv_wscale;
(...)
return new_win;
}
```

tcp_select_window(sk) is invoked in the tcp_transmit_skb() method when a TCP segment is sent (except for SYN and SYN-ACK segments) to specify the size of the transmit credit (i.e., the *advertised window*). The current advertised window size is initially specified by the tcp_receive_window(). Subsequently, the __tcp_select_window() function is used to see how much buffer space is available in the computer. This forms the basis for determining the new transmit credit offered to the partner instance. However, as specified in RFC 793, care should be taken not to reduce a previously granted credit.

Once the new advertised window has been computed, the credit is stored in the tcp_opt structure of the connection (tp->rcv_wnd). Also, the tp->rcv_wup is adapted; it stores the current value of the tp->rcv_nxt variable when computing and sending the new credit, known as *window update*. The reason is that each segment arriving after the advertised window has been sent has to be charged against the credit granted, just as happens in the tcp_receive_window() function.

In addition, another TCP algorithm is used in this method, namely an algorithm known as *window scaling*, which will be introduced in the next section. This algorithm had to be introduced to make it possible to work meaningfully with a 16-bit number for the transmit and receive windows. This *scaling factor* was introduced for this reason; it specifies the number of bits to move the window size to the left. With the value F in tp->rcv_wscale, this corresponds to an advertised window increase by factor 2^F.

tcp_receive_window()	including/net/tcp.4

```
/* Compute the actual receive window we are currently
 * advertising. Rcv_nxt can be after the window if the sending
 * peer pushes more data than the offered window.
 */
static __inline__ u32 tcp_receive_window(struct tcp_opt *tp)
{
        s32 win = tp->rcv_wup + tp->rcv_wnd - tp->rcv_nxt;
        if (win < 0)
                win = 0;
        return (u32) win;
}
```

This method calculates how much is left of the transmit credit granted in the last segment, taking the quantity of data received since then into account. Slightly rewriting the equation, we can clearly identify the objective of this computation:

```
s32 win = tp->rcv_wnd - (tp->rcv_nxt - tp->rcv_wup);
```

The difference in brackets is the data quantity received since the last window update was sent: the sequence number expected at the beginning of the next packet, minus the sequence number of the packet expected next when sending the credit, which was stored in the tp->rcv_wnd variable. This means that the resulting value, win, is the data quantity that can now be received against the credit granted last, corresponding to the actual size of the receive window.

__tcp_select_window()	net/ipv4/tcp_output.c

```
u32 __tcp_select_window(struct sock *sk)
{
    // free_space is being computed
    free_space = tcp_space(sk);
    (...)
    if (free_space < tp->ack.rcv_mss)
            return 0;

    window = tp->rcv_wnd;
    if (((((int) window) <= (free_space - ((int) mss))) ||
            (((int) window) > free_space))
            window = (((unsigned int) free_space)/mss)*mss;

    return window;
}
```

The __tcp_select_window() method is used to check how much memory of this connection is available for the receive buffer and what size can be selected for the receive window.

In the first step, tcp_space() determines how much buffer memory is available. After a few adaptations of the determined buffer space, it finally checks on whether there is enough buffer space for a TCP segment with maximum size (tp->ack.rcv_mss). If this is not the case, then this would mean that a *Silly Window Syndrome* (*SWS*) [Stev94a] has occurred. To avoid SWS, no credit smaller than the negotiated maximum segment size is granted in such a case.

If the available buffer space is larger than the maximum segment size, then the computation of the new receive window is continued. The window variable is set to the value of the credit last granted (tp->rcv_wnd). If the old credit is larger, or smaller by more than one segment size, than the available buffer, window, is set to the next smaller multiple of a maximum segment size (MSS) of the free buffer space (free_space). The value for window calculated in this way is returned as a recommendation for the new receive credit.

The Window-Scaling Option This option can be used to increase the value range for the flow-control transmit window from 2^{16} to $2^{16} \cdot 2^F$, where F is the exponent specified by this option. The window-based flow-control method used in the TCP protocol uses the 16-bit Window field in the TCP header. This field is used to grant transmit credits of up to 65535 bytes (the basic unit of the Window field is 1 byte, excluding window scaling). However, connections with a large path capacity (bandwidth times packet round-trip time) require a larger transmit credit to be able to send data continually. For example, if you consider a connection having transmission rate 10 Mbps and round-trip time 100 ms, then a constant data flow requires a transmit window of at least $10\ Mbps \cdot 100\ ms\ =\ 125000\ bytes$.

The *window-scaling* TCP option was introduced in [JaBB92] to solve this problem. Window scaling enlarges the TCP window by from 16 to 30 bits. To ensure backward compatibility, the size of the Window field remains 16 bits; instead, the option changes the basic unit of the Window field to 2^F. Figure 24–13 shows the packet-header format of the window-scaling option used by the TCP instances to negotiate the F parameter [Stev94a]. The Shift Count[2] field includes the scaling factor for the receive window. If the F value of the Shift Count field is unequal to zero, then the basic unit used to compute the receive window is 2^f rather than 1 byte.

The window-scaling option can be sent only in a SYN or SYN–ACK segment in the connection establishment phase—see Section 24.3:

- In a SYN segment, it assumes two tasks [JaBB92]: It shows that the TCP protocol instance can use window scaling both when sending and receiving, and it outputs the scaling factor for the receive window of this TCP instance.
- In a SYN–ACK segment, this option may be used only if it was specified in the SYN segment. To enable the use of window scaling, both TCP instances have to have the window-scaling option set in their SYN segments during the connection-establishment phase. This ensures that window scaling is used only provided that both instances are actually able to do so.

The maximum scaling factor is limited to 2^{14}, and the maximum byte sequence number is limited to $2^{16} \cdot 2^{14} = 2^{30} < 2^{31}$ to prevent byte-sequence-number overflow. The negotiated window-scaling value is stored in the `tp->rcv_wscale` variable.

Zero-Window Probing No minimum size for the advertised window is guaranteed, so it can happen that the sender has fully used up its advertised window while the receiver has no more new buffer space available. The consequence is that the sender receives

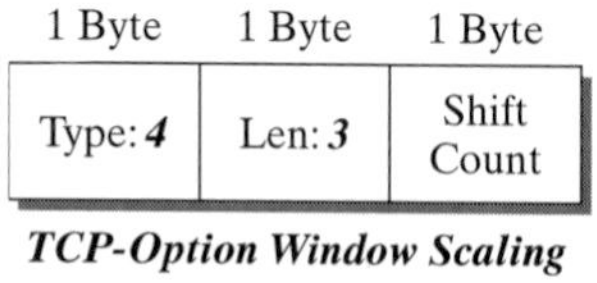

1 Byte	1 Byte	1 Byte
Type: *4*	Len: *3*	Shift Count

FIGURE 24–13
Format of the window-scaling TCP option.

TCP-Option Window Scaling

---

[2]Field name as used in [JaBB92].

an acknowledgement with a new advertising window having size **null**, which means that it must not send more data.

The problem is now that it can receive a new window size (i.e., a new transmit credit) only together with a new packet. There is no additional acknowledgement, because it cannot send more data, which means that the sender now depends on whether the other end sends data. If the receiver does not have data to send, or if it was also granted a window having size **null**, then the two communicating partners would wait eternally to be able to continue sending data.

To solve this problem, the Transmission Control Protocol includes a mechanism known as *zero-window probing*. This mechanism is based on an additional timer, the *probe timer*. When this timer expires, a TCP packet is sent even the advertising window has size **null**. This packet consists only of a packet header; it does not carry payload, because data must not be transmitted in this situation.

The communication peer acknowledges this packet, and, if the other end was able to remove its congestion, at least to some extent, in the meantime, then a window larger than **null** is granted together with this acknowledgement, so that the transmission of data can be resumed. If the window size **null** occurs again, then the communication peers have to wait until the probe timer expires to send another probing packet.

tcp_probe_timer()	net/ipv4/tcp_timer.c

```
static void tcp_probe_timer(struct sock *sk)
{
        (...)
        if (tp->probes_out > max_probes) {
                tcp_write_err(sk);
        } else {
                /* Only send another probe if we didn't close things
                   up. */
                tcp_send_probe0(sk);
        }
}
```

tcp_probe_timer(sk) is the handling routine for the zero-window probe timer, if it leads to a timeout. The routine initially checks on whether the peer has offered a meaningful transmit window over a lengthy period. If several (more than max_probes[3]) window probes were sent unsuccessfully, then an error message is output to announce that there are serious problems in the TCP connection (tcp_write_err()) and to close this connection by tcp_done().

If the maximum number of window probes has not yet been reached, tcp_send_probe0() sends a TCP segment without payload, and the acknowledgment segment will then, it is hoped, grant a credit (advertised window) larger than **null**.

tcp_send_probe0()	net/ipv4/tcp_output.c

---

[3]The value for max_probes is initialized to 15 and can be set in the proc file /proc/sys/net/ipv4/tcp_retries2.

```
void tcp_send_probe0(struct sock *sk)
{
        struct tcp_opt *tp = &(sk->tp_pinfo.af_tcp);
        int err;

        err = tcp_write_wakeup(sk);

        if (tp->packets_out || !tp->send_head) {
                /* Cancel probe timer, if it is not required. */
                tp->probes_out = 0;
                tp->backoff = 0;
                return;
        }
        if (err <= 0) {
                tp->backoff++;
                tp->probes_out++;
                tcp_reset_xmit_timer(sk, TCP_TIME_PROBE0,
                             min(tp->rto << tp->backoff, TCP_RTO_MAX));
        } else { (...) }
}
```

tcp_send_probe0(sk)() uses tcp_write_wakeup(sk)() to generate and send a zero-window probe packet. If the probe timer is no longer needed, as can be seen from the fact that there is currently nothing to be sent (tp->send_head == NULL), or if there are still packets currently under way and their ACKs could contain new credits, then it is not restarted, and the probes_out and backoff parameters are reset.

Otherwise, these parameters are incremented after a probe packet has been sent, and the zero-window probe timer is restarted, so that it expires again after some time. This time is tp->rto*2$^{tp->backoff}$ or a maximum of TCP_RTO_MAX (120 seconds).

tcp_write_wakeup()	net/ipv4/tcp_output.c

```
int tcp_write_wakeup(struct sock *sk)
{
        (...)
        if ((skb = tp->send_head) != NULL &&
                before(TCP_SKB_CB(skb)->seq, tp->snd_una+tp->snd_wnd))
        {
                (...)
                /* We are probing the opening of a window
                 * but the window size is != 0
                 * must have been a result SWS avoidance ( sender )
                 */
                (...)
                err = tcp_transmit_skb(sk, skb_clone(skb, GFP_ATOMIC));
                (...)
        }
        else
        {
                return tcp_xmit_probe_skb(sk);
```

```
        }
                    (...)
}
```

`tcp_write_wakeup(sk)` checks for whether the transmit window is of size null and for whether the beginning of the data segment in `skb` is still within the transmit window range (`snd_una + snd_wnd`). In the case of a zero-window problem discussed so far, the transmit window has null size, so the `tcp_xmit_probe_skb()` method is invoked in the `else` branch. It generates the desired zero-window probe packet.

However, if the above condition is met, and if there is at least one packet in the transmit queue that is within the transmit window range, then we probably have a *silly window syndrome* situation. A packet that corresponds to the requirements of the current transmit window is generated and sent by `tcp_transmit_skb()`.

`tcp_xmit_probe_skb()`	net/ipv4/tcp_output.c

```c
/* This routine sends a packet with an out of date sequence
* number. It assumes the other end will try to ack it.
*/
static int tcp_xmit_probe_skb(struct sock *sk, int urgent)
{
        (...)
        skb = alloc_skb(MAX_TCP_HEADER, GFP_ATOMIC);
        (...)
        /* Reserve space for headers and set control bits. */
        skb_reserve(skb, MAX_TCP_HEADER);
        skb->csum = 0;
        TCP_SKB_CB(skb)->flags = TCPCB_FLAG_ACK;
        TCP_SKB_CB(skb)->sacked = urgent;
        /* Use a previous sequence. This should cause the other
        * end to send an ack. Don't queue or clone SKB, just send it.
        */
        TCP_SKB_CB(skb)->seq = urgent ? tp->snd_una : tp->snd_una - 1;
        TCP_SKB_CB(skb)->end_seq = TCP_SKB_CB(skb)->seq;
        TCP_SKB_CB(skb)->when = tcp_time_stamp;
        return tcp_transmit_skb(sk, skb);
}
```

`tcp_xmit_probe_skb(sk, urgent)` creates a TCP segment without payload, because the transmit window has size **null**, and data currently must not be sent. `alloc_skb()` procures a socket buffer having length `MAX_TCP_HEADER`. As mentioned above, no payload is sent, and the packet consists only of the TCP packet header.

The trick of this routine utilizes the fact that an old sequence number (i.e., a previously acknowledged sequence number) is written to the packet. `tp->snd_una` holds the first, so far unacknowledged sequence number, which means that `tp->snd_una - 1` meets this purpose. The old sequence number causes the counterpart to send an acknowledgement. Together with this ACK, it also sends the current transmit window size, which is now, it is hoped, larger than **null**.

In the next line, the last sequence number is set to the first sequence number of this packet, which results in the payload size end_seq - seq = 0. Subsequently, a timestamp is added to the segment, and the segment is sent by tcp_transmit_skb().

`tcp_ack_probe()`	`net/ipv4/tcp_input.c`

```
static void tcp_ack_probe(struct sock *sk)
{
        struct tcp_opt *tp = &(sk->tp_pinfo.af_tcp);

        /* Was it a usable window open? */
        if (!after(TCP_SKB_CB(tp->send_head)->end_seq, tp->snd_una +
                                tp->snd_wnd)) {
                tp->backoff = 0;
                tcp_clear_xmit_timer(sk, TCP_TIME_PROBE0);
                /* Socket must be waked up by subsequent tcp_data_snd_check().
                 * This function is not for random using!
                 */
        } else {
                tcp_reset_xmit_timer(sk, TCP_TIME_PROBE0,
                                min(tp->rto << tp->backoff, TCP_RTO_MAX));
        }
}
```

tcp_ack_probe(sk, ack) is invoked in tcp_ack() when a TCP segment with the ACK flag set is received and if it is suspected to be a reply to a zero-window probe segment. Depending on whether the segment opens the receive window (the first packet in the transmit queue affects the transmit window), tcp_clear_xmit_timer() stops the zero-window probe timer or tcp_reset_xmit_timer() restarts this timer.

Protection Against Wrapped Sequence Numbers (PAWS)   The PAWS mechanism prevents a byte-sequence-number overflow, which would lead to inconsistencies, from occurring in connections with too large a bandwidth/delay product (i.e., when there is an excessive amount of data "in the pipe").

The byte-sequence numbers of a TCP connection are of length 32 bits. With a sufficient transmission rate and an accordingly large packet round-trip time, byte-sequence numbers can reach the end of the byte-sequence-number range within the time that a segment is delayed in router queues and thereby cause a byte-sequence-number overflow. In this case, the byte-sequence numbers take the initial values of the byte-sequence-number range. In this situation, the TCP protocol cannot identify delayed segment duplicates if their byte-sequence numbers are within the receive window and consequently cannot drop these duplicates.

The PAWS mechanism was introduced to solve this problem. It uses the Timestamp option, to protect the TCP protocol within a connection from problems caused by several segments' having the same byte-sequence numbers. The PAWS mechanism operates basically by attaching timestamps to TCP segments and dropping a segment as a duplicate if its timestamp is smaller than the timestamp of the segment received last, which cause the receive window to move forward. (See Section 24.4.1.)

All segments arriving over an established connection are subject to the following checks by the PAWS algorithm [JaBB92]:

▨ The RST flag should not be set.

▨ The TCP partner instance should have received a valid Timestamp option (i.e., the tp->ts_recent variable contains a valid value).

▨ If an incoming segment contains the Timestamp option, and if its timestamp, tp->rcv_tsval, is actually smaller than the timestamp stored last, tp->ts_re-cent, then this segment should be dropped. This check is done in the tcp_paws_discard() function shown below, which is invoked in Slow Path in the tcp_rcv_established() function. (See Section 24.2.1.)

```
extern __inline__ int tcp_paws_discard(struct tcp_opt *tp, struct sk_buff
  *skb)
{
  return ((s32)(tp->ts_recent - tp->rcv_tsval) > TCP_PAWS_WINDOW &&
          xtime.tv_sec < tp->ts_recent_stamp + TCP_PAWS_24DAYS &&
          !tcp_disordered_ack(tp, skb));
}
```

The second condition checks the validity of the tp->ts_recent timestamp. There is a very small probability that an extremely long time has passed since the time when the timestamp was taken from a received segment, which is stored in the tp->ts_recent_stamp variable. This means that, if more than 24 days have passed since this time, the ts_recent timestamp is considered invalid. [Stev94b] includes an example for such a situation.

If the TCP connection is not in the ESTABLISHED state, then the PAWS check on incoming packets is done in the tcp_paws_check() method (net/ipv4/tcp_input.c).

The *PAWS* mechanism requires the use of the *timestamp* option and the time-stamp property as monotonically increasing values. In addition, it requires that the timestamp increase at least once per window and that the time in which it repeatedly takes the same value is greater than the maximum segment lifecycle.

The *timestamp* option is a prerequisite for the PAWS algorithm and additionally is used to determine the packet round-trip time and the *retransmission timeout*; we will introduce it next.

The Timestamp Option   This option offers TCP instances a way to continually probe and adapt the packet *round-trip time (RTT)* of a connection. The timestamp option allows you to set a timestamp in each segment. The receiver returns this timestamp in the acknowledgement segment, allowing the sender to compute the round-trip time for each acknowledgement received. A timestamp is a monotonically increasing value taken from a timer. Figure 24–14 shows the format of the *timestamp* option in the TCP packet header [JaBB92].

The *timestamp* option was introduced to make possible a more exact measure-ment of the packet round-trip time. When setting a segment, the sender sets the current

1 Byte	1 Byte	4 Bytes	4 Bytes
Type: *8*	Len: *10*	Timestamp value (TSval)	Value of timestamp received (TSecr)

FIGURE 24–14
Format of the timestamp option in the
TCP packet header.

TCP Timestamp Option

timestamp in the TSval field. The receiver returns this timestamp in the TSecr field of the ACK segment, together with the timestamp it set. Because the receiver returns the timestamp it received together with the acknowledgement for data it accepted to the sender without considering the timestamp's value, the timestamp unit is not relevant for the receiver. In particular, no timer synchronization between the communicating TCP instances is required [Stev94a]. This means that the sender can compute the packet round-trip time for each acknowledgement it received; this calculation is done in the method tcp_rtt_estimator() method of the TCP instance in the Linux kernel.

Notice that only a single timestamp variable per connection is used, to minimize the number of states the communicating TCP instances have to maintain. The value of this variable is updated by the following algorithm:

▨ TCP holds the value for the timestamp to be sent in the next acknowledgement in the tp->ts_recent parameter.

▨ When an incoming TCP segment with the *timestamp* option set in the tcp_rcv_established() method is handled, then the routine tcp_ts_replace_recent() checks on whether the tp->rcv_tsval timestamp contained in the tp->ts_recent variable should be accepted. If so, this is done by the tcp_store_ts_recent() method. In *fast path*, acceptance of the timestamp is checked directly.

▨ Whenever a TCP segment with the timestamp option should be sent, the value of the timestamp received is copied from the tp->ts_recent variable to the TSecr field when the packet header is assembled in tcp_transmit_skb().

The above algorithm shows the following behavior when segments are delayed or lost:

▨ When acknowledgements are delayed by the receiver, the timestamp in the acknowledgement refers to the first of the segments being acknowledged.

▨ When an incoming segment belongs to the current window, but arrives out of order (which implies that an earlier segment was lost), the timestamp of the earlier segment is returned as soon as it arrives, rather than the timestamp of the segment that arrived out of order.

Figure 24–15 shows an example for the use of the *timestamp* option [JaBB92]. The *timestamp* option can be negotiated by the same principle used for the *window scaling* option during the connection-establishment phase. A TCP instance can set the *timestamp* option in the initial SYN segment (i.e., in a segment with the SYN bit set and

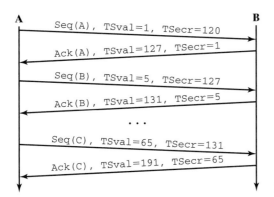

FIGURE 24–15
Example using the timestamp option.

the ACK bit not set), and it may set this option in other segments only provided that it received them in the initial SYN segment for this connection.

24.4.2 Detecting, Avoiding, and Handling Congestions

The flow-control mechanisms introduced in Section 24.4.1 ensure that only that amount of data is sent to a receiving TCP instance that this instance can accommodate, to avoid packet losses in the receiving end system. However, buffer overflows can occur in the forwarding systems—more specifically, in the queues of the Internet Protocol—when they are not emptied fast enough and more data arrives than can be sent over a network adapter. This situation is called *congestion*.

Detecting a Congestion   Congestions occur mainly in the IP instances in forwarding systems. The question is now how a loss by the TCP instances in the end systems can be detected. The reason is that the TCP instances suffer from such a congestion, and have to retransmit their data. In addition, they have to reduce their transmission rates, initially to resolve the congestion and then to avoid additional congestions. Unfortunately, the Internet Protocol does not respond to congestions.

This means that recognizing a congestion is a basic prerequisite for using the congestion-handling and -prevention methods. The TCP protocol has several mechanisms to detect congestions and uses various algorithms to respond to a congestion:

- A *retransmission timer* waits for a certain period of time for an acknowledgement once a packet has been sent. If no acknowledgement arrives, it is assumed that a congestion caused the packet to be lost. The initial response to a lost packet is the slow-start phase, which, from a certain point on, is replaced by the congestion-avoidance algorithm. Both methods will be introduced in the following section.
- The *receipt of duplicate acknowledgements* (*dupacks*) is an indication that a data segment was lost, because, although subsequent segments arrive, they cannot be acknowledged, because of cumulative ACK segments. In this case, it is normally not assumed that a serious congestion occurred, because subsequent segments were actually received. For this reason, the more recent TCP versions (TCP Reno, TCP New Reno) do not respond to a loss by means of the slow-start phase,

but instead by means of the *fast retransmit* and *fast recovery* methods, which will be introduced further along.

Slow-Start and Congestion Avoidance   The slow-start algorithm is used once a connection has been initialized and the retransmission timer has expired. It serves for stepwise approximation of the transmitted data volume to the transmission capacity available in this connection. The slow-start algorithm is normally implemented together with the congestion-avoidance algorithm.

At the beginning of a connection, or after a congestion, the minimum transmission capacity is assumed; subsequently, it is increased exponentially until segments are lost or a threshold value is reached, representing an approximate measure for the available capacity. The following parameters are defined:

- The *congestion window* (snd_cwnd) denotes the number of bytes that may be under way at a certain point in time (without acknowledgement). This means that, in addition to the normal transmission window of the sliding-window mechanism, it defines a second credit, which also has to be available and sufficient to be able to send data.

  The congestion window is initialized to at most one segment at the beginning of the slow-start phase (i.e., only one segment, and that of minimum size, can be sent). Subsequently, the congestion window is increased by one byte for each arriving acknowledgement of a byte. This corresponds to doubling the congestion window when the data volume of the entire window has been fully sent and acknowledged.

- The *slow-start threshold* (ssthresh) limits the exponential growth of the slow-start phase when the available transmission capacity is approximately known. At the beginning of a connection, the threshold is set to the maximum value, to ensure that the slow-start phase will be able to test for the available capacity. If a packet loss occurs, then the threshold value is set to half the size of the current congestion window, to limit the exponential growth of the slow-start phase.

The *congestion avoidance* algorithm starts once the threshold value for the congestion window has been reached in the slow-start phase. This algorithm represents a measure for the available transmission capacity. For this reason, the congestion window still increases linearly during the congestion-avoidance phase, as shown in Figure 24–16. This value increases by one once n acknowledgements have arrived, where n corresponds to the size of the current congestion window. This means that the TCP instance increases its transmission rate only slowly, but still in a strictly monotone way. Naturally, the total data volume that can be sent corresponds to the minimum from the transmission window of the sliding-window algorithm and the congestion window, whichever is less.

Figure 24–16 also shows how the two mechanisms cooperate. The slow-start algorithm operates at the beginning of a data transmission. It terminates its exponential growth as soon as a congestion occurs, which is detected by the fact that the retransmission timer expires. According to the approach described above, the slow-start threshold, snd_ssthresh, is set to half of the current congestion window (i.e., 20 segments, in the above figure). Consequently, snd_cwnd takes the value 1 (2, in the Linux kernel), because the congestion was identified by the expiration of the retransmission timer. Next,

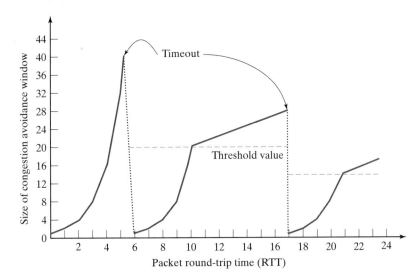

FIGURE 24–16
Operation of the slow-start and congestion avoidance mechanisms.

the TCP instance returns to the slow-start phase, which continues until snd_cwnd reaches the value snd_ssthresh. Subsequently, the congestion-avoidance algorithm is used until another congestion occurs at a window size of 28 segments; finally, this congestion is handled by the same approach.

The following example shows how the two mechanisms described above are implemented in the TCP instance of the Linux kernel:

tcp_v4_init_sock()	net/ipv4/tcp_ipv4.c

```
static int tcp_v4_init_sock(struct sock *sk)
{
        struct tcp_opt *tp = &(sk->tp_pinfo.af_tcp);
        (...)
        /* So many TCP implementations out there (incorrectly) count the
         * initial SYN frame in their delayed-ACK and congestion control
         * algorithms that we must have the following bandaid to talk
         * efficiently to them. -DaveM
         */
        tp->snd_cwnd = 2;

        /* See draft-stevens-tcpca-spec-01 for discussion of the
         * initialization of these values.
         */
        tp->snd_ssthresh = 0x7fffffff; /* Infinity */
        tp->snd_cwnd_clamp = ~0;
        tp->mss_cache = 536;
        (...)
}
```

Parameters for a TCP connection are initialized in the `tcp_v4_init_sock()` method, which is defined as an `init()` function of the `proto` structure. The most important parameters for congestion control are as follows:

- The size of the initial congestion window (`tp->snd_cwnd`) is set to the value two.
- The threshold value for the exponential growth (`tp->snd_ssthresh`) is set to "infinite" (the largest value that can be represented by an `int` variable).

The reason why the congestion window size is initialized to two and not to one (as by default) is as follows (as in many other places in the source text):

- This is an efficient way to avoid *errors in the TCP implementations of other operating systems*, ensuring smooth operation. In this case, some TCP instances count the SYN packet, even though the slow-start algorithm should not become active before the connection has been successfully established (as with all congestion avoidance and flow-control algorithms).

The following source-code fragment of the TCP instance shows how the congestion window grows exponentially during the slow-start phase and how the subsequent linear increase during the congestion-avoidance phase is implemented in the Linux kernel.

`tcp_cong_avoid()`	**net/ipv4/tcp_input.c**

```
/* This is Jacobson's slow start and congestion avoidance.
* SIGCOMM '88, p. 328.
*/
static __inline__ void tcp_cong_avoid(struct tcp_opt *tp)
{
        if (tp->snd_cwnd <= tp->snd_ssthresh)
        { /* In 'safe' area, increase. */
          if (tp->snd_cwnd < tp->snd_cwnd_clamp)
             tp->snd_cwnd++;
        }
        else
        { /* In dangerous area, increase slowly.
           * In theory this is tp->snd_cwnd += 1 / tp->snd_cwnd
           */
        if (tp->snd_cwnd_cnt >= tp->snd_cwnd)
        {
                if (tp->snd_cwnd < tp->snd_cwnd_clamp)
                        tp->snd_cwnd++;
                tp->snd_cwnd_cnt=0;
        }
        else
                tp->snd_cwnd_cnt++;
        }
}
```

`tcp_cong_avoid(tp)` implements the congestion window growth in the slow-start and congestion-avoidance algorithms. `tcp_cong_avoid()` is invoked when an incoming TCP segment with valid acknowledgement (ACK) is handled in `tcp_ack()`. (See Section 24.2.1.)

Initially, the code checks for whether the TCP connection is still in the slow-start phase or is already in the congestion-avoidance phase:

- The congestion window is increased by one in the *slow-start phase* (i.e., when the current value of the congestion window `tp->snd_cwnd` is not yet bigger than the current threshold value `tp->snd_ssthresh`). However, it must not exceed the upper limit value, `tp->snd_cwnd_clamp`. This means that, in this phase, the congestion window is increased by one upon each incoming acknowledgement. In practice, this means that the amount of data that can be sent doubles each time. This behavior corresponds to the exponential growth shown in Figure 24–16.

- In the *congestion-avoidance phase*, the congestion window will be increased by one only if *n* acknowledgements have been previously received, where *n* corresponds to the current congestion-window value.

To implement this behavior, the additional variable `tp->snd_cwnd_cnt` is introduced; it is incremented by one upon each incoming acknowledgement (i.e., upon each call of `tcp_cong_avoid()` in the congestion-avoidance phase). Next, when the congestion-window value `tp->snd_cwnd` is reached, `tp->snd_cwnd` can finally be increased by one, and `tp->snd_cwnd_cnt` is reset. This method makes linear growth achievable.

In summary: There is initially an exponential increase of the congestion window, but, once the threshold value has been reached, there is only a linear growth, as shown in Figure 24–16. Notice at this point that the congestion window increases continually in `tcp_cong_avoid()`. It increases until the criteria for a congestion are met, which will then cause it to reduce in the function described next.

`tcp_enter_loss()`	**net/ipv4/tcp_input.c**

```
void tcp_enter_loss(struct sock *sk, int how)
{
        struct tcp_opt *tp = &sk->tp_pinfo.af_tcp;
        (...)
        /* Reduce ssthresh if it has not yet been
             made inside this window. */
        if ((tp->ca_state <= TCP_CA_Disorder)
                    || (tp->snd_una == tp->high_seq)
                    || (tp->ca_state == TCP_CA_Loss && !tp->retransmits))
        {
             tp->prior_ssthresh = tcp_current_ssthresh(tp);
             tp->snd_ssthresh = tcp_recalc_ssthresh(tp);
        }
```

```
tp->snd_cwnd = 1;
tp->snd_cwnd_cnt = 0;
tp->snd_cwnd_stamp = tcp_time_stamp;
(...)
```

tcp_enter_loss(sk, how) is invoked in the handling routine of the
retransmission timer (tcp_retransmit_timer). This timer triggers whenever a transmitted data segment has not been acknowledged by the time the *retransmission timeout (RTO)* expires. It is assumed that the data segment or its acknowledgement was
lost. In modern networks, except wireless networks, packet losses occur only in congestion situations, and packets have to be discarded in forwarding systems to handle
buffer overflows.

In such a situation, which is detected either because no acknowledgement arrives
or because duplicate acknowledgements arrive, the TCP congestion-handling routine
has to ensure that the data flow of the TCP connection involved is reduced.

Initially, the threshold value for exponential growth in the slow-start phase is set to
a new value, which is computed by the tcp_recalc_ssthresh() method. Before this
value is computed, the current threshold value is stored in the tp->prior_ssthresh
variable. Subsequently, the other congestion-control variables—primarily the congestion
window—are reset. tp->snd_cwnd is set to a maximum segment, which causes the TCP
connection to start the next transmission in the slow-start phase again.

tcp_recalc_ssthresh()	include/net/tcp.h

```
/* Recalculate snd_ssthresh, we want to set it to:
*
* one-half the current congestion window, but no
* less than two segments
*/
static inline __u32 tcp_recalc_ssthresh(struct tcp_opt *tp)
{
        return max(tp->snd_cwnd>>1, 2);
}
```

The threshold value for the exponential growth in the slow-start phase is recalculated in tcp_recalc_ssthresh(tp) as soon as a congestion situation is detected.
Consequently, the current size of the congestion window, tp->snd_cwnd, is reduced to
half as soon as the congestion is detected and is returned as the new threshold value.
However, care is taken only that the threshold value not be smaller than two.

Fast Retransmit and Fast Recovery   The fast-retransmit algorithm was integrated in
the TCP protocol for fast detection of single packet losses. Previously, the only way to
detect packet losses was the expiry of the retransmit timer, and TCP responded to this
by reducing the transmission rate in the slow-start phase.

The new fast-retransmit algorithm enables TCP to detect a packet loss before the
retransmit timer expires—that is, when a single segment out of a series of many segments is lost. The receiver responds to incoming segments with one segment missing by

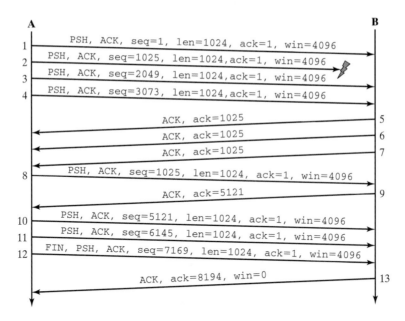

FIGURE 24–17
Detecting a single packet loss by duplicate acknowledgements (segments 5 to 7) and
handling by fast retransmit.

sending duplicate acknowledgements, because it is now receiving packets out of order.
Figure 24–17 shows such a situation.

The sender can see from the duplicate acknowledgements it received that a segment must have been lost, but that other segments still made their way to the receiver.
This means that a massive congestion is very unlikely. The sender retransmits the data
segment that follows the sequence number of the duplicate acknowledgements without
waiting for the retransmission timer to trigger.

A new slow-start phase would be the normal response to a packet loss; that reaction
would significantly reduce the transmission rate. Given duplicate acknowledgements,
however, TCP detects that there is no serious congestion. For this reason, the fast-recovery
method was introduced as an extension of the fast-retransmit algorithm. After a fast retransmit, the congestion window is not set to a minimum value, but instead cut in half, and,
subsequently, increased linearly directly in the congestion-avoidance phase.

We will next describe how these two algorithms cooperate in the TCP instance of
the Linux kernel[4]:

■ When three acknowledgement duplicates are received, the variable
tp->snd_ssthresh is set to half of the current transmit window. The missing segment is retransmitted, and the congestion window tp->snd_cwnd takes the value
tp->ssthresh + 3 * *MSS*, where *MSS* denotes the maximum segment size.

---

[4]We will keep our discussion short, because the implementation of these two algorithms is extensive and is
distributed over many positions within the TCP instance.

- Each time that a duplicate acknowledgement is received, the congestion window tp->snd_cwnd increases by the value of the maximum segment size, and an additional segment is sent (if permitted by the transmit window size).

- When the first acknowledgment of new data arrives, then tp->snd_cwnd takes the original value of tp->snd_ssthresh, which was stored in tp->prior_ssthresh. This acknowledgement should acknowledge the data segment that was originally lost. In addition, it should acknowledge all segments sent between the lost packet and the third acknowledgement duplicate.

24.4.3   Congestion Avoidance

The TCP protocol could produce considerable load, even when a relatively small amount of data is sent. This effect is due to the size of the TCP packet header, which comprises 20 bytes. If we add the IP packet header and an Ethernet packet header to this, the protocol-control information sent with each packet adds up to more than fifty bytes. With scarcely filled data packets or frequent acknowledgement packets (consisting of packet headers only), a large amount of bandwidth is wasted on packet headers. The two methods described below are aimed at minimizing these circumstances.

Delayed Acknowledgements   The principle of *delayed acks* enables the TCP protocol to delay an acknowledgement for a segment. The acknowledgement is delayed so as to eventually be sent together with the data (which is also called *piggybacking*) and so as to enable TCP to accumulate several acknowledgements. The delayed transmission of acknowledgements is implemented by using the *delack* timer, which will be introduced in Section 24.5.

Nagle Algorithm   John Nagle's algorithm, also known by the name *small-packet-avoidance algorithm*, serves to avoid excessive network load due to a large number of small TCP packets. For this purpose, the data to be sent is held back as long as possible, because two complete TCP packets would have to be sent for each payload byte in the worst case: the first packet to transport the data, and the second packet, which is sent by the receiver, to acknowledge the first one.

This worst case occurs when data to be sent accumulate more slowly than they can be sent (e.g., in a Telnet connection, where the data to be transmitted is transported very slowly—a few characters per second—to the TCP instance. The TCP instance would pack each character in a packet and send these packets separately. The packet-header overhead created by this approach was described above.

To avoid high loads in the network due to these many small segments, ones smaller than the negotiated maximum segment length (MSS), the Nagle algorithm [Nagl84] introduces the limitation that at most one segment in a connection may be unacknowledged before other segments are sent. The algorithm says that small segments should be retained pending arrival of an acknowledgement in the case of sent and unacknowledged segments. The data contained in these small segments are grouped into a larger segment. However, if an application (e.g., Telnet) wants to avoid packet delays, for some specific reason, then it can use the socket option TCP_NODELAY to disable the Nagle algorithm.

The following fragment shows the complete source text of the Nagle algorithm. These few lines are sufficient to achieve the behavior discussed above.

tcp_nagle_check()	include/net/tcp.h

```
static __inline__ int tcp_nagle_check(struct tcp_opt *tp,
                      struct sk_buff *skb, unsigned mss_now)
{
    return (skb->len < mss_now &&
        !(TCP_SKB_CB(skb)->flags & (TCPCB_FLAG_URG|TCPCB_FLAG_FIN))
        && (tp->nonagle == 2 ||
            (!tp->nonagle &&
            tp->packets_out &&
            tcp_minshall_check(tp))));
}
```

The Nagle algorithm (i.e., the tcp_nagle_check() method) is asked in tcp_snd_test() whether the existing segment may be sent. If it wants to prevent the segment from being sent at this time, then tcp_nagle_check() returns the value true. If there are reasons for immediate transmission of this data, then it returns false.

The first check is for whether there is a sufficient amount of data to fill a complete segment. If this is the case, then there is no reason to delay its transmission further. Consequently, the segment length (skb->len) collaborates with mss_now to determine the amount of data than can be sent at once.

The next check is to see whether there are particularly important control packets (e.g., FIN or URG packets). These packets have to be sent immediately, and Nagle's algorithm must not delay them.

The next line checks for whether the socket option TCP_CORK was activated (tp-nonagle == 2). It forces that only complete packets will be sent.

If all checks done so far have resulted in false, the next step checks for whether the Nagle algorithm has been disabled by the socket option TCP_NODELAY. If so, then tp->nonagle would have the value one, and tcp_nagle_check() would return false, which means that the segment can be sent.

However, if the Nagle algorithm is still active, then tcp_minshall_check() (described later) checks for whether small and incompletely filled packets are on their, way (i.e., packets that have not yet been acknowledged). If there are no small and unacknowledged packets in the connection, this data packet may be sent; otherwise, it has to be delayed.

The previous line checks for whether any acknowledgements for packets are still missing. Only one variable has to be checked here, so this query is much faster than the method call in the next line (tcp_minshall_check(tp)). *Lazy evaluation* saves time, because the slower method has to be invoked only if the fast query has not yet returned a result.

tcp_minshall_check()	include/net/tcp.h

```
static __inline__ int tcp_minshall_check(struct tcp_opt *tp)
{
        return after(tp->snd_sml,tp->snd_una) &&
               !after(tp->snd_sml, tp->snd_nxt);
}
```

24.5   TIMER MANAGEMENT IN TCP

In closing, this section briefly discusses how timers are managed in TCP. Timers are used in different positions within the TCP protocol to control retransmissions and to limit the hold time for missing packets.

24.5.1 Data Structures

`struct timer_list`	**include/linux/timer.h**

```
struct timer_list {
        struct list_head list;
        unsigned long expires;
        unsigned long data;
        void (*function)(unsigned long);
        volatile int running;
};
```

The basis for each timer is the `jiffies` variable. As described in Chapter 2, it is updated by Linux every 10 ms.

A timer structure includes a function pointers that takes a behavior function when initialized. This function is invoked when the timer expires. The time at which it expires depends on the `expires` field. This field takes an offset (in the `jiffies` unit) for the current time (also in the `jiffies` unit). The behavior function is invoked when this value is reached.

TCP maintains seven timers for each connection:

▪ SYNACK timer This timer is used when a TCP instance changes its state from LISTEN to SYN_RECV. The TCP instance of the server initially waits three seconds for an ACK. If no ACK arrives within this time, then the connection request is considered outdated.

▪ Retransmit timer Because the TCP protocol uses only positive acknowledgements, the sending TCP instance has to see for itself whether a segment was lost. It does this by use of the `retransmit` timer, the expiry of which indicates that a segment could have been lost, causing its retransmission.

The exponential backoff method assumes that retransmissions are caused by a congestion. When segments are retransmitted, the timer value is increased exponentially so as to be able to detect segment losses.

The `retransmit` timer determines when packets have to be retransmitted during a data transmission phase. This value depends on the round-trip time and normally is within the range from 200 ms to two minutes.

This timer is also used during the establishment of a connection. It is initialized to three seconds. Upon expiry of this time, the backoff mechanism is used five times.

- ▨ `Delayed ACK` timer This timer delays the transmission of ACK packets. The value is smaller than 200 ms.

- ▨ `Keepalive` timer This timer is used to test whether a connection is still up. It is invoked for the first time after nine hours. Subsequently, nine probes are sent every 75 seconds. If all probes fail, the connection is reset.

- ▨ `Probe` timer This timer is used to test for a defined time interval, to see whether the zero window still applies. The value depends on the round-trip time.

- ▨ `FinWait2` timer The expiry of this timer switches the connection from the FIN_WAIT2 state into the CLOSED state, if no FIN packet from the partner arrives.

- ▨ `TWKill` timer This timer manages the interval in the TIME_WAIT state. The value is twice the maximum segment lifecycle, which is 60 seconds.

24.5.2 Functions

This section first introduces all general timer functions.

`tcp_init_xmit_timers()`	net/ipv4/tcp_timer.c

`tcp_init_xmit_timers(sk)` initializes the set of various timers. The `timer_list` structures are hooked, and the function pointers are converted to the respective behavior functions.

`tcp_reset_xmit_timer()`	include/net/tcp.h

The function `tcp_reset_xmit_timer(sk, what, when)` sets the timer specified in `what` to the time `when` (i.e., to the time `jiffies + when`).

`tcp_clear_xmit_timer()`	include/net/tcp.h

The function `tcp_clear_xmit_timer(sk)` removes all timers set for a connection from the linked list of `timer_list` structures.

SYNACK Timer   The actions of the SYNACK timer are implemented in the function `tcp_synack_timer(sk)`   (include/linux/tcp_timer.c). This timer walks through a list of all connections with unacknowledged SYNACK packets and deletes all connections for which the timeout value `min ((TCP_TIMEOUT_INIT << req->retrans), TCP_RTO_MAX)`, has expired. Subsequently, the `keepalive` timer is started for a new connection and initialized by `TCP_SYNQ_INTERVAL`.

There are various functions to manage the `keepalive` timer:

`tcp_delete_keepalive_timer()`	**net/ipv4/tcp_timer.c**

The function `tcp_delete_keepalive_timer(sk)` removes the keepalive timer from the list of `timer_list` structures.

`tcp_reset_keepalive_timer()`	**net/ipv4/tcp_timer.c**

The function `tcp_reset_keepalive_timer(sk,  len)` sets the timer to the value `jiffies + len`.

`tcp_keepalive_timer()`	**net/ipv4/tcp_timer.c**

The function `tcp_keepalive_timer(data)` is the behavior function for the `keepalive` timer. When this function is invoked, the state of the connection is checked to decide whether this connection should be terminated. This function implements various logically separated TCP timers. In addition to the SYNACK timer described here, it implements the timeout in the FIN_WAIT_2 state and the actual `keepalive` timer.

Retransmit Timer   The client's TCP instance sends a SYN packet to the server and waits for an answer (with SYN and ACK set) while the connection-establishment phase is active. At the same time, `tcp_connect()` (in `net/ipv4/tcp_output.c`) and the function `tcp_reset_xmit_timer(sk,  TCP_TIME_RETRANS,  tp->rto)` are used to set the retransmit timer to the value `TCP_TIMEOUT_INIT`. `TCP_TIMEOUT_INIT` is set to the value 3*HZ in the file `include/net/tcp.h`.

The `retransmit` timer is also used when the connection is established and running. The duration of the timeout is doubled, in the `tcp_retransmit_timer()` function (`net/ipv4/tcp_timer.c`), upon each retransmission, until it has arrived at the maximum and the connection is reset:

```
tp->rto = min(tp->rto << 1, TCP_RTO_MAX);
    tcp_reset_xmit_timer(sk, TCP_TIME_RETRANS, tp->rto);
    if (tp->retransmits > sysctl_tcp_retries1)
        __sk_dst_reset(sk);
```

The retransmit timer is initialized to the retransmission timeout (RTO), which is recalculated by use of various helper functions:

`tcp_set_rto()`	**net/ipv4/tcp_input.c**

This function computes the RTO (retransmission timeout) from the round-trip time values.

| tcp_bound_rto() | net/ipv4/tcp_input.c |

The function `tcp_bound_rto(tp)` limits the value range for RTO to a fixed interval.

| tcp_ack_saw_tstamp() | net/ipv4/tcp_input.c |

The function `tcp_ack_saw_tstamp(sk, tp, seq, ack, flag)` computes and sets the RTO and terminates the retransmission mode, if applicable.

| tcp_ack_packets_out() | net/ipv4/tcp_input.c |

In the retransmission mode, the function `tcp_ack_packets_out(sk, tp)` continues to send packets from the retransmission queue and updates the `retransmit` timer.

Delayed ACK Timer The `Delayed` ACK timer is implemented in the function `tcp_delack_timer()`.

| tcp_delack_timer() | net/ipv4/tcp_timer.c |

This function is invoked when the `TCP_TIME_DACK` timer expires. It resets the `Delayed` ACK timer and sends an ACK packet.

| tcp_send_delayed_ack() | net/ipv4/tcp_output.c |

This function is invoked by `tcp_ack_snd_check()` (`include/linux/tcp_input.c`) when an incoming packet should be acknowledged and when no direct ACK is required.

The function `tcp_send_delayed_ack()` uses the `mod_timer` (`&tp->delack_timer, timeout`) call to set the Delayed ACK timer. When this timer expires, the function `tcp_send_delayed_ack(sk)` sends a delayed ACK packet, and the Delayed ACK timer restarts.

Keepalive Timer The actual keepalive timer is implemented in the function `tcp_keepalive_timer()`, which serves to test a connection that has not been used over a lengthy period of time. When this timer expires, the function `tcp_write_wakeup(sk)` uses the function `tcp_xmit_probe_skb()` (both in `net/ipv4/tcp_output.c`) to send a probe packet. Subsequently, the variable `tp->probes_out` is incremented until the maximum number of probes, defined in `sysctl_tcp_keepalive_probes`, is reached.

Probe Timer Zero-window probing was described in Section 24.4.1; we mention it here only for the sake of completeness.

FinWait2 Timer   The keepalive timer is also used to implement the timeout when waiting for a FIN packet in the FIN_WAIT2 state. In this case, it is used to compute the timeout duration. During calling of the function tcp_time_wait(), the connection state changes to TIME_WAIT. The connection is closed when the timeout expires, at the latest.

TWKill Timer   The timeout in the TIME_WAIT state is implemented by the function tcp_tw_schedule() (net/ipv4/tcp minisocks.c), which is invoked by the function tcp_time_wait() when the connection is torn down.

24.5.3 Configuration

To be able to use the TCP/IP support, we have to activate the option TCP/IP networking in the kernel-configuration menu.

In addition, when creating a socket, you can use optional settings to influence the behavior. These settings are defined as constants in the file /include/linux/tcp.h. All available settings are listed in Table 24–1.

TABLE 24–1   Socket options for the Transmission Control Protocol.

Socket Options	
TCP_NODELAY	Disables the Nagle algorithm.
TCP_MAXSEG	Limits the maximum segment size.
TCP_CORK	Only segments with max. size are sent.
TCP_KEEPIDLE	Initial value for keepalive probes.
TCP_KEEPINTV	Interval between keepalive probes.
TCP_KEEPCNT	Number of keepalives.
TCP_SYNCNT	Number of SYN retransmissions.
TCP_LINGER2	Timeout duration in the FIN_WAIT2 state.
TCP_DEFER_ACCEPT	Notify only when data is received.
TCP_WINDOW_CLAMP	Limit the receive window.
TCP_INFO	Information about the current connection.
TCP_QUICKACK	Activate or deactivate Quick ACKs.
TCP_OPT_TIMESTAMPS	Activate or deactivate the timestamp option.
TCP_OPT_WSCALE	Activate or deactivate the window scaling option.
TCP_OPT_ECN	Activate or deactivate the ECN (Explicit Congestion Notification).

User Datagram Protocol (UDP)

25.1 INTRODUCTION

The *User Datagram Protocol* (*UDP*) is described in RFC 768 [Post80] and represents a minimal transport protocol. It runs on top of the Internet Protocol (IP) and essentially offers the same functionality as IP itself: an unreliable, connectionless datagram service. In this case, unreliable means that there are no mechanisms to detect and handle lost or duplicate packets. However, packets can be optionally protected against bit errors by using a checksum, which covers both the packet header and the payload of each packet, in contrast to IP. Otherwise, there is only one additional option, compared to IP: Port numbers can be used to address different applications in a specific end system.

On the one hand, UDP is used for transaction-oriented applications, such as the *Domain Name System* (*DNS*), where only one request and the relevant reply have to be transmitted, so that it is not worthwhile establishing a connection context, which would mean, for example in TCP, that three additional messages for the establishment and four messages for the tear-down were required. On the other hand, UDP is also used where the reliability of a transmission plays a secondary role, because one is primarily interested in transmitting data easily and quickly. For example, it is normally not a problem if some packets are lost when audio streams are transmitted in small packets. On the contrary, an automatic flow and error control with retransmission of lost packets would often be disturbing to the smooth playback of the stream.

25.1.1 Packet Format

Figure 25–1 shows the format of UDP packets. The header fields are briefly described below.

- *Source port*: The source port is the port number used by the sending process, in the range from 1 to 65535; normally, the receiver of a request sent over UDP will

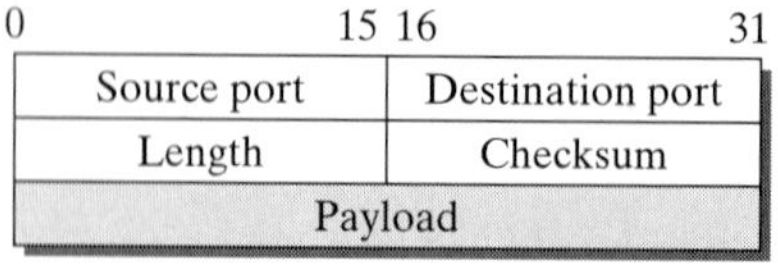

FIGURE 25–1
UPD packet format.

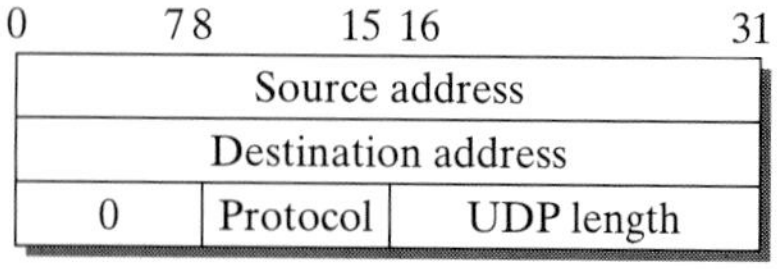

FIGURE 25–2
Pseudo header format for checksum calculation.

direct its reply to this port. RFC 768 specifies that giving the source port number is optional, and the field can have the value zero, if it is not used. However, for UDP over the socket programming interface in Linux (see Chapters 26 and 27), this is not possible, because a port number different from zero is automatically assigned to each socket, if the user does not state one.

▨ *Destination port*: The destination port is used to address the application in the destination system that is to receive a UDP packet.

▨ *Length*: The length is specified in octets and refers to the entire UDP packet, consisting of packet header and payload. The smallest possible length is therefore eight octets, and the largest possible UDP packet can transport 65535 − 8 = 65527 payload octets.

▨ *Checksum*: As in TCP, the calculation of the checksum includes a pseudo header, in addition to the packet header and the payload. The format of this pseudo header is shown in Figure 25–2. It includes the IP source and destination addresses, the UDP protocol identifier (17), and the length of the UDP packet. The checksum is computed as a 16-bit ones complement of the ones-complement sum over the data mentioned above, where a zero octet is appended if the octet number is uneven. This method can be implemented efficiently for all processor types (as described in RFCs 1071, 1141, and 1624 [BrBP88, MaKu90, Rijs94]). If the computation results in the checksum zero, the all-1-bit value is transmitted instead, which is equivalent in ones-complement arithmetic. A zero in the checksum field means that the sender has not computed a checksum.

25.2   DATA STRUCTURES

The implementation of UDP in the Linux kernel does not require any additional or particularly complex data structures. This section describes the data structure used to pass payload at the socket interface, the UDP datagram itself, which is included in the general socket buffer structure, and the data structure instances used to integrate the protocol into the network architecture.

25.2.1   Passing the Payload

The payload is given for the sendmsg() system call at the socket interface in the form of an msghdr structure, which is checked by the socket interface and copied into the kernel (except for the actual payload that initially remains in the user address space). Otherwise, the structure is passed, as is, to the udp_sendmsg() function for sending UDP packets.

`struct msghdr`	`include/linux/socket.h`

```
struct msghdr {
        void                    *msg_name;
        int                     msg_namelen;
        struct iovec            *msg_iov;
        __kernel_size_t         msg_iovlen;
        void                    *msg_control;
        __kernel_size_t         msg_controllen;
        unsigned                msg_flags;
};
```

For sending of UDP packets, msg_name is not really a name, but a pointer to a sockaddr_in structure (see Section 27.1.1), which contains an IP address and a port number; msg_namelen describes the length of this structure. The msg_iov pointer refers to an array of iovec structures, which reference the payload. This means that this payload can be present in a series of individual blocks, where each block is denoted in an iovec structure by its initial address (iov_base) and its length (iov_len):

```
struct iovec
{
        void                    *iov_base;
        __kernel_size_t         iov_len;
};
```

The buffer specified by msg_control and msg_controllen can be used to pass protocol-specific control messages. We will not discuss the format of these messages; see detailed information in the recv() system call manpage.

The msg_flags element can be used to pass different flags both from the user process to the kernel and in the opposite direction. For example, the kernel evaluates the following flags:

- MSG_DONTROUTE specifies that the destination must be in the local area network and that, for this reason, the datagram should not be sent over a router to its destination.
- MSG_DONTWAIT prevents the system call from blocking if, for example, there are no data to be received.
- MSG_ERRQUEUE means that no packet should be fetched, but instead a detailed error message, which might be available at the socket.

The following flag is an example of flags returned by the kernel to the user process:

- MSG_TRUNC indicates that the buffer space provided for receiving was insufficient, so that some of the packet data were lost.

The flags discussed above are only some examples; we will not describe all possible flags and their meanings here. Readers can find more information in the system calls' manpages.

25.2.2 The UDP Datagram

`struct udphdr`	**include/linux/udp.h**

The `union` element h of the `sk_buff` structure includes a pointer, `struct udphdr *uh`, which references the UDP header within the packet data. The udphdr structure is declared as follows, based on the packet format shown in Figure 25–1:

```
struct udphdr {
        __u16 source;
        __u16 dest;
        __u16 len;
        __u16 check;
};
```

`struct udpfakehdr`	**net/ipv4/udp.c**

When sending a packet and computing the checksum, as required, the data structure used is somewhat more complex. In addition to a udphdr structure, where the packet header is built, and from which it is copied into the packet later, it also includes the other data required to create the pseudo IP packet header:

```
struct udpfakehdr
{
        struct udphdr uh;
        u32 saddr;
        u32 daddr;
        struct iovec *iov;
        u32 wcheck;
};
```

The IP source and destination addresses are stored in saddr and daddr, the payload can be reached over the iovec structure, and the checksum is computed in wcheck during the sending.

25.2.3 Integration of UDP into the Network Architecture

As a transport protocol, UDP has two interfaces: one "downwards" to the network layer (the Internet Protocol) and one "upwards" to the application layer. The latter is formed by the sockets described in Chapter 26—more specifically, by the sockets of the PF_INET protocol family. (See Section 26.3.1.)

Interface to the Application Layer   The socket implementation uses the `proto` structure, which is defined in `net/ipv4/udp.c` for UDP, to access the functionality of transport protocols:

```
struct proto udp_prot = {
        name:                   "UDP",
        close:                  udp_close,
        connect:                udp_connect,
        disconnect:             udp_disconnect,
        ioctl:                  udp_ioctl,
        setsockopt:             ip_setsockopt,
        getsockopt:             ip_getsockopt,
        sendmsg:                udp_sendmsg,
        recvmsg:                udp_recvmsg,
        backlog_rcv:            udp_queue_rcv_skb,
        hash:                   udp_v4_hash,
        unhash:                 udp_v4_unhash,
        get_port:               udp_v4_get_port,
};
```

The elements missing here (e.g., `bind` and `accept`), compared to the complete `proto` structure shown in Section 26.3.1, are initialized to zero, which means that no transport-protocol-specific handling of the corresponding events is done.

Socket-state information is stored in the `sock` data structure mentioned in Section 26.3.1. The simplicity of UDP means that no protocol-specific additional data is required, so there is no UDP-specific part of the `tp_pinfo` field.

Most of the functions referenced in the `proto` structure are not very complex, so we will discuss them here only briefly:

- `udp_close()`: During the closing of a UDP socket, only the function `inet_sock_release()` (`net/ipv4/af_inet.c`), which is the same for all `PF_INET` sockets, is invoked to release the socket data structure. From there, `udp_v4_unhash()` is invoked (as described later).
- `udp_connect()`: UDP is a connectionless protocol, so the `connect()` system call at the application layer interface, which is used in connection-oriented protocols to establish a connection, has a slightly different meaning: It can be used to define the destination of all UDP packets subsequently sent over a socket, so that it doesn't have to be specified each time. Accordingly, the destination address and destination port are stored in the `sock` data structure within `udp_connect()`. The fact that this optional definition has taken place is registered by entering the state identifier `TCP_ESTABLISHED`, which is "borrowed" from TCP, in the `state` field of the `sock` structure. In addition, a routing cache entry is constructed by using `ip_route_connect()` and stored in the `sock` structure. This entry is used when packets are being sent, so that some overhead is avoided.
- `udp_disconnect()`: The state is set to `TCP_CLOSE`, the destination address and destination port are deleted, and a stored routing cache entry is released.

- udp_ioctl(): The ioctl() system call can be used here to poll the lengths of transmit and receive queues.

- ip_setsockopt() and ip_getsockopt(): There are no socket options on the UDP level, so these two entries refer directly to the general handling routines of the IP level. (See also man setsockopt.)

- udp_sendmsg() and udp_recvmsg(): These two functions implement the sending and receiving of UDP packets. Section 25.3 will discuss them in more detail.

- udp_queue_rcv_skb(): This function will be discussed together with the description of udp_recvmsg() in Section 25.3.2.

- udp_v4_hash(): During the receiving of UDP packets, a decision must be made about which socket these packets should be assigned to, so that they can be placed in that socket's receive queue to be fetched by the user process later. To facilitate this assignment to a socket, the sock structures of all UDP sockets are registered in a hash table, struct sock *udp_hash[UDP_HTABLE_SIZE]. The port number modulo UDP_HTABLE_SIZE is used as hash value.

  Within the proto structure, the hash entry could actually reference a function that enters a socket into the hash table. However, the socket had already been entered into the table by udp_v4_get_port() (described later) when the port number was assigned in UDP, so udp_v4_hash() actually is not needed and is never used.

- udp_v4_unhash(): This function is invoked when a socket is released, to remove the sock structure from the hash table.

- udp_v4_get_port(): This function is invoked by the PF_INET implementation in net/ipv4/af_inet.c whenever a local port number has to be assigned to a socket. The desired port number passed here can also be zero. In this case, a free port is selected, with a position in the hash table where as few sockets as possible are linked.

Interface to IP   The interface used to accept UDP packets received by the IP layer is defined by the inet_protocol structure described in Section 14.2.5 in connection with the function inet_add_protocol() and shown in Figure 14–5. It is contained in net/ipv4/protocol.c for UDP and all protocols running directly on top of IP, appearing as follows:

```
static struct inet_protocol udp_protocol = {
        handler:          udp_rcv,
        err_handler:      udp_err,
        next:             IPPROTO_PREVIOUS,
        protocol:         IPPROTO_UDP,
        name:             "UDP"
};
```

The function udp_rcv() serves to receive incoming packets; Section 25.3.2 will discuss it in more detail. udp_err() handles ICMP error messages communicated by the IP layer.

To send packets over IP, UDP uses the function ip_build_xmit() from net/ipv4/ip_output.c. In contrast to ip_queue_xmit(), this function does not take the complete IP payload as parameter, but instead a callback function, which it can use to request this data. In addition, it uses a routing cache entry, also provided as a parameter, instead of handling the routing itself.

25.3   SENDING AND RECEIVING UDP DATAGRAMS

The sending of UDP packets, starting from the system call at the socket interface and running all the way until the completed packet is added to the output queue of the network interface, is handled in just one pass, but the receiving of UDP packets requires two separate steps: Once a packet has been received, udp_rcv() first allocates it to a socket in bottom-half context and places it into that socket's receive queue. From there, the packet is fetched via system call of a user process, which is mapped to udp_recvmsg().

Sending UDP Datagrams

udp_sendmsg()	net/ipv4/udp.c

The function udp_sendmsg() is invoked over the socket interface whenever a UDP packet has to be sent: The different kinds of systems calls all lead to this single function's being called. Its parameters are a sock structure with the state of the sending PF_INET socket, a pointer to a msg structure that specifies the receiver and payload, and the payload length in octets.

First, a locally created udpfakehdr structure takes the destination address and the destination port from the msg_name element of the msg structure. The destination doesn't have to be specified explicitly only if a default destination address has previously been assigned to this socket via udp_connect(). In this case, the information from the sock structure is used instead. The source address and the source port always derive from the sock structure. Additionally, they are stored in an ipcm_cookie structure. This structure, which we will not describe here in detail, serves later on to pass the addresses, the device identifier, and the IP options (if applicable) to the Internet Protocol.

Any control messages in the msg_control element of the msghdr structure are processed by calling the function ip_cmsg_send(), and the results are registered in the ipcm_cookie structure. Control messages can be used to modify the source address or to pass IP options, which will then also be registered in the ipcm_cookie structure. If no IP options are specified, then the IP options stored in the sock structure, if applicable, will be used.

A routing cache entry has to be procured, so it is also necessary to handle the source routing IP options beforehand; the address of the first intermediate station might need to be used instead of the destination address.

If the socket had previously obtained a routing cache entry by udp_connect(), and if the corresponding destination address has not yet been changed in the process of udp_sendmsg(), then this routing cache entry is now checked. If this check produces a negative result, or if the destination address was changed, then ip_route_output() is used to procure a new routing cache entry (which is then stored in the sock structure).

Eventually, the transmission of data is initiated by calling ip_build_xmit(), where either udp_getfrag() or udp_getfrag_nosum() is provided as the callback function for getting data, depending on whether the checksum in the packet header should include the payload.[1] The parameters used here also include the udpfakehdr and ipcm structures, the routing cache entry, the flags from the msghdr structure, and the total length of the UDP packet.

The following discussion considers only udp_getfrag(), because udp_getfrag_nosum() provides the same functionality, but is simpler for omitting the checksum calculation.

udp_getfrag()	net/ipv4/udp.c

For each IP fragment it generates, ip_build_xmit() invokes the callback function udp_getfrag() to get the required payload. A pointer to the udpfakehdr structure filled by udp_sendmsg() is one of the parameters passed here, in addition to the desired destination address, the fragment offset, and the desired data quantity.

The actual bulk of the work is done by the function csum_partial_copy_fromiovecend(), defined in net/core/iovec.c. This function not only copies the data referenced by the iovec structure directly from the user-address space to the desired location, but also computes the checksum. The result of the checksum calculation is stored in the wcheck element of the updfakehdr structure in each such step. The next step uses this intermediate result as a starting value, so that the checksum eventually extends over the entire data.

The first fragment has to be created last, because it contains the UDP header with the checksum. It is left to ip_build_xmit() to ensure the correct order; udp_getfrag() recognizes the first fragment only by the offset value zero. It extends the checksum calculation to the packet header and the IP pseudo header, and eventually it completes the packet header by inserting the checksum, before it finally copies it to the beginning of the packet.

Receiving UDP Datagrams

udp_rcv()	net/ipv4/udp.c

Once IP has received a UDP packet, it passes this packet in the form of an sk_buff pointer to udp_rcv() for further processing. After the packet length has been checked and the checksum has been computed over the pseudo IP header (if the packet header includes no checksum, or if the checksum was previously computed by the interface hardware, this is registered in the sk_buff), udp_rcv() directly forwards multicast and broadcast packets to udp_mcast_deliver(), which is described further later on.

The most important task is now to allocate the packet to a socket, so that it can be placed into that socket's queue until it is fetched by the user. This task is handled by the function udp_v4_lookup() (or udp_v4_lookup_longway()) invoked by udp_rcv(). This function looks up the udp_hash table and selects the socket with the most specific

---

[1]A checksum is computed if the flag no_check in the sock structure is null, which is the case by default. This flag can be set via the socket option SO_NO_CHECK on the SOL_SOCKET level.

information with regard to addresses, destination port, and input interface from the sockets linked in the entry and matching the packet.

When a socket has been found, then `udp_queue_rcv_skb()` is called and in turn invokes `sock_queue_rcv_skb()`, which inserts the packet into that socket's receive queue. Otherwise, an ICMP error message is generated, provided that the checksum calculation can be completed successfully. No ICMP messages are generated for packets with faulty checksums.

`udp_mcast_deliver()`	**net/ipv4/udp.c**

Like `udp_v4_lookup()`, `udp_mcast_deliver()` searches for a matching receiver socket. However, it does not select the single socket matching best, but all sockets with a matching destination port and—if this information is included—with matching addresses and input interface and correspond to the packet. All these sockets receive a copy of the packet. The copies are created by using `skb_clone()` and delivered as in `udp_rcv()` by `udp_queue_rcv_skb()`.

`udp_recvmsg()`	**net/ipv4/udp.c**

If a user process uses one of the system calls to receive packets, then the socket interface maps it to a call of the function `udp_recvmsg()`. This function removes an `sk_buff` structure from the receive queue of the socket passed as a parameter, interprets it as UDP packet, and returns the payload contained (and information from the packet header, if necessary) in the form of an entry in an `msghdr` structure passed by reference. If the receive queue is currently empty, then either the process has to be set to waiting state, or the call has to be terminated with an appropriate feedback, depending on the specification.

The process of fetching `sk_buff` structures from receive queues, of waiting for their arrival, and of copying the data are part of not only the UDP, are also required in several other places. Therefore, the file `net/core/datagram.c` contains generic functions for these purposes, which are used by `udp_recv_msg()`:

- `skb_recv_datagram()` serves to fetch an `sk_buff`. This is done by using `skb_dequeue()` (or `skb_peek()`, if the provided flags show that the packet should merely be read, but not be removed). If an `sk_buff` is actually available, then it is returned; otherwise, if blocking is permitted, the function `wait_for_packet()` implemented in the same file is invoked. It registers the process as a waiting process with the socket and finally invokes `schedule()` to temporarily obtain control.

- `skb_copy_datagram_iovec()` or `skb_copy_and_csum_datagram_iovec()` are invoked by `udp_recvmsg()` to copy the payload from the packet into the `msg_iov` element of the `msghdr` structure and to compute and verify the checksum in the process, if applicable.

- `skb_free_datagram()` is used to release the `sk_buff` structure after the address information has been copied in `udp_recvmsg()` and, for example, IP options have been taken over into a control message (by calling the function `ip_cmsg_recv()`).

CHAPTER 26

The Concept of Sockets

26.1 INTRODUCTION

The abstraction of sockets was introduced (based on the BSD version of UNIX, where this interface was used for the first time; also called BSD sockets) to facilitate programming of networked applications. An application can use this uniform interface to send or receive data over a network. This interface looks alike for all protocols, and the desired protocol is selected to match three parameters: family, type, and protocol. Chapter 27 gives a complete overview of all available protocol families (family). It also discusses how applications can use the socket interface. In contrast, this chapter gives an overview of the socket implementation in the Linux kernel.

Figure 26–1 gives an overview of how the socket support is integrated into the protocol implementations in the Linux kernel. The BSD socket interface provides a uniform interface upwards to the applications; underneath the interface, however, different protocol families are distinguished by protocol-specific sockets. Currently, one of the most important protocol families, PF_INET (protocol family internet) will be described in the following section. In addition, PF_PACKET sockets in more recent Linux versions provide an elegant way to send data packets by directly accessing a network device. For example, the use of the packet socket was introduced in Chapter 9. Section 26.3.2 describes the packet socket in more detail. In contrast, the Netlink sockets do not serve for data transmission over a network, but to configure various parts of the Linux network architecture. The part to be configured is selected over the parameters NETLINK_* of the socket's protocol variable, as shown in Figure 26–1. The third part of this chapter describes the PF_NETLINK sockets.

26.2 BSD SOCKETS

The Linux kernel offers exactly one socket-related system call, and all socket calls of applications are mapped to this system call. The function asmlinkage long sys_socketcall(int call, unsigned long *args) is defined in net/socket.c. Moreover, a

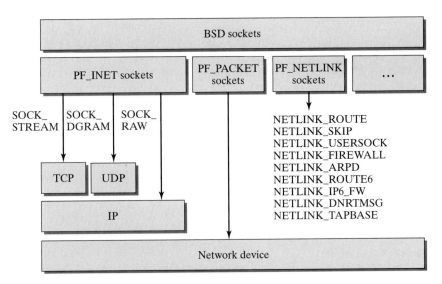

FIGURE 26–1
Structure of the socket support in the Linux kernel.

number is assigned in `include/asm/unistd.h` (#define __NR_socketcall 102) and added to a table with system calls in `arch/i386/kernel/entry.S`. The socket function to be addressed can be stated in the `call` parameter of a call. The admissible parameters are defined in `include/linux/net.h`:   SYS_SOCKET,   SYS_BIND,   SYS_CONNECT, SYS_LISTEN, SYS_ACCEPT, SYS_GETSOCKNAME, SYS_GETPEERNAME, SYS_SOCKET-PAIR,   SYS_SEND,   SYS_RECV,   SYS_SENDTO,   SYS_RECVFROM,   SYS_SHUTDOWN, SYS_SETSOCKOPT, SYS_GETSOCKOPT, SYS_SENDMSG, SYS_RECVMSG. From within libraries in the user space, the `sys_socketcall()` call with a specific parameter is mapped to an independent function (e.g., sys_socketcall(SYS_SOCKET,...) becomes the call socket(...)).

`sys_socketcall()`	**net/socket.c**

The function to be called is selected in the kernel by using a `switch` command in the function `sys_socketcall()`, and the command `copy_from_user()` is used to first copy the function's arguments into a vector, `unsigned long a[6]`:

```
...
if copy_from_user(a, args, nargs[call]))
      return -EFAULT;

a0=a[0];
a1=a[1];

switch(call)
      {
      case SYS_SOCKET:
            err = sys_socket(a0,a1,a[2]);
            break;
```

```
        case SYS_BIND:
                err = sys_bind(a0,(struct sockaddr *)a1, a[2]);
                break;
        case SYS_CONNECT:
                err = sys_connect(a0, (struct sockaddr *)a1, a[2]);
                break;
        case SYS_LISTEN:
                err = sys_listen(a0,a1);
                break;
        ...
        }
    ...
```

The most important structure within the BSD socket support is `struct socket`. It is defined in `include/linux/net.h`:

```
struct socket {
        socket_state            state;
        unsigned long           flags;
        struct proto_ops        *ops;
        struct inode            *inode;
        struct fasync_struct    *fasync_list; /* Asynchronous wakeup list*/
        struct file             *file;        /* File back pointer for gc*/
        struct sock             *sk;
        wait_queue_head_t       wait;

        short                   type;
        unsigned char           passcred;
};
```

This structure is slightly reduced, compared to that in earlier kernel versions. The socket state stored in `state` can take the following values (`include/linux/net.h`): SS_FREE (not busy), SS_UNCONNECTED (not connected), SS_CONNECTING (currently being connected), SS_CONNECTED (connected), SS_DISCONNECTING (currently being disconnected). The `flags` are required to synchronize accesses. The `ops` pointer references the protocol operation of the connected protocol (e.g., TCP or UDP) after the initialization. Just as there is an `inode` for each file in Linux, an `inode` is assigned to each BSD socket. A pointer to the `file` structure is stored in `file`; this structure is connected to the socket and can also be used to address it. If any process is waiting for events at this `file`, then that process can be reached over `fasync_list`.

A matching `sock` structure can be used via the `sk` pointer. However, this structure is initialized by protocol-specific sockets underneath the BSD sockets (e.g., PF_INET sockets) and connected to this pointer. The `wait` entry serves to implement synchronous (blocking) receipt. The `type` field serves to store the second parameter by the same name of the socket call in the user space. The admissible parameters are defined in `include/asm/socket.h`: SOCK_STREAM, SOCK_DGRAM, SOCK_RAW, SOCK_RDM, SOCK_SEQPACKET, and SOCK_PACKET. (The last should no longer be used.)

Now let's see how all of this works in the Linux kernel when `socket()` is invoked by an application. As was mentioned, this call is passed within the function `sys_socketcall()` in `net/socket.c` by invoking the function `sys_socket()`.

sys_socket()	net/socket.c

This function initializes the socket structure and allocates an `inode` and a `file` descriptor by calling the functions `sock_create()` and `sock_map_fd()`.

sock_create()	net/socket.c

In this function, the first step checks on whether the protocol family specified in the `family` parameter is available. An attempt may be made to load the corresponding module. Subsequently, the `type` field of the socket structure is described, and two additional functions are invoked: `sock_alloc()`, to provide a socket, and `net_families[family]->create()`. The function `sock_alloc()` is described further later on. `net_families[family]->create()` executes the `create()` function of the lower-layer socket. For this purpose, the respective protocols register themselves with the vector `static struct net_proto_family *net_families[NPROTO]` when the system starts or when the appropriate module is loaded by the `sock_register()` function (`net/socket.c`). They also pass the name of the protocol family and a pointer to the `create()` function. In case of the PF_INET socket, for example, this is done by the `sock_register(&inet_family_ops)` (`net/ipv4/af_inet.c`) call, which exports the `inet_create()` function. The control flow leaves the BSD socket area and is passed to the implementation of the lower-layer socket.

sock_alloc()	net/socket.c

This function is initially invoked by `sock_create()`; it reserves a new `inode` and allocates a socket structure. The fields of the socket structure are initialized to null, or `state` is initialized to SS_UNCONNECTED.

sock_map_fd()	net/socket.c

This function uses a number of helper functions to allocate a file descriptor to the socket, which is used to address this socket. It is also called a socket descriptor, but there is no difference from other file descriptors. This is the reason why you can also use the `read()` and `write()` I/O calls to read or write over a socket. The `file` entry for the socket structure is also set in the `sock_map_fd()` function.

The `create()` function of the lower-layer socket, which is invoked by `net_families[family]->create()`—as described above—now has to fill the other fields of the socket structure with entries—in particular, the `ops` pointer, which references the `proto_ops` (`include/linux/net.h`) structure. This structure serves to supply the BSD socket with the functions of a lower-layer socket. It includes a variable, which is stored in the socket family, and a number of function pointers:

```
struct proto_ops {
int        family;
int        (*release)      (...);
int        (*bind)         (...);
int        (*connect)      (...);
```

```
int          (*socketpair)    (...);
int          (*accept)        (...);
int          (*getname)       (...);
unsigned int (*poll)          (...);
int          (*ioctl)         (...);
int          (*listen)        (...);
int          (*shutdown)      (...);
int          (*setsockopt)    (...);
int          (*getsockopt)    (...);
int          (*sendmsg)       (...);
int          (*recvmsg)       (...);
int          (*mmap)          (...);
ssize_t      (*sendpage)      (...);
};
```

Notice that not all of these functions have to be fully implemented; in such a case, however, an error message should be returned.

This also makes the sending of data over a BSD socket easily understandable: For example, when an application sends data over the sendto() socket call, then the function sys_socketcall() executes sys_sendto() in net/socket.c. There, a message consisting of the transmit data, the address, and control fields is composed. Finally, the function sock_sendmsg() uses sock->ops->sendmsg() to invoke the transmit function of the respective lower-layer protocol-specific socket.

BSD sockets support many different protocols, so a general address structure, sockaddr (include/linux/socket.h), was defined. It consists of a protocol-family identifier and the corresponding address:

```
struct sockaddr {
        sa_family_t   sa_family;      /* address family, AF_xxx */
        char          sa_data[14];    /* 14 bytes of protocol address */
};
```

26.3   PROTOCOL-SPECIFIC SOCKETS

The central structure of all protocol-specific sockets underneath the BSD sockets is struct sock. This structure was oriented to TCP/UDP and IP in earlier kernel versions. Along with the addition of other protocols (e.g., ATM), the sock structure was extended, and other entries were partially removed from the structure. Initially, this created an extremely unclear construction having a number of entries needed for only a few protocols. Together with the introduction of the three union structures (net_pinfo, tp_pinfo, and protinfo), each of which contains a reference to protocol options of the matching layer, this situation should gradually improve, and the structure should become easier to understand. The structure is still rather extensive, but we will introduce only the entries of interest in the following sections.

26.3.1   PF_INET Sockets

This section describes the initialization on the level of PF_INET sockets when an application uses a socket() call.

| inet_create() | **net/ipv4/af_inet.c** |

As has been mentioned, this function is invoked by the function sock_create() to initialize the sock structure. Initially, the state of the BSD socket is set to SS_UNCONNECTED, and then the function sk_alloc(), which was described in Chapter 4, allocates a sock structure. The protocol family can only be PF_INET at this point, but we still have to distinguish by type and protocol. This is now done by comparing against the information in a list, struct inet_protosw inetsw_array, which is created by inet_register_protosw() (net/ipv4/af_inet.c) when the kernel starts.

Next, the ops field of the BSD socket structure can be filled. The sk pointer connects the BSD socket to the new sock structure, and the latter is connected to the BSD socket by the socket pointer. (See sock_init_data() in net/core/sock.c.) Similarly to the proto_ops structure, the proto structure supplies the functions of the lower-layer protocols:

```
struct proto {
void          (*close)          (...);
int           (*connect)        (...);
int           (*disconnect)     (...);
struct sock*  (*accept)         (...);
int           (*ioctl)          (...);
int           (*init)           (...);
int           (*destroy)        (...);
void          (*shutdown)       (...);
int           (*setsockopt)     (...);
int           (*getsockopt)     (...);
int           (*sendmsg)        (...);
int           (*recvmsg)        (...);
int           (*bind)           (...);
int           (*backlog_rcv)    (...);
void          (*hash)           (...);
void          (*unhash)         (...);
int           (*get_port)       (...);
char          name[32];
              struct {
                      int inuse;
                      u8 __pad[SMP_CACHE_BYTES - sizeof(int)];
              } stats[NR_CPUS];
};
```

Consequently, the proto structure represents the interface from the socket layer to the transport protocols. The hash() and unhash() functions serve to position or find a sock structure in a hash table.

Finally, inet_create() invokes the inet() function for the identified protocol from the proto structure, if it exists. For example, this would be the function tcp_v4_init_sock() (net/ipv4/tcp_ipv4.c) in case of TCP. A similar function exists in net/ipv4/raw.c for direct access to IP (SOCK_RAW). The other protocol functions are now available over the sock structure in these init() functions.

In TCP, the structure `tcp_func` (defined in `include/net/tcp.h` in `net/ipv4/tcp_ipv4.c`) is filled with TCP-specific functions and made available to the sock structure over the entry `tp_pinfo.af_tcp.af_specific`.

The transmit function of TCP (`tcp_transmit_skb()`—see Chapter 24) accesses the transmit function `ip_build_xmit()` (described in Chapter 14) available from the IP layer (network layer). However, this approach is not uniform (e.g., UDP does not implement an `init()` function, but accesses `ip_build_xmit()` directly).

26.3.2 PF_PACKET Sockets

The PF_PACKET sockets represent a type of socket created to allow applications to access a network device directly. The basic idea was to let an application state a packet type at a PF_PACKET socket (e.g., PPPoE connection-management packets with the type ETH_P_PPP_DISC). This means that all incoming packets of this type are delivered directly to this socket; and, vice versa, all packets sent over this socket are sent directly over the specified network device. Consequently, no protocol processing occurs within the kernel, so you can implement network protocols in the user space. At the socket interface, the application sets the family field to PF_PACKET. Formerly, PF_INET had to be selected, and the type SOCK_PACKET had to be specified.

As for PF_INET sockets, a `create()` function is exported when the PF_PACKET support starts (the function `packet_create()` (`net/packet/af_packet.c`), in this case). This function registers the functions of the PF_PACKET socket with the BSD socket. In addition, the functions `register_netdevice_notifier()` and `packet_notifier()` are used to invoke the function `dev_add_pack()` (`net/core/dev.c`) for all packet types registered with the PF_PACKET socket. This means that a handler is installed in the specified network device for all incoming packets of the desired packet type. This handler forwards the packets to the `packet_rcv()` function for processing, as was described in Chapter 5.

In the following, we will briefly introduce the transmit and receive functions.

`packet_sendmsg()`	**net/packet/af_packet.c**

Pointers to the sock structure and the message to be sent are passed to this function. Next, the network device that should be used for this transmission has to be selected. This can be done by using the source address specified at the socket, unless the device had already been added to the field `protinfo.af_packet->ifindex` of the sock structure as a consequence of a previous `bind()` call. Subsequently, the message is copied to an skb and directly sent to the network device by the function `dev_queue_xmit()`, without using protocols underneath the PF_PACKET socket.

`packet_rcv()`	**net/packet/af_packet.c**

When data of the registered packet type is received, the network device passes a pointer to the sk_buff that contains the receive data to the `packet_rcv()` function. The next step fills other fields of the sk_buff structure. Subsequently, the function `__skb_queue_tail()` inserts sk_buff in the receive queue of the associated sock structure. Next, the process waiting for a packet at the socket has to be notified. This is done by the function pointer data_ready() of the sock structure, which was bound to the function sock_def_readable() when the structure was initialized.

sock_def_readable()	**net/core/sock.c**

This function informs a process that data have been received. For this purpose, two cases have to be distinguished: If the application is in blocking wait at the socket, wake_up_interruptible() is used to add the relevant process to the list of executable processes. In case of nonblocking wait, the field of the descriptor that probes the relevant process has to be converted. This is done by the function sk_wake_async() (include/net/sock.h), which accesses the fasync_list of the BSD socket, as mentioned earlier.

26.3.3 PF_NETLINK Sockets

PF_NETLINK sockets are used to exchange data between parts of the kernel and the user space. The protocol family to be stated here is PF_NETLINK, and the type is SOCK_RAW or SOCK_DGRAM. The protocol can be selected from among a number of options (see include/linux/netlink.h): NETLINK_ROUTE (interface to the routing and the network), NETLINK_USERSOCK (reserved for protocols that run in the user space), NETLINK_FIREWALL (interface to the firewall functionality), NETLINK_ARPD (management of the ARP table), NETLINK_ROUTE6 (IPv6 routing), NETLINK_IP6_FW (IPv6 firewall), and others.

A header containing information about the length and content of the message is appended to data to be sent from the user space to the kernel. The format of this header is defined as struct nlmsghdr (include/linux/netlink.h):

```
struct nlmsghdr {
        __u32           nlmsg_len;      /* Length of message including header */
        __u16           nlmsg_type;     /* Message content */
        __u16           nlmsg_flags;    /* Additional flags */
        __u32           nlmsg_seq;      /* Sequence number */
        __u32           nlmsg_pid;      /* Sending process PID */
};
```

The field nlmsg_type can take any of three values: NLMSG_NOOP, NLMSG_ERROR, and NLMSG_DONE. Other valid values for nlmsg_flags are also available in include/linux/netlink.h.

This general Netlink interface is now used for communication between the user space and different parts of the kernel. For further adaptation to the respective application purpose, additional values for nlsmg_type were defined (e.g., for NETLINK_ROUTE6 in include/linux/ipv6_route.h and for NETLINK_ROUTE in include/linux/rtnetlink.h).

In addition to the PF_NETLINK sockets, there is another Netlink interface over a character device (see net/netlink/netlink_dev.c), but it is still included for reasons of backward compatibility only. We will mainly discuss the so-called RT Netlink interface below. RT Netlink sockets are actually `PF_NETLINK` sockets with the `NETLINK_ROUTE` protocol option set. These are currently the most interesting for network implementation, so we will continue describing the `PF_NETLINK` sockets with emphasis on this type.

PF_NETLINK sockets reside underneath the BSD sockets, where they register themselves exactly as do `PF_INET` sockets. For registering `PF_NETLINK` sockets over the function `sock_register(&netlink_family_ops)`, the function `netlink_create()` (both in `net/netlink/af_netlink.c`) is first registered as `create()` function with the BSD socket. The latter function handles all initializations required and registers the `proto_ops` structure.

Now, when data is sent to the kernel over a `PF_NETLINK` socket, the function `netlink_sendmsg()`   (`net/netlink/af_netlink.c`)   invokes   the   function `netlink_unicast()`. The vector `struct sock *nl_table[MAX_LINKS]` serves to manage sock structures that use a common `protocol` (e.g., `NETLINK_ROUTE` sock structures having the same `protocol` are distinguished by the process ID of the requesting application, which is copied into the `protinfo.af_netlink->pid` field of the sock structure).

`netlink_unicast()`	**net/netlink/af_netlink.c**

This function uses the function `netlink_lookup()` to access the `sock` structure that contains the desired value in its `protocol` field (e.g., NETLINK_ROUTE) and belongs to the requesting process. Subsequently, it has to wait until the field `protinfo.af_netlink->state` is deleted (access synchronization). Next, the `sk_buff` structure is positioned in the receive queue of the `sock` structure, and, finally, `sk->data_ready()` is used to access the respective `input()` function.

In the case of RT Netlink sockets, the function `rtnetlink_rcv()` is invoked here. This function was loaded by `rtnetlink_init()` (`net/core/rtnetlink.c`) when the system started: `rtnetlink_init()` uses `rtnetlink_kernel_create()` to set the function pointer `data_ready()` of the `sock` structure for NETLINK_ROUTE to the function `netlink_data_ready()` (`net/netlink/af_netlink.c`) and the entry `protinfo.af_netlink->data_ready()`   to   the   function   `rtnetlink_rcv()` (`net/core/rtnetlink.c`). At first sight, the naming convention of this function is confusing, because it is used for transmission, from the socket's view, but it serves to receive data from the user space, from the kernel's view.

On   the   basis   of   the   values   defined   for   `nlmsg_type`   in `include/linux/rtnetlink.h`, the elements to be addressed within the kernel are now selected. Once again, we distinguish by `family` and `type`. `type` is identical to the type specified at the BSD socket (as mentioned above, RT_NETLINK defines additional types, which are exported from `include/linux/rtnetlink.h`); the RT_NETLINK support defines new, peculiar message formats and allocates them to a family (e.g., `rtm_family` to manage the routing table, `tcm_family` for traffic control messages). Each of these families defines its own structure, which determines the format of messages. These RT_NETLINK messages are within the data range of a PF_NETLINK message, which means that they are transparent for a PF_NETLINK socket.

A vector, `static struct rtnetlink_link link_rtnetlink_table[RTM_MAX-RTM_BASE+1]`, is used to enable kernel elements, such as the traffic control element, to allocate functions to messages of their families. The structure `rtnetlink_link` (include/linux/rtnetlink.h) has two entries:

```
int (*dolt)(struct sk_buff*, struct nlmsghdr*, void *attr);
int (*dumpit)(struck sk_buff*, struct netlink_callback *cb);
```

An appropriate function can be allocated to each function pointer. The function `doit()` passes a command; the function `dumpit()` is used to read an existing configuration. For example, the following allocation is done for traffic control (net/sched/sch_api.c), among other things:

```
link_p[RTM_GETQDISC-RTM_BASE].dolt = tc_get_qdisc;
link_p[RTM_GETQDISC-RTM_BASE].dumpit = tc_dump_qdisc
```

As was mentioned earlier, the function `rtnetlink_rcv()` is used as an `input()` function. It invokes the function `rtnetlink_rcv_skb()` for each skb. The latter function uses the function `rtnetlink_rcv_msg()` (all in net/core/rtnetlink.c) to discover the type of a Netlink message and the family of the RT Netlink message and eventually invokes either `doit()` or `dumpit()`.

Layer V—Application Layer

C H A P T E R   2 7

Network Programming with Sockets

27.1 INTRODUCTION

An application programming interface (API) is required to enable application programmers to access the network functionality implemented in the operating system. One of the most common interfaces to access transport protocols in the UNIX domain is *Berkeley sockets* or *BSD sockets*, which obtained their names from the UNIX variant *Berkeley Software Distribution*, where they were implemented for the first time.

The design of Berkeley sockets (in the following discussion called sockets for short) follows the UNIX paradigm: Ideally, map all objects that are read or write accessed to files, so that they can be processed by use of the regular file write and read operations. Sending or receiving in a communication relationship can be easily mapped to write and read operations. The objects manipulated by such operations in the context of transport protocols are the endpoints of a communication relationship; these are represented by sockets.

27.1.1 Socket Addresses

A communication endpoint in the transport layer is described by three parameters in the Internet: the protocol used, an IP address, and a port number. These parameters therefore have to be allocated to a socket, before it can be used for communication. In building a communication relationship, we additionally have to specify the communication partner's endpoint address.

struct sockaddr	/usr/include/sys/socket.h

The data structure used to represent socket addresses was kept quite general, because the socket interface can also support other protocols, in addition to Internet protocols:

```
typedef unsigned short sa_family_t;

struct sockaddr
{
        sa_family_t             sa_family;
        char                    sa_data[14];
};
```

The sa_family element registers the address family (e.g., AF_INET for the family of Internet protocols). The exact address format is not yet defined in detail in the general sockaddr structure. For this reason, there is a more specific variant for Internet addresses, called sockaddr_in.

struct sockaddr_1n	/usr/include/netinet/in.h

```
struct in_addr {
                __u32 s_addr;
};

struct sockaddr_in {
  sa_family_t             sin_family;     /* Address family: AF_INET   */
  unsigned short int      sin_port;       /* Port number               */
  struct in_addr          sin_addr;       /* Internet address          */

  /* Pad to size of 'struct sockaddr'. */
  unsigned char sin_zero[sizeof (struct sockaddr) -
                    sizeof (sa_family_t) -
                    sizeof (uint16_t) -
                    sizeof (struct in_addr)];
};
```

The address family is at the same position as above, and the IP address is stored as a 32-bit number in the element sin_addr.s_addr. The 16-bit port number is in the sin_port element. The remaining free space is not used. Notice that the addresses and port numbers have to be specified in the *network byte order*; see Section 27.2.3.

27.1.2 Socket Operations

Sockets are represented by normal file descriptors at the programming interface. These file descriptors can be used to perform write and read operations. However, the establishment of a communication relationship is different from opening a file, so, from the application's view, additional system calls are available for sockets.

Figure 27–1 shows the system calls employed during use of a socket—and their order. We distinguish between the client role (left) and the server role (right). This distinction does not refer to the payload transfer, but merely to the establishment of a communication relationship: A client actively initiates the establishment of a communication

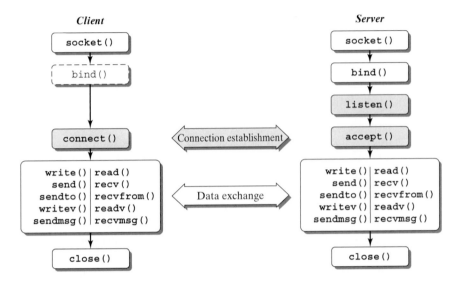

FIGURE 27–1
System calls at the socket interface; grayed calls are not required for connectionless protocols (e.g., UDP).

relationship, but a server initially remains passive, waiting for incoming communication requests.

We will briefly explain the meaning of each of these calls below:

▪ A new socket is initially created by the socket() system call, which requires information about the protocol to be used (TCP or UDP in the Internet). The result of this operation is a file descriptor, which is used in the further course to identify the socket and which has to be specified in all subsequent calls.

▪ bind() is used to allocate a local address to the socket. For Internet sockets, this address consists of the IP address of a network interface of the local system and a port number. Clients can do without bind() call, because their exact address often does not play any role; an address is then allocated to them automatically.

▪ The listen() call is used by a server to inform the operating system that connections should be accepted at the socket. This is meaningful only for connection-oriented protocols (currently, for TCP only, where it causes transition of the protocol state machine into the LISTEN state—see Section 24.3).

▪ An active connection establishment (e.g., in TCP) to an address passed as parameter is initiated by the connect() call. For connectionless protocols (e.g., UDP), connect() can be used to specify a destination address for all packets subsequently transmitted.

▪ accept() is used by a server to accept a connection, provided that it had previously received a connection request. Otherwise, the call will block until a connection request has been received.

The socket is copied when a connection is accepted: The original socket remains in the LISTEN state, but the new socket is in the CONNECTED state. A new file descriptor for the second socket is returned by the accept() call. This duplication of sockets during the accepting of a connection allows a server application to continue accepting new connections without having first to close previous connections.

Notice that accept() is not used by sockets for connectionless protocols.

■ Now that a communication relationship has been established, data can be transmitted. If a connection exists, or if connect() defined the destination address for a connectionless protocol, then the write() and read() file operations are applicable. Otherwise, the functions sendto() and recvfrom() can be used, which require a destination address to be specified for each data unit to be sent or supply a source address for each data unit received.

■ When a socket is no longer needed, then the descriptor can be released by close(). This function also closes the connection, if one is still open.

The following section discusses each of these system calls for the socket interface in more detail.

27.2   FUNCTIONS OF THE SOCKET API

This section gives an overview of the most important functions for the socket application programming interface. The original TCP/IP implementation of the BSD UNIX version, which the socket API is derived from, used only the six system calls of the input and output interface for file operations to communicate over networks. Only the next version added the whole number of additional operations that will be discussed below.

27.2.1 Functions for Connection Management

The functions described in this section serve to manage communication relationships: to create and delete sockets, to open and close connections, and so on.

```
int socket (int family, int type, int protocol)
```

Berkeley sockets, or sockets for short, are the basis for communication relationships over the socket interface. A socket represents the endpoint of a communication relationship in an end system and forms the interface between the network protocols and applications. This means that, in a communication using the TCP protocol, the two sockets in the two communicating end systems form the endpoints for this communication. In a multicast communication, more than two sockets normally participate in a communication.

An application can use the socket() system call to cause the operating system to create a socket, always the first step in communicating over networks. In the creating of a socket, the required resources are reserved in the operating system, and the type of communication protocol to be used is determined (e.g., TCP or UDP).

The result of a socket() system call consists of the socket descriptor—an integer number that uniquely identifies the socket. This descriptor has to be used in all subsequent system calls to identify the socket.

The following parameters are passed with the `socket()` system call:

- `int family` denotes the protocol family used and thus, mainly, the address type used. Constants for the following address families (`AF_...`) are defined:

  - ▷ `AF_UNIX`: Sockets for interprocess communication in the local computer.
  - ▷ `AF_INET`: Sockets of the TCP/IP protocol family based on the Internet Protocol Version 4.
  - ▷ `AF_INET6`: TCP/IP protocol family based on the new Internet Protocol, Version 6. (See Chapter 23.)
  - ▷ `AF_IPX`: IPX protocol family.

- `int type` denotes the type of the desired communication relationship. Within the TCP/IP protocol family, we mainly distinguish the following three types:

  - ▷ `SOCK_STREAM` (*stream socket*) specifies a stream-oriented, reliable, in-order full duplex connection between two sockets.
  - ▷ `SOCK_DGRAM` (*datagram socket*) specifies a connectionless, unreliable datagram service, where packets may be transported out of order.
  - ▷ `SOCK_RAW` (*raw socket*).

- `int protocol` selects a protocol for the specified socket type, if several protocols with the specified type properties are available. In the `AF_INET` address family, TCP is always selected for the `SOCK_STREAM` socket type, and UDP is always used as the transport protocol for `SOCK_DGRAM`.

  If the socket type in itself uniquely identifies a protocol, then the protocol argument in the `socket()` system call can be set to zero.

Application Example: A TCP socket should be set up. The first parameter is set to `AF_INET`, the second to `SOCK_STREAM`. The third parameter is not required; therefore, it is initialized to 0.

```
#include <sys/types.h>
#include <sys/socket.h>
int          sockfd;

sockfd = socket(AF_INET, SOCK_STREAM, 0);
if (sockfd < 0)
        printf("ERROR: Error when creating the socket.");
```

`int close (int sockfd)`

The normal UNIX system call `close()` is used to close a socket. When the socket is closed, the system has to ensure that data waiting in kernel buffers ready to be sent (be acknowledged) is actually sent (acknowledged). Normally, the system returns immediately after a close() system call, while the kernel still tries to handle data waiting in the queues.

The only parameter of the close() function is the following:

▩ int sockfd is the descriptor of the socket that should be closed. A process that terminates and releases all open sockets automatically.

Application Example:

```
#include <sys/socket.h>
int    sockfd;

/* Creating a socket. */

/* Communication operations. */
close(sockfd);
```

```
int bind(int sockfd, struct sockaddr *mAddress, int AddrLength)
```

A newly created socket has no allocation to local addresses or port numbers. On the client side, user programs do not necessarily have to care about the local addresses they use, because they can be allocated automatically. In contrast, server processes have to specify the port they are working at, because this port is used to address the corresponding service. This means that the server has to bind a new socket to a local address and a port; this binding is the task of the bind() system call.

The bind() system call requires the following parameters:

▩ int sockfd is a socket descriptor.

▩ struct sockaddr *mAddress is a pointer to a structure with the address the socket is to be bound to.

▩ int AddrLength specifies the size of the address structure provided in the second parameter. The size of the address structure has to be specified, because different address families use different address formats.

The bind() system call is used in three cases:

▩ Servers register their own addresses within the system. They inform the system about the kind of packets to be forwarded at this socket, e.g., packets with a specific port number. Server applications use special globally defined port numbers, the so-called *well-known ports*. They are assigned by IANA upon request and listed in the file /etc/services.

▩ A client itself can store a specific address.

▩ A connectionless client has to ensure that the system creates an individual address for it, so that the other end of the communication relationship has a valid return address for replies.

Application Example: A TCP server registers its own address (IP address and port number) and declares itself ready to receive arbitrary client requests. The constant INADDR_ANY is used for the IP address, which tells the system that an appropriate local IP address should be used. This 32-bit value has to be brought into the network byte order (see Section 27.2.3) by htonl(). The port number should be a value higher than 1024, to avoid collisions with well-known ports. The port number is a 16 bits in size, so it is initially brought into the network byte order by htons(). Notice that it is a good idea to have previously initialized the entire address structure with zero values.

```
#include <sys/types.h>
#include <sys/socket.h>

#define SERVER_TCP_PORT 2001

int sockfd;
struct sockaddr_in serv_addr;

/*  Initialize address area. */
memset(&serv_addr, 0, sizeof(serv_addr));
serv_addr.sin_family = AF_INET;
serv_addr.sin_addr.s_addr = htonl(INADDR_ANY);
serv_addr.sin_port = htons(SERVER_TCP_PORT);

/*  Since a sockaddr_in structure was used above for the address,
    it has to be transformed to the more general sockaddr
    before using it as second parameter of the bind call. */
bind(sockfd, (struct sockaddr*) &serv_addr, sizeof(serv_addr));
```

int listen(int sockfd, int backlog)

The listen() system call enables a server to prepare a socket for incoming connections. The socket is switched into a passive mode and is then ready to accept connections. In addition, the operating system is informed that the protocol instance should order incoming requests in a queue.

listen() is normally used after the socket() and the bind() system calls and immediately before accept(). listen() is suitable only for connection-oriented socket types (e.g., SOCK_STREAM).

The listen() system call takes two parameters:

- ▪ int sockfd is a socket descriptor.
- ▪ int backlog denotes the number of possible connection requests (the maximum number of connection requests that can be placed in the queue). This is done while the system is waiting for the accept() call to be executed by the server process. This value is normally given as 5, corresponding to the current maximum value. Requests beyond this value are denied.

Application Example: A server process calls the `listen()` routine after it has used `bind()` to announce the port number it uses:

```
#include <sys/socket.h>

/* Create a socket and bind it to an address. */

listen(sockfd, 5);
```

```
int accept(int sockfd, struct sockaddr *Peer, int *AddrLength)
```

Once a connection-oriented server process has executed the `listen()` call described above, the server has to wait for a connection, using the `accept()` call. It blocks the process until a connection request arrives.

As soon as a connection request arrives, the address of the requesting client is stored in the data structure named `Peer`. The length of this address is stored in `AddrLength`. Subsequently, the system creates a new socket, which is connected to the client, and returns the descriptor of this socket as result of the `accept()` system call. A negative value is returned if an error occurs.

The `accept()` call takes the following parameters:

- `int sockfd` is a descriptor of the ready-to-receive socket.
- `struct sockaddr *Peer` is a pointer to a previously reserved memory space for the address of the communication partner. This address is entered in this structure when a connection request arrives.
- `int *AddrLength` specifies the length of the reserved memory space in bytes before the call. Once `accept()` has returned, this parameter shows the actual address length (in bytes).

Application Example: A successful `accept()` call has returned, and the server starts a child process to continue communication with the client in this new process. The parent process can close the new socket or wait for other client connection requests.

```
#include <sys/types.h>
#include <sys/socket.h>

int newsockfd, clilen;
struct sockaddr_in cli_addr;
clilen = sizeof(cli_addr);

/* socket, bind, listen, ... */

newsockfd = accept(sockfd, (struct sockaddr *) &cli_addr, &clilen);
if (newsockfd < 0)
        printf("ERROR: Creating new socket");
```

```
if (childpid = fork()) < 0)
        printf("ERROR: Creating child process");
else if (childpid == 0)
{
            /* Child process */
        close(sockfd);                 /* Parent socket */
        doit(newsockfd);               /* Handle client request */
        exit(0);
}
close(newsockfd);                      /* Parent closes the new socket */
```

```
int connect(int sockfd, struct sockaddr *ServAddr, int AddrLength)
```

A newly created socket is not connected (i.e., it is not associated with a destination address or a communication partner). However, a user program has to establish a connection before data can be sent over a reliable connection. Once a connection has been successfully established, no destination address needs to be specified to transmit data in a connection-oriented communication (e.g., SOCK_STREAM). Sockets for connectionless datagram services don't have to be connected; they can transmit directly.

For the connection-oriented TCP protocol, the connect() system call results in the actual setup of a connection from the local system to a (remote) communication partner.

The following parameters are required to open a connection:

- int sockfd: Socket descriptor.
- struct sockaddr *ServAddr: Pointer to a structure that specifies the destination address to which the socket should be connected.
- int AddrLength: Length of the address structure in bytes.

Application Example: Once it has opened a socket, the client fills the data structure for the server address. If the IP address is available in dotted decimal notation, it can be converted by the inet_addr function. The port number of the server is brought into network byte order by the htons() routine. Again, it is useful to first initialize the entire address memory.

```
#include <sys/types.h>
#include <sys/socket.h>

#define SERVER_TCP_PORT 2001
#define SERVER_HOST_ADDR "129.13.35.77"

struct sockaddr_in serv_addr;

/* A sockfd was already created ... */
/* Initialize data space. */
memset(&serv_addr, 0, sizeof(serv_addr));
```

```
/* Enter address family in address structure. */
serv_addr.sin_family = AF_INET;

/* Set IP address. */
serv_addr.sin_addr.s_addr = inet_addr(SERVER_HOST_ADDR);

/* Set port number. */
serv_addr.sin_port = htons(SERVER_TCP_PORT);

/* Establish connection to server. */
connect(sockfd, (struct sockaddr*) &serv_addr, sizeof(serv_addr));

/* Transmit data ... */
```

27.2.2 Functions for Data Transmission

`write(), send(), sendto()`

The following are some of the system calls available for transmitting data over a socket:

- `size_t write(sockfd, buffer, length)`
- `int send(sockfd, buffer, length, flags)`
- `int sendto(sockfd, buffer, length, flags, destaddr, addrlen)`

send() and write() can be invoked only when a socket is in the connected state; sendto() can be invoked at any time.

These calls take the following parameters:

- `int sockfd`: socket descriptor.
- `void *buffer`: starting address of a buffer, which contains a sequence of bytes that should be sent.
- `size_t length`: length of the byte sequence to be sent in the buffer (in bytes).
- `int flags`: transmission control. (See details in [Come00].)
- `struct sockaddr *destaddr`: pointer to a sockaddr structure with the destination address.
- `int addrlen`: length of the destination address structure.

All four functions return the length of the data that was actually sent.

`read(), recv(), recvfrom()`

In analogy to the transmit functions described above, the following functions are available for receiving data:

- `size_t read(sockfd, buffer, length)`
- `int recv(sockfd, buffer, length, flags)`
- `int recvfrom (sockfd, buffer, length, flags, fromaddr, addrlen)`

The parameters these functions take are similar to those for transmit operations. All three functions return the length of data received.

readv(), writev(), sendmsg(), recvmsg()

As their arguments, the transmit and receive functions discussed so far each took a pointer to a single memory area that had to be transmitted or was to take in the data received, respectively. This is different with the following functions:

- int readv(int sockfd, const struct iovec *vector, size_t count)
- int writev(int sockfd, const struct iovec *vector, size_t count)
- int sendmsg(int sockfd, const struct msghdr *msg, int flags)
- int recvmsg(int sockfd, struct msghdr *msg, int flags)

The vector pointer in the readv and writev system calls (that otherwise behave like read and write) references an array of iovec structures. In turn, each of these structures references a memory location (iov_base) and specifies its length (iov_len):

```
struct iovec {
        void *iov_base;    /* Starting address */
        size_t iov_len;    /* Number of bytes */
};
```

The specified memory locations are used one after the other for sending or receiving data. The benefits of this behavior can be used when messages are composed of several parts.

The sendmsg and recvmsg system calls receive a reference to a msghdr structure, which also contains an iovec pointer. In addition, this structure can accommodate addresses for communication over unconnected sockets, and it makes possible the delivery of specific control messages to the transport protocol instance. (See also Section 25.2.1.)

27.2.3 Byte Ordering Methods

Unfortunately, not all computer architectures store the individual bytes of multibyte values in the same order. We distinguish between *little-endian* and *big-endian* orders. (See Figure 27–2.)

For this reason, we have to define a fixed byte order to ensure correct communication. In the TCP/IP protocol family, this is the big-endian format for 16-bit and 32-bit integer values. (The protocols handle only integer sizes.) The protocol has no influence on and no control of the format of data transmitted by an application over the network. The protocol defines the format only for the fields it manages itself.

htonl(), htons(), ntohl(), ntohs()

To enable computers with different byte orders (big endian or little endian) to communicate, the so-called *network byte order* (big endian) was defined for transmissions in

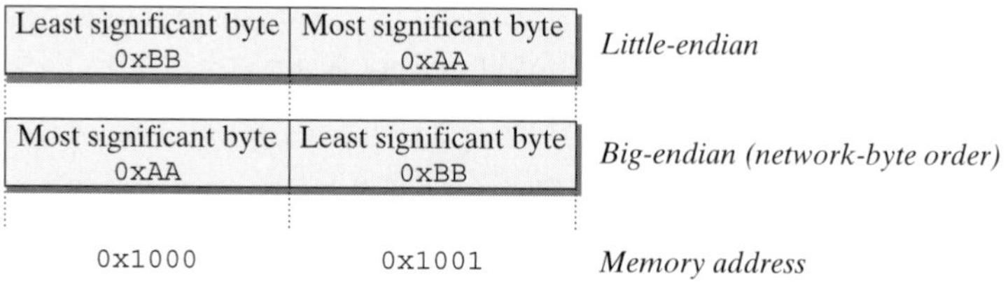

Least significant byte	Most significant byte
0xBB	0xAA

Little-endian

Most significant byte	Least significant byte
0xAA	0xBB

Big-endian (network-byte order)

0x1000   0x1001   *Memory address*

FIGURE 27–2
Little-endian and big-endian orders of 16-bit structures, using the number 0xAA BB as an example.

the Internet. The following functions are available to convert 16-bit and 32-bit values from the local format (*host byte order*) into the network byte order and vice versa:

- `unsigned long htonl(unsigned long hostlong)`: host → network (32 bits)
- `unsigned short htons(unsigned short hostshort)`: host → network (16 bits)
- `unsigned long ntohl(unsigned long netlong)`: network → host (32 bits)
- `unsigned short ntohs(unsigned short netshort)`: network → host (16 bits)

27.2.4 Functions to Handle Internet Addresses

Because the socket interface also supports protocol families, other than TCP/IP (e.g., the ISO/OSI protocols), handling IP addresses and DNS names is not as simple as it might seem. The most frequently needed functions are introduced below.

To handle 32-bit IPv4 addresses or socket addresses (IP address plus TCP/UDP port), the socket-programming interface defines the data structures described in Section 27.1.1, `struct sockaddr` and `struct sockaddr_in`.

All socket functions expect address information as parameters in the form of a generic `sockaddr` structure. However, this structure serves merely as a placeholder for one of the protocol-specific address formats (e.g., `sockaddr_in`, `sockaddr_x25`). This is the reason why a type conversion is normally required when calling these functions:

```
struct sockaddr_in *localaddr;

error = bind (sockfd,(struct sockaddr*)localaddr,addrlen)
```

`inet_addr()`, `inet_aton()`, `inet_ntoa()`, `inet_ntop()`, `inet_pton()`

IPv4 addresses are normally written in dotted decimal notation, e.g., `192.25.10.72`. The following functions can be used to convert formatted character strings into in_addr structures and vice versa. The parameters are actually self-explanatory:

- `int inet_aton(const char *cp, struct in_addr *inp)`
- `char *inet_ntoa(struct in_addr in);`
- `unsigned long int inet_addr(const char *cp)`

The following two functions can be used instead of `inet_ntoa()` and `inet_aton()`. Their benefit is that they support several address families, mainly AF_INET and AF_INET6. It is, therefore, recommended to use `inet_ntop()` and `inet_pton()`.

- `int inet_pton(int af, const char *src, void *dst)`
- `const char *inet_ntop(int af, const void *src, char *dst, size_t cnt)`

`int getpeername(int sockfd, struct sockaddr *name. int *namelen)`

The function `getpeername()` serves to find out the IP address of the communication partner with a connected socket. The following parameters are passed:

- `int sockfd`: Socket descriptor.
- `struct sockaddr *name`: Pointer to a previously reserved memory location for the communication partner's address.
- `int *namelen` contains the length of the reserved memory location in bytes before the call. After the call, `namelen` shows the address length in bytes.

If an error occurs, the functions do not return a value called "unequal null," but some integer value that is not equal to ϕ (the exact value is determined by the type of error. If everything went okay, then the functions return ϕ.

`int gethostname(char *name, size_t len)`

The function `gethostname()` serves to find out the DNS name (*not* the IP address) of the local computer:

- `char *name`: Pointer to a previously reserved memory location for the name.
- `size_t len`: Length of the reserved memory location. The call fails if the length is insufficient.

If an error occurs, then the value *unequal null* is returned.

`struct hostent *gethostbyname(const char *name)`

If the name of the communication partner is known, the function `gethostbyname()` can find its address. The name of the computer it looks for is passed in the `name` parameter.

`gethostbyname()` supplies a pointer to a `hostent` structure, which is defined in the header file `<netdb.h>`:

```
struct hostent {
    char    *h_name;            /* Official name of host. */
    char    **h_aliases;        /* Alias list. */
    int     h_addrtype;         /* Host address type. */
    int     h_length;           /* Length of address. */
```

```
    char      **h_addr_list;          /* List of addresses from name server. */
    #define   h_addr h_addr_list[0]   /* Address, for backward compatibility. */
};
```

The field h_addr_list contains a list with valid addresses, where the end of this list is denoted by an entry consisting of all zero bits. For IPv4, the list contains IP addresses in the form of 32-bit binary values, which can be copied into a data structure of the type in_addr—for example, by the memcopy() function.

27.3   EXAMPLES

The source text for a complete small sample application, where a client and a server communicate over TCP, is included in Appendix G. A much more detailed description of network programming in UNIX operating systems, including many examples, is found in, for example, [Stev90].

Appendices

APPENDIX A

The LXR Source-Code Browser

The Linux kernel in Version 2.4.9 consisted of 9,837 files, totaling to approximately 3,857,319 lines of source code. Even modifications from one version to the next comprise several megabytes. This volume of Linux source code makes it difficult to navigate to the desired place right away.

To facilitate working with the source code of the Linux kernel, the University of Oslo developed the LXR source-code browser[1] (http://lxr.linux.no). This browser is Web-based and represents the source code of the Linux kernel in HTML (HyperText Markup Language). The benefit of HTML, compared to normal source code, is the possibility of integrating hyperlinks that let you reference further information at specific positions, so that navigation between related source-code sections becomes very easy.

A.1 FUNCTIONALITY

The LXR source-code browser creates a reference file for existing C/C++ source texts. This reference file stores links between different parts of the source code. For initializing of the LXR, the source files are searched for certain keywords, and an index of these keywords is created. The following elements of a C program are recognized as keywords, and their functions are interpreted accordingly:

- Functions and function prototypes;
- global variables;
- type definitions (`typedef`);
- structure definitions (`struct`);
- variant definitions (`union`);
- enumeration types (`enum`); and
- preprocessor macros and definitions (`#define`).

---

[1]LXR is short for Linux Cross (X) Reference.

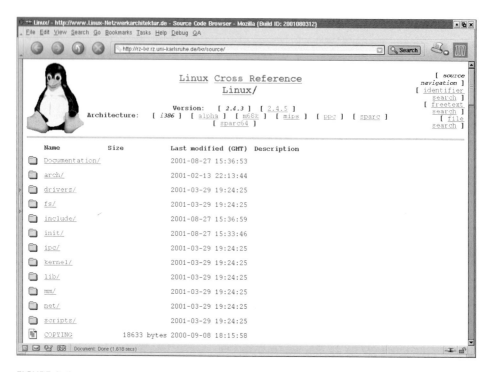

FIGURE A–1
Browsing the Linux kernel in the LXR source-code browser.

Subsequently, all keywords occurring in the source code are stored in an index file.

When a Web browser requests one of the source files, a Web page consisting of the original source-code file with all keywords emphasized by hyperlinks (see Figure A–2) is created. By clicking one of the links, another page is generated, which shows all information about this keyword. (See Figure A–3.) When a function is called, for example, the location (file and line number) of the function declaration, the actual function itself, and all locations where this function is invoked are displayed. Hyperlinks offer an easy way to jump to these locations. Figure A–2 uses the `ip_rcv()` function as an example, to show how this works.

Consequently, rather than creating static HTML pages, the LXR source-code browser generates the pages anew upon each request. Though this approach is somewhat slower than static pages, it does not modify the source code. In addition, the volume of static pages would probably be too big and take too much memory space.

We will briefly describe the possibilities of the LXR source-code browser below. Readers who want to use the LXR source-code browser can find both the source code of the current kernel versions and the LXR packet for installation at `http://lxr`.`linux.no`. You can also easily install the LXR source-code browser on your local computer, if you have a Web server and Perl.

The functionality of LXR is currently under revision. Reference information should no longer be stored in one single file in the future, but in a database (e.g., `mySQL`).

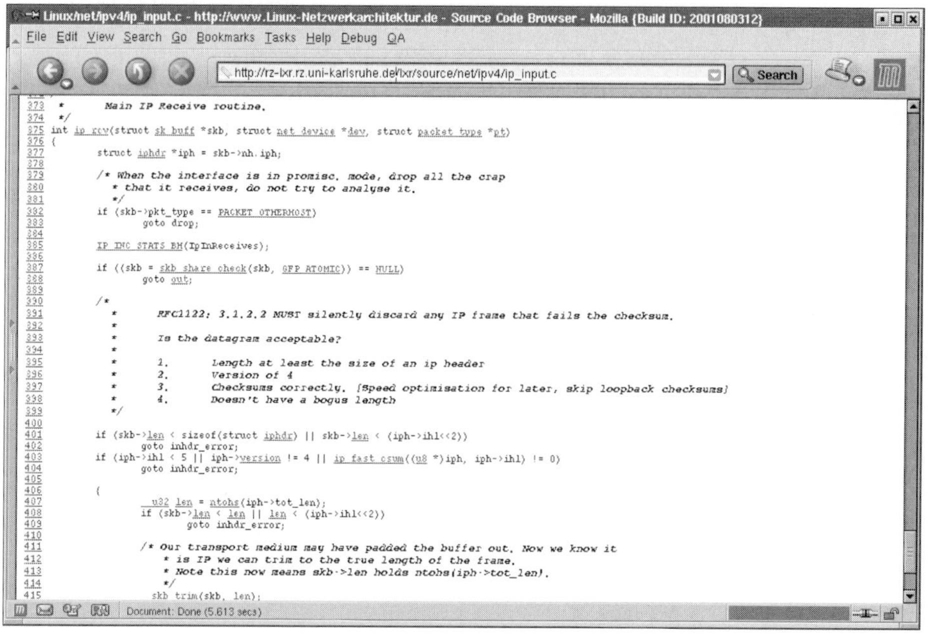

FIGURE A-2
Browsing the Linux kernel in the LXR source-code browser, using the `ip_rcv()` function as example.

Information about the current development in the beta stage is available at `http://lxr.sourceforge.org`.

A.1.1   Navigation through the source code

The entry point into the LXR source-code browser is shown in Figure A-1. This is the root directory for source files of the Linux kernel. From this page, you have the following possibilities:

- *Browsing to a specific file of the kernel sources*: You can click your way to a desired file by clicking the corresponding directories. If you know the file path, you can abbreviate it by directly typing the path in the URL. The path of the desired file is simply written after `/source/` in the URL. Figure A-2 shows this by the example of the file `net/ipv4/ip_input.c`.

- *Searching for a file*: If you don't know the name of the desired file, you can search for it on the `file search` page.

- *Searching for a keyword*: When working with the Linux source code, we are mainly interested in functions and data structures (i.e., what was defined as keywords above).

Keywords are stored in the reference file of the LXR source-code browser. This file also includes all information about the use of a keyword. Clicking a keyword emphasized as hyperlink or explicitly searching for a keyword on the `identifier`

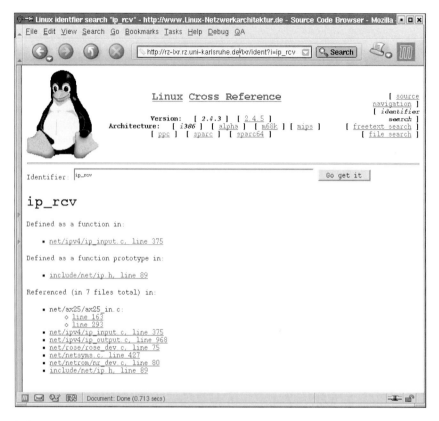

FIGURE A–3
Showing information stored for the keyword `ip_rcv`.

`search` page causes a Web page similar to the one shown in Figure A–3 to be displayed. For example, the stored information shown in Figure A–3 is output for the `ip_rcv()` function:

▷ *Definition of the function*: The location (file and line) of the `ip_rcv()` function, including statements, in the source code.

▷ *Definition of the function prototype*: The location where `ip_rcv()`, including its header file, was defined as function prototype. This information helps, for example, when searching for a header file to be included when you want to use this function.

▷ *Calls of the function*: All positions where either the `ip_rcv()` function is invoked or its address is assigned are displayed.

Naturally, this page with stored information varies, depending on the type of keyword. For examples, no prototype definition is shown for variables.

This information can be used to navigate easily through the kernel. Relations and processes can easily be tracked and analyzed.

■ *Various architectures*: The particularities of various architecture-specific parts of the kernel are considered in the creating of the index. Selection of the desired architecture (top of the Web page) causes the respective source code parts to be displayed.

■ *Various source-code versions*: You can use the LXR source-code browser to index several kernel versions or several software projects concurrently. Selection of the version or project (top of the Web page) causes the source code of the corresponding project to be displayed.

A.2   INSTALLATION

Installing the LXR source-code browser is relatively easy for an experienced Linux user. Problems or suggestions for improvement can be published in a mailing list. The following components are required to install the LXR source-code browser:

■ The *LXR package* with the scripts to generate the source-code index and the HTML pages. The version currently most stable is lxr-0.3. It can be downloaded from http://lxr.sourceforge.org.

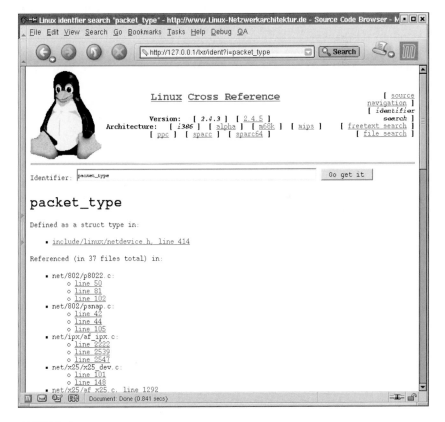

FIGURE A–4
Information stored for the C structure packet_type.

- A *Web server* that can work with CGI (Common Gateway Interface) scripts. We recommend the Apache Web server (http://www.apache.org).
- Perl is required to run the scripts. Mainly, the possibilities of regular expressions in Perl are used for the functionality of the LXR source-code browser.
- Glimpse can be used to extend the functionality of the LXR source-code browser. It allows you to search the entire source code of the Linux kernel for full-text search. This is useful mainly when one is searching for certain source-code identifiers the LXR parser was unable to identify. In addition, when you are searching for full text, Glimpse lets you display the corresponding lines of the source code, thereby simplifying and accelerating your search.
- A *Web browser* (e.g., Mozilla, Netscape, Konqueror) is needed for navigation through the pages generated by LXR.
- Finally, you need the *source code of the Linux kernel*. Notice that you can index several kernel versions or source texts of other programs concurrently.

Once you have installed the LXR scripts by the attached Makefile (read the INSTALL instruction included in the package), you first have to edit the configuration file lxr.conf. This file stores most settings of the LXR source-code browser. You also find details about the configuration of lxr.conf in the INSTALL instruction, included in the LXR package.

Subsequently, you have to create the source-code index for various kernel versions or other software projects. To create such an index, you use the Perl script genrefx, which is *very* time-consuming. Finally, you have to configure the Web server so that it recognizes and executes the Perl scripts in the directory $(LXR-INSTALL)/http. Experience has shown that this is the most delicate point in the LXR installation. Please also consult the literature for the Web server you use.

Naturally, readers who don't want to bother with the installation of the LXR source-code browser can easily access the pages of Oslo University at http://lxr.linux.no.

APPENDIX B

Debugging in the Linux Kernel

Debugging is a helpful step when writing reliable software. This is normally not a big problem when one writes simple applications. There are appropriate tools, such as the gdb debugger and its graphic variant, ddd, and other useful tools (e.g., `strace`), to track system calls.

However, the prerequisites are different for debugging an operating-system kernel. Remember that it is the very task of an operating system to provide a sufficient environment to run applications and to catch as many exceptions as possible to ensure that the work of other applications is not at risk. Probably the best known error in programs is a NULL pointer that references the memory position NULL rather than a valid memory address. When an application wants to access this page or run the statement at this location, the operating system should catch this error and output a message (i.e., `segmentation fault` or `memory protection violation`). The faulty application can then be checked step by step in a debugger to find the faulty places in the source code.

Unfortunately, it's not so easy to check an operating itself for errors. The reason is that, when a NULL pointer occurs in the system itself, there is no way to stop the computer from crashing. It is often impossible to find the exact location of an error or even the faulty component. Despite these circumstances, this chapter introduces several ways to track the process of a component in the kernel to discover potential sources of error.

In addition to prevent NULL pointer dereferences, it is also important to obtain information about the functionality of algorithms and kernel components at runtime, to be able to check for correct operation. In the selecting of an operating system, its correct operation is as important as its stability.

B.1 LOG OUTPUTS FROM THE LINUX KERNEL

One of the most common debugging techniques is the output of certain messages at strategic program positions—meaningful screen outputs are simply inserted (ideally before and after) at potential sources of error. This helps us to track the kernel's behavior and how it progresses. Of course, we could also output variable values and similar useful things.

Though this rather simple but useful fault-tracing variant often helps, there can be cases where an error in the operating-system kernel causes the entire computer to crash, leaving no way to store or read log information. These cases often occur when function pointers are wrongly initialized or are due to accesses beyond array boundaries. Some of these errors can be caught with the well-known "kernel Ooops," but some lead inevitably to a crash.

The following sections introduce several helpful methods to create outputs from the kernel and make them visible to the programmer or user.

B.1.1   Using printk() to Create Log Outputs

The `printf()` function is normally used in conventional writing of C programs—and the Linux kernel is actually not different—to output messages at a text console. `printf()` is a function of the standard input/output library (`<stdio.h>`), which is not available in the Linux kernel. For this reason, the Linux developers simply simulated `printf()` and integrated it into the kernel as the `printk()` function. Other functions borrowed from the standard libraries help the handling of character strings (`lib/string.c`):

printk()	**kernel/printk.c**

`printk()` offers almost the same functionality as `printf()` and has a similar syntax. A special property of `printk()` is the classification of messages to be output, by different debugging levels. The `syslogd` and `klogd` daemons can be used to store and output kernel messages or send them to specific addresses.

Altogether, there are eight debugging levels, from KERN_DEBUG, which is the lowest level (normal debugging messages) to KERN_EMERG—the highest level (system unusable). These debugging levels are defined in `<linux/kernel.h>`. Depending on the DEFAULT_CONSOLE_LOGLEVEL variable, messages are output on the current console. The administrator can use the command `syslogd -c` to modify the value appropriately.

`printk()` itself uses the `printf()` function to generate the output string. This is the reason why the syntax of the two functions and parametrizing of the variables to be output are identical. `sprintf()` will be introduced in Section B.2.

B.1.2   The syslogd Daemon

While the operating system is running, there are often situations where programs have to log error messages or specific information. An application in text mode outputs these messages simply at the console (`stdout` or `stderr`). A popup window is normally created for window-based applications (X11). The operating system kernel and processes working directly for it, such as daemons or child processes of the `init` process, have no direct allocation to a console.

Now, where should error and log messages be output? The standard output (`stdout`) of these processes uses the `/dev/console` console. In the X-Windows system, this is the `xconsole` window.

This approach can cause problems in a multiuser environment. On the one hand, messages can be read by anyone; on the other hand, the person in charge (normally the administrator) might be looking at something else and not pay attention to the message window. Another problem is that these screen outputs cannot easily be stored, which means that they are very volatile.

To solve these problems, we use the `syslogd` daemon. Daemons or other system programs outside the kernel have the possibility to generate messages for `syslogd`, which receives these messages over the `/dev/log` device and processes them. Within the kernel, log messages are simply created by the `printk()` function. If you additionally have started the `klogd` daemon, then the messages are also forwarded to `syslogd`. Section B.1.1 described how `printk()` works.

The messages mentioned above are accepted automatically after `syslogd` has started. The file `/etc/syslog.conf` defines how these messages should be further handled (i.e., in what files and by what criteria they should be stored).

The syslogd Configuration File /etc/syslog.conf   This file defines the rules for the processing of log messages by the `syslogd` daemon. If this file needs to be modified, then we first have to terminate the daemon and restart it afterwards.

`syslog` messages are distinguished by two criteria: by their *creator* and by their *priority*.

Priorities for `syslog` messages: There are eight different priorities. These are identical to the priorities defined for `printk` in `linux/kernel.h` (i.e., emerg corresponds to KERN_EMERG). The following priorities are sorted in descending order by urgency:

- `emerg`: System unusable—crash.
- `alert`: Serious error that has to be dealt with immediately.
- `crit`: Critical situation.
- `err`: Error notification.
- `warning`: Warning.
- `notice`: Special-situation notification.
- `info`: Regular messages within routine operation.
- `debug`: Fault-tracing messages.

Origin of `syslog` messages: Messages for `syslogd` can be generated by the following areas:

- `kern`: Messages from the kernel (`printk()`).
- `auth`: Messages from the area of security, authentication (`login`, …).
- `mail`: Messages from the mail system.
- `news`: Messages from the news system.
- `lpr`: Messages from the print daemon.
- `cron`: Messages from the cron daemon.
- `syslog`: Messages from the syslog daemon.
- `daemon`: Messages from any daemon.
- `user`: Messages from application programs.
- `local0-7`: Message areas that can be freely assigned.

Processing messages: There are various ways to store and to deliver messages, which can be configured depending on the priority and origin of messages. The file /etc/syslog.conf always defines actions to be done in the following syntax:

origin.priority{;origin.priority}* action*

Each line outputs a processing rule, consisting of a sequence of message types (origin.priority), separated by a semicolon, and an action. Both the origin and the priority of a message type can be replaced by a wildcard (*). The following actions are possible:

- The message can be written to a file. To write a message to a file, we state the file name with the absolute path (starts always with a "/").
- The message can be sent to one or several users. The user names (login names) have to be stated in a list (separated by commas). The message is displayed only for those users who are logged in at the time of the event. You can use a wildcard (*) to send a message to all users currently logged in.
- A message can be sent to the syslog daemon of another computer, which is specified with a leading "at" character (e.g., @tux.icsi.Berkeley.edu).

Example for a syslogd configuration file—comments begin with #:

```
# /etc/syslog.conf - Configuration file for syslogd(8)
#
# print most on tty10
kern.warn;*.err;authpriv.none   /dev/tty10
*.emerg                         *
#
# all email messages in one file
#
mail.*                          -/var/log/mail
#
# all news messages
news.crit                       -/var/log/news/news.crit
news.err                        -/var/log/news/news.err
news.notice                     -/var/log/news/news.notice
# enable this, if you want to keep all news messages
# in one file
#news.*                         -/var/log/news.all
#
# Warnings in one file
*.warn                          /var/log/warn
#
# save the rest in one file
#
*.*;mail.none;news.none         /var/log/messages
#
# All messages with priority emerg and higher will be sent to the
# users, who are logged in. They will also be sent to syslogd on
# host tux.icsi.Berkeley.edu.
*.emerg                         *
```

```
*.emerg                              @ tux.icsi.Berkeley.edu
# All messages with priority alert and higher will be sent to the
# administrator, if he/she is logged in.
*.alert                              root
```

B.1.3 Using console_print() for direct outputs

There can always be situations where the kernel gets stuck and no more output is possible. This is usually the case when `printk()` has written a message to the buffer, but klogd hasn't been invoked by the scheduler yet. In such cases, it is recommended to use the `console_print()` function for outputs. It outputs a specific string immediately at the current console.

`console_print()`	`kernel/printk.c`

In contrast to `printk()`, `console_print()` merely outputs a string, but does not convert variables into characters. In such cases, the output string should have been created previously by `sprintf()`. Naturally, we first have to reserve a byte array.

The use of `console_print()` is extremely helpful, but only provided that it is absolutely required to always output to the current console. This is conceivable only for temporary debugging or really important exceptions. Otherwise, unexpected outputs at the console can be disturbing and confusing for the regular user.

B.2 CREATING STRINGS IN THE KERNEL

This section introduces several useful functions to create debugging messages. As was mentioned earlier, they are somewhat similar to the functions provided by standard C libraries.

`sprint()`	`lib/vsprintf.c`

`sprintf(buffer, str, arg1, ...)` is a function very useful for converting certain variable types into strings. Its functionality is almost identical to that of the `sprintf()` function in the C library `<stdio.h>`. `sprintf()` also supports the formatting options known from `printf()`.

The character string `str` consists of regular characters and control characters, if present. Instead of control characters that begin with a % sign and end with a type descriptor (`c`, `s`, `p`, `n`, `o`, `x`, `X`, `d`, `i`, `u`), variable values are inserted according to the formatting specification. The *n*th formatting specification refers to the *n*th argument in the `str` string. The created string is written to the `buffer`, and the set of written characters (including the closing null byte) is returned as the result.

The formatting options of `sprintf()` are as follows: A format specification begins with the % sign and ends with one of the type descriptors mentioned. Between these two characters, there may be the following format specifications (in this order):

▫ `Blank`—No leading plus sign is used for a positive number, but instead a blank. A minus sign is inserted for negative numbers. This enables positive and negative numbers to appear aligned (if they have the same length).

- −—This argument is inserted left-justified in the string.
- +—A plus sign is inserted if the argument is positive.
- #—If the octal system (o) was selected as the output form, then a leading null is added to the argument; 0x or 0X are inserted for the hexadecimal system (x or X).
- min, max—The numbers min and max specify the minimum or maximum length of an output. min or max can be omitted if the respective option is not desired. If min begins with a null, then the output is padded with zeros to the minimum format length.
- h, l, or L—denote that a variable is of short or long type.
- type—A formatting specification ends with the type of variable to be output. The following types are available:

  - c (*character*)—The character arg is output.
  - s (*string*)—The string arg is output to the first null byte (unless limited by the maximum format length).
  - p (*pointer*)—The pointer address is output in hexadecimal system.
  - o (*integer*)—The number arg is output in octal system.
  - x, X (*integer*)—The number arg is output in hexadecimal system.
  - d, i (*integer*)—The leading sign for the number arg should be considered in the output.
  - u (*integer*)—The number arg is considered to be an unsigned number.

The formatting options described correspond to the options of printk(), because printk() itself uses sprintf() to format an output string. However, sprintf() is useful not only in connection with printk(), but also to generate outputs in the proc directory.

As was described in Section 2.8, the output is recreated upon each read operation on the proc directory. This is not different from a string that includes output data. We can use sprintf() to output not only fixed text blocks, but also formatted contents of variables and memory addresses.

String Operations   lib/string.c

The Linux kernel has several functions for simple (and familiar) work with strings. These functions are similar to the string operations of the C library. We will briefly introduce them here:

- *Copying strings*

  - strcpy(dest, src) copies the string src, including the closing null byte, to the address dest. strcpy() returns the dest pointer.
  - strncpy(dest, src, count) copies a maximum of count bytes from the src string to the address dest. If the original string was longer than count bytes, then no closing null byte is appended. dest is also returned here.

▶ strcat(s1, src) extends the string s1 by the string s2, which is appended to the end of s1.

▶ strncat(s1, s2, count) works like strcat, but copies a maximum of count bytes.

Comparing strings

▶ strcmp(s1, s2) compares two strings and returns 0 if the strings are equal. Otherwise, it returns a positive value if s1 is lexicographically larger than s2, but a negative value if s1 is lexicographically smaller than s2.

▶ strncmp(s1, s2, count) compares a maximum of count bytes of two strings. The return values correspond to those of the strcmp() function.

▶ strnicmp(s1, s2, count) also compares the first count characters of two strings, s1 and s2, but ignores lowercase and uppercase.

Searching in strings

▶ strchr(str, ch) searches for the first occurrence of the character ch in the string str. If it was successful, it returns the memory location of the first occurrence; otherwise, null.

▶ strrchr(str, ch) searches for the last occurrence of the character ch in the string str. If it was successful, it returns the memory location of the last occurrence; otherwise, null.

▶ strpbrk(str, ch_str) finds the first occurrence of a character from the string ch_str in the string str.

▶ strtok(str, tok_str) returns the first string from str that does not contain any character from the string tok_str.

Length of strings

▶ strlen(str) returns the length of the string str (excluding null bytes).

▶ strnlen(str, count) returns the length of the string str or count, if the string is longer than count.

▶ strspn(str, ch_str) computes the length of that initial part of the string str in which only characters from the string ch_str occur, beginning from the first character in str.

Functions for memory locations

▶ memset(ptr, ch, count) fills count bytes of memory (starting from the ptr location) with the value of the ch parameter.

▶ memcpy(dest, src, count) copies count bytes from the memory location src to the memory location dest.

▶ memcmp(ptr1, ptr2, count) compares count bytes of two memory locations, prt1 and prt2. The return values correspond to those of the strcmp function.

Entries in the /proc/sys/net/core Directory

- `rmem_default`: Default value for the memory space used for incoming socket buffers (in bytes).
- `rmem_max`: Maximum size for incoming socket buffers (in bytes).
- `wmem_max`: Maximum size for outgoing socket buffers (in bytes).
- `message_burst`: Parameters limiting the number of warning or log messages created by the network implementation (number of messages per second). This is necessary to limit the consequences of denial-of-service attacks.

Entries in /proc/sys/net/ipv4/   This directory holds the most important information and configuration options for the TCP/IP protocols. Most of these entries work as switches. Specifically, if a 1 is written to the file, then a specific functionality is enabled; if a 0 is written to the file, this functionality is disabled.

- `icmp_echo_ignore_all` or `icmp_echo_ignore_broadcasts`, respectively, suppresses a reply to all *echo requests* directed to the host or to multicast/broadcast addresses.
- `icmp_` ... can be used to specify, for various ICMP message types, how often at most an ICMP packet may be sent. This value is stated in packets per second.
- `ip_autoconfig` shows whether the computer should be configured automatically (e.g., by RARP, BOOTP, DHCP, or similar mechanisms).
- `ip_dynaddr` specifies whether IP addresses may be dynamically allocated.
- `ip_forward` enables or disables packet forwarding: 1 means that packets will be forwarded and that the computer behaves like a router; 0 means that the computer behaves like a *host*. "Toggling" this switch sets the default parameters as specified in RFC 1122 (for hosts) and RFC 1812 (for routers).
- `ip_default_ttl` holds the default value for the Time-To-Live (TTL) field in the IP packet header. This parameter normally is initialized to 64.
- `ip_mask_debug` enables or disables debugging messages in masquerading.
- `ip_no_pmtu_disc` disables the path MTU discovery mechanism.
- `ipfrag_high_thresh` specifies the maximum memory used for IP packet defragmenting. If this threshold value is exceeded, then the kernel starts dropping fragments until the bottom threshold value, `ipfrag_low_thresh`, is reached. (See Chapter 14.)
- `ipfrag_low_thresh`—see `ipfrag_high_thresh`.
- `ipfrag_time` is the interval (in seconds) an IP fragment is held in memory. If the rest of the fragmented packet does not arrive by the time this interval expires, then the fragment is dropped.

The following parameters concern the TCP transport protocol only:

- `tcp_syn_retries`: Number of attempts to establish a TCP connection (sending the initial SYNs). This value should not be greater than 255.
- `tcp_keepalive_time` specifies how long keepalive packets are sent, if `keepalive` is active.

- `tcp_keepalive_probes`: Number of *KeepAlive probes* sent by TCP before the connection is declared to have failed.
- `tcp_retries1`: Number of acknowledgements for a packet before it is given up.
- `tcp_retries2`: Maximum number of attempts to send a packet.
- `tcp_fin_timeout`: The wait time for the acknowledgement of a connection-teardown request before the connection is aborted.
- `tcp_max_syn_backlog`: Number of TCP connection-establishment requests to be buffered for a socket.
- `tcp_window_scaling` enables or disables the scaling of TCP windows (as specified in RFC 1323).
- `tcp_timestamps` enables or disables the *TCP timestamp* (as specified in RFC 1323).
- `tcp_sack`: Switch for *select acknowledgements* (TCP ACK).
- `tcp_sturg`: Enables *urgent* priority data, as specified in RFC 793.
- `tcp_retrans_collapse`: Several TCP stacks in printers are faulty. You can activate this option to work around this problem.
- `ip_local_port_range` specifies the range for local ports of the TCP and UDP protocols. The first number specifies the beginning of the interval, the second specifies the end.

/proc/sys/net/ipv4/conf The `/proc/sys/net/ipv4/` directory is subdivided; let's first look at the `conf` subdirectory. It contains, in turn, several subdirectories: one each for each registered network device, and one named `all`. All of these directories include the same entries, which are introduced here:

- `accept_redirects` shows whether *ICMP redirects* are accepted. This option is disabled by default in routers, but enabled in end systems.
- `accept_source_route` enables or disables accepting of source-route packets. This option normally is enabled in routers, but disabled in end systems.
- `forwarding` enables or disables the forwarding of packets on this network device.
- `log_martians` enables or disables the logging of "impossible" addresses (including class-E addresses in IP).
- `mc_forwarding` enables or disables multicast routing. If activated, the `CONFIG_MROUTE` option should additionally be compiled for the kernel, and a multicast routing daemon should be installed.
- `proxy_arp`: Support for an ARP proxy.
- `rp_filter`: Checking the sender IP address can be disabled.
- `secure_redirects` enables or disables the option that *ICMP redirect* messages are accepted only by routers present in the default gateways list.

/proc/sys/net/ipv4/route

- `error_burst, error_cost`: These parameters are used to limit the log messages of the routing code in the kernel. The larger that `error_cost` is, the earlier that log messages will be created. `error_burst` limits the rejection of warning messages.

- ush: Accessing this file causes the routing cache to be deleted.
- gc_elastic, gc_interval, gc_min_interval, gc_thresh, gc_timeout: These parameters control the automatic *garbage collection* of the routing table (i.e., how soon and how strictly old entries will be removed from the table).
- max_size specifies the size of the routing cache. Older entries are removed as soon as this size is reached.
- max_delay, min_delay: Delays for deleting the entire routing cache.
- redirect_load, redirect_number: These factors specify how many ICMP redirect packets may be sent. No more redirects are sent as soon as redirect_load or redirect_number is exceeded.
- redirect_silence is the timeout value for redirect packets. Once this interval expires, redirect packets that have not yet been acknowledged are retransmitted. This process runs even when redirects were disabled because redirect_load or redirect_number was exceeded.
- max_size: Maximum number of entries in the routing cache. If this number is exceeded, the least-used entries are overwritten.

/proc/sys/net/ipv4/neigh/[net dev]   The following parameters denote the immediate *network neighbors*; they are located in the /proc/sys/net/ipv4/neigh/[net dev] directory of the respective network device:

- base_reachable_time: A value used to compute the *random reachable time.* (See RFC 2461.)
- retrans_time: The time between two consecutive *neighbor solicitation* packets, used for address resolution and for checking the reachability of a local computer. This time is specified in ticks.
- unres_qlen: Specifies the maximum queue length for (higher-layer) packets waiting for the resolution of a specific address. (See Chapter 15.)
- ucast_solicit: Maximum number of packets sent to resolve a unicast address.
- mcast_solicit: Maximum number of attempts to resolve a multicast address.
- delay_first_probe_time: Wait time, after the expiry of which a valid *neighbor* entry is checked again. (See gc_stale_time.)
- locktime: An entry in an ARP/neighbor table will be replaced by a new one provided that the old entry is locktime ticks old.
- proxy_delay: The maximum wait time for the reply to an ARP request, which has an entry in the ARP proxy.
- proxy_qlen: Maximum length of the queue for a delayed ARP proxy timer. (See proxy_delay.)
- arp_solicit: Specifies the number of requests sent to the ARP daemon (on user level).
- gc_scale_time: Specifies the intervals in which the ARP table is checked for old entries (state = NUD_STALE). If an entry is in the NUD_STALE state, then an initial attempt is made to check it directly (by using a unicast packet). If this attempt fails, and if mcast_solicit > 0, a broadcast ARP request is used to find the computer.

B.4   USING A DEBUGGER WITH THE LINUX KERNEL

A debugger is a tool that allows you to stop a program under development during its execution and to execute it step by step to monitor the program state—the values of variables and the contents of memory locations—and to modify it, if necessary. A debugger can also be used for development in the Linux kernel. However, there is no way of stopping or stepwise running, because stopping the kernel would immediately cause the entire system to become unusable. Reading global variables and other memory locations is possible while the kernel is running, and it can often be helpful for better understanding active processes.

Interface Between Kernel and Debugger   Debuggers normally offer a way to edit a so-called core file instead of a running program. Such a file can be created automatically when a program is terminated by an illegal memory access. It contains a copy of the memory locations occupied by this program. We can use a debugger, after reading a core file, to check the program state when the crash happened.

The core file, as interface between the debugger and the program state, can also be used to monitor the Linux kernel. To this end, the file /proc/kcore maps the entire main memory of the system to the format of a core file. So, if we give this file to a debugger as a core file, we can use the debugger tools to check the current state of the entire system.

Compiler Options   In addition to a core file, a debugger requires a file with the executable program. In case of the Linux kernel, this file is available under the name vmlinux in the directory in which the kernel was compiled. When compiling a program to be debugged, the compiler should have been instructed to embed debugging information (e.g., the full names of variables in text form and references to the relevant places in the source code). If this information is available, the debugger lets you (for example) query variables by their names.

The C compiler gcc lets you use the -g option to embed debugging information during compilation. This option has to be entered in a make file at the appropriate position to ensure that it will be used when the Linux kernel is compiled. If we want to achieve this for the entire kernel, we can add this option to the definition of the CFLAGS variable in the main make file in the top directory of the source-code tree. If we want to check only limited kernel areas in the debugger, it is sufficient to add one EXTRA_CFLAGS = -g line each to the make files in the directories that contain the files for each of these areas. For example, this would be net/ip4/Makefile if we were to check routing.

gdb and ddd   One of the most popular debuggers in the UNIX world is the gdb debugger, developed under the auspices of the Free Software Foundation (FSF). gdb offers only a text interface to the user, so it is universal, but not comfortable to use. More recently, several front ends have been developed to remove this drawback (e.g., by offering a graphical user interface). Two representatives of this kind were also developed by FSF: the Data Display Debugger, ddd, and the Grand Unified Debugger (gud) mode of the emacs text editor. ddd has options for graphic representation of data structures, which make it suitable particularly to check such data structures in the Linux kernel.

A detailed description of how these tools work would go beyond the scope and volume of this book. Detailed instructions are included in each of the distribution packages.

Example   Figure B–1 shows an example for the graphic representation of data structures in ddd. This example uses a fragment from a concrete variant of data structures to represent some of the routing tables described in Chapter 16.

The entry point is a global array, `fig_tables`, the 254th element of which is the `fib_table` structure of the routing table `main`. The `fn_hash` structure (reachable as `* (struct fn_hash *) fib_tables[254]->tb_data`) is appended to the `main` table. The `fn_hash` structure has a number of pointers to `fn_zone` structures for prefix lengths 0 through 31 in its `fn_zones` array. The figure represents the data structure for the zone with prefix length 8. An explicit type conversion is required to display the hash table referenced there, because the hash table size cannot be derived from the pointer type, `fz_hash`. Specifically, we have to give the expression that describes this pointer a leading (`struct fib_node *[16]`) * to make the hash table visible, as shown in the figure. The eighth element of the hash table is unequal null and refers to a `fib_node` structure for the prefix 10.0.0.0/8 (where the prefix length can be derived from the `fn_zone` structure further up). The figure also represents the associated `fib_info` structure, and the `fib_prefsrc` element of that structure contains the source address 10.0.0.1 in hexadecimal representation (in network byte order) and the hooked `fib_nh` structure.

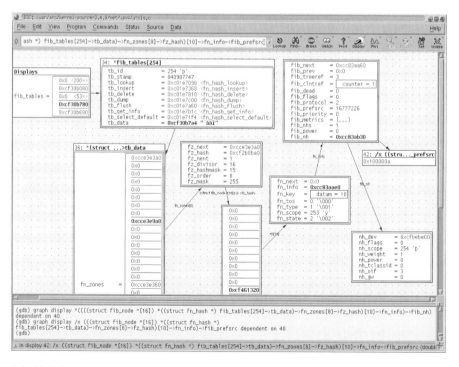

FIGURE B–1
Example using ddd: Checking routing-table data structures. (See Chapter 16.)

To use ddd in this example, we inserted the mentioned line, EXTRA_CFLAGS = -g, in the file net/ipv4/Makefile before compiling the Linux kernel. Next, we installed the kernel prepared in this way; then we used the command ddd /usr/src/linux/vmlinux /proc/kcore to start ddd.

Notice that gdb, upon which ddd is based, cannot see later modifications to the data structures itself, because such modifications normally do not occur in core files. We can use the gdb command core /proc/kcore to make the debugger reread the core file, so that the displayed values are updated.

Tools and Commands for Network Operation

The sections of this appendix introduce tools and commands to manage, configure, and control the network functionality in Linux. We will explain the most important operations and their parameters for each command. More detailed information about the exact syntax of a command and additional options are described in the respective man pages.

C.1 USING `ifconfig` TO MANAGE NETWORK DEVICES

The command `ifconfig` is available in Linux to configure a network device. It serves mainly to activate, deactivate, and configure a network device and its physical adapters. This tool lets you modify both protocol-specific parameters (address, subnet mask, etc.) and interface-specific parameters (I/O port, interrupts, etc.). `ifconfig` can also be used to modify the flags of a registered network device (ARP, PROMISC, etc.).

To be able to use it, a network device has to first be activated in `ifconfig`. To this end, the adapter has to be known to the kernel and be present in the list of network devices. (See Chapter 5.)

Syntax

```
ifconfig      [-a] [-i] [-v] interface [[family] address]
              [add address[/prefixlen]] [del address[/prefixlen]]
              [tunnel aa.bb.cc.dd] [[-]broadcast [aa.bb.cc.dd]]
              [[-]pointopoint [aa.bb.cc.dd]]
              [netmask aa.bb.cc.dd] [dstaddr aa.bb.cc.dd]
              [hw class address][metric NN] [mtu NN]
              [[-]trailers] [[-]arp] [[-]allmulti] [[-]promisc]
              [multicast] [mem_start NN] [io_addr NN] [irq NN]
              [media type] [up] [down]
```

- `interface` denotes the network device to be configured (e.g., `eth0`, `ppp1`).
- `family` denotes the protocol family of the network-layer protocol used. Depending on the address family, the addresses specified here have different address formats (e.g., `inet` (TCP/IPv4 protocols), `inet6` (TCP/IPv6 protocols), `ax25` (Packet Radio), `ddp` (Apple), `ipx` (Novell)). `inet` is the default choice, so it does not have to be selected.
- `address` is the address of the network device in the address format of the address family. IP addresses are written in the usual dotted decimal notation, `a.b.c.d`.

If `ifconfig` is started with the name of a network device, then only the configuration of this interface is output on the console. If you start it without parameters, it lists all currently configured interfaces. The option -a can be used to additionally display network devices known to the kernel, but not yet activated.

Example

```
root@tux # ifconfig
eth0    Link encap:Ethernet HWaddr 00:90:27:44:D9:89
        inet addr:129.13.25.10 Bcast:129.13.25.255 Mask:255.255.255.0
        UP BROADCAST RUNNING MTU:1500 Metric:1
        RX packets:879876 errors:1 dropped:0 overruns:0 frame:11
        TX packets:706287 errors:0 dropped:0 overruns:0 carrier:0
        collisions:45793 txqueuelen:100
        Interrupt:11 Base address:0xe800

lo      Link encap:Local Loopback
        inet addr:127.0.0.1 Mask:255.0.0.0
        UP LOOPBACK RUNNING MTU:3924 Metric:1
        RX packets:130 errors:0 dropped:0 overruns:0 frame:0
        TX packets:130 errors:0 dropped:0 overruns:0 carrier:0
        collisions:0 txqueuelen:0
```

- The fields `MTU` and `Metric` show the current values for Maximum Transfer Unit (MTU) and the metrics of the interface. The metrics can be used by routing protocols to make a choice when several routes having the same cost lead over two different network devices.
- The flags displayed by `ifconfig` correspond more or less to the names of command parameters and will later be explained further.
- The RX (Receive) and TX (Transmit) information shows how many packets have been received or sent over the network device.
- `errors` gives the number of errors that occurred.
- `overruns` shows the number of faulty packets. Among other reasons, errors can occur that are due to an overrun of the receive queue. An *overrun* occurs in a computer when more packets arrive than the kernel can process. The input queues reach their maximum (`max_backlog`), and all packets arriving additionally will be dropped. (See Chapter 6.)

The following list describes the parameters of the ifconfig command (with the names of the relevant flags in brackets). Some of these parameters enable certain modes of the network device (e.g., the ARP capability). These modes can be disabled by a leading minus ($-$) sign.

- up activates a network device. When you use this command to state an address, then up is taken as the default option. If up is called without additional parameters, ifconfig initializes the network adapter to the default values (e.g., the IP address to 0.0.0.0, which won't make much sense). The up option sets the flags UP and RUNNING.

- down deactivates a network device. However, this device remains in the list of registered network devices, so that it can be reactivated later. At the same time, all routes in which this network device participated are removed from the routing table.

- netmask *mask* assigns a subnet mask to the network device.

- pointopoint *address* is used for a point-to-point connection that directly connects two computers. Examples include SLIP and PLIP network connections. This parameter is used to set the IP address of the peer system. ifconfig shows the presence of a point-to-point peer by the flag POINTOPOINT.

- broadcast *address* sets the broadcast address of the network device. It normally is built from the network address and the appropriate address class. All bits of the host part are set to one. However, the broadcast address can also be set explicitly. The presence of a broadcast address is shown by the flag BROADCAST.

- mtu *bytes* sets the Maximum Transfer Unit (MTU) (i.e., the maximum size of a MAC frame) to the specified size. The default value is 1500 bytes for Ethernet adapters, 296 bytes for SLIP connections.

- arp enables the Address Resolution Protocol for network devices that use broadcast technologies (Ethernet, token ring, etc.) to allocate logical layer-3 addresses to physical MAC addresses. This option is set by default for broadcast networks. ifconfig shows the flag NOARP if ARP was deactivated.

- -arp disables the use of the Address Resolution Protocol and sets the NOARP flag.

- promisc moves the network adapter into the *promiscuous* mode. For broadcast-capable networks, this mode causes all packets to be received by the network interface and to be forwarded to the higher layers, regardless of whether they are addressed to this computer. This allows us to monitor the network traffic in a local area network. Of course, this mode should be used for analysis purposes only, which is often extremely useful. The tcpdump tool uses the promiscuous mode to analyze the traffic in a local area network. The promiscuous mode is shown by the flag PROMISC.

- -promisc disables the promiscuous mode.

- multicast enables the receipt of multicast packets addressed to groups at which the computer is registered as a member.

- -multicast disables the receipt of multicast packets.

- allmulti enables the receipt of all multicast packets, including multicast packets from groups of which the computer is not a member. This mode is used by multicast routers, among others.

- -allmulti disables the *allmulti* mode.
- irq, io_addr, and mem_start set the number of the interrupt, the I/O address, and the memory address of a network adapter.

C.2 USING ping TO TEST THE REACHABILITY

ping is the first tool generally used when a computer is not reachable, to check the network connection. ping sends an ECHO_REQUEST packet to the specified computer and expects an ECHO_REPLY. (See Section 24.4.) In addition, ping outputs statistical values about the connection. It is also possible to use the IP option *record route* to track the route of packets.

Syntax

```
ping [-DdfLnqRrv] [-c number] [-I address] [-i time]
     [-1 number] [-p pattern] [-s size] [-t ttl] [-w time]
     computer
```

ping has the following options:

- -c *number*: ping sends only number packets, then terminates. Normally, ping runs forever until the process is stopped.
- -f runs a so-called *flood ping*. This means that ping sends as many packets as it received replies, or at least a hundred per second. This option can be used to check the behavior of a network or end system under high load.
- -I *address* specifies the network device (by the IP address) that should be used to send echo packets.
- -i *time* specifies the wait time between two sent *echo request* packets. This value is normally one second.
- -1 *number* sends number packets at maximum speed. Subsequently, ping switches into the normal transmit mode.
- -n prevents the resolution and output of DNS names. IP addresses are written in dotted decimal notation.
- -p *pattern* fills sent *echo* packets with the specified pattern. This allows you to check the behavior of packets with certain contents.
- -q is the *quiet* mode, which outputs statistics only when the program is closed.
- -R enables the IP option *record route*. (See Section 14.4.) It outputs all routers visited, if these routers support the *record route* option.
- -s *size* sets the ICMP packet to size bytes. Normally, an echo packet is of size 56 bytes. Together with the ICMP header (8 bytes), the size is then 64 bytes.
- -t *ttl* sets the value of the Time-To-Live field in the packet header to ttl, which allows you to limit the reach of an *echo request*.
- -w *time* sets the maximum wait time for a reply to an *echo request* to time seconds. The normal wait time for an outstanding reply to an *echo request* is ten seconds.

Example

```
root@tux # ping www.Linux-netzwerkarchitektur.de
PING www.Linux-netzwerkarchitektur.de (192.67.198.52): 56 data bytes
64 bytes from 192.67.198.52: icmp_seq=0 ttl=246 time=4.589 ms
64 bytes from 192.67.198.52: icmp_seq=1 ttl=246 time=3.481 ms
64 bytes from 192.67.198.52: icmp_seq=2 ttl=246 time=3.271 ms
64 bytes from 192.67.198.52: icmp_seq=3 ttl=246 time=3.785 ms
--- www.Linux-netzwerkarchitektur.de ping statistics ---
4 packets transmitted, 4 packets received, 0% packet loss
round trip min/avg/max = 3.271/3.781/4.589 ms
```

C.3   USING netstat TO VIEW THE NETWORK STATE

netstat is an extensive tool for viewing the network state. For example, you can use netstat to display the routing table and the state of the socket currently created.

Displaying routing tables   If you start it with the -r option, netstat outputs the routing tables of the kernel. This corresponds broadly to the result of the route command. The option -n is used to output the IP addresses of computers instead of their DNS names.

```
root@tux # netstat -nr
Kernel routing table
  Destination      Gateway         Genmask         Flags MSS Window Use Iface
  129.13.42.0      0.0.0.0         255.255.255.0 U     0   0      478 eth0
  127.0.0.0        0.0.0.0         255.0.0.0       U     0   0      50  lo
  0.0.0.0          129.13.42.233 0.0.0.0           UG    0   0      238 eth0
```

The first column of this output shows the route destination. The column *Flags* shows the type of destination (i.e., *Gateway* (G) or *Host* (H)), to better explicate the entry in the first column.

If the destination is a gateway (router), the second column shows the IP address of that router (or, more exactly, the IP address of the adapter where the packet arrives in that router). If the route does not lead across a gateway, then the second column shows the value 0.0.0.0.

The third column shows the *reach* of a route. In routes with a (sub)network as the destination, the entry in the third column corresponds to the network mask; the value 255.255.255.255 is output for routes to computers (H). The default route has the mask 0.0.0.0.

All entries in the routing table are sorted so that the more special routes (long network masks) are listed before the more general routes (short network masks). When searching for a matching route, the kernel takes the bit-by-bit AND of the destination address and the network mask and compares the result with the route's destination.

The fourth column shows various flags that provide more information about a route. As has been mentioned, these flags specify the type of destination (gateway or host), among other things:

- G: The next hop is a router (gateway). This means that the packet is sent with the router's MAC address.
- U shows that the network device is enabled (UP).
- H: The next hop is an end system, addressed directly by its MAC address in the MAC layer.
- D: This entry was created dynamically, either by an *ICMP redirect* packet or by a routing protocol.
- M: The route was modified by an *ICMP redirect*.

The last column shows the output interface for a route.

Viewing Interface Statistics   We can start netstat with -i to output current statistics about active network devices. This option can be used together with the option -a to show inactive network devices in addition to active network devices. The output from netstat -i looks like an output of the ifconfig command and uses the same parameters.

Active Connections and Sockets   netstat supports a number of options we can use to list active and passive sockets. The arguments -t, -u, -w, and -x show active TCP, UDP, RAW, and UNIX sockets. We can additionally use the option -a to list all sockets currently waiting for an incoming connection. This shows all open server sockets.

```
root@tux # netstat -ta
Active Internet connections (including servers)
Proto Recv-Q Send-Q  Local Address          Foreign Address       (state)
tcp       0      0  localhost.4261         localhost.sunrpc      TIME_WAIT
tcp       0      0  sioux.1023             cocopah.1017          ESTABLISHED
tcp       0    280  sioux.22               tpc17.telemat.873     ESTABLISHED
tcp       0      0  localhost.4254         localhost.2301        TIME_WAIT
tcp       0      0  localhost.4255         localhost.2301        TIME_WAIT
tcp       0    217  tmnis.domain           tmins.4263            ESTABLISHED
tcp       0      0  sioux.4257             tlps17.print-sr       SYN_SENT
tcp       0      0  sioux.4259             tlps17.print-sr       SYN_SENT
tcp       0      0  *.printer              *.*                   LISTEN
tcp       0      0  *.dnacml               *.*                   LISTEN
tcp       0      0  *.1027                 *.*                   LISTEN
udp       0      0  sioux.domain           *.*
udp       0      0  *.908                  *.*
udp       0      0  *.987                  *.*
udp       0      0  *.1017                 *.*
```

This example of a netstat -ta output shows that most sockets either are in the LISTEN state (waiting for incoming connections) or already have an existing TCP connection (ESTABLISHED). Previously closed connections remain in the TIME_WAIT state for a little while before the sockets are deleted and so can be reused. (See Chapter 24.)

The first two columns of the output show the current number of packets in the input queue (Recv-Queue) and the output queue (Send-Queue). The fourth and fifth columns show the socket addresses (IP address / DNS name, and port) of the two communication peers. An asterisk next to connections that don't yet exist means that there is no communication peer yet, so that no address can be specified. `*:ssh` means that the computer waits for connections incoming at port `ssh`. The allocation of port addresses to protocols is defined in `/etc/services`.

C.4   USING route FOR ROUTING INFORMATION

The `route` command serves to set and manage routing information in a computer. The `route` command knows exactly two options; one to set, and one to delete, static routes. Dynamic routes are set by routing protocols.

Syntax

```
route add [-A family] [-net|-host] address [gw gateway] [netmask mask]
          [mss MSS] [dev interface]
route del address
```

- `-A` *family* specifies the address family (`inet`, `inet6`, etc.).
- `-n` shows addresses in dotted decimal notation and does not attempt to resolve them into DNS names.
- `-e` specifies the routing table in `netstat` format.
- `-ee` shows all information of the routing table.
- `-net` means that the specified address denotes a (sub)network and not a computer.
- `-host` shows that the address denotes a computer.
- `-F` shows the *Forwarding Information Base* (routing table). The options `-e` and `-ee` can be used to specify a format for the output.
- `-C` shows the current routing cache of the kernel.
- `del` deletes the specified route.
- `add` adds a route to the routing table.
- `address` specifies the route destination. This can be a (sub)network or a computer. The address can be written in dotted decimal notation or as a DNS name.
- `netmask` *mask* is the network mask for the new route.
- `gw` *gateway* specifies a gateway (router). All packets on this route are sent over this router, which knows the further path. Before it can be used as gateway for some destination, a computer has to know the route to it; either we must previously have set a static route, or the destination should be reachable over the default route.
- `metric` *metric* sets the metrics for this entry in the routing table.
- `mss` *MSS* sets the maximum segment size of TCP to MSS bytes. The default value is 536 bytes.
- `dev` *interface* specifies that packets on this route should always be output over the specified network device. If no device is specified, then the kernel attempts to find a network device to be used from other routes.
- `default` denotes the default route for all routes that do not have a matching entry in the routing table.

The output of the route command corresponds largely to the output of netstat. (See Section C.3.)

Examples

- root@tux # route add -net 127.0.0.0

  sets the entry for the loopback network device. Because no network mask was specified, the default network mask for a class-A network is assumed (255.0.0.0).

- root@tux # route add -net 129.13.42.0 netmask 255.255.255.0 dev eth0

  forwards the route for all addresses in network 129.13.42.0 to the network eth0. Packets are sent directly to the computers in network 129.13.42, not over a router.

- root@tux # route add default gw router-icsi.Berkeley.edu

  sets the default route to router router-icsi. All packets that have no matching route in the routing table are sent over this gateway. In IP computers, a default gateway should always be specified, because no computer stores the routes to all computers in the Internet.

C.5   USING tcpdump FOR NETWORK ANALYSIS

tcpdump is a high-performing tool for monitoring the packet streams in local area networks. tcpdump -i *interface* can be used to log and output all activities in a LAN. The actions of the local area network can be fully logged only provided that it is a broadcast-capable medium, such as Ethernet or token ring, and that the network card supports the promiscuous mode. In switched LANs, we cannot log packets that are not actually sent to the adapter.

Syntax

```
tcpdump    [ -deflnNOpqStvx ] [ -c <counter>] [ -F <file> ]
           [ -i <interface> ] [ -r <file>] [ -s <length> ]
           [ -w <file> ] [<expression>]
```

If tcpdump is started without specifying options, it outputs all packets received by the specified network device. This is normally a large number of packets; hence, the output can become unclear. For this reason, we can specify a logical <expression> to limit the number of logged packets. This logical printout helps make the output more clear.

We can use tcpdump for extremely useful studies. On the other hand, it can be misused by intruders to eavesdrop on communication in a LAN. For example, an intruder could log and evaluate the contents of communication connections. The intruder could then easily filter passwords transmitted in cleartext in Telnet or Rlogin sessions. For this reason, tcpdump can be executed only by administrators (root).

Parameters

- -c *counter*: The analysis of tcpdump ends after receipt of counter packets.
- -d *expression*: The expression is evaluated and output, and the program is terminated.
- -e: The MAC header is output explicitly for each packet (i.e., the MAC sender address, the MAC destination address, and the protocol type).
- -f disables the DNS name resolution. If computers are not listed in /etc/hosts, their IP addresses will not be resolved.
- -F *file*: The logical expression (see option -d) is read from file, and expressions in the command line are ignored.
- -i *interface* specifies the network device for which the packets should be logged. Without this option, tcpdump always selects the first element from the internal list of active network adapters (except the loopback network device).
- -l buffers the output line by line. Without this option, each character is output immediately.
- -n disables the name resolution. IP addresses are not converted into DNS names; similarly with the allocation of ports.
- -N omits the domain names in addresses (i.e., www instead of www.linuxnetzwerkarchitektur.de).
- -O disables the internal optimization of the qualification expression.
- -p means that tcpdump does not activate the promiscuous mode. However, a network device may be in this mode for other reasons, so there is no guarantee that the promiscuous mode is disabled.
- -q outputs abbreviated messages and less protocol information.
- -r *file* reads the packets to be checked from the specified file. The file should previously have been created by tcpdump, as is achieved by using the option -w.
- -s *length* sets the number of bytes that tcpdump handles as protocol header at the beginning of a packet. Normally, these are 68 bytes, which is sufficient for IP, ICMP, TCP, and UDP. For NFS and DNS packets, this value may truncate information.
- -S outputs absolute instead of relative TCP sequence numbers.
- -t suppresses the timestamp output.
- -tt outputs the timestamp in unformatted form. This enables faster processing, because the time information does not have to be converted. However, the readability of the output suffers.
- -v enables more detailed outputs. For example, this option additionally outputs the *TTL* values and the *TOS* field values of IP packets.
- -vv enables outputs that are even more detailed.
- -w *file* causes unprocessed packet information to be written to the specified file. Subsequently, you can use the option -r to edit and analyze this information. This option is recommended when tcpdump has problems handling a large number of packets.

▓ -x causes each packet (except the LLC header) to be output in hexadecimal form. The number of output bytes can be defined by the option -s (default = 68). You can use an expression to output only packets of the LAN that meet this expression.

Expressions   Expressions consist of one or several primitives. A primitive, in turn, is built from a qualification parameter and a value (name or number).

There are three types of qualification parameters:

▓ Types define the type to be qualified. Three types are available: host, net, and port; host is the default if no type is specified.

▓ The *direction* defines the transmit direction of the packet to be analyzed. The direction can be either src, dst, src or dst, and src and dst. src stands for incoming packets and dst for transmitted packets. src or dst is assumed if nothing is specified.

▓ The *protocol* specifies that only packets of a specific protocol type should be analyzed. Some of the protocols that can be specified are ether, fddi, ip, arp, rarp, tcp, and udp.

If several protocols should be analyzed, then the types can be OR-linked. If no special protocol is specified, then all protocols matching the specified type are analyzed.

Examples

▓ src tux: All packets from computer tux.

▓ (src tux) and (ip or arp): All packets from tux, but only IP or ARP packets.

▓ port 80: All packets of the TCP or UDP protocols where the port is equal 80.

Notice that keywords and arithmetic expressions can be used in addition to this syntax. Complex conditions are achieved by AND, OR, and NOT linking (e.g., host tux AND NOT port 80 AND NOT port 21).

Other Conditions

▓ less *length*: Only packets with the a maximum of the specified length are considered.

▓ greater *length*: Only packets with at least the specified length are considered.

▓ broadcast: The packet must be a broadcast message.

▓ multicast: The packet must be a multicast message.

Arithmetic Conditions

▓ *Expression RelOp expression*: The expression is an arithmetic integer expression and may include one of the following three operators:

▷ Binary operators (as in the programming language C: + − * / & |).

▶ If a *length operator* len occurs, then it is replaced by the packet length.

▶ An *access operator*, which can be used to access data in a packet.

Data in a packet is accessed as follows:

Protocol [offset : length]

The [and] characters must be stated; they are not used for optional specifications here.

Protocol is one of the keywords ether, fddi, ip, arp, rarp, tcp, udp, or icmp and denotes the network protocol. Offset can be one of the valid arithmetic expressions. Length is optional; it denotes the field size. Possible values are 1 (byte), 2 (short integer), and 4 (long integer), where 1 is the default when nothing is specified.

Examples

▪ ether[0] & 1 != 0 analyzes all of the multicast traffic.
▪ ip[0] & 0xf != 5 intercepts all IP packets with options.

Primitives can be grouped within brackets. The complete expression might have to be written between exclamation signs or be otherwise marked to prevent the shell from interpreting the information. Grouped or single expressions can be negated and logically AND or OR linked:

▪ ! or not: Negation.
▪ && or and: logical AND.
▪ || or or: Logical OR.

If a value is specified without qualification parameter, then the last of the specified keywords is assumed. For example, not host A and B is identical with not host A and host B, and should not be confused with not (host A or B).

The outputs of tcpdump are extremely complex and require a detailed explanation of the network protocols, in addition to a detailed description, which would go far beyond a regular syntax description.

C.6   USING traceroute TO TRACE PACKETS

traceroute can be used to trace the route of IP packets through the Internet. traceroute not only outputs a list with IP nodes (routers or end systems); it also determines the quality of the connection to each of these nodes by measuring the time to reach these routers.

Syntax

```
traceroute    [-m maxttl] [-n] [-p port] [-q query] [-r] [-s hostadr]
              [-t tos] [-w delay] host [packet size]
```

You can use `traceroute` to identify the route that packets actually take to the specified computer (host). Within local area networks, the path is only one hop, because the communication peer itself can be within this LAN—it is simply the next hop. In contrast, the communication relationships in larger networks (e.g., in the Internet) use much larger routes (as in the accompanying example).

Another benefit of `traceroute` is that it is suitable for analyzing connection problems. For example, if a computer in the Internet is not reachable, you can use `traceroute` to list all reachable routers on the path to this computer. If one of the intermediate systems does not respond, then it is easy to find the source of error.

To identify a router on the way to the desired destination computer, `traceroute` applies a trick rather than using the IP option *record route*. Specifically, it creates IP packets with the destination address of the specified computer and sends these packets to that computer. The trick is that the TTL value in the IP packet header is initially set to one. This means that the packet, on its way to the destination computer, has to be dropped in the first router, because its maximum time to live (TTL) has expired. According to the IP standard, the router has to return an ICMP message to the sender. From this ICMP message, the sender learns the IP address of the router and so can identify the first switching node. This method is repeated—each time with a TTL value larger by one—until the destination computer is reached.

Example: Connection in a LAN—Directly Connected Station

```
root@tux # traceroute www
    traceroute to www.Linux-netzwerkarchitektur.de (129.13.42.100),
    30 hops max, 40-byte packets

    1 www.Linux-netzwerkarchitektur.de (129.13.42.100) 13 ms 9 ms 9 ms
```

Example: Connection in the Internet

```
root@tuc # traceroute www.tux.org
 traceroute to www.tux.org (207.96.122.8), 30 hops max. 40 Byte packets
 1   router1. linux-netzwerkarchitektur.de (129.13.42.244) 10 ms 20 ms 20 ms
 2   141.3.1.1 (141.3.1.1) 10 ms 10 ms 10 ms
 3   Karlsruhe1.BelWue.de (129.143.167.5) 10 ms 10 ms 10 ms
 4   ZR-Karlsruhe1.WiN-IP.DFN.DE (188.1.174.1) 10 ms 10 ms 10 ms
 5   ZR-Hannover1.WiN-IP.DFN.DE (188.1.144.177) 30 ms 30 ms 30 ms
 6   IR-New-York1.WiN-IP.DFN.DE (188.1.144.86) 280 ms 130 ms 290 ms
 7   dfn.ny1.ny.dante.net (212.1.200.65) 260 ms 120 ms 270 ms
 8   * * *
 9   501.ATM3-0.XR2.NYC4.ALTER.NET (152.63.22.6) 280 ms 270 ms 120 ms
10   192.ATM2-0-0.BR1.EWR1.ALTER.NET (146.188.176.53) 260 ms 280 ms 290 ms
11   UUNET-EWR-1-PEER.cw.net (137.39.23.66) 280 ms 140 ms 130 ms
12   corerouter1.WestOrange.cw.net (204.70.9.138) 290 ms 130 ms 130 ms
13   core4.Washington.cw.net (204.70.4.105) 280 ms 290 ms 290 ms
14   fe0-1-0.gw1.spg.va.rcn.net (207.172.0.5) 140 ms 300 ms 270 ms
15   gwyn.tux.org (207.96.122.8) 160 ms 270 ms 270 ms
```

When `traceroute` doesn't receive a reply from the queried systems, it outputs *. If no connection to this system can be established, then several * signs appear, and `traceroute` eventually aborts. This gives one reason to assume that the famous digger cut a cable, or the cleaning person arranged the cables by color :-). If you do get a reply from the queried system despite several asterisks, this could mean that the system or the connected links are under heavy load.

If no parameters are specified, `traceroute` sends data packets having length 38 bytes to the destination computer. At most 30 stations are addressed by packets with limited TTL values before it is assumed that a packet has not arrived. `Traceroute` uses the port range between 33,434 and 33,434 + max stations - 1 (i.e., 33,434 to 33,463 in the normal case). For each station, at most three attempts are made to get a reply, and each attempt waits at most three seconds for a reply.

Parameters

- `host` is the DNS name or the IP address of the computer to which the route should be identified. The usual DNS mechanisms for name resolution are used.
- `-m maxttl` sets the maximum TTL value of request packets to `maxttl`, which means that a maximum of `maxttl` stations will be checked.
- `-l` specifies the remaining time to live (TTL) of each packet.
- `-n` specifies addresses in dotted decimal notation (i.e., no name resolution is done).
- `-p port` sets the basic port (i.e., the port number from which test packets should be sent). The default is 33,434. The port range depends on the number of participating stations.
- `-q queries` is the number of attempts to obtain a reply (default 3).
- `-r` means that routing tables will be ignored. A locally connected computer is addressed directly. An error is output, if the computer is a computer not locally reachable. This option can be used to test the routing situation or a computer without the existence of a route.
- `-s hostadr` uses the specified IP address as the sender address for packets for computers with several IP addresses.
- `-t tos` sets the value of the TOS field in the IP packet header.
- `-w delay` is the wait time in seconds for each attempt to address a computer (default 3).
- `-s packet size` specifies a different size for data packets (default 38 bytes).

C.7 OTHER TOOLS

In addition to the tools introduced in the previous sections, which have been available since the early days of Linux, there are several new programs that can be used to check and monitor networks. We will introduce three of these tools. Detailed information about these tools is found in the relevant manual pages or URLs.

■ bing is a tool to identify the bandwidth currently available between two computers. bing uses ICMP packets with different sizes and tries to work out the current bandwidth from identified packet round trips.

bing uses numerous options, which are described in the manual page (man bing). The following example shows how a 54-kbps modem line can be measured.

```
root@tux # bing 213.7.6.95 141.25.10.72
BING      www.linux-netwerkarchitektur.de (213.7.6.95)
          and 1701d.tm.uka.de (141.25.10.72)
          44 and 108 data bytes
1024 bits in 0.000ms
1024 bits in 20.123ms: 50887bps. 0.019651ms per bit
1024 bits in 10.103ms: 101356bps. 0.009866ms per bit
1024 bits in 10.138ms: 101006bps. 0.009900ms per bit
1024 bits in 10.557ms: 96997bps. 0.010310ms per bit
1024 bits in 19.966ms: 51287bps. 0.019498ms per bit
1024 bits in 19.174ms: 53406bps. 0.018725ms per bit
1024 bits in 19.314ms: 53019bps. 0.018861ms per bit
1024 bits in 19.510ms: 52486bps. 0.019053ms per bit

-- 213.7.6.95 statistics --
bytes   out   in   dup  loss   rtt (ms): min        avg        max
   44    51   51         0%               0.049      0.053      0.078
  108    51   51         0%               0.023      0.024      0.025

-- 141.25.10.72 statistics --
bytes   out   in   dup  loss   rtt (ms): min        avg        max
   44    51   50         1%              99.644    112.260    147.178
  108    50   50         0%             119.154    127.578    199.999

-- estimated link characteristics --
   warning: rtt big host1 0.023ms < rtt small host2 0.049ms
   estimated throughput 52486bps
   minimum delay per packet 86.182ms (4523 bits)

   average statistics (experimental):
   packet loss: small 1%, big 0%, total 0%
   warning: rtt big host1 0.024ms < rtt small host2 0.053ms
   average throughput 66849bps
   average delay per packet 98.793ms (5185 bits)
   weighted average throughput 66188bps
```

■ ntop shows information about the current utilization of connected networks. It logs all packets received over the network adapters and creates various statistics. Figure C–1 shows an example of the current distribution of the protocols used. We can see that ntop is browser-based (i.e., it represents its information in the form of Web pages). There is also a text-based version, which is similar to the top tool used to display current processes and their computing load.

Information about the use of ntop is available in the manual page or at http://www.ntop.org.

■ ethereal is another tool for studying the data traffic in local area networks. In contrast to ntop, which is more suitable for creating statistics and studying the load distribution in local area networks, ethereal is used for detailed analysis of certain data streams. It captures the current data streams in a local area network and interprets the packet contents or the relevant protocol processes. Figure C–2 shows an example of how ethereal captures an HTTP request to a Web server, http://www.tux.org.

Information about ethereal is available in the manual page (man ethereal) or at http://www.ethereal.com.

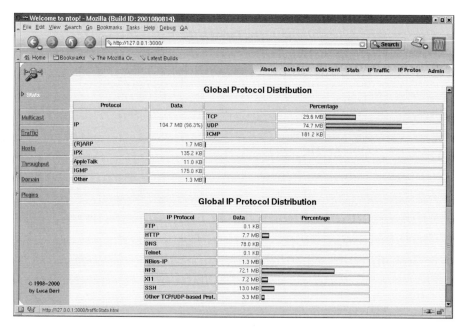

FIGURE C–1
Using ntop to analyze the network traffic in local area networks.

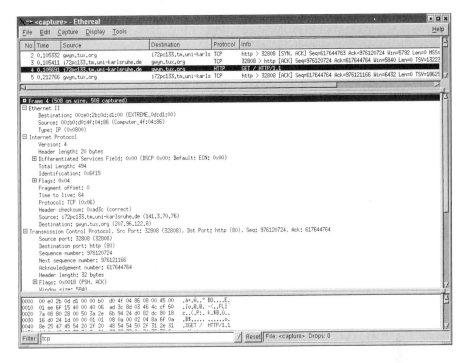

FIGURE C–2
Using ethereal to analyze data streams.

Example for a Kernel Module

```
/**********************************************************
* Example of a kernel module
* Compile:
* gcc -I/lib/modules/'uname -r'/build/include -c module.c
**********************************************************/
#ifndef __KERNEL__
#define __KERNEL__
#endif
#ifndef MODULE
#define MODULE
#endif
#ifndef EXPORT_SYMTAB
#define EXPORT_SYMTAB
#endif

#include <linux/module.h>
#include <linux/kernel.h>
#include <linux/init.h>
#include <linux/proc_fs.h>
MODULE_AUTHOR("Test Author (klaus@Linux-netzwerkarchitektur.de)");
MODULE_DESCRIPTION("This is an example module for the book
            Linux Network Architecture.");

/*******************************************/
/* Example variables for module parameters */
/*******************************************/
unsigned int variable1;
unsigned long variable2[3] = {0,1,2};

/* Example function; will be exported as symbol. */
void methode1(int test1, char *test2)
{
      // do anything
}
```

```c
EXPORT_SYMBOL (variable1);
EXPORT_SYMBOL (variable2);
EXPORT_SYMBOL (methode1);

MODULE_PARM (variable1, "i");
MODULE_PARM_DESC (variable1, "Description for the integer");

MODULE_PARM (variable2, "1-31");
MODULE_PARM_DESC (variable2, "Description for the array of longs");

/*********************************************************/
/* Function to create the output from proc files. */
/*********************************************************/

#ifdef CONFIG_PROC_FS
struct proc_dir_entry *test_dir, *entry;

int test_proc_get_info(char *buf, char **start, off_t offset, int len)
{
        len = sprintf(buf, "\n This is a test module\n\n");
        len += sprintf(buf+len, " Integer: %u\n", variable1);
        len += sprintf(buf+len, " Long[0]: %lu\n", variable2[0]);
        len += sprintf(buf+len, " Long[1]: %lu\n", variable2[1]);
        len += sprintf(buf+len, " Long[2]: %lu\n", variable2[2]);
        return len;
}

int test_proc_read(char *buf, char **start, off_t off, int count, \
                        int *eof, void *data)
{
        unsigned int      *ptr_var1 = data;

        return sprintf(buf, "%u\n", *ptr_var1);
}

int test_proc_write(struct file *file, const char *buffer, \
                        unsigned long count, void *data)
{
        unsigned int      *ptr_var1 = data;

        printk(KERN_DEBUG "TEST: variable1 set to: %s", buffer);

        *ptr_var1 = simple_strtoul(buffer, NULL, 10);
        return count;
}

register_proc_files()
{
        test_dir = proc_mkdir("test_dir", &proc_root);
        if (!create_proc_info_entry("test", 0444, test_dir, test_proc_get_info))
        printk(KERN_DEBUG "TEST: Error creating /proc/test.");

        entry = create_proc_entry("test_rw", 0644, test_dir);

        entry->nlink = 1;
        entry->data = (void *) &variable1;
```

```
        entry->read_proc = test_proc_read;
        entry->write_proc = test_proc_write;
}

unregister_proc_files()
{
        remove_proc_entry("test", test_dir);
        remove_proc_entry("test_rw", test_dir);

        remove_proc_entry("test_dir", NULL);
}
#endif /* CONFIG_PROC_FS */

/*****************************************/
/* Initialization function of the module */
/*****************************************/

int skull_init(void)
{
        /* Register the functionality of the module, */
        /* e.g., register_netdevice, inet_add_protocol, dev_add_pack, etc. */

        #ifdef CONFIG_PROC_FS
        register_proc_files();
        #endif /* CONFIG_PROC_FS */

        return 0;
}

/***********************************************/
/* Function to clean up the module context */
/***********************************************/

void skull_cleanup(void)
{
        /* Unregister the functionality of the module, */
        /* e.g., unregister_netdevice, inet_del_protocol, dev_remove_pack, etc. */

        #ifdef CONFIG_PROC_FS
        unregister_proc_files();
        #endif /* CONFIG_PROC_FS */
}

/* Alternative function names for init_module() and cleanup_module() */

module_init(skull_init);
module_exit(skull_cleanup);
```

Example for a Network-Layer Protocol

```c
/*********************************************************
* Example for a network-layer protocol
* Compile:
* gcc -I/lib/modules/'uname -r'/build/include -c file.c
*********************************************************/

#ifndef __KERNEL__
#define __KERNEL__
#endif
#ifndef MODULE
#define MODULE
#endif

#include <linux/module.h>
#include <linux/version.h>
#include <linux/kernel.h>
#include <linux/init.h>
#include <linux/skbuff.h>
#include <linux/in.h>
#include <linux/netdevice.h>

MODULE_AUTHOR("Test Author (fixme@Linux-netzwerkarchitektur.de)");
MODULE_DESCRIPTION("Module with a layer-3 test protocol");

#define TEST_PROTO_ID 0x1234

int test_pack_rcv(struct sk_buff *skb, struct net_device *dev, struct
  packet_type *pt);

static struct packet_type test_protocol =
{
        __constant_htons(TEST_PROTO_ID),
        NULL,
        test_pack_rcv,
```

```
        (void *) 1,
        NULL
};

int test_pack_rcv(struct sk_buff *skb, struct net_device *dev, struct
  packet_type *pt)
{
        printk(KERN_DEBUG "Test protocol: Packet Received with length: %u\n",
              skb->len);
        return skb->len;
}

int init_module(void)
{
        dev_add_pack(&test_protocol);
        return 0;
}

void cleanup_module(void)
{
        dev_remove_pack(&test_protocol);
}
```

Example for a Transport Protocol

```
/****************************************************************
* Example for a transport protocol
* Compile:
* gcc -I/lib/modules/'uname -r'/build/include -c file.c
****************************************************************/

#ifndef __KERNEL__
#define __KERNEL__
#endif
#ifndef MODULE
#define MODULE
#endif

#include <linux/module.h>
#include <linux/version.h>
#include <linux/kernel.h>
#include <linux/init.h>
#include <linux/skbuff.h>
#include <linux/in.h>
#include <net/protocol.h>

MODULE_AUTHOR("Test Author (fixme@Linux-netzwerkarchitektur.de)");
MODULE_DESCRIPTION("Module with a layer-4 test protocol");

int test_proto_rcv(struct sk_buff *skb);

static struct inet_protocol test_protocol =
{
        &test_proto_rcv,      /* protocol handler */
        NULL,                 /* error control */
        NULL,                 /* next */
        IPPROTO_TCP,          /* protocol ID */
```

```
        0,                      /* copy */
        NULL,                   /* data */
        "Test_Protocol"         /* name */
};

int test_proto_rcv(struct sk_buff *skb)
{
        printk(KERN_DEBUG "Test protocol: Packet Received with length: %u\n",
                skb->len);
        return skb->len;
}
int init_module(void)
{
        inet_add_protocol(&test_protocol);
        return 0;
}
void cleanup_module(void)
{
        inet_del_protocol(&test_protocol);
}
```

Example for Communication over Sockets

G.1 SERVER

```
/*******************************************************************
* Socket example: Chat application, server component comm_s.c
*
* Compilation: gcc -o comm_s comm_s.c
*
* comm_s <port> is used to start a server on each end system,
* and comm_c <destination system> <port> is used to start an
* arbitrary number of clients.
* All messages written in the client are displayed at the respective
* destination server.
*******************************************************************/

#include <stdio.h>
#include <sys/types.h>
#include <sys/socket.h>
#include <netinet/in.h>
#include <signal.h>
#include <string.h>

/* Macro for easier output of IP addresses with printf() */
#define NIPQUAD(addr) \
          ((unsigned char *)&addr)[0], \
          ((unsigned char *)&addr)[1], \
          ((unsigned char *)&addr)[2], \
          ((unsigned char *)&addr)[3]

#define BUFSIZE 1024
char buf[BUFSIZE + 1];
```

```c
/* Signal handler to accept the SIGCHLD signal when terminating
 * child processes; otherwise, these zombie processes would remain.
 */
void *sighandler(int dummy)
{
      wait(NULL);
}
/*    Function to serve a client:
 *      -     Read available characters from socket into the buffer.
 *      -     Search for end-of-line character; if found, or if buffer full:
 *            output message, move the rest forward, and repeat.
 *      -     Abort, if error, or connection closed.
 */
void serve(int s, struct sockaddr_in *peer)
{
      int space, n;
      char *p, *q;
      q = p = buf; space = BUFSIZE;
      while (1) {
            if ((n = read(s, p, space)) <= 0) break;
            p += n; space -= n;
            while ((q < p) && (*q != '\n')) q++;
            while ((q < p) || !space) {
                  *q = 0;
                  printf("message from %d.%d.%d.%d %d: %s\n",
                  NIPQUAD(peer->sin_addr.s_addr), ntohs(peer->sin_port), buf);
                  if (q < p) q++;
                  memmove(buf, q, p - q);
                  n = q - buf; // Number of characters "done"
                  p -= n; space += n;
                  q = buf;
                  while ((q < p) && (*q != '\n')) q++;
            }
      }
      if (n < 0) perror("read");
      else if (p > buf) { // Output rest
            *p = 0;
            printf("message from %d.%d.%d.%d %d: %s\n",
                  NIPQUAD(peer->sin_addr.s_addr), ntohs(peer->sin_port), buf);
      }
}

/* Main program:
 * -    Process arguments
 * -    Open socket and wait for connections
 * -    Start separate process for each new connection
 */
int main(int argc, char *argv[])
{
```

```
        int s;
        struct sockaddr_in myaddr;
        int optval;

        if (argc != 2) {
                fprintf(stderr, "Usage: %s <port>\n", argv[0]); exit(1);
        }
        if ((s = socket(AF_INET, SOCK_STREAM, 0)) < 0) {
                perror("socket"); exit(1);
        }
/*      Socket option SO_REUSEADDR: Allow bind(), even when old
        protocol instances are still using the address. */
optval = 1;
if (setsockopt(s, SOL_SOCKET, SO_REUSEADDR, &optval, sizeof(optval))) {
        perror("setsockopt"); exit(1);
}

memset(&myaddr, 0, sizeof(myaddr));
myaddr.sin_family = AF_INET;
myaddr.sin_port = htons(atoi(argv[1]));
myaddr.sin_addr.s_addr = INADDR_ANY;

if (bind(s, (struct sockaddr *) &myaddr, sizeof(myaddr))) {
        perror("bind"); exit(1);
}

if (listen(s, SOMAXCONN)) {
        perror("listen"); exit(1);
}

/* Install signal handler for SIGCHLD signal */
if (signal(SIGCHLD, (sig_t) sighandler) == SIG_ERR) {
        perror("signal"); exit(1);
}

while (1) {
        int new_s;
        struct sockaddr_in claddr;
        int claddrlen;

        claddrlen = sizeof(claddr);
        if ((new_s = accept(s, (struct sockaddr *) &claddr, &claddrlen)) < 0) {
                perror("accept"); continue;
        }

        if (fork()) { /* Parent process */
                close(new_s); /* New socket is used by child process only. */
        }
        else { /* Child process */
                close(s); /* Old socket is used by parent process only. */
                printf("connection from %d.%d.%d.%d %d\n",
```

```
                NIPQUAD(claddr.sin_addr.s_addr), ntohs(claddr.sin_port));
        serve(new_s, &claddr);
        printf("connection from %d.%d.%d.%d %d closed\n",
                NIPQUAD(claddr.sin_addr.s_addr), ntohs(claddr.sin_port));
        exit(0);
        }
    }
}
```

G.2   CLIENT

```
/***********************************************************************
* Socket example: Chat application, client component comm_c.c
*
* Compilation: gcc -o comm_c comm_c.c
***********************************************************************/
#include <stdio.h>
#include <sys/types.h>
#include <sys/socket.h>
#include <netinet/in.h>
#include <string.h>

#define BUFSIZE 1024
char buf[BUFSIZE+1];

/* Main program:
* -    Process arguments.
* -    Open socket and establish connection to server.
* -    Read text line by line and send it over this connection.
* -    Close connection at end of entry (Ctrl-D).
*/

int main(int argc, char *argv[])
{
        int s;
        struct sockaddr_in addr;
        char *p;

if (argc != 3) {
        fprintf(stderr, "Usage: %s <address> <port>\n", argv[0]); exit(1);
}

memset(&addr, 0, sizeof(addr));
addr.sin_family = AF_INET;
addr.sin_port = htons(atoi(argv[2]));
addr.sin_addr.s_addr = inet_addr(argv[1]);

if ((s = socket(AF_INET, SOCK_STREAM, 0)) < 0) {
        perror("socket"); exit(1);
}
```

```
if (connect(s, (struct sockaddr *) &addr, sizeof(addr))) {
        perror("connect"); exit(1);
}

buf[BUFSIZE] = 0;
while (fgets(buf, BUFSIZE, stdin) != NULL) {
        if (write(s, buf, strlen(buf)) == 0) {
                perror("write"); break;
        }
}
close(s);
exit(0);
}
```

Bibliography

[Alme01]   Werner Almesberger. *Traffic Control: Next Generation.*
            http://tcng.sourceforge.net. (Visited on December 23, 2003.)

[Bake95]   Fred Baker. *Requirements for IP Version 4 Routers*, Internet Engineering
            Task Force (IETF), Requests for Comments (RFC) document series,
            RCF 1812, June 1995. *http://www.faqs.org/rfcs/rfc1812.html.* (Visited on
            December 23, 2003.)

[BBDK+01]   Michael Beck, Harald Böhme, Mirko Dziadzka, Ulrich Kunitz et al.
            Linux Kernel Programming. Boston: Addison-Wesley, 3d ed., 2002.

[BoBu01]   Uwe Böhme and Lennert Buytenhenk. *Linux BRIDGE-STP-HOWTO.*
            http://www.tldp.org/HOWTO/BRIDGE-STP-HOWTO. (Visited on
            December 23, 2003.)

[BlAl01]   Mitchell Blank, Werner Almesberger et al. "Project: ATM on Linux:
            Summary," *SourceForge.net.* *http://sourceforge.net/projects/linux-atm.*
            (Visited on January 9, 2003.)

[BoCe00]   Daniel P. Bovet and Marco Cesati. *Understanding the Linux Kernel.*
            Beijing and Cambridge, MA: O'Reilly, 2000.

[Brad89]   R. Braden. *Requirements for Internet Hosts—Communication Layers*,
            Internet Engineering Task Force (IETF), Requests for Comments
            (RFC) document series, RCF 1122, October 1989.
            http://www.faqs.org/rfcs/rfc1122.html. (Visited on December 23, 2003.)

[BrBP88]   R. Braden, D. Borman, and C. Partridge. *Computing the Internet
            Checksum*, Internet Engineering Task Force (IETF), Requests for
            Comments (RFC) document series, RCF 1071, September 1988.
            http://www.faqs.org/rfcs/rfc1071.html. (Visited on December 23, 2003.)

[Buyt01]   Lennert Buytenhenk. *Linux Bridge Utilities.* Sources at
            http://bridge.sourceforge.net, 2001. (Visited January 9, 2004.)

[ChBe94]   William R. Cheswick and Steven M. Bellovin. *Firewalls and Internet
            Security: Repelling the Wiley Hacker.* Reading, MA: Addison-Wesley,
            1994.

[Come00]   Douglas E. Comer. *Principles, Protocols, and Architecture*, vol. 1 of
            Internetworking with TCP/IP. Upper Saddle River: Prentice Hall, 4th
            ed., 2000.

[Deer86]   Stephen E. Deering. *Host Extensions for IP Multicasting*, Internet En-
            gineering Task Force (IETF), Requests for Comments (RFC) docu-
            ment series, RCF 988, July 1986.
            http://www.faqs.org/rfcs/rfc988.html. (Visited on December 23, 2003.)

[Deer91]   Stephen E. Deering. Multicast Routing in a Datagram Network. PhD dissertation, Stanford University, Palo Alto, CA, December 1991.

[Drak00]   Joshua Drake. *Networking Howto. http://www.linuxdoc.org/HOWTO /Net-HOWTO*. (Visited on December 23, 2003.)

[Fenn97]   W. Fenner. *Internet Group Management Protocol, Version 2*, Internet Engineering Task Force (IETF), Requests for Comments (RFC) document series, RCF 2236, November 1997.
http://www.faqs.org/rfcs/rfc2236.html. (Visited on December 23, 2003.)

[FeSe00]   Paul Ferguson and Daniel Senie. *Network Ingress Filtering: Defeating Denial of Service Attacks which Employ IP Source Address Spoofing*, Internet Engineering Task Force (IETF), Requests for Comments (RFC) document series, RCF 2827, May 2000.
http://www.faqs.org/rfcs/rfc2827.html. (Visited on December 23, 2003.)

[FLYV93]   Vince Fuller, Tony Li, Jessica Yu, and Kannan Varadhan. *Classless Inter-Domain Routing (CIDR): An Address Assignment and Aggregation Strategy*, Internet Engineering Task Force (IETF), Requests for Comments (RFC) document series, RCF 1519, September 1993.
http://www.faqs.org/rfcs/rfc1519.html. (Visited on December 23, 2003.)

[FMMT84]   R. Finlayson, T. Mann, J. C. Mogul, and M. Theimer. *Reverse Address Resolution Protocol*, Internet Engineering Task Force (IETF), Requests for Comments (RFC) document series, RCF 903, June 1984.
http://www.faqs.org/rfcs/rfc903.html. (Visited on December 23, 2003.)

[Foru95]   ATM Forum. The ATM Forum Technical Committee, *LAN Emulation over ATM Specification, Version 2*. AF-LANE-0084.000.
ftp://ftp.atmforum.com/pub/approved-specs/af-lane-0084.000.pdf.
(Visited on December 23, 2003.)

[Gren00]   Mark Grennan. *Firewall and Proxy Server HOWTO v0.83*.
http://www.grennan.com/Firewall-HOWTO.html. (Visited on December 23, 2003.)

[Grou01]   Bluetooth Special Interest Group. *The Official Bluetooth Membership Site. http://www.bluetooth.org*. (Visited on December 23, 2003.)

[Hase97]   Michael Hasenstein. IP Network Address Translation. Undergraduate thesis, Technical University at Chemnitz, Germany, 1997.
http://www.suse.de/~mha/HyperNews/get/linux-ip-nat.html.

[Hein93]   Juha Heinanen. *Multiprotocol Encapsulation over ATM Adaptation Layer 5*, Internet Engineering Task Force (IETF), Requests for Comments (RFC) document series, RCF 1483, July 1993.
http://www.faqs.org/rfcs/rfc1483.html. (Visited on December 23, 2003.)

[HiDe98a]   R. Hinden and S. Deering. *Internet Protocol, Version 6 (IPv6) Specification*, Internet Engineering Task Force (IETF), Requests for Comments (RFC) document series, RCF 2460, December 1998.
http://www.faqs.org/rfcs/rfc2460.html. (Visited on December 23, 2003.)

[HiDe98b]   R. Hinden and S. Deering. *IP Version 6 Addressing Architecture*, Internet Engineering Task Force (IETF), Requests for Comments (RFC) document series, RCF 2373, July 1998. *http://www.faqs.org/rfcs/rfc2373.html*. (Visited on December 23, 2003.)

[ISO93]   International Organization for Standardization. Information Technology—Telecommunications and Information Exchange between Systems—High-Level Data Link Control (HDLC) Procedures. ISO/IEC 13239:2003

[ITU-94]   ITU-T. Information Technology—Open Systems Interconnection— Basic Reference Model: The Basic Model. ISO/IEC 7498-1:1994

[JaBB92]   V. Jacobson, R. Braden, and D. Borman. *TCP Extensions for High Performance*, Internet Engineering Task Force (IETF), Requests for Comments (RFC) document series, RCF 1323, May 1992. *http://www.faqs.org/rfcs/rfc1323.html*. (Visited on January 8, 2004.)

[Jaco90a]   Van Jacobson. "4BSD TCP Header Prediction." *Computer Communications Review* 20(2), 1990.

[Jaco90b]   Van Jacobson. *Compressing TCP/IP Headers for Low-Speed Serial Links*, Internet Engineering Task Force (IETF), Requests for Comments (RFC) document series, RCF 1144, February 1990. *http://www.faqs.org/rfcs/rfc1144.html*. (Visited on January 8, 2004.)

[Kuzn99]   Alexey N. Kuznetsov. *IP Command Reference. http://linux-ip.net/gl/ip-cref*. (Visited on January 10, 2004.)

[Kuzn01]   Alexey Kuznetsov. IProute2 and the tc tools. *http://tcng.sourceforge.net/*

[Laub94]   M. Laubach. *Classical IP and ARP over ATM*, Internet Engineering Task Force (IETF), Requests for Comments (RFC) document series, RCF 1577, January 1994. *http://www.faqs.org/rfcs/rfc1577.html*. (Visited on January 8, 2004.)

[LGLK+96]   M. Leech, M. Ganis, Y. Lee, R. Kuris, D. Koblas, and L. Jones. *SOCKS Protocol Version 5*, Internet Engineering Task Force (IETF), Requests for Comments (RFC) document series, RCF 1928, March 1996. *http://www.faqs.org/rfcs/rfc1928.html*. (Visited on January 8, 2004.)

[MaKu90]   T. Mallory and A. Kullberg. *Incremental Updating of the Internet Checksum*, Internet Engineering Task Force (IETF), Requests for Comments (RFC) document series, RCF 1928, January 1990. *http://www.faqs.org/rfcs/rfc1928.html*. (Visited on January 8, 2004.)

[Malk98]   Gary S. Malkin. *RIP Version 2*, Internet Engineering Task Force (IETF), Requests for Comments (RFC) document series, RCF 2453, November 1998. *http://www.faqs.org/rfcs/rfc2453.html*. (Visited on January 8, 2004.)

[McSp95]   D. E. McDysan and D. L. Spohn. *ATM Theory and Application*. New York: McGraw-Hill. 1995.

[MLEC+99]   L. Mamakos, K. Lidl, J. Evarts, D. Carrel, D. Simone, and R. Wheeler. *A Method for Transmitting PPP over Ethernet (PPPoE)*, Internet

Engineering Task Force (IETF), Requests for Comments (RFC) document series, RCF 2516, February 1999. *http://www.faqs.org/rfcs/rfc2516.html*. (Visited on January 8, 2004.)

[Nagl84]   John Nagle. *Congestion Control in TCP/IP Networks*, Internet Engineering Task Force (IETF), Requests for Comments (RFC) document series, RFC 896, January 1984. *http://www.faqs.org/rfcs/rfc896.html*. (Visited on January 8, 2004.)

[NBBB98]   K. Nichols, S. Blake, F. Baker, and D. Black. *Definition of the Differentiated Services Field (DS Field) in the IPv4 and IPv6 Headers*, Internet Engineering Task Force (IETF), Requests for Comments (RFC) document series, RFC 2474, December 1998. *http://www.faqs.org/rfcs/rfc2474.html*. (Visited on January 8, 2004.)

[ObWe01]   Vincent Oberle and KlausWehrle. A High Resolution Programmable Timer for the Linux OS. *http://www.oberle.org/apic_timer.html*

[Ostr01]   Michael Ostrowski. PPPoE for Linux 2.4. *http://www.roaringpenguin.com/pppoe/*

[OtWi96]   Thomas Ottmann and Peter Widmayer. *Algorithmen und Datenstrukturen*. Springer Publishing, Heidelber, Germany 1996.

[Pete00]   Larry L. Peterson and Bruce S. Davie. *Computer Network: A Systems Approach*. San Francisco: Morgan Kaufmann Publishers. 2000.

[Post80]   Jon Postel. *User Datagram Protocol*. Internet Engineering Task Force (IETF), Requests for Comments (RFC) document series, RCF 768, August 1980. *http://www.faqs.org/rfcs/rfc768.html*. (Visited on January 10, 2004.)

[Post81a]   Jon Postel. *Assigned Numbers*, Internet Engineering Task Force (IETF), Requests for Comments (RFC) document series, RCF 790, September 1981. *http://www.faqs.org/rfcs/rfc790.html*. (Visited on January 10, 2004.)

[Post81b]   Jon Postel. *Internet Control Message Protocol*, Internet Engineering Task Force (IETF), Requests for Comments (RFC) document series, RCF 792, September 1981. *http://www.faqs.org/rfcs/rfc792.html*. (Visited on January 10, 2004.)

[Post81c]   Jon Postel. *Internet Protocol DARPA Internet Program Protocol Specification*, Internet Engineering Task Force (IETF), Requests for Comments (RFC) document series, RCF 791, September 1981. *http://www.faqs.org/rfcs/rfc791.html*. (Visited on January 10, 2004.)

[Pusa00]   T. Pusateri. *Distance Vector Multicast Routing Protocol Specification*, Internet Draft, draft-ietf-idmr-dvmrp-v3-10.txt (work in progress*)*. *http://www1.ietf.org/mail-archive/ietf-announce/Current/msg08997.html*

[ReLi93]   Yakov Rekhter and Tony Li. *An Architecture for IP Address Allocation with CIDR*, Internet Engineering Task Force (IETF), Requests for Comments (RFC) document series, RCF 1518, September 1993. *http://www.faqs.org/rfcs/rfc1518.html*. (Visited on January 10, 2004.)

[RePo94]   J. Reynolds and J. *Postel. Assigned Numbers*, Internet Engineering Task Force (IETF), Requests for Comments (RFC) document series, RCF 1700, October 1994. *http://www.faqs.org/rfcs/rfc1700.html*. (Visited on January 10, 2004.)

[Rijs94]   Anil Rijsinghani. *Computation of the Internet Checksum via Incremental Update*, Internet Engineering Task Force (IETF), Requests for Comments (RFC) document series, RCF 1624, May 1994. *http://www.faqs.org/rfcs/rfc1624.html*. (Visited on January 10, 2004.)

[RMKG+96]   Yakov Rekhter, Robert G. Moskowitz, Daniel Karrenberg, Geert Jan de Groot, and Eliot Lear. *Address Allocation for Private Internets*, Internet Engineering Task Force (IETF), Requests for Comments (RFC) document series, RCF 1918, February 1996. *http://www.faqs.org/rfcs/rfc1918.html*. (Visited on January 10, 2004.)

[Roar01]   Roaring Penguin Software, Inc. *Roaring Penguins PPPoE Software*. *http://www.roaringpenguin.com/products/rp-pppoe/index.php*. (Visited January 10, 2004.)

[Romk88]   J. Romkey. *A Nonstandard for Transmission of IP Datagrams over Serial Lines: SLIP*, Internet Engineering Task Force (IETF), Requests for Comments (RFC) document series, RCF 1055, June 1998. *http://www.faqs.org/rfcs/rfc1055.html*. (Visited on January 10, 2004.)

[RuCo01]   Alessandro Rubini and Jonathan Corbet. *Linux Device Drivers*. Sebastopol, CA: O'Reilly & Associates, 2d ed., 2001.Online version at *http://www.oreilly.com/catalog/linuxdrive2/index.html*. (Visited on January 10, 2004.)

[Russ00a]   Paul "Rusty" Russell. *Linux IPCHAINS-HOWTO v1.0.8*. *http://www.tldp.org/HOWTO/IPCHAINS-HOWTO.html*. (Visited January 13, 2004.)

[Russ00b]   Paul "Rusty" Russell. Linux Kernel Locking HOWTO, March 2000. *http://www.kernel.org/pub/linux/kernel/people/rusty/kernel-locking/*

[Russ00c]   Paul "Rusty" Russell. *Unreliable Guide to Hacking the Linux Kernel*. *http://netfilter.gnumonks.org/unreliable-guides/kernel-hacking/lk-hacking-guide.html*. (Visited on January 13, 2004.)

[Russ00d]   Paul "Rusty" Russell. "Writing a Module for Netfilter." *Linux Magazine* (6), June 2000.

[Russ01a]   Paul "Rusty" Russell. *Linux 2.4 NAT HOWTO v1.18*. *http://www.netfilter.org/documentation/HOWTO/NAT-HOWTO.html*. (Visited on January 13, 2004.)

[Russ01b]   Paul "Rusty" *Russell. Linux 2.4 Packet Filtering HOWTO v1*.26. *http://www.netfilter.org/documentation/HOWTO/packet-filtering-HOWTO.html*. (Visited on January 13, 2004.)

[Simp94a]   William Allen Simpson. *The Point-to-Point Protocol (PPP)*, Internet Engineering Task Force (IETF), Requests for Comments (RFC) document series, RCF 1661, July 1994. *http://www.faqs.org/rfcs/rfc1661.html*. (Visited on January 13, 2004.)

[Simp94b]   William Allen Simpson. *PPP in HDLC-like Framing*, Internet Engineering Task Force (IETF), Requests for Comments (RFC) document series, RCF 1662, July 1994. *http://www.faqs.org/rfcs/rfc1662.html*. (Visited on January 13, 2004.)

[SrHo99]   Pyda Srisuresh and Matt Holdrege. *IP Network Address Translator (NAT) Terminology and Considerations*, Internet Engineering Task Force (IETF), Requests for Comments (RFC) document series, RCF 2663, August 1999. *http://www.faqs.org/rfcs/rfc2663.html*. (Visited on January 13, 2004.)

[Stal98]   William Stallings. *Cryptography and Network Security: Principles and Practice*. Upper Saddle River, NJ: Prentice Hall, 2d ed., 1998.

[Stev90]   W. Richard Stevens. *UNIX Network Programming*. Upper Saddle River, NJ: Prentice Hall, 1990.

[Stev94a]   W. Richard Stevens. *The Protocols*, vol. 1 of *TCP/IP Illustrated*. Reading, MA: Addison-Wesley, 1994.

[Stev94b]   W. Richard Stevens. *The Implementation* , vol. 2 of *TCP/IP Illustrated*. Reading, MA: Addison-Wesley, 1994.

[Tane95]   Andrew S. Tanenbaum. *Modern Operating Systems*. Upper Saddle River, NJ: Prentice Hall, 1995, 2001 (2d ed.)

[Tane97]   Andrew S. Tanenbaum. *Computer Networks*. Upper Saddle River, N.J: Prentice Hall, 3d ed., 1997.

[WaPD88]   D. Waitzman, C. Partridge, and S. Deering. *Distance-Vector Multicast Routing Protocol*, Internet Engineering Task Force (IETF), Requests for Comments (RFC) document series, RCF 1075, November 1998. *http://www.faqs.org/rfcs/rfc1075.html*. (Visited on January 13, 2004.)

[Wehr01b]   Klaus Wehrle. "An open Architecture for Evaluating Arbitrary Quality of Service Mechanisms in Software Routers,". in *Proceedings of IEEE International Conference on Networking (ICN 2001)*, Colmar, France, June 2001

[WeRi00]   Klaus Wehrle and Hartmut Ritter. "Traffic Shaping in ATM and IP Networks Using Standard End Systems," in *Proceedings of Conference on High Performance Switching & Routing, Joint IEEE/ATM Workshop 2000 and 3d International Conference on ATM*, Heidelberg, Germany, May 2000.

[WeRW01]   Klaus Wehrle, Hartmut Ritter and Lars Wolf. "Improving the Performance of TCP on Guaranteed Bandwidth Connections," in *Tagungsband der Konferenz KiVS 2001 (Kommunikation in verteilten Systemen)*, Hamburg, Germany, February 2001

Index